MW00787679

A Frequency Dictionary of Contemporary American English

A Frequency Dictionary of Contemporary American English is an invaluable tool for all learners of American English, providing a list of the 5,000 most frequently used words in the language.

The dictionary is based on data from a 385-million-word corpus—evenly balanced between spoken English (unscripted conversation from radio and TV shows), fiction (books, short stories, movie scripts), more than 100 popular magazines, ten newspapers, and 100 academic journals—for a total of nearly 150,000 texts.

All entries in the rank frequency list feature the top 20–30 collocates (nearby words) for that word, which provide valuable insight into the meaning and usage. Alphabetical and part of speech indexes are provided for ease of use. The dictionary also contains 31 thematically organized and frequency-ranked lists of words on a variety of topics, such as family, sports, and food. New words in the language, differences between American and British English, and grammar topics such as the most frequent phrasal verbs are also covered.

A Frequency Dictionary of Contemporary American English is an engaging and efficient resource enabling students of all levels to get the most out of their study of vocabulary. It is also a rich resource for language teaching, research, curriculum design, and materials development.

Mark Davies is Professor and **Dee Gardner** is Associate Professor, both at the Department of Linguistics and English Language, Brigham Young University at Provo, Utah.

Routledge Frequency Dictionaries

Other books in the series

A Frequency Dictionary of Arabic (forthcoming)
A Frequency Dictionary of Chinese
A Frequency Dictionary of French
A Frequency Dictionary of German
A Frequency Dictionary of Portuguese
A Frequency Dictionary of Spanish

A Frequency Dictionary of Contemporary American English

Word sketches, collocates, and thematic lists

Mark Davies and Dee Gardner

Routledge
Taylor & Francis Group

LONDON AND NEW YORK

First edition published 2010
by Routledge
2 Park Square, Milton Park, Abingdon Oxon OX14 4RN

Simultaneously published in the USA and Canada
by Routledge
711 Third Avenue, New York, NY 10017

Routledge is an imprint of the Taylor & Francis Group, an informa business

© 2010 Mark Davies and Dee Gardner

Typeset in Parisine by Graphicraft Limited, Hong Kong

British Library Cataloguing in Publication Data
A catalogue record for this book is available from the British Library

Library of Congress Cataloging in Publication Data
Davies, Mark, 1963 Apr. 22
  A frequency dictionary of contemporary American English : word sketches, collocates,
  and thematic lists / Mark Davies, Dee Gardner.—1st ed.
      p. cm.—(Routledge frequency dictionaries)
  Includes bibliographical references and index
  English language—Word frequency—Dictionaries. I. Gardner, Dee. II. Title.
  PE1691.D35 2010
  423'.1—dc22
                                                                  2009031322

ISBN 13: 978-0-415-49064-1 (hbk)
ISBN 13: 978-0-415-49063-4 (pbk)
ISBN 13: 978-0-203-88088-3 (ebk)

Printed and bound in the United States of America
By Edwards Brothers Malloy on sustainably sourced paper.

Contents

Thematic vocabulary lists

Series preface

Frequency information has a central role to play in learning a language. Nation (1990) showed that the 4,000–5,000 most frequent words account for up to 95 percent of a written text and the 1,000 most frequent words account for 85 percent of speech. Although Nation's results were only for English, they do provide clear evidence that, when employing frequency as a general guide for vocabulary learning, it is possible to acquire a lexicon which will serve a learner well most of the time. There are two caveats to bear in mind here. First, counting words is not as straightforward as it might seem. Gardner (2007) highlights the problems that multiple word meanings, the presence of multiword items, and grouping words into families or lemmas, have on counting and analysing words. Second, frequency data contained in frequency dictionaries should never act as the only information source to guide a learner. Frequency information is nonetheless a very good starting point, and one which may produce rapid benefits. It therefore seems rational to prioritize learning the words that you are likely to hear and read most often. That is the philosophy behind this series of dictionaries.

Lists of words and their frequencies have long been available for teachers and learners of language. For example, Thorndike (1921, 1932) and Thorndike and Lorge (1944) produced word frequency books with counts of word occurrences in texts used in the education of American children. Michael West's *General Service List of English Words* (1953) was primarily aimed at foreign learners of English. More recently, with the aid of efficient computer software and very large bodies of language data (called corpora), researchers have been able to provide more sophisticated frequency counts from both written text and transcribed speech. One important feature of the resulting frequencies presented in this series is that they are derived from recently collected language data. The earlier lists for English included samples from, for example, Austen's *Pride and Prejudice* and Defoe's *Robinson Crusoe*, thus they could no longer represent present-day language in any sense.

Frequency data derived from a large representative corpus of a language brings students closer to language as it is used in real life as opposed to textbook language (which often distorts the frequencies of features in a language, see Ljung, 1990). The information in these dictionaries is presented in a number of formats to allow users to access the data in different ways. So, for example, if you would prefer not to simply drill down through the word frequency list, but would rather focus on verbs for example, the part of speech index will allow you to focus on just the most frequent verbs. Given that verbs typically account for 20 percent of all words in a language, this may be a good strategy. Also, a focus on function words may be equally rewarding—60 percent of speech in English is composed of a mere 50 function words. The series also provides information of use to the language teacher. The idea that frequency information may have a role to play in syllabus design is not new (see, for example, Sinclair and Renouf, 1988). However, to date it has been difficult for those teaching languages other than English to use frequency information in syllabus design because of a lack of data.

Frequency information should not be studied to the exclusion of other contextual and situational knowledge about language use and we may even doubt the validity of frequency information derived from large corpora. It is interesting to note that Alderson (2007) found that corpus frequencies may not match a native speaker's intuition about estimates of word frequency and that a set of estimates of word frequencies collected from language experts varied widely. Thus corpus-derived frequencies are still the best current estimate of a word's importance that a learner will come across. Around the time of the construction of the first machine-readable corpora, Halliday (1971: 344) stated that "a rough indication of frequencies is often just what is needed." Our aim in this series is to provide as accurate as possible estimates of word frequencies.

Paul Rayson and Mark Davies
Lancaster and Provo, 2008

References

Alderson, J.C. (2007) Judging the frequency of English words. *Applied Linguistics*, 28(3): 383–409.

Gardner, D. (2007) Validating the construct of "word" in applied corpus-based vocabulary research: A critical survey. *Applied Linguistics* 28, 241–265.

Halliday, M.A.K. (1971) Linguistic functions and literary style. In S. Chatman (ed.) *Style: A Symposium*. Oxford University Press, Oxford, 330–365.

Ljung, M. (1990) *A Study of TEFL Vocabulary*. Almqvist & Wiksell International, Stockholm.

Nation, I.S.P. (1990) *Teaching and Learning Vocabulary*. Heinle & Heinle, Boston.

Sinclair, J.M., and Renouf, A. (1988) A lexical syllabus for language learning. In R. Carter and M. McCarthy (eds) *Vocabulary and Language Teaching*. Longman, London, 140–158.

Thorndike, E.L. (1921) *Teacher's Word Book*. Columbia Teachers College, New York.

Thorndike, E.L. (1932) *A Teacher's Word Book of 20,000 Words*. Columbia Teachers College, New York.

Thorndike, E.L. and Lorge, I. (1944) *The Teacher's Word Book of 30,000 Words*. Columbia Teachers College, New York.

West, M. (1953) *A General Service List of English Words*. Longman, London.

Acknowledgments

We are indebted to a number of students from Brigham Young University who helped with this project: Athelia Graham, Andrea Bowden, Amy Heaton, Tim Wallace, Tim Heaton, Kyle Jepson, Timothy Hewitt, Mikkel Davis, Jared Garrett, Teresa Martin, Billy Wilson, and Dave Ogden, and several student employees at Brigham Young University's English Language Center. A special thanks to Brigham Young University's English Language Center, the College of Humanities, the Department of Linguistics and English Language, and the Data-Based Research Group for their financial support.

Abbreviations

The following are the part of speech codes for the 5,000 headwords in the dictionary.

Code	No. of Words	Explanation	Examples
a	11	article	the, a, your
c	38	conjunction	if, because, whereas
d	34	determiner	this, most, either
e	1	existential	there
g	1	genitive	'
i	96	preposition	with, instead, except
j	839	adjective	shy, risky, tender
m	36	number	seven, fifth, two-thirds
n	2558	noun	bulb, tolerance, slot
p	46	pronoun	we, somebody, mine
r	333	adverb	up, seldom, fortunately
t	1	to + infinitive	to
u	12	interjection	yeah, hi, wow
v	992	verb	modify, scan, govern
x	2	negation	not, n't

Introduction

The value of this frequency dictionary of English

"I don't know that word." "What does that word mean?" "How is that word used?" These are some of the most common pleas for help by language learners—and justifiably so.

Not knowing enough words, or the right words, is often the root cause of miscommunication, the inability to read and write well, and a host of related problems. This fundamental need is compounded by the fact that there are simply so many words to know in any language, but especially in English, which may contain well over two million distinct words (Crystal, 1995)—and growing fast. Thirty years ago, who would have thought that we would be "surfing" in our own homes, or that "chips" would be good things to have inside our equipment, or that we would be excited "to google this" and "to google that."

Without belaboring the obvious, it is little wonder that learners, teachers, researchers, materials developers, and many others are interested in establishing some sense of priority and direction to what could easily become vocabulary chaos. Our frequency dictionary is designed for this very purpose. We wanted to know which of the vast number of English words to start with, and we also wanted to know which other words these words "hang out with"—their neighbors (or collocates)—which provide crucial information about the meaning and use of these words. Perhaps even more importantly, we wanted to know this for our current day, not for some English of the past, when punch cards were used to program computers, and when surfing was only done at the beach. In short, we offer *A Frequency Dictionary of Contemporary American English* with the hope that it will benefit those who are trying to learn our current mother tongue, as well as for those who desire to assist them.

As a final introductory note, we might mention that if you find this dictionary valuable and would like a similar electronic version (fewer collocates, but more of other features), feel free to visit http://www.americancorpus.org/dictionary.

What is in this dictionary?

This frequency dictionary is designed to meet the needs of a wide range of language students and teachers, as well as those who are interested in the computational processing of English. The main index contains the 5,000 most common words in American English, starting with such basic words as *the* and *of*, and quickly progressing through to more intermediate and advanced words. Because the dictionary is based on the actual frequency of words in a large 385-million-word corpus of many different types of English texts (spoken, fiction, magazines, newspaper, and academic), the user can feel comfortable that these words are very likely to be encountered in the "real world."

In addition to providing a listing of the most frequent 5,000 words, the entries provide other information that should be of great use to the language learner. Each entry shows the main collocates for each word, grouped by part of speech and in order of frequency. These collocates provide important and useful insight into the meaning and usage of the word, following the idea that "you can tell a lot about a word by the other words that it hangs out with." The entries also show where each of the collocates occur with regards to the head word (before, after, or both), which denotes whether they are subject, object, and so on. Finally, the entries indicate whether the words are more common in one genre of English (e.g. spoken or academic) than in the others.

Aside from the main frequency listing, there are also indexes that sort the entries by alphabetical order and part of speech. The alphabetical index can be of great value to students who, for example, want to look up a word from a short story or newspaper article, and see how common the word is in general. The part of speech indexes could be of benefit to students who want to focus selectively on verbs, nouns, or some other part of speech. Finally, there are a number of thematically related lists (clothing, foods, emotions, etc.) as well as comparisons of vocabulary across genres and over time, all of which should enhance the learning experience. The expectation, then, is that this frequency dictionary will significantly support the efforts of a wide range of students and teachers who are involved in the acquisition and teaching of English vocabulary.

Comparison to other frequency dictionaries of English

Historically, most frequency dictionaries (also referred to as *word books* and *word lists*) have been created to meet educational needs, with many designed specifically to meet the needs of foreign- and second-language learners of English. Prominent among these are: *The Teacher's Word Book of 30,000 Words* (Thorndike and Lorge, 1944)—based on 4.5 million words from general English texts, magazines, and juvenile books; *The General Service List of English Words* (West, 1953)—a list of the 2,000 highest frequency words (with semantic distinctions and counts) based on visual inspections by semanticists of 5 million words from various sources (encyclopedias, magazines, textbooks, novels, etc.); the *Brown Corpus* list (Francis and Kučera, 1982)—based on 1 million words of written American English; and its British English counterpart—the *LOB corpus* list (Johansson and Hofland, 1989).

For many purposes, these latter two replaced the older lists of Thorndike and Lorge. Additionally, there are several more specialized school lists, such as: the *American Heritage Word Frequency Book* (Carroll, Davies, and Richman 1971)—based on 5 million running words of written school English (grades 3 through 9); the *Academic Word List* (Coxhead, 2000)—570 academic word families based on 3.5 million running words of academic texts; and the very early *A Basic Vocabulary of Elementary School Children* (Rinsland, 1945)—based on 6 million running words of actual children's writing samples.

A great debt is owed to the pioneering scholars who generated these and other frequency lists to facilitate English vocabulary learning, research, and description. Building on these earlier efforts, *A Frequency Dictionary of Contemporary American English* addresses several vocabulary needs in the field of English language education. First, and perhaps most obvious, it is based on contemporary American English, thus making it more ecologically valid in educational and research settings where American English is the target, and where many are still relying on the nearly 30-year-old Brown Corpus (Francis and Kučera, 1982) for frequency information about American English vocabulary. (Note: the actual texts for the Brown Corpus were from 1961.) Second, unlike the Brown Corpus (1 million words of written English only), the frequency counts in this dictionary are based on a very large and balanced corpus of both written and spoken materials (385 million words from five major genres), thus adding confidence that the highest frequency words have indeed been determined and properly ranked, and that these words have a high degree of utility across major genres of importance to English language learners (spoken, fiction, newspapers, magazines, and academic).

Third, the inclusion of collocates (by part of speech) for each of the 5,000 high-frequency node words adds a semantic richness to the dictionary that is often lacking when only the forms of words are tallied without consideration of their potential meanings (Gardner, 2007). The tightness of some of these node-collocate relationships (*big deal, bad habit, make sense, trash talk*, etc.) also highlights the phrasal nature of many English vocabulary items (Cowie, 1998). Such collocational knowledge is a crucial component of what it means to know a word (Nation, 2001) and has also been recognized as a characteristic difference between native and non-native language abilities (Nesselhauf, 2005). Therefore, language learners and their teachers should benefit from the rich semantic and pragmatic information the collocates provide, thus taking us one step closer to Read's (2000) call for new high-frequency word lists that are based on large electronic corpora, but which also account for the many meanings that language learners need to negotiate. Although semantic frequency is not fully realized in this dictionary, the collocates do provide some support for semantic interpretations, and will certainly aid in determining which meanings of a word form to teach or learn.

Finally, the 30 call-out boxes in this dictionary are packed with useful vocabulary information for language learners and their teachers, including words that make up many of the basic semantic sets of the language (*animals, body, clothing, colors, emotions, family, food*, etc.), words that characterize a specific genre of the language (spoken, fiction, academic, etc.), words that are new to American English, words that tend to be characteristically American or British, productive suffixes and the actual content words they are found in (nouns and adjectives), and the highest frequency phrasal verbs of American English. (Compare with Gardner and Davies, 2007, which lists the highest frequency phrasal verbs of British English.) These and other call-out boxes in the dictionary can be used for self-study, teaching, assessment, materials development, and research purposes.

To our knowledge, there is only one other publicly accessible frequency dictionary of English that is based on a large mega-corpus—*Word Frequencies in Written and Spoken English* (Leech, Rayson, and Wilson, 2001). However, our dictionary is quite different in at least three major respects. First, the Longman frequency dictionary represents British, not American, English, and it bases its word-frequency information on the British National Corpus (BNC). Second, most of the texts in the BNC are at least 20 years old, while texts in the Corpus of Contemporary American English (COCA) are current through late 2008. Third, while both corpora are balanced for genre (e.g. spoken, fiction, newspaper, and academic), COCA (385 million words as of 2008, currently 400 million and growing by 20 million per year) is nearly four times as large as the BNC (100 million words), allowing us to have more confidence in determining the words that should "make the list" and in finding their meaningful neighbors.

In addition to the differences in focus, age, and sampling size between the two dictionaries, there are also differences in the presentation formats. The Longman dictionary is mainly composed of straight frequency lists of words and lemmas, while this dictionary is oriented specifically to language learners, supplementing the frequency listings with the unique features previously mentioned: (a) frequency-ranked collocates (co-occurring words) for each headword in the frequency dictionary—which can help learners and their teachers better understand the *meanings* and *uses* of the high frequency words; and (b) the more than 30 thematically oriented vocabulary lists (call-out boxes) for particular semantic, grammatical, or lexical categories that would be helpful for language training purposes.

The corpus

A frequency dictionary is only as good as the corpus on which it is based. The Corpus of Contemporary American English (COCA) is the largest balanced corpus of American English, and the largest balanced corpus of any language that is publicly available (http://www.americancorpus.org). In addition to being very large (currently over 400 million words; 20 million words each year 1990–2008), the corpus is also balanced evenly between spoken (unscripted conversation from 150+ radio and TV shows), fiction (e.g. books, short stories, movie scripts), 100+ popular magazines, ten newspapers, and 100+ academic journals—for a total of 150,000+ texts.

The more than 150,000 texts come from a variety of sources:

- *Spoken*: (79 million words) transcripts of unscripted conversation from more than 150 different TV and radio programs (e.g. *All Things Considered* (NPR), *Newshour* (PBS), *Good Morning America* (ABC), *Today Show* (NBC), *60 Minutes* (CBS), *Hannity and Colmes* (Fox), *Jerry Springer*, etc.). (See notes on the naturalness and authenticity of the language from these transcripts.)
- *Fiction*: (76 million words) short stories and plays from literary magazines, children's magazines, popular magazines, first chapters of first edition books 1990–present, and movie scripts.
- *Popular magazines*: (81 million words) nearly 100 different magazines, with a good mix (overall, and by year) between specific domains (news, health, home and gardening, women, financial, religion, sports, etc.). A few examples are *Time, Men's Health, Good Housekeeping, Cosmopolitan, Fortune, Christian Century, Sports Illustrated*, etc.
- *Newspapers*: (76 million words) ten newspapers from across the US, including: *USA Today, New York Times, Atlanta Journal Constitution, San Francisco Chronicle*, etc. In most cases, there is a good mix between different sections of the

newspaper, such as local news, opinion, sports, financial, etc.

- *Academic journals*: (76 million words) nearly 100 different peer-reviewed journals. These were selected to cover the entire range of the Library of Congress classification system (e.g. a certain percentage from B (philosophy, psychology, religion), D (world history), K (education), T (technology), etc.), both overall and by number of words per year.

In summary, the corpus is very well balanced at both the "macro" level (e.g. spoken, fiction, newspapers) and the "micro" level (i.e. the types of texts and the distribution of the sources) within each of these macro genres.

Annotating and organizing the data from the corpus

In order to create a frequency dictionary, the words in the corpus must be tagged (for part of speech) and lemmatized. Tagging means that a part of speech is assigned to each word—noun, verb, and so on. Lemmatization means that each word form is assigned to a particular "head word" or "lemma", such as *go, goes, going, went,* and *gone* being marked as forms of the lemma *go*.

The tagging and lemmatization was done with the CLAWS tagger (Version 7), which is the same tagger that was used for the British National Corpus (http://www.natcorp.ox.ac.uk/) and for other important corpora of English as well. One of the most difficult parts of tagging, of course, is to correctly assign the part of speech for words that are potentially ambiguous. In cases such as *computer, disturb, lazy,* or *fitfully,* these are unambiguously tagged as noun, verb, adjective, and adverb, respectively. But in a case such as *light,* the word can be a noun (*he turned on the light*), verb (*should we light the fire?*), or adjective (*there was a light breeze*). In these circumstances, the tagger looks at the context in which the word occurs in each instance to determine the correct part of speech. While the CLAWS tagger is very good, it does produce errors. We have tried to correct for most of these, but there are undoubtedly still some that remain.

It of course makes sense to provide separate entries in the dictionary for words with different parts of speech, such as noun and verb. For example,

the word *beat* as a noun has collocates such as *hear, miss, steady, drum,* and *rhythm.* As a verb, however, it takes collocates such as *heart, egg, bowl, severely,* or *Yankees.* Even in cases where the word appears as a noun and an adjective (*magic, potential, dark, veteran*), the collocates for the two parts of speech are very different, and it would probably be too confusing to conflate them into one entry. Perhaps the most problematic are function words such as *since,* which appear up to three times in this dictionary. In the case of *since,* for example, it appears as preposition (*he's been here since 1942*), adverb (*several other schools have since been constructed*), and conjunction (*since they won't be here until 5 pm, we'll just leave for a minute*). In these cases, we have simply followed the output of the tagger. If it says that there are multiple different parts of speech, then the word appears under each of those parts of speech in the dictionary.

Frequency and dispersion

After the tagging and lemmatization of the 400 million words in the corpus, our final step was to determine exactly which of these words would be included in the final list of the 5,000 most frequent words (or lemmas). One approach would be to simply use frequency counts. For example, all lemmas that occur 5,000 times or more in the corpus might be included in the dictionary. Imagine, however, a case where a particular scientific term was used repeatedly in engineering articles or in sports reporting in newspapers, but it did not appear in any works of fiction or in any of the spoken texts. Alternatively, suppose that a given word is spread throughout an entire register (spoken, fiction, newspaper, or academic), but that it is still limited almost exclusively to that register. Should the word still be included in the frequency dictionary? The argument could be made that we should look at more than just raw frequency counts in cases such as this, and that we ought to look at "dispersion" as well, or how well the word is "spread across" all of the registers in the entire corpus.

In our dictionary, we have used Juilland's "D dispersion index". A score of 1.00 means that the word is perfectly spread across the corpus, so that if we divided the corpus into one hundred equally sized sections (each with 4 million words, in the case

Table 1 Contrast between frequency and dispersion

Good dispersion				Poor dispersion			
Frequency	Lemma	PoS	Dispersion	Frequency	Lemma	PoS	Dispersion
3134	convincing	j	0.96	4653	healthcare	n	0.56
3107	sensible	j	0.95	4282	electron	n	0.58
3041	honesty	n	0.96	4181	skier	n	0.43
3033	unusually	r	0.95	4113	compost	n	0.31
3020	confusing	j	0.97	3685	watercolor	n	0.41
3014	exaggerate	v	0.96	3769	ski	v	0.47
2950	distraction	n	0.95	2028	nebula	n	0.46
2922	resent	v	0.96	2547	palette	n	0.57
2891	wrestle	v	0.95	2536	angle	v	0.55
2876	urgency	n	0.96	2479	algorithm	n	0.52
2873	hint	v	0.96	2437	pastel	n	0.25
2842	obsessed	j	0.95	2388	socket	n	0.60
2833	genuinely	r	0.96	2350	nasal	j	0.44
2813	respected	j	0.95	2281	cache	n	0.43

of our nearly 400 million word corpus), the word would have exactly the same frequency in each section. A dispersion score of .10, on the other hand, would mean that it occurs a lot in a handful of sections, and perhaps not at all or very little in the other sections.

As a clear example of the contrast between "frequency" and "dispersion", consider Table 1. All of the words in this table have essentially the same frequency—an average of about 3,000 occurrences in the corpus. The words to the left, however, have a "dispersion" score of at least 0.95, which means that the word has roughly the same frequency in all of the 100 sections of the corpus that we used for the calculation. The words to the right, on the other hand, have a much lower dispersion score. Most would easily agree that the words shown at the left would be more useful in a frequency dictionary, because they represent a wide range of texts and text types in the corpus. Therefore, as we can see, frequency alone is probably not sufficient to determine whether a word should be in the dictionary.

The final calculation

The calculation to determine which words are included in this frequency dictionary was a fairly straightforward one. The formula was simply:

$$score = frequency * dispersion$$

For example, consider the words near 3210 in the frequency dictionary (see Table 2). The word *furthermore* has a higher frequency (9594 tokens) than the other two words, but it has lower dispersion (.86). *Orange*, on the other hand, has a lower frequency (8881 tokens) but it has better dispersion across the corpus. *Taxpayer* (frequency of 9140 and dispersion of .90) is in the middle of both of these. But with the formula that takes into account both frequency and dispersion, these three words end up having more or less the same score.

Table 2 Frequency and dispersion

ID	Lemma	PoS	Frequency	Dispersion	Score
3207	orange	j	8881	0.93	8270
3209	taxpayer	n	9140	0.90	8256
3213	furthermore	r	9594	0.86	8235

The 5,000 lemmas with the top score (frequency * dispersion) are those that appear in this frequency dictionary.

Collocates

A unique feature of this frequency dictionary is the listing of the top collocates (nearby words) for each of the 5,000 words in the frequency listing. These collocates provide important and useful insight into the meaning and use of the keyword. To find the collocates, we did the following. First, we decided which parts of speech to group together in order to rank the collocates and show the most frequent ones. In the case of verbs, we grouped noun collocates (subject: *the evidence supports what she said*, and object: *this supports the claim*), and all other collocates were grouped as miscellaneous (e.g. *with*, *directly*, *difficult*, and *prepare* for the verb *deal*). For nouns, we looked for adjectives (*green grass*), other nouns (*fire station*), and verbs (e.g. *desire to succeed*). For adjectives, we looked for nouns (*fast car*) and all other collocates were grouped as miscellaneous (*completely exhausted, willing to stay, black and white*). Finally, for adverbs and other parts of speech, we see collocates from all parts of speech listed together (*sharply reduce, fewer than, except for*).

To find the collocates for a given word, a computer program searched the entire 385-million-word corpus and looked at each context in which that word occurred. In all cases, the context (or "span") of words was four words to the left and four words to the right of the "node word". The overall frequency of the collocates in each of those contexts was then calculated, and the collocates were examined and rated by at least four native speakers.

Obviously, common words such as *the, of, to,* etc. were usually the most frequent collocates. To filter out these words, we set a Mutual Information (MI) threshold of about 2.5. The MI calculation took into account the overall frequency of each collocate, so that common words were usually eliminated from the list.

Using MI is sometimes more an art than a science. If the MI is set too low, then high frequency "noise words" show up as collocates, whereas if it is set too high, then only highly idiomatic collocates are found. As an example, the most frequent collocates of *break* as a verb—when the MI score is set high at 5.5—are: *deadlock, logjam, monotony, and stranglehold*. These are quite idiomatic and don't really show well the "core meaning" of *break*. On the other hand, the most frequent collocates

when the MI threshold is set very low at 1.0 are *down, into, up*, and *off*, which again do not provide a good sense of its meaning. Finally, however, when we set the MI threshold to 2.5, we find the most frequent collocates are: *heart, silence, rules, loose, leg, and barriers*, which (for native speakers, at least), probably do relate more to the core meaning and usage of *break*. But getting the MI threshold set just right for each of the 5,000 headwords was a bit daunting, to say the least. We hope that the data found here agree with your intuitions of what these words mean and how they are used.

The main frequency index

The main index in this dictionary is a rank-ordered listing of the top 5,000 words (lemma) in English, starting with the most frequent word (the definite article *the*) and progressing through to *parish*, *rejection*, and *mutter*, which are the last three words in the list. The following information is given for each entry:

> rank frequency (1, 2, 3, . . .), **lemma**, *part of speech*
>
> **collocates, grouped by part of speech and ordered by frequency**
>
> raw frequency, dispersion (0.00 – 1.00), (indication of register variation)

As a concrete example, let us look at the entry for the verb *break*:

> **501 break** *v*
> *n* .law, heart, news, .rule, silence, story, .ground, .barrier, leg, bone, .piece, .neck, arm, .cycle, voice.
> *misc* .into, .away, .free, .apart, .loose
>   **up** marriage, .fight, boyfriend, meeting., girlfriend, union, band, pass, .demonstration, .monotony
> **down** .into, .barrier, car., .cry, .door, .tear, talk., enzyme., completely, negotiation. **out** war., fight., fire., sweat, fighting., riot, violence., .laugh, .hive
> **off** piece, talk, .engagement, negotiation, branch, abruptly, .relation
> 72917 | 0.97

This entry shows that word number 501 in our rank order list is the verb *break*. The last line of the entry shows the raw frequency for the lemma (72,917 tokens) and the dispersion (.97 in this case). The collocates are given in the intervening lines. As can be seen, they are partially grouped by part of speech. In the case of verbs, we see the noun collocates and then other parts of speech (miscellaneous).

Note also that for some collocates, there is an indication of the placement of the collocate. When the [.] is before the collocate, this means that the node word (headword) is typically found before that collocate (**break** the _law_, **break** into _pieces_). When the [.] is after the collocate, this means that the node word is typically found after the collocate (_her voice_ **broke**, all _hell_ **broke** loose). This symbol can provide useful information, for example, on whether the collocates are subjects or objects of a given verb, or whether the node word noun acts as a subject or object of the verbal collocate. (Note, however, that with passives and relative clauses, the noun that is object of a verb will occur before the verb, which does confuse things a bit.) In order to display the [.] symbol, 80 percent or more of the tokens of a given collocate had to occur either before or after the node word. In the case of ADJ / NOUN and NOUN / ADJ, word order is typically so consistent (_blue house_, never *_house blue_) that the [.] is not used to show placement.

Finally, as is seen above, in the case of some verbs that can act as phrasal verbs (_break up_, _turn down_, _cut off_, etc.), these are listed in bold (with their own collocates) at the end of the regular collocates list for verbs. Phrasal verbs are only listed when they have a frequency of at least 1,000 in the corpus, and when there are at least three collocates with a frequency of at least five occurrences each.

Let us consider one other example:

3404 hypothesis _n_
_j_ null, following, consistent, alternative, working, general, initial, original, theoretical, competing _n_ study, support., result, test, research, testing, evidence, analysis, method, set _v_ .predict, suggest, reject, examine, confirm, base, develop, formulate, .state, .explain
9282 | 0.82 A

This entry is for _hypothesis_ (word #3404 in our list). As before, the collocates are listed in frequency order and grouped by part of speech. In this case, however, note that there is an [A] at the end of the entry. This indicates that the lemma _hypothesis_ occurs at least twice as frequently in the Academic genre as it does overall in the corpus (Spoken, Fiction, Magazines, Newspapers).

Thematic vocabulary ("call-out boxes")

Placed throughout the main frequency-based index are 31 "call-out boxes", which serve to display in one list a number of thematically related words. These include thematic lists of words related to the body, food, family, weather, professions, nationalities, colors, emotions, and several other semantic domains There are also lists of words that are much more common in each of the five main genres (spoken, fiction, popular magazines, newspapers, and academic) than overall, as well as comparisons of American and British vocabulary, as well as new words in the language. Finally, there are lists related to word formation issues, such as irregular past tense and irregular plurals, and common suffixes to create nouns, adjectives, and verbs. In each case, the entries are, of course, ordered by frequency.

Alphabetical and part of speech indexes

The alphabetical index contains all of the words listed in the frequency index. Each entry includes the following information: 1) lemma 2) part of speech, and 3) rank order frequency. The part of speech index contains the 5,000 words from the frequency index and the alphabetical index. Within each of the categories (noun, verb, adjective, etc.) the lemma are listed in order of descending frequency. Because each entry is linked to the other two indexes via the rank frequency number, each of the entries in this index contains only the rank frequency and lemma.

Electronic version

As was noted in the first section, if you find this dictionary valuable and would like to have a similar electronic version (somewhat fewer collocates, but more of other features), feel free to visit http://www.americancorpus.org/dictionary.

Delimitations and Notes

1 Frequency is form-based (lemma), not semantically based (homographs—_bank_, _run_; heterophones—_lead_ "metal" vs. _lead_ "be in front", _contract_ vs. _contract_, etc.). But our approach is an improvement over many similar frequency listings because the collocates give some indication of potential variant meanings. For example, take a look at the entries for _lead_ (n) [entry 1605] and _bow_ (n) [entry 4147]. For _lead_, there are collocates for the two meanings "metal" and "in front" and for _bow_ there are collocates for _bow_ in the context of "ship, arrow, hair, and violin".

2 Except in the case of high-frequency phrasal verbs, only single-word nodes were included. When a lemma occurs almost exclusively in a given multi-word expression (*as far as, in charge of, lots of*), that multi-word expression is listed as part of the entry.

3 All collocates are single-word collocates. In cases such as *in terms of, by means of*, etc., each of the collocates is listed separately.

4 The most frequent form of a given collocate lemma may be an inflected form, not the head word form as listed (e.g. *long* as a collocate of *no* almost always appears as *longer* in the corpus).

5 In general, proper nouns were not included in the dictionary, either as node words or collocates. However, a few highly salient proper noun collocates were included for certain node words (e.g. *Iraq* as a collocate of *invade*; *China* as a collocate of *export*).

References

Carroll, J.B., Davies, P., and Richman, B. (1971) *The American Heritage Word Frequency Book*. New York: American Heritage Publishing Co., Inc.

Cowie, A.P. (ed.) (1998) *Phraseology: Theory, Analysis, and Applications*. Oxford: Clarendon Press.

Coxhead, A. (2000) A new academic word list. *TESOL Quarterly*, 34(2): 213–238.

Crystal, D. (1995) *The Cambridge Encyclopedia of the English Language*. New York: Cambridge University Press.

Francis, W.N., and Kučera, H. (1982) *Frequency Analysis of English Usage: Lexicon and Grammar*. Boston: Houghton Mifflin.

Gardner, D. (2007) Validating the construct of "word" in applied corpus-based vocabulary research: A critical survey. *Applied Linguistics*, 28(2): 241–265.

Gardner, D., and Davies, M. (2007) Pointing out frequent phrasal verbs: A corpus-based analysis. *TESOL Quarterly*, 41(2): 339–359.

Johansson, S., and Hofland, K. (1989) *Frequency Analysis of English Vocabulary and Grammar: Based on the LOB Corpus: Volume 1: Tag Frequencies and Word Frequencies*. Oxford: Clarendon Press.

Leech, G., Rayson, P., and Wilson, A. (2001) *Word Frequencies in Written and Spoken English: Based on the British National Corpus*. London: Longman.

Nation, I.S.P. (2001) *Learning Vocabulary in Another Language*. Cambridge: Cambridge University Press.

Nesselhauf, N. (2005) *Collocations in a Learner Corpus*. Amsterdam: John Benjamins Publishing Company.

Read, J. (2000) *Assessing Vocabulary*. Cambridge: Cambridge University Press.

Rinsland, H.D. (1945) *A Basic Vocabulary of Elementary School Children*. New York: The Macmillan Company.

Thorndike, E.L., and Lorge, I. (1944) *The Teacher's Word Book of 30,000 Words*. New York: Columbia Teachers College.

West, M. (1953) *A General Service List of English Words*. London: Longman.

Frequency index

Format of entries

Rank frequency (1, 2, 3, . . .), **lemma**, *part of speech*

Collocates

Raw frequency | dispersion (0.00 – 1.00), (indication of register variation: Spoken, Fiction, Magazines, Newspapers, Academic)

Note that the collocates are grouped by part of speech and ordered by frequency (most frequent first). The [•] symbol indicates pre/post placement with regards to the headword.

---

1 the *a*
of, first, year, most, •world, over, •same, day, end, between, •United States, next, during•
20431716 | 0.99

2 be *v*
there, if, many, •able, long, always, likely, since, never, sure, often, •available, •aware, afraid
14338665 | 0.99

3 and *c*
her, their, other, up, between•, •then, both, back, over, year, down, off, family, friend
9893569 | 0.99

4 of *i*
out•, because•, front•, instead•, terms•, way, top•, ahead•, outside•, favor•, place, charge•, light, spite•
9585500 | 0.97

5 a *a*
•lot, •few, while, month, •single, •minute, •chance, •bit, •series, hour, •variety, •huge, •dozen, mile
8159297 | 0.99

6 in *i*
which, year, new, way, place, •world, life, school, country, case, •area, city, •United States, •fact
6475319 | 0.98

7 to *t*
in, want•, try•, back•, need•, able•, lead•, return•, allow•, enough•, continue, listen•, close•, refer•
5842936 | 0.99

8 have *v*
noun •trouble, •knack, •qualm, •repercussion, •recourse, •inkling, misgiving, •foresight *misc* already, •been, •done, •shown, •begun, •seen
4557421 | 0.98

9 to *i*
in, want•, try•, back•, need•, able•, lead•, return•, allow•, enough•, continue, listen•, close•, refer•
3561680 | 0.99

10 it *p*
think•, so, because, •seem, even, hard, •easy, •clear, whether•, •difficult, •possible, sound, worth, •impossible
3585308 | 0.97

11 I *p*
•think, know, like, •mean, •believe, love, guess, sure, myself, •remember, sorry, •wonder, wish, afraid
3655790 | 0.94 S F

12 that *c*
fact, believe•, suggest•, indicate•, argue•, realize•, note•, clear•, evidence•, ensure•, aware•, notion•, stuff, •correct
3174256 | 0.97

---

1. Animals

Note that several of these animals are also the mascot for sports teams or have figurative meaning (e.g. *pig, mole*), which would increase their overall frequency, and most of these are marked with parentheses in the following list.

[Top 80] dog *n* 49897, fish *n* 41277, bird 35610, horse 30042, chicken 23955, cat 20463, (bear) *n* 19980, fox 17303, turkey 15445, wolf 14452, deer 11259, (duck) *n* 11003, (tiger) 10210, cow 9755, mouse 9697, (eagle) 9395, snake 9387, lion 9260, rat 8115, (pig) 8048, (buffalo) 7678, cattle 7636, (hawk) *n* 7587, whale 6750, sheep 6172, bee 6148, shark 6035, rabbit 5927, monkey 5611, elephant 5562, goat 5330, worm *n* 5112, crab 4873, butterfly 4869, turtle 4667, crow *n* 4398, oyster 4328, frog 4304, goose *n* 4137, spider 4122, mosquito 4010, elk 3925, dolphin 3913, ant 3904, coyote 3850, lobster 3784, owl 3657, (falcon) 3626, mule 3111, (panther) 2972, (penguin) 2923, dove *n* 2906, squirrel 2832, camel 2825, (raven) 2673, (beetle) 2612, hog *n* 2298, moose 2231, pigeon 2225, ape 2203, pony 2194, swan 2059, donkey 1920, beaver 1895, (mole) 1860, gorilla 1694, alligator 1588, hare 1502, parrot 1456, crocodile 1426, bison 1327, leopard 1286, toad 1266, sparrow 1252, antelope 1168, quail 1122, ox 1117, raccoon 1092, gull 1068, heron 1057

13 for *i*
.year, reason, wait., need., while, support, .month, .minute, .hour, search., responsible., account., .second, prepare.
3024819 | 0.98

14 you *p*
know, if., get, think, want, see, tell, me, thank., ask, let, .need, mean, talk
2836681 | 0.92 S

15 he *p*
say, when., tell, like, ask, feel, before, himself, believe, though., .write, .add, speak, die
2676895 | 0.95 F

16 with *i*
deal., associate., fill., relationship., compare., contact., charge., interview., consistent., familiar., conversation., cope., .exception, comfortable.
2467038 | 0.99

17 on *i*
base., .side, focus., street, .floor, .ground, depend., .basis, effect., rely., impact., .list, attack., .page
2289891 | 0.99

18 do *v*
noun .homework, harm, me, .laundry, .talking, .disservice, .bidding, .housework, .push-up *misc* you, what, .not, .know, .think, want, why., mean, .believe, .care, .mind
2379017 | 0.95 S

19 's *g*
mother, father, nation., America., .office, China., driver., Japan., CNN., Saddam., ABC., Alzheimer., Hussein., Iran.
1990870 | 0.97

20 say *v*
noun official., expert., spokesman, analyst, critic., prosecutor., spokeswoman, diplomat *misc* .goodbye, .quietly, .softly, needless., .aloud, .proudly, .flatly, suffice., quoted
1767682 | 0.95

21 they *p*
because., so, .want, like, before, believe, themselves, once, decide, realize, eat, insist, .perceive, .deserve
1730878 | 0.97

22 this *d*
.year, .country, .case, .week, point, .morning, early., .season, month, .article, .stuff, .weekend, .summer, .particular
1741794 | 0.96 S

23 but *c*
.also, .for, .rather, nothing., necessarily, .nonetheless, .now, .reason, everything., truth, .moment, wear., .sake, whole
1634790 | 0.98

24 at *i*
look., .time, .university, .point, .end, .home, .level, stare., .center, .moment, .age, PM, .top, professor.
1625953 | 0.98

25 we *p*
.go, know, think, so., .see, our, .need, .talk, .want, .hear, before, believe, .learn, ourselves
1685647 | 0.94 S

26 his *a*
hand, .own, .head, .wife, .eye, father, face, arm, .mother, shake., .son, .brother, .career, .shoulder
1657234 | 0.95 F

27 from *i*
range., different, remove., prevent., benefit., suffer., across, emerge., separate., derive., mile., .perspective, distance., .beginning
1509499 | 0.99

28 that *d*
fact., believe., suggest., indicate., argue., realize., note., clear., evidence., ensure., aware., notion., stuff, .correct
1580403 | 0.94 S

29 not *x*
.only, .enough, .yet, .sure, or., whether., simply, certainly., .necessarily, .mention, .anymore, .proofread, .surprising, .merely
1520589 | 0.98

30 n't *x*
do., can., .know, .want, .any, why, .anything, really, .enough, .understand, .care, .anymore, .worry, .matter
1505529 | 0.94

31 by *i*
own, cause., surround., back, influence., affect., .inch, accompany., replace., publish., inspire., mark, fund, dominate.
1386130 | 0.96

32 or *c*
either., whether., minute., hour, .whatever, month, search, modify., .otherwise, sooner., mile., .depending
1271634 | 0.97

33 she *p*
her, say, like, herself, before, realize, cry, marry, soon, whisper, pregnant, reply, asleep, softly
1345504 | 0.91 F

34 as *c*
well, such., much., long., such., far., same., .result, .part, .though, soon., serve., .possible, describe.
1197642 | 0.98

35 what *d*
do, know., about, .happen, tell, like, .mean, .call, exactly., matter, .wrong, wonder., .hell, .supposed
1090516 | 0.95 S

36 go *v*
noun .bed, .bathroom, .mile, .nut, .berserk, jail
misc .through, let., .home, .away, .happen, .ahead, .beyond, .sleep, .anywhere, .crazy
on what., .inside, list., .forever, hell, fighting., .length, .usual, heck., .indefinitely **off** bomb., alarm., siren., beeper., bulb., pager., .tangent, firework., flashbulb., firecracker. **back** let., .home, .forth, .sleep, .inside, .upstairs, .downstairs, .jail **up** .flame, .smoke, curtain., cheer., eyebrow., .dramatically, roar., .chimney **down** sun., .tube, swelling., .breakfast, Titanic **out** .dinner, .public, party, breakfast
1059397 | 0.93 S

37 their *a*
.own, child, .life, .home, parent, .ability, .daughter, .counterpart, .peer, .identity, .neighbor, .respective, relative, .participation
999740 | 0.97

38 will *v*
able, continue, probably, soon, hope, likely, tomorrow, eventually, forget, predict, bet, hopefully, forever, ultimately
994085 | 0.97

39 who *p*
people., those., man., one., woman., .live, someone., person., guy., anyone., care, individual., somebody., anybody.
940258 | 0.98

40 can *v*
you, not, help, afford, anything, imagine, easily, anyone, handle, possibly, achieve, trust, anybody, anywhere, hardly
913100 | 0.98

41 get *v*
noun .job, chance, trouble, .call, help, message, .sleep, .impression *misc* better, .home, .rid, .ready, .marry, .involved, .sick, .closer, .married, worse
  out .there, .vote, .alive, ahead, .safely, .underneath, wallet, .handkerchief, bail, .checkbook **back** .home, .together, .normal, .track, .basic, .touch, till, eager., anxious. **up** .walk, .early, .speed, slowly, .nerve, .courage, .dawn, .pace, abruptly **off** .bus, .easy, .ass, .butt, .lightly, .scot-free, .duff
912273 | 0.95 S

42 if *c*
.you, even., ask, wonder., .ever, .anything, .necessary, mind., .somebody, .desire, lucky, .convict, .correctly
862083 | 0.97

43 all *d*
after., well, above., .sort, .along, while, .stuff, virtually., equal, .ingredient, .due
824478 | 0.98

44 would *v*
probably, otherwise, prefer, predict, surely, normally, dare, differently, someday, tolerate, presumably, inevitably
826270 | 0.97

45 her *a*
she, .she, hand, mother, .eye, .husband, .own, .head, tell., .face, .father, hair, arm, .daughter
873868 | 0.91 F

46 make *v*
noun decision, .sense, money, .difference, .mistake, point, choice, change, effort, statement, progress, movie, sound, .love, deal *misc* .sure, .feel, .easy, .clear, .possible, .difficult, .impossible, .worse
  up .mind, .percent, .story, .own, group, .difference, .lost, try., .majority, mostly **out** can., .word, barely., check, .shape, .bandit
788981 | 0.98

47 about *i*
talk., what, think., how, tell., worry., something, question., write., hear., care., learn., information., story.
804060 | 0.96 S

48 my *a*
.mother, .father, life, .own, .friend, hand, .head, .eye, .wife, .mind, .husband, .brother, .son, .name
835092 | 0.93 F

49 know *v*
noun guy, truth, stuff, hell, .certainty, whereabouts, .bound *misc* you., do., .what, .how, everyone, .exactly, everybody, nobody., anybody, .firsthand, instinctively, .intimately, collectively
816733 | 0.93 S

50 as *i*
well, such., much., long., such., far., same., .result, .part, .though, soon., serve., .possible, describe.
765651 | 0.95 A

51 there *e*
.no, .lot, .nothing, .something, .little, .reason, .evidence, .difference, .enough, .doubt, .plenty, .significant, .wrong, .sign
732394 | 0.96 S

52 one *m*
no., .thing, .day, only., .most, another, .another, only., .reason, .side, least., .person, each, example
710388 | 0.99

53 up *r*
pick., come., grow., set., give., end., .to, show., stand., wake., hold., bring., open., catch.
731495 | 0.96

54 time *n*
adj long, short, hard, tough, prime, present, given, spare *noun* year, period, day, minute, lot., week, amount., space, couple. *verb* spend., waste., cook, devote, .elapse, shorten.
705209 | 0.99

55 year *n*
adj old, past, new, recent, previous, fiscal, following, married, junior, coming *noun* time, school, percent, couple., age, .prison *verb* spend., die, pass, serve, last., publish, born, sentence., average, precede
714235 | 0.96 N

56 so *r*
.much, .many, .far, why, .long, and., .forth, fast, .hard, thanks., .badly, .excited, .proud, .glad
692883 | 0.95 S

57 think *v*
noun people, thing, lot, reason, moment, mistake, nonsense, coincidence, retrospect *misc* I., you, do., we, .about, what, well, really, .important, maybe, probably, ever, everybody, anybody, frankly
  through .problem, carefully, .consequence, .implication, .situation, opportunity. **up** .idea, .name, .excuse, whoever. **back** when, .over
712569 | 0.92 S

58 see *v*
noun face, .table, ID, .picture, movie, .note, mirror, .listing, neighbor, .image(s), .caption, .hardcopy, .outline, .silhouette, daylight *misc* never., ever., .again, anyone, nice., clearly, .tomorrow, surprised., glad., rarely.
646789 | 0.96

59 which *d*
.mean, .include, .turn, extent., .allow, .require, produce, determine, describe, .represent, .contain, .occur, .involve, feature
637504 | 0.96

60 when *c*
.come, even., home, ago., especially., .arrive, .finally, .finish, pregnant, asleep
626830 | 0.98

61 some *d*
.kind, .sort, .extent, .degree, .critic, .analyst, .instance, .advice, .mile, .observer
625074 | 0.98

62 them *p*
tell., give., help., let., put., keep., among., bring., allow., behind., watch., send., teach., kill
627443 | 0.97

63 people *n*
adj other, young, American, poor, ordinary, native, homeless, innocent, elderly, gay *noun* lot., thing, way, number., group., thousand. *verb* .live, kill, .die, .vote, encourage., hire, employ, trust, attract, interview
640236 | 0.95 S

64 take *v*
noun .place, .care, .look, .step, .advantage, action, .break, picture, .account, .risk, position, month, .responsibility, .course, approach *misc* long, .away, .seriously, home, .deep
   off .clothes, .shoe, plane., .hat, .shirt, .coat, .jacket, .glass, career. **out** .loan, .ad, pocket, .wallet, .garbage, .cigarette, .trash, .handkerchief, .full-page **on** .role, .responsibility, .meaning, .task, .challenge, .significance, ready., .importance **up** .space, .residence, .position, .arm, .cause, .slack, .challenge, .golf **over** communist., instinct., .CEO
618291 | 0.98

65 me *p*
tell., let., give., ask, go, help., feel, excuse., remind., please, next, bother., front., strike.
651474 | 0.92 F

66 out *r*
.there, come., find., point., turn., figure., pull., carry., check., .window, reach.
624776 | 0.96

67 into *i*
turn., .room, move., fall., walk., break., step., transform., .account, divide., translate., throw., enter., .space
616067 | 0.97

68 just *r*
.as, .about, let, .few, .minute, .moment, .month, case, second, hour, .fine, .below, .plain, .mile
620284 | 0.95 S

69 him *p*
tell., see., give., look, ask., want, let., call., behind., help., around, leave, keep, love.
623094 | 0.93 F

70 come *v*
noun .term, .conclusion, minute, .grip, .stop, .rescue, .stair, me, .realization, announcement., verdict, reply, .fruition, knock, .prominence
misc .from, when., .here, .home, next, .together, .along, .close, .forward, soon, .surprise, .closer, .alive, .clean, tomorrow
   up .next, sun., .short, graphics, .empty-handed, .renewal, .parole **out** .clean, .support, toothpick., .favor, .publicly, paperback **down** .pike, .aisle, .breakfast, .chimney **on** oh., honey, aw., .sweetheart **back** when., .haunt, .anytime
580705 | 0.96

71 your *a*
.own, .life, .hand, .body, .friend, .father, .mind, .name, call, .heart, .arm, .doctor, .search, .husband
599233 | 0.93 M

72 now *r*
right., from, by, year, join., until., month, OK., minute, till.
562129 | 0.95 S

73 could *v*
n't, hear, anything, imagine, easily, wish, possibly, afford, anyone, hardly, handle, barely, smell, anywhere
551669 | 0.96

74 than *c*
more., less., rather., better., year, much., any, rather., other., high., percent, far., .ever, .million
534727 | 0.97

75 like *i*
look., feel., something., sound., seem., look., feel., anything., she, act., kind, treat., smell., sort
522132 | 0.96

76 other *j*
noun people, hand, thing, side, word, country, group, day, member, area, part *misc* any, among, such, unlike, ethnic, relative, apart, countless
507990 | 0.98

77 then *r*
back, again, .turn, since., until, minute., .suddenly, second., pause, .slowly, hesitate., first., .sudden, briefly
502369 | 0.95 F

78 how *r*
do, know, about, .much, .many, .long, .feel, learn., show., matter., understand., wonder., explain, teach.
493994 | 0.97

79 its *a*
.own, because, despite., share, .ability, .original, .neighbor, .content, .annual, .nuclear, .citizen, .ally, .mission, .root
499968 | 0.95

80 two *m*
.year, .week, .three, between., day, .ago, .month, .hour, .later, .decade, past., minute, .hundred, separate
472824 | 0.99

81 our *a*
.own, .society, .guest, .culture, .understanding, .tonight, .goal, .web, focus, .discussion, conversation, .studio, .troop, .ally
482025 | 0.97

82 more *r*
.than, even., become., much., .likely, .important, less, far., .often, .difficult
476489 | 0.97

83 these *d*
.day, .guy, result, .finding, .factor, none., .item, .folk, .works, .variable, .circumstance, characteristic, .allegation, .creature
476474 | 0.95 A

84 want *v*
noun me, anytime., .millionaire, .revenge, mommy, .assurance, .autograph, .reassurance, .gratification, .companionship *misc* I., do, what, if, know, really., something, .talk, .hear, anything, sure, whatever., .stay, .marry, desperately
474852 | 0.95 S

85 way *n*
adj only, best, long, different, better, easy, wrong, effective *noun* people, life, thing, .thinking, variety., harm. *verb* find., change, act, pave., behave, explore, clear., interpret, block, alter
433369 | 0.98

86 no *a*
there., .one, .idea, .reason, .question, .matter, .what, need, .evidence, .doubt, oh., .know, .difference, .sign
430839 | 0.98

87 look *v*
noun eye, window, face, picture, shoulder, .mirror, .watch, sky, foot, .clock, .ceiling, me, .clue *misc* .at, .like, .forward, .pretty, .ahead, .closely, .straight, beautiful, .carefully, .surprised
   up .at, .smile, suddenly, .startle, .surprise, .sharply, barely., .briefly **out** .window, .over, .onto, balcony, .rear, .windshield, .porthole **down** .at, .upon, .nose, .barrel, balcony, railing, aisle **around** nervously, .wildly, frantically, .desperately, .suspiciously, anxiously **back** .forth, pause., .fondly, .nostalgically **on** .helplessly, .amazement, .approvingly
451967 | 0.93 F

88 first *m*
.time, year, .place, since, .step, .month, .week, .lady, .half, .amendment, .season, .round, .quarter, .visit
427866 | 0.98

89 also *r*
but., .include, .provide, .note, .available, .indicate, .contribute
429795 | 0.96

90 new *j*
noun year, world, technology, book, way, life, system, job, law, idea, product, development *misc* create, build, whole, introduce, relatively, entirely, exciting
403451 | 0.97

91 because *c*
.of, part, .its, simply., partly., afraid, interesting., precisely., part., largely., .lack, partly., mainly., .nature
404444 | 0.96 S

92 day *n*
adj single, past, final, following, sunny, previous, very, present, given *noun* time, hour., night, school, couple., work, .care, election *verb* spend., remember, arrive, last., miss, wake, celebrate, rain, .dawn
398807 | 0.97

93 more *d*
.than, .year, much., any, .million, little., .information, percent, .money, spend., .half, nothing., lot., .hour
386475 | 0.97

94 use *v*
noun word, method, technique, term, data, technology, computer, drug, force, model, tool, material, test, approach, measure *misc* instead, standard, widely, commonly., frequently, multiple
   up .all, more, .energy, .resource, .oxygen, already., quickly, minute, .half, reserve
388459 | 0.95 A

95 man *n*
adj young, old, black, white, dead, tall, rich, unidentified, handsome *noun* woman, way, face, family, group, kind, sex, .basketball *verb* .name, .wear, marry, .accuse, enlist., shout, date, rape, wound, rob
379282 | 0.95 F

96 here *r*
come., right., over., live., around., stay., sit., .tonight, minute
381190 | 0.93 S

97 find *v*
noun .way, study., body, .evidence, .document, difference, .topic, researcher., .solution, .answer, survey., .spot, jury., poll., investigator. *misc* try., .himself, .themselves, .myself, hard, difficult, .similar, easy, .guilty, .yourself, .ourselves, surprised.
   out .what, .about, how, if, when, .who, .where, .why, .whether, later
361174 | 0.98

98 give *v*
noun money, .opportunity, .birth, name, information, .look, .credit, .sense, advice, .idea, speech, .rise, attention, .example, .choice *misc* .away, willing., .quick, .extra, .damn, .time, freely, charitable, generously
   up never., .hope, .run, finally., willing., refuse., .control, ready., .fight, .hit **out** .information, award, knee., ticket, .condom **in** finally., .temptation, refuse.
355233 | 0.99

99 thing *n*
adj other, good, only, whole, bad, important, right, different, best, certain *noun* kind., people, lot., way, sort., number., couple. *verb* do, .happen, change, learn, accomplish, fix, .bother, straighten, complicate., amaze
368950 | 0.95 S

100 well *r*
as, very., might., yeah, yes, oh., pretty., .enough, .certainly, OK, .guess, .obviously, .suit, extremely.
381873 | 0.91 S

101 many *d*
as, so., .people, how., .other, .year, too., .American, including, .whom, .hour, .expert, .species, .resident
357909 | 0.97

102 only *r*
not., .one, .few, .percent, .month, .half, .minute, .hour, .recently, second, .slightly, .handful, .mile, .fraction
351851 | 0.98

103 those *d*
.who, among., especially., similar., particularly., .whom, .responsible, .circumstance, comparable.
348615 | 0.97

104 tell *v*
noun story, .truth, mother, friend, .reporter, doctor, police, tale, mom, .joke, lie, dad, .jury, investigator, secret *misc* .me, .us, .about, something, anyone, .exactly, please., somebody, anybody, far., repeatedly, reportedly.
358443 | 0.94 F

105 very *r*
.much, .good, .well, .important, .difficult, .little, .different, .hard, .few, .close, .strong, .clear, .nice, .interesting
364993 | 0.92 S

106 one *p*
no., .thing, .day, only., .most, another, .another, only., .reason, .side, least., .person, each, example
341358 | 0.98

107 even *r*
.more, before, maybe., perhaps., sometimes.,
.harder, .bother, possibly., .faster, .modest,
.remotely
332970 | 0.98

108 her *p*
she, .she, hand, mother, .eye, .husband, .own, .head,
tell., .face, .father, hair, arm, .daughter
360798 | 0.89 F

109 back *r*
go., come., then, look., bring., turn., .home, .forth,
.again, pull., welcome., step., send.
338105 | 0.94 F

110 any *d*
.other, than, more, without., .kind, .idea, far, .sense,
.given, evidence., .particular, nor., .chance, .sort
323350 | 0.98

111 good *j*
noun morning, thing, news, time, night, idea,
job, evening, luck, reason, friend, man *misc* very,
feel, pretty, bad, enough, sound, welcome,
excellent
326515 | 0.96 S

112 us *p*
tell., join., give., our, let., help., bring., allow., rest.,
.morning, remind., thanks., teach., none.
324563 | 0.95 S

113 through *i*
run., pass., .door, walk., .window, process, air,
.interpreter, .glass, hole, .crowd, .gate, .forest,
.wood
312803 | 0.98

114 woman *n*
adj young, old, white, pregnant, beautiful, married,
sexual, single, poor, elderly *noun* man, group,
percent, .age, role, number., lot., .movement, voice,
sex *verb* .wear, marry, dress, rape, date, exclude,
abuse, murder, portray, .undergo
316521 | 0.96

115 life *n*
adj real, whole, human, personal, daily, everyday,
private, normal, entire *noun* way, people, rest.,
quality., family, .death, .insurance, .expectancy
verb live, save., change, spend., improve., risk.,
affect., enjoy., .depend, enrich.
307607 | 0.98

116 child *n*
adj young, gifted, poor, foster, healthy, educational,
elementary, pregnant, emotional, unborn
noun parent, school, care, woman., age, wife.,
.abuse, education, health, need *verb* raise., .learn,
teach, protect., adopt, .attend, educate., treat, bear,
encourage
310257 | 0.94

117 there *r*
out., right, over., sit., stand., stay., somewhere, troop.,
Hi, nobody
306070 | 0.93 S

118 down *r*
sit., come., look., put., break., shut., slow., turn.,
bring., lay., walk., pull., calm., settle.
303634 | 0.94 F

119 work *v*
noun way, hour, project, artist, employee., strategy.,
scientist., factory, engineer, .shift, crew, .magic,
consultant, nurse, wage *misc* .hard, how., .together,
best, .toward, .closely, .harder, willing.
   out thing., detail, deal, problem, everything., gym,
agreement, arrangement, .fine, kink **up** .sweat,
.courage, .nerve, .appetite
292598 | 0.98

120 after *i*
year, .all, day, month, year, week, hour, .war, shortly.,
day, .death, minute, few, month
286751 | 0.98

121 call *v*
noun name, police, information, phone, .attention,
doctor, meeting, .help, .shot, witness, telephone.,
.cop, critic., technique., reservation *misc* .himself,
.themselves, sometimes., please., .quit, commonly.,
.toll-free, repeatedly, affectionately., jokingly.
   out .name, voice., .help, wave, .greeting, .softly,
.warning, .loudly, cheerfully, announcer. **in** military,
listener., caller., .investigate, .advise **up** reserve,
reservist, .image, .memory, somebody
285031 | 0.97

122 may *v*
able, although, suggest, contain, affect, occur,
whatever, prove, contribute, reflect, due, useful,
herein, vary, ultimately
289764 | 0.95

123 world *n*
adj new, large, real, whole, outside, wide, natural,
modern, developing, entire *noun* .war, .trade,
.center, rest., .series, .bank, .cup, .championship,
.organization, view *verb* enter., travel., explore.,
dominate, rule, compete, transform, conquer.,
shock.
282318 | 0.97

124 over *i*
.year, all., .past, .last, .next, control., .head, .period,
.heat, .decade, debate., .shoulder, .month, .course
277010 | 0.98

125 should *v*
noun priority, caution, precedence, hindsight,
wake-up *misc* why, maybe, whether, able, consider,
therefore, encourage, aware, emphasize, interpret,
resign, publish, ideally, ashamed
276994 | 0.98

126 still *r*
.alive, .ahead, .exist, large, .struggle, .plenty,
.asleep, .intact, perfectly., .unknown, .unclear,
.reel, .pending, .infancy
273411 | 0.97

127 try *v*
noun .luck, trick, tribunal, doorknob, juvenile,
.treason, .acupuncture, hypnosis *misc* .get, .find,
keep, again, .figure, stop, .explain, .kill, decide,
.avoid, .convince, .save, .catch, .imagine
   out .new, .idea, .different, .various, chance.,
opportunity., .recipe, .variety, exercise, eager.
271536 | 0.96

128 in *r*
come., .addition, .part, general, .particular, bring.,
move., .short, .public, .common
263029 | 0.98

129 school *n*
adj high, public, elementary, middle, private, medical, secondary, junior *noun* student, year, .district, teacher, law., .system, .counselor, .board *verb* attend., teach, graduate., drop, finish., enter, enroll
279025 | 0.92

130 as *r*
.well, .much, .many, just., .possible, might., .usual, twice., .early, .important, .fast, almost., .quickly
259848 | 0.98

131 last *m*
.year, .week, .night, .month, over., .season, day, .few, .summer, .fall, during., .decade, game, .five
267650 | 0.95 N

132 ask *v*
noun question, .help, doctor, participant, respondent, .permission, reporter, judge, mom, .advice, .opinion, .forgiveness, favor, questionnaire, neighbor *misc* if, .about, why, .whether, .yourself, .nod, specifically, frequently., .shrug, quietly, repeatedly, politely, dare., .rhetorically
  around .about, .find, so., start., after, .town **out** girl, .date, never.
262196 | 0.95

133 too *r*
.much, .many, far, .late, .long, little, .often, .bad, .soon, .fast, .busy
258435 | 0.96

134 need *v*
noun .help, money, information, support, skill, attention, assistance, .protection, assessment, surgery, improvement, sleep, .repair, educator., .approval *misc* we., more, really., something, understand, someone, care, desperately., .address, somebody, realize, badly
251436 | 0.98

135 three *m*
.year, two., .time, .day, .four, .month, .week, .ago, about., .hour, .later, five, least., past.
246708 | 0.98

136 feel *v*
noun way, pain, .need, sense, .pressure, heart, presence, .heat, foot, relief, guilt, stomach, emotion, breath, .warmth *misc* .like, make., .good, .better, really, .comfortable, .bad, .sorry, .guilty, .safe, .strongly
253108 | 0.95

137 when *r*
time., come, day., happen., start, remember., moment., night., occur., die, .arrive, period., month., arise
245736 | 0.97

138 become *v*
noun .part, .friend, .player, .citizen, .reality, .symbol, .victim, .target, .partner, .focus, .chairman, .champion, habit, .hit, .priority *misc* .more, .increasingly, .clear, .less, .important, .aware, .apparent, .popular, .involved, soon., quickly., .available, .familiar
240927 | 0.97

139 state *n*
adj federal, local, western, current, united, eastern, mental, African, northern, sovereign *noun* secretary., law, government, new, court, official, .park, agency, .legislature *verb* require, declare, adopt, impose, regulate, grant, approve, enact, sue, prohibit
246927 | 0.94

140 never *r*
.see, .before, .again, .hear, .anything, .forget, .mind, .happen, .meet, .able, .anyone, .quite, .anybody, .fully
?41641 | 0.96

141 between *i*
difference., .two, relationship., connection., distinction., relation., link., gap., correlation., significant., line, conflict., tension., interaction.
244066 | 0.94 A

142 high *j*
noun school, level, rate, price, cost, score, risk, standard, pressure, foot, quality, degree *misc* low, graduate, above, relatively, attend, extremely, all-time, pile
235590 | 0.95

143 something *p*
about, like, there., .else, .happen, .wrong, .different, other, maybe, .special, somebody, .terrible, .strange, ought
234865 | 0.95

144 really *r*
.want, like, .good, .need, never., .care, .matter, .hard, .nice, .interesting, no., .appreciate, nobody., .kind
241772 | 0.92 S

---

2. Body

Note that some of the most frequency terms for parts of the body also have extensive use in more general meanings, e.g. *head, face, back,* etc.

(hand) *n* 216096, eye *n* 164906, (head) *n* 153507, (face) *n* 121890, (back) *n* 119858, (arm) *n* 81390, hair 66086, leg *n* 45525, shoulder *n* 42413, finger *n* 40336, (mouth) *n* 39330, ear 28370, (foot) *n* 27547, knee *n* 24805, neck *n* 24789, lip 24015, breast 21781, chest 21475, nose *n* 21357, tooth 19531, stomach *n* 13306, cheek 12673, hip *n* 12354, tongue *n* 11308, heel *n* 10079, toe 9079, elbow *n* 8571, thumb *n* 8261, wrist 7855, forehead 7677, chin 7558, belly 7515, fist 7443, ankle 7080, thigh 6261, waist 6064, eyebrow 5878, beard 5641, (calf) 3869, nostril 1970, armpit 896, toenail 660, moustache 585, collarbone 504

145 most *r*
one., .important, .thing, .part, .likely, .recent,
perhaps., .popular, for., .common, the., among,
.powerful, .often
228469 | 0.96

146 another *d*
one, one., yet., .person, .reason, .example, .minute,
month, .hour, .factor, .round, .option, .edition,
.aspect
222798 | 0.99

147 much *d*
as, so., too., how., that, very., thank., .more, spend.,
.money, pretty., love, thanks., .less
226091 | 0.97

148 own *d*
their., his., her., its., my., your., our., life, .experience,
mind, .personal, .identity, .version, .sake
222619 | 0.98

149 family *n*
adj whole, extended, royal, entire, poor, nuclear,
immediate, wealthy, middle-class, low-income
noun member, friend, child, life, .history, support,
parent, .planning *verb* live, raise, own, visit, gather,
feed., belong, extend, reunite, .flee
222823 | 0.96

150 out *i*
(out of) .of, get., come., way, run., pull., .door,
.control, .car, walk., .business, .bed, .sight, step.
223561 | 0.96

151 house *n*
adj empty, safe, halfway, two-story, haunted,
Victorian, suburban, single-family, Republican,
neat *noun* white., .committee, .representative,
Senate, speaker, .night, leader, chairman, majority,
opera. *verb* build, leave., buy., pass, sell, enter.,
clean., burn, .vote, paint
223341 | 0.96

152 leave *v*
noun .room, .house, .office, .message, .town, .mark,
note, photograph., hour, .impression, .trail,
.apartment, foot, gap, .wake *misc* .behind, before,
.alone, .home, without, .open, soon, pack.
  over .from, money., enough., whatever., plenty.,
energy., material., debris. **out** feel., detail, feeling.,
.key, completely., .critical, conveniently.
221568 | 0.96

153 put *v*
noun .hand, .money, .arm, .pressure, .foot, .finger,
.risk, .position, effort, .perspective, .hold, .gun, .jail,
.emphasis, .clothes *misc* .together, .away, .aside,
.behind, .forward, simply, .forth
  down .root, .phone, .fork, .pen, .rebellion,
.gun, .weapon, .knife **out** .fire, .hand, .statement,
.cigarette, .album, press, .flag, .flame **on** .clothes,
.weight, .suit, dress, .uniform, .clean, .fresh, .brave
up .fight, .money, .sign, willing., .sale, .fence, .poster,
.adoption
219537 | 0.96

154 old *j*
noun year, man, woman, friend, day, age, house, lady,
boy, world, school, building *misc* enough, tired, plain,
wise, wooden, fashioned, dear, faithful
218220 | 0.96

155 on *r*
go., what., come., take., move., put., hold., hang.,
keep., later., carry., .board, early.
218932 | 0.95

156 while *c*
.other, wait, .maintain, .simultaneously, alive, .retain,
.await, asleep, .pregnant, .latter
215613 | 0.97

157 mean *v*
noun .disrespect, compliment *misc* really, .anything,
.nothing, necessarily., exactly, absolutely, obviously,
literally, deal, basically, .harm, though., interpret.,
phrase, insult
222520 | 0.93 S

158 let *v*
noun .look, minute, .break, .hook, .temperature, pan,
oven., .steam, .imagination, caller *misc* .me, .go,
.him, just, .us, .ask, .talk, .tell, .start, .alone, .face,
please., .listen, .forget, .cool
  out .breath, .sigh, .long, .scream, school., .little,
.cry, .deep, .whoop, .loud
222257 | 0.93 S

159 why *r*
.do, that, so, ask, .shall, reason., explain., understand.,
wonder., .choose, .anyone, .bother, explanation.
217080 | 0.95 S

160 president *n*
adj past, elected, incumbent, outgoing, interim,
executive, Republican, advisory, loyal, incoming
noun vice., year, office, .CEO, college *verb* elect., sign,
support, announce, appoint, name, .propose, declare,
.veto, urge
226653 | 0.91 S

161 keep *v*
noun .eye, .mind, .track, .secret, record, .pace,
.mouth, promise, .peace *misc* .out, try, .alive, .off,
.away, .open, enough., .warm, .close, .low, .safe,
.quiet, .busy, .clean, order.
  up .with, can., try., .good, .demand, struggle., able.
on just., .until, .walk, .fight, hit, .push, .roll, .tick
212682 | 0.97

162 same *d*
.time, .as, .thing, .way, much., .kind, .period, exactly.,
share., .true, .amount, apply, .size, exact.
206339 | 0.99

163 great *j*
noun deal, thing, power, number, job, idea,
place, opportunity, story, depression, guy, success
misc significantly, lesser, all-time, horned, seeing,
vastly, all-around
207716 | 0.97

164 begin *v*
noun year, process, career, month, season, series, trial,
construction, journey, .video, .clip, investigation,
painting, search, minute *misc* before, already., soon,
immediately, .cry, .wonder, slowly, .realize
203712 | 0.98

165 big *j*
noun deal, problem, thing, man, company, city,
question, difference, business, house, issue, game
misc enough, ten, fat, bold, at-large, bid, hairy,
accounting
207702 | 0.95

166 seem _v_
noun moment, idea, surface, glance, argument, possibility, solution, comparison, .eternity, consensus, odds, .verge _misc_ always., almost, though, .likely, everything, .clear, everyone, .quite, .unlikely, .notice, suddenly, .happy, strange, .obvious, somehow
204008 | 0.97

167 group _n_
adj small, ethnic, different, social, various, local, terrorist, nonprofit, working, experimental _noun_ member, .people, age., control., interest., advocacy. _verb_ form, join, support, represent, compare, organize, belong, divide., .consist, .oppose
212763 | 0.93 A

168 country _n_
adj other, developing, European, foreign, developed, African, whole, industrialized, Asian, entire _noun_ people, world, .club, .music, region, home, rest., .road, population, house _verb_ travel., flee., defend., cross., divide, rebuild., invade, vary., rule, occupy
207668 | 0.94

169 talk _v_
noun .phone, hour, .politics, reporter, .stranger, neighbor, .me, trash, counselor, .nonsense, .specific, .whisper, .smack, pollster, headset _misc_ .about, let., listen, someone, everybody, nobody., somebody, anybody, willing., refuse., welcome., .anymore, .openly, .loud, .publicly
211571 | 0.92 S

170 problem _n_
adj big, serious, real, social, major, environmental, economic, potential, medical, financial _noun_ solution, health., behavior, .solving, drug, lot., kind., heart., approach, answer. _verb_ solve., face, address., deal., create, resolve, fix., pose, .arise, .exist
203641 | 0.96

171 where _c_
.live, area., room., exactly., town., spot., near., .belong, hotel., neighborhood., kitchen., .born, locate, bedroom.
197189 | 0.98

172 turn _v_
noun head, light, .attention, eye, face, .page, .corner, .radio, .television, wheel, key, camera, .profit, tide, .volume _misc_ .away, .toward, slowly, quickly, .red, .left, .upside, suddenly
   up .heat, .volume, .nose, search., collar, .thermostat, .notch, unexpectedly, mysteriously. **down** .offer, .request, .volume, .invitation, .thermostat, .promotion, .alley, politely. **out** .light, .differently, voter, .badly, .cheer, .drove, impeccably. **over** document, .rein, .confidential, .day-to-day, voluntarily **off** .heat, .ignition, switch, .flashlight, microphone **around** slowly, .troubled, abruptly, urge., .struggling **back** .toward, .clock, tide
203724 | 0.94 F

173 student _n_
adj black, female, special, medical, male, physical, educational, fellow, diverse, doctoral _noun_ school, teacher, college, university, group, class, graduate., learning, parent, number. _verb_ .learn, help., teach, provide, allow., .receive, require, encourage, .attend, .participate
229864 | 0.83 A

174 every _a_
.day, .time, .year, .night, .week, almost., .single, .morning, .month, .minute, hour, nearly., once, virtually.
195342 | 0.97

175 hand _n_
adj other, right, left, free, upper, outstretched, warm, soft, steady, wet _noun_ head, .shoulder, arm, man, finger, .pocket, .mouth, palm, woman, chest _verb_ hold, put., shake, raise., reach, place., wave., wash., touch, grab
207369 | 0.92 F

176 help _v_
noun .student, .concept, document., topic., other, teacher, .victim, .client, foot, .balance, neighbor, .me, .chore, .learner _misc_ can., .us, .understand, .develop, .create, .build, similar., .discuss, .below, .explain, .overcome, .rebuild
   out .with, there, around, friend, .lot, volunteer., willing., able., neighbor, glad.
194798 | 0.97

177 against _i_
.wall, war, lean., fight., charge., press., proofread., vote., check., .track, protect., game., action., .Iraq
194244 | 0.97

178 start _v_
noun year, business, season, fire, career, month, engine, minute, foot, beginning, conversation, shooting, fight, rumor, bidding _misc_ before., .again, .walk, .cry, .laugh, immediately, .sing, slowly, .scream, .crying, .scratch, singing
   up .again, car, engine, .conversation, motor, .trail, .ladder, furnace **out** .as, .slowly, .slow, .innocently, .promisingly **over** .again, .scratch, .somewhere **off** .down, .slow, .badly
195922 | 0.96

179 American _j_
noun people, association, history, society, culture, life, public, woman, study, troop, company, art
200408 | 0.94

180 part _n_
adj large, important, integral, only, better, various, hardest, essential, spare _noun_ .life, body, .country, .process, time, .history, .town, .brain, auto., .package _verb_ become., play., form., consist, divide., constitute., assemble, concur, stem, comprise
192302 | 0.98

181 show _v_
noun study., figure, poll., table, .sign, research., result, picture, record., data., evidence, .interest, .difference, image, photograph _misc_ .little, recent., .significant, clearly, consistently
   up people, just., .work, .late, fail, .unannounced, cop., bother., .everywhere, regularly **off** proudly., eager., .talent, proud.
191859 | 0.98

182 about _r_
.year, .percent, just., .minute, .million, only., .mile, .hour, .half, .ago, bring., .three, .five, .month
192185 | 0.97

183 over _r_
take., .year, .there, turn., .again, walk., hand., all., .shoulder, million, roll., pull., lean.
192431 | 0.96 F

184 might *v*
noun possibility, clue *misc* able, expect, consider, suggest, otherwise, wonder, whatever, imagine, afraid, affect, useful, suspect, someday
186641 | 0.98

185 such *d*
.as, as, .thing, other., issue., factor., activity., .exist, .behavior, food, organization., measure, disease, product.
193197 | 0.95 A

186 place *n*
adj right, only, better, wrong, safe, special, dangerous, perfect *noun* time, people, work, kind, meeting., hiding. *verb* take., occupy, earn., lock., secure, rent, frequent, trash, fasten, stink
185886 | 0.98

187 again *r*
and, once., over., then, never., time, back., start., ever., laugh., .tomorrow, nod, pregnant.
191013 | 0.94 F

188 city *n*
adj inner, entire, industrial, holy, ancient, coastal, rural, crowded, municipal, surrounding *noun* new., .council, .hall, street, .official, center, police, mayor, capital., resident *verb* visit, locate, approve, rebuild, flee., sue, host, found, bomb, flood
188307 | 0.94 N

189 case *n*
adj particular, criminal, civil, involved, extreme, legal, sexual, rare, classic, pending *noun* court, .study, .point, number., law, murder., .manager, prosecution., abuse *verb* .involve, report, present, handle, argue, discuss, settle, investigate, prove, review
187170 | 0.95

190 most *d*
.people, .American, .case, spend., .agree, .whom, .likely, .expert, unlike., .observer, .folk, .analyst, .instance, .respondent
183226 | 0.97

191 few *d*
a., .year, .day, only., .ago, .minute, .week, .month, after, .later, last., next., .hour, past.
181443 | 0.97

192 system *n*
adj solar, political, immune, legal, nervous, current, educational, economic, criminal, entire *noun* school., health., information., justice., computer., care., operating. *verb* develop, create, design, build, install, operate, establish, .fail, improve, control
188180 | 0.92 A

193 week *n*
adj past, recent, following, coming, final, previous, busy, holy, consecutive, intensive *noun* day., time, couple., hour., night., work, season, election, training *verb* spend., announce, visit, resign, average, unveil, cancel, rehearse, .progress, mail
183035 | 0.95 S

194 where *r*
know., place., point., live, situation., .stand, area., wonder., no., matter., .head, .hell, .belong, mile.
178895 | 0.97

195 company *n*
adj big, small, major, pharmaceutical, financial, foreign, holding, electric, independent, Canadian
noun insurance., oil., business, stock, drug., phone., executive, employee, record, tobacco. *verb* sell, .pay, own, .offer, .operate, .plan, found, .announce, force, form
190876 | 0.90 N

196 each *d*
.other, .year, one, they, .day, .side, different, .week, look., individual, four, .month, .person, item
181834 | 0.95 A

197 percent *n*
adj total, annual, gross, estimated, remaining, Asian, African-American, retail, maximum, 90-plus *noun* year, rate, .population, .people, woman, increase, tax, .chance *verb* rise., compare, account., fall., grow, drop.
182559 | 0.93

198 hear *v*
noun .sound, story, .word, music, door, .news, .noise, song, radio, .argument, .footstep, tape, minute., distance, conversation *misc* voice, never., ever., .anything, .scream, .sing, surprised., glad.
    back .from, never., wait., expect.
180517 | 0.94 F

199 so *c*
.can, me, OK., kind, touch, okay., mm-hmm.
176163 | 0.95 S

200 during *i*
.year, .period, .war, time, .day, .last, .week, .season, .month, .past, .summer, .early, .hour, .campaign
176653 | 0.95

201 question *n*
adj big, tough, interesting, key, serious, open, simple, difficult, quick, specific *noun* answer, people, research., lot., kind, .mark, number, comment, interview, reporter *verb* ask, raise, address, pose, remain, respond., .arise, face, .relate, beg.
177737 | 0.94 S

202 right *r*
all., .now, there, here, .away, .let, .next, .front, .middle, exactly
186147 | 0.90 S

203 program *n*
adj social, educational, nuclear, special, gifted, successful, physical, comprehensive, available, similar *noun* education., school, training, teacher, development, health, director, computer., community, college *verb* provide, develop, offer, include, design, create, implement, support, establish, fund
181977 | 0.92 A

204 work *n*
adj social, hard, recent, previous, dirty, creative, literary *noun* .force, day, .art, lot., life, artist, hour, kind., .ethic *verb* return., improve, complete, finish, perform, publish, ensure, admire, resume., concentrate
174084 | 0.96

205 run *v*
noun .president, business, .office, campaign, .risk, .finger, ad, .mile, .yard, race, candidate, operation, .Senate, ball, dog *misc* .into, .through, .away, home, .off, .across, hit., .fast, .deep, .wild, scream

down tear•, •face, •cheek, •hall, blood•, sweat•, •spine, •list, clock, battery **out** time, money, luck•, clock, patience, supply, benefit•, •onto, limitation• **up** •down, •against, debt, •spine, •deficit, •huge, •score, •credit, rating• **around** •scream, •naked, •circle
172718 | 0.96

206 number *n*
adj large, small, growing, total, increasing, significant, limited *noun* •people, phone•, year, time, •student, •thing, telephone• *verb* increase, reduce•, •dial, limit•, indicate, count•, double, estimate•, •divide, record
172392 | 0.96

207 small *j*
noun town, group, business, number, amount, company, size, child, room, part, piece, house *misc* large, relatively, rural, wooden, round, chop, medium, fairly, medium-sized
171234 | 0.97

208 government *n*
adj federal, local, central, Iraqi, Chinese, private, British, Israeli *noun* US•, state, •official, •agency, policy, •program, •office, •regulation, •spending *verb* support, form, •announce, elect, overthrow•, impose•, •regulate, demand, shut, issue
178353 | 0.93

209 play *v*
noun •role, game, •part, music, team, •basketball, •golf, •card, •football, •baseball, band, guy, season *misc* •important, •major, •key, hard, •significant, •crucial, •critical, •active, •vital
out drama, scene•, scenario•, story•, •public, fantasy, struggle•, •differently, tragedy•, •daily **down** •significance, seek•, •importance
173285 | 0.95

210 off *r*
take•, cut•, pay•, turn•, set•, pull•, start•, better•, show•, run•, drop•, lay•, fall•
169099 | 0.95 F

211 move *v*
noun •direction, lip, •apartment, leg, camera, troop, finger, •speed, shadow, muscle, cloud, traffic, storm•, furniture, •headquarters *misc* •into, •out, •toward, •forward, •away, •quickly, •slowly, •closer, •beyond, •fast, •ahead, •along, •faster
in •together, •closer, camera•, storm•, cloud•, •relative, tenant•, firefighter• **on** let•, before•, ready•, quickly, eager•, anxious• **down** •hall, •aisle, •hallway, •slope, •driveway **up** •ladder, •rank, runner•, •notch, steadily•
165957 | 0.96

212 like *v*
noun thing•, idea, guy, taste, me, •feel, tester•, •excerpt, acknowledgment•, •gratitude, •simplicity, •outdoors, •limelight *misc* I•, you, do, will•, really•, •best, everybody, nobody•, personally, •comment, pretend
168445 | 0.95 S

213 always *r*
there•, almost•, •seem, •love, •pleasure, •admire, •fascinate, •hungry, •lookout, •grateful, •polite
164652 | 0.96

214 night *n*
adj good, late, dark, previous, sleepless, starry, rainy, Arabian, drunk, lonely *noun* day, room•, middle•, •sky, hour, bed, •week, dinner, sleep, air *verb* spend•, stay•, wake, pray, awake, wander, sneak
171678 | 0.92 F

215 believe *v*
noun reason•, •God, expert•, official•, scientist•, researcher•, analyst•, investigator•, Jesus, observer•, •me, Christian•, •miracle, lie, •ghost *misc* really•, hard•, strongly, truly•, firmly•
in I, you, he, they, we, what, she
164840 | 0.96 S

216 today *r*
early•, news, •tomorrow, announce, alive•, guest, yesterday, Senate, poll
171285 | 0.93 S

217 hold *v*
noun hand, arm, •breath, meeting, position, court, •hostage, •hearing, view, baby, finger, •gun, •promise, bag, glass *misc* •together, •accountable, •onto, •responsible
out •hand, •hope, •arm, •promise, •possibility, •palm, •prospect, •wrist, luck• **up** •hand, •finger, •sign, •glass, mirror, •bottle, •traffic, •copy **on** •tight, each, OK, •dear, •tightly, struggle•, barely• **down** •job, •cost, •Fort, wage, •full-time, inflation **back** •tear, •any, •flood, •tide, •laughter
163983 | 0.97

218 point *n*
adj important, focal, certain, turning, whole, main, interesting, extra *noun* •view, time, percentage•, starting•, •guard, •rebound, case•, game, vantage• *verb* make, score•, reach•, average•, miss•, prove•, illustrate•, earn, stress, accumulate
163889 | 0.96

219 live *v*
noun people•, life, year, family, house, city, home, •area, parent, •street, •poverty, town, month, writer•, •mile *misc* who•, where•, •here, •there, long, •up, •together
out •life, •fantasy, •dream, •faith, •rest, •final, gospel, •ideal, •remainder **on** •less, enough•, •legacy, memory, spirit•, •forever, legend•, tradition• **in** we•, •house, world, •neighborhood, •town, •society, •building, today
162663 | 0.97

220 happen *v*
noun thing•, accident•, event•, stuff•, incident•, miracle•, tragedy•, •me, disaster•, •anytime *misc* something•, nothing•, never•, •again, really•, •next, anything•, ever•, whatever•, bad•, exactly•, everything•, actually•
168676 | 0.94 S

221 bring *v*
noun •boil, •attention, charge, •peace, •justice, suit, •memory, •tear, troop, bag, gift, pot, •joy, •focus, saucepan• *misc* •into, •together, •home, •along, •closer, •mind, •forth
about change, •peace, •improvement, •desired, •fundamental, •destruction, •downfall, •peaceful, •demise, •lasting **up** issue, •subject, •rear, interesting, topic, •short, glad•, •unpleasant **back** •memory, •fond, •draft, souvenir, specimen, •vivid, •crown **in** •question, •revenue, noise, harvest, outsider, catch, •heavyweight **down** •deficit, •curtain, •wrath, •inflation, •communism, •fever **out** •best, •flavor, •sweetness, •tray, waiter•
160394 | 0.98

222 next *m*
•to, •year, •day, •week, over•, •month, •morning, •few, •door, sit•, •step, •generation, hour, •her
162654 | 0.96

223 without *i*
.any, .word, .permission, .help, .support, .doubt,
whole., part., .warning, .prior, .fear, .knowledge,
.written, media.
159445 | 0.98

224 before *i*
get, day., year., long, even, hour, week., year., .leave,
long., minute., month., begin, .start
158938 | 0.98

225 large *j*
noun number, part, company, group, bowl, area, city,
amount, population, size, egg, scale *misc* small,
enough, loom, relatively, combine, urban, medium,
chop, fairly
162297 | 0.95

226 must *v*
noun teacher., educator., caution, employer.,
applicant., provider., plaintiff., military.
misc .understand, .consider, therefore, .recognize,
.address, realize, .admit, .accept, surely, .carefully,
.ensure, .careful, .aware
159805 | 0.96

227 all *r*
.right, at., .over, of, .sudden, once, .let, .same, .the
163433 | 0.93 S

228 war *n*
adj civil, cold, Korean, nuclear, holy, revolutionary,
global *noun* world., end., year, .terror, .terrorism,
.crime, veteran, drug, peace, prisoner. *verb* fight, win.,
wage., declare., oppose., survive., .rage, escalate,
.erupt, flee.
160220 | 0.94

229 home *n*
adj foster, mobile, single-family, suburban,
permanent, sweet, expensive, broken, ancestral,
nearby *noun* nursing., care, .office, .state, game,
country, computer *verb* run, live, build, buy., stay.,
sell, return., own.
156634 | 0.95

230 under *i*
.circumstance, .law, .condition, .control, .pressure,
.rule, .tree, .name, .arm, .fire, .age, cover, plan,
.attack
153399 | 0.97

231 room *n*
adj dark, empty, main, front, darkened, crowded, cool,
spare, outdoor *noun* living., dining., hotel., .night,
emergency., door, locker., .temperature, back.,
conference. *verb* leave., sit, walk., enter., fill, share,
cross., rent., step, clean
159860 | 0.92 F

232 fact *n*
adj simple, very, aware, basic, mere, proud, sad,
plain, objective, well-known *noun* matter, life,
point, fiction, statement, .sheet, nutrition.
verb accept., ignore., base., reflect., mention,
hide., overlook.
153769 | 0.95 S

233 area *n*
adj rural, urban, metropolitan, major, certain, remote,
particular, surrounding, residential, key *noun* study,
ski., metro., resident, park, subject., development,
wilderness., surface., population *verb* live., cover,
identify, locate, surround, populate., explore, expand,
search, concentrate.
154416 | 0.94

234 national *j*
noun park, security, health, center, service, league,
guard, radio, committee, forest, interest, director
misc public, democratic, international, local,
according, regional, African, historic
154640 | 0.94

235 write *v*
noun book, letter, story, song, article, paper, word,
novel, poem, .check, .column, name, piece, report,
essay *misc* .about, read., .extensively, .illustrate,
frequently, originally.
   down .name, .number, .everything, .word,
.thought, .address, .license, notebook., pencil.,
instruct. **out** .check, .list, .prescription, .address,
.receipt, instruction **off** debt, .entire, .portion
149765 | 0.97

236 money *n*
adj federal, extra, soft, additional, borrowed, hard-
earned, awful, unlimited, stolen *noun* lot., time,
amount., people, fund, bank, taxpayer., spending.,
.manager, sum. *verb* make, spend, give, raise., save.,
put., pay, need, lose., .buy
152069 | 0.95

237 right *n*
adj human, civil, constitutional, religious,
gay, individual, legal, equal, far, fundamental
noun woman, bill., .movement, property., group,
abortion, amendment *verb* protect, violate, deny.,
exercise., defend, reserve, recognize., advocate,
oppose, preserve
152882 | 0.95 S

238 story *n*
adj short, different, whole, top, interesting, sad
noun news, life, success., cover., love., .line, page,
horror. *verb* tell, hear, write, read, share., publish,
relate, recount, illustrate, .unfold
151053 | 0.96

239 water *n*
adj cold, hot, clean, warm, boiling, fresh, running
noun cup, .supply, food, air, system, surface, .quality,
glass, foot, river *verb* drink., add, pour, boil, .flow,
carry, splash, drain, pump, drip
151940 | 0.95

240 mother *n*
adj single, working, biological, foster, divorced,
adoptive, unmarried, widowed, drunk, adolescent
noun father, child, .daughter, sister, wife, house, son,
birth, grandmother, .nature *verb* .die, born, visit,
divorce, kiss, hug, inherit., murder, .sigh, beg
156206 | 0.92 F

241 different *j*
noun way, kind, people, thing, type, group, level, story,
place, view, part, culture *misc* from, very, something,
each, quite, completely, several, entirely
149823 | 0.96

242 young *j*
noun man, woman, people, child, girl, boy, adult,
age, lady, kid, son, mother *misc* name, beautiful,
handsome, healthy, bright, attractive, talented, gifted,
ambitious
146708 | 0.98

243 month *n*
adj past, recent, coming, previous, following, preceding, mere, fiscal, ensuing, shy *noun* week., time, couple., day, summer, winter., prison, dollar., jail *verb* take, spend., pay, last., die, end, wait, .pass, serve
149257 | 0.96 N

244 lot *n*
adj whole, awful, vacant, unanswered, abandoned, adjoining, wooded, deserted, used-car, pent-up, weedy *noun* .people, parking., .time, .thing, .money, .work, .fun, .stuff *verb* spend., hear., learn., save., cause., sound., cost., alienate.
155610 | 0.92 S

245 book *n*
adj new, recent, comic, late, best-selling, favorite, popular, forthcoming, rare, numerous *noun* author., child, history, page, review, picture, phone., article, title, magazine *verb* write, read, publish, buy., close, finish, sign, .entitle, promote., recommend
143224 | 0.97

246 eye *n*
adj blue, dark, black, brown, wide, open, green, bright, red, left *noun* hair, man, .contact, corner., look., mouth, nose, public., light, mind *verb* close, keep., roll., catch., meet, shut, stare, .widen, rub., smile
154400 | 0.89 F

247 study *n*
adj social, recent, American, current, previous, early, international, future, scientific, cultural *noun* result., case., woman, research, purpose., finding, group, participant, data, area *verb* .show, .find, use, conduct, .examine, .suggest, .indicate, report, publish, participate.
157521 | 0.87 A

248 job *n*
adj good, better, great, full-time, part-time, tough, odd, excellent *noun* day, .training, .satisfaction, worker, .security, .market, loss *verb* do, get., lose., create, quit., offer, land., generate, interview., compete.
142628 | 0.96

249 kind *n*
adj different, certain, various, particular, weird, old-fashioned, loving, silly, bizarre, sexy *noun* .thing, people, .person, man, .guy, .stuff, .work, .money *verb* create., engage., undergo., tolerate., envision, subject., retaliate., withstand.
144054 | 0.95 S

250 word *n*
adj other, key, final, single, written, spoken, exact, very, harsh, dirty *noun* .mouth, meaning, use., language, .processor, sound, choice, kind, .processing, war *verb* hear., speak, write, read, spread, .describe, utter, choose, repeat, search.
141504 | 0.96

251 issue *n*
adj important, social, environmental, real, major, key, economic, public, whole, legal *noun* health, policy, woman, security, abortion, number., concern, discussion, safety, .magazine *verb* address., raise, deal., discuss, focus., resolve, involve, .affect, debate, .arise
144572 | 0.94

252 side *n*
adj other, right, left, far, opposite, dark, upper, wrong *noun* .effect, head, .road, .street, door, minute, window, .bed, .dish, flip. *verb* stand., sit., lie., lay, place, hang., switch., press, scrape., slide
140622 | 0.97

253 four *m*
.year, three., .five, .day, .month, .ago, about., .hour, .week, each, six, .later, .season, least.
139158 | 0.97

254 business *n*
adj small, big, international, serious, successful, unfinished, profitable, risky, legitimate *noun* people, school, .community, family., .leader, world, .owner *verb* start, run, conduct, own, operate, mind., expand, generate, .boom, compete
144134 | 0.94

255 though *c*
even., as., .necessarily, .hardly, .rarely, .technically
139502 | 0.96

256 head *n*
adj bald, shaved, severed, ugly, round, blond, balding, *noun* back, side, .start, .shoulder, top., .state, hair, .neck, arm, department *verb* shake., turn, nod., tilt, lift., hit., raise., stick., bow, cock
146894 | 0.92 F

257 far *r*
so., .from, .than, .more, too, .away, by, .beyond, .less, thus., .enough
137354 | 0.98

258 long *j*
noun time, way, run, term, period, island, hour, day, hair, history, line, foot *misc* ago, before, short, wide, hard, narrow, thin, slow
137332 | 0.97

259 black *j*
noun man, woman, people, hair, hole, community, pepper, student, eye, child, family, American *misc* white, wear, Hispanic, red, ground, freshly, dress, blue
139404 | 0.94

260 million *m*
.year, more., than., .people, .dollar, spend., worth, nearly., cost., half., per, estimated.
143616 | 0.91

261 both *d*
.side, .party, .hand, thank., .parent, .sex, .candidate, .whom, common, thanks, .gender, .aisle, .Atlantic, equally
135116 | 0.97

262 little *j*
noun bit, girl, boy, thing, kid, while, man, house, guy, child, brother, town *misc* tiny, nice, cute, relatively, sweet, pretty, dirty, neat
138107 | 0.94 F

263 yes *u*
oh., right, .sir, no, answer., .course, .ma'am, yeah, OK, absolutely., .indeed, hello
145809 | 0.88 S

264 after *c*
year, .all, day, month, week, hour, .war, shortly., .death, minute, few,
131608 | 0.97

265 since c
have, .then, year, first, ever., long., .war, .early,
especially., month., .late, .beginning
130318 | 0.98

266 around i
.world, her, .country, arm., wrap., .neck, .corner, put.,
.room, walk., .table, area, build., .town
132434 | 0.96

267 long r
no., how., so., .ago, before, .enough, too., last, any,
live
130674 | 0.97

268 provide v
noun service, .information, .opportunity, .support,
student, care, program, .evidence, .assistance,
.insight, .access, .protection, benefit, experience,
food misc .additional, .better, necessary, .financial,
.adequate, .useful
139221 | 0.91 A

269 service n
adj social, public, national, secret, human, military,
armed, financial, medical, postal noun health., park.,
community, US., forest., reader., customer., .provider,
good., .card verb provide, offer, receive, attend.,
deliver, perform, improve
135570 | 0.93

270 important j
noun thing, issue, role, part, factor, question,
point, aspect, information, step, decision, difference
misc most, more, very, as, become, play, perhaps
133160 | 0.95 A

271 sit v
noun .chair, room, .bed, .desk, night, .side, .floor,
.kitchen, .couch, car, .edge, office, .porch, .sofa, .stool
misc .on, .down, .there, .here, .next, .front, .beside,
.behind, .wait
   down .talk, .next, .beside, .again, .write, .eat,
.dinner, .together **up** .straight, .bed, suddenly, slowly,
struggle., .late, abruptly **back** .down, .watch, .wait,
.enjoy, .relax, sigh
136358 | 0.92 F

272 away r
go., take., right., far., turn., walk., give., mile., run.,
put., throw., pull., drive., move.
133524 | 0.94 F

273 friend n
adj best, old, close, closest, longtime, dear, mutual,
male noun family, relative, school, member, house,
group, brother, childhood., help, sister verb tell, meet,
visit, invite, gather, introduce, date, greet, betray,
entertain.
130009 | 0.96

274 however r
professionally., transcribe., finding, .proofread, overall,
unlikely, unclear, .briefly
135875 | 0.92 A

275 power n
adj nuclear, political, military, economic, electric,
major, solar, electrical, western, European
noun .plant, .line, balance., source, air., struggle,
authority, wind., structure verb exercise, increase,
gain., wield, share, possess, seize., shift, .influence,
lack.
131566 | 0.94 A

276 no u
there., .one, .idea, .reason, .question, .matter,
.what, need, .evidence, .doubt, oh., .know,
.difference, .sign
137295 | 0.90 S F

277 yet r
not., .another, .proofread, better., quite, .despite,
ready, clear, .fully, .somehow, dead., .precisely,
.unknown, distinct
126219 | 0.98

278 father n
adj founding, biological, proud, holy, loving, putative,
heavenly, divorced noun mother, son, child, brother,
death, husband, daughter, grandfather, sister, .figure
verb .die, marry, inherit., found, murder, divorce, pray,
abuse, forgive, bury
133605 | 0.92 F

3. Clothing

General terms and parts of clothing

(pocket) n 22655, (button) 13028, clothing 11590, (hood) 6800, jewelry 6052, sleeve 5607, collar 5564, cuff 3276

Items of clothing

(suit) n 35280, shoe 26007, (ring) n 21069, shirt 20470, dress n 20389, hat 17462, (tie) n 17060, coat n 15297, jacket 14938,
boot n 14436, belt n 13966, pants 11412, glove 9852, uniform n 9809, skirt n 8858, jeans 8037, sock n 6486, sweater 5179,
robe 4751, shorts 4626, gown 4387, scarf n 3551, (slip) n 3545, vest 3313, blouse 3110, underwear 3037, necklace 2914,
diaper 2738, earring 2720, cloak 2624, bracelet 2394, bra 2378, apron 2205, sneakers 2181, stocking 2027, slipper 1943,
blazer 1932, pajamas 1491, bikini 1418, sweatshirt 1342, baseball cap 1087, nightgown 1031, high heels 985,
overcoat 979, parka 859, overalls 812, swimsuit 799, tights 729, (loafers) 677, raincoat 670, cardigan 611,
bow tie 593, halter 591, mitten 583, cowboy boot 561, tank top 553, underpants 489, leggings 442, undershirt 413,
suspenders 384, polo shirt 369, petticoat 364, pantyhose 329, trousers 283, pullover 271, leotards 254, camisole 164,
galosh(es) 111, sweatsuit 93, earmuffs 89

279 hour *n*
adj long, full, past, wee, extra, countless, endless, flexible, odd, awake *noun* .day, minute, mile., .week, couple., night, morning, .half, rush., number. *verb* spend., take, work, talk, wait, last., drive, .pass, arrive
128061 | 0.96

280 often *r*
more, too., most., quite, every., .refer, .difficult, stir., .associate, .overlook, .cite, .accompany
129872 | 0.95

281 until *c*
minute., wait., year, about, .after, .now, .recently, stir, up., cook., .then, heat., .tender, add
128867 | 0.95

282 political *j*
noun party, system, leader, power, science, process, issue, life, scientist, action, change, reform *misc* economic, social, military, cultural, religious, personal, legal, democratic
135970 | 0.90 A

283 line *n*
adj bottom, long, front, straight, fine, offensive, multiple, thin, hot *noun* phone., power., story., assembly., product, party., finish., .equation *verb* draw, cross., form, blur, step., divide, connect, stretch, mark, cast
126004 | 0.97

284 end *n*
adj other, far, defensive, dead, very, low, tight, front *noun* year, .day, .war, .world, .century, week, beginning., month, season, .result *verb* reach., mark., near., signal., .justify, trim, tuck., discard., dangle, prevail
123996 | 0.98

285 stand *v*
noun door, .side, .doorway, .line, moment, window, .chance, ground, .corner, .middle, guard, .trial, tree, .edge, kitchen *misc* .front, .behind, .before, .next, .outside, .beside, .watch, .around
up .walk, .against, .straight, hair., .front, slowly, .fight, .stretch, willing., please **out** .front, vein., particular., .sharp, .sharply, stark, .amid
130063 | 0.93 F

286 among *i*
.other, .them, .those, most, .group, .American, .member, difference., .themselves, common., rate., relationship., especially., leader
127451 | 0.94 A

287 game *n*
adj Olympic, all-star, final, fair, running, passing, previous, fun, complete, wild *noun* video., season, football., home, championship., player, baseball, basketball., .plan *verb* play, win., lose, watch., miss., attend., average, tie, finish, compete
134554 | 0.89 N

288 ever *r*
than., if., .see, .since, before, one., .hear, best., anything, .again, .happen, nobody., anyone
125145 | 0.96

289 lose *v*
noun .job, .weight, .money, .pound, game, .control, .sight, .interest, .mind, season, .thought, husband, .vote, .temper, .leg *misc* win., .million, .everything, risk., .billion, .forever, completely

out will., who., .because, .there, may., worker., best, both, consumer.
123521 | 0.97

290 bad *j*
noun thing, news, guy, time, day, idea, luck, weather, situation, boy, habit, shape *misc* good, too, enough, pretty, that, smell, necessarily, ugly
123592 | 0.97

291 member *n*
adj other, national, senior, individual, fellow, active, democratic, various, key, founding *noun* family, group, board, staff., faculty., team, council *verb* .vote, elect, .participate, encourage, appoint, recruit., invite, urge, interview, contact
124985 | 0.95

292 meet *v*
noun .need, .standard, eye, .requirement, .demand, .criterion, .goal, .challenge, friend, week, end., leader, .press, .expectation, official *misc* in, order., nice., someone, fail.
up .with, when., where., .again, .friend, .him, later, until, before.
120795 | 0.98

293 pay *v*
noun .attention, tax, price, .bill, money, fee, company., .debt, dollar, cost, .rent, insurance, salary, cash, wage *misc* .for, much, .million, willing., enough, agree., .close, .extra, afford.
off .debt, .loan, work., .mortgage, .card, .credit, effort., investment., .handsomely, gamble.
down .debt, .national, budget., credit, .mortgage, surplus.
123150 | 0.96

294 law *n*
adj federal, international, environmental, common, natural, criminal, constitutional, martial *noun* .enforcement, .school, state, .firm, professor, rule., .order *verb* pass, require, break., enforce., violate., allow, change, protect, apply, sign.
124932 | 0.93

295 almost *r*
.year, .every, .as, .always, seem, .certainly, .impossible, .immediately, .half, .entirely, .ago, .exclusively, .everyone
118469 | 0.98

296 car *n*
adj used, electric, parked, luxury, Japanese, light, stolen, armored, fancy, classic *noun* police., door, seat, .accident, sport., rental, driver, street, window, race *verb* drive, buy., pull, park, stop, sell, hit, steal, rent., roll
123703 | 0.93 F

297 later *r*
year., day., .on, month., few., week., minute., hour., three., moment., sooner., four., five., six.
117096 | 0.97

298 much *r*
.more, .than, very., so., as, how., .better, thanks., pretty., .less, too, .same, .large, .easy
116429 | 0.98

299 name *n*
adj real, full, familiar, middle, maiden, proper, given, holy *noun* .address, man, brand., family, father,

household., .recognition, character _verb_ give, call,
change, remember., mention, bear., sign., forget,
.withhold, clear.
117553 | 0.97

300 include v
noun program, study, group, list, information, item,
activity, survivor., plan, example., analysis, model,
data, feature, package. _misc_ whose., .both, .following,
expand., future, additional, please.
122716 | 0.93 A

301 five m
.year, four., .minute, .day, .six, .ago, about., after,
three, last., .month, .week, past., .hour
116383 | 0.97

302 center n
adj medical, national, cultural, senior, civic, day-care
noun world., research, trade., art, director.,
community., health, study, .disease, shopping.
verb locate, insert., establish, operate, house,
found, occupy, sponsor, situate
118990 | 0.95 N

303 once r
.again, at., for, all, .while, .week, .twice, every, least.,
.month, .upon
116659 | 0.97

304 university n
adj Catholic, prestigious, Hebrew, Methodist, Nigerian,
applied, agricultural, marine, institutional, cooperative
noun state., professor, college, school, student,
new, .press, center, study, law _verb_ teach, attend.,
graduate., publish, found, .specialize, recruit,
enroll
121090 | 0.93

305 continue v
noun trend, .discussion, break, .conversation,
tradition, search, .path, minute, struggle, journey,
dialogue, pace, cycle, mystery., revision. _misc_ .until,
.grow, .rise, .increase, .throughout, .expand
115494 | 0.97

306 least r
at., .one, .year, .two, .three, .hour, .once, .four, .five,
until, .million, .month, .six, .minute
114373 | 0.98

307 real j
noun estate, world, life, problem, people, time, name,
issue, question, story, reason, sense _misc_ quick, nice,
commercial, fast, live, imagined, virtual, imaginary
114856 | 0.98

308 white j
noun man, people, woman, shirt, hair, wine, student,
light, paper, dress, house, wall _misc_ black, wear, blue,
red, green, yellow, male, predominantly
116763 | 0.96

309 change v
noun .mind, life, way, world, name, .subject, rule,
behavior, .course, view _misc_ .since, dramatically,
quickly, rapidly, completely, radically
113625 | 0.98

310 set v
noun .record, standard, goal, stage, .fire, .foot, .tone,
.motion, .example, limit _misc_ .aside, within., current.,
.apart, .free, .forth, .straight

up system, .shop, help., .camp, .own, table,
.meeting, tent, trust, .appointment **off** .alarm,
.bomb, .chain, .explosion, .down, .bell, .wave,
.firework, spark **out** .prove, deliberately., .explore
in reality., winter., panic.
114003 | 0.98

311 several d
.year, .time, .day, .month, over., after, .week, .ago,
.hundred, .including, .hour, study, past., .thousand
115198 | 0.96

312 ago r
year., long., few., month., week., .when, about.,
decade., day., couple., several., century.
115962 | 0.95

313 information n
adj available, additional, personal, useful, specific,
detailed, financial, classified _noun_ .system,
.technology, source, service, access., center, amount.,
.age, data, nutrition. _verb_ provide., give, gather, share,
obtain, receive, collect, contain, acquire, exchange
118678 | 0.93 A

314 nothing p
there., but, .more, .than, .else, .happen, .wrong,
.change, .ever, .less, absolutely., .except, .compare,
.short
116813 | 0.94 F

315 community n
adj international, local, black, European, small,
Jewish, scientific, entire, medical, gay _noun_ .college,
member, service, school, .center, business., leader,
development, sense., intelligence. _verb_ build,
establish, organize, affect, attend, participate,
promote, engage, belong, divide
120945 | 0.91 A

316 best j
noun friend, way, thing, interest, time, player, team,
place, chance, effort, actor, practice _misc_ ever,
possible, probably, perhaps, available, despite,
brightest, defensive
114468 | 0.96

317 right j
noun back, thing, hand, time, side, way, place,
direction, arm, leg, foot, wing _misc_ that, all, exactly,
absolutely, wrong, left, choose, commercial, upper
116364 | 0.94 S

318 idea n
adj good, new, great, bad, whole, better, very, basic,
creative, musical _noun_ people, time, man, woman,
story, marketplace. _verb_ like., support., share, express,
reject., present, accept., discuss, promote, test
112430 | 0.97

319 lead v
noun team, road., door, effort, nation, .league,
development, path., event., .charge, step., trail.,
series, discussion, loss _misc_ eventually., .increased,
ultimately., .directly, inevitably
112811 | 0.97

320 body n
adj human, dead, whole, upper, entire, governing,
female, growing _noun_ part, .weight, mind, student.,
.image, .fat, .language _verb_ cover, lie, recover, burn,
bury, dump, drag, wrap, absorb, press
114841 | 0.95

321 learn *v*
noun student., lesson, thing, skill, .language, .lot,
experience, opportunity, teacher, .English, strategy,
classroom, concept, importance, .secret *misc* .how,
.read, later, quickly, hard, teach, soon.
113914 | 0.95

322 kid *n*
adj little, young, poor, smart, safe, healthy, sick,
married, fun, skinny *noun* school, parent, time,
college, thing, .age, wife., care, adult, street *verb* play,
love, teach., .grow, .learn, raise., send., educate.,
scream, yell
116112 | 0.93

323 minute *n*
adj final, full, extra, passing, spare *noun* hour, second,
couple., oven, preparation., pan, matter., word,
chicken, mixture *verb* wait., take., cook, bake., spend.,
simmer., last., .pass, cover
115028 | 0.94

324 table *n*
adj round, wooden, folding, nearby, periodic,
multiple, antique, outdoor, selected, changing
noun kitchen., coffee., chair, room, result, dinner.,
.figure, dining., data, analysis *verb* sit., see., show,
present, set, indicate, list, summarize, place, display
117605 | 0.92 A

325 whether *c*
.or, not, question., determine., ask., decide., .shall,
wonder., issue., debate., consider., decision.,
regardless., matter.
112810 | 0.96

326 understand *v*
noun need, .nature, .importance, .concept, culture,
.meaning, public, .implication, .significance, difficulty,
perspective, .complexity, .dynamics, educator.,
.evolution *misc* .how, .why, help., really., better,
important., fully., easy., difficult.
111685 | 0.97

327 team *n*
adj national, Olympic, special, all-star, legal,
winning, successful, opposing, ranked, investigative
noun member, player, US., football., league,
basketball., sport, baseball., season, research.
verb play, .win, lead, beat, join., coach, compete,
.finish, .score, head
120637 | 0.89 N

328 back *n*
adj far, running, defensive, upper, flat, sore, bare,
stiff, aching *noun* .door, head, .seat, hand, way.,
.room, .yard, .neck, .wall, arm *verb* turn, sit., lie.,
push, throw., lay., roll., bend, stretch, rest
115127 | 0.93 F

329 watch *v*
noun .TV, .television, .movie, .game, .show, night,
.news, kid, .video, .film, minute *misc* sit., stand.,
closely, .carefully, listen, tonight
   out .for, better., .each, warn., everybody, everyone,
sign, somebody, neighbor, .hidden **over** .shoulder,
angel., sister, carefully
115091 | 0.93 F

330 together *r*
put., work., come., bring., hold., live., piece., pull.,
spend., tie., gather., stir., bowl
109434 | 0.98

331 follow *v*
noun .lead, .rule, .path, .suit, trail, .instruction,
.direction, procedure, .order, .example, .advice,
.footstep, step, course, period *misc* closely,
immediately., .behind, soon, .along, brief
   up .with, .lead, patient, tip, fail., plan,
.telephone, investigator. **through** .promise,
.plan, .commitment, fail., actually., failure.
110178 | 0.97

332 around *r*
turn., look., .here, walk., move., sit., run., hang.,
spin., stick., drive.
113075 | 0.95 F

333 only *j*
noun thing, way, time, person, child, people,
reason, part, place, problem, man, woman
misc one, ever, whose, available, remaining,
known, truly, capable
108675 | 0.98

334 stop *v*
noun car, heart, .track, .violence, bus., traffic,
.crying, foot, truck, rain., train, fighting, .breathing,
second, driver *misc* try, before, .short, suddenly,
.front
   by .see, .visit, .talk, .pick, .check, visitor,
neighbor., appreciate, .chat, .lunch
112029 | 0.94 F

335 face *n*
adj red, pale, familiar, round, dark, pretty, smiling,
straight, handsome *noun* hand, look., smile.,
eye, man, hair, expression, woman, mask, mother
verb cover, stare, wipe., hide, wash., touch., slap.,
study., .flush, twist
117057 | 0.90 F

336 anything *p*
do, n't., can, about, if., .else, than, .like, never., want,
ever, .happen, .wrong, hear.
110885 | 0.95

337 public *j*
noun school, health, policy, service, radio, relation,
education, interest, system, life, official, land
misc national, private, attend, environmental,
initial, certified, elementary, widespread
111714 | 0.94

338 social *j*
noun security, worker, study, work, service,
science, support, life, skill, problem, change, issue
misc economic, political, cultural, academic, personal,
environmental, emotional, psychological
120120 | 0.87 A

339 already *r*
have, .begin, well, .under, .exist, .dead, .establish,
.way, .existing, .familiar, .underway, .asleep,
.evident
106221 | 0.98

340 parent *n*
adj single, foster, adoptive, biological, concerned,
involved, responsible, educational, married, proud
noun child, teacher, student, home, .company, group,
.involvement, relationship, birth., support *verb* live,
.divorce, involve, care, born, visit, communicate,
inform, educate, blame
109524 | 0.94

341 speak v
noun language, .English, word, voice, .condition, .interpreter, .mind, .truth, French, .phone, .volume, .tongue, .anonymity, minute, mouth. _misc_ generally., .directly, .softly, .publicly
out .against, .publicly, begin., .loud, .behalf, continue., afraid., .favor, .strongly, courage. **up** finally., afraid., courage., suddenly, rarely.
107937 | 0.96

342 create v
noun job, problem, .environment, system, program, opportunity, image, situation, condition, God, .sense, effect, market, .atmosphere, model _misc_ .new, newly., .equal, in, powerful, .additional
109142 | 0.95

343 office n
adj oval, public, congressional, front, regional, central, elected, outer _noun_ .building, post., attorney., box., home., doctor., budget, .counsel, district., door _verb_ run., leave., contact., open, enter., remove., head., elect., assume., occupy
106790 | 0.96

344 allow v
noun .student, law., system., .access, .user, technology., rule., freedom, .individual, judge, .researcher, software., employee, yard, citizen _misc_ refuse., .participate, vote, .escape, .cool, .operate, .dry, sufficient
105905 | 0.96

345 level n
adj high, low, different, local, national, federal, certain, personal, various, individual _noun_ education, grade., school, sea., skill, blood. _verb_ reach., rise, increase, raise., report., reduce., achieve., maintain., require, state
112394 | 0.91 A

346 read v
noun book, story, .newspaper, .article, .paper, letter, sign, magazine, text, novel, .Bible, .poem, .script, statement, .label _misc_ .write, .aloud, learn., carefully, widely
on .find, learn, .tip, .discover, .detail
105195 | 0.97

347 spend v
noun .time, .year, money, .day, .hour, .night, .week, .month, dollar, .life, amount, .minute, .rest, government., .weekend _misc_ billion, .less, .together, .half, .several, .million, .whole, .entire, .nearly
105364 | 0.97

348 person n
adj only, young, average, single, responsible, normal, nice, wrong, retired _noun_ kind., life, type., group, day, number., sort., business _verb_ .commit, trust, respect, injure, qualify, infect, exclude, punish, .impair, harm
105024 | 0.96

349 door n
adj front, closed, double, revolving, rear, French, wooden, locked, back _noun_ room, window, car, glass., side, knock., bedroom., screen., kitchen, bathroom. _verb_ open, close, walk., shut, slam, lock, stand, push, unlock, swing
114834 | 0.88 F

350 sure j
noun thing, kid, sign, hell, bet, recipe, winner, cure, indication, grip, footing _misc_ I, make, not, want, enough, oh, quite, understand
106368 | 0.95 S

351 add v
noun minute., heat., water, .onion, oil, salt, mixture, .garlic, pepper, sugar, value, color, .egg, butter, .tomato _misc_ until, .another, .cook, stir, .extra, .remaining, hot, quickly, gradually.
up all, number, cost, total, quickly, saving, fast, expense, .score, vote
107420 | 0.94 M

352 street n
adj narrow, quiet, busy, dark, residential, mean, safe, one-way, two-way, nearby _noun_ wall., people, city, main., side., corner, building, light, town, block _verb_ walk., cross., line, hit., head, wander., patrol., drag, clean, race
105946 | 0.95

353 such i
(such as) .as, as, .thing, other., issue., factor., activity., .exist, .behavior, food, organization., measure, disease, product.
109384 | 0.92 A

354 history n
adj American, natural, long, human, recent, modern, oral, medical, cultural, ancient _noun_ art, family., museum, world, book, culture, life, professor, science, course _verb_ teach, study., .repeat, record, trace., rewrite., review., shape, preserve, research.
106554 | 0.94 A

355 party n
adj democratic, political, communist, ruling, major, conservative, liberal, private, socialist, interested _noun_ member, leader, birthday., opposition., dinner., candidate, reform., .line, cocktail. _verb_ throw., join, attend, invite, form, vote, host, organize, switch., oppose
105025 | 0.95

356 grow v
noun child, plant, tree, economy., kid., population., hair, food, crop, .rate, grass., .size, vegetable, farmer., farm _misc_ .out, .old, continue., .rapidly, .faster, .strong, .increasingly
up .in, when., who., child., kid., .poor, generation., .fast, .poverty, .suburban
101064 | 0.96

357 reason n
adj good, only, main, real, political, simple, major, primary, various, personal _noun_ people, number., variety., lot, security., health, couple., .lack _verb_ .believe, cite, .guarantee, suspect, .doubt, compel, outline, speculate., .prevail, articulate
99388 | 0.97

358 morning n
adj good, early, following, sunny, chilly, rainy, awake, foggy, damp, brisk _noun_ news, hour, time, .edition, .sun, light, paper, .show _verb_ wake, join, spend., sleep, awaken, dress, greet, shave, .dawn, rain
106314 | 0.91 S

359 open v
noun door, eye, mouth, window, store, gate, box, season, office, .drawer, month, opportunity, elevator,

screen, theater *misc* .wide, .AM, slowly, schedule.,
.step, .daily, inside, shut, newly.
   up new, world, door, .possibility, market, .whole,
opportunity, space, .area, eye
102728 | 0.94 F

360 within *i*
.year, .day, .hour, search., .month, .few, .week,
.community, .context, .minute, .set, group, .each,
.current
103896 | 0.93 A

361 change *n*
adj social, major, significant, dramatic, global,
fundamental, positive, radical, rapid, cultural
noun climate., policy, attitude, regime., .heart, lifestyle,
pace, sea., agent, structure *verb* make, .occur, bring,
undergo., cause, affect, reflect, produce, result, effect.
103300 | 0.93 A

362 although *c*
however., .may, .text, transcribe., .generally, .initially,
somewhat, .rarely, .necessarily, widely, .occasionally,
.considerable, .latter, .statistically
102877 | 0.94 A

363 walk *v*
noun .street, .room, house, car, .mile, .hall, road,
.office, .dog, .step, .kitchen, .distance, .path, .block,
.store *misc* .into, .away, .through, .over, .toward
   up .down, .aisle, .driveway, .avenue, .sidewalk,
.ramp, .steep, .slope **down** .hall, .aisle, .hallway,
.sidewalk, .avenue, .alley, .block, .ramp **back** .toward,
.forth, .down, .towards, slowly, .downstairs **out** .onto,
.front, .protest, .onstage, calmly, delegation. **around**
.naked, mall, .downtown, .barefoot, .freely, .amongst
104959 | 0.92 F

364 news *n*
adj good, bad, local, daily, late, nightly, sporting
noun .conference, story, world, morning, .media, US.,
new, television., .summary, evening. *verb* .report,
hear., watch., deliver., spread, broadcast, welcome,
dominate., leak, greet
105858 | 0.91 S

365 health *n*
adj mental, public, environmental, human,
physical, social, poor, reproductive *noun* .care,
.service, .insurance, department, .problem, .system,
education, .plan, center *verb* provide, improve.,
protect., affect, promote., maintain., assess, link,
monitor, .deteriorate
105441 | 0.91

366 court *n*
adj Supreme, federal, high, superior, criminal,
appellate, lower *noun* US., state, appeal, .decision,
case, district., .justice, .ruling, .order, circuit.
verb .rule, hold, .decide, .uphold, file, overturn,
.reject, challenge, settle, apply
104109 | 0.92

367 force *n*
adj military, American, special, driving, political,
powerful, economic, full, multinational, Soviet
noun air., task., work., security., police., use., labor.,
.base, coalition. *verb* join., fight, enter, withdraw,
attack, deploy, maintain., market., threaten, capture
102504 | 0.93

368 early *j*
noun year, day, century, morning, stage, childhood,
age, hour, spring, period, education, summer

misc late, during, since, twentieth, nineteenth,
modern, twenties, thirties, seventies
100406 | 0.95 A

369 himself *p*
he, find., kill., pull., force., throw., describe., defend.,
distance., introduce., pour., remind., .mirror, pride.
101249 | 0.94 F

370 air *n*
adj fresh, clean, cold, hot, cool, warm, thin, open
noun .force, .base, .pollution, water, .bag, .quality,
.conditioning, .conditioner, .traffic *verb* fill, breathe,
fly, hang., blow, smell, gasp., rise, suck., sniff.
98647 | 0.96

371 low *j*
noun level, rate, price, cost, heat, score, vision,
income, voice, wage, temperature, self-esteem
misc high, relatively, reduce, simmer, extremely,
cook, due, all-time
100465 | 0.95 A

372 before *c*
get, day., year., long, even, hour, week., .leave, long.,
minute., month., begin., .start
99034 | 0.96

373 art *n*
adj fine, American, African, contemporary, modern,
visual, liberal, western, cultural *noun* museum,
.education, center, gallery, history, work., .form,
works. *verb* teach, study., master., collect, feature,
imitate, practice, inspire, fund, house
110038 | 0.86 A

374 result *n*
adj current, similar, significant, present, direct,
previous, preliminary, negative, mixed, net
noun .study, search., research, end., survey, election,
difference, factor, poll, .investigation *verb* show,
.indicate, produce., .suggest, report, yield., achieve,
base, .support, .reveal
104309 | 0.91 A

375 moment *n*
adj long, very, brief, silent, quiet, particular,
defining, remaining, given, present *noun* .break,
time, silence, .history, .truth, .notice, summary.,
.hesitation *verb* wait, pause., hesitate., arrive, enjoy.,
capture., seize., imagine, recall
100837 | 0.93 F

376 offer *v*
noun service, program, .opportunity, company.,
course, .advice, job, .support, .view, option,
explanation, .benefit, class, .chance, .insight
misc .free, little, following, .additional, .unique
   up prayer, .name, .own, long, .another, .such,
.advice, piece, .best, defense
98155 | 0.96

377 both *r*
.female, .male, .within, .private, .inside, .terms,
.outside, .positive, .negative, .physically, .domestic,
.internal, .politically, .external
98086 | 0.95 A

378 remember *v*
noun .name, .detail, dream, .incident, grandmother,
birthday, .smell, .saying, grandma, classmate, .clarity,
thrill, kindness, old-timer., .motto *misc* I., .when,
.how, always, important., long., suddenly., vividly
98466 | 0.94 F

379 research *n*
adj future, previous, recent, scientific, medical, current *noun* center, .development, institute, study, .project, group, program, education, .question, area *verb* .show, conduct, .suggest, support, .indicate, base, .focus, .examine, fund, publish
103769 | 0.89 A

380 enough *r*
not., long., good., big., old., strong., sure., far., large., hard., fast.
96898 | 0.96

381 girl *n*
adj little, young, teenage, pretty, beautiful, nice, pregnant, gifted, lovely, blond *noun* boy, school, woman, baby, .scout, .basketball, .club, sex, .lady, grade *verb* .name, .wear, marry, dance, dress, kiss, rape, date, giggle, whisper
99673 | 0.93 F

382 boy *n*
adj little, young, teenage, golden, lost, dear, gifted *noun* girl, man, .scout, school, .age, baby, .basketball, .club, poster. *verb* .name, cry, molest., kiss, shout, yell, chase, abuse, murder, bully
99611 | 0.93 F

383 win *v*
noun .game, .championship, .award, year, .war, team., .election, .title, .prize, .medal, .race, .gold, chance., battle, vote *misc* .lose, .national, .super, .straight, easily
   over .voter, .fan, .skeptic, .audience, .critic, .conservative, .opponent, .Catholic, .lawmaker
   out .over, eventually., always., ultimately., truth., usually.
100752 | 0.92 N

384 food *n*
adj fast, healthy, organic, favorite, Chinese, Mexican, rich, fried, fatty, Italian *noun* .drug, water, .administration, .processor, .supply, .safety, .store, .service, health, .chain *verb* eat, bring, provide, buy., serve, cook, prepare, produce, contain, feed
98016 | 0.94

385 across *i*
.country, .street, .room, .United States, .border, .face, walk., .table, line, spread., .river, move., .floor, .America
96511 | 0.96 F

386 guy *n*
adj bad, good, nice, little, young, tough, smart, poor, regular, rich *noun* kind., lot, time, cable., thing, couple., bunch., type. *verb* like, .name, love, beat, date, marry, hire, hate, knock, chase
99870 | 0.92 S

387 second *m*
.half, .year, .floor, .war, .third, .round, during., .quarter, .term, .chance, .season, .thought, .wife, .language
95416 | 0.97

388 able *j*
noun advantage, learner, leverage, erection *misc* will, shall, may, might, never, better, identify, afford, handle, willing, achieve, barely
95112 | 0.97

389 toward *i*
attitude., move., turn., head., walk., step., .end, .door, point., policy., lean., direct., trend., .goal
97585 | 0.94 F

390 maybe *r*
or, think, .shall, .even, something, little, month, wrong, hour, minute, except., somebody, .ought, bit
99046 | 0.92 F

391 process *n*
adj political, due, whole, democratic, involved, decision-making, creative, entire, complex, slow *noun* peace., part., learning., development, selection., step, planning., design., healing., review. *verb* begin, involve, describe, repeat; occur, speed., improve, complete, facilitate, control
100342 | 0.91 A

392 off *i*
take., turn., cut., .coast, keep., .ground, .road, .street, foot, pull., throw., fall., .wall, .floor
95547 | 0.95

393 everything *p*
.else, but, change, .happen, almost., .fine, .possible, .except, own, .wrong, .OK, .okay, .perfect, .normal
94958 | 0.95

394 appear *v*
noun article., image., .television, star., .page, magazine, scene, .newspaper, sky, surface, .cover, column., .journal, glance, .print *misc* first, suddenly., frequently, bright, regularly
94035 | 0.96

395 age *n*
adj old, young, middle, early, average, golden, mean *noun* year, child, .group, people, gender, sex, ice., difference *verb* range, die., reach., increase, retire, vary, decrease., decline., differ, correlate
94870 | 0.95

396 policy *n*
adj foreign, public, economic, national, social, domestic, environmental, monetary, federal *noun* US., government, change, insurance., administration, .maker, health., trade., .decision, energy. *verb* implement, adopt, pursue, support, develop, affect, influence., promote, state, establish
100217 | 0.90 A

397 consider *v*
noun option, .possibility, Congress., .risk, alternative, proposal, legislation, context, .consequence, .implication, aspect, failure, .suicide, characteristic, educator. *misc* important, .themselves, .myself, seriously., generally., carefully, .following, .yourself, widely.
94252 | 0.95 A

398 including *i*
many, several., variety., various., factor., range., numerous., species, dozen., equipment, works, multiple, topic., prominent
94971 | 0.94

399 probably *r*
will, most, .best, .due, somewhere, .greatest, .hardest, .closer, .closest, .best-known, .inevitable, .coincidence
92304 | 0.96 S

400 education *n*
adj physical, special, public, national, general, environmental, social, gifted *noun* .program, teacher, art., school, music., student, department, health,

state, college _verb_ provide, receive, teach, improve, support, promote, relate, pursue., implement, .instill
104880 | 0.85 A

401 love v
noun kid, God, music, wife, movie, husband, dog, fan., .neighbor, daddy, baseball, .me, .smell, passion, tester. _misc_ I., you, her, .him, really., .other, .each, .hate, dearly, care, truly.
94085 | 0.94

402 actually r
not, .happen, .quite, pretty, .exist, funny, surprised, .decrease, .physically, .beneficial, .harmful
95678 | 0.92 S

403 buy v
noun .house, money., .car, company, .stock, .home, .ticket, .share, store, .product, .book, .land, .property, .clothes, .insurance _misc_ .sell, best., enough, cheap, afford., expensive, .organic, borrow, shop, retail, .fancy, legally
up .land, company, .property, .stock, .share, start., corporation, local **out** company, .partner, .contract, .share, .owner, offer., option
93317 | 0.94

404 wait v
noun .minute, .second, line, hour, moment, door, month, .answer, bus, .turn, call, while, .wing, train, crowd. _misc_ .for, .until, long, .till, .outside, patiently
out .storm, .weather, .winter, .market, .rain, .blizzard **around** .for, .until, .long, .hope
94249 | 0.93 F

405 die v
noun people., year, mother., day, father., .cancer, .heart, .age, month, death, .attack, wife., .AIDS, husband., son. _misc_ who., when, after, before, .ago, later, .suddenly
out species., .because, generation, completely, eventually., .danger, .dinosaur, gradually., quickly
down wind., fire., applause., laughter., flame., noise., controversy., quickly, eventually.
91585 | 0.96

406 human j
noun right, being, life, nature, health, service, resource, body, development, history, activity, experience _misc_ basic, international, natural, abuse, universal, fundamental, normal, fully
93519 | 0.93 A

407 send v
noun .message, letter, .e-mail, .troop, .signal, money, .kid, .copy, picture, son, Congress, army, soldier, sample _misc_ .home, .off, .away, please., .wrong, .jail, .fly, .via
out letter, message, .signal, .e-mail, .press, invitation, .resume, notice **back** .home, image, picture, data, .prison, .earth, .forth
89248 | 0.97

408 fee n
adj legal, annual, monthly, additional, flat, nominal, consulting, reasonable, modest, one-time _noun_ service, attorney., user., entry., tuition., registration., entrance. _verb_ pay, charge, collect, .range, impose, .vary, drop
91465 | 0.94

409 expect v
noun analyst., sales, earnings, profit, revenue, investor., observer., visitor, economist., .miracle, approval, announcement, ruling, astronomer., reply _misc_ might., .increase, .soon, anyone, fully., reasonably., reasonable., tomorrow, hardly.
88323 | 0.97

410 serve v
noun year, .purpose, minute., interest, food, .sentence, community, .function, .term, .board, army, sauce, meal, .need, dinner _misc_ .as, per, before., .immediately, hot, .warm, military, currently., fresh
91243 | 0.94

411 sense n
adj common, strong, real, perfect, broad, moral, general _noun_ .humor, .community, .self, .identity, .responsibility, .security, .purpose, .urgency, lot., .loss _verb_ make., give., feel, create., lose., develop., .belong, convey., contribute., possess.
88872 | 0.97

412 teacher n
adj elementary, special, English, professional, cooperating, individual, future, retired, positive, academic _noun_ student, school, education, classroom, parent, music., program _verb_ teach, help, .must, report, train, encourage, hire, assist, .implement, evaluate
106742 | 0.8 A

413 home r
go., come., get., back., when, bring., return., stay., drive., leave., send., work, walk., head.
90117 | 0.95 F

---

4. Colors

Comments: psychologists and linguists have noted that the more basic color distinctions (light/dark; white/black) and the primary colors (_red, yellow_, and _blue_) are lexicalized more frequently in languages of the world than secondary colors such as _orange_ or _purple_. The frequency data for these color terms shows the same tendency.

white 186826, black 168647, red 78285, green 64578, blue 58167, brown 55594, yellow 23789, gray 23335, (golden) 18959, pink 14458, orange j 9298, purple 7755, pastel 3900, (violet) 3494, (crimson) 1770, (tan) j 1532, (emerald) 1521, (khaki) 1361, beige 1297, (turquoise) 1270, burgundy 924, indigo 766, aqua 576, magenta 465, teal 454, mauve 383, chartreuse j 360, goldenrod j 348, azure 317, vermilion 309

414 market *n*
adj free, black, global, competitive, domestic, common *noun* stock., .share, .economy, US, world., price, .value, labor., farmer. *verb* open, enter., dominate, hit, expand, invest, gain, flood, .crash, decline
93505 | 0.91

415 stay *v*
noun .US, hotel, .course, .bed, month, .calm, .touch, .shape, apartment, guest, .motel, .inn, aunt, shelter, .midnight *misc* .here, .home, .there, long, .away, .tune
    up .night, .late, .all, .until, .watch, .later, .till, .past, .midnight, .dawn **out** .night, .late, .there, long, .until, .past, party, .till **on** long, .until, decide, light., .forever, .chairman, .indefinitely
89095 | 0.96

416 build *v*
noun house, home, system, company, plant, wall, bridge, road, community, .relationship, building, structure, plan., model, facility *misc* new, help., design., .strong, .nuclear
    up .over, .force, military, pressure, .strength, gradually., .muscle, slowly, .inside, .confidence
89178 | 0.96

417 nation *n*
adj other, European, African, top, western, Arab, entire, leading, foreign, developed *noun* talk., world, state, .capital, .security, .news, history, .council, .Islam, ambassador. *verb* lead, face, address., defend, divide, urge, sponsor, rebuild, sweep., shock.
90757 | 0.93

418 fall *v*
noun .love, .percent, price, .category, snow., rain., .ground, .floor, rate, hair., face, tree, stock., .knee, .victim *misc* .into, .asleep, .apart, .short, .behind, .below
    off .horse, .cliff, .chair, .bike, wheel., .ladder, .sharply, hat. **down** .dead, .well, drunk, bridge., .onto, pant., tear. **back** .into, .onto, head., .sleep, .asleep, .earth, .upon **out** hair., bottom., tooth., .onto, .clump, .patch
88948 | 0.95 F

419 oh *u*
.my, .God, .yes, .no, .yeah, .sure, .absolutely, .OK, .gosh, .boy, .thank, .please, .dear, .sorry
95808 | 0.88 S F

420 death *n*
adj sudden, scared, violent, tragic, premature, untimely, wrongful, civilian, near *noun* .penalty, life., .row, cause., .sentence, .rate, father, .toll *verb* die, shoot., face., beat., .occur, starve.
86806 | 0.97

421 plan *n*
adj economic, comprehensive, original, strategic, ambitious, future, five-year, individual, grand, immediate *noun* health., action, business., game., pension., lesson., retirement. *verb* develop, announce., include, implement, approve, draw, discuss., devise., lay, prepare
88360 | 0.96

422 interest *n*
adj special, national, best, public, low, economic, particular, political, vested, growing *noun* .rate, .group, term., conflict., student, business., .payment,

lack. *verb* .modify, show., serve, protect, lose., pay, express., represent., act., define
88506 | 0.94 A

423 someone *p*
.who, in, .else, love, kill, other, hire., close, .steal, .whom, trust, .shout, case., unless.
87261 | 0.95

424 experience *n*
adj personal, human, sexual, different, previous, past, educational, positive, early, religious *noun* year., student, life, learning., field., teaching., knowledge, training *verb* learn, share., provide, base., teach, gain, describe., draw, reflect, lack.
89900 | 0.92 A

425 cut *v*
noun tax, .piece, .cost, hair, budget, spending, tree, .deal, .slice, knife, .strip, .deficit, .corner, throat, .chunk *misc* .into, .through, .half, .short, peel., .loose, .thin, deeply, propose.
    back force., .spending, .forth, .production, .fat, sharply, drastically, .purchase, .salt, .travel **off** head, .supply, .aid, hair, .fund, completely, threaten., .escape, abruptly **out** work., .shape, cookie, .circle, tongue, .fat, biscuit, .middleman **down** tree, forest, .fat, .size, .net, .travel
89101 | 0.92

426 kill *v*
noun people, man, soldier, civilian, American, wife, father, son, person, police, husband, accident, animal, attack, bomb *misc* shoot., someone, .wound, somebody, threaten., nearly
    off by, .bacteria, .any, cell, character, cancer, .dinosaur, antibiotic., .entire, nearly
85730 | 0.95

427 behind *i*
.him, .her, door, leave., back, stand., hide., .bar, .scene, sit., wall, .wheel, .desk, close.
87372 | 0.93 F

428 reach *v*
noun hand, agreement, .point, .level, .conclusion, .goal, .age, .end, door, .top, .peak, arm, consensus, .height, .phone *misc* before., until., .across, finally., once., .beyond, forward, .critical
    out hand, .touch, .other, .grab, try, arm, .help, effort. **over** .touch, .pat, .grab, .shoulder, .squeeze, .gently, .stroke, .tap **up** .touch, .pull, .grab, .stroke, .brush, .rub, .pat, .grasp **down** .pick, .pull, .grab, .touch, .lift, .pet, .pat, .pluck
84993 | 0.96 F

429 six *m*
.month, .year, .week, five., after, about., .day, .ago, .seven, last., .foot, four, .hour, .eight
83613 | 0.97

430 local *j*
noun government, state, school, community, official, level, people, news, group, authority, station, police *misc* national, federal, regional, check, global, environmental, contact
85964 | 0.94

431 remain *v*
noun question, .mystery, second., challenge, .calm, minute., troop., decade, focus, core, doubt, .secret, priority, inflation., gap *misc* while, .until, .same, .silent, however, .open, .constant, .unchanged
84339 | 0.95

432 effect *n*
adj significant, main, negative, positive, special, possible, direct, profound, environmental, economic *noun* side., .size, health, study., cause., drug, change, interaction, sound., greenhouse. *verb* produce., examine., create, determine., investigate., indicate, predict, analyze., explore., estimate
88201 | 0.91 A

433 suggest *v*
noun study., evidence., research., result., finding., data., report., model, approach., possibility, factor, pattern, strategy, title, .presence *misc* recent., strongly., instead, previous., .otherwise
85793 | 0.93 A

434 use *n*
adj widespread, personal, effective, increased, illicit, efficient, extensive, steroid *noun* drug., .force, land., substance., alcohol, .technology, resource, water, energy, condom. *verb* make., reduce., report., require, associate, involve., support., encourage.
88244 | 0.90 A

435 control *n*
adj remote, internal, local, civilian, parental, complete, total, direct *noun* .group, center, disease., system, birth., gun., arm., .prevention, .room, quality. *verb* take., lose., gain., maintain., exercise., regain., seize.
84620 | 0.94 A

436 perhaps *r*
.most, .even, .more, .because, .important, .best, .greatest, except., .importantly, .surprising, bit, hundred, .famous, .due
81241 | 0.97

437 raise *v*
noun question, .money, .child, .hand, .tax, issue, .eyebrow, concern, .voice, .price, family, .rate, fund, .awareness, .glass *misc* born., .serious, billion, .minimum, .interesting, slowly
   up God., child, generation
80127 | 0.98

438 class *n*
adj middle, working, social, upper, special, whole, entire, ruling *noun* student, school, education., time, race, music., .size, .action *verb* teach, attend, offer, graduate., enroll., conduct, complete, divide, cook., belong.
84406 | 0.93 A

439 late *j*
noun afternoon, century, night, summer, spring, show, fall, husband, father, winter *misc* too, during, until, since, nineteenth, early, twentieth, twenties
80023 | 0.98

440 little *r*
a., .more, .bit, .than, .too, feel., .better, .less, .different, maybe, .later, .far, .long, .nervous
81488 | 0.95

441 major *j*
noun league, problem, city, change, role, issue, company, factor, player, source, area, concern *misc* play, represent, minor, metropolitan, urban, industrial, undergo, virtually
81592 | 0.95

442 yeah *u*
oh., well, right, OK, sure, yes, exactly, .guess
95029 | 0.81 S

443 else *r*
something., someone., anything., anyone., everyone., everything., than., somebody., nothing., everybody., one., no., anybody.
80932 | 0.95

444 pass *v*
noun bill, law, year, Congress, house, .test, legislation, Senate, resolution, car, hour., week, .generation, legislature, tax *misc* .away, .by, .along, .through, quickly, front, easily, .overhead
   out drunk., .leaflet, nearly., .flier, .condom, .pamphlet, .literature, .flyer, .candy **on** .generation, knowledge, gene, tradition, saving, .future, inheritance **over** .promotion, cloud., storm., .silence, .favor
79512 | 0.97

445 photo *n*
adj white, black, framed, black-and-white, still, glossy, autographed, graphic, accompanying, front-page *noun* .color, staff., illustration, .courtesy, collection., artist., family, image, .album, mug *verb* .omit, snap., pose, feature, print, display, picture, post, decorate, upload
88458 | 0.87 M

446 sell *v*
noun company, product, year, house, stock, .copy, share, store, car, home, book, business, ticket, drug, market *misc* million, buy., hard., .directly, cheap, retail, .used
   out game, .every, show, ticket, concert, quickly, stadium, tour., .less, completely
81890 | 0.94 N

447 themselves *p*
they, find., other, among., identify., protect., consider., defend., present., express., view., perceive., commit., define.
79533 | 0.96

448 field *n*
adj magnetic, playing, open, left, visual, electric, green, gravitational *noun* .goal, .study, track., .trip, oil., football., research, .experience *verb* enter., level., plow., dominate, cross, narrow., advance., sweep, overlook., border
80577 | 0.95

449 college *n*
adj junior, black, electoral, four-year, medical, technical *noun* community., student, university, school, year, education, .football, art, .campus, professor *verb* attend., teach, enter., earn, finish., complete, enroll, coach
87246 | 0.88

450 sometimes *r*
.even, wonder, hard, difficult, .forget, hour, .refer, .wish, funny, angry, .violent, painful, sad, .contradictory
78719 | 0.97

451 former *d*
.president, .Soviet, .United States, .secretary, .chief, .director, .member, .union, .governor, .executive, .official, .minister, .chairman, .senator
81629 | 0.93 N

452 development *n*
adj economic, professional, human, social,
sustainable, international, urban, late
noun research., program, child, community,
project, skill, stage., housing., policy, business.
verb promote., lead, support., contribute.,
encourage., focus, .occur, relate, influence.,
facilitate.
85506 | 0.89 A

453 require *v*
noun law, state, student, skill, change, level, rule.,
.attention, education, process, act., care, regulation,
use, action *misc* .less, special, far, additional, usually.,
physical
82624 | 0.92 A

454 along *i*
.with, .way, .line, .road, .river, .coast, walk., .border,
run., .street, .side, .wall, .edge, .path
78485 | 0.97

455 decide *v*
noun court., judge., jury., .fate, official., Congress.,
voter., election, administration., juror., commissioner.,
.punishment, guilt, lawmaker., merit *misc* .whether,
try, finally., .stay, .not, instead, whatever, ultimately.
77673 | 0.98

456 security *n*
adj social, national, economic, international, financial,
internal, collective *noun* .council, homeland., .force,
.guard, .system, .adviser, issue, threat, .resolution,
nation. *verb* provide., protect, improve, ensure.,
maintain., threaten, guarantee, enhance., tighten,
pose
81021 | 0.93

457 up *i*
.to, live., walk., .until, .stair, step, lead., .hill, stand.,
.point, add., .street, .road, pull.
79281 | 0.95

458 possible *j*
noun explanation, world, effect, solution, reason, use,
exception, cause, source, outcome, attack, extent
misc as, make, much, soon, best, quickly, whenever,
everything
79042 | 0.96 A

459 effort *n*
adj best, concerted, successful, collaborative,
serious, joint, conscious, cooperative, current,
extra *noun* time., government, war., research.,
reform., relief., lot., administration, support,
success *verb* make, require, lead, focus, fail,
coordinate., involve, concentrate, .address,
.achieve
80242 | 0.94 A

460 role *n*
adj important, major, key, active, significant, central,
crucial, critical *noun* .model, woman, government,
gender., leadership., teacher, play, sex., conflict, lead.
verb assume., define, perform., determine, fill,
examine., emphasize., .shape, reverse, adopt
81660 | 0.92 A

461 better *j*
noun way, job, life, understanding, chance, place,
thing, world, part, idea, health, care *misc* than,
much, any, bad, nothing, off
70900 | 0.98

462 rate *n*
adj high, low, annual, average, current, overall,
faster, alarming, metabolic *noun* interest., percent,
growth, heart., tax., exchange., unemployment.
verb increase, rise, raise., reduce., fall, lower., cut,
.drop, report, slow
81150 | 0.93 A

463 strong *j*
noun support, woman, sense, economy, feeling,
evidence, relationship, wind, case, family, position,
hand *misc* very, enough, remain, weak, pretty,
particularly, healthy, despite
77028 | 0.97

464 music *n*
adj classical, popular, pop, live, instrumental,
contemporary, loud *noun* .education, .teacher,
.educator, school, country., student, art, program,
video *verb* play, listen., hear, teach, dance, love,
perform, record, blare, select
95675 | 0.78 A

465 report *v*
noun news., study, percent, Washington, student,
result, case, participant., teacher, respondent., finding,
newspaper., correspondent., .use, patient *misc* likely.,
similar, recently, .significantly, previously.
81154 | 0.92 A

466 leader *n*
adj religious, democratic, military, black, local,
national, Palestinian, Soviet, Iraqi, civil *noun* majority.,
Senate., world, party, business., community, minority.
verb elect., recognize, urge, rush, accuse, invite,
.oppose, criticize, arrest, convince
79582 | 0.94

467 light *n*
adj red, bright, green, blue, yellow, fluorescent,
visible, natural, soft, ultraviolet *noun* .bulb, day,
window, morning, shadow, traffic., city, dark, speed.,
sun *verb* turn, shed., shine, flash, reflect, cast, dim,
catch, .flicker, .burn
80950 | 0.92 F

468 whole *j*
noun thing, lot, life, world, time, family, story,
process, idea, body, country, system *misc* new,
spend, damn, apart, cup, ahead, fucking, damned,
practically
77505 | 0.96

469 voice *n*
adj low, soft, deep, loud, quiet, familiar, male,
female, hoarse, husky *noun* woman, man, tone.,
.mail, mother, father, .whisper, village., ear, .recorder
verb hear, speak, raise., .sound, lower., .rise, listen.,
sing, recognize, .break
81800 | 0.91 F

470 color *n*
adj different, bright, light, dark, primary, favorite,
vibrant, vivid, cool, brilliant *noun* photo., skin,
people., .page, shape, hair, texture, illustration,
image, .scheme *verb* add, change, paint, choose,
mix, match, apply, fade, blend, print
88116 | 0.84 M

471 heart *n*
adj human, broken, artificial, healthy, lonely, bleeding,
tender, generous, damaged, respiratory *noun* .attack,
.disease, .rate, risk., mind, .failure, .soul, .problem,

blood, cancer _verb_ break, die., .beat, stop, .pound,
suffer., win., .race, lie, .sink
77705 | 0.95

472 care _n_
adj medical, foster, primary, long-term, managed,
intensive, better, prenatal _noun_ health., child, day.,
.system, patient, home, cost, quality., service,
education _verb_ take., provide, receive, improve,
seek., deliver, afford.
81285 | 0.91

473 police _n_
adj local, military, secret, armed, metropolitan,
uniformed, mounted _noun_ .officer, .department,
chief, .force, .station, .car, city, new. _verb_ call, tell,
.arrest, report, state, .arrive, .investigate, shoot,
.search, .respond
79307 | 0.93 S

474 economic _j_
noun growth, development, policy, reform,
problem, activity, system, crisis, issue, power,
condition, sanction _misc_ political, social,
cultural, military, environmental, international,
global, current
83625 | 0.88 A

475 wife _n_
adj pregnant, beautiful, future, estranged, lovely,
dear, beloved _noun_ .child, husband, .daughter,
man., mother, .son, .kid, survivor. _verb_ kill, .die,
include., meet, marry, murder, survive., beat.,
divorce, sleep
77029 | 0.95

476 show _n_
adj popular, live, daily, favorite, syndicated, one-man,
light, freak, greatest, magic _noun_ talk., TV., radio.,
television., .host, .business, reality. _verb_ watch.,
.feature, enjoy., steal., tape, air, attend., cancel,
organize, star
79776 | 0.92 S

477 mind _n_
adj human, open, fresh, blank, conscious, sharp,
brilliant, rational, unconscious, subconscious
noun body, people, state., heart, eye, doubt.,
peace., thought, frame. _verb_ keep., change., bear.,
lose., read., cross., speak., .wander, enter., .race
76497 | 0.96

478 report _n_
adj special, recent, annual, final, full, financial,
medical, live, preliminary, previous _noun_ news.,
world., .card, commission, police., committee,
consumer., credit. _verb_ issue, contribute., release,
write, file, read., publish, .indicate, prepare,
.suggest
77459 | 0.95

479 finally _r_
when., until., break, .decide, .reach, .arrive, .tonight,
.realize, .settle
75609 | 0.97

480 drug _n_
adj new, illegal, illicit, available, experimental,
intravenous, used, harsh, expensive, safe _noun_ alcohol,
prescription., .administration, food., .dealer, .abuse,
.company, .user, war _verb_ use, sell, deal, test, treat,
approve, develop, prescribe, fight, reduce
78879 | 0.93

481 less _r_
.than, or., more, .likely, much., become., far.,
.expensive, .important, little., often, care., lot.,
.effective
76648 | 0.95

482 return _v_
noun .call, .work, .home, week, .phone, starter,
month, .earth, .trip, .fire, hour, questionnaire,
.favor, .yard, refugee _misc_ when., after, before.,
later, soon
75289 | 0.97

483 according _i_
(according to) .to, .report, year., .study, .national,
.official, .recent, .survey, .source, .record, .research,
.department, .data, .estimate
77135 | 0.94

484 pull _v_
noun hand, .trigger, hair, door, .chair, .gun, .plug,
.string, pocket, bag, shoulder, bed, troop, camera,
station _misc_ .into, .away, her, .together
    up car., .front, .chair, truck., .next, .beside, .outside,
.behind, bus., .alongside **off** .road, .upset, .glove,
.shirt, shoe, .highway, .boot, .miracle **back** .reveal,
hair., camera., .curtain, lip., slowly, .onto, troop
out pocket., .gun, bag, drawer, troop, .chair, box,
.wallet **down** .pant, hat., shade, cap., .rebound
80028 | 0.90 F

485 decision _n_
adj final, right, important, difficult, tough, major,
informed, conscious, key, wrong _noun_ court.,
.maker, policy., judge, process, business., investment.,
.making, action, choice _verb_ make, base, affect,
influence., reach, face, announce, appeal., reverse,
accept
76755 | 0.94

486 explain _v_
noun .difference, theory, factor., variance,
.situation, behavior, .phenomenon, .purpose,
.detail, variable, .origin, variation, .importance,
.significance, mystery _misc_ .why, how, try., help.,
hard., attempt., fully
74717 | 0.96

487 carry _v_
noun yard, .bag, .gun, .weight, .weapon, .load, baby,
.message, burden, .passenger, .gene, pound, shoulder,
.sign, .tradition _misc_ .away, heavy, .forward, concealed,
.along, .extra
    out attack, study, order, .mission, research,
.task, operation, .duty, .function, .responsibility
on .conversation, .tradition, .affair, .legacy, .fight
73994 | 0.97

488 develop _v_
noun program, system, .skill, student, plan,
technology, relationship, model, strategy, process,
.weapon, research, product, ability, .understanding
misc new, help., .own, .nuclear, fully
78843 | 0.91 A

489 view _n_
adj different, political, clear, better, spectacular,
religious, panoramic, broad, rear, differing
noun point., world, mountain., people, field.,
.life, ocean, river _verb_ express, hold, share,
offer., change, support., reflect, block.,
hide., echo
75670 | 0.95 A

490 free *j*
noun trade, agent, market, speech, time, press, hand, throw, man, world, election, will *misc* set, offer, break, available, fair, under, relatively, completely, unrestricted, truly
74532 | 0.96

491 hope *v*
noun official., scientist., researcher., organizer., .glimpse, .miracle, supporter., planner., NASA. *misc* I., .will, we, certainly., .enjoy, .pray, .someday
74716 | 0.96

492 even *c*
(even if, even though) .though, .if, .when, .disagree, persist., .technically, unpopular
72593 | 0.98

493 drive *v*
noun car, .mile, truck, night, hour, .town, street, cost, .nut, bus, .airport, .wedge, driver, .influence, license *misc* .home, .down, .through, .away, .crazy, .past, .across
  up .price, .cost, car., .down, .rate, demand, .coast, .driveway **down** .price, .highway, .cost, .wage, .avenue, .boulevard, competition., .freeway **off** car., truck., .down, .bridge, van., cab., ambulance. **out** competition, Taliban, .competitor, .demon
74262 | 0.96

494 son *n*
adj young, old, only, eldest, teenage, native, married, favorite *noun* daughter, father, wife., mother, .bitch, husband, death, birth., king, infant. *verb* kill, .die, lose, raise., .born, send, murder, coach, .inherit, bury
74476 | 0.96

495 arm *n*
adj right, left, upper, strong, nuclear, outstretched, open, bare, wide, thin *noun* leg, hand, shoulder, .control, head, side, .length, .embargo, body, .sales *verb* put., hold, grab., raise, wrap, lift, cross, fold, throw., pull
78121 | 0.91 F

496 department *n*
adj interior, athletic, English, academic, agricultural, administrative, clinical, conservation, editorial, cabinet-level *noun* justice, police., US., health, education, defense, .store, fire., agriculture, energy *verb* .report, state, investigate, head, .announce, issue, contact., conduct, .estimate, oversee
75130 | 0.95

497 true *j*
noun story, dream, nature, believer, opposite, self, meaning, statement, identity, spirit, faith *misc* love, religion
73173 | 0.97

498 price *n*
adj high, low, average, retail, reasonable, median, natural, heavy, domestic *noun* oil, stock., gas., market, .tag, increase, share., percent, .range, food *verb* pay, rise, fall, raise., drive., drop, set, lower., offer, reduce
77951 | 0.91

499 military *j*
noun force, action, service, officer, base, personnel, power, operation, leader, official, police, presence

misc American, political, against, civilian, economic, Soviet, Iraqi, Israeli
80792 | 0.88

500 federal *j*
noun government, court, law, state, agency, judge, commission, program, tax, official, fund, budget *misc* reserve, under, local, require, receive, according, grand
76465 | 0.92 N

501 break *v*
noun .law, heart, news, .rule, silence, story, .ground, .barrier, leg, bone, .piece, .neck, arm, .cycle, voice. *misc* .into, .away, .free, .apart, .loose
  up marriage, .fight, boyfriend, meeting., girlfriend, union, band, pass, .demonstration, .monotony **down** .into, .barrier, car., .cry, .door, .tear, talk, enzyme., completely, negotiation. **out** war., fight., fire., sweat, fighting., riot., violence., .laugh, .hive **off** piece, talk, .engagement, negotiation, branch, abruptly, .relation
72917 | 0.97

502 action *n*
adj affirmative, military, political, legal, collective, environmental, civil, necessary, appropriate, disciplinary *noun* course., plan, government, .program, class., committee, .research, responsibility., decision *verb* take, support, justify., miss., file, perform, defend., initiate., influence, direct
74890 | 0.94 A

503 value *n*
adj social, traditional, human, low, democratic, total, religious, personal, daily, shared *noun* family., market., .system, property, stock, face., dollar, culture, society, core. *verb* add, base, place, increase, reflect, teach, share, recognize., represent, compare
77244 | 0.91 A

504 thank *v*
noun .God, US., .goodness, gentleman, .me, author., Lord, .heaven, .reviewer, madam, compliment, admiral, blessing, .hospitality, update *misc* .you, .much, .very, so, join, .both, all, like.
81968 | 0.86 S

505 relationship *n*
adj sexual, close, personal, significant, social, positive, strong, working, human, special *noun* family, people, kind., nature, variable, power, business, type, peer, partner *verb* develop, examine., establish., build., maintain., .exist, describe., explore., cultivate., emphasize.
77024 | 0.91 A

506 town *n*
adj small, little, whole, southern, nearby, rural, tiny, entire *noun* city, house, .hall, .meeting, center, home, mile, part. *verb* leave., drive., visit, head, arrive., ride., overlook, skip., dot, border
73258 | 0.96

507 better *r*
.than, get, know, feel., much., even., understand, lot., little., .able, .yet, perform., .prepare, serve
71981 | 0.98

508 building *n*
adj federal, tall, public, main, downtown, commercial, green, abandoned, two-story, burning *noun* office., apartment., .block, street, school, .material, brick.,

government., floor, center *verb* .house, design, enter., construct, own, .collapse, surround, blow, occupy, burn
73021 | 0.96

509 receive *v*
noun .attention, letter, .call, treatment, support, information, service, .training, benefit, percent, .degree
misc million, .little, .less, .federal, .special, medical
74021 | 0.95 A

510 society *n*
adj American, civil, historical, democratic, modern, human, free, astronomical, humane *noun* member, people, state, woman, culture, science., cancer., .whole, individual, institution *verb* exist, reflect, contribute, transform, function, integrate., benefit, impose, shape, evolve
76447 | 0.92 A

511 difference *n*
adj significant, big, individual, only, important, major, mean, ethnic, huge, fundamental *noun* gender., group, age, sex, time, similarity, score, .opinion, level, .rate *verb* make., show., .exist, reveal., indicate., explain., examine., notice., identify, .emerge
76474 | 0.91 A

512 church *n*
adj Catholic, Methodist, Christian, Episcopal, Presbyterian, orthodox, Lutheran *noun* member, Baptist., .leader, service, separation., pastor, teaching, council *verb* attend., build, .state, .teach, sing, belong, preach, organize, rebuild, violate.
78027 | 0.89

513 full *j*
noun time, moon, day, year, life, range, house, name, circle, potential, hour, force *misc* half, ahead, empty, partial, devote, diplomatic, frontal, chock, head
71340 | 0.98

514 join *v*
noun .morning, .force, group, .club, .army, .team, .studio, other, .phone, party, .conversation, .rank, union, organization, .staff *misc* .us, .now, .live, today, .tonight, .together
  in other., everyone., too, soon, .sing, voice, everybody
74889 | 0.93 S

515 road *n*
adj long, main, paved, winding, two-lane, dusty, straight, icy, impassable, flat *noun* side., dirt., mile, car, .map, .trip, country., mountain, block, .bike *verb* drive, .lead, build, walk, hit., travel, cross, head, line, wind
74410 | 0.93

516 because *i*
(because of) .of, part, .its, simply., partly., afraid, interesting., precisely., part., largely., .lack, partly., mainly., .nature
71389 | 0.97

517 international *j*
noun community, law, organization, airport, trade, relation, agency, fund, study, system, center, conference *misc* national, monetary, domestic, economic, human, financial, environmental, criminal
75688 | 0.91 A

518 model *n*
adj new, standard, theoretical, available, conceptual, linear, alternative, medical, various, mathematical

noun role., computer., year, development, business., program, regression., variable, use, analysis
verb provide, develop, base, serve., test, build, .predict, offer, create, present
76219 | 0.90 A

519 position *n*
adj strong, better, current, difficult, key, official, top, unique, awkward, upright *noun* power, leadership, government, president, .issue, starting., .paper, sitting. *verb* take, hold, change., occupy., support, assume., maintain., place, .repeat, defend
72064 | 0.95

520 tax *n*
adj high, federal, flat, corporate, total, huge, fair, luxury, marginal, minimum *noun* .cut, income., property., .increase, .rate, .credit, sales. *verb* pay, raise., reduce, support, file., propose, finance, fund, gain., promise
75006 | 0.91 S

521 director *n*
adj national, athletic, managing, assistant, associate, medical, artistic, public, regional *noun* executive., board., .center, program, research, deputy., film, marketing, communication, .office *verb* serve., rate., name, appoint., hire, contact., elect, scout, nominate, .oversee
73960 | 0.93 N

522 early *r*
as, year, .on, .morning, month, week, .today, mention., century, .season
69883 | 0.98

523 agree *v*
noun expert., court., party., official., judge, deal, scientist., .principle, contract, majority, analyst., settlement, observer., scholar., economist.
misc most., everyone., strongly, .pay, .disagree, finally.
71247 | 0.95

524 matter *n*
adj bad, organic, dark, practical, simple, serious, private, legal, religious, ordinary *noun* fact, subject., .time, truth., day, policy, choice, family., .minute, .hour *verb* discuss., settle, deal, resolve, handle, relate, investigate., pursue.
69694 | 0.97

525 especially *r*
.when, .those, .since, .important, young, .among, now, .one, difficult, .light, .vulnerable, .useful, popular, .helpful
70559 | 0.96

526 form *n*
adj other, new, different, various, human, social, final, common, pure, particular *noun* art., life, .government, consent., shape, tax, .communication, function, .cancer, behavior *verb* take., fill, sign., complete, .update, exist, assume., file, engage., evolve
73363 | 0.92 A

527 record *n*
adj public, criminal, historical, previous, official, financial, winning, all-time, consecutive, congressional *noun* track., world., company, school., .number, court., .label *verb* set., show, keep, break., sell, tie., .indicate, review, state, compile.
71721 | 0.94 N

528 special *j*
noun education, interest, force, report, program, student, need, prosecutor, edition, effect, service, team *misc* something, require, receive, administrative, tonight, regular, welcome, deserve
70227 | 0.96

529 ground *n*
adj common, high, middle, fertile, solid, bare, sacred, firm *noun* foot, troop, force, .zero, .floor, .pepper, .war, cinnamon, .level, salt *verb* fall., hit., break., stand, cover, lose., gain., lie., touch., shake
69175 | 0.97

530 whose *d*
.name, .work, .include, family, only, parent, father, member, .son, .husband, wife, daughter, artist., .career
69861 | 0.96

531 hard *j*
noun time, drive, way, thing, rock, part, day, disk, look, evidence, question, currency *misc* it, very, work, find, really, believe, imagine
69150 | 0.97

532 pick *v*
noun draft, .tab, .fight, stock, .bag, wind., .winner, .spot, .ball, .newspaper, glass, fruit, .gun, .cotton, .flower *misc* .off, .choose, bend., .apart, carefully, .random, ring, .remote, ripe
   up .phone, where, .piece, .book, .speed, .tab, pace, .bag, wind., .newspaper
70476 | 0.95 F

533 paper *n*
adj white, local, brown, waxed, recycled, yellow, daily, technical, federalist *noun* piece., sheet., .towel, .bag,

toilet., morning, pencil, scrap., pen, .plate *verb* read., write, publish, present, sign, wrap., describe, print, cover, place
70426 | 0.95

534 official *n*
adj senior, local, elected, public, federal, top, American, military, Israeli, Chinese *noun* government., state, administration., city., department., school., health. *verb* .say, meet, .acknowledge, .insist, .estimate, .deny, .admit, elect., .discuss, .plan
74190 | 0.90 N

535 season *n*
adj regular, growing, dry, full, rainy, final, entire *noun* game., .salt, end, holiday., time, team, week, .pepper, .ticket, league *verb* play, open, finish, enter., last, mark, .progress
76544 | 0.87 N

536 wear *v*
noun clothes, .suit, .dress, man., .hat, woman., .shirt, shoe, .uniform, .jeans, .jacket, .pant, .mask, .coat, .glove *misc* .black, .white, .blue, .red, always.
   out .welcome, too, shoe, body., tired., quickly, boot, soon **off** novelty., shock., drug., .quickly, initial., euphoria., eventually **on** day, evening., afternoon., season., summer.
71314 | 0.93 F

537 event *n*
adj historical, recent, important, current, past, annual, main, traumatic, stressful, cultural *noun* life, world, .place, sporting., series., history, sport., week, sequence., turn. *verb* .occur, .lead, attend., win, .unfold, plan, organize, host, experience, surround
69644 | 0.95

---

5. Emotions

Negative

[Top 50] (sorry) $_{32861}$, afraid $_{26791}$, angry $_{20693}$, (crazy) $_{19380}$, guilty $_{17002}$, nervous $_{13551}$, scared $_{10335}$, desperate $_{9382}$, worried $_{8807}$, (bitter) $_{8041}$, (uncomfortable) $_{7381}$, anxious $_{6825}$, lonely $_{6594}$, (reluctant) $_{6587}$, disappointed $_{6446}$, (hostile) $_{6162}$, (uncertain) $_{5746}$, upset $_{5730}$, embarrassed $_{5443}$, depressed $_{5379}$, suspicious $_{5208}$, unhappy $_{4995}$, (awkward) $_{4687}$, troubled $_{4644}$, (grim) $_{4192}$, furious $_{4008}$, confused $_{3936}$, ashamed $_{3905}$, (useless) $_{3876}$, frightened $_{3867}$, shocked $_{3793}$, miserable $_{3662}$, bored $_{3614}$, jealous $_{3208}$, fearful $_{3165}$, helpless $_{2988}$, uneasy $_{2976}$, frustrated $_{2740}$, outraged $_{2573}$, impatient $_{2460}$, (hopeless) $_{2148}$, (rotten) $_{2005}$, annoyed $_{1968}$, stunned $_{1867}$, hysterical $_{1662}$, terrified $_{1603}$, (powerless) $_{1598}$, somber $_{1514}$, gloomy $_{1459}$, fed up $_{1423}$

Neutral

surprised $_{18138}$, shy $_{5563}$, (cautious) $_{4238}$, (thoughtful) $_{3644}$, (tense) $_{3174}$, puzzled $_{2616}$, (energetic) $_{2542}$, exhausted $_{2121}$, (shaky) $_{2110}$, unsure $_{2083}$, startled $_{1571}$, (serene) $_{1375}$, ambivalent $_{1305}$, (timid) $_{1127}$, (detached) $_{989}$, smug $_{955}$, (taken aback) $_{854}$, apologetic $_{690}$, (unsettled) $_{429}$, sheepish $_{359}$, contrite $_{274}$, (infatuated) $_{257}$, (bashful) $_{229}$, distracted $_{167}$, repentant $_{147}$, penitent $_{79}$, (rattled) $_{48}$

Positive

happy $_{49524}$, glad $_{14889}$, confident $_{10334}$, pleased $_{8194}$, excited $_{8103}$, satisfied $_{4514}$, hopeful $_{4372}$, loving $_{4362}$, passionate $_{4341}$, sympathetic $_{4336}$, enthusiastic $_{3941}$, humble $_{3201}$, (fond) $_{3193}$, delighted $_{2871}$, cheerful $_{2521}$, (compassionate) $_{2184}$, ecstatic $_{1294}$, (affectionate) $_{1009}$, (appreciative) $_{900}$, elated $_{622}$, thrilled $_{495}$, (genial) $_{455}$, euphoric $_{422}$, overjoyed $_{399}$, contented $_{392}$, jovial $_{325}$, gleeful $_{320}$, (touched) $_{147}$, worshipful $_{107}$

538 support *v*
noun family, evidence., research, president, study,
.effort, government, finding, hypothesis, data, .idea,
result., community, position, .claim *misc* strongly.,
fully., democratic, generally., financially
70392 | 0.94 A

539 space *n*
adj open, outer, public, empty, international, living,
available, green, deep *noun* time, .station, .shuttle,
.telescope, .program, .center, office., air., foot., .flight
verb create, fill, occupy, share., stare., fly., rent.,
design, define, transform
69223 | 0.95

540 player *n*
adj best, young, key, great, major, defensive, valuable,
better, greatest, pro *noun* team, football., basketball.,
baseball., league, CD., school, tennis., season, owner
verb sign, name, recruit, .score, earn, draft, compete,
trade, rush, scout
74983 | 0.88 N

541 everyone *p*
.else, know, .agree, almost., nearly., .laugh, .except,
.happy, surprise, virtually., please, .involved, hello.,
equal
68112 | 0.96

542 couple *n*
adj married, young, elderly, odd, interracial,
infertile, unmarried, middle-aged, royal, homosexual
noun .year, .day, .week, .time, .month, .hour, .minute
verb spend, marry, adopt, .file, dance, divorce, last.,
stroll, .wed, chat
68509 | 0.95

543 end *v*
noun war, year, season, month, career, marriage, week,
relationship, .video, .divorce, .clip, quarter., period.,
.videotape, .violence *misc* fiscal., soon, abruptly,
eventually., effectively., .badly, officially., .happily
   up .with, will., .like, might., .pay, .dead, .jail, .cost,
usually., eventually.
67329 | 0.97

544 base *v*
noun decision, study, data, research, system,
information, .experience, model, value, result,
evidence, .principle, theory, finding, .race
misc .upon, largely, .solely, primarily
70237 | 0.93 A

545 project *n*
adj large, public, special, involved, federal, joint,
various, ambitious, current, proposed *noun* research.,
development, housing., construction., .manager,
director, pilot., genome. *verb* work, include, complete,
fund, .involve, support, undertake, finance, plan,
participate.
69629 | 0.93 A

546 produce *v*
noun .result, .effect, product, plant, image, energy, oil,
film, food, change, material, good, cell, electricity,
crop *misc* enough, .significant, similar, capable.,
.positive, locally
69105 | 0.94 A

547 site *n*
adj historic, archaeological, online, sacred, holy, grave,
specific, various, historical, potential *noun* web.,
Internet., construction., waste., test., park, crash.,

visit, landing. *verb* .offer, check., locate, .contain,
identify, select, clean, maintain, launch, access
69287 | 0.93

548 situation *n*
adj bad, difficult, current, similar, political, social,
economic, dangerous, whole, particular *noun* people,
kind., family, security., emergency., type., response.,
hostage., variety. *verb* change, create, improve,
handle., face, deal., describe, explain., .involve, occur
67816 | 0.95

549 hit *v*
noun ball, .head, .ground, shot, car, .target, .road,
.wall, .button, .floor, plane., bullet, rock, hurricane,
storm. *misc* .home, .hard, before., .bottom, hardest,
harder, somebody, kick, straight
67484 | 0.94

550 industry *n*
adj private, pharmaceutical, entire, heavy, nuclear,
chemical, automotive *noun* oil., tobacco., auto.,
music., insurance., entertainment., airline., .analyst
verb develop, regulate, dominate, affect, employ,
promote, deregulate, attract, invest, spawn
68750 | 0.93

551 half *d*
than., about., .hour, more., year, .dozen, two., only.,
.million, .century, nearly., over, cut., .ago
65437 | 0.97

552 activity *n*
adj physical, other, sexual, economic, human, social,
criminal, illegal, various, terrorist *noun* student, level,
school, group, program, kind., teacher, leisure.,
education, brain *verb* engage., include, participate.,
involve, support, perform, plan, promote, conduct,
focus
71827 | 0.89 A

553 American *n*
adj native, average, native-born, patriotic, first-
generation, overworked, provident *noun* percent.,
majority., number., way, lot., thousand. *verb* believe,
kill, .live, die, understand, .spend, .support, afflict,
emulate, overrun
67727 | 0.94

554 eat *v*
noun food, .lunch, meal, .dinner, .breakfast, .meat,
fish, .fruit, dog, .vegetable, restaurant, .sandwich,
chicken, .egg, animal *misc* drink, sleep, enough,
.healthy, exercise, cook
   up .by, .all, more, cost, .mile, .every, debt., inflation,
.profit, easily. **out** when., .restaurant, meal,
.frequently, afford.
67606 | 0.94 F

555 itself *p*
manifest., within, present., lend., process., defend.,
repeat., reveal., nature., transform., pride., upon,
express., bill.
66722 | 0.95 A

556 need *n*
adj special, social, specific, urgent, educational,
desperate, economic, personal, immediate, particular
noun student, child, people, family, community,
health, teacher, interest, individual, population
verb meet., feel., .change, address., eliminate.,
recognize., satisfy., serve., emphasize.
68745 | 0.92 A

557 figure *n*
adj public, political, human, central, female, major, historical, key, available, male *noun* graph., diagram., table., father., authority., map., .page, action. *verb* see., show, illustrate, represent, present, depict, indicate, emerge, paint, carve
70277 | 0.90 A

558 cost *n*
adj high, low, total, average, social, economic, environmental, additional, marginal, annual *noun* care, health, percent, production, labor, energy, .saving, service *verb* reduce., cut., pay, cover., rise, increase, estimate, include, lower., add
68990 | 0.92

559 easy *j*
noun way, access, task, target, answer, part, chair, money, solution, decision, reach, step *misc* relatively, quick, that, pretty, forget, fairly, imagine, spot
65691 | 0.96

560 quite *r*
.a, not., .as, .different, .bit, never., .few, .frankly, .sure, often, .clear, actually., .while, .right
65048 | 0.96

561 face *v*
noun problem, challenge, issue, .charge, question, threat, dilemma, .death, situation, .reality, difficulty, nation, risk, .competition, obstacle *misc* up, other, turn., let., .each, .tough, serious
63730 | 0.98

562 picture *n*
adj big, best, clear, whole, complete, pretty, accurate, overall, beautiful *noun* motion., book, .window, wall, family, word, .frame, camera, magazine, page *verb* take, see., look, paint., draw., send, snap., present, hang, .emerge
64568 | 0.96

563 clear *j*
noun sky, water, message, evidence, day, picture, lake, view, night, plastic, understanding, idea *misc* it, that, make, very, become, whether, quite, pretty, blue
63629 | 0.98

564 cover *v*
noun .story, .cost, face, water, insurance, area, wall, head, plastic, ground, body, .expense, floor, reporter., .mouth *misc* until, .cook, simmer, .entire, completely, .refrigerate, enough., tightly
up try., .crime, lie, .fact, attempt., something, .evidence, effort., .mistake, .murder
63957 | 0.97

565 describe *v*
noun article, word., process, .experience, term, situation, .relationship, paper, event, section, model, scene, report, behavior, condition *misc* .as, how, .above, best., .himself, accurately, previously, similar
66241 | 0.93 A

566 image *n*
adj public, digital, visual, negative, positive, mental, additional, still, graphic, familiar *noun* body., mirror., color, screen, video, quality, computer, star, film, satellite. *verb* create, produce, project, .appear, capture, conjure., present, form, improve., .reveal
66924 | 0.92 A

567 teach *v*
noun student, school, child, class, teacher, course, skill, lesson, year, university, .kid, music, education, college, experience *misc* .how, learn, .basic, .elementary, .respect, effective, effectively, currently., Catholic, .proper, .advanced
66658 | 0.92 A

568 wall *n*
adj white, far, concrete, opposite, outer, blue, dark, green, yellow, front *noun* .street, stone., back., brick., window, glass, hole., painting, city, rock *verb* hang., lean., build, cover, hit., line, stand, face, push, surround
65253 | 0.94 F

569 doctor *n*
adj medical, primary, sick, primary-care, ill, Cuban, prescribed, reluctant, optimistic, honorary *noun* patient, hospital, .nurse, .office, family, visit, drug, health, appointment, treatment *verb* ask, .prescribe, .treat, .recommend, check, .perform, .diagnose, consult., refer, trust
64925 | 0.94

570 recent *j*
noun year, study, month, research, report, history, book, week, survey, day, poll, interview *misc* most, more, show, during, according, suggest, despite, indicate, relatively
65145 | 0.94

571 product *n*
adj new, domestic, finished, final, natural, available, agricultural, industrial, specific, cultural *noun* company, consumer, line, food, dairy., .development, quality, technology *verb* sell, use, buy., produce, market, develop, .contain, create, offer, introduce
66463 | 0.92 M

572 data *n*
adj available, demographic, recent, raw, scientific, qualitative, empirical, electronic *noun* analysis, .collection, study, system, table, source, information, survey, set, computer *verb* collect, use, .show, provide, analyze, gather, .indicate, base, .suggest, obtain
70493 | 0.87 A

573 practice *n*
adj social, private, religious, common, best, current, medical, clinical, standard, sexual *noun* law, theory., policy, business., management, skill, .medicine, teacher, education, .session *verb* engage., teach, improve, adopt, reflect, implement, encourage, examine, influence, inform
67369 | 0.91 A

574 phone *n*
adj cellular, mobile, local, cordless, portable, prepaid, rotary, high-speed, nearest, hand-held *noun* .call, cell., .number, .company, .line, .ring, .service, .book, .conversation, address. *verb* pick., answer., use, talk., hang., dial, receive., return., check, connect
65324 | 0.93

575 piece *n*
adj small, little, large, single, tiny, short, missing, particular, bite-size, favorite *noun* .paper, .evidence, .legislation, bit., .information, .equipment, .wood, .furniture, .cake, .land *verb* cut., write, pick., break., fall, buy., place, tear., fit, publish
63628 | 0.96

576 certain *j*
noun thing, amount, way, kind, time, type, point, area, level, group, extent, condition *misc* such, almost, absolutely, fairly, under, from, virtually
62856 | 0.97

577 either *r*
.or, interest., .search, .modify, .directly, choice., .negative, assign., .indirectly, classify., randomly., .explicitly, .unwilling, .physically
62432 | 0.97

578 oil *n*
adj crude, hot, foreign, essential, offshore, domestic, imported, used *noun* price, .company, .gas, tablespoon., cup, vegetable., heat, .industry, olive., teaspoon *verb* add, .spill, drill, produce, sell, cook, pour, increase, reduce, sesame.
67264 | 0.90 M

579 simply *r*
not, .because, put, rather., quite., .matter, .true, .ignore, than., .enough, .disappear, .afford, .vanish, .impossible
62154 | 0.97

580 test *n*
adj standardized, nuclear, positive, diagnostic, genetic, medical, comprehensive, physical, specific, ultimate *noun* .score, result, blood., achievement., drug., DNA., litmus. *verb* pass., .show, conduct, perform, fail, administer, .determine, measure, .indicate, .reveal
65135 | 0.92 A

581 personal *j*
noun life, computer, experience, relationship, information, responsibility, trainer, communication, level, history, problem, interest *misc* own, professional, social, political, close, financial, private, individual
62727 | 0.95

582 star *n*
adj bright, young, red, brightest, massive, rising, excellent, hot, extraordinary, central *noun* movie., .war, rock., .trek, film, cluster, neutron., light, pop., basketball. *verb* form, .shine, rise, orbit, explode, observe, surround, twinkle, earn, feature
68290 | 0.88 M

583 land *n*
adj public, private, federal, holy, promised, agricultural, native, dry *noun* .use, acre., water, .mine, area, .management, forest, .reform, sea, resource *verb* own, buy., sell, protect, purchase, acquire, clear, .belong, control, surround
63801 | 0.94

584 third *m*
.world, second., .year, .party, .quarter, about., .fourth, .grade, .floor, finish., .base, .season, .baseman, .person
61853 | 0.96

585 general *j*
noun attorney, manager, motor, office, public, education, counsel, assembly, population, election, accounting, hospital *misc* electric, former, assistant, united, vice, specific, elementary, cognitive, linear, theoretical
63479 | 0.94 A

586 computer *n*
adj personal, digital, portable, sophisticated, interactive, handheld, used, complex, high-speed, faster *noun* .system, .screen, .program, .software, technology, .science, network, .game, .model *verb* use, buy, connect, generate, link, check, install, store, operate, display
63867 | 0.93 M

587 movie *n*
adj favorite, classic, popular, scary, famous, upcoming, violent, animated, silent, made-for-TV *noun* .star, .theater, television, scene, studio, home., show, .house, video, horror. *verb* see, watch., love, direct, feature, film, rent, inspire, portray, review
64171 | 0.93

588 worker *n*
adj social, American, skilled, united, temporary, foreign, hard, average, postal, medical *noun* health, job, construction., factory., care, farm., migrant., aid. *verb* hire., employ, lay, train, .earn, protect., represent, rescue., fire, expose
64599 | 0.91

589 open *j*
noun door, space, window, eye, mouth, market, question, house, mind, field, forum, air *misc* leave, British, remain, swing, win, wide
61429 | 0.96

590 catch *v*
noun .eye, .breath, fish, .glimpse, .attention, .fire, .sight, .ball, yard, light, .middle, arm, camera, .bus, .act *misc* before, finally., .cold, .myself, .steal, .off-guard, hurry., .red-handed, occasionally., .unawares
up .in, .with, get., finally., hurry., .sleep, eventually., .gossip, .paperwork, .academically
on quickly, finally., .fast, slow., eventually., .wildfire, instantly, slower.
62569 | 0.94 F

591 type *n*
adj different, other, certain, various, specific, particular, common, similar, basic, sexual *noun* .thing, .diabetes, people, .person, personality, body., blood., .error, material, sport *verb* identify., represent, determine., depend., vary, relate, distinguish., select, engage., classify.
63528 | 0.93 A

592 support *n*
adj social, financial, public, strong, political, emotional, international, popular, military *noun* .group, family, child., .system, service, community, life., lack., network *verb* provide., need, receive, offer., win., show., gain., lend., maintain, obtain
63548 | 0.93 A

593 north *n*
adj far, communist, due, temperate, near, indigenous, magnetic, frozen, industrialized, tropical *noun* south, mile., state, .side, east, west, .trade, .shore, coast, .agreement *verb* head., move., drive., travel., migrate., extend, invade, flee.
61959 | 0.95

594 love *n*
adj romantic, tough, unconditional, lost, brotherly, passionate *noun* life, .affair, .story, song, .letter, sex, marriage, .scene, labor., respect *verb* fall., make.,

share, express., declare., inspire, profess., .conquer, bind, confess.
62109 | 0.94

595 step n
adj important, small, necessary, major, final, giant, positive, significant, logical, simple *noun* .direction, process, back, porch, number., baby., stone., couple., dance., hall *verb* take., walk., follow, climb., retrace., represent., .ensure, descend., complete
60883 | 0.96

596 attention n
adj special, close, national, public, medical, particular, full *noun* media., lot., people, .detail, .deficit, .disorder, .span, center. *verb* pay., get., draw., focus, turn., give, receive., attract., call., catch.
60161 | 0.97

597 technology n
adj new, advanced, modern, available, digital, medical, nuclear, assistive *noun* information., science., company, use., computer, education, development, communication, transfer, advance. *verb* develop, .allow, improve, .enable, invest., incorporate, integrate, adopt, .exist, combine
63679 | 0.92 A

598 organization n
adj other, international, national, nonprofit, political, social, religious, professional, terrorist, large *noun* world., health., news., group, community, trade., woman, right., service, government *verb* support, represent, join, form, found, .promote, .dedicate, .operate, manage, belong
63144 | 0.92 A

599 baby n
adj little, healthy, newborn, beautiful, tiny, unborn *noun* .boomer, mother, girl, .boy, birth, .boom, parent, .sister, .food, .brother *verb* .born, hold, cry, .die, deliver., carry, kill, sleep, feed, adopt.
63081 | 0.92

600 source n
adj other, major, primary, reliable, important, main, only, potential, light, available *noun* information, energy, water, power, food, data, .income *verb* provide, identify, cite, reveal, quote, locate, .research, confirm, derive., obtain
62135 | 0.93 A

601 draw v
noun .attention, line, conclusion, .breath, .picture, .crowd, blood, plan, distinction, experience, paper, circle, .fan, knee, weapon *misc* .from, .between, .upon, .close, .closer, .away, .together
up plan, will, .list, paper, agreement, contract, constitution, document, .guideline, .blueprint
out long, .implication, pocket., .syllable, .juice
60142 | 0.96

602 cause v
noun problem, damage, disease, death, pain, .trouble, .cancer, injury, loss, harm, virus, heart, condition, drug, fire *misc* .by, may., .serious, severe, likely., .significant, .massive
60064 | 0.96

603 tree n
adj tall, small, large, fallen, bare, nearby, dark, native, mature, beautiful *noun* Christmas., branch, palm., trunk, oak., pine., apple., family. *verb* grow, plant,

cut, climb., hang, line, hide, surround, decorate, remove
62040 | 0.93 F

604 film n
adj independent, short, thin, animated, foreign, silent, upcoming, photographic, gay, low-budget *noun* .festival, director, feature., .critic, television, star, .industry, .maker, .version *verb* watch., direct, produce, shoot, release, capture, view, depict, review, portray
62093 | 0.92 N

605 choose v
noun word, option, reason., color, path, site, .career, subject, candidate, method, individual, participant., freedom., route, topic *misc* .between, right, .among, carefully, pick., .ignore
59236 | 0.97

606 evidence n
adj physical, scientific, strong, empirical, clear, hard, circumstantial, anecdotal, available *noun* piece., DNA., body., lack., kind, lot., rule. *verb* find., .suggest, provide., show, .support, present, .indicate, base, gather, .point
60918 | 0.94

607 Republican n
adj conservative, moderate, fellow, prominent, leading, registered, lifelong *noun* .party, Democrat, house, senator, .candidate, .committee, .leader *verb* vote, win, elect, control, oppose, accuse, propose, criticize, favor, defeat
65057 | 0.88 S

608 difficult j
noun time, situation, task, question, problem, decision, issue, case, job, position, choice, circumstance *misc* it, very, more, make, find, most, become
59582 | 0.96

609 century n
adj early, late, previous, mid, coming, Ottoman, preceding, bloody, Portuguese, influential *noun* turn., end., half., quarter., decade., beginning., middle., world, woman, art *verb* date., enter., survive., last., span., evolve, found, persist, .progress, invent
61799 | 0.92 A

610 nearly r
.year, .all, .as, .million, .percent, .every, .two, .half, .three, .ago, .decade, .billion, .month, .four
59262 | 0.96

611 red j
noun pepper, cross, light, wine, hair, eye, onion, flag, face, blood, carpet, tape *misc* white, blue, green, yellow, wear, black, bright, hot
60466 | 0.94 F

612 look n
adj closer, quick, hard, close, better, fresh, serious, puzzled, critical *noun* .face, .eye, thing, life, kind, .surprise, .mirror, exchange, .faraway. *verb* take., give, let., shoot., cast., sneak., steal.
60801 | 0.93 F

613 point v
noun finger, gun, evidence., sign, critic., toe, camera, arrow., foot, .sky, poll., telescope, .spot, .importance, pistol *misc* to, .toward, .straight, .directly, .upward

out as., also., however, important, correctly.,
rightly., .error, scholar., .flaw, proudly.
58087 | 0.98

614 window *n*
adj front, rear, broken, narrow, round, huge, wide,
arched, French, floor-to-ceiling *noun* door, glass,
car, light, bedroom., kitchen., .opportunity, picture.
verb look, open, stare., stand, watch, roll, close,
break, lean, peer.
63090 | 0.90 F

615 park *n*
adj national, public, industrial, nearby, regional,
grand, conservation, marine, proposed, protected
noun .service, state., city, theme., amusement.,
mountain., street, .system, forest, college.
verb preserve, visit, establish, overlook, contact,
surround, stroll, encompass, jog., roam.
64483 | 0.88 N

616 period *n*
adj long, short, early, extended, brief, colonial,
five-year, three-year, postwar, two-year *noun* time,
year, month, war, study, transition, class., growth,
grace. *verb* .end, enter., extend, last, experience,
characterize, .range, date., span, coincide
60958 | 0.93 A

617 culture *n*
adj popular, political, native, dominant, traditional,
mass, corporate, contemporary, common, modern
noun history, language, art, society, pop., religion,
.war, material., aspect., politics *verb* understand,
define, represent, study, influence, promote,
preserve., shape, celebrate, dominate
62520 | 0.90 A

618 hair *n*
adj black, long, dark, blond, brown, gray, white,
red, short, thick *noun* eye, face, head, skin, color,
strand., makeup, .loss, .cell, .dryer *verb* cut, pull, wear,
comb, brush, .fall, grow, stroke., wash., .hang
62955 | 0.89 F

619 listen *v*
noun .music, .radio, .edition, ear, hour, silence,
.recording, .wind, .speech, .jazz, .lecture, while,
breath, speaker, album *misc* .to, talk, .carefully, sit.,
watch, .intently
in let., .conversation, phone, .call, able., someone,
else., FBI., .briefly **up** okay., everyone, guy, folk, hey.
59950 | 0.94 F

620 chance *n*
adj good, better, best, only, fair, excellent, fat,
reasonable, rare *noun* percent., people, .success, life,
.survival, peace, fighting. *verb* have., get, give., take.,
.win, stand., increase., offer.
57808 | 0.97

621 less *d*
(less than) .than, percent, .year, much., .hour,
nothing., .minute, cost, .half, .month, far., .money,
spend., .week
57222 | 0.96

622 available *j*
noun information, data, resource, service, option,
store, technology, material, evidence, space, product,
source *misc* make, become, readily, widely, best, only,
currently, commercially
58717 | 0.93 A

623 brother *n*
adj old, young, big, little, elder, Muslim, like, eldest,
dear *noun* .sister, father, mother, twin., baby., kid,
half. *verb* .die, visit, marry, murder, inherit, tease,
hug, spare, glare, betray
57793 | 0.95 F

624 summer *n*
adj late, hot, early, past, warm, previous, following
noun day, .camp, spring., winter, night, month,
.program, .vacation, end, heat *verb* spend.,
attend., last, bloom., cool, swim, plant, rain, rent,
.progress
57454 | 0.95

625 realize *v*
noun .potential, .dream, .mistake, .importance,
vision, gain, .extent, .danger, ambition, .error,
retrospect, ideal, panic *misc* .that, .how, when.,
then., suddenly., begin.
56631 | 0.97

626 private *j*
noun sector, school, collection, life, company,
property, government, practice, land, business,
insurance, firm *misc* both, hire, attend, personal,
religious, nonprofit, corporate, public
57460 | 0.95

627 no *r*
matter., .how, .doubt, can., means
56030 | 0.97

628 science *n*
adj social, political, natural, environmental, modern,
medical, human, basic *noun* .technology, .monitor,
art, .fiction, math, center, professor, .education,
computer., .teacher *verb* teach, advance, integrate.,
major., specialize, .progress, reshape
60485 | 0.90 A

629 letter *n*
adj open, recent, anonymous, scarlet, pastoral, angry,
handwritten, bold, featured, written *noun* .editor,
number, president, love., call, name, phone, .writer,
e-mail, reader *verb* write, send, receive, read, sign,
contain, mail, .arrive, answer., state
56226 | 0.97

630 congress *n*
adj national, democratic, federal, continental,
Republican, divided, partisan, ruling, regulatory,
representative *noun* member., president, year, US.,
house, people, party, law, administration, power
verb pass, approve, .enact, .vote, testify., elect,
control, authorize, urge, lobby.
59336 | 0.91 S

631 condition *n*
adj economic, human, medical, social,
environmental, physical, certain, living, necessary,
working *noun* weather., .anonymity, health.,
control., heart, treatment, participant, market.,
disease, variety. *verb* improve, create, speak.,
meet, affect, cause, .exist, describe, treat,
impose
59008 | 0.92 A

632 short *j*
noun time, story, term, period, hair, life, distance, run,
break, supply, list, while *misc* fall, stop, long, cut,
relatively, ago, nothing, wear, tall, fairly
55624 | 0.97

633 likely *j*
noun candidate, voter, result, scenario, effect, outcome, impact, explanation, cause, source, target, consequence *misc* more, less, than, as, seem, much, most
57746 | 0.93 A

634 opportunity *n*
adj new, equal, great, economic, educational, unique, available, better, ample, rare *noun* student, people, employment., job., business, window., teacher, photo., .commission, practice *verb* give., provide., offer., create, present, miss., seize., afford., open, explore
57255 | 0.94 A

635 rule *n*
adj new, general, federal, military, colonial, proposed, international, golden, democratic, authoritarian *noun* .law, .game, exception., .thumb, .regulation, set., change, .procedure, ground., majority. *verb* follow., break., apply, play., .require, .govern, violate., .allow, enforce, .prohibit
57102 | 0.94

636 choice *n*
adj best, right, personal, free, individual, tough, hard, multiple, obvious, available *noun* school, people, career., freedom., word, matter, draft., food, decision *verb* make, give., offer., face, limit, influence., affect, reflect, narrow., inform.
55581 | 0.97

637 single *j*
noun mother, day, woman, parent, person, word, year, thing, man, family, mom, layer *misc* every, most, large, important, married, greatest, rather, European
55164 | 0.97

638 place *v*
noun .hand, emphasis, .order, side, bowl, pan, table, sheet, call, ad, oven, plate, .bet, position, .blame *misc* .on, .under, best., .within, .upon, carefully, .near, strategically.
55901 | 0.95

639 patient *n*
adj ill, clinical, elderly, mental, psychiatric, sick, female, normal, positive, surgical *noun* care, doctor, cancer., percent., AIDS., number., .right, drug, heart, health *verb* treat, .receive, .undergo, .die, .experience, .suffer, identify, diagnose, discharge, test
67634 | 0.79 A

640 floor *n*
adj top, concrete, wooden, main, bare, flat, carpeted, bottom, shiny *noun* room, foot, dance., wall, Senate, ground., ceiling, tile, kitchen., .plan *verb* sit., fall., lie., lay, drop., hit., reach, scrub., spread, knock
57715 | 0.92 F

641 term *n*
adj long, select, short, general, near, economic, practical, technical, uncertain, simple *noun* .interest, document., use., president, prison., .office, meaning, life, .agreement, .paper *verb* come., serve., describe, limit, define, coin, .refer, apply, seek., accept.
56829 | 0.94 A

642 material *n*
adj raw, nuclear, genetic, organic, radioactive, natural, fissile, basic, advanced, explicit *noun* quote., building., use, source., resource, .culture, amount., construction,

product, science *verb* contain, provide, include, produce, read, develop, teach, collect, gather, remove
58547 | 0.91 A

643 mile *n*
adj square, long, extra, downtown, nautical, distant, frequent, mere, due, round *noun* .north, .south, .west, .east, .day, thousand., city *verb* go., drive., walk., run., travel., live., locate., swim, wind, separate
56860 | 0.93

644 administration *n*
adj federal, national, senior, current, previous, democratic, civil, educational, presidential, successive *noun* .official, drug., food., policy, US, business., security., health., safety., aviation. *verb* .propose, criticize, .seek, .announce, argue, .fail, .approve, .insist, accuse, defend
57075 | 0.92 S

645 well *i*
(as well as) as, .one, individual, physical, cultural, emotional, practical, spiritual, .numerous, overall, technical, psychological, visual, personnel
56538 | 0.93 A

646 course *n*
adj main, introductory, online, required, due, short, physical, traditional, normal, remedial *noun* golf., .action, education, college, study, history, .work, university, teacher, obstacle. *verb* take., teach, offer, change., run., stay., complete, follow, require, chart.
57843 | 0.91 A

647 defense *n*
adj national, legal, criminal, civil, environmental, strategic, aggressive, joint, defensive, immune *noun* secretary, .attorney, .lawyer, missile., minister, .fund, .team, .system, US., .budget *verb* play, .argue, rush, score, mount., testify, attack, deploy, strengthen., .rest
56373 | 0.93

648 plant *n*
adj new, nuclear, native, chemical, potted, aquatic, green, industrial, growing, tall *noun* power., animal, species, treatment., .life, tree, manufacturing., processing. *verb* grow, build, produce, close, operate, shut, feed, collect, water, generate
58750 | 0.89 M

649 energy *n*
adj renewable, solar, atomic, nuclear, alternative, total, kinetic *noun* source, time., .efficiency, use, .policy, price, .resource, cost, .conservation, amount. *verb* save., produce, reduce, focus, spend, increase, expend, conserve., burn, measure
57086 | 0.92

650 campaign *n*
adj presidential, political, military, successful, negative, primary, senatorial *noun* .finance, .reform, ad, election., .trail, .contribution, issue, .manager *verb* run, launch., wage, mount., conduct, organize., contribute., .aim, .feature, engage
57423 | 0.91 S

651 population *n*
adj large, general, total, local, entire, growing, human, diverse, civilian, rural *noun* percent., .growth, world., student, US., segment., size, rate, .density, majority. *verb* .grow, serve, reduce, decline, estimate, represent, double, control, affect, study
58499 | 0.89 A

652 fire *n*
adj friendly, heavy, warm, machine-gun, anti-aircraft, rapid *noun* .department, police, forest., firefighter., .station, line, .truck, .escape *verb* set., .burn, start, open., catch., light., build., fight., destroy, kill
55188 | 0.95

653 close *v*
noun eye, door, .gap, hand, window, mouth, book, deal, office, store, stock., month, poll., lid, .loophole *misc* .behind, open, .enough, .together, .by, slowly, .lock, tightly, lean, inside.
in .around, wall., winter, police., camera., darkness., quickly, fog. **down** .operation, plant, factory, shop, facility, .newspaper, industrial., stock. **up** .shop, Dow., throat., average., .tight
55989 | 0.93 F

654 daughter *n*
adj young, old, teenage, beautiful, eldest, adopted *noun* son, mother., wife., father, husband, life, sister, marriage, baby, birth *verb* marry, raise., .born, visit, .attend, adopt, bury, .graduate, divorce, hug
54836 | 0.95

655 involve *v*
noun case., issue, process, student, study., activity, .use, project., research, parent, effort, decision, step, analysis, procedure. *misc* usually., complex, directly, physical, actively., typically., .hundred
55342 | 0.94 A

656 husband *n*
adj late, future, estranged, abusive, loving, devoted, beloved *noun* wife, child, father, woman, son, family, daughter, death, sister *verb* .die, kill, meet., lose, marry, divorce, share, murder, sleep, cheat
54734 | 0.95

657 wrong *j*
noun thing, way, place, time, side, direction, answer, person, message, reason, turn, number *misc* what, something, there, nothing, anything, right, prove, maybe
54515 | 0.95 S

658 certainly *r*
.not, well., almost., most, .hope, .true, .lot, .worth, .aware, .is, .entitle, .understandable, .plausible
55619 | 0.93 S

659 increase *v*
noun number, .risk, rate, year, tax, price, cost, .amount, production, .chance, .likelihood, population,

pressure, .size, power *misc* dramatically, significantly, continue., greatly., substantially
56165 | 0.92 A

660 future *n*
adj near, foreseeable, bright, uncertain, better, immediate, distant *noun* past, child, country, vision., present., hope., wave., market, energy, prospect. *verb* .hold, plan., predict., face., shape., build., determine., .depend, worry., promise
53959 | 0.95

661 south *n*
adj black, deep, rural, suburban, segregated, upper, tropical, polar, temperate, agricultural *noun* north, mile., .side, west, city, new, street, area, .pole, .end *verb* head., move., live., drive., travel., face, locate., host, drift., .secede
54674 | 0.94

662 medical *j*
noun center, school, care, association, treatment, service, record, doctor, examiner, research, student, problem *misc* American, receive, seek, chief, scientific, British, regional, dental
55101 | 0.93

663 call *n*
adj close, long-distance, tough, quick, incoming, repeated, frantic, urgent, domestic, numerous *noun* phone., telephone., wake-up., information., conference., roll., house, .center *verb* make, get., take., receive., give., return., answer.
54282 | 0.95

664 board *n*
adj national, advisory, federal, editorial, medical, governing, diving, cutting, wooden, online *noun* member, school., .director, .education, bulletin., chairman, county. *verb* serve., .meet, approve, .vote, cut, .decide, join., appoint, elect, state
54600 | 0.94 N

665 anyone *p*
.who, can, .else, than., want, never., tell, ever, why., before, anything, better., hurt, care
53317 | 0.96

666 deal *v*
noun .problem, .issue, drug, .situation, .blow, .crisis, matter, .reality, .stress, .threat, card, crime, .loss, .violence, .aspect *misc* .with, how., difficult, .directly, effectively, prepare.
53382 | 0.96 S

6. Family

child ₃₂₃₀₀₅, mother ₁₆₃₂₈₂, father ₁₄₀₁₇₆, (kid) ₁₂₆₀₅₄, parent ₁₁₅₃₃₉, wife ₈₀₃₈₀, son ₇₇₈₄₈, (baby) ₆₅₆₁₅, brother ₆₀₇₅₃, husband ₅₇₆₂₅, daughter ₅₇₅₅₁, sister ₄₅₉₀₄, mom ₃₉₀₂₁, dad ₃₄₃₆₄, uncle ₁₈₀₉₁, twin ₁₅₀₇₃, aunt ₁₃₁₈₄, grandmother ₁₃₀₄₅, daddy ₁₂₇₄₈, cousin ₁₁₆₄₀, mama ₁₀₈₃₈, grandfather ₁₀₆₆₃, ancestor ₆₃₃₆, sibling ₅₈₆₄, bride ₅₆₇₇, (widow) ₅₂₆₅, grandparent ₅₁₄₇, grandchildren ₄₈₄₆, grandma ₄₅₂₉, papa ₄₀₀₇, (guardian) ₃₇₅₅, groom ₃₄₅₈, nephew ₃₀₆₆, grandson ₂₈₅₃, grandpa ₂₈₁₀, orphan ₂₄₀₃, niece ₂₃₅₇, granddaughter ₁₈₇₁, ex-wife ₁₆₁₇, granny ₁₅₄₇, brother-in-law ₁₃₁₂, ex-husband ₁₂₆₀, mother-in-law ₁₂₅₃, godfather ₁₁₅₁, fiancé ₁₀₅₆, son-in-law ₉₂₁, sister-in-law ₈₆₃, fiancée ₈₁₅, father-in-law ₈₁₂, grandchild ₇₈₅, daughter-in-law ₆₅₆, triplet ₆₂₈, (widower) ₅₈₀, foster child ₄₇₀, godmother ₄₀₉

667 hospital *n*
adj medical, local, mental, psychiatric, public, military, nursing, nearby, regional, not-for-profit *noun* child., doctor, .room, patient, .bed, care, center, state, emergency, home *verb* admit., treat, rush., visit, release, arrive., enter., discharge, volunteer, .diagnose
54778 | 0.93

668 rest *n*
adj eternal, well-deserved, well-earned, prolonged, much-needed, fitful, deserved *noun* .life, .world, day, .country, .room, .season, hour, .society, .history, minute *verb* spend., lay., separate., enjoy., compare., isolate., devote.
52316 | 0.97

669 seek *v*
noun .help, information, .support, .advice, .treatment, .refuge, .solution, .approval, .care, .assistance, justice, .term, .shelter, .truth, .employment *misc* actively., professional, .avoid, .establish, desperately.
    out .new, people, .help, woman, actively., .opportunity, .destroy, .advice, .enemy, aggressively.
54039 | 0.94 A

670 myself *p*
I, find., tell., feel, ask., consider., kill., remind., force., imagine., introduce., throw., convince., enjoy
54892 | 0.92 F

671 county *n*
adj rural, surrounding, neighboring, urban, metropolitan, coastal, elected, historic, populous, fastest-growing *noun* school, city, .sheriff, district, .office, .official, .commissioner, .board, court, .attorney *verb* .vote, approve, locate, file, sue, contact., elect, appoint, reside., populate.
58889 | 0.86 N

672 fight *v*
noun war, battle, .terrorism, .fire, force, soldier., army, .crime, troop, drug, .cancer, enemy, .disease, American, .tear *misc* .against, other, hard, .each, continue., die
    off .infection, .attack, .disease, .attempt, .attacker, .cancer, ability., .virus, .sleep, successfully. **back** .tear, .against, try, decide., industry., urge, ready., smile, courage.
52567 | 0.96

673 subject *n*
adj human, academic, favorite, male, female, particular, normal, various, healthy, sensitive *noun* .matter, study, .area, group, school, test., number, knowledge, .debate, interest *verb* change., teach, discuss, broach., relate, .range, address, .participate, approach., obtain
58051 | 0.87 A

674 risk *n*
adj high, great, increased, low, developing, serious, significant, relative, greatest *noun* .factor, cancer, .disease, health, .heart, breast, .assessment, .behavior, .management, .injury *verb* take., reduce., increase., run., put., associate, pose, involve, minimize., consider.
55137 | 0.92 A

675 order *n*
adj social, political, restraining, international, economic, natural, tall, moral, alphabetical, descending *noun* world., court., law., executive., thing, mail., .business *verb* give, issue, follow., place., maintain., restore, sign., determine, .prevent
52744 | 0.96

676 west *n*
adj wild, far, due, arid, coastal, Antarctic, industrialized, intermediate, prosperous, mountainous *noun* .bank, .coast, east, .side, .street, .point, mile., south, north, key.
verb move., head., travel., locate., sail., flow., migrate., situate.
53141 | 0.95

677 economy *n*
adj global, political, local, strong, national, growing, weak, booming, domestic, healthy *noun* world., US., fuel., state, country, sector., growth, nation, .scale, society *verb* .grow, slow, improve, stimulate., affect, .recover, hurt, expand, boost., .depend
54930 | 0.92

678 quickly *r*
as, very., move., more., .become, too., .possible, turn, learn, away, change, grow, act., .enough
51995 | 0.97

679 throw *v*
noun .ball, .hand, .arm, .party, head, rock, .money, door, stone, .yard, window, .punch, light, .ground, floor *misc* .into, .away, .back, .down, .around
    out court, judge., case, .window, ballot, appeal, conviction, .arm, lawsuit **up** .hand, .arm, bathroom, barrier, dust, sick., barricade **off** .balance, .timing, .robe
53233 | 0.95 F

680 bed *n*
adj asleep, empty, double, ready, warm, narrow, four-poster, unmade, king-size, separate *noun* night, hospital., side., foot., edge., time, breakfast, sheet, flower., chair *verb* go., get., sit., lie., lay., sleep, fall, climb.
55810 | 0.90 F

681 officer *n*
adj chief, military, financial, senior, commanding, young, top, retired, medical, naval *noun* police., executive., army., operating., law., intelligence., enforcement. *verb* serve, shoot, train, .arrive, arrest, enlist, respond, .charge, hire., appoint
53661 | 0.93 N

682 represent *v*
noun .text, group, .percent, equation., lawyer., .interest, attorney., figure, organization, change, line., union, value, character., district *misc* each, .significant, .claim, total, accurately., adequately.
54477 | 0.92 A

683 soon *r*
will, as, .after, too., .possible, .become, may., pretty., .enough, begin, anytime., follow, .realize, home
51960 | 0.96

684 top *n*
adj very, green, flat, tall, tight, convertible, sleeveless, matching, rounded, spinning *noun* .head, .list, .bottom, page, .percent, tank., mountain, .stair, table, .hour *verb* reach., rank., climb., finish., rise., sprinkle, cover, blow., spread, pour
52867 | 0.94 M

685 fill *v*
noun room, water, air, .gap, eye, form, space, .void, glass, tear, hole, tank, box, seat, role *misc* .with, enough., empty, quickly, entire, suddenly., completely

out .form, .application, .questionnaire, .paperwork, .card, .survey, paper, .tax, .online **up** room, .tank, space, gas, water, car, quickly, .fast, .tear
52313 | 0.95

686 author n
adj best-selling, favorite, prize-winning, award-winning, principal, primary, contemporary, prolific, abstract, published _noun_ .affiliation, .book, study, article, editor, novel, writer, life, professor, report _verb_ write, .thank, note, .acknowledge, .wish, .conclude, .contribute, publish, photograph., review
53280 | 0.94 M

687 past j
noun year, decade, week, month, day, season, century, president, couple, experience, summer, research _misc_ over, two, few, during, three, five, several, four
51970 | 0.96

688 upon i
base., depend., call., once., rely., dependent., draw., build., agree., focus., act., .return, fall., impose.
52990 | 0.94 A

689 goal n
adj ultimate, primary, common, main, long-term, social, personal, environmental, clear, stated _noun_ field., program, .orientation, policy, life, achievement, career., .setting, project, strategy _verb_ achieve., set, meet., reach., accomplish., score., pursue.
54097 | 0.92 A

690 behavior n
adj sexual, social, human, aggressive, disruptive, appropriate, antisocial, bad, inappropriate, positive _noun_ problem, student, child, attitude, pattern, change, risk., parent _verb_ engage., influence, exhibit, affect, control., predict., identify, determine, examine, focus
58018 | 0.85 A

691 drop v
noun .percent, school, bomb, hand, price, rate., charge, .floor, ball, temperature., head, ground, level, jaw., .pound _misc_ .into, .down, .onto, .below, .dead, .dramatically
off .sleep, .passenger, .dramatically, .bag, .sharply, .considerably, .laundry, cleaning **out** student., .because, before, likely., bottom., .graduation, abruptly., runner. **by** thanks., .visit, appreciate, .check, .chat, neighbor.
51864 | 0.95 F

692 nature n
adj human, very, fundamental, changing, sexual, essential, complex, exact, spiritual, competitive _noun_ mother., man, law, thing, relationship, force., state, science, .center, extent _verb_ understand., change., reflect., determine., reveal, recognize., explore., imply, grasp., endow
53837 | 0.92 A

693 agency n
adj federal, environmental, other, international, free, regulatory, social, various, official, responsible _noun_ government., state, protection., intelligence., US., enforcement., law., news. _verb_ .report, .charge, .issue, hire, oversee, monitor, .conduct, .operate, .regulate, fund
53143 | 0.93

694 plan v
noun year, company., .trip, .attack, activity, project, lesson, strategy, event, official., retirement, wedding, vacation, meeting, operation _misc_ .spend, .ahead, .build, .stay, carefully
out .there, life, well, attack, everything, future, really., whole.
51384 | 0.96

695 recently r
more., until., most., only., as., .publish, .announce, .release, .complete, .discover, .sign, .introduce, researcher
51896 | 0.95

696 second n
adj split, close, final, distant, mere, brief, silent, extra, finished, flat _noun_ minute, time, foot., couple., fraction., meter., .thought, matter., kilometer. _verb_ take, wait., hold., finish, last., .pass, .remain, count, tie., pause.
51141 | 0.96

697 store n
adj available, retail, general, antique, health-food, online, select, independent, federated, Asian _noun_ grocery., department., food., convenience., hardware., liquor., .owner, video. _verb_ sell, buy, open, walk., own, close, .carry, hit., visit, enter.
52163 | 0.94

698 foreign j
noun policy, minister, language, investment, country, US, affair, relation, aid, ministry, government, committee _misc_ American, domestic, speak, Soviet, military, direct, Russian, French
53808 | 0.91 A

699 current j
noun result, study, system, state, level, research, situation, law, policy, practice, rate, issue _misc_ set, within, under, former, economic, future, base, narrow
52724 | 0.93 A

700 performance n
adj academic, poor, overall, better, economic, athletic, actual, financial _noun_ student, level, school, music, test, measure, task, skill, standard, job. _verb_ improve., affect., enhance, base, evaluate., assess., increase, indicate, result, reflect
55276 | 0.89 A

701 bank n
adj central, national, federal, large, commercial, international, reserve, foreign, major, outer _noun_ world., .account, loan, river, money, investment., credit, development, fund, saving _verb_ rob., buy, .lend, own, .fail, finance, charge, issue, borrow, operate
52366 | 0.93

702 sound n
adj soft, loud, faint, familiar, distant, strange, muffled, digital _noun_ voice, music, .bite, .system, sight., word, .effect, .wave, island., quality _verb_ make, hear., listen, produce, .echo, wake, record, fade, scream, utter.
52792 | 0.93 F

703 push v
noun .button, door, .limit, .envelope, .chair, price, hair, .cart, wall, .agenda, .glass, administration, crowd,

.legislation, finger _misc_ .into, .out, .through, .away, her, .down, .aside, .forward
  back .chair, .hair, .against, up, date, hat, .hard, cap
51229 | 0.95 F

704 focus v
noun attention, study., research., eye., effort, program., education, energy, article., development, .aspect, activity, goal, project, skill _misc_ instead, primarily, tend., .exclusively
  on we., shall., need, .how, just, want., only
51735 | 0.94 A

705 reduce v
noun .risk, .heat, .cost, .number, .emission, .rate, .amount, tax, .deficit, .size, .stress, effort., .pollution, pressure, energy _misc_ help., .low, significantly., greatly., .simmer, dramatically., substantially.
52650 | 0.92 A

706 note v
noun report, difference, court., author, researcher, official., article, observer., critic., historian, review, participant., .importance, trend., .absence _misc_ .that, important., .above, worth., interesting.
52745 | 0.92 A

707 before r
have, never., see., than., year., ever., day., night., hear., week., happen., month., once., anything.
51209 | 0.95 F

708 fine j
noun art, line, museum, print, point, hair, wine, job, detail, example, restaurant, dining _misc_ just, everything, perfectly, OK, along, okay, long, suit, mighty
50843 | 0.96

709 near i
.end, home, live., .border, park, stand., anywhere., town, center, river, city, area, .top, street
50854 | 0.95

710 than i
(other than, rather than) more., less., rather., better., year, much., any, other., high., percent, far., .ever, .million
51693 | 0.94 A

711 movement n
adj social, political, environmental, Islamic, feminist, democratic, conservative, nationalist, growing, gay _noun_ right., woman., labor., reform., leader, freedom., liberation., democracy _verb_ control, track., organize, restrict, limit, facilitate., monitor., detect., inspire, .arise
52014 | 0.93 A

712 common j
noun sense, ground, problem, law, cause, practice, interest, goal, denominator, theme, language, knowledge _misc_ most, more, among, become, less, increasingly, quite
51850 | 0.93 A

713 other p
(each other) each., .than, look., talk., against., love., anything., something., face, no., none., any., stare., fight.
50441 | 0.96 F

714 billion m
.year, than., .dollar, over, spend, cost., worth, revenue, nearly., sales, total., per
53579 | 0.90

715 blood n
adj red, cold, dried, fresh, holy, mixed _noun_ .pressure, .vessel, .cell, .test, .sugar, .flow, .level, heart _verb_ draw, cover., cause, drip, reduce, stain, .clot, drink., .pour, .rush
51693 | 0.93

716 page n
adj opposite, front, editorial, yellow, blank, previous, printed, double, facing, revised _noun_ web., color., story, top, home., box., table, newspaper, article, figure. _verb_ see., turn., show, read, face., appear., flip., fill, list, contain
51595 | 0.93 M

717 concern n
adj environmental, major, great, big, public, main, primary, social, growing, particular _noun_ issue, health, security, safety, area., cause., matter., lot., lack _verb_ express., raise, address., share., voice., reflect., focus, .arise, ignore, balance.
51279 | 0.94 A

718 poor j
noun people, country, child, woman, man, family, health, performance, neighborhood, condition, thing, kid _misc_ rich, standard, working, rural, because, urban, elderly, fair
49997 | 0.96

719 enter v
noun .room, .world, .house, student, door, .market, .office, .college, .building, force, .race, data, .plea, .profession, .period _misc_ .into, before., once., upon, soon., .overall, exit, .final, illegally
50573 | 0.95

720 share v
noun information, .experience, view, .story, room, idea, .concern, power, .knowledge, .thought, .responsibility, .feeling, .secret, belief, .characteristic _misc_ .with, same, .common, .similar, willing.
49286 | 0.97

721 each p
(each other) .other, .year, one, they, .day, .side, different, .week, look., individual, four, .month, .person, item
49785 | 0.96 F

722 series n
adj special, whole, popular, occasional, three-part, ongoing, endless, continuing, two-part _noun_ world., TV., game, television., championship, .event, time, article, .question, test _verb_ win., begin, produce, publish, conduct, .feature, design, present, launch., consist
50427 | 0.95 N

723 usually r
.involve, .require, .occur, .associate, .reserve, .refer, .accompany, symptom, expensive, .sufficient, mild, .fatal
49654 | 0.96

724 natural j
noun resource, gas, history, world, museum, selection, disaster, environment, science, law, system, process _misc_ human, such, cultural, preserve, organic, born, perfectly, man-made
51179 | 0.93 A

725 hot *j*
noun water, dog, day, spot, summer, spring, air, pepper, sauce, tub, sun, oil *misc* too, cold, serve, until, red, add, dry, humid
50063 | 0.95

726 race *n*
adj presidential, human, different, close, tight, gubernatorial, mixed, three-way *noun* gender, class, .relation, car, issue, .ethnicity, Senate., sex *verb* win., run, base., enter., finish, divide, transcend., dominate, .tighten
49890 | 0.95

727 language *n*
adj foreign, English, native, common, whole, official, written, spoken *noun* culture, body., .art, use, .skill, sign., .barrier *verb* speak, learn., understand, teach, translate, study, contain, preserve, convey, .resonate
51892 | 0.91 A

728 river *n*
adj scenic, mighty, muddy, frozen, slow, coastal, raging, flowing, winding, free-flowing *noun* water, bank, lake, side., mile, .basin, bridge, mouth, town, road *verb* cross., flow, overlook., float., swim, .flood, fish, wind, span., meander
50211 | 0.94

729 dead *j*
noun man, body, end, tree, animal, fish, baby, husband, leaf, zone, center, living *misc* alive, shoot, already, bury, drop, grateful, lie, lay
50739 | 0.93 F

730 act *n*
adj sexual, terrorist, criminal, final, very, simple, homosexual, creative, specific, individual *noun* air., .violence, right., water., species., freedom., protection., balancing., education., reform. *verb* commit, pass, .require, perform, catch., clean., engage., .prohibit, protect, violate
50907 | 0.92 A

731 significant *j*
noun difference, effect, change, number, relationship, group, role, correlation, amount, interaction, impact, result *misc* there, no, between, statistically, most, find, show, reveal
54017 | 0.87 A

732 no *p*
(no one) there., .one, .idea, .reason, .question, .matter, .what, need, .evidence, .doubt, oh., .know, .difference, .sign
49313 | 0.95 F

733 response *n*
adj positive, emotional, immune, appropriate, correct, sexual, immediate, initial, strong, quick *noun* student, .rate, time, item, participant, emergency., scale, kind., frequency., difference. *verb* receive, indicate, elicit., base, .range, compare, provoke., trigger., evoke., generate
52116 | 0.90 A

734 rise *v*
noun price, rate, year, sun., cost, voice., water, stock., temperature, air *misc* .from, .above, .fall, .high, continue., slowly
up .from, .against, again, smoke., voice., .protest, anger, .overthrow, .revolt, .rebellion
49331 | 0.95

735 decade *n*
adj past, recent, early, previous, coming, following, later, preceding, communist, lost *noun* .century, year, end., time, war, life, couple., half, reform, increase *verb* spend., follow, span., last., .pass, emerge, decline., enter, exist., reverse.
49657 | 0.94

736 article *n*
adj recent, original, related, following, numerous, front-page, scientific, excellent *noun* .copyright, magazine, section, journal, newspaper., book, series, page, purpose., author *verb* write, read., publish, describe, .appear, discuss, .examine, .provide, present, contain
50550 | 0.92 A

737 thus *r*
.far, .reduce, .eliminate, .hypothesis, .reinforce, increasing, potentially, discourse, .effectively, .vulnerable, respectively., .subject, validity, .indirectly
53663 | 0.87 A

738 seven *m*
.year, .day, six., .month, .eight, .week, after, five, about., .ago, last, hour, game, four
48004 | 0.97

739 shoot *v*
noun gun, .head, .death, film, .look, police, .back, scene, movie, officer, video, ball, soldier, rifle, picture *misc* .kill, .dead, someone, somebody, .through, fatally., accidentally.
up .percent, hand., price., eyebrow., rate., flame., pain., stock., suddenly., sales. **down** plane, .over, helicopter, aircraft, pilot., missile, Iraqi, fighter, jet **out** hand., flame., window, arm, tire, light, .grab
48903 | 0.95

740 east *n*
adj middle, big, far, upper, near, volatile, Persian, mid, mediterranean, municipal *noun* .coast, west, .side, mile., peace, south, street, .bay, river *verb* head., drive., face, travel., rise, locate., flow
48916 | 0.94

741 animal *n*
adj other, wild, small, large, stuffed, domestic, live, endangered, exotic, various *noun* plant, human, .right, species, life, farm *verb* kill, eat, feed, treat, study, hunt, test, stuff., slaughter, evolve
49296 | 0.93

742 away *i*
.from, take., her, move., turn., stay., walk., .home, far., keep., run., pull., back., shy.
47870 | 0.96 F

743 similar *j*
noun topic, result, situation, way, study, problem, pattern, program, experience, case, effect, finding *misc* find, those, very, below, help, report, face, quite, remarkably
49739 | 0.92 A

744 save *v*
noun .life, .money, .energy, dollar, God., effort., .face, .soul, .retirement, .marriage, .taxpayer, month, file, .planet, .seed *misc* try., enough, order., in., .yourself, .million, .hundred, .invest, .billion, .ourselves, literally, .endangered, desperate., .restore, sacrifice
up .for, have., money, .enough, .buy, some, dollar, month, vacation, .summer
47520 | 0.97

745 factor *n*
adj other, important, major, key, environmental, significant, social, economic, critical, contributing
noun risk•, •analysis, number•, item, loading, growth, •structure, score, •development, race *verb* •influence, •contribute, •affect, consider, identify, determine, examine, suggest, base, depend•
52549 | 0.87 A

746 central *j*
noun park, government, bank, role, system, intelligence, city, issue, committee, office, command, region *misc* American, eastern, nervous, Asian, European, grand, southern, northern
48924 | 0.93 A

747 occur *v*
noun change•, event•, year, problem•, death•, process, incident•, result, accident•, injury•, period, loss•, •patient, •month, error• *misc* when, •during, never•, naturally, •within
49486 | 0.92 A

748 committee *n*
adj national, Olympic, advisory, foreign, international, congressional, central, special
noun Senate•, house•, member, chairman, judiciary•, service•, ethics• *verb* chair, form, •meet, •vote, approve, •investigate, appoint, establish, head, •recommend
48842 | 0.93

749 serious *j*
noun problem, injury, question, threat, issue, crime, business, consequence, health, illness, concern, trouble *misc* about, very, more, most, face, cause, raise, suffer
46788 | 0.97

750 sport *n*
adj professional, physical, competitive, major, Olympic, pro, organized, female, extreme, traditional
noun team, •car, woman, athlete, participation, •fan, •utility, game•, •medicine *verb* play, participate•, coach, compete, associate, dominate, engage•, feature, perceive, excel•
53983 | 0.84 N

751 lie *v*
noun •bed, •side, night, •ground, •oath, heart, •wait, •Congress, sun, jury, dog•, •surface, •bottom, core, •middle *misc* •under, •ahead, beyond, •awake, dead, •outside, •near
   down •on, bed, •sleep, •again, •beside, •next, •die, •rest, •front, •flat
47888 | 0.95 F

752 beyond *i*
go•, far•, move•, extend•, reach, •control, •doubt, •scope, •reasonable, anything, •border, •limit, above•, lie
46708 | 0.97

753 exactly *r*
•what, know•, •how, right, •same, •where, •happen, mean, •why, sure, •kind, almost•, •opposite
48314 | 0.94 S

754 despite *i*
•fact, •effort, yet•, •difference, •recent, •success, •lack, •evidence, •claim, strong, •concern, •warning, •attempt, •opposition
47312 | 0.96

755 happy *j*
noun day, birthday, life, ending, year, family, holiday, hour, marriage, Thanksgiving *misc* very, healthy, everyone, everybody, wish, sad, perfectly, pretty
47427 | 0.95

756 eight *m*
•year, •month, six•, seven•, •hour, about•, •day, after•, •ago, •week, last, •nine, four, •foot
46585 | 0.97

757 protect *v*
noun right, •child, interest, law, •environment, •health, •privacy, amendment, •citizen, •property, effort•, resource, •public, species, consumer *misc* •against, •themselves, help•, •yourself, design•, order•, in•, necessary•
46698 | 0.96

758 list *n*
adj long, short, disabled, complete, injured, endangered, growing, partial *noun* top•, name, waiting•, people, wine•, time, wish•, price, item, best-seller• *verb* include, add•, provide, compile, read, contain, join•, present, mail•, rank
46697 | 0.96

759 size *n*
adj small, large, different, average, various, right, available, similar, sheer, minimum *noun* shape, effect•, sample•, class•, time•, body•, population *verb* reduce•, increase•, range, grow•, double•, vary, determine, shrink•, compare, matter
47989 | 0.94

760 quality *n*
adj high, environmental, poor, better, low, overall, personal, improved *noun* •life, water•, air•, •care, •education, service, •control, product, quantity, standard *verb* improve•, provide, affect•, produce, maintain•, enhance•, ensure•, reduce, relate, vary
48527 | 0.93 A

761 pressure *n*
adj high, political, low, intense, international, public, social, increasing, enormous, tremendous
noun blood•, lot•, time, group, air•, temperature, peer•, kind• *verb* put•, feel•, keep, apply, increase, exert, face, reduce, lower•, •build
47613 | 0.94

762 accept *v*
noun •responsibility, •fact, •offer, •invitation, •idea, •position, •challenge, •gift, •role *misc* refuse•, willing•, widely•, generally•, force•, prepare•, ready•
46289 | 0.97

763 ready *j*
noun bed, dinner, access, action, minute, use, answer, smile, supply, availability, cash, harvest *misc* get, until, stand, yet, quite, fight, willing
46618 | 0.96

764 approach *n*
adj new, different, traditional, similar, comprehensive, alternative, effective, holistic, basic, integrated
noun education, study, management, learning, teaching, kind•, •life, assessment, team, theory *verb* take, use, adopt, develop, suggest, teach, involve, •focus, emphasize, •deal
49477 | 0.91 A

765 sign n
adj good, early, sure, clear, vital, positive, visible, encouraging, hopeful, growing *noun* warning., street., .language, road, neon., stop., .symptom *verb* show., read, post, point, hang, carry., recognize., warn, .indicate, notice.
45970 | 0.97

766 attack n
adj terrorist, nuclear, recent, deadly, massive, chemical, biological, future, direct, British *noun* heart., terror., missile., suicide., air., risk., panic., week, bomb. *verb* launch., die., prevent., suffer., plan., .occur, cause, survive., mount., order
47768 | 0.94

767 individual n
adj social, private, particular, certain, personal, single, likely, wealthy, unique, involved *noun* group, life, family, right, organization, number., education, institution, ability, relationship *verb* identify, allow., involve, affect, .experience, .engage, seek, indicate, choose, .participate
50474 | 0.89 A

768 career n
adj political, long, professional, successful, entire, military, academic, whole *noun* life, woman, .choice, college, .development, .path, .goal, stage, record, opportunity *verb* begin, start, pursue., end, spend., launch., build., choose., .span, plan
47532 | 0.94 N

769 answer n
adj correct, simple, right, easy, short, wrong, obvious, possible, quick, definitive *noun* question, student, man, no, kind, .prayer, .sheet *verb* know., give, find., provide., wait., .lie, seek., receive, search., .depend
46231 | 0.97

770 dog n
adj hot, little, mad, top, stray, sled, yellow, barking, sleeping, spotted *noun* cat, day, .food, prairie., owner, family, guide, animal *verb* .bark, walk., eat, train, love, kill, feed., .sniff, chase, shoot
47704 | 0.93 F

771 media n
adj national, mass, mainstream, local, electronic, major, liberal, popular *noun* news., .coverage, .attention, .attribution, .company, center, .outlet *verb* use., .report, .cover, .focus, portray, control, blame, mix., ignore, influence
47935 | 0.93

772 thought n
adj final, negative, very, serious, modern, positive, deep, rational, suicidal, conscious *noun* mind, school., .process, .action, train., food., line., behavior, .prayer *verb* give, lose., share., express, .occur, finish., .cross, bear., collect., .drift
47133 | 0.94 F

773 whatever d
or., .want, .happen, .reason, .may, .might, .else, .choose, .necessary, .cause, .outcome, .hell, willing., .merit
46402 | 0.96

774 determine v
noun study., factor, test., .effect, .extent, .difference, analysis., court., size, outcome, rate, price, .cause,

.amount, .future *misc* .whether, .if, .how, help., .not, difficult., order., conduct., largely.
48449 | 0.92 A

775 television n
adj national, public, local, independent, live, digital, worldwide *noun* .show, radio, .station, .news, network, cable., .program, movie, .set *verb* watch., appear., broadcast, own, air, switch, dominate, ban, depict, tape
47333 | 0.94

776 meeting n
adj annual, recent, private, open, secret, initial, professional, regional, nice, senior *noun* town., .place, board., council, committee, summit., hall *verb* hold, attend., discuss, set, schedule, arrange., organize, plan, convene, host
46253 | 0.96

777 scene n
adj political, whole, final, familiar, famous, nude, contemporary, domestic, graphic, funny *noun* crime., movie, sex, music., murder, art., love., opening. *verb* arrive., set, describe, shoot, depict, paint, survey., view, .unfold, fade
47028 | 0.94

778 success n
adj great, academic, economic, critical, commercial, financial, huge, future, limited, long-term *noun* .story, .failure, .rate, student, key., chance., school, measure., secret., factor *verb* achieve, enjoy., .depend, attribute, ensure., contribute., experience, limit, influence, assess.
46975 | 0.94

779 prepare v
noun student, food, meal, report, teacher, dinner, plan, college, dish, .future, training., career, statement, .battle, lunch *misc* better., help., .deal, .accept, fully.
45519 | 0.97

780 identify v
noun student, problem, study, factor, area, source, research, need, teacher, individual, participant, .type, characteristic, analysis, researcher. *misc* .as, .themselves, help., able., .specific, clearly., correctly., easily.
49220 | 0.90 A

781 press n
adj free, national, popular, mainstream, foreign, western, tabloid *noun* .conference, .secretary, .release, time, .corps, freedom, .coverage, .club, reporter, printing. *verb* meet., report, hold, publish, announce, leak., criticize, distribute, brief, portray
47033 | 0.94

782 particularly r
.those, .important, area, .among, .since, .interested, .difficult, .strong, .vulnerable, .useful, .interesting, .regard, .concerned, .one
46559 | 0.95 A

783 resource n
adj natural, human, available, financial, scarce, economic, public, local, valuable, additional *noun* water., use, management, .center, department, energy., community, land, .council, .defense *verb* provide, allocate, develop, devote, protect, manage, .support, share, control, focus
49316 | 0.89 A

784 amount n
adj small, large, certain, tremendous, enormous, huge, significant, fair _noun_ •time, •money, •information, •water, •energy, •work, dollar, •material _verb_ spend, reduce•, pay, increase•, require, produce, receive, contain•, limit•, save
46269 | 0.95

785 argue v
noun case, critic•, other•, court, lawyer•, defense•, official•, article•, attorney•, scholar•, theory, proponent•, advocate•, Democrat, opponent• _misc_ •against, persuasively, convincingly, successfully, •strongly
47116 | 0.93 A

786 recognize v
noun •need, •importance, •right, voice, name, •value, court•, •difference, leader, ability•, •sign, marriage, individual, authority, failure _misc_ must•, important, fail•, widely•, immediately, internationally•
46191 | 0.95 A

787 treatment n
adj medical, effective, special, preferential, wastewater, residential, equal, fair, ethical _noun_ drug•, •program, •group, patient, •plant, cancer, water•, •center, •facility _verb_ receive, provide, require, seek•, undergo•, develop, refuse•, compare, respond•, improve
49110 | 0.89 A

788 left j
noun hand, side, arm, foot, leg, knee, eye, shoulder, wing, field _misc_ his, your, right, top, above, upper, below, alone
46262 | 0.94

789 degree n
adj high, varying, great, certain, advanced, lesser, doctoral, various, significant, baccalaureate

noun master•, bachelor•, college•, law•, education, •program, science, graduate•, engineering, business _verb_ earn•, receive•, hold•, preheat•, complete•, require, pursue•, indicate•, reach•, determine•
46923 | 0.93 A

790 stock n
adj mutual, common, foreign, individual, average, financial, hot, preferred, total, restricted _noun_ •market, •price, •exchange, company, fund, •option, new•, share, value, investor _verb_ buy•, sell, trade, •fall, own, invest•, •rise, •drop, •soar, •plunge
51662 | 0.84 M N

791 indicate v
noun result•, study•, research•, student, data•, finding•, score, respondent•, analysis•, percent, evidence•, number, participant, •difference, teacher _misc_ •that, high, significant, clearly•, •whether, low
49282 | 0.88 A

792 growth n
adj economic, rapid, annual, strong, personal, human, future, explosive _noun_ rate, population•, year, percent, •fund, development, job, earnings•, •hormone, •stock _verb_ slow, promote•, experience•, stimulate•, encourage•, •occur, achieve, control•, reflect, accelerate
47841 | 0.91 A

793 simple j
noun thing, question, way, life, fact, reason, answer, solution, matter, task, rule _misc_ very, as, that, relatively, enough, quite, pure, complex
45061 | 0.96

794 ability n
adj cognitive, athletic, physical, academic, natural, perceived, intellectual, uncanny, unique

7. Foods

General, meals, and implements

(cup) 51027, dinner 33218, (plate) 23725, lunch 22657, meal 20630, (knife) 15345, breakfast 14337, (fork) 7978, (spoon) 7165, (grill) n 5256, snack 4553, supper 4016, picnic 3871, napkin 2700, toothpick 812

Specific foods (note that many of these are also the names of animals, where they are used frequently in a non-culinary sense)

(fish) n 46247, (ice) n 30754, salt 27021, egg 26964, sugar 24060, (chicken) 23955, fruit 21875, pepper 20166, meat 19421, rice 19300, vegetable 18592, (cream) 18207, apple 17812, milk 17529, cheese 16549, bread 16113, (turkey) 15445, sauce 15180, potato 15028, bean 14520, butter 14219, tomato 14211, corn 13326, cake 13155, onion 13054, (roll) n 12556, chocolate 11995, salad 11623, olive 11527, garlic 10859, honey 10709, soup 10173, lemon 9507, nut 9322, (salmon) 8932, orange n 8912, sandwich 8704, pie 8624, beef 8543, pizza 6829, (mushroom) 6650, olive oil 6592, cherry 6451, dessert 6101, pork 5806, pasta 5742, carrot 5436, (lamb) 5422, toast 5394, steak 5326, banana 5218, grape 5153, peanut 5067, (trout) 4941, (crab) 4873, pea 4481, lime 4236, burger 4168, strawberry 4157, peach 4084, (lobster) 3784, cereal 3435, sausage 3277, yogurt 3189, lettuce 3057, pear 2862, cabbage 2739, almond 2669, hamburger 2578, jelly 2560, pancake 2559, plum 2486, broccoli 2303, pecan 2156, biscuit 2076, cucumber 2057, (cod) 2032, pudding 1949, hot dog 1940, asparagus 1860, pickle n 1780, pineapple 1757, spaghetti 1663, doughnut 1663, melon 1607, vegetable oil 1568, margarine 1486, (blackberry) 1480, taco 1418, bagel 1320, waffle 1231, custard 866, lentil 824, cauliflower 695, legume 625, kiwi 544, cashew 427, sunflower seed 337, pepperoni 291, jello 149

noun student, child, level, people, skill, confidence., government, knowledge, individual, .achievement
verb lose., develop, limit., affect., demonstrate., improve., .control, enhance., .communicate, .perform
47389 | 0.91 A

795 dollar *n*
adj federal, top, silver, weak, additional, strong, multi-million, constant, falling, hard-earned
noun thousand., .year, tax, cent, .bill, value, taxpayer., .month, money *verb* spend, pay, make, cost., give, buy, save, lose, help, pour
45260 | 0.96

796 union *n*
adj civil, international, monetary, same-sex, gay, patriotic, striking, municipal, collective, postal
noun state., labor., worker, member, trade., .leader, .address, liberty., credit., teacher. *verb* join, represent, organize, form, fight, oppose, .collapse, negotiate, vote, preserve.
46796 | 0.92

797 disease *n*
adj infectious, chronic, cardiovascular, transmitted, coronary, deadly, fatal, certain, vascular *noun* heart., .control, center., risk., cancer, .prevention, patient, diabetes, treatment, death *verb* cause, prevent., die., treat., develop, spread, affect, cure., diagnose., fight.
48003 | 0.90 M

798 everybody *p*
know, .else, want, talk, love, .agree, everything, welcome, .happy, hi., kind, .laugh, hate, thanks.
47348 | 0.91 S

799 wonder *v*
noun observer., critic., awe., viewer, skeptic., amazement, pundit. *misc* I., .if, .what, she, .how, .why, .whether, begin.
46444 | 0.93 F

800 election *n*
adj presidential, general, federal, democratic, local, special, primary, close, multiparty, Iraqi *noun* year, day, .campaign, result, week, candidate, month, .official, .commission, midterm. *verb* win., lose., vote, steal, participate., influence., conduct, contest., organize, sweep
46982 | 0.92 S

801 loss *n*
adj net, total, significant, potential, heavy, tragic, terrible, devastating, key, consecutive *noun* weight., hearing., .life, job, memory., vision, sense., hair., bone *verb* suffer., cause, result, lead, report., experience, prevent., mourn., .occur, post.
45699 | 0.94

802 box *n*
adj cardboard, black, wooden, empty, light, rectangular, safe-deposit *noun* .office, .page, ballot., lunch, music., dialog, shoe., boom. *verb* open, .contain, fill, carry, check, place, pack, hand, grab., line
45632 | 0.94

803 deal *n*
adj great, big, good, new, real, better, whole, raw, fair, five-year *noun* .time, money, budget., business., book., peace., .attention *verb* make, cut., sign., strike, spend., close, negotiate., announce, seal., involve
45217 | 0.95

804 herself *p*
she, her, find., pull., allow., throw., force., kill., smile, remind., .mirror, push., introduce., imagine.
47988 | 0.89 F

805 fund *n*
adj mutual, federal, international, monetary, public, legal, private, available, general, environmental
noun stock, trust., pension., hedge., .manager, bond., defense., year *verb* raise, invest, receive, manage, establish, support, sell, allocate, contribute, state
50551 | 0.85 M

806 miss *v*
noun .game, .point, .opportunity, .chance, .beat, season., mark, .cut, month, .boat, .deadline, plane, foot, .start, throw *misc* never., narrowly., completely, barely., .terribly, .entirely
   out .on, .some, .opportunity, may., .something, might., afford., stuff, .valuable
44536 | 0.96

807 pretty *r*
.good, .much, .well, .soon, .sure, .bad, .clear, actually, guy, .close, .tough, .quickly
45846 | 0.93 S

808 region *n*
adj different, central, economic, entire, southern, northern, administrative, geographic, particular, various *noun* country, state, city, border., mountain., economy, peace., stability., troop., presence.
verb vary., dominate, locate, divide, spread., populate, destabilize., inhabit, occupy, concentrate.
47374 | 0.90 A

809 feeling *n*
adj strong, bad, personal, negative, hard, positive, warm, mixed, general, strange *noun* people, thought, guilt, child, gut., kind, fear, attitude, .stomach, depression *verb* express., share., experience, describe., reflect., shake., overwhelm, stir, enhance, sense
44054 | 0.97

810 lay *v*
noun .bed, .hand, .egg, .foundation, .groundwork, head, .claim, .eye, table, plan, .blame, blanket, track, female., snow *misc* there, .across, .ahead, .beside, .bare, .upon, .awake
   out plan, .case, .vision, .agenda, .detail, clothes, clearly, carefully., .scenario **down** .law, .arm, rule, .beside, .sleep, .next, .weapon, condition, guideline **off** worker, employee, .thousand, fire, .hundred
45367 | 0.94 F

811 training *n*
adj military, formal, basic, professional, medical, vocational, on-the-job *noun* .program, .camp, education, teacher, job., spring., .session, .center
verb provide, receive., require, offer, complete., attend., focus, undergo., enhance, .consist
46068 | 0.92 A

812 message *n*
adj clear, strong, wrong, mixed, simple, positive, powerful, brief *noun* e-mail., people, phone, .board, text., president, machine, kind., .hope *verb* send., get, leave., deliver, receive, convey, carry., communicate, spread., intend
43978 | 0.96

813 arrive v
noun day, police., hour, morning, minute, week, moment, month, guest., letter., immigrant, officer., .hospital, evening, afternoon *misc* before, after, .early, .late, finally.
43791 | 0.97

814 standard n
adj high, national, new, double, federal, international, environmental, low, academic, weekly *noun* living, quality, gold., performance, safety., industry., music, art, teacher *verb* meet., set, establish, apply, raise., require, develop, maintain., exceed., state
46396 | 0.91 A

815 outside i
.home, .door, stand., .window, .house, .city, inside., area, .office, .room, town, park, .United States, .building
43031 | 0.98

816 fail v
noun test, system., government., effort, attempt, bank., administration., Congress, mission, .grade, agreement, .exam, .duty, .significance, bid *misc* .meet, often., .provide, .recognize, .understand
43861 | 0.96

817 trade n
adj international, federal, foreign, economic, global, fair, increased *noun* world., .center, .agreement, US, .policy, .deficit, .union, .organization, .group, .commission *verb* promote, ply., expand, negotiate, free., regulate, .flow, oppose, lower, crash.
46908 | 0.90 A

818 staff n
adj joint, medical, senior, general, professional, entire, administrative, editorial, paid *noun* chief., .member, .writer, house., faculty., office, hospital, .development, coaching. *verb* .contribute, support, join., hire, train, .handle, employ, monitor, review, interview
45369 | 0.93 N

819 benefit n
adj social, great, potential, public, full, environmental, medical, additional, added, significant *noun* health., cost, security., .doubt, drug., retirement., welfare., unemployment., worker, care *verb* provide, receive, offer., reap., cut, outweigh, enjoy., derive, .accrue, produce.
45190 | 0.93 A

820 character n
adj main, fictional, female, moral, central, literary, Chinese, unique *noun* cartoon., actor, cast., issue, role, .trait, .education, title. *verb* play, create, .represent, .convert, base, portray, define, identify, reveal, feature.
45708 | 0.92

821 army n
adj Iraqi, Israeli, Red, Soviet, British, retired, German, Russian, Swiss, regular *noun* US., .corps, .officer, force, .engineer, general, salvation., war, soldier, unit *verb* join., serve, fight, enlist., train, command, attack, .march, retire, order
45936 | 0.92

822 association n
adj national, medical, international, professional, psychological, athletic, psychiatric, civic, historical

noun school, president, bar., education, trade, industry, member, director, college, health *verb* represent, form, state, establish, .estimate, examine., sponsor, .recommend, organize, found
45448 | 0.93 A

823 operation n
adj military, special, covert, major, international, successful, joint, entire, foreign, peacekeeping *noun* year, .desert, director., rescue, company, .center, business, manager, chief, sting. *verb* run, perform, conduct, oversee., support, launch, plan, expand., undergo., .restore
44633 | 0.94

824 present v
noun table, evidence, case, problem, information, .challenge, result, paper, opportunity, data, study, article, award, view, research *misc* .themselves, .annual, united, following, .unique, standard, originally., scientific
46060 | 0.91 A

825 crime n
adj violent, organized, serious, guilty, federal, juvenile, international, tough, heinous, white-collar *noun* .scene, war., .rate, .bill, drug, victim, hate., violence *verb* commit, charge., reduce., solve., convict., fight., accuse., report, .occur, rise
44730 | 0.94 S

826 name v
noun president, .editor, player, director, executive, .honor, daughter, baby, coach, .publisher, manager, chief, .chairman, secretary, minister *misc* .after, .few, aptly., .vice, recently., senior, decline., appropriately.
43781 | 0.96

827 cup n
adj remaining, empty, steaming, drained, rinsed, extra, measuring, covered *noun* coffee, sugar, world., water, oil, tablespoon, teaspoon, flour, .tea, butter *verb* chop, add., win., dice, pour., slice, drink.
48207 | 0.87 M

828 island n
adj Caribbean, tiny, main, remote, British, tropical, entire, deserted, outer *noun* new, sea, mile, coast, beach, barrier., .sound, home, treasure., .nation *verb* visit, surround, locate, arrive., own, land., explore, invade., dot, swim
44509 | 0.94

829 analysis n
adj statistical, final, multivariate, economic, significant, detailed, content, critical, comparative, careful *noun* data, factor., result, regression., .variance, table, variable, system, method, policy *verb* conduct, .show, include, .reveal, perform, base, .indicate, .suggest, .examine, require
49404 | 0.85 A

830 check v
noun .track, .watch, .web, box, .record, .listing, .e-mail, .account, hospital, bag, phone, computer, minute, .pulse, hour *misc* .against, .audio, your, sure, .local, carefully, please, online, regularly, periodically, tire, .vital
out .site, .web, book, library, worth., online, .website, tip, recipe, .blog **in** .with, let., .periodically, regularly
44210 | 0.94

831 answer *v*
noun .question, .phone, .call, .door, prayer, voice, .letter, .ad, .telephone, respondent, .e-mail, item, participant, .questionnaire, reporter *misc* before, refuse, correctly, difficult, directly, please, immediately
43905 | 0.95 F

832 photograph *n*
adj black-and-white, framed, still, digital, historic, detailed, classic, naked, faded, stunning *noun* page, .author, color, time, family, collection, .courtesy, .right, photo, image *verb* show, pose, feature, display, depict, illustrate, document, accompany, snap, frame
48003 | 0.87 M

833 glass *n*
adj broken, stained, empty, magnifying, clear, tall, wire-rimmed, looking, round *noun* wine, water, .door, window, wall, bottle, plate, .milk, metal, juice *verb* wear, .pour, .put, .drink, hold, fill, raise, break, shatter, pick
45824 | 0.91 F

834 forward *r*
look, move, go, come, step, lean, put, push, foot, bend, leap, backward, carry, pull
43605 | 0.95

835 authority *n*
adj local, political, moral, central, public, legal, religious, civil, regional, leading *noun* state, power, government, port, housing, .figure, position, enforcement, transit, *verb* exercise, challenge, grant, arrest, question, seek, .investigate, assert, undermine, recognize
44239 | 0.94 A

836 earth *n*
adj greatest, flat, dry, soft, wet, bare, scorched, damp, round, planetary *noun* .day, life, surface, .atmosphere, planet, mother, orbit, heaven, place, sun *verb* return, fall, save, exist, strike, observe, crash, inherit, .rotate, .spin
45048 | 0.92

837 stage *n*
adj early, final, various, different, initial, later, developmental, late, advanced, critical *noun* center, life, .development, world, career, planning, .manager, production, actor, screen *verb* set, reach, walk, enter, perform, share, step, dance, mark, consist
42871 | 0.96

838 one *n*
adj loved, only, old, small, big, young, lucky, similar, existing, previous *noun* plastic, zero, metal, glass, cotton *verb* get, know, go, make, see, say, love, replace, survive, .benefit
42150 | 0.98

839 act *v*
noun way, Congress, force, .interest, American, .manner, ability, authority, individual, .faith, .concert, adult, .behalf, .catalyst, .intermediary *misc* .as, .like, .upon, .quickly, .alone, fail, .responsibly
   out .fantasy, .story, child, .scene, .role, sexual, student, .part, play, drama **up** .again, AIDS, asthma.
42216 | 0.97

840 sort *n*
adj different, various, strange, very, odd, middling, weird, bizarre, peculiar, exotic *noun* .thing, .way, man, .person, .stuff, place, woman *verb* engage, undergo, tolerate, resort, subject, exert, withstand.
43527 | 0.94 S

841 station *n*
adj local, public, international, central, naval, commercial, generating, biological, nursing, busy *noun* radio, space, gas, police, television, train, TV, .wagon *verb* own, build, broadcast, operate, arrive, tune, air, acquire, monitor, install
43232 | 0.95

842 clearly *r*
very, show, .define, United States, understand, .indicate, quite, .demonstrate, .visible, .identify, .establish, .mark, .evident
42855 | 0.96

843 little *d*
very, as, there, .more, .than, so, too, .attention, .evidence, .interest, pay, .effect, .possible, offer
42212 | 0.97

844 compare *v*
noun study, group, student, result, rate, data, score, performance, .control, level, cost, .note, price, test, analysis, *misc* .other, .those, small, .contrast, billion, .favorably, relatively, .previous, current
44259 | 0.92 A

845 indeed *r*
very, may, yes, rare, strange, fortunate, odd, impressive, inevitable, ironic
43318 | 0.94 A

846 public *n*
adj American, general, open, available, British, aware, broad, traveling, wider, flying *noun* .opinion, .eye, .school, .access, poll, information, media, company, interest, court, *verb* educate, understand, inform, protect, .support, convince, accept, close, mislead, respond
43157 | 0.95

847 knowledge *n*
adj scientific, common, environmental, best, human, prior, basic, indigenous, content, personal *noun* skill, student, .base, experience, attitude, lack, teacher, body, *verb* acquire, gain, share, require, apply, increase, teach, test, reflect, measure
46646 | 0.87 A

848 state *v*
noun law, court, police, report, member, article, letter, goal, rule *misc* clearly, simply, explicitly, publicly, .obvious
44322 | 0.92 A

849 blue *j*
noun eye, sky, light, jeans, Jay, shirt, cross, chip, hair, water, suit, color *misc* white, red, wear, green, out, dark, pale, yellow
43762 | 0.93 F

850 example *n*
adj good, classic, prime, perfect, best, recent, excellent, early *noun* case, student, kind, .type, other, number, .approach, couple, textbook, literature *verb* give, provide, set, .include, follow, cite, show, offer, illustrate, consider
43912 | 0.92 A

851 strategy n
adj effective, different, economic, military, successful, long-term, environmental, various, global, overall noun student, development, management.. marketing.. teaching.. teacher, intervention.. exit.. change verb use, develop, adopt, employ, learn, implement, include, pursue, follow, involve
45136 | 0.90 A

852 mountain n
adj rugged, distant, northern, steep, tall, western, remote, beautiful, wild, surrounding noun .bike, .view, stone.. .park, .range, road, .lion, top, man, peak verb climb, rise, hike, ride, surround, head, cross, overlook, .loom, locate
45044 | 0.90 M

853 guess v
noun question, .answer, luck misc I.. so, well.. just, yeah.. sort, .kind, OK, okay, .depend, lucky, correctly
44674 | 0.91 S

854 sister n
adj old, young, little, dear, elder, eldest, beloved, pretty, loving, perpetual noun brother.. mother, father, twin.. baby.. daughter, wife, husband, mom, kid verb .die, marry, visit, murder, kiss, hug, rape, tease, beg, babysit
43622 | 0.93 F

855 force v
noun government, company, .smile, change, pressure.. .turnover, .sex, .bankruptcy, budget, thousand, attempt.. .exile, injury.. resident, .fumble misc .out, .pay, .resign, .sell, .accept, .close
41557 | 0.97

856 gun n
adj smoking, top, loaded, hired, illegal, German, silent, Gatling, automatic, stolen noun machine.. .control, hand, .head, .law, barrel, .owner, .violence, .battle, drug verb carry.. fire, point, put.. hold., shoot, pull.. draw, buy.. aim
44017 | 0.92

857 various j
noun group, way, form, time, type, level, kind, part, aspect, stage misc including, among, such, ethnic, throughout, cultural, religious, associate
43639 | 0.92 A

858 laugh v
noun joke, audience.. mouth, crowd.. smile, .tear, .delight, uncle, hyena, dancing, .irony, grin, .disbelief, .glee, astonishment misc start.. .again, everyone.. .hard, burst.
45147 | 0.89 F

859 environment n
adj natural, social, physical, safe, hostile, different, political, global, urban, economic noun learning.. health, school, work.. home.. development, classroom.. family, impact.. energy verb create.. protect.. provide, build.. improve, affect, control.. promote, operate, establish
44633 | 0.90 A

860 design n
adj intelligent, interior, experimental, original, simple, basic, industrial, graphic, computer-aided noun system, study, art, research.. .process, product, engineering, .construction, .team, analysis

verb .protect, help, .reduce, improve, .prevent, allow, provide, incorporate, employ, influence
45091 | 0.89 M A

861 sun n
adj hot, bright, full, rising, blazing, tropical, cool noun morning.. ray, moon, afternoon.. light, setting.. star, sky, summer.. heat verb .shine, .rise, .set, watch.. burn, warm, .beat, dry, orbit.. block.
43823 | 0.92 F

862 lawyer n
adj young, legal, criminal, civil, corporate, private, prominent, involved, female, outside noun defense.. trial.. case, doctor, plaintiff.. client, court, right, law, president verb .represent, hire.. .argue, .defend, sue, advise, .handle, .specialize, contact, appoint
45134 | 0.89

863 sex n
adj oral, opposite, casual, safe, sexual, unprotected, female, consensual, premarital noun .life, .offender, age, .education, difference, .partner, drug, race, violence, .scandal verb talk.. engage.. perform.. involve, enjoy.. force.. trade.. abstain.. practice.
44228 | 0.91

864 rather r
but.. .like, much.. .quickly, .unusual, .limited, .strange, .odd, .obvious, manner, unique, .narrow, .remarkable, ordinary
41874 | 0.96

865 artist n
adj American, young, contemporary, local, creative, visual, various, fine, graphic, famous noun collection.. work, painting, writer, makeup.. studio, woman.. portrait, con.. performance. verb create, .paint, represent, draw, feature, record, inspire, depict, explore, invite
50315 | 0.8 M

866 club n
adj local, social, private, exclusive, rotary, athletic, nuclear, civic noun country.. golf, member, health.. book.. night, boy.. player, .owner, press. verb join.. swing.. belong.. form, own, host, sponsor, found, contact, honor
43365 | 0.92 N

867 prove v
noun .point, case, evidence.. test.. .innocence, .worth, .existence, prosecution.. challenge, prosecutor.. document.. exception, .guilt, .mettle, DNA. misc may.. difficult, .wrong, .effective, .useful, .successful
41024 | 0.97

868 section n
adj special, following, final, previous, main, separate, cesarean, upper, criminal, technical noun article, cross.. business, news, .report, .feature, page, food, science, wall verb discuss, describe, divide.. present, contain, .examine, explore, consist, devote, list
46528 | 0.86 A

869 skill n
adj social, necessary, academic, technical, important, cognitive, physical, special, personal, effective noun knowledge, level, development, communication.. motor.. language.. teacher verb learn, develop.. teach, use, require, acquire, improve, hone.. read, enhance
46142 | 0.86 A

870 truth *n*
adj whole, simple, absolute, scientific, historical, sad, honest, naked *noun* .matter, .commission, moment., search., claim, justice, .reconciliation, lie, beauty, reality *verb* tell., speak., reveal, learn., discover, seek., face., hide, expose, confront.
41581 | 0.96

871 set *n*
adj new, different, whole, particular, complex, full, specific, common *noun* television., .rule, TV., data, .value, .standard, movie, skill, .circumstance *verb* develop., complete., present., consist, perform, define, repeat, rest, generate, feature
41686 | 0.95

872 ok *r*
.so, .let, right, .now, well, all, here, yeah, .thanks
50770 | 0.78 S

873 manager *n*
adj general, assistant, senior, middle, top, regional, professional, female, financial, alcoholic *noun* fund., campaign., money., project., program., case., sales. *verb* hire, fire, name, promote, appoint, .oversee, interview, inform, resign, rate
43246 | 0.92 N

874 executive *n*
adj chief, top, corporate, national, senior, legislative, retired, financial, female, key *noun* .director, president, .officer, .branch, .producer, .editor, chairman., .committee, .order *verb* name, appoint, hire, elect, resign, retire, exercise, .testify, recruit, .oversee
44242 | 0.90 N

875 district *n*
adj congressional, federal, historic, financial, southern, central, poor, northern, unified, eastern *noun* school., .attorney, .court, state, .judge, county, US., .office, business., water. *verb* represent, file, order, sue, elect, implement, redraw, vary, .encompass, house
44552 | 0.89 N

876 claim *v*
noun right, .responsibility, .victory, .credit, land, official, critic., .victim, authority, lawsuit., .title, .success, expert, .deduction, identity *misc* .represent, file., .violate, .innocent, falsely, .rape
41086 | 0.96

877 forget *v*
noun name, moment, past, minute, .birthday, incident, .root, .promise, horror, excitement, pill, me, .sunscreen, homework, .umbrella *misc* .about, never., almost., ever, sometimes., easy., completely.
41974 | 0.94 F

878 hang *v*
noun .wall, head, .air, .ceiling, .side, arm, door, hair., window, picture, clothes, painting, .shoulder, hook, sign *misc* .around, .over, .above, .onto, .open
  on .wall, .every, .second, .dear, barely., manage., minute, clothes., cross, .nail **up** .phone, after., before, .coat, caller., .dial, .receiver, .telephone, .immediately, .jacket **out** .together, .window, .dry, tongue., .shingle, gang, laundry, teenager
42811 | 0.92 F

879 entire *j*
noun life, world, family, system, body, country, population, community, process, career, class, nation

misc spend, throughout, cover, almost, across, devote, fill
40452 | 0.98

880 leg *n*
adj right, left, long, hind, low, broken, front, short, strong, thin *noun* arm, foot, knee, pant., side, head, muscle, body, chair, hip *verb* break, cross, stretch, move, stand, lift, pull, swing, lose., extend
43576 | 0.91 F

881 enough *d*
n't., not., there., get, .money, .time, .water, provide., pay, .food, .evidence, .room, .information, buy
40785 | 0.97

882 design *v*
noun program, system, study, measure, building, architect, project, course, .use, policy, intervention, computer, engineer., curriculum, software *misc* .help, specifically, .build, .provide
42632 | 0.93 A

883 close *j*
noun friend, relationship, family, attention, tie, call, proximity, look, relative, range, race, contact *misc* to, very, as, too, up, keep, pay, behind
40158 | 0.98

884 study *v*
noun student., year, .art, .effect, researcher., .history, scientist., .face, college, music, science, subject, .behavior, culture, method *misc* carefully, .hard, closely, extensively, intently
41448 | 0.95

885 since *i*
have, .then, year, first, ever., long., .war, first., .early, especially., year, month., .late, .beginning
41994 | 0.94 N

886 environmental *j*
noun protection, health, agency, issue, group, problem, education, impact, law, policy, concern, program *misc* economic, social, national, global, such, international, local, federal
47767 | 0.82 A

887 establish *v*
noun .relationship, program, government, system, standard, law, rule, community, goal, policy, .relation, center, fund, research, foundation *misc* .between, help., already., firmly., international, seek., clearly.
43022 | 0.91 A

888 democratic *j*
noun party, candidate, convention, leader, committee, senator, state, president, government, society, process, primary *misc* national, presidential, liberal, political, former, social, vote, free
42862 | 0.91 S

889 remove *v*
noun .heat, .pan, .oven, water, .office, skin, body, seed, .barrier, .shoe, piece, material, .hat, doctor., cover *misc* .from, stir, carefully., .discard, immediately, completely., easily., slot
41140 | 0.95

890 main *j*
noun effect, reason, street, thing, road, course, character, room, source, point, concern, goal

misc three, significant, off, down, along, whose, drag, onto
40636 | 0.96

891 professor *n*
adj associate, assistant, emeritus, clinical, English, visiting, distinguished *noun* university, law, college, science, history, psychology, student, .medicine, study, economics *verb* .teach, hire, .specialize, retire, appoint., .lecture, chair
41556 | 0.94

892 financial *j*
noun aid, service, support, institution, market, officer, resource, company, statement, planner, crisis, system *misc* chief, provide, international, personal, receive, global, emotional, technical
42301 | 0.92 N

893 enjoy *v*
noun .life, .support, .success, freedom, music, .benefit, .moment, .view, .show, advantage, .meal, .ride, .popularity, .fruit, privilege *misc* really., hope., each, .yourself, relax., thoroughly.
40344 | 0.97

894 network *n*
adj social, national, global, terrorist, vast, extensive, neural, private, nationwide, commercial *noun* cable., television, news, computer, TV, support, communication, show *verb* build, create, develop, establish, connect, form, link, censor., operate, broadcast
41850 | 0.93

895 sound *v*
noun voice., alarm, word, music, note, bell, .fun, ear, horn, warning, song, siren, theme, trumpet, cry *misc* .like, it., .good, may., .familiar, .pretty
   out .word, .each, .letter, .syllable **off** .about, there., .today
41328 | 0.94 F

896 discuss *v*
noun issue, .document, topic, article, problem, .matter, case, .detail, section, meeting, .plan, idea, .possibility, official., strategy *misc* help., meet., .early, decline, refuse., previously
41571 | 0.94 A

897 form *v*
noun group, .basis, .part, company, .alliance, star, coalition, .partnership, party, relationship, organization, shape, community, planet, galaxy *misc* together., .own, newly., fully., combine., soft, recently., stiff., eventually., perfectly.
41426 | 0.94 A

898 final *j*
noun day, decision, word, year, analysis, report, stage, game, question, round, week, thought *misc* before, during, until, third, complete, issue, fourth, fifth
40261 | 0.97

899 trial *n*
adj clinical, fair, criminal, Olympic, civil, controlled, successful, mock, speedy, separate *noun* .lawyer, murder, court, jury, time, case, .judge, .error *verb* begin, stand., await., conduct, testify., cover., face, .end, schedule, .involve
41905 | 0.93 S

900 legal *j*
noun system, right, service, issue, action, defense, status, fee, expert, battle, fund, problem

misc political, illegal, ethical, moral, perfectly, financial, yellow, constitutional
41522 | 0.94

901 help *n*
adj little, professional, financial, medical, outside, extra, psychological *noun* people, friend, government, student, kind, cry., call., plea., offer. *verb* need., get, ask., seek., provide, receive
39957 | 0.97

902 cold *j*
noun war, water, air, weather, night, day, winter, wind, morning, temperature, blood, rain *misc* during, hot, wet, warm, rinse, end, hard, dark
41100 | 0.95 F

903 above *i*
.all, head, foot., rise., high., level, .average, .ground, .water, hang., .sea, .else, floor, sky.
40791 | 0.95

904 rock *n*
adj hard, red, flat, solid, hot, volcanic, classic, molten *noun* .roll, .star, .band, music, wall, water, castle., .climbing, .concert, .formation *verb* throw, climb, hide, carve., collect, crash, land, kick, jut, slip
41289 | 0.94

905 that *r*
.is, .much, .far, .say, really., .early, .simple, .bad, best, worse
40209 | 0.96

906 seat *n*
adj front, empty, rear, hot, congressional, available, front-row, cheap, permanent, legislative *noun* back., .belt, car, passenger., driver., window., toilet., chair, bench, .cushion *verb* take., sit., win., lose., fill, lean, slide., shift., pick., return.
40706 | 0.94 F

907 weapon *n*
adj nuclear, automatic, secret, concealed, deadly, military, heavy, lethal, Iraqi, conventional *noun* .program, assault., .system, .inspector, murder., war, proliferation, .inspection, gun, material *verb* use, carry., develop., build., fire, acquire., produce., sell, draw
40994 | 0.93 S

908 song *n*
adj favorite, popular, pop, traditional, sad, original, beautiful, famous, definitive, sweet *noun* folk., theme., album, lyric, dance, title, country, hit, movie *verb* sing, write, play, hear, record, perform, listen., love, accompany, echo
41885 | 0.91

909 expert *n*
adj leading, military, financial, international, outside, top, forensic, foreign, independent, scientific *noun* .system, health., industry., .field, .witness, advice, security., law, opinion, .testimony *verb* .say, .agree, .believe, .recommend, .suggest, .predict, .estimate, testify, hire, consult
40783 | 0.94

910 radio *n*
adj public, local, two-way, commercial, portable, syndicated, amateur, Christian *noun* .station, .show, television, talk, .host, .program, news, .wave, music, .broadcast *verb* listen., hear, turn., play, .report, tune, own, switch., blare, crackle
40565 | 0.94

911 nice *j*
noun guy, thing, people, man, day, place, way, girl, house, job, person, morning *misc* very, see, really, meet, little, real, oh, pretty, clean
41132 | 0.92 S

912 avoid *v*
noun way., .problem, .eye, .conflict, .contact, .tax, .mistake, effort., situation, .risk, .confrontation, .pitfall, .injury, attempt., .fate *misc* try., help., in., order., possible, seek., able.
39561 | 0.96

913 memory *n*
adj recent, early, vivid, short-term, collective, long-term, historical, happy, distant, personal *noun* childhood, .loss, .card, experience, problem, computer, system, mind, .chip *verb* bring., fade, store, share., improve, honor., erase., commit., refresh., flood
40013 | 0.95

914 management *n*
adj environmental, federal, top, senior, financial, effective, middle, upper *noun* .system, resource, program, waste., company, .team, land., office., emergency., .plan *verb* improve, focus, oversee, promote, adopt, hire, integrate, facilitate, specialize, consult
42017 | 0.90 A

915 charge *n*
adj criminal, free, guilty, federal, serious, extra, additional, lesser, electric, electrical *noun* murder, service, drug., felony., assault, misdemeanor., sales. *verb* take., face., file, bring, lead., drop, deny, .relate, .stem, avoid.
39751 | 0.95

916 spring *n*
adj early, hot, late, warm, cold, past, following, deep *noun* .training, .summer, day, fall, winter., water, .break, season, flower, .semester *verb* plant, publish., bloom, release, feed, graduate, last., celebrate, melt, flow
40446 | 0.93 N

917 card *n*
adj wild, green, smart, calling, flash, yellow, fake, playing, get-well, holy *noun* credit., reader., service., business., report., .table, game, .company, Christmas. *verb* play., use, .accept, send, hold, hand., buy, carry, issue, receive
40005 | 0.94

918 maintain *v*
noun .control, .level, .relationship, .balance, system, .position, .contact, .status, .standard, .integrity, .weight, interest, ability, force *misc* order, help., able., .healthy, .strong
40563 | 0.93 A

919 theory *n*
adj social, general, political, literary, economic, critical, cognitive, evolutionary, feminist, contemporary *noun* .practice, conspiracy., development, research, relativity, evolution, quantum., learning, string. *verb* base, develop, explain, .suggest, support, apply, test., .predict, propose, prove
42507 | 0.89 A

920 care *v*
noun people, American., voter., nurse., .infant, physician, provider, .pet, .whit, .Alzheimer, mama, .grandchildren, orphan, caregiver., hospice *misc* do., .about, .for, who., .what, really., much
39326 | 0.96

921 visit *v*
noun .site, .web, friend, year, information., .home, week, city, mother, .museum, hospital, parent, .website, town, relative *misc* often, recently, regularly, invite., .upon, please., frequently
39055 | 0.96

922 imagine *v*
noun moment, .scene, .scenario, possibility, .surprise, shock, horror, .happening, .excitement, analogy., .delight, .disappointment *misc* can., I., .how, hard., try., might, difficult., anyone, .myself, easy., .yourself, impossible., easily.
39929 | 0.94 F

923 finish *v*
noun year, .school, season, .job, work, .point, .sentence, team., book, game, .college, project, race, .drink, hour *misc* just., after., before, .second, last
off .last, .glass, .beer, .bottle, drink, .meal **up** just., here, work, .paperwork, .dish, .homework
39763 | 0.94

924 statement *n*
adj financial, written, following, strong, clear, joint, official, recent, brief, general *noun* mission., opening., policy, impact., fashion., bank., income., response *verb* make, issue., read, release, include, agree., sign, indicate, reflect, base
39782 | 0.94

---

8. Materials

These refer to materials from which things can be made.

paper 73045, glass 49632, wood 36555, stone *n* 35007, gold 31573, plastic 23456, metal 22444, (lead) *n* 22372, silver 19448, steel 17080, leather 10605, cotton 10239, fabric 9929, brick 8800, silk 7059, rubber 6927, aluminum 6293, copper 5066, (marble) 5064, bronze 4979, brass 4802, ink 4702, ceramic 4639, silicon 4239, tin 4207, cement 4005, wool 3999, linen 3535, cardboard 3489, ivory 3336, granite 2762, tar *n* 2194, nickel 2146, acrylic 2025, limestone 1662, denim 1453, titanium 1261, sandstone 1011, cobalt 931, cashmere 928, polyester 870, chromium 540, formica 509, burlap 442, Teflon 383

925 firm *n*
adj private, big, financial, foreign, local,
architectural, top, pharmaceutical, commercial,
industrial *noun* law., investment., research.,
accounting., partner, company, business, brokerage.,
security., management *verb* hire, represent,
.specialize, join, own, account, invest, .operate,
.handle, found
42171 | 0.89 N

926 huge *j*
noun amount, number, problem, difference, crowd,
success, fan, tree, impact, increase, profit, sum
misc wooden, massive, loom, potentially, atop,
concrete, underground, hairy, incredibly
38891 | 0.96

927 respond *v*
noun student, need, .request, participant., .survey,
police., .demand, chance., opportunity., ability.,
letter, .criticism, .situation, officer, .concern
misc how., quickly, fail., immediately, .positively,
.differently
38955 | 0.96

928 popular *j*
noun culture, music, vote, support, program, show,
book, song, art, form, science, movement *misc* most,
become, very, among, increasingly, remain, contrary,
especially, wildly
39541 | 0.94

929 hard *r*
work., so., how., very., try, as., hit., too., find, .enough,
push., press, play., fight.
39133 | 0.95 F

930 physical *j*
noun education, activity, health, teacher,
fitness, educator, evidence, program, abuse,
class, therapy, condition *misc* mental, emotional,
psychological, social, such, sexual, teach,
spiritual
47006 | 0.79 A

931 talk *n*
adj small, tough, straight, direct, middle, cheap,
bilateral, late-night, high-level, Israeli *noun* .show,
.nation, radio, peace., .host, hour., kind. *verb* let.,
hear., listen., resume, engage., stall, .collapse
39888 | 0.93 S

932 traditional *j*
noun value, way, role, family, method, culture,
approach, system, practice, form, music, school
misc more, such, Chinese, modern, religious, beyond,
African, cultural
40499 | 0.92 A

933 contain *v*
noun material, information, quote., table, product.,
percent, article, .item, food, .error, book, box.,
.element, .amount, word *misc* each., .herein,
.within, .less, barely.
39815 | 0.93 A

934 peace *n*
adj international, quiet, lasting, inner, comprehensive,
relative, regional, permanent *noun* .process, .talk, war,
world, .corps, .agreement, justice, .mind, .conference,
.treaty *verb* make., bring., keep., live., sign, achieve,
rest., resume, reject., .prevail
39932 | 0.93

935 green *j*
noun onion, bean, light, eye, pepper, tea, grass, card,
space, tomato, party, salad *misc* red, blue, white,
yellow, dark, wear, chop, bright
39558 | 0.94

936 thanks (PL) *n*
adj special, sincere, heartfelt, generous, deepest,
effusive, hearty, profuse *noun* time, .call, year., guy,
day., man, pleasure, gentleman, world. *verb* .join,
.watch, appreciate, welcome, express., nod., extend,
deserve., owe., murmur
42160 | 0.88 S

937 control *v*
noun government, .cost, system, ability., .behavior,
effort., Congress, party, variable, computer, .access,
.effect, process, movement, .flow *misc* .by, .over,
able., tightly., carefully., difficult., unable., own.,
effectively.
39094 | 0.95 A

938 Democrat *n*
adj liberal, conservative, moderate, top, senior,
incumbent, lifelong *noun* Republican, house, Senate,
Congress, party, percent, time *verb* vote, .win, support,
control, .oppose, elect, accuse, favor, blame, defeat
42221 | 0.88 S

939 base *n*
adj military, naval, economic, broad, industrial, solid,
democratic, conservative *noun* air., knowledge., data.,
power, home., .camp, tax., .price *verb* build.,
establish, steal., cover, expand., reach., touch.,
operate, attack, secure
38430 | 0.96

940 impact *n*
adj environmental, economic, negative, significant,
positive, big, great, potential, major *noun* study,
.student, health, .statement, .environment, .economy,
.crater, assessment, project, point *verb* have., assess.,
reduce., examine., minimize., consider.
39915 | 0.92 A

941 structure *n*
adj social, political, organizational, large, economic,
complex, basic, internal, existing, narrative
noun power, family., system, factor., .function,
process, knowledge, force., class., building *verb* build,
create, change, form, determine, examine., establish,
alter., maintain, define
41126 | 0.90 A

942 tonight *r*
us., here., news., show, report., story, join., finally.,
tomorrow, dinner, summary.
43161 | 0.85 S

943 note *n*
adj accompanying, mental, final, personal,
handwritten, positive, promissory, brief, cautionary,
additional *noun* editor., .text, program., author.,
suicide., page, ransom., type., thank-you., letter
verb take., write, leave, read, send., compare., hit.,
strike., record, issue
41349 | 0.89

944 direction *n*
adj opposite, right, different, wrong, future, general,
positive, spiritual *noun* step., change, wind, sense.,
policy, speed, stage., pasta., move. *verb* give., head.,
follow., point., provide., face, pull., push., match
38040 | 0.97

945 fly *v*
noun plane, bird., flag, pilot., airplane, helicopter, .face, jet, mission, aircraft, airline, door, .space, spark., hour *misc* .over, .into, .out, .through, .away
in .from, plane, bird., helicopter, .California, .Paris, guest. off .shelf, .handle, bird, hat., cap., .hinge
38581 | 0.95

946 onto *i*
out., back, hold., .floor, step., turn., .street, .road, fall., drop., climb., pull., .bed, .side
39777 | 0.92 F

947 king *n*
adj future, ancient, undisputed, divine, reigning, Persian, Egyptian, wise, homecoming, evil
noun .queen, burger., man, lion., son, father, .mackerel, Lord, .pop *verb* .live, welcome., kill, crown., rule, honor., celebrate, declare, march, .command
39179 | 0.94

948 reveal *v*
noun study., analysis., .difference, result., secret, test., information, data., research., .detail, effect, truth, survey., pattern, identity *misc* .that, .significant, open., .itself, .themselves, clearly, fully
39261 | 0.93 A

949 cell *n*
adj embryonic, white, solar, healthy, dead, terrorist, fat, living, individual *noun* .phone, stem., fuel., blood., cancer., brain, .research., .membrane, jail. *verb* use, produce, cause, kill, contain, destroy, .divide, form, remove, generate
40694 | 0.90 M

950 religious *j*
noun belief, group, leader, right, freedom, organization, community, practice, tradition, faith, institution, experience *misc* political, ethnic, cultural, secular, social, moral, spiritual, deeply
42604 | 0.86 A

951 ball *n*
adj foul, rubber, wrecking, loose, inaugural, pro, fast, wooden, straight, solid *noun* game, golf., tennis., crystal., player, soccer., .field, bowling. *verb* hit, play., throw., roll, catch., drop, run, bounce, kick., toss.
39778 | 0.92

952 particular *j*
noun case, time, interest, group, area, problem, issue, way, attention, place, kind, situation *misc* any, within, no, focus, specific, historical, religious
39324 | 0.93 A

953 employee *n*
adj public, full-time, local, total, current, female, civilian, part-time, disgruntled, retired *noun* company, government., employer, benefit, job, business, customer, city., office, manager *verb* .work, hire, allow, lay, require, fire, .receive, train, state., treat
40341 | 0.90 N

954 head *v*
noun .door, .south, .north, .west, .east, car, team, street, .office, department, committee, road, town, .hill, .kitchen *misc* .toward, .into, .down, .home, before., .straight
down .hall, .hallway, .aisle, .trail, highway, .avenue, .driveway, .steep back .toward, turn., before., around., .home, .towards up .investigation, .trail, walk,

.towards, driveway, .canyon, .aisle out before., .sea, boat., lunch, .search off before., .down, .college
38249 | 0.95

955 suddenly *r*
then., feel, .become, stop, .realize, seem, turn, .appear, eye, .remember, face, die., voice, .aware
40590 | 0.90 F

956 apply *v*
noun law, rule, principle, pressure, standard, .job, theory, .knowledge, concept, model, court, skill, paint, color, .coat *misc* .equally, directly, similar, generally, successfully
39306 | 0.93 A

957 shake *v*
noun .head, hand, shoulder, voice., arm, finger, .fist, ground, leg, hair, foot, pan, confidence, .foundation, .disgust *misc* smile, slowly, laugh, .sadly, .violently
off .excess, try., flour, .water, .feeling, .thought, .sign, .chill, .injury up really., little, pretty., .staff, .politics out .hair, cigarette, .match
41403 | 0.88 F

958 cultural *j*
noun difference, identity, value, center, heritage, diversity, context, group, study, history, tradition, change *misc* social, political, economic, historical, religious, ethnic, within, racial
41871 | 0.87 A

959 chair *n*
adj folding, rocking, wooden, easy, electric, empty, vice *noun* table, back, desk, department, arm, lawn., leather., committee, leg, bed *verb* sit., lean., pull., push., rise., .face, settle., slump., throw, swivel.
39829 | 0.91 F

960 PM *r*
.today, open
46955 | 0.77 N

961 justice *n*
adj criminal, chief, social, juvenile, environmental, international, economic, military *noun* court., .system, US., peace, obstruction, law, .official, opinion, minister *verb* bring., serve, obstruct., seek, appoint, demand, achieve, promote., .prevail
38766 | 0.94

962 discover *v*
noun scientist., researcher., truth, .secret, astronomer., doctor., evidence, planet, cancer, gene, species, joy, .talent, object, investigator. *misc* recently, newly., quickly, surprised., suddenly.
37533 | 0.96

963 measure *n*
adj large, dependent, economic, preventive, necessary, self-report, specific, additional, objective, similar *noun* security., control, performance, outcome., study, .success, use, score, scale, health *verb* take, design, provide, pass, develop, adopt, .reduce, .protect, .prevent, propose
40750 | 0.88 A

964 politics *n*
adj American, national, domestic, international, inside, democratic, local, presidential, involved

noun religion, world., economics, power, party, culture, history, policy, identity, role. *verb* talk., play, dominate, enter., cover., discuss., engage., analyze., motivate., interfere
38854 | 0.92 A

965 manage v
noun .care, company, money, fund, resource, .smile, land, project, ability., organization, .affair, .growth, agency, investment, career *misc* finally., .escape, .stay, effectively, successfully, .billion
37131 | 0.97

966 treat v
noun people, patient, child, .disease, .respect, drug, doctor., .cancer, hospital, condition, .illness, .depression, .disorder, infection, antibiotic *misc* .as, .like, .differently, .fairly, .equally, .unfairly
37430 | 0.96

967 yourself p
you, your, find., ask., protect., care., kill., enjoy., save., hurt., imagine., prepare., push., treat.
38403 | 0.93

968 pain n
adj chronic, severe, physical, growing, sharp, abdominal, joint, excruciating, emotional *noun* back., chest, patient, .suffering, relief, lot., .medication, .management *verb* feel, cause, suffer, ease., experience, relieve., inflict, reduce., shoot, avoid
38233 | 0.94

969 evening n
adj good, early, late, previous, quiet, entire, following *noun* .news, morning, dinner, hour, .post, summer., afternoon., .sky, .gown, .meal *verb* spend., join, enjoy, gather, feature, dance, schedule, light, host, .progress
37931 | 0.94

970 rather i
(rather than) .than, one, individual, focus, .later, sooner., .simply, rule, rely, specific, exception, .risk
38663 | 0.92 A

971 unit n
adj small, special, national, basic, mobile, separate, individual, functional, astronomical, neonatal *noun* care., research, army, family., housing, police., business. *verb* include, build, form, operate, consist, assign, deploy, cost, complete, measure
38541 | 0.93 A

972 affect v
noun .life, factor., decision, issue., change, policy, health, .performance, behavior, .ability, disease, condition, .quality, community, level *misc* .by, how., adversely., directly., significantly., negatively.
38426 | 0.93 A

973 play n
adj big, fair, foul, double, free, musical, final, key, defensive, dramatic *noun* child, game, role, school., power., .area, character *verb* come., write, watch., perform, produce, direct, resume, engage, .shape, suspect
38270 | 0.93 N

974 production n
adj mass, agricultural, industrial, domestic, increased, cultural, total, artistic *noun* oil., company, cost, food., process, energy., .line, film, consumption, .facility

verb increase, reduce, stimulate., boost., expand, .decline, control, affect, result, estimate
39125 | 0.91 A

975 bit n
adj little, tiny, slight, extra, wee, browned, fair, broken, brown, digital *noun* .piece, .time, .information, .money, .history, .paper, drill., .part, .luck, .advice *verb* talk., add., bite., blow., scrape., upset, chomp., champ., frighten, shock
38260 | 0.93 S

976 inside i
.house, .head, look., .room, deep., .door, .building, body, .car, box, wall, .Iraq, bag, hide.
37517 | 0.95 F

977 far j
noun end, side, back, right, cry, corner, wall, reach, distance, edge, bank, shore *misc* off, thus, left, wide, eastern, away, near, distant
37056 | 0.96

978 range n
adj wide, broad, full, whole, close, wider, long, front, normal, possible *noun* price., mountain., age, .issue, .motion, .activity, size, .option, temperature, missile *verb* offer., cover., provide., extend, represent., expand., shoot., limit, span, score.
38292 | 0.93 A

979 top j
noun official, priority, player, executive, story, floor, speed, aide, nation, team, job, leader *misc* among, left, including, former, military, bottom, secret, tonight, rank
37884 | 0.94 N

980 worry v
noun parent., official., .safety, expert., critic., analyst., investor., observer., environmentalist., .inflation, prospect. .fate, privacy, .me, shyness *misc* do., .anymore, constantly, .aloud, terribly, .dear, overly
   about what, thing, .how, nothing., need., something, anything
36966 | 0.96

981 perform v
noun .task, function, analysis, test, student., work, music, surgery, service, procedure, .duty, abortion, operation, act, doctor. *misc* .well, .better, able., .poorly, traditional, .significantly, unable., effectively, successfully, .complex
38301 | 0.92 A

982 necessary j
noun skill, condition, step, change, information, action, force, resource, part, means, knowledge, measure *misc* if, may, provide, absolutely, whatever, deem, achieve, protect, maintain
38074 | 0.93 A

983 conference n
adj national, international, annual, western, Catholic, recent, athletic, professional *noun* press., news., .room, peace., .call, .table, .center, week, .committee *verb* hold, attend., win, .announce, organize, sponsor, host, convene, conduct, .feature
37695 | 0.94

984 individual j
noun student, group, right, difference, member, level, need, case, investor, freedom, account, responsibility

misc each, within, than, rather, base, collective, personal
39346 | 0.90 A

985 candidate *n*
adj presidential, democratic, other, political, leading, likely, potential, major, independent, possible *noun* Republican., party, .president, election, campaign, Senate, .governor, .office, teacher., issue *verb* run., win, choose, endorse., elect, nominate., select, .replace, .promise, attack
38338 | 0.92 S

986 museum *n*
adj national, American, metropolitan, historical, private, maritime, living, native, archaeological *noun* art, history, collection, new, director, gallery, science, curator, exhibition, exhibit *verb* open, visit., house, display, feature, acquire, found, travel, .devote, donate.
40210 | 0.88 M

987 specific *j*
noun area, information, question, group, issue, problem, need, goal, type, skill, behavior, activity *misc* very, such, each, identify, within, focus, address, require
39323 | 0.90 A

988 best *r*
at, know, as., how., work., win, .suit, .place, like., .describe, perhaps., .serve, .ever, among
36566 | 0.96

989 throughout *i*
.world, .country, .year, .day, .history, .life, .United States, .region, .career, spread., city, .Europe, .entire, area
37312 | 0.95 A

990 hall *n*
adj great, front, main, empty, future, juvenile, narrow, hallowed, downtown *noun* .fame, city., town., concert., room, music., door, end., dining., meeting *verb* walk., fill, enter., induct., head, wander., cross., hurry., ring, honor
37412 | 0.94

991 past *n*
adj recent, present, distant, future, historical, colonial, glorious, ancient, painful, violent *noun* .year, .game, memory, history, .century, mistake., link., connection., nation, relic. *verb* forget, confront., preserve, dwell., haunt, connect., bury, shape, escape., relive.
36716 | 0.96

992 fish *n*
adj big, small, fresh, dead, tropical, grilled, freshwater *noun* .wildlife, water, game, species, meat, .oil, chicken, sauce, river, bird *verb* catch, eat, .swim, feed, kill, cook, smell, contain, spawn, clean
38596 | 0.91 M

993 trip *n*
adj long, round, recent, short, quick, whole, frequent, entire *noun* field., road., business., fishing., return., camping., family., shopping., weekend, bus. *verb* make., take, plan., cancel., enjoy., organize, .cost, book., accompany, hike
37011 | 0.95

994 mention *v*
noun name, article, fact, letter, .possibility, text, respondent, .beginning, incident, .passing, Bible,

topic, column, .introduction, paragraph *misc* not., never., .above, already., previously, fail.
36499 | 0.96

995 edge *n*
adj leading, sharp, outer, competitive, top, western, hard, eastern, very, southern *noun* cutting., .bed, water, .town, city, field, river, cliff, forest, wood *verb* sit., stand., cut, push., lose., reach., perch., teeter., soften., roll
37769 | 0.93 F

996 trouble *n*
adj big, serious, real, deep, little, financial, legal, foul *noun* lot., people, time, kind., sign., .spot, school, heart., .sleeping, .breathing *verb* have., get, cause., run., stay, spell., avoid., stir., .concentrate, blame
36530 | 0.96

997 interview *n*
adj recent, exclusive, personal, structured, live, individual, rare, initial, numerous *noun* telephone., week, television, request, job., police., question, phone., teacher, official *verb* conduct, give, base., grant., decline., complete, .reveal, .last, tape, obtain
37439 | 0.94

998 style *n*
adj personal, musical, traditional, architectural, unique, cognitive, particular, classic, various, distinctive *noun* learning., life, management., teaching, leadership, thinking, type, parenting., color, substance *verb* learn., develop, cope., change, teach, reflect, describe, define, fit, suit
37725 | 0.93

999 middle *j*
noun school, class, age, student, ground, ear, finger, name, income, manager, level, linebacker *misc* eastern, elementary, upper, throughout, poor, rich, urban, Islamic
37373 | 0.93

1000 cause *n*
adj common, leading, probable, major, natural, underlying, lost, main, primary, just *noun* .death, .effect, root., .concern, disease, .cancer, .action, .celebration, .consequence, behavior *verb* die., support., determine., advance., identify., champion., address., search, list, cite
36444 | 0.96

1001 ten *m*
.year, .minute, .ago, about., .day, after, .thousand, big., .later, .foot, five., .percent, .commandment, .old
37326 | 0.93 F

1002 weight *n*
adj heavy, light, healthy, extra, full, dead, free, ideal *noun* .loss, body., pound, .gain, height, .training, .room, size, .control, .lb *verb* lose., carry., put., feel., keep, shift.
38565 | 0.90 M

1003 adult *n*
adj young, old, healthy, responsible, sexual, mature, gifted, average, active, juvenile *noun* child, .life, percent., .education, .male, age, year, .population, program, world *verb* treat., accompany, smoke, expose, aim., interact, interview, function, behave, appeal.
37246 | 0.93 A

1004 dream n
adj American, true, bad, wild, sweet, impossible, lifelong, alive, wet, recurring *noun* night, .team, hope., world, .house, .reality, girl, pipe., .job, .nightmare *verb* .come, live., .become, realize., pursue., wake, remember, fulfill., chase., sleep
36609 | 0.95

1005 fear n
adj bad, greatest, constant, unknown, growing, irrational, deep, sudden, widespread, deepest *noun* people, hope, anxiety, .death, .failure, .crime, pain, .factor *verb* live., express, overcome., confirm, face, allay., cause, strike, .anger, experience
35736 | 0.97

1006 dark j
noun hair, eye, side, room, night, matter, sky, light, skin, cloud, suit, glass *misc* brown, blue, wear, green, black, white, red, gray, cold, thick
38455 | 0.90 F

1007 sign v
noun .contract, agreement, president, bill, treaty, .law, paper, letter, .name, .autograph, agent, document, .petition, player, book *misc* free, recently., refuse., .dated, .onto
 up .for, .class, before, customer, already., .online, volunteer, subscriber, worker, employee. **on** .play, sponsor, eventually, refuse., originally.
36535 | 0.95 N

1008 method n
adj traditional, different, scientific, effective, alternative, various, common, current, appropriate, modern *noun* .participant, study, research, teaching, .subject, data, analysis, .course, use, assessment *verb* develop, teach, employ, provide, describe, apply, determine, .produce, .assess, .involve
39601 | 0.88 A

1009 somebody p
.who, .else, if., something, kill, maybe, shoot, other, hurt, .steal, unless., please, somewhere, blame
38294 | 0.91 S

1010 magazine n
adj weekly, literary, monthly, online, glossy, pornographic, conservative, quarterly, mainstream, outdoor *noun* time., editor, newspaper, article, cover, book, new., issue., news., page *verb* read, publish, appear, report, feature, sell, pick, launch, edit, .devote
36361 | 0.95

1011 reflect v
noun light, change, value, view, .fact, difference, .concern, .reality, policy, attitude, price, mirror, interest, level, pattern *misc* may., .upon, accurately., .off, cultural, simply.
37716 | 0.92 A

1012 heavy j
noun metal, rain, cream, load, door, weight, burden, equipment, traffic, industry, snow, drinking *misc* too, carry, wear, lift, hang, thick, hot, wooden
36195 | 0.96

1013 soldier n
adj American, young, wounded, dead, military, Japanese, fellow, French, female, Soviet *noun* war, army, .field, foot., child., officer, enemy., marine,

battle, unit *verb* kill, .die, .fight, send, capture, shoot, .wound, return, carry, train
37120 | 0.93

1014 property n
adj private, intellectual, personal, public, physical, local, commercial, residential, cultural, common *noun* .tax, .right, .owner, value, damage, land, protection, piece., rental., ownership *verb* own, buy., sell, protect., acquire, purchase, seize, .belong, define
37124 | 0.93

1015 beautiful j
noun woman, girl, day, place, child, eye, face, house, city, wife, hair, color *misc* most, young, ever, blue, absolutely, wonderful, bright, rich, elegant
36757 | 0.94 F

1016 writer n
adj American, senior, free-lance, young, editorial, famous, British, prolific, contributing, female *noun* staff., freelance., artist, editor, woman., fiction, science., director, letter., author *verb* .live, .base, .contribute, travel, e-mail, .specialize, portray, .reside, chronicle, compile
36528 | 0.95

1017 stuff n
adj good, right, serious, fun, hot, crazy, tough, weird, funny *noun* lot., kind., people, kid, sort., .legend, food., bunch., .sack *verb* buy., .happen, love, sell, throw, eat, strut., pack, clean, store
36934 | 0.93 S

1018 camera n
adj hidden, digital, infrared, still, candid, live, light, hand-held, advanced, planetary *noun* .club, television, .crew, surveillance., lens, security. *verb* use, move, .follow, capture, .roll, set, .record, catch, point, carry.
38159 | 0.90

1019 improve v
noun .quality, .life, .performance, .health, condition, skill, education, effort., situation, .efficiency, relation, .ability, economy, chance, technology *misc* help., significantly, dramatically, greatly., continue., economic
37022 | 0.93 A

1020 shoulder n
adj right, left, broad, bare, wide, cold, thin, heavy, sore, thick *noun* hand., arm., head., back, .blade, neck, bag, strap, face, .injury *verb* look, shrug., touch., glance., stand, pat., lift, shake, sling., tap.
38852 | 0.89 F

1021 bar n
adj full, local, gay, wet, parallel, wooden, topless, crowded, uneven, trendy *noun* restaurant, candy., chocolate., hotel, state., snack., .grill, drink, .stool, window *verb* sit, raise, hang, grab, lean., tend., lower., dance, feature, slide
36593 | 0.94 F

1022 hotel n
adj grand, luxury, downtown, five-star, cheap, expensive, fancy *noun* .room, restaurant, night, suite, lobby, resort, bar, casino, guest, beach *verb* stay., check., return., own, arrive, book, operate, lodge, .overlook, .cater
36591 | 0.94 N

1023 instead *r*
focus, choose, rely, opt, prefer, concentrate, argue, propose, .merely, .reward, altogether.
35599 | 0.96

1024 hill *n*
adj rolling, steep, green, pleasant, southern, nearby, surrounding, eastern, auburn, gentle *noun* chapel., .country, road, top., town, forest, oak., crest., tree, mountain *verb* climb., walk, .overlook, roll, head., rise, surround, ride, dot, perch.
35944 | 0.95

1025 exist *v*
noun difference., problem., relationship., evidence., condition., form, possibility., society, opportunity., culture, universe, tension., earth, literature, structure. *misc* no., .between, still., only, such, long., already.
36600 | 0.94 A

1026 sea *n*
adj open, deep, blue, shining, green, inland, vast, heavy *noun* .level, .lion, .turtle, island, water, .salt, black., dead., red., .change *verb* rise, sail, swim, head., float., drown., cross., overlook., blow, crash
36577 | 0.94

1027 institution *n*
adj other, financial, high, political, educational, social, public, international, religious, democratic *noun* education, government, society, research, university, art., college, law, marriage, policy *verb* build, establish, support, attend, state, strengthen., operate, transfer., lend, shape
38779 | 0.88 A

1028 purpose *n*
adj primary, political, present, main, sole, specific, public, common, real, whole *noun* .study, sense., life, .article, research, intent., discussion, meaning., tax, .investigation *verb* serve., use, explain., achieve, test., accomplish., suit., establish, defeat.
37395 | 0.92 A

1029 pattern *n*
adj similar, different, consistent, general, complex, cultural, changing, familiar, certain, typical *noun* behavior, change, color, weather., movement, relationship, development, response, difference, growth *verb* follow., show, .emerge, create, reveal, fit., reflect, establish, identify, repeat
37609 | 0.91 A

1030 detail *n*
adj great, small, fine, specific, full, personal, final, technical, graphic, vivid *noun* attention., story, page, .news, plan, security., work, .summary, level., photograph *verb* describe., provide, discuss., reveal., add, remember., explain., examine., focus., .emerge
35573 | 0.96

1031 machine *n*
adj answering, military, flying, automatic, heavy, complex, well-oiled, expensive, smart *noun* .gun, washing., time, fax., slot., sewing., message, .tool *verb* vend., build, buy, operate, install, test, replace, invent, measure, feed
36132 | 0.94

1032 challenge *n*
adj new, big, real, greatest, major, legal, serious, tough, economic, environmental *noun* court,

problem, week, kind., security, century, design, response., .authority, .future *verb* face, meet., pose, present., accept., address., rise., issue., prepare, mount.
36184 | 0.94 A

1033 owner *n*
adj new, small, private, previous, original, principal, current, proud, rightful, sole *noun* business., property., store., team., shop., player, restaurant, gun., building *verb* sell, hire, compensate, .complain, convince., sue, contact, advise., negotiate, notify.
36704 | 0.93 N

1034 agent *n*
adj federal, secret, special, undercover, literary, foreign, double, independent, Soviet, British *noun* estate., travel., insurance., government, intelligence., enforcement., .orange, police, drug, player *verb* sign, act, arrest, .investigate, hire, .search, .banish, contact, .testify, pursue
35666 | 0.95

1035 tough *j*
noun time, question, guy, decision, job, law, issue, choice, love, situation, problem, crime *misc* really, face, enough, pretty, smart, very, extremely
36387 | 0.94 S

1036 ahead *r*
go., look., straight., still., move., day., year., lie., plan, stare., far., week., road.
36994 | 0.92 S

1037 generation *n*
adj new, young, old, previous, whole, early, current, entire *noun* people, power., woman, child, parent, .leader, electricity, boom., .gap, boomer *verb* pass., represent, .born, produce, inspire., belong., hand., influence., train, attract.
35642 | 0.95

1038 commercial *j*
noun break, bank, development, fishing, use, estate, interest, success, fisherman, market, building, product *misc* welcome, continue, right, join, residential, real, industrial
38932 | 0.87 S

1039 whom *p*
many., most., man., those., .meet, both., person., friend., .speak, .love, someone., .share, name, .marry
35158 | 0.96

1040 fall *n*
adj great, late, early, free, past, cool, previous, light, following, backward *noun* spring, rise., summer., .winter, season, day, election, .semester *verb* break, publish, plant, release, schedule., survive., launch
35454 | 0.96

1041 down *i*
.road, .street, walk., .stair, .hill, way., back, run., .step, .hall, .side, .corridor, .line, .path
36448 | 0.92 F

1042 surface *n*
adj smooth, flat, floured, hard, lunar, entire, outer *noun* water, earth, .area, .temperature, work., planet, skin, soil, moon, painting *verb* cover, break., scratch., rise., reach., float., skim., apply, measure, spread
36864 | 0.91 M

1043 budget *n*
adj balanced, federal, annual, congressional, military, total, current, tight *noun* .deficit, year, office, .cut, defense., president, percent, .amendment, tax, .committee *verb* balance., pass, reduce, increase, submit, approve, state, sign, double, exceed
36509 | 0.92

1044 senator *n*
adj democratic, senior, junior, conservative, incumbent, bipartisan, vice, moderate, distinguished, influential *noun* Republican, state., US., .Democrat, new, president, time, congressmen *verb* thank, .vote, agree, support, introduce, welcome, elect, .oppose, propose, sponsor
39231 | 0.85 S

1045 bag *n*
adj brown, full, heavy, mixed, overnight, punching, zipper-lock, athletic *noun* plastic., air., sleeping., paper., shopping., garbage., duffel. *verb* carry., put, pack, hold, fill, pull, open, grab., drop, pick.
36465 | 0.92 F

1046 reality *n*
adj virtual, political, social, economic, harsh, physical, objective, historical, ultimate *noun* .show, .check, .TV, dream., perception., fantasy, sense., television, truth *verb* become., face., reflect., deal., accept., confront., ignore., exist, experience, transform
35501 | 0.94 A

1047 editor *n*
adj managing, senior, associate, assistant, contributing, medical *noun* magazine, .note, executive., letter., news, newspaper, .chief, writer, publisher, author *verb* contribute., name., appoint., retire, resign, edit, .reserve, .applaud, .commend
39799 | 0.84 N

1048 tend *v*
noun people., garden, individual., American., .bar, female., male., attitude, athlete., voter., minority, adolescent., plot, personality, .flock *misc* .toward, .focus, .less, .view
35315 | 0.94 A

1049 address *v*
noun .issue, .problem, question, .concern, study., research, program., article., letter, topic, policy, .nation, .correspondence *misc* need, directly, social, specific, specifically.
36227 | 0.92 A

1050 civil *j*
noun right, war, society, liberty, movement, union, service, servant, law, case, leader, group *misc* American, during, against, political, criminal, federal, military, file
35492 | 0.94

1051 step *v*
noun room, foot, .line, moment., .effort, .elevator, .ladder, .shadow, .toe, .hall, .doorway, .bus, .stage, .plane, .microphone *misc* .into, .forward, .onto, .aside, .inside, .outside, .over
   up .effort, .pressure, .attack, .onto, .campaign, .enforcement, .pace, .production **down** .chief, .chairman, force., .CEO, .onto, speaker, intention., voluntarily **in** government., .fill, military., fate., legislature., .rescue, .broker, .regulate **out** .into, door,

.onto, .behind, .front, .public **back** .inside, .pace, .admire, .survey, startle
35747 | 0.93 F

1052 discussion *n*
adj public, open, serious, general, online, detailed, following, brief, present *noun* group, issue, result, class., topic, student, panel., debate, subject, purpose *verb* continue., include, lead, focus, join., engage., participate., involve, conclude., .center
36661 | 0.90 A

1053 test *v*
noun hypothesis, drug, model, student, system, study, water, .theory, sample, effect, product, skill, ability, .limit, subject *misc* .positive, design., .determine, currently., thoroughly, empirically, .evaluate, fully., successfully
   out .new, chance., as, just, .idea, .its
35465 | 0.93 A

1054 mom *n*
adj single, stay-at-home, working, full-time, divorced, scared, teenage, foster, adoptive, part-time *noun* .dad, kid, time, house, soccer., sister, home, car, birth, birthday *verb* tell, love, .die, cry, yell, hug, kiss, sigh, shop, divorce
36781 | 0.90 F

1055 violence *n*
adj domestic, political, sexual, sectarian, physical, ethnic, racial, random *noun* act., scene, .woman, sex, school, drug, crime, victim., threat., level. *verb* stop., end., prevent., .occur, reduce., erupt, commit, involve, cause, threaten
35531 | 0.93

1056 total *j*
noun number, percent, fat, score, cost, population, time, return, amount, value, sample, carbohydrate *misc* sit, million, saturated, increase, per, estimate, reduce, annual, less
35790 | 0.92 A

1057 skin *n*
adj white, pale, dark, smooth, dry, soft, brown, thin, thick, light *noun* color, hair, .cancer, bone, .tone, .cell, surface, layer, .care, muscle *verb* remove, cause, peel, burn, protect, touch, rub, break, wear, stretch
36190 | 0.91 F M

1058 heat *n*
adj medium, high, medium-high, low, medium-low, intense, dead *noun* oil, skillet., minute, pan., boil., saucepan., oven, summer, water, .onion *verb* reduce., .add, remove., cook, turn, feel., increase.
36450 | 0.91 M

1059 council *n*
adj national, American, economic, foreign, advisory, governing, international, legislative, Supreme, tribal *noun* security., city., member, .resolution, president, research., nation., meeting, education, .relation *verb* .meet, .vote, approve, pass, .decide, elect, .adopt, form, appoint, attend
35382 | 0.93

1060 notice *v*
noun thing, .change, .difference, .sign, foot, absence, .improvement, reader., .smell, .expression, .similarity, .ring, neighbor, observer., .odor *misc* seem., .something, never., hardly., barely.
35630 | 0.93 F

1061 beat *v*
noun egg, heart., team, sugar, .death, drum, .butter,
white, .odds, .wife, mixture, police, flour, vanilla,
cream *misc* .until, hard, lightly., badly
  up .on, get., kid, guy, .wife, pretty, someone,
badly, cop, threaten. **down** sun., .door, rain.,
.upon **out** issue., decliners, .advancer,
.competition
35222 | 0.93

1062 nor *c*
neither., .any, .ever, .anyone, .deny, .necessarily,
confirm., fully, entirely, .merely, sufficient, surprising,
.inclination, desirable
34818 | 0.95 A

1063 modern *j*
noun art, world, time, museum, history, life, society,
technology, science, state, era, medicine *misc* early,
ancient, traditional, western, industrial, thoroughly,
urban, democratic, European
35754 | 0.92 A

1064 vote *n*
adj electoral, popular, final, presidential, single, close,
unanimous, total, necessary *noun* percent., Senate,
majority., Republican, election, .confidence, Congress,
count, candidate, number *verb* get., cast, win, lose.,
receive, support, delay., tally
36477 | 0.90 S

1065 sing *v*
noun song, voice, music, choir, bird., .praise, .tune,
hymn, church, .anthem, .blue, love, heart, singer.,
gospel *misc* .along, together, softly, musical, .sweet,
shout, .loudly, .favorite, .Spanish, chant, beautifully,
accompany
35859 | 0.92

1066 cancer *n*
adj ovarian, cervical, pancreatic, colorectal, testicular,
terminal, endometrial *noun* breast., risk, prostate.,
lung., .patient, disease, woman, colon., .cell,
treatment *verb* die., cause., diagnose., prevent.,
develop., treat., .spread, cure., kill, reduce
36767 | 0.89 M

1067 finger *n*
adj long, little, middle, left, cold, tiny, thin, bony,
gloved, broken *noun* hand, index., .lip, hair, ring.,
thumb, tip., eye, .toe, arm *verb* point, put., run., hold,
snap., touch, keep., stick., press, lift.
37148 | 0.88 F

1068 lake *n*
adj great, clear, nearby, frozen, shallow, freshwater,
man-made, artificial, arctic, sparkling *noun* salt., .city,
water, river, shore, forest, area, mile, mountain, view
verb overlook., swim, head, surround, fish, flow., feed,
drain, .freeze, .dry
35614 | 0.92

1069 wish *v*
noun .luck, author., birthday, reader, .harm, .happiness,
holiday, educator., instructor., retrospect., .fulfillment,
hindsight., .farewell, .grandpa, majesty. *misc* I, .can,
well, .thank, sometimes., someone, anyone
34575 | 0.95 F

1070 marriage *n*
adj gay, same-sex, happy, previous, interracial,
traditional, arranged, legal, civil, failed *noun* year,
child, family, .divorce, couple, sex., relationship,
love, daughter, institution *verb* end, .last, save., ban.,
recognize, fail, oppose., enter, define, perform
34739 | 0.94

1071 victim *n*
adj alleged, sexual, innocent, potential, female, dead,
violent, intended, helpless, sacrificial *noun* family,
crime, rape, abuse, murder., accident, police, AIDS,
disease *verb* become., fall., help., blame., kill, identify,
claim., treat, .suffer, shoot
34313 | 0.95

1072 task *n*
adj difficult, easy, daunting, simple, specific, complex,
impossible, challenging, joint, main *noun* .force,
performance, time, .hand, group, .orientation,
teacher, difficulty, type, activity *verb* perform.,
complete, accomplish., face, .require, assign, set,
.involve, carry, undertake
36492 | 0.90 A

---

9. Nationalities

Note that many of these words may also refer to languages: English, Chinese, Russian, German, etc.

[Top 80] American 278042, Indian 41558, English 38009, French 37332, African 36181, British 33924, Chinese 33374,
Russian 30042, German 29115, Japanese 28757, Iraqi 25042, Israeli 24824, Arab 23866, Palestinian 23689, Jewish 19412,
Mexican 17571, Italian 16418, Spanish 15707, Canadian 15542, Latin 15443, Korean 10619, Irish 10570, Greek 9748,
Cuban 8424, Polish 7858, Native American 6941, Iranian 6656, Dutch 6449, Egyptian 5640, Australian 5240,
Turkish 4350, South African 4238, Brazilian 4238, Bosnian 4168, Vietnamese 4116, Swiss 3804, Pakistani 3270,
Haitian 3177, Czech 3174, Swedish 3109, Syrian 3090, Serbian 2876, Lebanese 2747, Serb 2736, Kuwaiti 2721, Thai 2689,
Dominican 2425, Danish 2293, Puerto Rican 2292, Portuguese 2285, Scottish 2271, Norwegian 2202, Albanian 2196,
Indonesian 2042, Hungarian 2008, Colombian 1849, Austrian 1820, Jordanian 1795, Belgian 1736, Lithuanian 1720,
Argentine 1713, Filipino 1707, Nigerian 1682, Yugoslav 1647, Croatian 1643, Ethiopian 1630, Somali 1543, Chilean 1487,
Croat 1471, Spaniard 1466, Armenian 1444, Ukrainian 1417, Taiwanese 1352, Welsh 1346, Peruvian 1338,
Jamaican 1320, (Georgian) 1212, Arabian 1205, Romanian 1120, Finnish 1113

1073 yard *n*
adj front, total, cubic, rushing, passing, wide, square, receiving, net, combined *noun* .touchdown, back., .trimming, pass., .game, tree, season, side, school, play *verb* rush, carry, run., throw., catch, gain.
36190 | 0.90 N

1074 kitchen *n*
adj open, tiny, outdoor, cramped, dirty, darkened, remodeled *noun* .table, room, door, .window, .floor, .counter, .sink, .cabinet, soup. *verb* sit., walk., stand, enter., cook, return, head., clean, .smell, gather
36076 | 0.90 F

1075 item *n*
adj other, personal, individual, single, specific, big-ticket, luxury, various, expensive, additional *noun* scale, response, number, factor, test, food., table, questionnaire, line., news. *verb* include, consist., contain., buy, .relate, respond., identify, comprise, remove
36726 | 0.89 A

1076 responsibility *n*
adj personal, social, individual, primary, moral, full, fiscal, corporate *noun* sense., government, right., family, .action, role., job, authority, freedom, accountability *verb* take., assume., accept., bear., claim., share., carry, .protect, .ensure
34645 | 0.94 A

1077 mouth *n*
adj full, dry, wide, gaping, pink, toothless, round, smiling, wider, loose *noun* hand., word., eye, corner., nose, river, tongue, finger., taste., tooth *verb* open, shut, keep., close, cover., wipe., hang, fill, .drop, .twist
36865 | 0.88 F

1078 agreement *n*
adj international, general, collective, interim, prenuptial, final, tentative, mutual, regional *noun* trade., peace., budget., term., bargaining., .tariff, development., plea., arm. *verb* reach, sign, negotiate, nod., enter., end, violate., conclude, announce, fail
36137 | 0.90 A

1079 attorney *n*
adj general, assistant, criminal, civil, senior, prosecuting, court-appointed, associate, managing *noun* district., defense., .office, US., state., county., deputy., city. *verb* .represent, hire, .argue, .file, prosecute, appoint, .handle, .specialize, .defend, contact
35304 | 0.92 S

1080 capital *n*
adj social, human, foreign, political, financial, private, international, cultural, long-term *noun* .gain, .city, .punishment, nation., investment, venture., .market *verb* raise., cut, invest, attract., reduce, .flow, finance, accumulate, lack., found
34958 | 0.93

1081 threat *n*
adj serious, real, nuclear, potential, military, terrorist, greatest, major, perceived, immediate *noun* security, death., health, war, .violence, terrorism, bomb., .peace, perception *verb* pose, face, receive., represent., perceive., deal., present, reduce., warn, exaggerate
34394 | 0.94

1082 smile *v*
noun eye, head, face, mouth, .camera, lip, shoulder, ear, joke, tear, grin, wave, .relief, .satisfaction, .greeting *misc* .back, nod, again, shake, .broadly, .slightly
38074 | 0.85 F

1083 gas *n*
adj natural, electric, hot, cheap, atmospheric, interstellar, ionized, clean, used, burning *noun* oil., .station, greenhouse., .price, emission, tank, tear., .mask *verb* run, produce, reduce, buy, pump., fill, burn, hit, emit, contain
34675 | 0.93

1084 instead *i*
(instead of) .of, use, .usual, .traditional, hour, .rely, cash, plastic, milk, butter, concentrate, stair., .elevator
33300 | 0.97

1085 positive *j*
noun attitude, effect, relationship, result, change, outcome, way, thing, experience, impact, response, feedback *misc* negative, more, very, test, between, toward, significant, both
35902 | 0.90 A

1086 track *n*
adj audio, fast, right, wrong, dead, inside, Olympic, short, fresh, beaten *noun* .record, .field, railroad., race, .team, sound., car, title., .athlete *verb* keep., check., lose., stop., run, follow, cover., cross, train, feature
33798 | 0.95

1087 investment *n*
adj foreign, private, real, direct, long-term, initial, chief, minimum, personal *noun* .firm, capital, .bank, .banker, company, fund, return., trade, .banking, business *verb* make, require, increase, encourage., attract., protect, reduce, manage, promote, recoup.
35803 | 0.90

1088 account *n*
adj personal, private, current, detailed, historical, medical, receivable, various, joint, taxable *noun* bank., retirement., saving., checking., number, eyewitness., news. *verb* take., open., read., offer, close, publish, handle, .differ, withdraw, cancel
34181 | 0.94

1089 break *n*
adj commercial, short, quick, big, fast, lucky, clean *noun* moment., tax., back, spring., lunch., coffee., summer, .room, Christmas. *verb* take., give., .welcome, let, continue, deserve., mark., chat
38422 | 0.84 S

1090 rich *j*
noun people, man, country, history, tax, color, nation, source, soil, gap, kid, tradition *misc* poor, famous, powerful, deep, strike, dark, cultural, brown
33209 | 0.97

1091 citizen *n*
adj senior, American, private, ordinary, fellow, average, law-abiding, local, individual, free *noun* US., state, right, group, nation, community, .action, .committee, .suit, participation *verb* become., protect., allow, treat., .vote, .participate, educate., encourage, urge, defend
34103 | 0.94

1092 audience *n*
adj large, wider, broad, mass, captive, live, wide, huge
noun member, studio., television., target., stage,
reaction, applause, .share, viewing., laughter *verb* tell.,
reach., attract., .laugh, draw., address., .applaud,
remind., .respond, perform
33919 | 0.94

1093 lady *n*
adj old, young, fat, nice, leading, fair, lovely, beautiful,
elderly *noun* .room, man, friend, church, .bird,
volleyball., luck, cleaning., Lord., bag. *verb* .enter,
.sing, welcome, .host, excuse, dance, seat, escort.,
.skate, .faint
35436 | 0.90 F

1094 dinner *n*
adj nice, formal, sit-down, quiet, romantic, black-tie,
four-course, complete, expensive, lavish *noun* lunch.,
.table, .party, night, family, breakfast., restaurant,
Thanksgiving., .plate, evening *verb* eat., cook., serve,
sit, invite., prepare, finish., plan, .honor, feature
34252 | 0.93

1095 western *j*
noun state, country, world, culture, hemisphere,
civilization, society, nation, conference, art, tradition,
diplomat *misc* European, eastern, modern, reserve,
central, traditional, cultural, northern
34820 | 0.92 A

1096 debate *n*
adj public, political, national, presidential, heated,
current, open, ongoing *noun* issue, policy, side.,
discussion, subject., Senate, Congress, matter,
abortion, reform *verb* continue, .rage, spark., engage.,
end, .focus, .surround, provoke., dominate., enter.
34218 | 0.93 S

1097 consumer *n*
adj American, average, available, individual, Japanese,
willing, growing, potential, concerned, online
noun product, price, .group, .good, .confidence,
.electronics, .protection, .advocate, company
verb .buy, .pay, .spend, protect, sell., benefit, cost.,
.purchase, save, .demand
35188 | 0.91

1098 majority *n*
adj vast, overwhelming, great, large, democratic,
simple, clear *noun* .leader, Senate., .people, house,
Republican, .American, .student, .vote, .population,
minority *verb* win., support, indicate, represent.,
constitute., .favor, oppose, account., form, adopt
34212 | 0.93 A

1099 interesting *j*
noun thing, question, story, point, way, study, case,
idea, part, finding, aspect, character *misc* very, more,
most, because, find, really, something
34314 | 0.93 S

1100 prevent *v*
noun .disease, .attack, .cancer, .injury, law., .heart,
.infection, .damage, .loss, .spread, effort., .abuse,
.violence, .pregnancy, .crime *misc* .from, help., try.,
.far, order., in., .future, treat, effective., necessary.,
intend., effectively.
33741 | 0.94

1101 travel *v*
noun .mile, .world, distance, .Europe, car, .south,
.north, .west, train, .east, speed, month, space,

American., .Africa *misc* .through, .around, far,
.across, .along, .hundred
32848 | 0.97

1102 born *v*
noun child., baby., year, son., daughter., month,
star., infant., July., .wedlock, .June, .Germany,
.Chicago, .Brooklyn, .poverty *misc* before., after,
.raise, where., since., .breed, healthy, .prematurely,
newly.
32761 | 0.97

1103 relate *v*
noun issue., problem, question., factor., information,
activity, story, experience, variable, health, use, level,
education, development, performance *misc* directly.,
closely., significantly., positively.
35866 | 0.88 A

1104 assume *v*
noun .role, .responsibility, .position, .control,
.leadership, model., .form, .risk, .duty, .presidency,
theory., .command, .posture, researcher., function
misc always., everyone, reasonable., safe.,
automatically., generally.
33412 | 0.95 A

1105 none *p*
.these, .other, all, .business, .ever, .matter, .above,
.whom, .whatsoever, violence, second., .exist,
absolutely., virtually.
32578 | 0.97

1106 admit *v*
noun .hospital, official., .mistake, patient, evidence,
.guilt, .wrongdoing, .defeat, .error, affair, .failure,
fault, immigrant, testimony, .oath *misc* must., later,
finally., readily., freely., willing., hate., refuse., force.,
publicly
32598 | 0.97

1107 front *i*
(in front of) .of, .her, stand., .me, right., .house, sit.,
stop., .camera, .face, .mirror, car, table., .TV
34300 | 0.92 F

1108 figure *v*
noun .way, guy, scientist., hell, genius., .odds,
analyst., engineer., trick, coverlet *misc* .prominently,
hard., finally., .transcribe, .illustrate, .depict,
harder., .importantly, .correctly, .summarize,
kinda.
   out .how, .what, try., can., .way, who, .why, .where,
.whether, .exactly
32786 | 0.96

1109 coach *n*
adj assistant, offensive, male, first-year,
winningest, opposing, interim, active, professional
noun player, football., basketball., team, college.,
head., season, sport, parent, track. *verb* hire, pitch.,
name, fire, recruit, yell, resign, train, perceive,
impress.
37489 | 0.84 N

1110 partner *n*
adj sexual, managing, senior, general, male,
equal, corporate, multiple, romantic, longtime
noun business., sex., trading., firm, law, coalition.,
life, marriage, investment, behavior *verb* become.,
choose, engage, date., trust, dance, trade.,
communicate, satisfy, perceive
34479 | 0.91

1111 shot *n*
adj long, best, cheap, single, wide, better, final, clear, various *noun* mug., flu., jump., tee., gun, .glass, warning. *verb* get., take., fire, give., hit, hear, miss, .kill, .ring, score
34051 | 0.92

1112 scientist *n*
adj political, social, senior, planetary, concerned, chief, natural, mad, top, Soviet *noun* university, research, year, computer., group., team., rocket., science *verb* .believe, .study, .discover, .develop, .hope, .agree, .argue, conduct, .measure, enable.
34991 | 0.89 M

1113 senior *j*
noun official, president, citizen, year, editor, officer, fellow, analyst, correspondent, member, center, adviser *misc* vice, high, military, junior, former, associate, Iraqi, chief
33579 | 0.93 N

1114 suffer *v*
noun people., .loss, injury, child., .damage, pain, .disease, .depression, .consequence, .stroke, patient., American., .effect, .setback, .fate *misc* .from, .severe, .serious, die, likely., .broken
32238 | 0.97

1115 alone *r*
live., let., stand., sit., home., walk., act., travel., eat., dark, sleep., .account, .enough, .sufficient
32348 | 0.96

1116 collection *n*
adj private, large, permanent, extensive, vast, entire, impressive, corporate, native *noun* data., .artist, museum, art, story, .essay, .analysis *verb* include, publish, house, contain, display, assemble, present, feature, amass., edit
35581 | 0.87 M

1117 successful *j*
noun program, career, business, effort, company, school, campaign, strategy, woman, performance, businessman, outcome *misc* most, more, very, become, highly, prove, less, quite
32962 | 0.94 A

1118 speech *n*
adj free, public, recent, commercial, religious, famous, protected, inaugural *noun* freedom., president, right, acceptance., night, language, .recognition, stump. *verb* give, deliver, protect, listen., prepare, finish., restrict., regulate., declare, outline
32996 | 0.94

1119 eventually *r*
will, .become, .lead, may, .reach, .return, hope, .settle, .force, .replace, .result, .succeed, .altogether
31982 | 0.97

1120 key *j*
noun word, issue, role, player, element, question, point, factor, component, area, part, thing *misc* play, several, such, identify, following, strategic, congressional, organizational
32927 | 0.94 A

1121 mission *n*
adj military, impossible, primary, diplomatic, humanitarian, educational, peacekeeping, future,

foreign, original *noun* .statement, space, .control, school, church, college, rescue., .district, shuttle., combat. *verb* accomplish, fly, carry, complete, send, support, define, fulfill., perform, plan
32717 | 0.94

1122 score *n*
adj high, mean, low, total, average, overall, composite, significant, final, possible *noun* test., student, scale, difference, subscale, table, achievement, factor, grade, measure *verb* .indicate, sit., .range, compare, base, receive., report, improve, .reflect, tie
36069 | 0.86 A

1123 newspaper *n*
adj local, daily, weekly, British, independent, tabloid, conservative, regional, English, mainstream *noun* magazine, editor, .article, ad, story, reporter, page, publisher, .headline, column *verb* read., publish, .report, appear., sell, buy, own, pick., quote, subscribe.
35365 | 0.87 N

1124 wind *n*
adj solar, strong, high, cold, prevailing, hot, warm, light, sustained, powerful *noun* .power, rain, gust, water, energy, .turbine, .speed, direction, tree, snow *verb* .blow, .whip, carry, .pick, catch, .howl, .shift, .die, drive, knock
33294 | 0.93 F

1125 reform *n*
adj economic, political, social, democratic, educational, constitutional, agrarian, military, recent *noun* welfare., health., campaign., finance., care., .party, education, tax., immigration., .effort *verb* pass, implement, support., push., enact, promote, oppose., .fail, seek, .aim
34153 | 0.90 A

1126 concerned *j*
noun issue, parent, citizen, safety, scientist, official, public, individual, lack, consumer, educator, well-being *misc* about, as, far, more, very, less, primarily, particularly
32121 | 0.96

1127 professional *j*
noun development, sport, school, life, organization, woman, association, career, teacher, athlete, service, team *misc* personal, seek, academic, hire, amateur, medical, educational, highly, technical
33434 | 0.92 A

1128 relation *n*
adj public, foreign, international, social, sexual, diplomatic, civil-military, economic, human, political *noun* race., power, country, council., labor., community, trade., gender., history., .firm *verb* improve, establish., maintain., normalize., bear., examine., affect, strain, define, strengthen
34877 | 0.88 A

1129 troops (PL) *n*
adj American, Iraqi, British, Soviet, Israeli, Russian, military, foreign, German, allied *noun* ground, withdrawal, army, force, war, scout., combat, government., .border, movement *verb* send., withdraw, bring, pull, kill, support., fight, commit, order., .arrive
34021 | 0.90 S

1130 garden *n*
adj botanical, botanic, Japanese, formal, secret, English, private, green, organic, wild *noun* square., rose., house, vegetable., home., plant, flower, city, .center, .hose *verb* create, tend, design, visit, surround, overlook., feature, weed., water, bloom
35281 | 0.87 M

1131 access *n*
adj easy, equal, free, open, direct, full, limited *noun* Internet, .information, service, .health, market, people, .care, .resource, public., .education *verb* have., provide., gain., give., allow., deny., restrict.
32729 | 0.94 A

1132 publish *v*
noun book, article, paper, story, report, university, letter, result, work, issue, volume, list, data, collection, science *misc* .by, recently., originally., previously., short, widely
32649 | 0.94 A

1133 recall *v*
noun day, moment, memory, event, .conversation, .detail, .interview, .incident, meeting, scene, .childhood, .visit, governor, reader., occasion *misc* later, vividly, fondly, .correctly, vaguely.
32288 | 0.95

1134 Soviet *j*
noun union, republic, state, leader, president, troop, force, army, government, system, economy, empire
35385 | 0.86

1135 cost *v*
noun dollar, .money, .taxpayer, .cent, .lot, .thousand, .fortune, drug., project., fuel., insurance., ticket., transaction., health-care, capital. *misc* .more, .than, much, .about, .less, .per, .million, estimate., .effective, .billion, nearly, .hundred
32509 | 0.94

1136 southern *j*
noun university, state, part, city, town, hemisphere, region, border, district, end, accent *misc* northern, Baptist, eastern, along, central, African, Christian, European
32739 | 0.93

1137 senate *n*
adj democratic, full, Republican-controlled, representative, divided, partisan, Democratic-controlled *noun* .committee, house, .leader, state., US., Republican, .majority, chairman, member., floor *verb* pass, run., approve, confirm, win, elect., testify., control, reject, ratify
33994 | 0.90 S

1138 opinion *n*
adj different, personal, strong, popular, legal, professional, dissenting, favorable, concurring, honest *noun* public., .poll, court, difference., majority., justice, world., expert, survey *verb* express, ask., write, change, offer., voice., form., entitle., influence., .differ
32068 | 0.95

1139 option *n*
adj other, available, only, best, military, viable, various, open, limited, nuclear *noun* stock., treatment., range., .share, policy., price, response., career., cost,

investment. *verb* give, offer, consider, exercise., choose, include, provide, explore., weigh., .exist
32357 | 0.94

1140 judge *n*
adj federal, superior, chief, appellate, administrative, retired, municipal, liberal, presiding, independent *noun* court., district., US., case, trial., lawyer, state, decision, jury, circuit. *verb* .rule, ask, .decide, appoint, allow, .dismiss, agree, .issue, .throw, approve
32870 | 0.93 S

1141 original *j*
noun plan, version, broadcast, idea, sin, article, design, owner, form, text, source, intent *misc* return, reflect, identical, restore, accurately, audio, preceding
31916 | 0.95

1142 customer *n*
adj potential, regular, corporate, satisfied, loyal, happy, retail, paying, willing, commercial *noun* .service, company, business, .satisfaction, .base, information, price, market, .support, cost *verb* pay, .buy, serve., offer, attract., sell, charge, satisfy, .order, improve.
33738 | 0.90 N

1143 critical *j*
noun thinking, issue, role, mass, point, skill, factor, question, analysis, success, condition, information *misc* most, reach, highly, absolutely, particularly, historical, creative, increasingly, sharply
33036 | 0.91 A

1144 corner *n*
adj far, right, dark, left, upper, remote, quiet, right-hand *noun* street, .eye, .room, .mouth, table, store, .office, building, back, desk *verb* turn., stand., sit., round., cut., tuck., disappear, hang
32607 | 0.93 F

1145 basic *j*
noun skill, principle, need, right, research, question, service, training, problem, education, law, concept *misc* most, human, provide, such, teach, lack, simple, fundamental
32495 | 0.93 A

1146 income *n*
adj low, net, high, annual, capita, average, median, personal, federal, gross *noun* .tax, family, percent, household., level, source., growth, rate, security, distribution *verb* pay, earn, rise, increase, provide, report., generate, raise., supplement., .fall
32954 | 0.92

1147 directly *r*
.into, .relate, .indirectly, .affect, speak., address, .front, link, .involved, lead., .behind, either., deal., connect
31632 | 0.95 A

1148 own *v*
noun company, land, family, property, house, .home, business, stock, car, .share, right, .gun, father., team, bank *misc* .by, privately., .operate, already., publicly.
  up will., want., one, must., even., when
32076 | 0.94 N

1149 release *v*
noun report, year, hostage, .prison, statement, information, hospital, data, .jail, department, figure, police, amount, version, fish *misc* recently., early, finally., newly., .yesterday
31342 | 0.96

1150 restaurant n
adj Chinese, fast-food, local, Italian, best, favorite, fine, Mexican, French, popular *noun* hotel, bar, shop, food, owner, dinner, business, chain, city *verb* open, eat, .serve, own, .offer, close, dine, feature, enter., operate
32875 | 0.92 N

1151 neighborhood n
adj old, poor, residential, urban, working-class, tough, quiet, middle-class, suburban *noun* city, school, street, kid, park, resident, group, .association, center, store *verb* live, .surround, attend, organize, destroy, patrol, mix, revitalize., search, house
32112 | 0.94 N

1152 effective j
noun way, program, strategy, treatment, teacher, method, use, system, intervention, means, teaching, control *misc* more, most, very, as, prove, less, provide
33172 | 0.90 A

1153 labor n
adj cheap, organized, hard, forced, manual, skilled, physical *noun* .force, .market, .day, .union, child., cost, .party, .law, .movement, US. *verb* organize, reduce, enter., rise, perform, employ, hire, induce, demand, exploit.
32601 | 0.92 A

1154 nobody p
.know, .ever, .want, .else, .really, .anything, .talk, .care, .believe, sure, .notice, hurt, .attention, .bother
31846 | 0.94 S

1155 stare v
noun eye, face, .ceiling, moment, head., .space, .screen, door, wall, floor, glass, .disbelief, .sky, foot, .horror *misc* .at, .into, .back, .straight, .ahead, .blankly, .across
out .window, .at, .over, eye., sit., .across, .sea, .windshield **down** .at, .barrel, window.
36063 | 0.83 F

1156 immediately r
.after, almost., serve., .follow, begin, start, recognize, .upon, respond, .apparent, notice, available
30514 | 0.98

1157 achieve v
noun .goal, .objective, success, result, .level, student, effect, .end, means., .balance, .status, peace, outcome, .independence, reduction *misc* help., order., in., able., difficult., necessary, .desired
32829 | 0.91 A

1158 forest n
adj national, tropical, old-growth, dense, ancient, thick, dark, central, southern, western *noun* .service, rain., tree, park, land, US., .fire, pine., acre, .floor *verb* preserve, cut, protect, save, destroy, manage, burn, clear, surround, disappear
33132 | 0.90

1159 dad n
adj proud, stay-at-home, divorced, biological, suburban, loving, drunk, full-time, devoted *noun* mom., mother, thing, way, house, brother, deadbeat., mum. *verb* love, .die, yell, shout, divorce, borrow, inherit, .remarry, adore, .molest
32669 | 0.92 F

1160 hurt v
noun feeling, back, economy, .chance, knee, leg, stomach., ear, chest., .career, .me, neck, throat, .fly *misc* really., never., .bad, badly, anyone
31677 | 0.94

1161 video n
adj digital, interactive, live, online, instructional, funny, pornographic, full-motion, educational, amateur *noun* .game, .camera, .clip, music, home., .screen, image *verb* watch., show, play, begin., end., shoot, produce, capture, feature, order.
32055 | 0.93

1162 strike v
noun deal, .balance, .chord, lightning, court., .blow, .pose, .conversation, .law, .heart, .match, .note, .gold, bullet, disaster. *misc* .by, .against, particularly, suddenly., supreme., .rich
down court., .law, Supreme., .state, federal, decision., appeal., ruling. **out** .batter, three, hit, innings, five, .seven, .swing **up** .conversation, band, .friendship, .relationship
30727 | 0.97

1163 safety n
adj public, occupational, environmental, strong, personal, concerned, patient, relative, physical *noun* health, food., .net, issue, concern, .board, .administration, highway., security, .standard *verb* ensure., provide, improve., protect, guarantee., fear., increase., address, relate
31541 | 0.95

1164 absolutely r
no, right, .nothing, sure, .necessary, .correct, .certain, .essential, .wrong
33915 | 0.88 S

1165 therefore r
shall, must, .likely, surprising, necessary, purpose, finding, .subject, .essential, appropriate, hypothesis, reasonable, .unlikely, .crucial
33553 | 0.89 A

1166 freedom n
adj religious, academic, political, human, economic, individual, personal *noun* .speech, right, press, .expression, .act, democracy, .choice, .information, .religion, degree. *verb* give., allow, enjoy, protect, fight., .choose, defend., restrict., experience, violate
31938 | 0.93 A

1167 version n
adj new, early, different, original, final, modified, late, revised, updated *noun* film., .event, movie., .article, software, .history, test, stage., language, play *verb* offer, create., produce., develop., present, release, introduce, publish, differ, install
31616 | 0.94

1168 like c
look., feel., something., sound., seem., look., anything., she, act., kind, treat., smell., sort
32085 | 0.93 S F

1169 plane n
adj small, private, military, Iraqi, British, allied, commercial, horizontal, orbital, Japanese
noun .crash, air, fighter., .ticket, pilot, flight,

passenger, cargo., airport, spy. _verb_ fly, land, .hit, shoot, board., .carry, catch, die., drop, step.
31306 | 0.95

1170 attitude _n_
adj positive, negative, environmental, different, social, public, sexual, general, favorable, significant _noun_ behavior, student, change, knowledge, people, belief, teacher, .education, scale, perception _verb_ reflect, develop, influence, affect, express, adopt., relate, maintain., reveal, improve
33261 | 0.89 A

1171 sexual _j_
noun harassment, abuse, behavior, orientation, activity, woman, assault, relationship, intercourse, experience, partner, relation _misc_ engage, report, physical, female, unwanted, male, associate, emotional
39231 | 0.76 A

1172 refer _v_
noun term., patient, article, doctor, title., client, text, statement, reader, physician, concept, item, context, category, literature _misc_ .to, .as, often., sometimes., commonly., specifically, whom., usually.
31791 | 0.93 A

1173 fresh _j_
noun air, water, juice, fruit, vegetable, lemon, basil, leaf, parsley, food, cilantro, tomato _misc_ chop, chopped, mince, cup, frozen, green, finely, minced, dried, grate
32380 | 0.92 M

1174 involved _j_
noun process, case, activity, issue, project, politics, community, parent, drug, effort, decision, sport _misc_ get, become, actively, directly, deeply, heavily, everyone
31211 | 0.95

1175 powerful _j_
noun force, man, tool, woman, state, group, nation, interest, influence, computer, drug, effect _misc_ most, more, very, become, enough, rich, less, politically
30707 | 0.96

1176 bird _n_
adj small, migratory, wild, dead, early, rare, blue, exotic, wading, native _noun_ species, .flu, .nest, animal, wing, tree, .prey, dog, lady., .feeder _verb_ .fly, .sing, watch, kill, feed, shoot, migrate, catch, chirp, attract.
31966 | 0.92

---

10. Professions

General

president 235969, director 76735, official _n_ 76466, worker 67399, manager 44945, expert 43032, employee 41559, (agent) 36955, researcher 33448, (chief) _n_ 29249, investigator 14753, boss _n_ 13949, administrator 13688, specialist 12708, operator 9075, (clerk) _n_ 7032, coordinator 6202

Government

senator 43458, governor 33305, representative _n_ 24599, vice president 22519, politician 19773, prime minister 12705, congressman 10923, ambassador 10123

Military

soldier 38539, (general) _n_ 26218, (captain) _n_ 17799, commander 14114, colonel 7221

Specific (top 100)

teacher 112654, doctor 67219, author _n_ 56468, artist 52568, professor 48014, lawyer 46516, editor 41284, coach _n_ 38968, writer 37999, attorney 36708, scientist 36445, secretary 36041, judge _n_ 34099, reporter 29464, actor 23819, athlete 23137, farmer 22761, pilot 19597, engineer 19478, producer 19129, nurse _n_ 18901, journalist 16245, priest 14527, designer 13579, historian 13151, singer 13046, counselor 12375, baker 12258, detective 10757, poet 10513, musician 10222, economist 10103, publisher 9791, chef 9589, photographer 9363, actress 9019, painter 8823, architect 8686, police officer 8640, surgeon 8280, contractor 7414, dancer 7399, social worker 7207, therapist 7099, businessman 7025, pastor 6889, performer 6648, cook _n_ 6571, fisherman 6154, mechanic 5890, banker 5616, vendor 5361, technician 5225, sailor 5077, diplomat 5019, butler 4909, seller 4896, monk 4855, philosopher 4812, psychiatrist 4637, interpreter 4614, firefighter 4467, waiter 4244, astronaut 4085, miner 3980, nun 3939, gardener 3938, salesman 3911, carpenter 3765, prostitute 3597, accountant 3591, maid 3495, waitress 3327, dentist 3181, barber 3061, translator 2843, laborer 2735, security guard 2416, referee _n_ 2178, sculptor 2120, pianist 2068, fireman 1786, nanny 1777, receptionist 1450, coroner 1386, pharmacist 1374, magistrate 1283, cashier 1179, business owner 1160, horseman 1063, illustrator 1034, cartoonist 978, dermatologist 961, plumber 942, cameraman 925, valet _n_ 839, electrician 833, chauffeur 810, blacksmith 810, personal trainer 729

1177 touch v
noun hand, .arm, .shoulder, .face, finger, .hair, .ground, foot, .cheek, .heart, lip, story., .base, knee, nose *misc* her, him, reach., never., almost., lightly, barely., gently
  down plane., tornado., helicopter., wheel., .near, tornadoes., jet., twister., flight., chopper. **off** .wave, crisis, .storm, .series **up** makeup, .paint, .root
32084 | 0.92 F

1178 variety n
adj wide, great, available, wider, rich, infinite, endless, broad, resistant *noun* .way, .reason, .source, .activity, .food, .factor, .show, .style, .material, .form *verb* use., offer., include, provide., produce, develop, .range, perform., represent.
31904 | 0.92 A

1179 deep j
noun breath, water, voice, inch, space, sleep, pocket, trouble, end, throat, snow, root *misc* take, blue, draw, wide, dark, red, brown, purple
30888 | 0.95 F

1180 text n
adj preceding, accompanying, literary, original, written, biblical, full, religious, cultural *noun* note., .message, image, reader, reading, book, page, meaning, history, graphics *verb* .check, represent., read, convert., produce, accompany, interpret, translate, print, mention
34853 | 0.84 A

1181 wide j
noun range, variety, receiver, eye, world, foot, array, mouth, area, smile, door, arm *misc* long, across, spread, open, enough, awake, tall, deep
30767 | 0.95

1182 credit n
adj extra, full, academic, partial, preceding, cheap, stolen, closing, proper, online *noun* .card, tax., line, bank, company, .union, number, .report, debt, reservation. *verb* give., get., take., use, deserve., .accept, pay, receive., claim., include
31112 | 0.94

1183 nine m
.year, .month, eight., .day, after, out, about., .ago, .old, .ten, .hour, seven, five, .o'clock
30383 | 0.97

1184 sleep v
noun night, bed, hour, day, baby, morning, bedroom, wife, dog, husband, tent, dream, trouble., foot, .cot *misc* back, eat, .together, .soundly, better, drift.
  in .room, .bedroom, .until, .weekend, .Sundays
32186 | 0.91 F

1185 investigation n
adj criminal, federal, ongoing, internal, independent, congressional, present, thorough *noun* police, department, result., murder, government, research, subject., justice, office, crime *verb* conduct, begin, continue, lead, launch., .reveal, complete, .determine, cooperate., focus
31405 | 0.93 S

1186 hope n
adj high, only, best, greatest, faint, renewed, dashed, vain *noun* .future, people, fear, glimmer., sense.,

.peace, faith, message., reason., sign. *verb* give., offer., hold., lose, raise, bring, express., pin.
30012 | 0.97

1187 announce v
noun .plan, president, company., government., decision, .intention, official., .retirement, department, result, Monday, administration., .candidacy, .resignation, agreement *misc* recently., yesterday, early, publicly, formally., officially.
30798 | 0.95 N

1188 by r
.now, go., .far, .no, .means, stand., come., .large, pass., .most, stop., walk., drop., .about
30207 | 0.96

1189 completely r
.different, almost., .out, change, cover, until., lose, understand, ignore, cool., agree, .forget, rack, .destroy
29825 | 0.98

1190 vote v
noun people., Republican, election, Democrat, right., candidate, house., Senate., Congress., percent, board., voter., .resolution, primary, .impeachment *misc* .for, .against, register., .favor, likely., .unanimously
  on .by, Congress, today, debate., actually., award **down** proposal, council., Senate, .amendment, committee **out** committee, .article, .incumbent
31969 | 0.91 S

1191 conduct v
noun study, research, survey, interview, test, investigation, experiment, business, group *misc* .by, .determine, similar, recent., .extensive
31930 | 0.91 A

1192 conflict n
adj ethnic, armed, potential, Arab-Israeli, internal, military, violent, civil, religious, direct *noun* .interest, resolution, role, family, management, situation, source., class., value *verb* resolve., avoid., .arise, create, end, lead, involve, cause, deal., .occur
32441 | 0.90 A

1193 replace v
noun system, .one, window, worker, column., coach, equipment, machine, candidate., .receiver, fuel, unit, engine, .bulb, roof *misc* .by, .old, .traditional, repair, .current
30334 | 0.96

1194 attend v
noun .school, .college, .meeting, student., .university, .class, child., .conference, .church, .service, .event, .funeral, .session, .workshop, .ceremony *misc* high, .public, plan., .private, regularly
30648 | 0.95

1195 participant n
adj high, active, female, male, low, sexual, potential, likely, individual, significant *noun* study, method., group, number, program, sample, condition, research, table, data *verb* ask, .complete, indicate, include, .receive, .respond, select, require, assess, present
36167 | 0.8 A

1196 argument n
adj closing, strong, oral, legal, moral, compelling, persuasive, main, powerful, convincing *noun* court,

defense, line., sake, kind., justice, merit, lawyer, debate, quality *verb* make, hear., present, support, reject., advance, buy., accept., extend, persuade
31029 | 0.93 A

1197 object *n*
adj small, large, inanimate, faint, celestial, distant, natural, sacred, African, various *noun* art, subject, .desire, space, material, museum, painting, star, .lesson, sex. *verb* create, produce, identify, view, observe, contain, display, .illustrate, locate, discover
32888 | 0.88 A

1198 please *r*
me, your, us, .let, .tell, .contact, information., far., help, no, God, .send, stop, .stay
31607 | 0.92 F

1199 nuclear *j*
noun weapon, power, program, plant, war, reactor, waste, bomb, energy, test, missile, material *misc* its, develop, build, biological, Soviet, chemical, produce, strategic, Korean
32091 | 0.90

1200 sky *n*
adj dark, gray, black, bright, cloudless, eastern, starry, western *noun* night., star, cloud, light, sun, evening., earth, color, morning, .telescope *verb* fall, watch, fill, darken, rise, fly, point., .clear, scan., shoot
32630 | 0.89 F

1201 along *r*
come., get., all., move., bring., pass., walk., .line, ride, far., sing., follow., .road
30218 | 0.96

1202 afternoon *n*
adj late, good, early, hot, recent, sunny, previous *noun* morning., .sun, time, .evening, summer., .tea *verb* spend., arrive, visit, schedule, gather, .fade, light, rain, ring, relax
30891 | 0.93 F

1203 hundred *m*
.year, one., two., .dollar, several., .thousand, three., few., more, than., five., .mile, .yard, four.
30885 | 0.93

1204 encourage *v*
noun student, child, teacher, .development, government, program., parent, .use, policy., .participation, .investment, member, .growth, incentive., practice *misc* support, design., strongly., actively
30816 | 0.93 A

1205 perfect *j*
noun example, time, place, world, day, sense, match, storm, game, timing, condition, opportunity *misc* everything, fit, nearly, from, nobody, absolutely, beautiful
30113 | 0.96

1206 possibility *n*
adj real, open, endless, strong, future, human, remote, distinct, very, intriguing *noun* life, .war, world, range., .parole, realm., number, hope *verb* consider., .might, raise., explore., offer., suggest., rule., discuss., face., .exist
30300 | 0.95 A

1207 turn *n*
adj left, wrong, sharp, right, short, quick, unexpected, dramatic, sudden *noun* .century, .event, twist., .phrase, .signal, .millennium, mind, quarter. *verb* take., .lead, wait., .affect, .increase, carve., miss., .contribute, await., .inspire
30593 | 0.94

1208 British *j*
noun government, minister, troop, force, museum, army, empire, soldier, airway, official
30742 | 0.93

1209 once *c*
.you, .get, .start, .reach, .realize, .arrive, .complete, .decide, .finish, .past, .inside, .establish, .settle, figure
29624 | 0.97

1210 examine *v*
noun study., research., .relationship, .effect, article., student, issue, .difference, analysis., researcher., factor, .role, .impact, doctor, paper. *misc* .whether, closely, carefully, future, possible, conduct., in, order, .sexual, critically
32387 | 0.89 A

1211 conversation *n*
adj private, casual, normal, brief, interesting, polite, lively, intimate, recorded, friendly *noun* phone., telephone., topic., series., dinner, kind., minute, piece *verb* continue., join., engage., listen., strike., carry., remember., record, overhear, recall.
29783 | 0.96

1212 generally *r*
more, .speak, .consider, .agree, .low, .accept, .regard, .view, .accepted, .support, .available, .recognize, .positive, .less
30963 | 0.92 A

1213 beginning *n*
adj very, humble, auspicious, inauspicious, promising, shaky *noun* .end, .year, .century, time, war, .teacher, .season, .era, .career, student *verb* mark., signal., mention., trace., quote., coincide., cite.
29631 | 0.96

1214 secretary *n*
adj assistant, general, interior, foreign, legal, personal, chief, principal, executive *noun* .state, defense, treasury, press., deputy., president, education, commerce, labor *verb* serve., .thank, announce, name, appoint., act, resign, welcome, order, direct
30917 | 0.92 S

1215 experience *v*
noun student., problem, woman., .difficulty, pain, patient., stress, level, change, .growth, symptom, feeling, event, individual., person. *misc* never., ever., likely., .significant, report., personally
30947 | 0.92 A

1216 beach *n*
adj long, white, empty, deserted, nude, tropical, Caribbean, clean, coastal, remote *noun* palm., house, pebble., sand, state, island, .boy, mile, .resort, hotel *verb* walk., head., hit., swim, land, overlook., stroll., stretch, line, race
30168 | 0.94

1217 safe *j*
noun place, haven, house, environment, water, sex, distance, area, harbor, bet, drinking, passage

misc feel, keep, provide, effective, enough, sure, stay, perfectly
29328 | 0.97

1218 spirit _n_
adj holy, human, kindred, entrepreneurial, dead, creative, competitive, alive _noun_ world, body, mind., soul, Christmas, community, team., holiday, .possession, gift _verb_ lift, capture., break, embody, possess, reflect, violate., .soar, communicate, haunt
30439 | 0.93

1219 weekend _n_
adj long, past, nice, busy, final, entire, three-day _noun_ .edition, day., .news, night, holiday, evening, game, summer, labor., trip _verb_ spend., open., enter., visit, plan, enjoy, schedule., invite, .feature, .mark
30837 | 0.92 S

1220 date _n_
adj later, blind, early, due, late, certain, exact, effective _noun_ time, birth, name, .rape, expiration., court., release. _verb_ set, bring., last, check, record., mark, arrange, list, confirm, fix
29133 | 0.97

1221 define _v_
noun term, role, identity, culture, relationship, goal, value, boundary, interest, behavior, success, space, character, individual, act _misc_ .as, .by, clearly., .themselves, broadly, narrowly
31608 | 0.90 A

1222 feature _n_
adj important, key, common, unique, best, certain, central, regular, striking, major _noun_ .film, section., design, safety., .story, .article, face, model, water, surface. _verb_ include, add, offer, share, identify, incorporate., combine., lack., distinguish, direct
30820 | 0.92 A

1223 global _j_
noun warming, economy, change, system, market, climate, issue, network, trade, community, positioning, environment _misc_ economic, environmental, local, regional, international, financial, increasingly, truly
31793 | 0.89 A

1224 very _j_
noun beginning, moment, end, nature, thing, people, day, existence, fact, idea _misc_ whose, difficult, threaten, itself, indeed, serious, tough
29501 | 0.96

1225 element _n_
adj key, important, essential, critical, certain, finite, heavy, crucial, various, central _noun_ design, .culture, .surprise, .society, music, process, .analysis, core., style, nature _verb_ include, add., contain., combine, incorporate., identify, introduce., involve, constitute, mix.
30919 | 0.91 A

1226 attempt _n_
adj failed, early, unsuccessful, desperate, serious, recent, successful, previous, futile, repeated _noun_ suicide., coup., assassination., government, reform, goal., yard, critic., rescue. _verb_ make, fail, represent., .change, block, .avoid, resist., .escape, .gain, survive.
29041 | 0.94 A

1227 slowly _r_
move., then., walk, very., turn, down, begin, head, .toward, start, hand, grow, rise, away
31079 | 0.90 F

1228 governor _n_
adj democratic, provincial, Republican, incumbent, elected, regional, royal, liberal, fellow, territorial _noun_ state, new, lieutenant., .office, year, race, .mansion, candidate., campaign _verb_ run., elect., appoint, sign, support, .propose, .declare, .announce, veto, endorse
31257 | 0.90 S

1229 through _r_
go., get., come., follow., pass., break., until., fall., heat., walk., cook.
29327 | 0.96

1230 concept _n_
adj basic, whole, key, important, abstract, simple, very, traditional, general, original _noun_ topic., .document, idea, skill, development, .car, design, knowledge, use, practice _verb_ help., understand., develop, introduce., apply, teach, base, learn, relate, support.
31624 | 0.89 A

1231 sorry _j_
noun sir, state, mom, ma'am, honey, ass, mess, bout, excuse, sight, tale, shape _misc_ I, feel, so, oh, really, no, ahead, interrupt
31448 | 0.89 F

1232 easily _r_
can., as, more., .accessible, quickly, win, fit, .available, .identify, quite., .remove, .imagine, .dismiss, fairly.
29299 | 0.96

1233 battle _n_
adj legal, uphill, major, fierce, bloody, losing, bitter, pitched, constant _noun_ war, line, court., custody., gun., .cancer, .cry, .flag, scene, .plan _verb_ fight, win, lose, wage, face., .rage, kill., die., .erupt, .last
29557 | 0.95

1234 league _n_
adj national, American, minor, little, urban, junior _noun_ .baseball, team, player, major., football., game, season, hockey., record, .championship _verb_ play, lead., win, join., sign, coach, name., form, organize, dominate
32134 | 0.87 N

1235 camp _n_
adj terrorist, armed, overnight, opposing, British, makeshift, temporary, squalid, advanced, forced _noun_ training., refugee., summer., concentration., day, boot., base., prison. _verb_ set, attend., send., return, visit., break., arrive., operate, ride, survive.
29498 | 0.95

1236 introduce _v_
noun bill, year, legislation, .concept, friend, product, .guest, idea, model, evidence, technology, Congress, .element, reform, senator _misc_ new, let., .myself, recently., plan., .yourself, formally., newly.
29151 | 0.96

1237 status _n_
adj social, socioeconomic, marital, legal, economic, low, current, special _noun_ .quo, woman, health., power, education, change, minority.,

age, nation, .symbol _verb_ maintain., achieve.,
grant., enjoy., improve., gain., indicate, affect, reflect,
define
30871 | 0.90 A

1238 insurance _n_
adj private, medical, social, long-term-care,
supplemental, cheap, dental _noun_ health., .company,
life., .policy, .industry, .coverage, .premium, .plan,
cost, .program _verb_ pay, cover, buy., provide, sell, offer,
purchase., guarantee, .insure, file
30309 | 0.92

1239 complete _v_
noun student., .questionnaire, study, participant.,
work, task, project, survey, course, program, .degree,
process, teacher, .assignment, week _misc_ after.,
before, each, recently., successfully., require., nearly.,
return, final
30071 | 0.92 A

1240 stick _v_
noun .head, .hand, .tongue, .finger, hair., .mind,
.nose, leg, needle, .neck, plan, arm, wall, knife, piece
misc .together, .inside, .close, .straight, .forever, fast,
firmly
  around .long, .enough, .while, decide., plan.,
agree., please., .forever **out** his, her, .hand, .tongue,
.like, head, hair., leg
29394 | 0.94 F

1241 solution _n_
adj possible, simple, only, best, political, peaceful,
easy, long-term, diplomatic, real _noun_ problem,
.crisis, .conflict, government, kind., need, challenge,
search., software, percent. _verb_ find., offer., provide,
seek., propose, require, develop, implement, present,
apply
29560 | 0.94 A

1242 web _n_
adj available, complex, tangled, intricate, semantic,
worldwide, seamless, vast _noun_ .site, .page, world.,
information, company, spider., e-mail, .browser,
.address, food. _verb_ visit., check., surf., create, offer,
post., spin., .contain, publish, feature
30091 | 0.92

1243 vision _n_
adj low, peripheral, shared, common, moral, double,
blind, artistic, original, monocular _noun_ .future,
world, loss, field., night., .rehabilitation, .service,
.thing, .statement _verb_ share., blur, create, offer,
develop, articulate., present, realize, clear,
experience
29510 | 0.94 A

1244 stone _n_
adj large, cold, gray, ancient, huge, unturned, blue,
massive, carved, crushed _noun_ .wall, .mountain,
house, .age, building, .floor, wood, .step, brick, kidney.
verb throw, set, build, carve, place, drop, cast., mark,
surround, etch.
29797 | 0.93 F

1245 lack _n_
adj better, general, total, complete, relative,
apparent, perceived, utter _noun_ .interest, .support,
.knowledge, .information, .experience, .evidence,
.control, .understanding, .resource, education
verb show., suffer., cite., reflect., indicate., explain.,
complain., limit, hamper., account
29575 | 0.93 A

1246 driver _n_
adj drunk, drunken, designated, illegal, race-car,
dangerous, fellow, aggressive, unlicensed, suspended
noun .license, truck., car, .seat, bus., taxi., cab., .side
verb pull, race, hire., lean, obtain., shout, .swing, slow,
.speed, honk
29170 | 0.94

1247 normal _j_
noun life, people, thing, level, person, range,
circumstance, activity, cell, condition, process, stress
misc back, return, under, perfectly, within, everything,
human, healthy
29022 | 0.95

1248 truck _n_
adj light, big, armored, flatbed, Mexican, moving,
refrigerated, giant, heavy-duty, used _noun_ pickup.,
car., .driver, back., fire., delivery., tow., bed
verb drive, pull, stop, park, load, .carry, hit, pass,
buy, climb
29455 | 0.93 F

1249 minister _n_
adj prime, foreign, interior, Baptist, ordained,
Methodist, Presbyterian, European _noun_ defense,
deputy., government, cabinet., justice, information
verb meet, become., .announce, appoint, name,
resign, .visit, .warn, .declare, elect.
30048 | 0.91 S

1250 handle _v_
noun case, .situation, .problem, issue, job, matter,
.pressure, .stress, lawyer., .crisis, material, task, media,
firm., .ball _misc_ can., how., able., enough., easy.,
properly, .differently, cool., capable., equip., design.
28459 | 0.96

1251 hole _n_
adj black, gaping, deep, tiny, full, huge, dark, final
noun bullet., .wall, .ground, water, ozone, watering.,
bottom, par, ball., putt _verb_ dig, drill, fill, punch, play,
cut, poke., bore., cover, shoot
29780 | 0.92 M

1252 front _j_
noun door, page, line, seat, porch, yard, row, window,
step, room, office, end _misc_ sit, through, walk, stand,
open, toward, up
29514 | 0.93 F

1253 fan _n_
adj big, huge, loyal, female, avid, electric, longtime,
devoted, adoring, casual _noun_ sport., baseball., game,
team, .base, ceiling., music, .club, football., media
verb .love, draw., cheer, hit., .attend, boo, attract.,
.blow, wave, .gather
30074 | 0.91 N

1254 spot _n_
adj hot, bright, favorite, soft, red, sweet, black, right,
white _noun_ trouble., parking., playoff., .price, .market,
vacation., TV., sun, fishing., top _verb_ find., mark., hit.,
pick., earn., point., fill, choose, touch., hide
28748 | 0.95

1255 crisis _n_
adj economic, financial, political, current,
international, major, global, fiscal, constitutional
noun time., energy., health., identity., missile., oil.,
hostage., .management _verb_ face, deal., resolve,
solve., respond., handle., address., .occur, affect, avoid
29410 | 0.93

1256 supposed *j*
noun link, beneficiary, evil, superiority, cure, expertise, intention, glory, aphrodisiac, marker, epidemic, deficiency *misc* be, to, what, I, protect, last
28505 | 0.96

1257 refuse *v*
noun court., government., .request, offer, official., .treatment, judge., Congress., .order, administration., interview, authority, .permission, .invitation, .entry
misc .any, .accept, .allow, .pay, .answer
28120 | 0.97

1258 drink *v*
noun .water, .beer, .coffee, .wine, .tea, .glass, .milk, .alcohol, night *misc* eat, smoke, sit., .heavily, hot, .plenty
  up all, water, boy, .juice, .money, night
29336 | 0.93 F

1259 researcher *n*
adj other, future, leading, academic, interested, senior, previous, educational, various, independent
noun university, study, group, data, research, field, team., number, cancer., finding *verb* .find, .use, .report, .believe, suggest, .examine, allow., conduct, .determine, .agree
31545 | 0.86 M A

1260 tradition *n*
adj religious, long, cultural, oral, Christian, western, ancient, strong, literary, rich *noun* family, culture, history, art, custom, faith, practice, language
verb continue, follow., carry., break., maintain, preserve., draw, .date, steep., combine
29943 | 0.91 A

1261 communication *n*
adj personal, federal, effective, mass, electronic, international, sexual, oral, better, clear *noun* .skill, .system, director, technology, network, line, form., satellite, .university *verb* improve., open, facilitate., establish, develop, enhance., own, maintain., enable, monitor
29396 | 0.92 A

1262 distance *n*
adj long, short, great, safe, far, middle, certain
noun time, .learning, mile, .education, yard, earth, sun, .runner, speed, striking. *verb* keep., walk., travel, measure., cover, maintain., close, separate, stretch, approach
28843 | 0.94

1263 ship *n*
adj tall, alien, British, naval, tight, French, Iraqi, sunken, Russian, giant *noun* cruise., captain, cargo, crew, passenger, deck, pirate., mother., plane, sailing.
verb sail, sink, .carry, build, jump., send, board., arrive, abandon., .head
29877 | 0.91 F

1264 gain *v*
noun .weight, .access, .control, experience, .understanding, .pound, .insight, knowledge, .support, .ground, .momentum, student., .advantage, .confidence, .strength *misc* lose, nothing, order., in., hope., .better, quickly
28436 | 0.95

1265 express *v*
noun .concern, view, opinion, .interest, .feeling, .desire, .support, .frustration, .anger, sentiment,

.emotion, .gratitude, thought, need, .appreciation
misc .themselves, .strong, similar, .deep, clearly, .myself, .terms
29112 | 0.93 A

1266 independent *j*
noun counsel, variable, state, school, group, news, study, television, film, contractor, nation, candidate
misc become, newly, free, appoint, establish, fiercely, dependent
29063 | 0.93 A

1267 ice *n*
adj thin, cold, polar, dry, Arctic, Antarctic, crushed, glacial *noun* .cream, water, .cube, .age, snow, sheet, .hockey, sea. *verb* melt, break, eat., serve, cover, form, fill, freeze, crack, drain
28746 | 0.94

1268 scale *n*
adj large, small, 5-point, Likert-type, global, grand, different, full, five-point *noun* item, score, rating., time, economy., response, attitude, .model, pay.
verb use, .range, measure, rate., develop, .assess, tip., indicate, .consist, complete.
31467 | 0.86 A

1269 brain *n*
adj human, normal, living, developing, fetal, aging, electronic, organic, sensory *noun* cell, part., .damage, .tumor, .injury, .function, activity, blood., area, .surgery *verb* cause, die, suffer., affect, blow., pick., control, rack., study, .swell
29469 | 0.91 M

1270 winter *n*
adj cold, long, late, early, warm, mild, hard, past
noun summer, day, .month, .spring, fall., .Olympics, night, .game, snow, season *verb* spend., survive., freeze, last, store, feed, plant, .approach, compete, hibernate.
28757 | 0.94 M

1271 commission *n*
adj national, international, European, regulatory, special, joint, regional, bipartisan *noun* security., exchange., state, trade., report, member, communication., chairman, US., election.
verb .investigate, create, appoint, .recommend, establish, pay, receive, head, .approve, .study
29038 | 0.93 N

1272 wood *n*
adj dark, solid, deep, polished, dead, carved, dry, painted, dense, wild *noun* piece., .chip, .floor, metal, fire, .stove, .product, block, tree, stone *verb* walk., cut, carve, burn, hide, chop., knock., gather, cook, stack
29051 | 0.93 F M

1273 increase *n*
adj significant, large, dramatic, substantial, huge, rapid, sharp, average, slight *noun* percent, tax., rate, price, .number, population, cost, wage, spending, production *verb* show., lead., report., result., cause, experience., indicate., .occur, vote, observe
29158 | 0.92 A

1274 return *n*
adj total, annual, average, low, safe, diminishing, five-year, past, joint, expected *noun* tax., rate, .investment, percent, .trip, punt., .address *verb* file., receive, expect., earn., demand., produce., await.
28848 | 0.93

1275 division *n*
adj airborne, armored, marine, racial, central, criminal, deep, eastern, upper, Iraqi *noun* infantry•, •labor, team, service, •title, school, director, series, news•, wildlife *verb* win•, create, reflect, clinch•, overcome•, compete•, heal•, contact, oversee, transfer
29230 | 0.92 N

1276 species *n*
adj endangered, other, different, native, human, rare, invasive, various, common, alien *noun* plant, bird, animal, •act, fish, number, habitat, tree, population, diversity *verb* threaten, protect, identify, list, evolve, represent, introduce, save•, vary, •survive
32667 | 0.82 M A

1277 AM *r*
•PM, morning, daily, today, yes•, really•, weekday
30659 | 0.87 N

1278 roll *v*
noun •eye, window, ball, sleeve, head, •dough, side, •back, car, camera•, bed, •dice, floor, tape, hill *misc* •into, •off, •onto, •away, •across, •past, ready.
   up sleeve, window, eye•, shirt, pant, shirtsleeve, •carpet, cuff **down** •window, tear•, •cheek, •face, sweat•, driver, •highway, •sleeve **out** •dough, carpet, red, ball, •pastry, •welcome, pie **over** •onto, bed, vehicle, groan
28821 | 0.93 F

1279 hide *v*
noun face, •fact, •view, tree, bush, wall, truth, bed, hair, wood, weapon, •smile, identity, corner, feeling *misc* •behind, try•, •under, away, where•, •inside, nothing•, •beneath
   out •in, there, •here, while, •until, place•, somewhere, home, might•, along
28507 | 0.94 F

1280 middle *n*
adj thick, excluded, crowded, exact, hollow, mushy, expanding, swollen *noun* •night, •school, •room, •century, •street, •road, •class, •floor, •field, town *verb* stand•, sit•, catch•, wake•, stop•, stick•, split•, plant•, interrupt•, •shrink
27829 | 0.96

1281 client *n*
adj potential, corporate, prospective, private, legal, individual, Hispanic, elderly, wealthy, regular *noun* service, lawyer, need, company, list, treatment, group, interest, attorney, agency *verb* •include, help•, represent•, meet, serve, advise•, protect, identify, encourage, attract•
30901 | 0.87 A

1282 resident *n*
adj local, longtime, permanent, black, rural, poor, urban, medical, lifelong, low-income *noun* city, area, county, home, community, neighborhood, official, nursing•, village, park *verb* •live, •complain, •vote, force, evacuate, •oppose, urge•, •fear, •flee, encourage
29422 | 0.91 N

1283 contract *n*
adj social, long-term, five-year, three-year, lucrative, one-year, four-year, two-year, private, exclusive *noun* government, service, •extension, term, worker, •negotiation, labor, breach•, record *verb* sign•, win•,

award, negotiate•, •expire, offer, enter•, renew, extend, guarantee
28924 | 0.92 N

1284 gold *n*
adj Olympic, yellow, solid, pure, pale, heavy, liquid *noun* •medal, silver, •mine, •rush, •standard, •medalist, •chain *verb* win•, wear•, strike•, pan, paint•, earn•, shine, flash, dangle, gleam
28228 | 0.94

1285 future *j*
noun research, generation, study, development, direction, plan, growth, teacher, need, president, use, success *misc* shall, current, include, prevent, examine, predict, possible, economic
28890 | 0.92 A

1286 potential *j*
noun problem, benefit, impact, threat, risk, effect, conflict, source, customer, buyer, candidate, danger *misc* identify, because, future, reduce, environmental, actual, assess, negative
28743 | 0.93 A

1287 presence *n*
adj military, strong, physical, human, mere, continued, very, foreign, significant, constant *noun* US, •absence, troop, police•, •mind, woman, other, •region, stage• *verb* feel, indicate•, maintain•, sense•, establish•, detect•, reveal•, signal, demonstrate•, alert•
28416 | 0.94 A

1288 institute *n*
adj national, American, international, urban, medical, military, technical, independent *noun* research, •health, •technology, art, study, director, policy, cancer•, science, enterprise• *verb* fund, found, sponsor, establish, head, •estimate, attend•, graduate, direct, •recommend
28475 | 0.93

1289 screen *n*
adj big, small, blank, giant, tiny, flat *noun* computer•, •door, TV•, television•, image, radar•, video•, movie *verb* appear•, show, fill, stare•, flash, display, watch, open, hit, flicker
28532 | 0.93 F

1290 run *n*
adj long, short, earned, winning, presidential, successful, dry, wild *noun* home•, hit, •kick, game, touchdown•, record, average, mile, salmon, bull• *verb* make•, score, drive•, allow•, break•, •fail, end, finish, earn
28805 | 0.92 N

1291 Chinese *j*
noun government, people, official, woman, leader, restaurant, food, student, culture, immigrant
29659 | 0.90 A

1292 horse *n*
adj white, wild, dark, Trojan, dead, rocking, wooden, pretty *noun* race, man, •farm, rider, cart, sea•, leg, •manure, iron•, animal *verb* ride, pull, lead, mount•, gallop, shoot, feed, •rear, kick, tie
28781 | 0.92 F

1293 European *j*
noun union, country, community, state, nation, market, power, culture, commission, ally
29332 | 0.90 A

1294 target n
adj easy, military, prime, specific, primary, favorite, main, moving, likely, Iraqi *noun* attack, .group, .audience, .area, .population, .behavior, price, .practice, store, .market *verb* hit., become., set, meet., reach., identify, miss.
27852 | 0.95

1295 willing j
noun risk, participant, worker, buyer, partner, seller, ally, accomplice, victim, suspension, executioner *misc* to, pay, take, more, give, accept, able, spend
27431 | 0.97

1296 survey n
adj national, recent, geological, annual, nationwide, comprehensive, informal, completed *noun* result, data, percent, student, respondent, question, research, response, .instrument, health *verb* conduct, .show, .find, complete, .indicate, include, report, base, respond., .reveal
29806 | 0.89 A

1297 interested j
noun party, reader, art, person, politics, science, researcher, sport, individual, sex, scholar, topic *misc* more, very, become, seem, really, particularly, less
27018 | 0.98

1298 chief n
adj assistant, Indian, tribal, senior, paramount, principal, acting *noun* .staff, police, bureau., commander., chairman., house., deputy., editor., crew., fire. *verb* name, appoint., elect., hail., resign, promote., .oversee, .preside, phone
28088 | 0.94

1299 crowd n
adj large, small, huge, wild, angry, enthusiastic, silent, cheering, standing-room-only, thick *noun* people, street, noise, cheer, home, roar, .control, sellout., .pleaser *verb* .gather, draw., attract., walk, push, .wait, scan., address., join, shout
28145 | 0.94 F

1300 prison n
adj federal, private, secret, maximum-security, juvenile, Israeli, minimum-security, Vietnamese, visiting, nearby *noun* year., life, state., .sentence, time, .system, inmate, .term, month *verb* serve, send., release., spend., face., build, operate, house, commit, impose
28082 | 0.94 S

1301 terms i
(in terms of) .of, both, define., cost, measure., value, difference, .economic, .relationship, .quality, impact, .ability, express., performance
28708 | 0.92 S A

1302 obviously r
well, very, mean, quite, concerned, .pleased, .upset, disagree, .drunk, .intelligent, talented
28720 | 0.92 S

1303 basis n
adj regular, daily, case-by-case, individual, day-to-day, weekly, scientific, legal *noun* .race, case., decision, .evidence, .fact, discrimination., day, cost, .comparison, point *verb* provide., form., become., serve., select., judge, establish, discriminate., lay., define
28663 | 0.92 A

---

11. Sports and recreation

General and equipment (note that many of the most frequent terms are used much more in a non-sports context)

(point) n 170808, game 141129, team 129169, (win) 115765, (record) n 74769, (score) 57699, (shoot) 53006, ball 42625, league 34639, competition 27747, bike 17795, championship 15352, (uniform) 13288, stadium 12186, tournament 12089, (medal) 8740, (final) n 8514, Olympics 7884, gym 6916, bicycle 6354, (saddle) 4543, trophy 4128, athletics 2921, World Cup 2898, golf club 1670, rink 1316, (freestyle) 1293, puck 1073, sailboat 966, gymnasium 938, finish line 880, golf ball 736, cleat 697, racquet 447, ice skates 349, surfboard 282, racecar 136, hockey stick 118

Participant

(player) 78188, coach 54225, (crowd) n 34255, athlete 23137, (captain) 17799, (opponent) 15287, champion 13783, quarterback 10079, (pitcher) 8815, (rookie) 5844, (batter) 5125, (spectator) 4500, skier 4320, (boxer) 3183, golfer 3071, referee 2178, diver 2095, jockey 2074, swimmer 2065, umpire 1677, cyclist 1660, skater 1617, surfer 1233, goalie 701, gymnast 654, weight lifter 96, ice skater 73

Specific sports

baseball 27717, football 24265, golf 20336, basketball 20136, fishing 17500, tennis 9837, soccer 8876, hockey 5926, swimming 5527, skiing 5369, boxing 4099, wrestling 2731, volleyball 2310, cycling 2228, bowling 2148, diving 1928, (sailing) 1438, gymnastics 1395, lacrosse 975, rowing 845, rugby 776, jogging 670, badminton 381, field hockey 307, racquetball 241, windsurfing 156, mountain climbing 117, motocross 77, horse racing 48

1304 apartment *n*
adj small, two-bedroom, one-bedroom, tiny, empty, high-rise, one-room *noun* .building, .complex, .night, house, door, new, street, block, floor, window *verb* live., move., rent., leave., share, build, enter., buy, .overlook, .smell
28453 | 0.92 F

1305 farm *n*
adj large, organic, collective, nearby, commercial, working, urban, abandoned, corporate, industrial *noun* family, .worker, animal, dairy, fish., .bill, tree., .subsidy, .boy *verb* live., buy., own, sell, raise, visit., operate, bet., plant, convert
27764 | 0.94

1306 flight *n*
adj long, commercial, short, direct, daily, connecting, manned, powered, cheap, canceled *noun* .attendant, airline., .stair, space., air, hour, plane, .deck, .crew, .path *verb* cancel, catch., fly, board., book., miss., arrive, climb., .land, check
27453 | 0.95

1307 shape *n*
adj good, bad, better, different, great, dark, simple, various, terrible, physical *noun* size, color, body, form, thing, variety., kind., tree, design, weight *verb* take., help., change., stay., cut, determine, bend., assume., fit, retain.
28083 | 0.93 M

1308 demand *n*
adj growing, increased, increasing, strong, public, domestic, popular, global, physical, pent-up *noun* supply, energy, consumer., market, price, oil, world, .product, growth, increase *verb* meet., create, reduce., place, satisfy., respond., rise, face, exceed, generate
28548 | 0.91 A

1309 strength *n*
adj physical, military, greatest, full, economic, inner, financial, muscular, individual *noun* .weakness, .training, muscle, .endurance, size, source., arm, courage, .character, speed *verb* give., gain., build., increase., draw., gather., regain., combine, possess, enhance
27335 | 0.95

1310 village *n*
adj small, little, remote, global, nearby, tiny, Olympic, entire, whole *noun* town, home, fishing., street, mountain, life, .voice, mile, resident, chief *verb* live, return., visit, destroy, surround, travel., arrive, attack, settle, flee
28249 | 0.92

1311 operate *v*
noun company., system, program, plant, facility, .level, force., market, center, organization., store, vehicle, machine, principle, site *misc* .under, .within, continue., .independently, .efficiently
27477 | 0.94

1312 reporter *n*
adj investigative, unidentified, foreign, western, regional, veteran, female, top, consistent, fellow *noun* news, newspaper, new, editor, TV, question, post, television., court., camera *verb* tell., ask, talk, .cover, speak., .write, interview, .visit, answer, .travel
28429 | 0.91 N

1313 share *n*
adj fair, large, total, outstanding, disproportionate, foreign, equal, mutual, additional, growing *noun* market., cent., .price, company, percent, stock, lion., earnings., fund, option. *verb* sell, buy., hold., pay., own., increase, receive., gain., earn, .compare
29211 | 0.89 N

1314 guard *n*
adj national, old, armed, senior, junior, left, red, private, rear, offensive *noun* security., coast., point., prison., .troop, border., .unit, air., .duty, honor. *verb* stand, shoot, kill, .protect, hire, .patrol, post, order, approach, surround
27846 | 0.93

1315 observe *v*
noun student, behavior, teacher, change, star, astronomer., .site, researcher., phenomenon, object, .session, telescope, condition, interaction, earth *misc* directly, closely, carefully, frequently, .record, easily.
28656 | 0.90 A

1316 deliver *v*
noun message, speech, service, .baby, .news, address, .promise, food, lecture, .good, paper, mail, report, package, ability. *misc* able., fail., .directly, personally
26685 | 0.97

1317 count *v*
noun vote, .number, ballot, .money, second, .blessing, minute, hour, census, sperm., machine, breath, income, .sheep, voter *misc* .on, .among, .hundred, .lucky, .dozen, .heavily, accurately
26653 | 0.97

1318 inside *r*
go., .out, .outside, back., door, step., turn, both., deep., once., stay., peer., trap., window
28237 | 0.91 F

1319 advantage *n*
adj competitive, great, full, big, political, comparative, unfair *noun* .opportunity, home., .disadvantage, people, technology, .situation, tax, cost, price, number *verb* take., offer., gain., provide, enjoy, seek., confer, press., outweigh, .accrue
27183 | 0.95

1320 wild *j*
noun animal, card, thing, man, horse, turkey, mushroom, rice, bird, salmon, plant, place *misc* run, grow, crazy, scenic, domestic, woolly, edible, truly
27074 | 0.95

1321 previous *j*
noun year, study, research, experience, day, finding, generation, month, night, result, work, week *misc* than, during, consistent, suggest, base, compare, indicate, support
27575 | 0.93 A

1322 average *j*
noun age, year, rate, price, person, cost, income, number, score, percent, fund, size *misc* than, annual, American, per, high, about, above
27643 | 0.93

1323 emerge *v*
noun pattern., theme., leader, picture., difference., figure, .data, consensus., form, evidence., .bankruptcy,

analysis, decade, minute, .bathroom *misc* .from,
begin., later, finally., recently, clearly
27174 | 0.94 A

1324 contribute *v*
noun factor., .report, writer., .development, staff.,
.article, money, .understanding, process, community,
.campaign, author., .sense, researcher., .decline
misc .to, also., may., significantly, .million, greatly,
directly, thus., environmental
27786 | 0.92 A

1325 leadership *n*
adj political, democratic, national, strong, military,
effective, educational, moral, congressional
noun .role, position, party, .skill, style, community,
quality, .conference, change, church *verb* provide.,
assume., develop, exercise., demonstrate, maintain,
.emerge, define, assert., display
27868 | 0.92 A

1326 boat *n*
adj small, swift, wooden, bass, electric, tiny,
recreational, inflatable, flying, marine *noun* fishing.,
people, river, owner, dock, .ride, charter., party., show
verb rock, build, sail, miss., buy., row, sink, float, push,
drift
29680 | 0.86 M

1327 facility *n*
adj nuclear, medical, public, large, correctional,
nursing, composting, military, residential, private
noun care., treatment., research., health., storage.,
service, production., training. *verb* build, operate,
locate, close, house, own, process, construct, expand,
maintain.
28185 | 0.90 A

1328 present *j*
noun study, time, result, day, finding, purpose,
system, state, research, situation, moment, value
misc examine, past, clear, indicate, tense, future,
investigate, physically
28698 | 0.89 A

1329 earn *v*
noun money, .degree, .living, income, .reputation,
percent, .respect, college, profit, point, company.,
dollar, .right, worker., wage *misc* .more., .than, .million,
.less, high, enough, average, .per, .billion, .extra
27186 | 0.94 N

1330 highly *r*
.regard, .unlikely, most., .successful, value, .visible,
.skilled, .competitive, .train, .effective, .publicized,
.significant
27442 | 0.93 A

1331 vehicle *n*
adj armored, electric, sport-utility, military, off-road,
recreational, all-terrain, four-wheel-drive, light,
commercial *noun* motor., utility., sport., fuel,
emission, mile, emergency., tank *verb* use, drive,
armor., operate, build, park, .travel, reduce, crash,
own
27157 | 0.94

1332 pound *n*
adj heavy, overweight, square, British, cooked, excess
noun .year, foot, inch, .week, .cake, ground,
thousand., cup, .month, cent. *verb* weigh., lose.,
gain., drop., carry, shed., add, .cut, produce, eat
27561 | 0.92 M

1333 tiny *j*
noun bit, room, town, hand, fraction, piece, light,
island, house, village, apartment, baby *misc* white,
little, red, blue, inside, green, yellow, pink
27325 | 0.93 F

1334 understanding *n*
adj better, great, human, clear, deeper, mutual, basic,
common, full, cultural *noun* student, people,
knowledge, way, process, lack., .nature, .relationship,
.concept, .culture *verb* gain., develop., provide.,
require, contribute., increase., promote., enhance.,
base., deepen.
28674 | 0.89 A

1335 settle *v*
noun case, .dispute, dust., .lawsuit, court, issue,
.chair, matter, suit, score, .seat, .claim, immigrant,
.difference, .couch *misc* .into, .back, before, finally.,
.less, eventually.
   down before., thing., finally., ready., marry, until,
start **in** once., next, .behind, comfortably, .beside,
dusk.
26572 | 0.96

1336 unless *c*
.you, .something, .otherwise, .course, change, .note,
.someone, .count, .willing, .indicate, .Congress,
.absolutely, .somebody, is
25994 | 0.98

1337 tomorrow *r*
will, .night, .morning, today., back., again., tonight,
until., join., .evening, maybe, break., .afternoon
28220 | 0.90 S

1338 foundation *n*
adj national, private, solid, nonprofit, legal,
international, strong, charitable, educational, very
noun science., research, heritage., family, grant,
president, art, director, community, education
verb lay., provide, build, establish, form., support,
fund, serve, shake., sponsor
26977 | 0.94

1339 quick *j*
noun question, fix, break, look, glance, way, response,
answer, tip, trip, smile, step *misc* take, give, real, easy,
point, pretty, slow, relatively
26513 | 0.96

1340 block *n*
adj large, concrete, wooden, entire, square,
huge, solid, residential, fundamental, massive
noun building., street, road, city., stumbling., .grant,
kid., wood, couple., cinder. *verb* walk., live., build,
park., locate., stretch., circle.
26724 | 0.95

1341 light *j*
noun color, weight, truck, source, rail, hair, sugar,
fixture, eye, skin, rain, touch *misc* brown, blue, until,
dark, green, red, fluffy, gray
27375 | 0.92 M

1342 reader *n*
adj young, avid, modern, familiar, poor, Catholic,
dear, average, voracious, potential *noun* .service,
.card, circle., book, text, story, writer, letter,
response, mind *verb* remind., invite, share,
.respond, inform., encourage, .recognize, draw,
address, refer
28994 | 0.87 A

1343 collect v
noun data, information, sample, money, tax, water, evidence, study, fee, art, food, .signature, plant, amount, site *misc* .during, million, .analyze, demographic, .organize, cool, additional, used, systematically, .store
26734 | 0.95 A

1344 guest n
adj special, frequent, honored, invited, uninvited, regular, female, favorite, musical, male *noun* .room, house, .worker, .speaker, party, .list, .star *verb* join, .arrive, include, thank, introduce, invite, welcome, serve, greet, entertain.
27220 | 0.93 S

1345 living n
adj daily, independent, decent, healthy, assisted, comfortable, everyday *noun* .room, standard, way, cost, country, house, life, dining, family, kitchen *verb* make, earn, eke, assist, scratch, scrape.
26622 | 0.95 F

1346 tool n
adj new, powerful, useful, effective, available, valuable, best, educational, diagnostic, necessary *noun* power, hand, assessment, machine, .kit, .trade, stone, marketing, development *verb* use, provide, .help, develop, create, employ, apply, .enable, .assess, .measure
27558 | 0.92 A

1347 protection n
adj environmental, equal, legal, federal, constitutional, special, adequate, extra *noun* .agency, right, .act, law, consumer, child, bankruptcy, health, .program, amendment. *verb* provide, offer, need, afford, seek, file, require, extend, receive, guarantee
27329 | 0.92 A

1348 fair j
noun share, amount, trial, game, trade, play, election, price, value, question, number, market *misc* think, free, balanced, poor, pretty, accurate, equitable, impartial, reasonable
26259 | 0.96

1349 additional j
noun information, research, cost, study, resource, image(s), support, tax, reference, percent, benefit, need *misc* provide, also, million, add, require, each, include, billion, offer
27262 | 0.92 A

1350 promote v
noun .development, program, .growth, policy, effort, .health, interest, government, .use, .democracy, idea, activity, organization, .book, community *misc* .economic, social, design, .human, .positive, actively.
27257 | 0.92 A

1351 equipment n
adj new, medical, heavy, military, electronic, standard, digital, special *noun* piece, computer, supply, material, manufacturer, training, use, plant, office, facility *verb* need, buy, require, sell, purchase, install, carry, cost, load, own
26529 | 0.94

1352 mostly r
.because, .white, .black, young, consist, .male, poor, .empty, .Muslim, crowd, neighborhood, compose, .rural, .female
25816 | 0.97

1353 order v
noun court, judge, president, doctor, .drink, food, test, .troop, .pizza, .coffee, .beer, police, .copy, department, official *misc* .pay, short, federal, .online, immediately, .destroy, .evacuate
25998 | 0.96

1354 painting n
adj large, abstract, early, famous, completed, Chinese, French, finished, final, religious *noun* oil, .sculpture, artist, drawing, landscape, wall, surface, photograph, watercolor, technique *verb* begin, create, sell, hang, depict, complete, finish, study, exhibit, inspire
36681 | 0.68 M

1355 feed v
noun .family, animal, baby, fish, .dog, bird, .interest, cattle, mouth, cow, livestock, chicken, river, .cat, .diet *misc* hungry, house, .clothe, .raise, enough, directly, dress, .homeless, .lower
   on adult, bacteria, caterpillar, both, nothing.
off .energy, crowd, team
26093 | 0.96

1356 principle n
adj basic, general, fundamental, guiding, moral, political, constitutional, organizing, international, religious *noun* law, practice, matter, set, policy, .justice, rule, agreement, management, action *verb* apply, base, follow, violate, establish, guide, agree, accept, .govern, operate
27874 | 0.89 A

1357 bowl n
adj super, large, small, medium, pro, orange, shallow *noun* mixing, water, sugar, soup, game, egg, ingredient, serving, .mixer, salt *verb* .combine, .add, .stir, place, set, .whisk, pour, transfer, fill, eat.
27907 | 0.89 M N

1358 claim n
adj legitimate, federal, territorial, moral, competing, religious, environmental, medical, similar, scientific *noun* court, land, truth, insurance, .fame, health, product, worker, baggage, property *verb* make, file, support, lay, stake, pay, deny, reject, involve, .violate
26884 | 0.93 A

1359 technique n
adj new, different, traditional, effective, various, specific, modern, instructional, proper, advanced *noun* management, material, assessment, teaching, painting, relaxation, research, practice, strategy, development *verb* use, develop, learn, teach, employ, apply, .allow, .involve, demonstrate, .produce
27794 | 0.90 A

1360 limit v
noun .number, .ability, use, power, study, .amount, .access, law, .scope, option, activity, emission, .growth, effort, effect *misc* severely, strictly, extremely, somewhat.
26873 | 0.93 A

1361 identity n
adj national, ethnic, cultural, social, personal, collective, racial, sexual, religious *noun* sense, group, gender, development, .theft, .crisis, culture, formation, politics *verb* define, establish, create, lose, maintain, reveal, protect, determine, express, struggle
28301 | 0.88 A

1362 title *n*
adj national, consecutive, major, official, main, original, popular, working, back-to-back, honorary *noun* book, .game, world, .division, song, .role, conference., .track, .page, .character *verb* win., hold., defend., suggest, earn., claim., .refer, retain., state., bear.
26728 | 0.93 N

1363 critic *n*
adj literary, outspoken, harsh, cultural, vocal, conservative, leading, longtime, tough, frequent *noun* film., art., music., movie., book., media., administration, theater., TV., policy *verb* .say, .argue, .call, .charge, write, .point, .claim, .accuse, praise, respond
26629 | 0.93

1364 survive *v*
noun .year, .war, .wife, .attack, .winter, ability., .crash, species., cancer, .attempt, plant., .month, patient., struggle., marriage. *misc* only, long, .without, able., order., in., manage.
25615 | 0.97

1365 cry *v*
noun baby, mother, night, tear, boy, voice, girl, .pain, .help, .wolf, mom, hour, .foul, minute, daddy *misc* start., begin., hear., laugh, hard, break
   out for, she., .loud, .pain, hear., voice, .help, again, suddenly
27605 | 0.90 F

1366 border *n*
adj Mexican, national, southern, northern, Canadian, international, eastern, western *noun* .patrol, side., state, US, security, town, .agent, area, mile, .crossing *verb* cross., secure., close, open, control, protect., share., straddle., define, extend
26470 | 0.94

1367 lift *v*
noun .head, hand, arm, weight, .embargo, ban, leg, foot, sanction, eye, shoulder, spirit, .finger, body, ground *misc* .off, .heavy, toward, slowly, gently, slightly, carefully, herself
26988 | 0.92 F

1368 path *n*
adj shining, different, narrow, right, beaten, spiritual, wrong *noun* career., bike., flight., garden, development, dirt., gravel., road, .resistance *verb* follow., .lead, cross, walk., choose, block., clear., trace., cut, .wind
25854 | 0.96

1369 aspect *n*
adj other, important, various, different, social, certain, positive, technical, key, particular *noun* .life, .work, .experience, .process, business, .relationship, .education, .society, art, .policy *verb* focus., emphasize., consider, discuss., examine., address., explore., deal., involve
27331 | 0.90 A

1370 marry *v*
noun man, woman, year, daughter, girl, mother, father, wife, couple, sister, month, husband, guy, prince, brother *misc* want., her, before, never., young, .again
   off .daughter, girl, young, .child
26276 | 0.94 F

1371 shop *n*
adj local, antique, pro, retail, available, tiny, closed, one-stop, empty, outdoor *noun* coffee., gift., .owner, window, body., barber. *verb* set., open, sell, close, run., buy, own, walk, visit, enter
26227 | 0.94

1372 failure *n*
adj renal, mechanical, academic, respiratory, complete, total, catastrophic, past, dismal *noun* success., heart., rate, kidney., market., fear., bank., risk. *verb* die, cause, result, doom., .occur, recognize, explain, experience., end., .comply
26482 | 0.93 A

1373 ride *v*
noun .bike, horse, bus, .bicycle, day, horseback., .wave, train, .mile .motorcycle, coaster, .elevator, road, .town, .subway *misc* .down, .along, .off, .away, .around, .across
   up .down, elevator, skirt., dress., pant.
28059 | 0.88

1374 responsible *j*
noun person, government, death, behavior, action, party, agency, parent, care, citizen, member, decision *misc* for, hold, those, socially, environmentally, largely, partly, directly
25789 | 0.96

1375 gather *v*
noun information, data, people., crowd, family, group, evidence, friend, intelligence, .table, material, .strength, .dust, .momentum *misc* .around, .together, .outside, enough, everyone., .front, .round, hunt., pause., .pray, regularly
25473 | 0.97

1376 jump *v*
noun .percent, car, .conclusion, .bandwagon, .ship, .fence, price., .rope, .gun, heart., truck, .chair, .seat, rate., hoop *misc* .down, .back, run, .around, .ahead, suddenly., nearly, .front, quickly, ready., .board, .forward, scream, shout, yell
   up .down, .run, scream, shout, suddenly., .grab, yell, .onto **out** .window, .behind, .front, grab, cop.
   in swim, .rescue, .defend, .beside
26239 | 0.94 F

1377 sample *n*
adj small, large, representative, random, total, present, entire, free *noun* .size, student, blood., table, data, analysis, population, participant, method., water. *verb* collect, include, .consist, test, obtain, .report, provide, draw, base, send
29309 | 0.84 A

1378 affair *n*
adj foreign, public, international, internal, Indian, national, military, current, legal, political *noun* state., love., department, committee, president, world., veteran., bureau., family., ministry. *verb* manage., handle., conduct., admit, meddle., deny., intervene., .last, dominate, arrange
25640 | 0.96

1379 result *v*
noun loss, .death, change, problem, reduction, .increase, outcome, injury, effect, process, improvement, level, action, policy, failure *misc* .from, may., increased, .significant, likely.
27403 | 0.89 A

1380 worth *i*
it, .more, well., .note, .billion, .effort, risk, .money,
dollar, share., .price, consider, anything, .cost
25540 | 0.96

1381 fit *v*
noun model, .description, .profile, .need, piece, size.,
.pattern, .bill, .category, data, .mold, .definition,
clothes., .blade, shoe *misc* .into, .together, .perfectly,
best, enough., .neatly
   in how., try., .well, want, easily, quite., struggle.,
.perfectly, .nicely, .anywhere
25676 | 0.95

1382 chairman *n*
adj vice, national, democratic, federal, general,
honorary, past, tribal *noun* committee, board, house,
.CEO, .executive, .chief, party, president, commission,
campaign *verb* become., serve., name., elect.,
appoint., resign, .announce, succeed., testify, oust.
26993 | 0.91 N

1383 until *i*
minute., wait., year, about, .after, .now, .recently, stir,
up., cook., .then, heat., .tender, add
25092 | 0.97

1384 lesson *n*
adj important, valuable, private, moral, painful, daily,
flying, English, basic, developmental *noun* history,
teacher, life, music., piano., class, experience, hour,
object., .planning *verb* learn, teach, take., give., draw,
provide, plan, offer., apply, present
26308 | 0.93

1385 Christmas *n*
adj merry, white, traditional, wonderful, favorite,
Victorian, classic *noun* .tree, .eve, day, .present, .party,
.season, .card *verb* spend., celebrate., buy, sing.,
decorate, shop, feature, glow
26196 | 0.93

1386 insist *v*
noun official., administration., .anonymity, minister.,
critic., spokesman., aide., supporter., ally, .condom.,
ministry., feminist., .secrecy, Catholicism, .confidentiality
misc .on, .upon, continue., instead, repeatedly
25277 | 0.96

1387 anybody *p*
do, can, .who, .else, know, think, want, than., never.,
tell, ever, anything, hurt, better.
26705 | 0.91 S

1388 folk *n*
adj old, white, ordinary, traditional, common, poor,
rich, regular, nice, plain *noun* .art, .music, .song,
home, .tale, .hero, .culture, .artist, .singer, museum
verb thank, sing, .gather, .celebrate, bother., .line,
.flock, cater., energize.
26335 | 0.92 S

1389 band *n*
adj rubber, big, marching, live, narrow, elastic, marine,
regional, dark, yellow *noun* rock., member, school.,
music, jazz., .orchestra, .director, wedding., brass.,
leader *verb* play, form, join., .perform, sing, feature,
strike, march, hire, front
26984 | 0.90

1390 ear *n*
adj middle, left, right, inner, deaf, sympathetic,
external, pointed, tiny, floppy *noun* eye, hand,

.infection, nose, hair., phone., .corn, music, .canal,
mouth *verb* whisper., ring, cover., fall., listen, press,
pull, reach., scratch., close
27140 | 0.90 F

1391 procedure *n*
adj standard, surgical, medical, experimental, proper,
simple, normal, civil, criminal, certain *noun* rule.,
policy., participant, assessment., study, operating.,
control., evaluation, use, result *verb* follow, perform,
develop, require, repeat, establish, .involve, undergo.,
test, conduct
27430 | 0.89 A

1392 associate *v*
noun use, level, change, drug, stress, outcome, type,
rate, increase, violence, score, depression, substance,
alcohol, peer *misc* .with, high, often., closely.,
significantly.
27695 | 0.87 A

1393 inch *n*
adj tall, wide, thick, high, square, deep, short, cubic,
extra, mere *noun* foot., diameter, height, .water,
.collection, .museum, depth., pound, face, .page
verb measure., grow., stand., give, move., leave, add
28095 | 0.86 M

1394 warm *j*
noun water, air, day, weather, temperature, room,
night, spring, color, body, summer, sun *misc* keep,
serve, feel, cool, stay, dry, until, soft
26142 | 0.92 F M

1395 African *j*
noun American, art, country, student, state, culture,
nation, community, government, history, leader,
man
30848 | 0.78 A

1396 French *j*
noun fry, revolution, quarter, government, door,
president, bread, toast, woman, minister, restaurant,
company
25668 | 0.94

1397 baseball *n*
adj professional, major-league, pro, minor-league,
organized, amateur, big-league *noun* league., .player,
.team, game, .cap, .bat, football, .fan, basketball,
season *verb* play., wear., watch., love, throw, sign,
attend., bet.
26663 | 0.90 N

1398 demonstrate *v*
noun study., student, research., .ability, .skill,
result., teacher, .effect, .commitment, power, .level,
.relationship, .knowledge, behavior, .importance
misc clearly., .significant, .strong, recent., order., in.,
.effective, convincingly
26954 | 0.89 A

1399 foot *n*
adj square, high, long, bare, left, right, cubic, deep,
big, small *noun* hand, ground, water, floor, leg, .bed,
.space, .air, head, man *verb* get., stand., put., set.,
rise., look, keep, move, sit, walk
25912 | 0.93 F

1400 Christian *j*
noun church, faith, community, tradition, life, right,
group, school, theology, Democrat
27812 | 0.87

1401 approach *v*
noun way., car, .door, .subject, .significance, officer, foot, footstep, .task, deadline., election, storm., guard, birthday, .gate *misc* slowly, rapidly., cautiously, .billion, .differently, closely
25304 | 0.95

1402 competition *n*
adj international, foreign, fierce, intense, global, increased, stiff, tough, economic *noun* market, year, level, price, .law, .policy, .act, industry, sport, resource *verb* face., win, increase, enter., promote., reduce, lessen., intensify, engage., organize
26941 | 0.89 A

1403 measure *v*
noun scale, test, level, item, success, performance, .distance, .foot, study, instrument., variable, rate, progress, .change, value *misc* .by, .up, use, .against, difficult., accurately, directly
26558 | 0.91 A

1404 afraid *j*
(afraid of) *noun* dark, death, height, dog, flying, AIDS, snake, failure, commitment, needle, retaliation *misc* I, because, might, lose, anything, die, little, suddenly
25824 | 0.93 F

1405 spread *v*
noun word, arm, hand, disease, leg, wing, cancer., virus, rumor, .mixture, .message, finger, smile., blanket *misc* .over, .across, .through, .throughout, .wide, .among, .around, quickly, .evenly
   out .over, .before, .across, .below, .around, .along, .front, arm, map, blanket
25020 | 0.96

1406 ignore *v*
noun .fact, .warning, .advice, .reality, .evidence, media, .need, .order, .sign, rule, .pain, .plea, concern, .call, critic *misc* try., largely., simply., choose., completely, tend.
24867 | 0.96

1407 soft *j*
noun voice, drink, tissue, money, light, skin, spot, sound, hair, snow, landing, power *misc* until, hard, white, warm, brown, form, sweet, blue
25703 | 0.93 F

1408 annual *j*
noun meeting, rate, report, percent, income, budget, conference, revenue, year, festival, growth, award *misc* its, average, hold, during, second, present, total
26091 | 0.92 N

1409 wonderful *j*
noun thing, life, people, time, man, place, way, story, world, job, book, person *misc* really, most, oh, thank, absolutely, beautiful, sound, strange
25747 | 0.93 S

1410 threaten *v*
noun species, security, force, interest, action, Iraq, .neighbor, violence, .stability, existence, .survival, peace, future, weapon, letter *misc* feel., .kill, very, .sue, .destroy
24866 | 0.96

1411 commit *v*
noun crime, .suicide, murder, act, sin, atrocity, person., troop, .perjury, violence, fraud, .adultery, force, conspiracy., individual. *misc* .themselves, violent, remain., already., deeply., fully.
25010 | 0.96

1412 deny *v*
noun .right, charge, .access, request, .allegation, official., government, court, .wrongdoing, .existence, .involvement, judge., freedom, justice, motion *misc* .any, no., .ever, .anything, confirm., nor., vehemently., neither., categorically.
25007 | 0.96

1413 intelligence *n*
adj military, national, artificial, American, human, foreign *noun* .agency, US., .community, .committee, .official, .service, .officer, director., .report, information *verb* gather, share, base, collect, .indicate, insult., measure, confirm, possess, assess
25943 | 0.92

1414 regular *j*
noun season, basis, classroom, education, class, school, teacher, exercise, guy, game, interval, meeting *misc* during, physical, special, addition, attend, fairly, unleaded, aerobic
25044 | 0.95

1415 influence *n*
adj political, great, strong, positive, significant, powerful, major, considerable *noun* power, sphere., culture, family, factor, money, peer, .alcohol, kind., environment *verb* exert., exercise., examine., wield., drive., reflect., gain., extend, affect, .shape
26303 | 0.91 A

1416 general *n*
adj retired, top, commanding, marine, Iraqi, four-star, British, civil, allied, Haitian *noun* attorney., surgeon., inspector., army, US, major., lieutenant., force, brigadier., office *verb* thank, order, .announce, command, agree, appoint, .issue, accuse, .recommend, capture
25385 | 0.94 S

1417 past *i*
her, walk., .hour, minute., drive., move., push., .window, slip., door, half., street., road., month
25999 | 0.92 F

1418 reaction *n*
adj chemical, allergic, negative, initial, emotional, public, positive, immediate, natural, knee-jerk *noun* chain., .time, people, kind., .force, audience, .event, polymerase., response *verb* cause., trigger., produce., .occur, provoke., describe., elicit., experience, examine., fear
24984 | 0.95

1419 cross *v*
noun .line, .border, .street, arm, leg, .bridge, .river, .mind, path, road, .boundary, .threshold, .chest, look., thought. *misc* .over, once, illegally, attempt., .busy
25314 | 0.94 F

1420 master *n*
adj grand, open, modern, British, Dutch, Japanese, acknowledged, spiritual, certified, Spanish *noun* .degree, .bedroom, .plan, .teacher, .program, .suite, .ceremony *verb* earn., win, receive., serve., study., finish, copy., .swim, appoint., obey.
25016 | 0.95

1421 suit *n*
adj black, bathing, blue, white, dark, civil, gray, strong, class-action, red *noun* man., .tie, business., .jacket, .shirt, court, .coat, space., citizen. *verb* wear., file, follow., bring, dress., settle, buy., .claim, dismiss, .seek
25245 | 0.94 F

1422 blow *v*
noun wind., whistle, air, .nose, .smoke, breeze., .face, hair, .kiss, head, window, horn, .candle, .mind, storm.
misc .away, .through, .across
out .candle, window, .breath, air, wind., .smoke, .knee, tire, .match **up** .building, plot., bomb, plane, car, bridge, wind., threaten. **off** .steam, head., roof., leg.
25299 | 0.94 F

1423 destroy *v*
noun life, home, fire, weapon, building, missile, cell, evidence, Iraq, enemy, bomb, property, document, economy, record *misc* completely., nearly, threaten., totally., seek.
24513 | 0.97

1424 gift *n*
adj special, greatest, perfect, wonderful, precious, charitable, rare, lavish, spiritual, corporate
noun .shop, Christmas., .certificate, holiday., card, wedding., birthday., museum., food
verb give, receive, buy, bring, accept., send, offer, bear., .total, pile
24895 | 0.95

1425 coffee *n*
adj hot, black, strong, instant, fresh, cold, steaming
noun cup, .table, .shop, tea, pot, mug, morning, house, .bean, sip. *verb* drink., pour, bring, serve, buy, finish., grab, stare, boil, invite.
25853 | 0.92 F

1426 anyway *r*
die., thanks, ahead, matter., anymore., dead., stupid.
25810 | 0.92 F

1427 belief *n*
adj religious, political, strong, popular, Christian, cultural, common, widespread, firm, general
noun .system, value, practice, people, attitude, set., other, core., action, nature *verb* hold, base., share, reflect., express., support, reinforce., influence, confirm., state
26284 | 0.90 A

1428 comment *n*
adj public, helpful, early, positive, final, following, general, quick, recent, critical *noun* question, student, call., .article, .draft, .suggestion, feedback, reviewer., kind., request. *verb* make, hear, reach., send., decline., seek., return., offer., receive, .suggest
25167 | 0.94

1429 apparently *r*
.willing, .healthy, .unaware, .unable, .random, suicide, .contradictory, .unrelated, .oblivious, response, .unwilling, unknown, .endless, .irresistible
24554 | 0.96

1430 twice *r*
.as, once., .week, than., about, year, more., .much, .day, .many, least., .likely, nearly., .month
24408 | 0.97

1431 background *n*
adj different, ethnic, cultural, educational, cosmic, socioeconomic, racial, historical, religious, economic
noun .check, .information, music, family, .noise, experience, microwave., .radiation *verb* provide., require, fade., conduct., share, paint, .qualify, lurk., vary, match
24931 | 0.94 A

12. Time

General

now $_{601657}$, early $_{177101}$, ago $_{120614}$, age $_{106495}$, moment $_{105210}$, period $_{62979}$, (date) *n* $_{43094}$, schedule $_{27870}$, delay $_{17809}$, phase $_{16796}$, clock $_{12601}$, hurry $_{11213}$, o'clock $_{6766}$, quarter of $_{6487}$, interval $_{5574}$, calendar $_{5037}$, urgency $_{3011}$, quarter to $_{595}$, (intermission) $_{404}$

Days of the week (in chronological order)

Sunday $_{35024}$, Monday $_{21647}$, Tuesday $_{19036}$, Wednesday $_{15623}$, Thursday $_{16636}$, Friday $_{28361}$, Saturday $_{26973}$, weekday $_{2122}$, weekend $_{32073}$

Months (in chronological order; some are also women's names)

January $_{24895}$, February $_{17725}$, (March) *n* $_{43594}$, (April) $_{30734}$, (May) *n* $_{34799}$, (June) $_{36159}$, July $_{33013}$, August $_{22850}$, September $_{27614}$, October $_{22998}$, November $_{22629}$, December $_{21374}$

Seasons (in chronological order)

Spring *n* $_{42390}$, Summer $_{61526}$, Autumn $_{4750}$, (Fall) *n* $_{30693}$, Winter $_{32288}$

Parts of the day (morning to night)

dawn *n* $_{11289}$, sunrise $_{2459}$, morning $_{109770}$, noon $_{7006}$, afternoon $_{32034}$, evening $_{39323}$, eve $_{8948}$, sunset $_{5877}$, dusk $_{3558}$, night $_{178134}$, midnight $_{8121}$

Intervals (short to long)

second *n* $_{53610}$, minute $_{122119}$, hour $_{133415}$, day $_{431461}$, week $_{191038}$, fortnight $_{249}$, month $_{155762}$, season $_{80369}$, year $_{741980}$, decade $_{51825}$, generation $_{37109}$, century $_{64107}$, millennium $_{4232}$

1432 quarter n
adj French, living, close, past, fiscal, cramped, private, final, Jewish, tight *noun* .century, year, percent, .mile, .dollar, .hour, earnings, revenue, .moon, .inch *verb* .end, cut., drop, account., cost., decline, peel., confine., toss, comprise.
25089 | 0.94 N

1433 review n
adj national, judicial, recent, favorable, institutional, environmental, comprehensive, independent, physical, extensive *noun* literature, book, .board, law., .process, article, new., research, peer., study *verb* write, conduct, read, publish, base., receive., conclude, approve, present, obtain
25633 | 0.92 A

1434 faith n
adj good, Christian, religious, Catholic, strong, bad, personal, blind *noun* people, community, family, church, leap., article, matter, practice, act., tradition *verb* keep., lose., put., place., share, restore., test, sustain, convert., justify
25859 | 0.91

1435 move n
adj smart, bold, right, wrong, recent, risky, wise, strategic, unusual, unprecedented *noun* career., .direction, family, kind., series., business, dance., surprise. *verb* make., watch., follow, plan., .protect, oppose, announce, repeat, criticize, signal
24517 | 0.96

1436 speed n
adj high, low, top, full, medium, average, maximum, breakneck *noun* .limit, mixer, .mph, .light, power, wind., .mile, sound, size, direction *verb* beat, increase, pick., move., run, reduce., set, travel., slow, fly
25662 | 0.91 M

1437 engage v
noun .activity, student, .behavior, .sex, .conversation, .kind, .discussion, .dialogue, individual., community, .debate, effort, .research, person., participant. *misc* .in, .sexual, actively., likely., fully., directly
25515 | 0.92 A

1438 broad j
noun range, shoulder, spectrum, support, sense, daylight, category, smile, term, area, definition, array *misc* across, cover, tall, flat, encompass, narrow, thick, deep
24965 | 0.94 A

1439 perspective n
adj different, historical, theoretical, broad, global, unique, cultural, critical, multiple, proper *noun* thing., student, life, time, woman, sense, experience, article, value, health *verb* put., provide, offer., keep., change, view, gain., share, represent, adopt
26056 | 0.90 A

1440 slightly r
.than, only., .different, .more, .less, .high, head., .large, bend., .low, until., forward
24660 | 0.95

1441 growing j
noun number, season, population, concern, body, demand, problem, interest, economy, market, pain, evidence *misc* fastest, among, rapidly, reflect, despite, economic, face, contribute
24788 | 0.94

1442 view v
noun other, American., teacher, participant., .context, society, object, behavior, .videotape, .video, lens, .suspicion, film, culture, scene *misc* .as, .themselves, tend., widely., generally., likely., .differently
25308 | 0.92 A

1443 function n
adj important, different, discriminant, primary, normal, cognitive, sexual, immune, specific, physical *noun* brain., form, structure., body, role., school, cell, lung., management *verb* perform, serve., improve, vary., fulfill., affect, attend., identify, relate, assess
26526 | 0.88 A

1444 construction n
adj new, social, cultural, commercial, residential, heavy, proposed, complex *noun* .worker, .site, .project, .company, building, .industry, road, design., material, cost *verb* begin, complete, finance., oversee., halt, supervise., fund., approve., slow
25041 | 0.93

1445 egg n
adj large, beaten, hard-boiled, fertilized, fried, raw, green, golden, hot, female *noun* .white, cup, .yolk, sugar, milk, nest., mixture, bowl, chicken, vanilla *verb* beat, lay., add., eat., whisk., hatch, stir, combine, remove, throw.
25378 | 0.92 M

1446 charge v
noun .murder, fee, .crime, price, critic., company, police., .count, battery, agency., .assault, bank, prosecutor., interest, customer *misc* .with, arrest., highly., emotionally., politically.
24384 | 0.95

1447 wave n
adj new, tidal, gravitational, huge, light, recent, current, crashing, successive, gentle *noun* shock., radio., heat., sound., .future, water, brain., crime. *verb* ride., send., hit, break, .sweep, .crash, roll, create, catch., cause
24486 | 0.95

1448 female j
noun student, athlete, body, figure, voice, participant, character, role, member, coach, player, subject *misc* male, both, sexual, athletic, traditional, genital, mostly, predominantly
25627 | 0.91 A

1449 murder n
adj attempted, guilty, mass, first-degree, second-degree, brutal, double, bloody *noun* .case, trial, charge, rape, .weapon, crime, .rate, degree, .victim, death *verb* commit, convict., accuse., solve., arrest., .occur, investigate., link., plead, connect.
25704 | 0.90 S

1450 tape n
adj audio, red, yellow, adhesive, scotch, electrical, magnetic, secret, measuring *noun* proofread., .recorder, duct., video., cassette., .recording, masking., broadcast, piece., .player *verb* play, listen., hear, watch., record, catch., roll, send, wrap, bind
24983 | 0.93 S

1451 burn v
noun fire., house, eye, fuel, body, candle., flag, light., .ground, sun, coal, .death, face, oil, .fat *misc* .off, hot, .away, badly, .alive

out fire., before, bulb., light., candle., quickly, motor, .fast, completely **down** house, fire, building, home, candle., church, threaten., barn **up** .phone, .fever, .inside
24472 | 0.95 F

1452 means *n*
adj other, standard, effective, only, necessary, available, economic, possible, military, peaceful *noun* .deviation, end, table., .communication, way., .production, difference, goal, .support, .transportation *verb* use, provide., .achieve, justify., offer., serve., seek, lack.
25237 | 0.91 A

1453 aware *j*
(aware of) *noun* fact, need, danger, situation, public, risk, importance, reader, existence, possibility, consequence, potential *misc* of, that, become, more, well, shall, fully, acutely, problem, issue, presence
23666 | 0.97

1454 mistake *n*
adj big, terrible, serious, bad, common, huge, fatal, honest, tragic *noun* people, .past, kind., error, number, policy, rookie., consequence, accident, share. *verb* make., learn., admit., avoid., repeat., correct, realize., acknowledge., .assume, .cost
23916 | 0.96

1455 quiet *j*
noun time, room, voice, street, moment, place, man, life, peace, neighborhood, town, corner *misc* keep, very, stay, remain, relatively, suddenly, nice, except
24616 | 0.93 F

1456 connection *n*
adj direct, strong, personal, political, social, emotional, close, high-speed, intimate, spiritual *noun* Internet., family, network, kind., sense., brain, .land, love., cell *verb* make., establish., draw, break, maintain., sever., deny., form, miss., .exist
24209 | 0.95 A

1457 shoe *n*
adj black, running, white, red, athletic, brown, blue, high-heeled, sensible, expensive *noun* pair., tennis., leather, .store, .box, size, shirt, .company, pant, suit *verb* wear, put., buy., walk, tie., kick., fill, remove., sell, .drop
24750 | 0.93 F

1458 clothes (PL) *n*
adj new, old, clean, dirty, wet, civilian, nice, casual *noun* woman, shoe, food, hair, work., change., street., bag, closet, pile. *verb* wear, take., buy., put., wash., dress., hang, throw, pull, .fit
24899 | 0.92 F

1459 promise *v*
noun president., tax, return, official., benefit, reform, future, administration, aid, candidate., ad., minister., contract, .voter, dollar *misc* deliver, repeatedly., .cooperate, originally., publicly
23737 | 0.96

1460 religion *n*
adj different, organized, religious, free, traditional, major, civil, particular, popular, comparative *noun* politics, culture, world, race., freedom., science, role, practice *verb* teach, promote, argue, establish, study., relate, define, .prohibit, belong, endorse.
26004 | 0.88 A

1461 complete *j*
noun control, list, picture, guide, set, game, stranger, data, lack, understanding, sentence, works *misc* without, provide, almost, available, nearly, accurate, total, from
23731 | 0.96

1462 united *j*
noun nation, Church, state, airline, Way, resolution, front, service, force, organization, press *misc* Kingdom, Methodist, international, general, according, Iraqi, peacekeeping, democratic, European, western
24973 | 0.91 N

1463 context *n*
adj social, historical, cultural, political, large, broad, specific, particular, global, contemporary *noun* school, culture, relationship, history, meaning, community, family, use, discussion, sport *verb* provide., understand, place., occur, consider, examine, view., relate, influence, shape
26615 | 0.86 A

1464 active *j*
noun role, duty, member, participant, life, participation, ingredient, learning, community, involvement, part, church *misc* more, become, very, most, sexually, remain, physically
24597 | 0.93 A

1465 focus *n*
adj primary, main, major, special, central, narrow, sharp *noun* .group, study, .attention, research, education, area, .edition, article, section., .discussion *verb* become., keep., bring., lose., maintain., improve
24525 | 0.93 A

1466 youth *n*
adj American, black, at-risk, homeless, urban, inner-city, troubled *noun* child., program, group, .sport, center, service, .age, .culture, development, .league *verb* serve, participate, experience, educate., coach., target., attract, assist, benefit, inspire
24912 | 0.91 A

1467 location *n*
adj different, various, remote, geographic, specific, exact, central, geographical, particular, undisclosed *noun* time, map., area, size, number, name., date, game., assistant., mile *verb* show., pinpoint., determine, identify., choose, mark., shoot., vary
24256 | 0.94

1468 neighbor *n*
adj good, next-door, Arab, nearest, close, closest, Asian, northern, southern, friendly *noun* friend, house, family, door, child, relative, street, yard, police, peace *verb* call, help, ask, love., hear, talk, live, watch, threaten., meet
23607 | 0.96

1469 dress *v*
noun man, woman, .clothes, .suit, .jeans, girl, morning, .costume, .uniform, .shirt, hair, bed, boy, .dinner, lady *misc* .like, fully., casually, neatly, quickly
up .as, like, all., get., woman, .costume, .dinner, fancy, .nowhere, actor
24391 | 0.93 F

1470 Internet *n*
adj high-speed, broadband, fast, mobile, faster, secure, unlimited *noun* access, .service, .site, company,

.provider, .connection, .user _verb_ use., connect., surf.,
search, download, post., link, .enable, .explode
24740 | 0.92

1471 category _n_
adj different, broad, social, various, following, certain,
racial, main, separate, traditional _noun_ response,
product, age., .hurricane, number, .storm, price,
analysis, score, data _verb_ fall., include, divide., fit.,
create, identify, belong., group., list, indicate
25414 | 0.89 A

1472 dangerous _j_
noun situation, place, world, thing, man, drug, work,
game, job, weapon, level, condition _misc_ very, more,
most, too, potentially, extremely, consider, less
23374 | 0.97

1473 extend _v_
noun .hand, arm, .life, leg, line, study, range, benefit,
.reach, research, period, .deadline, invitation,
protection, season _misc_ .beyond, .far, .across, .toward,
fully.
23906 | 0.95 A

1474 combine _v_
noun bowl., .ingredient, .flour, .sugar, cup, element,
oil, salt, .juice, data, mixture, sauce, saucepan., egg,
image _misc_ .with, large., until., small., stir.,
.remaining, .bake, .single, thoroughly, gently.
24526 | 0.92 M

1475 demand _v_
noun .attention, government, .money, .change,
.action, .return, .answer, leader, .payment, consumer.,
.response, public., Congress, customer, .accountability
misc .immediate, increasingly., supply, angrily,
constantly, confront., march., .unconditional, .instant,
outraged, overly., loudly
23410 | 0.97

1476 coast _n_
adj southern, central, northern, Mediterranean,
Caribbean, upper, opposite, marine _noun_ west., east.,
.guard, Gulf., north, south, US., island, mile, ivory.
verb travel., sail., strike., hug., land, cruise., rebuild.,
patrol.
23834 | 0.95

1477 relatively _r_
.small, .low, .new, .few, .high, .easy, .little, .short,
.large, .simple, .number, remain.
24591 | 0.92 A

1478 smile _n_
adj big, little, wide, broad, warm, slight, faint, wry,
bright, quick _noun_ .face, eye, lip, head, tooth, mouth,
nod, kind, girl, wave _verb_ give., look, flash., force.,
.fade, break, manage., wear, return, .spread
25887 | 0.87 F

1479 bus _n_
adj yellow, crowded, double-decker, express, clean,
chartered, serial, electric, passing, rapid _noun_ school.,
.driver, .stop, tour, .station, .ride, .service, shuttle.
verb take, wait, drive, board., .pull, catch., arrive,
.carry, head, miss.
24060 | 0.94

1480 hey _u_
say., .guy, .wait, thank, .listen, .minute, .thanks, .baby,
yell, .buddy, .dad, hi, .mom
25445 | 0.88 S F

1481 chief _j_
noun executive, officer, justice, operating, economist,
correspondent, engineer, judge, strategist, counsel,
investment, negotiator _misc_ financial, former,
medical, name, vice, supreme, appoint, senior,
administrative
24453 | 0.92 N

1482 following _j_
noun year, day, question, week, morning, section,
example, page, statement, month, way, information
misc include, consider, offer, describe, suggest, illustrate
24835 | 0.90 A

1483 depend _v_
noun life., success., future., survival., .type, .extent,
size, answer., economy., quality, amount, nature,
.condition, society., individual _misc_ .on, .upon, much,
.heavily, .largely, .entirely
23668 | 0.95 A

1484 key _n_
adj low, minor, spare, extra, golden, missing, magic,
indispensable _noun_ car, .success, lock, door, ignition,
pocket, house, room, set, piano _verb_ turn, hold.,
.unlock, hand., press., .open, hit., throw., grab., pull
23349 | 0.96

1485 hell _n_
adj sure, loose, living, mad, bloody, pure, like, eternal,
absolute, sheer _noun_ heaven., life, .angel, .earth, gate,
fire, kind, .kitchen _verb_ go, .break, scare., raise.,
wonder., beat., hurt., burn., figure, .freeze
24867 | 0.89 F

1486 visit _n_
adj recent, brief, official, regular, follow-up, frequent,
previous, short, initial, historic _noun_ doctor, state,
home, site, office, month, surprise., return.
verb make., pay., include, receive., arrange., plan.,
recall., enjoy., .update, .last
23020 | 0.97

1487 bone _n_
adj broken, temporal, human, strong, bare, tiny,
funny, pubic, fragile _noun_ .marrow, .density, skin,
muscle, loss, flesh, .mass, body, .transplant, fracture
verb break, remove, cut, build., cause, prevent,
increase, crack, maintain., snap
24411 | 0.91

1488 cook _v_
noun minute, food, .meal, .dinner, onion, chicken,
meat, rice, pasta, garlic, pepper. _misc_ .until, .about,
add., cover., stir, .tender, love., continue.
up .some, something, .fun, .storm, scheme, idea,
recipe, .batch, .story, .dish **over** .heat, .medium, .low,
cover., saucepan., pan.
24876 | 0.89 M

1489 fire _v_
noun shot, gun, missile, rocket, weapon, bullet, .job,
.round, police, rifle, soldier., officer, month, gunman.,
attorney _misc_ after, hire, ready., shoot, immediately,
threaten., refuse, .wildly, quit, aim, resign, allegedly
up get., all, engine, .grill, crowd, .stove, .computer,
.cigarette, barbecue, fan. **off** .letter, .round, .e-mail,
.question, .memo, .angry
23486 | 0.95

1490 direct _j_
noun contact, instruction, result, effect, investment,
evidence, link, observation, experience, control,

impact, connection _misc_ between, no, indirect, provide, foreign, avoid, simple, personal
24103 | 0.92 A

1491 native _j_
noun people, culture, language, plant, species, land, community, population, woman, student, country, speaker _misc_ American, Hawaiian, Indian, African, cultural, Asian, contemporary, traditional
25672 | 0.86 A

1492 cool _j_
noun air, water, night, temperature, thing, place, breeze, weather, color, hand, pan, head _misc_ let, really, keep, warm, pretty, until, completely, dry
23756 | 0.93 M

1493 cut _n_
adj deep, short, federal, final, quick, cold, across-the-board, clean, rough, additional _noun_ tax•, budget•, rate, pay•, program, capital, job•, hair•, gain _verb_ make, miss•, propose, reduce, announce, increase, suffer•, oppose•, vote, favor
23522 | 0.94

1494 remind _v_
noun •reader, •viewer, •audience, •voter, •listener, •colleague, •visitor, •importance, smell•, •childhood, grandmother, joke, aunt, tragedy•, •observer _misc_ •me, •us, •myself, constantly•, •ourselves, •yourself, •everybody, gently, continually•, daily, repeatedly
23170 | 0.95 F

1495 historical _j_
noun society, context, event, record, perspective, study, fact, figure, novel, art, development, experience _misc_ cultural, social, political, contemporary, within, base, particular, specific
25472 | 0.87 A

1496 moral _j_
noun value, issue, authority, obligation, judgment, ground, responsibility, principle, standard, question, character, sense _misc_ political, ethical, social, religious, legal, spiritual, human, strong
24857 | 0.89 A

1497 voter _n_
adj black, registered, democratic, American, white, likely, young, undecided, independent, conservative _noun_ percent•, •registration, •turnout, woman•, league•, party, number•, swing•, campaign, Democrat _verb_ approve, show, •decide, register, •cast, •reject, win, •choose, convince•, remind•
24361 | 0.91 S N

1498 appropriate _j_
noun time, behavior, way, response, level, action, use, education, measure, strategy, model, place _misc_ more, most, seem, provide, determine, consider, developmentally
24481 | 0.90 A

1499 famous _j_
noun world, people, man, writer, person, woman, case, line, author, artist, star, painting _misc_ most, become, rich, perhaps, name, infamous, French, justly
22876 | 0.96

1500 hire _v_
noun people, company, •worker, •lawyer, firm, consultant, teacher, employee, employer•,

staff, attorney, contractor, director, guy, police _misc_ •someone, private, •former, •illegal, recently•
on •as, other
23295 | 0.94 N

1501 victory _n_
adj major, military, decisive, straight, final, stunning, upset, electoral _noun_ war, margin, season, career•, election, party, defeat, bowl•, celebration, landslide• _verb_ win, claim•, declare•, score•, celebrate•, achieve, earn, mark, result, record•
24294 | 0.90 N

1502 contact _n_
adj direct, sexual, physical, close, personal, social, human, constant _noun_ eye•, information, point, •lens, •sport, group, •person _verb_ make•, come•, maintain•, avoid•, lose•, establish•, initiate•, result, facilitate, permit
23243 | 0.94 A

1503 fully _r_
•understand, more•, never•, yet•, •aware, develop, •appreciate, •expect, •realize, recover, •support, until
22903 | 0.96

1504 negative _j_
noun effect, impact, consequence, attitude, reaction, affect, feeling, image, ad, outcome, correlation, result _misc_ positive, between, toward, significant, both, associate, experience, indicate
24555 | 0.89 A

1505 medicine _n_
adj alternative, modern, internal, traditional, medical, preventive, herbal, clinical _noun_ school•, new, professor•, journal•, college•, food•, practice•, sport•, •cabinet _verb_ study, treat, prescribe, specialize•, •cure, deliver•, administer, revolutionize•, alleviate, supplement
23798 | 0.92 M

1506 participate _v_
noun •study, student•, •activity, •sport, school, child•, woman•, •process, opportunity•, teacher•, member•, •discussion, individual•, •research, parent• _misc_ •in, actively, invite•, agree•, allow•, fully
24285 | 0.90 A

1507 grade _n_
adj good, elementary, low, final, middle, early, better, poor, passing, steep _noun_ school, student, •level, teacher, child, class, •average, •point, kindergarten• _verb_ teach, receive, enter•, earn, complete, drop, finish•, repeat•, determine, achieve
24658 | 0.89 A

1508 eastern _j_
noun time, country, state, conference, part, shore, region, seaboard, bloc, side, district, edge _misc_ middle, European, central, western, southern, Soviet, former, along
23486 | 0.93

1509 supply _n_
adj short, medical, available, adequate, steady, limited, fresh, military, ample, endless _noun_ water•, food•, demand, oil, power•, blood•, energy• _verb_ cut, increase, buy•, provide, reduce, ensure•, carry•, exceed•, protect•, clean•
23177 | 0.94

1510 yesterday *r*
.morning, today, .afternoon, announce, late., before, since., die, official, release., conference, meeting, statement., attack
24567 | 0.89 S

1511 familiar *j*
noun face, name, voice, story, source, place, word, pattern, figure, phrase, sight, scene *misc* with, become, more, sound, already, less, anyone, vaguely
22534 | 0.97

1512 democracy *n*
adj liberal, political, American, human, economic, free, social, modern, constitutional, representative *noun* freedom, transition., right, movement, market, development, form, peace, capitalism, principle. *verb* promote., restore, support, build., establish, fight, defend., strengthen., define, .depend
24708 | 0.88 A

1513 pair *n*
adj extra, matched, perfect, oppositional, favorite, clean, unlikely, odd, opposite *noun* .shoe, .jeans, .boot, .pant, .eye, .glove, .sock, .glass, .scissors, .short *verb* wear., buy., pull., own., grab., slip., consist., fit, select, nest
23133 | 0.94

1514 drive *n*
adj hard, long, four-wheel, short, all-wheel, floppy, two-hour, DVD-ROM, front-wheel, scenic *noun* hour., disk., CD-ROM., sex., block., line., road, test., shore., petition. *verb* hit., launch., organize., install, park, shift, connect, spearhead., back, score
24126 | 0.90 M

1515 healthy *j*
noun people, child, food, life, lifestyle, baby, diet, woman, weight, body, eating, relationship *misc* keep, stay, happy, eat, young, strong, maintain, normal
23592 | 0.92 M

1516 front *n*
adj united, rear, popular, cold, democratic, domestic, eastern, diplomatic *noun* back, .house, liberation, home., car, side, store, shirt, .center, seat *verb* sit., stand., open, walk., park., fight, present., hang, attack
22635 | 0.96

1517 tie *v*
noun .knot, game, .record, rope, ribbon, end, .shoe, string, score, .back, .tree, .neck, .lead, piece, arm *misc* to, .together, .around, closely., .behind
up .end, .loose, .court, money, boat, .line, .traffic, hair, .knot, phone
22457 | 0.96

1518 birth *n*
adj live, multiple, out-of-wedlock, premature, natural, present, teenage, noble, painful *noun* .control, child, mother, .certificate, .defect, .rate, year, baby, date, .parent *verb* give., cause, die., celebrate., prevent, separate., await., peak
22474 | 0.96

1519 progress *n*
adj economic, significant, technological, real, social, human, educational, academic, scientific *noun* student, work., .report, assessment., child, goal, lack., sign., development, works. *verb* make, monitor., show., measure, follow., track., achieve, slow, discuss., demonstrate
22850 | 0.94 A

1520 damage *n*
adj environmental, serious, permanent, severe, extensive, compensatory, significant, physical, structural, monetary *noun* brain., property, .control, collateral., lot., tissue, nerve., injury, .award, .assessment *verb* cause, suffer., repair., inflict, prevent., assess., destroy, .occur, result, minimize.
22716 | 0.95

1521 exchange *n*
adj foreign, cultural, international, free, fixed, global, official, heated *noun* stock., .rate, security., new., .commission, information, .program, student, .idea *verb* trade, involve, facilitate., .occur, promote, list, participate., engage., initiate., obtain
23287 | 0.93 A

1522 bottom *n*
adj very, flat, removable, muddy, smooth *noun* top., pan, rock., side, page, river, sea, .stair, ocean, hole *verb* hit., reach., fall, cover, sink., drop, lie, stick., place, scrape.
22760 | 0.95 M

1523 daily *j*
noun life, basis, news, newspaper, activity, routine, value, living, show, dose, paper, practice *misc* almost, base, average, weekly, recommended, total, twice, normal
22999 | 0.94

1524 next *i*
(next to) .to, .year, .day, .week, over., .month, .morning, .few, .door, sit., .step, .generation, hour, .her
23615 | 0.91 F

1525 document *n*
adj similar, legal, Christian, official, internal, historical, classified, available, original, written *noun* .term, concept, .topic, court., government, page., science., information, report, company *verb* find., discuss., .help, .show, sign, release, obtain, produce, file, read
23699 | 0.91

1526 grand *j*
noun jury, slam, hotel, scale, piano, prize, opening, total, tour, plan, opera, scheme *misc* before, federal, central, old, national, win
22415 | 0.96

1527 journal *n*
adj medical, international, scientific, academic, literary, daily, quarterly *noun* street., article, new., .medicine, editor, study, issue., .entry, research, science *verb* publish, write, keep, report, read., appear., record, edit, .devote, quote
23320 | 0.92 A

1528 knee *n*
adj right, left, wounded, weak, sore, sprained, front, bended, injured, bony *noun* hand., .injury, surgery, foot, elbow, hip, leg, back, ankle, head *verb* bend, fall., drop., pull, bring., sit, .buckle, sink., hurt, raise
23680 | 0.90 F

1529 primary *j*
noun care, source, school, goal, reason, concern, purpose, focus, education, responsibility, physician, color *misc* whose, secondary, democratic, presidential, select, educational, visual, dependent
23794 | 0.90 A

1530 otherwise *r*
will, or., might, unless., .note, suggest., indicate, prove.,
.healthy, convince., .empty, .specify, .normal, afford
22062 | 0.97

1531 train *v*
noun teacher, student, force, dog, worker, program,
staff, officer, police, team, troop, doctor, employee,
personnel, volunteer *misc* highly., specially., properly,
equip, military, poorly.
22089 | 0.97

1532 grab *v*
noun .arm, hand, .hold, .phone, .wrist, .attention,
.gun, leg, .handful, back, .throat, boy, .headline,
.handle, .paper *misc* reach., .pull, .onto, .throw,
suddenly., quickly, push, forward., manage., .shove
24742 | 0.86 F

1533 circle *n*
adj inner, full, small, social, dark, vicious, wide, tight,
academic, perfect *noun* .reader, .service, .friend,
.eye, phone., .number, family, .light, fax., winner.
verb form., draw, sit., walk., cut., spin., close,
complete., surround, travel
23073 | 0.92

1534 lean *v*
noun head, window, door, table, side, car, .elbow,
seat, arm, .railing, face, tree, .forehead, cheek, bike
misc .against, .forward, .toward, .down, her, .close,
.across
   over .kiss, .whisper, .shoulder, .desk, bed, .pick,
.touch, .grab **back** .his, .chair, .against, close, smile,
sigh, .slightly
24580 | 0.87 F

1535 wine *n*
adj red, white, dry, fine, sparkling, sweet, French,
cheap, Italian, light *noun* glass, bottle, cup, beer, food,
.vinegar, .list *verb* drink., pour, add., serve, sip., taste,
produce, buy, sell, spill
24034 | 0.89 N

1536 minority *n*
adj ethnic, other, small, racial, national, white,
significant, tiny, vocal, underrepresented *noun* .group,
.student, woman, .leader, member, .community,
majority, .population, .business *verb* represent,
increase, protect., hire, recruit., belong., affect,
constitute, attract., vote
23240 | 0.92 A

1537 flower *n*
adj yellow, fresh, small, little, purple, dried, green,
delicate, edible, tall *noun* garden, plant, .bed,
bouquet., spring, petal, arrangement, .shop, girl,
summer *verb* grow, send., bring, .bloom, pick.,
produce, cut, smell, fill, place
23917 | 0.89 M

1538 device *n*
adj other, electronic, medical, explosive, nuclear,
small, assistive, handheld, mechanical, simple
noun control., safety., storage., communication.,
technology, vision., micro., drug., data, phone
verb use, design, develop, allow, build, measure,
install, test, produce, place
23196 | 0.91

1539 Iraqi *j*
noun force, government, people, army, troop, soldier,
official, leader, police, security
24448 | 0.87 S

1540 plate *n*
adj small, hot, tectonic, empty, photographic,
individual, top, flat, thin, thick *noun* license.,
glass, home., food, paper., dinner., metal., steel.
verb serve, step., place, set, transfer., eat, fill, push,
remove, pick
22805 | 0.93

1541 attack *v*
noun Iraq, force, .target, terrorist., police, Republican,
enemy, troop, aircraft, army, ad, defense, position,
opponent, bomber. *misc* .kill, vulnerable., directly,
ready., personally, .destroy
22326 | 0.95 S

1542 clean *j*
noun air, water, act, room, energy, clothes, slate,
technology, environment, fuel, sheet, towel
misc come, keep, wipe, white, fresh, safe, up, dry
22317 | 0.95

1543 alive *j*
noun memory, hope, dream, spirit, tradition,
possibility, streak, excitement, breathing, bee, inside,
cooking *misc* keep, still, come, stay, dead, well, today,
while
22263 | 0.95 F

1544 actor *n*
adj best, political, great, supporting, social,
international, famous, favorite, fine, talented
noun director, character, role, movie, .actress, writer,
film, stage, screen., award *verb* perform, .portray,
cast, star, feature., nominate, hire, train, .rehearse,
audition
22823 | 0.93

1545 hate *v*
noun God., .idea, .gut, Jew, .thought, daddy, cat, .me,
.sin, .sight, .smell, neighbor, .bastard, .passion, cop
misc I., him, because, love., really., .other, .each,
.myself, .admit, absolutely.
22778 | 0.93 F

1546 expression *n*
adj facial, artistic, free, religious, cultural, personal,
harsh, sexual, creative, musical *noun* face, freedom.,
form., gene, change, mode., means., .emotion,
anger, speech *verb* find., wear., .soften, pardon.,
notice., encourage, convey, excuse., judge.,
regard.
22971 | 0.92 A

1547 below *r*
discuss, similar., .concept, topic., help., see., down.,
far., above, .percent, level, fall., describe., .left
22873 | 0.92 M

1548 bright *j*
noun light, eye, color, star, sun, spot, future, day, side,
sky, morning, sunlight *misc* very, red, yellow, blue,
white, young, green, orange
23151 | 0.91 F

1549 press *v*
noun .button, hand, freedom, face, lip, finger, .charge,
head, back, side, body, palm, wall, arm, window
misc .against, .into, .down, .together, forward, continue.
22563 | 0.93 F

1550 tour *n*
adj guided, senior, grand, self-guided, free, available,
nationwide, driving, quick, historical *noun* bus, .guide,

year, .duty, world, book., group, .event, player,
.operator _verb_ give., offer, win, lead, walk., finish,
join., serve., feature, .promote
23151 | 0.91 N

1551 finding _n_
adj consistent, previous, significant, current, recent,
early, preliminary, interesting, surprising, major
noun study, research, implication, group, report,
analysis, survey, researcher, fact, conclusion
verb .suggest, .indicate, base, .show, present, confirm,
reveal, explain, publish
25260 | 0.83 A

1552 exercise _n_
adj free, aerobic, regular, physical, military,
moderate, daily, vigorous _noun_ .program, diet,
.power, training, minute, weight, class, intensity,
.routine, form. _verb_ .help, perform, include, increase,
involve, improve, conduct, complete, participate.,
engage.
24185 | 0.87 M

1553 plastic _n_
adj clear, white, black, blue, red, recycled, cheap,
thin, heavy, molded _noun_ .bag, .wrap, .surgery,
.surgeon, .bottle, .container, paper, sheet, metal,
.cup _verb_ cover, use, place, fill, carry, contain,
remove, wear.
22454 | 0.94 M

1554 danger _n_
adj real, great, potential, imminent, clear, greatest,
grave, immediate _noun_ life, .zone, sign, sense., kind,
.drug, threat, fire, level, public _verb_ pose, face, warn.,
.lose, recognize, present, avoid., .lurk, .lie, protect.
21674 | 0.97

1555 neck _n_
adj long, thick, stiff, broken, thin, slender, narrow,
tight _noun_ back., head., arm, shoulder, hand, face,
nape., hair, pain, chain. _verb_ crane., break., hang.,
wear, kiss, stick., grab., stretch, breathe., snap
23399 | 0.90 F

1556 valley _n_
adj central, dry, green, narrow, fertile, lush, broad,
isolated, historic, forested _noun_ river., mill.,
mountain, death., sun., hill, .floor, spring., center,
peak. _verb_ overlook., fill, surround, visit, spread,
stretch, flow, descend., nestle., climb
23045 | 0.91

1557 academic _j_
noun achievement, student, performance, year,
freedom, program, school, skill, success, community,
study, research _misc_ social, high, improve,
professional, poor, athletic, well, traditional
25664 | 0.82 A

1558 start _n_
adj good, fresh, early, slow, bad, very, fast, running
noun head., .season, year, program, .war, time, career,
.treaty, .menu, race _verb_ get., mark., wake., miss.,
signal., .finish, delay., doom.
22100 | 0.95

1559 application _n_
adj practical, specific, available, military,
medical, broad, clinical, various, direct, successful
noun technology, software, process, program, law,
land., .form, research, theory, job _verb_ use, include,
require, fill., submit, file, receive, develop, accept,
review
23987 | 0.88 A

1560 intend _v_
noun Congress., .use, God., pun., nature., purpose,
message, .audience, article., harm, meaning, .reader,
founder., legislature., voter _misc_ never., originally.,
whether., clearly.
21773 | 0.96

1561 male _j_
noun student, athlete, voice, counterpart, participant,
friend, figure, role, model, subject, partner, body
misc female, white, both, black, young, sexual,
mostly, gay
22951 | 0.91 A

13. Transportation

General

street [110685], (drive) [102651], road [77837], fly _v_ [49402], (station) _n_ [47403], driver [30480], flight [28289], traffic [20599], airport [20259], (pilot) [19597], highway [17976], passenger [16082], journey [13904], parking lot [7420], intersection [3642], freeway [3527], pedestrian [2323], one-way [1621], bus stop [1097], road trip [950], speed limit [772], RV [647], round trip [569], stop sign [520], stoplight [393]

Specific types of transportation

car [128671], train _n_ [43971], ship [38312], plane [32339], truck [31140], boat [31036], bus [25488], van [22988], bike [17795], jet [13873], helicopter [9660], airplane [8339], automobile [6652], bicycle [6354], cab [6320], (metro) [5776], taxi [4635], subway [4485], ferry [4455], ambulance [4020], motorcycle [3480], jeep [3364], tractor [3100], carriage [3049], SUV [2813], convertible [2048], limo [1810], pickup truck [1716], space shuttle [1634], limousine [1583], minivan [1512], police car [1509], scooter [1392], school bus [1346], spaceship [1119], sport car [1081], trolley [1038], sailboat [966], cruise ship [931], steamer [901], snowmobile [887], steamboat [785], streetcar [739], sport utility vehicle [420], rowboat [372], fire engine [344], cable car [300], dump truck [282], 18-wheeler [108]

1562 tall *j*
noun foot, man, tree, building, woman, grass, glass, window, tale, order, guy, pine *misc* stand, as, thin, six, grow, five, black, slender
22967 | 0.91 F

1563 shut *v*
noun door, eye, mouth, window, plant, engine, operation, camera, gate, bedroom, factory, lid, drawer, trap, jaw. *misc* keep., .behind, .off, slam., open, pull., squeeze., snap., .tight, close, tightly
down government, plant, system, operation, engine, production, factory, airport, completely, reactor **up** oh., .listen, please, .bitch
22809 | 0.92 F

1564 lots *p*
(lots of) .of, there., .people, .thing, park., .money, parking., .different, vacant., .fun, .stuff, drink., space, empty.
22009 | 0.95

1565 Indian *j*
noun tribe, people, woman, reservation, community, culture, government, art, nation, population
24753 | 0.84 A

1566 respect *n*
adj due, great, mutual, tremendous, deep, utmost, proper, similar *noun* people, lot., .right, lack., dignity, other, love, trust, admiration, .authority *verb* show., pay., treat., earn., deserve, gain., command.
21627 | 0.96

1567 colleague *n*
adj democratic, professional, close, senior, longtime, academic, dear, conservative, esteemed, scientific *noun* friend, student, Republican., work, Senate, patient, institute, finding, client, respect. *verb* .report, describe, .study, share, .discover, urge., .publish, discuss, .propose, remind.
22430 | 0.93

1568 writing *n*
adj creative, early, historical, critical, academic, popular, collaborative, selected, ancient, native *noun* student, process, reading, .skill, .program, letter, style, .wall, .desk, piece. *verb* read, teach, improve, influence, inspire, explore, emphasize, submit., .prompt, analyze
23148 | 0.90 A

1569 rain *n*
adj heavy, cold, light, tropical, pouring, driving, steady, freezing *noun* .forest, acid., wind, day, snow, inch., cloud, window, drop *verb* .fall, .stop, bring, .pour, wash, pelt, blow, listen., pray., smell.
22349 | 0.93 F

1570 fast *r*
as, so., too., .enough, how., move., run., very., grow., happen., hold.
21909 | 0.95 F

1571 football *n*
adj pro, professional, American, Canadian, high-school, collegiate, intercollegiate *noun* .player, .team, .game, college., .coach, .league, .field, school., basketball, baseball *verb* play., watch., win, throw., love, attend
23319 | 0.89 N

1572 welcome *v*
noun .show, gentleman, .guest, .visitor, .opportunity, arm, .reader, newcomer, move, stranger, guideline.,

.arrival, initiative, hero, announcement *misc* good, .home, everybody, .both, please., everyone, open, warmly, pleased.
back break., .talk, .our, .everybody, .everyone
23536 | 0.88 S

1573 domestic *j*
noun violence, policy, product, issue, market, politics, problem, abuse, agenda, production, program, economy *misc* foreign, gross, international, political, economic, both, well, external, imported
22809 | 0.91 A

1574 pool *n*
adj large, indoor, deep, outdoor, shallow, potential, heated, common *noun* swimming., water, .table, .blood, gene., .hall, car., edge *verb* swim, play., shoot., lie., dive, overlook, jump, surround, climb, drain
21700 | 0.95

1575 literature *n*
adj American, English, scientific, recent, current, professional, modern, existing, medical *noun* review, child., art, study, history, research, body., language, science, music *verb* .suggest, read, report., teach, describe, .indicate, .reveal, discuss, base, examine
24290 | 0.85 A

1576 extra *j*
noun time, money, hour, point, cost, pound, mile, weight, effort, work, credit, cash *misc* give, need, pay, little, add, few, provide
21807 | 0.94 M

1577 northern *j*
noun alliance, state, hemisphere, city, part, region, university, area, town, border, light, coast *misc* southern, central, across, along, near, western, eastern, Kurdish
22084 | 0.93

1578 desire *n*
adj sexual, strong, natural, burning, male, female, intense, overwhelming, genuine, sincere *noun* need, object., man, woman, heart., .change, expression., feeling, .revenge, lack. *verb* express., reflect., motivate., satisfy., drive, share, indicate., .avoid, .maintain, act
22213 | 0.92 A

1579 direct *v*
noun attention, film, effort, movie, program, question, research, .traffic, project, energy, policy, production, activity, anger, action *misc* .by, .toward, .against, .towards, specifically
21474 | 0.96

1580 fight *n*
adj big, tough, legal, bitter, fair, involved, huge, uphill, civil *noun* .terrorism, food., scene, street, title., .AIDS, .cancer, .song *verb* lead., win, pick., break, lose, continue, join., end, wage, .ensue
21340 | 0.96

1581 corporate *j*
noun executive, tax, culture, profit, world, sponsor, headquarters, governance, interest, manager, client, office *misc* vice, private, financial, top, global, individual, environmental, senior, average
22374 | 0.92 N

1582 session *n*
adj special, legislative, joint, question-and-answer, closed, final, single, individual, plenary, daily
noun training., Congress, group, practice., therapy., end., class., counseling. *verb* attend., hold, begin, conduct, include, follow, .last, complete, .focus, address
21974 | 0.93

1583 supreme *j*
noun court, justice, decision, state, leader, council, law, commander, appeal, power, authority, being
misc rule, before, today, uphold, decide, Soviet, overturn
22385 | 0.91 S

1584 studio *n*
adj live, digital, contemporary, photographic, downtown, spacious, makeshift, rival, decorated
noun new, movie, artist, recording., .audience, film, art, .apartment, .executive, painting *verb* record, build, open, paint, maintain., .welcome, visit, own, enter., rent.
22973 | 0.89

1585 Russian *j*
noun president, government, federation, people, republic, troop, official, parliament, church, force
22351 | 0.91

1586 nod *v*
noun .head, .agreement, .approval, .direction, .thanks, .understanding, .assent, guard, captain, .satisfaction, .expression, .greeting, uncle, silence, .tear *misc* ask., slowly, .vigorously, .slightly, .solemnly, .politely
   off she, .sleep, .during, before, .behind, start., while, .again, finally., yourself.
24821 | 0.82 F

1587 learning *n*
adj cooperative, high, social, active, lifelong, early, experiential *noun* student, .experience, .process, .environment, teaching., .style, .center, .disability
verb provide, teach, enhance, create, .occur, promote, facilitate., improve, support., assess.
25835 | 0.79 A

1588 climb *v*
noun .stair, .ladder, mountain, .tree, .step, car, .bed, .hill, .wall, .percent, .fence, seat, truck, price., road
misc .into, .out, .down, .over, .back, .high, .onto, .aboard
   up .ladder, .onto, down, tree, .top, .next, .steep, .beside
22451 | 0.91 F

1589 importance *n*
adj great, relative, particular, critical, utmost, strategic, economic, paramount, central *noun* issue, .education, value, .family, matter, factor, order., .relationship, woman, role *verb* emphasize., stress., recognize., understand., place, underscore., highlight., attach, realize.
22929 | 0.89 A

1590 somewhere *r*
.else, .between, there, around, .along, down, off., .near, read., .middle, probably, away, someone, maybe
21700 | 0.93 F

1591 expand *v*
noun program, business, market, company, opportunity, universe., effort, area, .base, plan., role, economy, .range, .scope, .horizon *misc* .into, .include, continue., .beyond, rapidly
21631 | 0.94

1592 fourth *m*
.quarter, July, third., .year, .grade, .fifth, .floor, finish., .season, .grader, .century, .street, .amendment, game
21371 | 0.95 N

1593 dry *j*
noun season, mouth, skin, wine, cleaner, land, valley, air, ingredient, cleaning, soil, weather *misc* pat, hot, wet, during, white, warm, until, cool
21779 | 0.93 M

1594 disappear *v*
noun night, .view, face, door, month, .sight, .darkness, tree, sun, smile., .crowd, forest, minute, species., hour
misc .into, .behind, watch., quickly, completely
21547 | 0.94 F

1595 abuse *n*
adj sexual, physical, verbal, domestic, emotional, mental, human, alleged *noun* child., substance., drug., alcohol., case, .power, .neglect, victim, problem, treatment *verb* report, prevent., suffer, .occur, investigate., experience, accuse., protect., charge., result
22047 | 0.92

1596 chicken *n*
adj fried, grilled, skinless, boneless, roast, roasted, cooked *noun* .breast, .broth, cup, .soup, salad, egg, .stock, piece, vegetable, fish *verb* add., cook, eat, serve, cut, place, remove., raise, taste, prepare
22113 | 0.92

1597 obtain *v*
noun information, data, result, study, consent, sample, .permission, service, .license, copy, .permit, .approval, patient, analysis, report
misc order., able., difficult., require., necessary, seek, easily., significant
22945 | 0.88 A

1598 map *n*
adj detailed, topographic, electoral, available, topographical, mental, green, genetic, inlaid
noun road., area, .figure, .location, world, star, .page, table, trail, information *verb* .show, draw, provide, study., read., produce, mark, .highlight, .pinpoint, .indicate
21792 | 0.93

1599 carefully *r*
very., look., listen., watch., choose, plan, consider, must., read, place, each, word, examine, study
21206 | 0.95 F

1600 close *r*
.to, come., get., as, too., .enough, .home, stay., source., hold., .million, face, stand., lean.
20904 | 0.96

1601 increasingly *r*
become., .important, grow., .difficult, .popular, .common, .complex, society, .clear, .sophisticated, .global, .concerned, .likely, .aware
21839 | 0.92 A

1602 greatest *j*
noun world, challenge, history, player, number, hit, threat, fear, risk, impact, achievement, gift *misc* one, ever, perhaps, single, among, probably, face, possible
20914 | 0.96

1603 complex *j*
noun system, issue, problem, process, relationship, structure, task, interaction, set, situation, pattern, carbohydrate *misc* more, very, most, require, far, involve, simple, increasingly
21938 | 0.92 A

1604 metal *n*
adj heavy, precious, cold, thin, corrugated, twisted, shiny, hot, gray *noun* .detector, glass, piece., wood, .door, plastic, sheet., .plate, .box, scrap. *verb* cover, contain, attach, place, replace, slide, touch, bend, rust, grab
21471 | 0.94 F

1605 lead *n*
adj early, commanding, female, huge, male, romantic, solid, molten, outstanding *noun* .role, .singer, level, .story, time, .paint, .poisoning, blood *verb* take., follow., hold., play, blow., build., contain., maintain.
21175 | 0.95

1606 above *r*
as., photograph., describe., note., color., .below, mention., discuss., .beyond, .right, cite., outline.
22301 | 0.90 M

1607 jury *n*
adj grand, federal, guilty, hung, impartial, runaway, unanimous, mock *noun* trial, .verdict, case, judge, .selection, testimony, .room, court, member, .decision *verb* .find, tell., .hear, .decide, believe, .convict, testify., convince., .indict, serve.
22688 | 0.89 S

1608 sweet *j*
noun potato, corn, pea, spot, onion, home, voice, pepper, girl, flavor, wine, tooth *misc* little, smell, sour, red, taste, soft, hot, fresh
21587 | 0.93 F

1609 proposal *n*
adj new, specific, legislative, original, economic, modest, recent, various, controversial, initial *noun* president, tax, reform, budget., administration., marriage, peace., plan *verb* reject., put, include, submit, consider, accept, support., .allow, present, .require
21554 | 0.93

1610 impossible *j*
noun mission, task, situation, dream, position, fiction, condition, goal, odds, choice, angle *misc* it, make, almost, nearly, find, virtually, difficult
20623 | 0.97

1611 scientific *j*
noun research, community, evidence, study, knowledge, method, data, information, theory, discovery, journal, inquiry *misc* technical, technological, social, base, cultural, medical, support, international, educational
22196 | 0.90 A

1612 ticket *n*
adj available, hot, one-way, democratic, speeding, round-trip, winning, average, presidential, first-class *noun* price, season., .sales, airline., lottery., plane.,

game, lift. *verb* buy., sell, call, purchase, pay, write., .cost, receive., hand., .range
21802 | 0.92 N

1613 leaf *n*
adj small, large, dead, dried, yellow, mint, brown, fallen, chopped, thick *noun* bay., green., lettuce, maple., basil., gold., tea., water, color, wind *verb* fall, chop, cover, add, remove, eat, pick, rake., pack., place
22244 | 0.90 M

1614 classroom *n*
adj regular, elementary, traditional, typical, middle, formal, empty, future, bilingual, separate *noun* teacher, student, school, education, music, .management, activity, behavior, instruction, .environment *verb* teach, learn, enter., conduct, occur, observe, visit., integrate, enhance, relate
25124 | 0.8 A

1615 surround *v*
noun issue, controversy., house, circumstance., wall, building, event, fence, water, mountain, star, .death, police, debate., island *misc* .yourself, central, completely., dark, tall, huge, immediately.
20627 | 0.97

1616 lunch *n*
adj free, open, light, subsidized, reduced, quick, leisurely, boxed, casual *noun* .dinner, breakfast., school, hour, day, time, .break, box *verb* eat., serve, meet., bring, pack., stop, buy., arrive, drink, cater.
21284 | 0.94

1617 alone *j*
noun apartment, universe, darkness, cabin, wilderness *misc* leave, not, me, left, spend, home, past, enough, hardly, please, afraid, completely
21319 | 0.94 F

1618 meaning *n*
adj new, real, symbolic, literal, original, deeper, personal, whole, special, multiple *noun* word, life, term, .purpose, value, text, context, phrase, search., understanding *verb* give., understand., lose., change, convey., construct, carry., interpret., seek., express
22496 | 0.89 A

1619 injury *n*
adj serious, spinal, personal, severe, physical, traumatic, major, key, bodily, internal *noun* knee., death, head., brain., risk., cord., back. *verb* suffer, cause, prevent., sustain, .occur, result, add., treat, avoid., involve
22210 | 0.90 N

1620 invite *v*
noun friend, .dinner, party, member, reader, guest, leader, .meeting, viewer, visitor, artist, audience, .comparison, birthday, participant *misc* .join, .participate, .visit, .attend
20394 | 0.98

1621 enemy *n*
adj bad, public, natural, political, common, potential, foreign, mortal, sworn, dangerous *noun* friend, .combatant, .line, .fire, force, .soldier, .territory, troop *verb* fight, kill, face, attack, destroy, defeat., love., strike, define, hate
20969 | 0.95

1622 repeat *v*
noun .time, word, process, history., question, position., procedure, .mistake, story, pattern, phrase,

step, cycle, voice, sequence _misc_ .over, again, same, .remaining, .until, often
20897 | 0.95

1623 bear v
noun .mind, .name, child, .resemblance, .responsibility, .burden, .fruit, .witness, .arm, cost, weight, .brunt, pressure, market, .relation _misc_ bring, little, .upon, .striking, heavy, hardly, .directly, unable.
   out .by, seem, fact, observation, prediction, finding, conclusion, claim, expectation **down** .on, .him, .them, .upon, hurricane, .hard, weight, sun.
20626 | 0.96

1624 lip n
adj low, upper, full, red, thin, bottom, dry, soft, blue, thick _noun_ eye, .service, .gloss, hand, tooth, nose, word, hair, .balm, color _verb_ bite, move, purse, lick, press, read, part, curl, pay, tremble
22772 | 0.87 F

1625 mayor n
adj black, current, incumbent, elected, vice, longtime, outgoing, unofficial _noun_ city, new, .office, governor, year, deputy, town, race, candidate, county _verb_ run, elect, appoint, .announce, .declare, .propose, complain, endorse, criticize, invite
21894 | 0.91 N

1626 award n
adj annual, Grammy, outstanding, prestigious, numerous, distinguished, top, punitive, literary, coveted _noun_ academy, year, .winner, book, achievement, .ceremony, music. _verb_ win, receive, present, earn, accept, honor, nominate, .recognize, attend, hand
21634 | 0.92 N

1627 attempt v
noun study, .suicide, government, researcher, article, theory, scientist, regime, .smile, pass, educator, .comeback, coup, difficulty, explanation _misc_ .explain, .create, .address, .determine
21209 | 0.93 A

1628 commitment n
adj strong, long-term, organizational, political, personal, financial, religious, serious, civil, deep _noun_ time, level, government, family, value, kind, goal, lack, policy, resource _verb_ make, require, demonstrate, maintain, honor, reaffirm, increase, fulfill, involve, .improve
21469 | 0.92 A

1629 consequence n
adj negative, unintended, serious, social, economic, political, possible, long-term, environmental, potential _noun_ action, health, decision, war, use, cause, act, tax, violence, responsibility. _verb_ suffer, face, consider, understand, result, deal, accept, fear, evaluate, arise
21555 | 0.92 A

1630 instruction n
adj effective, traditional, religious, public, basic, clear, written, special, formal, daily _noun_ student, teacher, classroom, music, curriculum, skill, language, art, method, quality. _verb_ give, follow, provide, receive, read, include, offer, improve, contain, emphasize
23222 | 0.85 A

1631 surprise n
adj big, great, pleasant, full, complete, total, nice, huge _noun_ .attack, element, .party, .visit, look, bit,

team, .guest, .announcement, birthday _verb_ come, take, catch, express, discover, imagine, blink, register, .await, .lurk
20511 | 0.96

1632 poll n
adj recent, late, public, tracking, nationwide, online, informal, scientific, internal, accurate _noun_ opinion, percent, .number, news, voter, week, exit, result, straw, post. _verb_ show, .find, .conduct, .indicate, .suggest, .close, .release, lead, vote, base
21952 | 0.90 S

1633 favorite j
noun food, place, song, book, movie, spot, part, restaurant, show, color, recipe, story _misc_ my, his, your, one, her, our, all-time, Italian
20917 | 0.94 M

1634 explore v
noun way, study, issue, .possibility, student, .relationship, research, opportunity, article, idea, .option, area, .difference, theme, experience _misc_ .between, far, .whether, .possible, fully
21441 | 0.92 A

1635 predict v
noun model, year, analyst, theory, .behavior, .outcome, expert, .performance, variable, level, hypothesis, regression, result, effect, weather _misc_ .future, difficult, hard, accurately, significantly, able.
21171 | 0.93 A

1636 adopt v
noun child, policy, state, approach, strategy, resolution, standard, rule, system, government, measure, program, law, .baby, model _misc_ .by, new, .similar, recently, widely.
21303 | 0.93 A

1637 sight n
adj plain, common, pretty, beautiful, familiar, strange, rare, mere _noun_ .sound, line, end, love, .smell, sense, land, touch, relief, .hearing _verb_ lose, catch, set, hide, drop, disappear, stay, .behold, stun, freeze
21086 | 0.93 F

1638 storm n
adj tropical, perfect, severe, powerful, violent, electrical, coming, approaching _noun_ desert, operation, .surge, .cloud, dust, wind, winter, water, ice, .drain _verb_ hit, weather, .move, .blow, .pass, ride, .rage, .sweep, survive, track
20886 | 0.94

1639 half n
adj other, bottom, low, upper, remaining, front, forgotten _noun_ year, .century, hour, .season, week, .life, minute, decade, month, mile _verb_ cut, place, complete, divide, shape, fold, separate, arrange, dominate, wrap
20344 | 0.97

1640 assessment n
adj national, environmental, educational, functional, comprehensive, accurate, initial, authentic, dynamic, general _noun_ student, risk, program, process, performance, teacher, .tool, method, technology, .procedure _verb_ include, need, provide, conduct, base, develop, agree, .determine, identify, indicate
24158 | 0.81 A

1641 weather *n*
adj bad, cold, hot, national, cool, dry, severe, wet, local, nice *noun* .condition, .service, .pattern, .report, .forecast, winter., news., change, .station *verb* .turn, predict, .permit, check., .warm, affect, .clear, .cooperate, fly, control.
20802 | 0.94 M

1642 pocket *n*
adj deep, front, inside, full, left, inner, rear, deeper, outside, secret *noun* hand., money, jacket, back., coat, shirt., breast., pant, key, change *verb* reach., pull, stuff, dig., slip., line., fill, pat., empty.
21573 | 0.91 F

1643 aid *n*
adj financial, foreign, federal, military, humanitarian, international, economic, visual, navigational, mechanical *noun* hearing., .program, state, .worker, food., student, .agency, government, .package, development *verb* give, provide., receive., cut., send, offer, enlist., reduce, grant, extend
21330 | 0.92

1644 reading *n*
adj oral, close, low, careful, accurate, required, suggested, repeated *noun* student, skill, book, .program, math, writing, text, test, score, level *verb* teach., base, suggest, improve, indicate, enjoy, promote., encourage, assess, record
21849 | 0.90 A

1645 thin *j*
noun air, layer, line, man, slice, hair, strip, face, lip, film, woman, skin *misc* very, too, tall, .wear, long, cut, white, stretch
21292 | 0.92 F

1646 soul *n*
adj human, poor, lost, very, living, immortal, single, gentle, troubled, lonely *noun* heart., body, .mate, .food, man, spirit, mind, music, .singer *verb* save., sell., lose, search, rest, bare., feed., bless., free, .depart
20805 | 0.94

1647 strange *j*
noun thing, man, way, place, world, land, woman, voice, feeling, look, creature *misc* very, seem, feel, something, sound, happen, little
21199 | 0.92 F

1648 married *j*
noun year, couple, woman, man, child, life, people, mother, daughter, wife, son, sister *misc* never, happily, live, single, young, stay, after, before
20613 | 0.95

1649 organize *v*
noun group, community, conference, party, union, exhibition, event, worker, effort, information, meeting, society, committee, .protest, team *misc* .by, help., .around, .themselves, highly., local, international
20894 | 0.93 A

1650 conclusion *n*
adj different, similar, foregone, logical, successful, final, obvious, opposite, inescapable, future *noun* study, result, finding, discussion, summary, .article, student, court, researcher, survey *verb* come., draw, reach., lead., jump., support, arrive., suggest, present, .emerge
21728 | 0.90 A

1651 fuel *n*
adj alternative, nuclear, spent, clean, better, liquid, premium, solar, light, synthetic *noun* fossil., .cell, .economy, price, .tank, .efficiency, oil, cost, diesel. *verb* use, burn, run, produce, reduce, add., save., cause, power, generate
21514 | 0.91 M

1652 urban *j*
noun area, development, center, school, housing, population, league, life, setting, community, city, environment *misc* rural, large, suburban, poor, major, especially, industrial, modern
21852 | 0.89 A

1653 belong *v*
noun family, community, .category, party, .class, .generation, individual, past, tribe, .grandmother, .grandfather, tradition, .genus, .realm, .clan *misc* .to, where., like., .exclusively, rightfully., originally.
20214 | 0.96

1654 salt *n*
adj kosher, remaining, coarse, seasoned, excess, warm, cracked, iodized *noun* .pepper, teaspoon, .city, tsp, season., water, cup, sugar, oil., tablespoon *verb* taste, add, sprinkle., stir, combine, mix, remove, contain, dissolve, dry
21872 | 0.89 M

1655 farmer *n*
adj small, poor, organic, white, rural, agricultural, commercial, individual, wealthy, French *noun* .market, land, family, dairy., water, worker, food, peasant., price, rice. *verb* .grow, help., sell, .plant, buy, own, protect, force, .harvest, encourage
21125 | 0.92

1656 straight *r*
up, go., .ahead, .out, look., .into, your, .down, head., keep., set., stare., sit.
20943 | 0.93 F

1657 advice *n*
adj good, best, legal, medical, financial, bad, practical, professional, sound *noun* expert, piece., people, doctor, .consent, information, word., lawyer, investment., bit. *verb* give, offer., take., follow., ask., seek., provide.
20284 | 0.96

1658 cover *n*
adj front, thick, heavy, tattered, protective, dense, outer *noun* .story, magazine, book, album., cloud., ground., .letter, forest., .girl *verb* pull, run., provide., appear., feature, remove, blow, dive.
20404 | 0.95

1659 balance *n*
adj delicate, right, better, proper, perfect, competitive, appropriate *noun* .power, .sheet, check., trade, .payment, account, sense., energy, budget *verb* keep., strike., maintain., lose., find., achieve., hang., tip., shift, restore.
20432 | 0.95

1660 temperature *n*
adj high, low, warm, cool, average, global, internal, ambient, constant, frigid *noun* room., .degree, water, body., air., surface., pressure, change, .humidity, range *verb* .drop, rise, serve, reach, raise., increase, maintain., reduce., lower., measure
21456 | 0.90 M

1661 empty *j*
noun room, space, house, bottle, seat, glass, street, chair, lot, table, stomach, box *misc* sit, except, nearly, stand, fill, almost, half
21424 | 0.90 F

1662 conclude *v*
noun study., report., court., researcher., author., agreement, research, article, .discussion, evidence, committee., review, treaty, series, deal *misc* lead., therefore, reasonable., recently., reasonably.
20839 | 0.93 A

1663 somehow *r*
.manage, seem, feel, yet., .survive, connect, notion., .escape, somewhere, sense, .involved, .responsible, familiar, alive
20505 | 0.94 F

1664 presidential *j*
noun candidate, election, campaign, race, year, debate, nomination, nominee, politics, party, palace, primary *misc* democratic, during, Republican, former, win, hopeful, vice
21184 | 0.91 S

1665 limit *n*
adj upper, legal, low, outer, human, certain, federal, physical, current, maximum *noun* time., speed., city., size, sky., .power, age., bag., .growth *verb* set, push., reach., impose, exceed., put., test., place, stretch., determine
20341 | 0.95

1666 prime *j*
noun minister, time, example, suspect, target, mover, rib, candidate, rate, spot, estate, source *misc* Israeli, former, British, Palestinian, Iraqi, Japanese, past
20717 | 0.93

1667 breast *n*
adj small, left, boneless, large, skinless, full, right, developing, bare, firm *noun* .cancer, chicken., woman, risk, .implant, .milk, .pocket *verb* diagnose., die, touch., remove, develop., cover, prevent., press, place, reveal
20953 | 0.92 M

1668 desk *n*
adj front, wooden, empty, cluttered, antique, messy, built-in *noun* chair, drawer, paper, office, .clerk, computer, phone, reception., .lamp, wall *verb* sit., stand, lean, reach, seat., cross, return., place, push, approach.
21658 | 0.89 F

1669 record *v*
noun song, album, data, tape, camera., history, number, conversation, information, music, event, studio, video, sound, response *misc* each, ever., secretly., live, observe., digital, daily, previously.
20514 | 0.94

1670 breath *n*
adj deep, long, fresh, short, bad, hot, slow, quick, warm, sharp *noun* .air, shortness., life, intake., .throat, .mint, baby., .test *verb* take., hold., catch., draw., let, gasp., suck., smell, blow, mutter.
22136 | 0.87 F

1671 theater *n*
adj musical, local, national, regional, public, live *noun* movie., .company, music, art, film, home., street, center, community, dance *verb* open, enter, arrive, study, attend., feature, release., restore, host, seat
21078 | 0.91 N

1672 under *r*
.way, child., just., .year, .pressure, percent, .condition, age, foot, free, already., .circumstance
19934 | 0.97

1673 acknowledge *v*
noun official., author., .problem, .role, .importance, .need, .presence, .existence, .contribution, .support, .mistake, .reality, administration, .assistance, failure *misc* refuse., gratefully., fail., publicly, widely.
20322 | 0.95

1674 theme *n*
adj common, major, central, main, recurring, dominant, broad, religious, general, consistent *noun* .park, .song, variation, .music, year, campaign, book, edition., category, .restaurant *verb* .emerge, identify, develop, explore, reflect, consider., focus, return., echo, base
20779 | 0.93 A

1675 fat *n*
adj saturated, total, low, excess, dietary, extra, visible *noun* protein, carbohydrate., .cholesterol, .mg, percent., body., gram., diet, .sodium, .percentage *verb* eat, cut, trim., reduce, burn., contain, skim., eliminate., convert, shed.
22790 | 0.84 M

1676 software *n*
adj available, free, educational, special, commercial, sophisticated, open-source, proprietary *noun* computer., company, hardware, .program, system, .package, application, .developer, maker, business *verb* use, develop, .allow, sell, install, create, write, include, buy., .enable
22665 | 0.85 M

1677 sugar *n*
adj brown, powdered, granulated, dietary, remaining, refined, simple, added, natural, raw *noun* cup, tablespoon, teaspoon, blood., salt, fiber., butter, egg, flour, water *verb* add, beat, stir, combine., .dissolve, sprinkle., mix, melt, sift, reduce
21768 | 0.88 M

1678 educational *j*
noun program, system, institution, student, opportunity, service, experience, level, research, reform, need, process *misc* provide, social, national, cultural, economic, develop, special, current
23326 | 0.82 A

1679 thousand *m*
hundred., .year, .dollar, several., two., more, than., ten., .people, five., few., three., .mile
20420 | 0.94

1680 code *n*
adj genetic, moral, penal, secret, military, uniform, criminal, internal, civil, cultural *noun* tax., zip., .ethics, .conduct, dress., building., area., .word *verb* break., write, require, enter., violate., crack., adopt, develop, enforce, specify
20461 | 0.94 A

1681 fear *v*
noun .safety, official., reason., death, other, .loss, expert., critic., leader., .attack, .consequence, resident., violence, scientist., opponent.
misc nothing., .lose, bad, .itself, hate, anger, .tread, respect, greatly.
19737 | 0.97

1682 connect *v*
noun computer, •dot, line, network, community, cable, other, wire, bridge•, road•, ability•, phone, web, machine, feeling *misc* •with, directly, closely•, intimately•, deeply•
20011 | 0.96

1683 yellow *j*
noun light, page, flower, eye, jacket, color, pepper, hair, ribbon, leaf, fever, onion *misc* red, blue, white, green, bright, black, pale, wear
20822 | 0.92 F

1684 instrument *n*
adj musical, different, scientific, financial, traditional, available, various, blunt, stringed, surgical *noun* survey•, assessment•, •panel, policy, study, use, validity, measurement, reliability, percussion• *verb* play, •measure, develop, design, •assess, carry, complete, contain, identify, •detect
22286 | 0.86 A

1685 Japanese *j*
noun company, government, market, car, American, people, woman, firm, garden, economy
21018 | 0.91

1686 panel *n*
adj solar, advisory, three-judge, intergovernmental, front, top, independent, bottom, legal, flat
noun control•, expert, member, •discussion, side•, instrument•, report, •change, •climate *verb* open, •recommend, review, install, appoint, join, convene, assemble, •conclude, select
20573 | 0.93

1687 library *n*
adj public, local, presidential, main, central, digital, extensive, virtual, academic, educational *noun* school•, book, university, research, museum, collection, program, branch, science, •card *verb* build, •contain, visit•, enter, house, access, search, browse•, stock, store
20718 | 0.92

1688 expensive *j*
noun car, system, home, equipment, drug, suit, treatment, item, model, restaurant, option, product *misc* more, most, less, very, too, than, least, buy
20038 | 0.95

1689 emotional *j*
noun support, problem, response, state, issue, experience, abuse, reaction, distress, need, development, stress *misc* physical, very, social, behavioral, mental, psychological, spiritual
20745 | 0.92 A

1690 engine *n*
adj powerful, four-cylinder, economic, main, standard, available, internal-combustion, clean, electronic, 4-cylinder *noun* search•, car, diesel•, jet•, fire•, •room, steam•, combustion• *verb* start, turn, run, drive, cut, shut, power, build, •roar, kill•
21600 | 0.88 M

1691 propose *v*
noun president•, plan, tax, model, theory, legislation, solution, change, administration•, idea, amendment, Republican, project, rule, approach *misc* •by, cut, alternative, •billion, originally•, recently•
20316 | 0.94 A

1692 mental *j*
noun health, illness, service, retardation, disorder, state, problem, hospital, professional, care, abuse, note *misc* physical, national, emotional, social, severe, suffer, serious, treat
21102 | 0.90 A

1693 difficulty *n*
adj great, technical, financial, economic, social, serious, major, emotional, practical, significant
noun student, level, task, learning, •breathing, language, degree•, relationship, behavior *verb* have•, face, experience•, encounter, cause•, create, overcome, •arise, report•, •identify
20810 | 0.91 A

---

14. Weather

Adjectives and verbs (note that the frequency refers to overall use, not just with respect to weather)

hot 52712, cold 51641, cool 35515, warm 34999, dry 32046, mild 6968, sunny 4941, damp 4711, icy 3083, chilly 1918, windy 1859, cloudy 1355, humid 1252, foggy 952, overcast 689, scorching 271, partly cloudy 74

Nouns and verbs or adjectives

rain 28596, snow 26192, flood 13093, (shower) 11357, (hail) 4419, thunder 4244, drizzle 1960

Nouns

season *n* 80369, sun 46227, (heat) 44781, wind *n* 40853, ice 30754, sky 30548, storm 24060, temperature 22386, cloud 20058, (dust) 17282, (climate) 16409, hurricane 11113, breeze 6379, (forecast) 6229, lightning 5628, (fog) 5307, drought 4243, rainbow 3848, sunshine 3223, (haze) 2413, avalanche 2120, tornado 2045, humidity 1960, pollen 1637, (thermometer) 1561, blizzard 1509, thunderstorm 1304, Fahrenheit 1259, precipitation 1125, (smog) 1067, (dew) 1045, snowflake 1022, Celsius 917, snowstorm 861, meteorologist 754, cyclone 733, (sunburn) 692, monsoon 670, downpour 564, raindrop 549, barometer 543, sleet 521, (slush) 495, rainstorm 469, heat wave 453, air pressure 346, meteorology 258, wind chill 242

1694 train *n*
adj high-speed, electric, runaway, elevated, express, moving, oncoming *noun* .station, car, track, freight., .wreck, .thought, commuter., .ride *verb* take, run, stop, .pull, .move, board., catch., travel, arrive, wait
20258 | 0.94 F

1695 brown *j*
noun hair, eye, sugar, paper, rice, bag, skin, dwarf, face, trout, leather, bear *misc* until, dark, golden, light, black, white, turn, wear
20699 | 0.92 F

1696 basically *r*
.same, .conservative, .sort, .unchanged, bunch, .decent, .harmless, .identical, intact, .irrelevant, .lazy
21463 | 0.88 S

1697 last *v*
noun .year, .day, .hour, .month, .minute, .week, .lifetime, marriage., war., period, .decade, session., trial., interview., relationship. *misc* long, will., .than, only, .about, .until, .forever
19548 | 0.97

1698 average *n*
adj national, industrial, grade-point, annual, long-term, daily, weighted *noun* percent, year, point, grade., batting., hour, state., score, month, industry. *verb* spend, compare, earn., pay., rise, fall, cost, drop, increase., receive
20567 | 0.92

1699 ring *n*
adj key, outer, concentric, polar, golden, inner, nice, familiar, dark *noun* phone., wedding., .finger, diamond., engagement., gold., bell *verb* wear., answer, form, remove., enter., surround, place, slip, step., blow.
20264 | 0.93 F

1700 mark *v*
noun .anniversary, year, .end, .beginning, .point, .spot, line, event, .change, .boundary, .start, moment, .location, sign, calendar *misc* .by, .first, .turning, clearly., .significant
    out path, boundary, territory, line, place **off** space, area, boundary **up** .price, .bill, .cost
19703 | 0.96

1701 locate *v*
noun area, city, town, community, source, .street, building, county, island, object, .target, gene, .origin, .prey, .relative *misc* .near, .within, .outside, centrally., able., conveniently., unable.
20170 | 0.94 A

1702 search *n*
adj desperate, thorough, extensive, quick, frantic, massive, nationwide, house-to-house, intrusive *noun* .result, .engine, .warrant, job., .truth, Internet., .team, talent., .committee *verb* modify., begin, conduct, .narrow, continue, launch., obtain., execute, .reveal, complete
20867 | 0.91

1703 largely *r*
.because, remain., .ignore, base, due, result, .responsible, depend., .determine, thanks, .unknown
20452 | 0.92 A

1704 possibly *r*
can., how., .even, quite., everything., .imagine, except., .due, .dangerous, thousand, hundred, soon, .illegal, .greatest
19355 | 0.97

1705 anymore *r*
do, not., want, talk., anything., care., around., nothing., nobody., matter., exist., hardly., worry., bother.
20087 | 0.94 F

1706 generate *v*
noun revenue, electricity, power, heat, .interest, energy, income, idea, money, job, business, information, force, field, ability. *misc* .more, .million, enough, economic, .additional, .significant
20596 | 0.91 A

1707 regional *j*
noun center, office, director, power, government, development, level, security, cooperation, conflict, company, organization *misc* local, national, global, economic, international, such, base, environmental
21475 | 0.88 A

1708 obvious *j*
noun reason, question, answer, way, problem, thing, difference, choice, example, fact, sign, solution *misc* most, become, seem, less, pretty, despite, quite
19452 | 0.97

1709 angry *j*
noun man, voice, woman, face, letter, mob, parent, crowd, word, voter, response, look *misc* get, very, feel, frustrate, sad, sometimes, sound, frustrated
19908 | 0.94 F

1710 analyst *n*
adj political, senior, military, financial, legal, retail, western, foreign, Chinese, top *noun* industry., news., policy., security, research, stock, company, intelligence. *verb* .believe, .predict, .estimate, .agree, .project, .forecast, .doubt, .cite, .blame, .attribute
21212 | 0.89 N

1711 accident *n*
adj fatal, serious, tragic, terrible, involved, nuclear, freak, unfortunate *noun* car., traffic., automobile., auto., scene, victim, rate, month, investigation, motorcycle. *verb* .happen, kill, die., cause, .occur, .involve, injure, prevent., investigate., suffer
19511 | 0.96

1712 trend *n*
adj current, recent, growing, general, economic, long-term, social, significant, major, downward *noun* year, population, industry, .line, analysis, fashion, change, development, use, rate *verb* continue, reverse., follow., reflect, identify, indicate, buck., .emerge, accelerate
20395 | 0.92 A

1713 like *j*
noun family, mind, manner, heaven, magic, chocolate, paradise *misc* feel, sound, it, what, taste, know, more, imagine, hey, wow, oh, rather
19781 | 0.95 S

1714 appearance *n*
adj physical, public, personal, outward, sudden, recent, rare, brief, final *noun* court., television, TV,

guest., tournament., bowl., .impropriety, show,
cameo. _verb_ make., give., change, .last, create.,
avoid., improve., maintain., .deceive, mark
19537 | 0.96

1715 currently _r_
.work, .available, .under, .about, .serve, .exist, .operate,
.employ, .professor, .enroll, .underway, .popular,
.involved
20028 | 0.94 A

1716 shadow _n_
adj long, dark, deep, gray, pale, warm, soft, faint,
mere, strange _noun_ light, eye, man, sun, .doubt,
moon, area, earth, pattern, .death _verb_ cast, move,
.fall, stand, live., watch, throw., emerge., hide.,
create
21052 | 0.89 F

1717 being _n_
adj human, living, spiritual, very, natural, rational,
divine, well, entire, Supreme _noun_ God, nature,
animal, earth, creature, dignity, core., machine,
universe, existence _verb_ treat, .possess, clone.,
transform, inhabit, deserve, evolve, distinguish,
murder, function
20208 | 0.93 A

1718 moon _n_
adj full, new, blue, bright, pale, waning, rising
noun sun, earth, star, planet, crescent., night, light,
surface, sky, phase _verb_ .rise, .pass, walk., .shine,
.hang, land., fly., shoot, orbit, discover
21622 | 0.86 F

1719 bridge _n_
adj covered, wooden, narrow, flying, key, swinging,
downtown, enclosed, burning _noun_ road, river, .nose,
street, building, highway, suspension., railroad., .club
verb build, cross., play., .span, .connect, jump., drive.,
burn., .link, form
19795 | 0.94

1720 but _i_
.also, .for, .rather, nothing., necessarily, .nonetheless,
.now, .reason, everything., truth, .moment, wear.,
.sake, whole
19260 | 0.97

1721 recommend _v_
noun doctor., expert., commission., committee., .use,
book, report., change, treatment, health, panel.,
.patient, stock, guideline, approach _misc_ highly.,
strongly., far, advisory., generally., additional,
specifically
19985 | 0.93 M

1722 hearing _n_
adj public, congressional, preliminary, fair,
conductive, normal, closed, televised, extensive
noun .loss, committee., Senate, .aid, confirmation.,
court, .room _verb_ hold., schedule, testify., conduct,
attend., .determine, plan., request., demand,
.last
20240 | 0.92 S

1723 fruit _n_
adj fresh, dried, ripe, whole, tropical, sweet, forbidden,
raw, rotten, colorful _noun_ .vegetable, tree, .juice,
flower, .salad, bowl, .fly, piece., citrus, food _verb_ eat.,
bear., pick, produce, enjoy., sell, contain, taste, ripen,
bore.
20496 | 0.91 M

1724 dance _n_
adj modern, traditional, slow, popular, square,
aerobic, creative, contemporary _noun_ .floor, music,
song, .company, education, .club, .class, .hall,
theater, sun. _verb_ perform, teach, feature, attend.,
choreograph, study., celebrate, accompany, spin,
sponsor
20305 | 0.92

1725 shift _v_
noun focus, .weight, .gear, attention, power, eye, gaze,
emphasis, .position, paradigm., .seat, burden, .chair,
wind. _misc_ .from, .away, .toward, .slightly,
.uncomfortably
19429 | 0.96

1726 comfortable _j_
noun life, chair, home, room, place, seat,
position, talking, shoe, environment, bed, skin
misc with, feel, more, make, very, most, become,
enough
19446 | 0.96

1727 struggle _v_
noun year, .foot, .control, team., .sense, .weight,
season, .breath, identity, economy, .balance, decade,
.survival, offense, .depression _misc_ .with, .against,
.keep, .find
19318 | 0.96

1728 revenue _n_
adj internal, annual, total, gross, lost, net, additional,
increased, significant, current _noun_ tax., percent, year,
.service, company, oil., .growth, source, advertising.,
.stream _verb_ generate, increase, raise., .rise, share,
.grow, lose, expect, .fall, report
21098 | 0.88 N

1729 notion _n_
adj whole, very, traditional, preconceived, popular,
romantic, western, vague, individual _noun_ .woman,
.art, community, .identity, culture, .truth, .freedom,
.reality, .democracy, .self _verb_ support., reject., base.,
challenge., accept., reinforce., dismiss., dispel.,
embrace., scoff.
20237 | 0.92 A

1730 okay _r_
say, .let, well, yeah, right, .so, oh., .thanks, .maybe,
yes, fine, nod
21976 | 0.84 F

1731 package _n_
adj economic, whole, total, comprehensive,
statistical, complete, entire, special _noun_ software.,
stimulus., part., .direction, aid., tax, reform, benefit
verb .include, offer, open, send, pass, sell, buy.,
.contain, receive., .drain
19588 | 0.95

1732 ought _v_
noun government., law, Congress., tax, Democrat.,
constitution., judgment, notion. _misc_ .to, think.,
.able, something, maybe., really.
20497 | 0.90 S

1733 traffic _n_
adj heavy, oncoming, rush-hour, increased,
commercial, vehicular, blocking _noun_ air., .jam, .light,
highway., .congestion, .control, street, .safety, road,
.controller _verb_ stop, stick., direct., reduce, cause,
slow, close., handle., .flow, speed
19684 | 0.94 N

1734 internal *j*
noun consistency, revenue, affair, control, reliability, medicine, security, conflict, investigation, structure, organ, problem *misc* external, own, political, within, both, bleeding, well, adequate
20602 | 0.90 A

1735 prefer *v*
noun other, term, American., customer., majority., consumer., soil, version, client, participant., solution, investor., gentleman., .shade, setting *misc* instead, .stay, .avoid, generally.
19294 | 0.96

1736 crew *n*
adj live, whole, entire, experienced, wrecking, two-man, fellow *noun* .member, .chief, camera., passenger, flight., film., ship, TV., rest. *verb* send, .arrive, .prepare, cast, hire, gather, clean, head, order, .survive
19491 | 0.95

1737 search *v*
noun eye, police., house, room, .face, area, home, .answer, Internet, car, .information, database, web, .evidence, .clue *misc* .for, .through, continue., frantically, desperately, online, pause.
19161 | 0.96

1738 profit *n*
adj high, big, net, huge, low, annual, gross, fourth-quarter, average, quick *noun* .margin, company, percent, year, loss, growth, .motive, market, oil *verb* make., turn., earn, increase, .rise, sell, report., share, maximize., expect
20533 | 0.90 N

1739 regulation *n*
adj federal, new, environmental, strict, proposed, current, public, stringent, international, tough *noun* government., state, rule., law, safety., industry, cost, effect, use, agency *verb* require, enforce., .govern, issue, allow, comply., impose, implement, violate., .protect
21170 | 0.87 A

1740 link *v*
noun evidence., system, study., network, site, computer, cancer, arm, web, death, health, disease, .crime, communication., behavior *misc* closely., directly, inextricably., intimately., common, strongly.
  up .with, .other, country, organization, eventually., company., .again, .dispersed, line.
19706 | 0.93 A

1741 thinking *n*
adj critical, wishful, creative, positive, current, higher-order, divergent, strategic, reflective, independent *noun* way., .skill, student, style, kind., process, type., ability *verb* remember., stop., change, develop, teach, influence., promote, stimulate., relate, define
19885 | 0.92 A

1742 hardly *r*
can., .any, .ever, seem, .at, .anyone, .notice, .believe, .all, .surprising, .anything, .wait, .matter, though.
19316 | 0.95

1743 airport *n*
adj international, national, busy, regional, intercontinental, commercial, municipal, crowded,

congested *noun* security, city, flight, plane, terminal, hotel, runway, .official, mile, hour *verb* drive., arrive., land., fly, build, close, head., shut, check, travel
19704 | 0.93 N

1744 human *n*
adj modern, basic, fellow, physical, similar, normal, living, genetic, capable, dangerous *noun* animal, .right, way, .resource, species, study, environment, relationship, space, service *verb* .remain, .live, .need, cause, create, eat, evolve, infect, test., treat
19900 | 0.92

1745 extremely *r*
.important, .difficult, .well, .high, .rare, .low, .dangerous, .hard, .popular, .sensitive, .valuable, .useful
19033 | 0.96

1746 sick *j*
noun people, child, day, man, stomach, person, kid, patient, leave, hospital, care, baby *misc* get, make, feel, tired, too, die, poor
19432 | 0.94 F

1747 capture *v*
noun .attention, .imagination, image, camera, .moment, .essence, soldier, force, .spirit, .heart, troop., light, picture, army, event *misc* try., kill, fail., order., perfectly, easily.
19320 | 0.95

1748 unique *j*
noun opportunity, way, experience, feature, need, situation, characteristic, position, history, perspective, style, challenge *misc* its, each, own, provide, offer, among, create, because
19616 | 0.93 A

1749 actual *j*
noun number, behavior, practice, experience, cost, event, performance, world, fact, data, size, work *misc* between, base, than, physical, rather, reflect, potential
19768 | 0.93 A

1750 chest *n*
adj bare, upper, broad, flat, wooden, hairy, muscular *noun* arm, pain, hand, head, shoulder, heart, .drawer, back, knee., hair *verb* open, fall, hit., fold., lift, clutch., touch, cross., beat., rise
20474 | 0.89 F

1751 meal *n*
adj hot, delicious, home-cooked, favorite, quick, easy, ready, light, fine, daily *noun* .day, family, evening., restaurant, .plan, fish, corn, .preparation, midday., hotel *verb* eat, prepare, serve, cook., include, enjoy., share, provide, finish, .consist
19633 | 0.93 M

1752 beauty *n*
adj natural, sleeping, physical, inner, sheer, feminine, scenic *noun* .beast, .queen, .pageant, .salon, .shop, .contest, .parlor, truth, nature, .product *verb* appreciate., enjoy., capture., admire., celebrate., reveal, discover., surround, experience., inspire
19302 | 0.95

1753 extent *n*
adj great, certain, large, lesser, full, possible, true, limited, considerable, maximum *noun* nature, .damage, power, .individual, .injury, participant,

.involvement, type, .drug, respondent _verb_ determine., depend., assess., examine., indicate., measure., reveal., realize., vary, rely
20356 | 0.90 A

1754 defend _v_
noun right, .country, .interest, position, .title, .action, .decision, lawyer,. .charge, .freedom, .territory, .policy, court, force, administration _misc_ .against, .themselves, .himself, .itself, .ourselves, .herself, .myself, .yourself, able., protect, successfully., prepare., vigorously
19112 | 0.95

1755 visitor _n_
adj foreign, frequent, first-time, regular, annual, casual, unique, unexpected, European, distinguished
noun .center, park, .bureau, year, convention., museum, number., tour _verb_ draw., allow., attract., greet., receive., offer, welcome., .enter, .arrive, invite
19826 | 0.92

1756 outside _r_
go., step., wait., inside, stand, walk, sit, play, hear, door, car, street, cold, rain
19815 | 0.92 F

1757 judge _v_
noun court,. other, success, .quality, contest, behavior, .distance, .character, panel _misc_ .by, .whether, .harshly, .yourself, difficult., .rule, .solely, fairly, .order
18928 | 0.96

1758 dozen _m_
a., half., more, than., two., about., .year, .other, least., several., few., three., nearly., couple.
19160 | 0.95

1759 declare _v_
noun .war, state, president, .emergency, .independence, court., .victory, .bankruptcy, government, law, .winner, Congress, republic, judge., .intention _misc_ .dead, .unconstitutional, officially., federal, publicly, openly., Soviet, formally.
19095 | 0.95

1760 emergency _n_
adj medical, federal, national, humanitarian, dire, complex, supplemental, spiritual, life-threatening, cardiac _noun_ .room, state., .service, .management, hospital, .response, .department, .agency, .care
verb declare., provide., respond, handle., prepare., deal, treat, .arise
19008 | 0.96

1761 ad _n_
adj negative, political, full-page, personal, classified, local, running, online, effective, help-wanted
noun campaign., TV., newspaper, television, .agency, radio., attack., .revenue _verb_ run, place, show, .feature, appear, answer., buy., sell, read, air
19503 | 0.93

1762 truly _r_
.believe, .love, .understand, yours., only., .remarkable, .amazing, .sorry, .global, .free, .appreciate, .happy, .effective
18718 | 0.97

1763 planet _n_
adj red, giant, entire, minor, distant, whole, lonely, blue _noun_ star, .earth, moon, surface, sun, orbit, atmosphere, home., formation, image _verb_ form,

save., discover, explore., destroy, study, circle, .shine, photograph, revolve
21762 | 0.83 M

1764 select _v_
noun student, school, study, teacher, participant, team, site, item, player, option, member, criterion, candidate, .basis, material _misc_ randomly., .because, each, .best, carefully., .appropriate, .random, .represent
19974 | 0.91 A

1765 ethnic _j_
noun group, minority, identity, cleansing, background, conflict, community, difference, diversity, study, line, member _misc_ racial, other, religious, cultural, different, among, between, political
21133 | 0.86 A

1766 nose _n_
adj long, runny, red, broken, bloody, sharp, straight, stuffy _noun_ eye, mouth, ear, bridge., face, lip, hair, .throat, tip., chin _verb_ blow., wrinkle., hold., break, wipe., turn, thumb., stick., touch, .bleed
19999 | 0.91 F

1767 loan _n_
adj federal, bad, small, real, low-interest, home-equity, low, personal, private, foreign _noun_ saving., bank, student., home., .program, percent, .guarantee
verb make, pay, repay, provide, offer, receive., secure, finance, qualify., default.
19858 | 0.91 N

1768 cash _n_
adj extra, hard, free, cold, ready, petty, quick
noun .flow, .register, company, stock, money, .payment, .crop, amount., .value, dollar. _verb_ pay, raise., buy, receive., generate, offer, carry, stash, convert, borrow
19618 | 0.92 N

1769 contribution _n_
adj significant, important, political, major, unique, valuable, positive, corporate, relative, greatest
noun campaign., study, .field, limit, money, woman, .development, employer, employee, .understanding
verb make, receive, recognize., include, acknowledge., accept., reduce, increase, influence, .total
19610 | 0.92 A

1770 slow _j_
noun motion, process, growth, pace, progress, start, speed, movement, rate, death, cooker, breath
misc too, very, steady, long, little, fast, deep
18858 | 0.96

1771 contrast _n_
adj sharp, stark, marked, striking, direct, dramatic, interesting, visual _noun_ color, study, group, image, effect, finding, comparison, brightness, shadow
verb stand., provide., draw, present, strike, enhance, adjust., sharpen., heighten.
20040 | 0.90 A

1772 bottle _n_
adj empty, little, broken, brown, blue, expensive, dark, French, unopened, chilled _noun_ wine, water, beer, glass, plastic., champagne, whiskey, cap _verb_ drink, open., hold., fill, throw, buy., bring., pick., grab., pour
19746 | 0.91 F

1773 launch _v_
noun .attack, .campaign, program, year, missile, .investigation, .career, satellite, company, war, rocket,

effort, business, operation, force *misc* .into, .new, .against, plan., recently.
19015 | 0.95

1774 novel *n*
adj new, historical, late, recent, best-selling, graphic, literary, autobiographical, previous, later *noun* story, author, character, romance., mystery., detective., reader, fiction, page, title *verb* write, read, publish, base, finish., .feature, adapt., complete., inspire, .explore
20743 | 0.87 A

1775 feature *v*
noun show., music, program, ad., series., story, .article, magazine, event., artist, art, festival., video, photo, performance *misc* prominently, local, special, live, musical, popular, original, contemporary, regularly.
19638 | 0.91 M N

1776 duty *n*
adj active, military, double, civic, moral, heavy, constitutional, patriotic *noun* tour., right., line., sense., officer, jury., guard., call. *verb* perform., report, include, .protect, carry., assign, assume., return., fulfill.
18740 | 0.96

1777 root *n*
adj square, cultural, historical, ginger, religious, ancient, Latin, shallow, common, southern *noun* .cause, tree, grass, .problem, .beer, .system, .vegetable, .cellar *verb* take., grow, trace., return., lie, dig, address., form, sink., spread
19114 | 0.94

1778 content *n*
adj fat, sexual, specific, academic, emotional, entire, recycled, intellectual *noun* table., .issue, course, form, moisture., curriculum, image(s)., water, knowledge, heart. *verb* teach, determine, relate, empty., examine., pour., analyze, vary, focus, reveal
19905 | 0.90 A

1779 component *n*
adj important, key, major, principal, essential, critical, various, different, social, individual *noun* system, program, analysis, part, education, factor, travel., teacher, skill, development *verb* include, .highlight, identify, add, consist, contain, describe, represent, involve, incorporate.
20592 | 0.87 A

1780 appreciate *v*
noun .fact, .value, morning, .effort, call, .help, opportunity, .beauty, .concern, .importance, insight, fan, audience, gentleman., reader *misc* we., .your, much, really., fully., understand., join, greatly.
18938 | 0.95 S

1781 circumstance *n*
adj certain, different, normal, difficult, special, similar, best, economic, social, unusual *noun* life, set., .death, family, fact, kind, pomp., victim., .birth *verb* .surround, change, depend., adapt., face, reflect, .permit, arise, imagine, justify
18962 | 0.95 A

1782 teaching *n*
adj effective, social, traditional, Christian, professional, direct, full-time *noun* student, .experience, .learning, year., teacher, method, practice, research, .strategy, job *verb* improve.,

develop, relate, focus, enhance, evaluate., reflect, emphasize, accept., enter.
22201 | 0.81 A

1783 paint *v*
noun .picture, wall, portrait, color, artist., house, face, scene, landscape, room, canvas, mural, image, figure, window *misc* .bright, brightly., draw, .dark, freshly.
22212 | 0.81 M

1784 matter *v*
noun thing., issue., size, race, character., opinion., detail., .me, .whit, .nationality *misc* do., it., what, really., .much, .how, .whether, no.
18701 | 0.96

1785 thick *j*
noun hair, inch, glass, air, layer, wall, smoke, skin, cloud, tree, fog, slice *misc* through, black, too, white, until, dark, cover, wear
19520 | 0.92 F

1786 cat *n*
adj black, fat, feral, stray, dead, gray, orange, cool *noun* dog, .scan, .food, .mouse, house, eye, animal, .hat, owner, .litter *verb* eat, kill, feed., .jump, chase, purr, pet., stroke., .lick, skin.
19463 | 0.92 F

1787 neither *r*
.nor, .I, .anyone, .deny, .confirm, .necessary, disagree, .male, .fully, .female, .entirely, .desirable, .practical, .sufficient
18788 | 0.95

1788 standard *j*
noun deviation, means, procedure, model, practice, score, time, equipment, error, oil, test, feature *misc* poor, use, mean, include, available, above, below, eastern
19472 | 0.92 A

1789 ourselves *p*
we, our, find., other, ask., must., protect., defend., allow., remind., each, commit., kid., prepare.
18625 | 0.96

1790 correct *j*
noun answer, response, number, way, word, position, percentage, decision, interpretation, name, term, sequence *misc* that, politically, yes, absolutely, prove, incorrect, quite, OK
19298 | 0.92 S

1791 warn *v*
noun official., president, .danger, expert., doctor., report, leader, analyst., Iraq, department., scientist., Congress, attack, .consequence, .American *misc* .that, .against, repeatedly, .away, fail, careful, recently
18533 | 0.96

1792 capacity *n*
adj human, excess, full, limited, mental, generating, total, nuclear, intellectual, productive *noun* carrying., percent, state, production., storage., power, plant, building, stadium., transmission. *verb* increase., develop, build, fill, reduce, expand., exceed, lack., measure, influence
19719 | 0.90 A

1793 challenge *v*
noun student, court, .authority, .assumption, law, .notion, idea, .view, policy, party, .status, lawsuit, rule,

Republican, practice _misc_ ∎traditional, directly, physically∎, seriously∎, successfully∎
18787 | 0.95 A

1794 convention _n_
adj national, democratic, international, annual, Baptist, constitutional, social _noun_ ∎center, Republican∎, party, ∎visitor, delegate, framework∎, speech, week, climate, nation∎ _verb_ attend∎, ratify, follow∎, address∎, cover∎, sign, nominate, adopt, violate∎, define
19520 | 0.91

1795 politician _n_
adj local, black, prominent, professional, popular, leading, Iraqi, Catholic, civilian, Japanese _noun_ party, state, journalist, bureaucrat, career∎, media, businessman, public, opposition∎, voter _verb_ elect, ∎seek, ignore, ∎promise, trust, debate, criticize, complain, favor, warn
19040 | 0.94

1796 pursue _v_
noun ∎career, policy, ∎goal, ∎interest, strategy, case, ∎dream, ∎degree, government∎, ∎education, ∎study, opportunity, ∎agenda, research, option _misc_ ∎own, continue∎, aggressively, decide∎, actively∎, vigorously
18700 | 0.95 A

1797 setting _n_
adj urban, social, different, natural, educational, rural, clinical, physical, academic, public _noun_ school∎, ∎sun, classroom∎, goal∎, student, education∎, community∎, group, teacher _verb_ provide, place∎, occur, adjust, apply∎, enhance, employ, function∎, prefer, emphasize
20182 | 0.88 A

1798 zone _n_
adj no-fly, free, green, dead, economic, red, demilitarized, coastal, hot, special _noun_ war∎, end∎, time∎, comfort∎, buffer∎, twilight∎, strike∎ _verb_ create, enter∎, establish, enforce∎, extend, expand, declare∎, patrol∎, define, cross
19038 | 0.93

1799 dress _n_
adj black, white, blue, red, pink, beautiful, green, short, yellow, traditional _noun_ ∎code, wedding∎, ∎shirt, silk∎, ∎shoe, ∎rehearsal, cotton∎, cocktail∎ _verb_ wear∎, buy, pull, hang, fit, slip, tear, sew∎, ∎drag, smooth∎
19457 | 0.91 F

1800 pilot _n_
adj American, commercial, private, automatic, military, experienced, allied, Iraqi, Chinese, downed _noun_ ∎program, ∎study, fighter∎, air, airline, ∎project, test _verb_ ∎fly, train, shoot, conduct, land, hire∎, earn, rescue, crash, capture
18592 | 0.96

1801 ensure _v_
noun ∎safety, ∎security, system, ∎success, ∎survival, effort∎, ∎quality, policy, step∎, ∎compliance, process, ∎access, ∎stability, ∎protection, measure∎ _misc_ ∎that, help∎, must∎, order∎, necessary∎, design∎, ∎adequate, ∎proper
19452 | 0.91 A

1802 ultimately _r_
may, ∎lead, ∎decide, decision, ∎prove, ∎result, ∎responsible, ∎fail, ∎determine, ∎depend, consumer, ∎successful, ∎reject
18754 | 0.95 A

1803 male _n_
adj white, black, American, unidentified, likely, adolescent, significant, gay, dominant, single _noun_ female, adult∎, difference∎, percent, number∎, ∎athlete, alpha∎, gender∎, sample, participant _verb_ compare, ∎tend, mate, differ, dominate, consist∎, compete, ∎participate, attract, observe
20497 | 0.87 A

1804 wake _v_
noun morning, sleep, sound, dawn, baby, ∎start, nightmare, nap, sun, noise, alarm, afternoon, midnight, ∎neighbor, noon _misc_ ∎early, later, asleep∎, suddenly, ∎realize, late, ∎cold, sleeping, loud∎, dream, doze∎, ∎abruptly
   up morning, one, day, next, ∎early, ∎realize, asleep∎, suddenly, ∎smell, tomorrow
19458 | 0.91 F

1805 shirt _n_
adj white, blue, red, striped, button-down, clean, Hawaiian _noun_ pant, ∎tie, ∎pocket, flannel∎, polo∎, collar, cotton∎, suit∎, sleeve, plaid∎ _verb_ wear∎, pull, tuck, unbutton, hang, buy, lift, lose∎, ∎reveal
19666 | 0.90 F

1806 influence _v_
noun factor∎, ∎decision, behavior, ∎policy, power∎, attitude, ∎development, perception, ∎outcome, variable∎, ability, ∎choice, ∎performance, experience, other _misc_ ∎by, may∎, strongly∎, heavily∎, greatly∎, directly∎
19872 | 0.89 A

1807 guide _n_
adj complete, practical, comprehensive, useful, spiritual, reliable, rough, native, blind _noun_ tour∎, field∎, teacher, dog, shopping∎, food∎, curriculum∎, ∎detail, buyer∎ _verb_ provide, serve∎, publish, offer, hire∎, list, act∎, travel, hike, consult∎
19113 | 0.92 M

1808 AIDS _n_
adj global, pediatric, experimental _noun_ ∎virus, people∎, ∎patient, ∎epidemic, case, hearing∎, research _verb_ die∎, cause∎, infect∎, fight∎, treat, develop, contract∎, spread, devastate, ravage
19212 | 0.92

1809 mix _v_
noun bowl∎, water, ingredient, color, flour, oil, sugar, salt, egg, juice, pepper, paint, salad, cheese, ∎drink _misc_ ∎with, ∎well, ∎together, until, add, thoroughly, racially∎
   up get∎, ∎with, ∎together, ∎batter, ∎workout, ∎routine, ∎drink **in** ∎with, sugar, ∎among, seed
19005 | 0.93 M

1810 slip _v_
noun hand, door, finger, ∎arm, bed, shoe, ∎crack, mind, glass, shoulder, floor, ring, note, ice, ∎seat _misc_ ∎into, ∎out, ∎away, ∎through, ∎back, ∎down, ∎under, let∎, ∎inside, ∎around
   out ∎back, ∎under, quietly **in** ∎out, ∎behind, ∎beside
19468 | 0.91 F

1811 steal _v_
noun car, money, ∎base, ∎show, ∎glance, thief∎, ∎food, election, idea, ∎secret, drug, ∎thunder, credit, store, stuff _misc_ ∎from, try∎, ∎away, anything, report∎, lie, sell, allegedly∎
18626 | 0.95

15. Opposites

The following table shows the frequency of contrasting adjectives. Note that some words have two meanings (*hard* = "not soft, not easy"; indicated with an asterisk) and so the overall frequency is divided between those two meanings. In addition, alternative pairings could have been made (*big* and *small*, rather than *big* and *little*). Also, note also that in most cases, the positive adjective is more frequent that the negative one.

A	B	Freq A	Freq B
new	old *	412599	176437
good	bad	340107	81546
big	little	170192	143787
large	small	106013	149164
young	old *	123335	176437
black	white	144769	121598
high	low	170119	58493
long	short	127704	51440
public	private	115783	59623
right *	left	121603	48762
right *	wrong	121603	56902
same	different	216686	156775
best	worst	119724	21565
early	late	82845	58174
easy	hard *	51416	72349
soft	hard *	24693	72349
better	worse	80561	25607
possible	impossible	82299	21448
hot	cold	48148	40989
true	false	75708	12469
poor	rich	47468	29900
strong	weak	63185	13467
dead	alive	52981	23234
open	closed	64245	7246
light *	dark	24285	40560
light *	heavy	24285	33698
positive	negative	37951	25934
happy	sad	45445	14764
modern	ancient	37188	19019
close	far	41992	14052
wide	narrow	32226	15893
beautiful	ugly	38432	8246
powerful	weak	32071	13467
interesting	boring	36026	4702
deep	shallow	32457	5891

1812 late *r*
as, .night, too., .last, .year, .afternoon, stay., day,
until., work., in., arrive., .week
18305 | 0.96

1813 frequently *r*
more., most., use, less., occur, stir., .cite, mention,
appear, .used
19160 | 0.92 A

1814 blame *v*
noun problem, .victim, government, death, other,
media, official, Congress, .failure, Republican,
Democrat, .lack, .loss, attack, critic *misc* .her, .him,
themselves, .everything
18312 | 0.96

1815 sheet *n*
adj white, clean, thin, prepared, single, top, blank,
baking, folded, soft *noun* .paper, balance., cookie.,
ice, .music, .metal *verb* place, cover, pull, lay, wrap,
remove., line, cut, contain, lie
18891 | 0.93

1816 estimate *v*
noun .percent, year, .number, official., study.,
model, earnings, expert., rate, value, analyst., size,
department., loss, researcher. *misc* .million, cost,
.about, .billion, total, .approximately
19041 | 0.92 A

1817 relief *n*
adj great, humanitarian, international, comic, federal,
temporary, welcome, sharp *noun* tax., sigh., .effort,
.worker, pain, .agency, disaster. *verb* provide., feel,
breathe., bring., seek., offer., express., .flood, .wash,
organize
18149 | 0.96

1818 combination *n*
adj different, various, possible, right, unique, rare,
unusual, perfect, powerful, strange *noun* .factor,
drug, color, .therapy, variable, .lock, method, speed,
.element, characteristic *verb* use., offer., involve.,
result, contain., test, consist, employ., mix
18592 | 0.94 A

1819 investor *n*
adj foreign, individual, institutional, small, private,
potential, real, long-term, financial, average
noun stock, fund, group, .confidence, share, bond,
value, interest, investment, estate. *verb* .buy, sell,
attract., own, seek, protect., recommend., advise.,
close., scare.
20674 | 0.85 M N

1820 due *i*
(due to) .to, may., .fact, .lack, high, change,
difference, part., loss, effect, largely., partly.,
increase, low
19540 | 0.89 A

1821 silence *n*
adj long, awkward, stunned, dead, uncomfortable,
sudden, total, complete, eerie, deafening
noun moment, minute, sound, code., second,
wall., conspiracy. *verb* break, sit., .follow, fall, fill,
stand., walk., listen, eat., drive.
19621 | 0.89 F

1822 manner *n*
adj good, similar, timely, consistent, bad,
appropriate, efficient, following, professional,

traditional *noun* table., bedside., .death, style, speech,
comedy., custom *verb* .speak, act., teach., behave.,
respond., mind., proceed., address, dress, handle
18618 | 0.94 A

1823 muscle *n*
adj abdominal, strong, low, smooth, skeletal, lean,
tight, pulled, increased, taut *noun* .group, back,
bone, body, heart, strength, .mass, tissue, arm, .cell
verb use, build., flex., relax, help, stretch, move,
strengthen., cause, contract
20417 | 0.85 M

1824 branch *n*
adj legislative, broken, olive, judicial, local, military,
dead, bare, various, green *noun* executive., tree,
.government, bank, .office, library, spring., .manager
verb open, hang, cut, close, remove, snap, bend,
swing, establish., extend
18239 | 0.96

1825 chain *n*
adj large, big, key, retail, fast-food, major, heavy,
complex, golden, nuclear *noun* food., store,
.command, .reaction, link, gold., restaurant, supply.,
.event *verb* break, set, pull, hang, wear., own, form,
attach, bind, dangle
18272 | 0.95

1826 long *c*
(as long as) as, for., stay, keep, .remember, live,
remain, continue, last, fine., month, hour, alive, care
17843 | 0.98

1827 telephone *n*
adj cellular, local, long-distance, mobile, regular,
unlisted, cordless, standard *noun* .number,
.company, .interview, .line, .service, .conversation,
.pole *verb* .call, use., .ring, talk, answer., pick.,
speak., receive., return., disconnect
18398 | 0.95

1828 investigate *v*
noun study., case, police., research., .effect,
committee., commission., .relationship, department,
.allegation, researcher., .crime, issue, .complaint,
.matter *misc* .whether, far, begin., .possible,
thoroughly, independent., fully
18608 | 0.93 A

1829 German *j*
noun government, shepherd, army, company,
chancellor, soldier, troop, state, unification, force,
society, Jew
19061 | 0.91 A

1830 percentage *n*
adj high, small, large, low, total, great, daily,
certain, significant, winning *noun* .point, .student,
table, .population, .people, time, .woman, rate,
increase, .respondent *verb* show., report, win.,
represent., indicate, spend, express., decline,
reflect., .range
19099 | 0.91 A

1831 outcome *n*
adj positive, negative, possible, important, successful,
desired, likely, final, better, academic *noun* student,
.measure, .variable, health., election, learning.,
treatment, program, performance, result *verb* affect.,
determine, predict., influence., achieve, produce.,
improve., lead., report, depend
20363 | 0.85 A

1832 estate *n*
adj real, commercial, entire, sprawling, taxable, royal, palatial, gated, marital *noun* .agent, .tax, .market, .investment, .developer, .broker, company, business, .trust, value *verb* sell, buy, own, invest, settle, manage, handle, repeal, preserve., acquire
18892 | 0.92 N

1833 forth *r*
back, so., set., put., bring., move., rock., .across, hold., pace., swing., walk.
18154 | 0.96

1834 stress *n*
adj high, post-traumatic, normal, physical, emotional, psychological, posttraumatic, environmental, chronic, acute *noun* level, .disorder, life, source., .management, .hormone, job, anxiety, factor, effect. *verb* reduce., cause, cope, experience, deal., relieve., increase, handle., affect, result
19658 | 0.88 A

1835 equal *j*
noun opportunity, right, protection, number, woman, amount, access, part, time, employment, footing, value *misc* all, create, great, roughly, approximately, less, separate
18554 | 0.93 A

1836 English *j*
noun language, teacher, class, word, literature, translation, department, professor, subtitle, proficiency, muffin
18560 | 0.93

1837 welfare *n*
adj social, public, federal, general, economic, corporate, human *noun* .reform, child, state, .system, .recipient, .program, health., .benefit, mother *verb* cut, end., receive, reduce, promote., sign, increase, force, depend, contribute.
19016 | 0.91

1838 typical *j*
noun day, student, family, school, case, example, home, pattern, response, fashion, behavior *misc* American, fairly, describe, pretty, male, suburban, normal
18354 | 0.94

1839 crazy *j*
noun people, thing, man, guy, Horse, idea, woman, kid, stuff, person, love, quilt *misc* go, drive, think, like, me, little, sound
18588 | 0.93 F

1840 except *i*
.for, all., .when, no., nothing., everything., anything., .few, .perhaps, every., .where, .maybe, everyone.
18133 | 0.95 F

1841 funny *j*
noun thing, way, story, guy, man, joke, face, movie, look, girl, name, stuff *misc* think, very, so, really, something, happen, pretty
18577 | 0.93

1842 meat *n*
adj red, fresh, raw, white, lean, dark, dead *noun* fish, .poultry, vegetable, piece., .product, bone, food, .loaf, chicken, milk *verb* eat., cook, add, sell, buy, remove, produce, cover, brown, taste
18474 | 0.94

1843 appeal *n*
adj broad, strong, popular, mass, universal, criminal, emotional, commercial, pending, final *noun* court, state, sex., board, right, .process, .panel, trial, .voter, audience *verb* file, hear, lose., uphold, overturn, reject, broaden., limit, issue, respond.
18316 | 0.94

1844 long-term *j*
noun care, effect, goal, interest, rate, relationship, problem, study, investment, contract, health, plan *misc* short-term, economic, require, financial, serious, environmental, ensure, immediate
18745 | 0.92 A

1845 official *j*
noun policy, government, language, record, agency, position, report, news, document, statement, church, history *misc* according, receive, despite, Soviet, unofficial, Chinese, involved, familiar, Catholic
18295 | 0.94

1846 eliminate *v*
noun .need, job, tax, problem, program, .possibility, .risk, .use, plan., process, .threat, .weapon, position, .barrier, .deficit *misc* reduce, completely, virtually., .altogether, entirely
18364 | 0.94

1847 used *j*
noun car, book, oil, equipment, computer, method, condom, technique, bookstore, vehicle, instrument, clothing *misc* to, get, most, widely, commonly, buy, frequently, sell
17653 | 0.97

1848 motion *n*
adj slow, circular, constant, forward, smooth, perpetual, major, orbital *noun* .picture, range., hand, .sickness, .control, .art, summary, fluid., .science, .sensor *verb* set., file, .dismiss, deny, grant., detect, measure., introduce, .proceed, induce
18468 | 0.93

1849 complain *v*
noun official, critic., .pain, parent., resident., patient., worker., police, neighbor., customer., .headache, .chest, mayor, .difficulty, .boss *misc* .that, .about, never, .bitterly, often, .loudly, nobody.
17795 | 0.96

1850 row *n*
adj front, neat, top, bottom, double, middle, green, orderly, parallel, bright *noun* death., year., .house, back., seat, .inmate, skid. *verb* sit., stand, line, walk., plant, arrange., fill, lay, hang, form
18067 | 0.95

1851 Jewish *j*
noun community, people, state, settlement, family, woman, center, group, identity, life, settler, population
18699 | 0.92

1852 kick *v*
noun door, .ass, leg, .butt, foot, .ball, .goal, .shoe, .habit, .heel, .gear, wind., season, boot, wall *misc* .out, .scream, .hard, punch, hit
off .shoe, season, .campaign, tour, .series, festival, .boot, .sandal, tomorrow **up** dust, wind., .heel, .cloud, dirt, storm, .sand, .fuss, breeze. **in** until, instinct., engine., hormone., coverage., insurance., machine., adrenaline.
18347 | 0.93 F

1853 snow *n*
adj white, heavy, deep, fresh, cold, soft, wet, light, falling, packed *noun* ice, foot, rain, winter, wind, inch., mountain, .ground, .pea, storm *verb* .fall, melt, cover, blow, watch, pile, drift, swirl, fill, lie
19283 | 0.89 F M

1854 producer *n*
adj large, independent, senior, leading, associate, foreign, commercial, primary, Japanese, organic *noun* executive., director, show, film, oil., television., writer, TV., record. *verb* compete, benefit, enable., team, credit, co-write, nominate, subsidize, import, collaborate
18514 | 0.92

1855 solve *v*
noun .problem, mystery, case, .crime, puzzle, .crisis, .murder, .riddle, .dilemma, .conflict, approach., technology *misc* help., try., able., .environmental, difficult, alone, quickly, order., easily
17867 | 0.96

1856 just *j*
noun day, thought, hope, war, wish, cause, society, money, business, compensation *misc* I, me, more, maybe, than, sort, fair, sorry
18122 | 0.94 S

1857 issue *v*
noun .statement, report, order, .warning, permit, court., government, president., company, department, subpoena, judge., press, .ruling, decision *misc* .by, public, recently., civil., state, newly., official, refuse., .release, immediately., .declare, .following
18018 | 0.95

1858 opposition *n*
adj political, strong, public, main, organized, growing, direct, serious *noun* .party, leader, .group, government, force, .war, .movement, .candidate, regime, support *verb* face., lead, express., meet., voice., reach., encounter., .claim, mount, accuse
18871 | 0.90 A

1859 basketball *n*
adj professional, pro, Olympic, greatest, collegiate, high-school, indoor *noun* .team, .player, .game, college., .coach, woman., football, .court, man., school *verb* play., watch, love, shoot, dribble, bounce, dunk., retire
19420 | 0.88 N

1860 rely *v*
noun system, court, method, industry, technique, strategy, computer, approach, .judgment, resource, agency, analysis, .memory, firm., .help *misc* .heavily, .upon, instead, must., .solely, often.
on can., people, must., many, when, come., company, only, American, trust
18056 | 0.94 A

1861 conservative *j*
noun Republican, party, group, Democrat, estimate, movement, leader, court, member, view, government, voter *misc* more, very, most, liberal, political, Christian, religious, moderate
18208 | 0.93

1862 trust *v*
noun God, government, .instinct, .judgment, banker., bank, voter, .gut, politician, .intuition, .stranger, .secret, physician, investor. *misc* can., .me, .him,

never., someone, .anyone, learn., .other, .each, enough, whom., .anybody, completely
17761 | 0.96

1863 back *v*
noun .claim, car, government, file, door, .corner, force, plan, truck, .wall, step, administration, Republican, .threat, loan *misc* .by, .away, .out, .down, .against, .toward
up .claim, right., .against, data, traffic, evidence, truck, .file, slowly, .assertion **off** .bit, slowly, immediately, ought.
17771 | 0.95

1864 address *n*
adj inaugural, public, full, presidential, televised, forwarding, postal, known *noun* e-mail., name., state., number, union., .phone, .book, radio., .correspondence *verb* give., deliver, include., send, list, mail., check., .concern, contain, type
17987 | 0.94

1865 mirror *n*
adj primary, rear-view, full-length, secondary, one-way, two-way, tiny, side-view, outside *noun* rearview., .image, face, reflection, bathroom., wall, side, telescope, view., glass *verb* reflect, hold, stare, check, hang, glance., adjust, place, shatter, flash
18611 | 0.91 F

1866 tank *n*
adj septic, Israeli, full, Iraqi, Soviet, heavy, empty, external, holding, Russian *noun* fuel., gas, water, think., .top, storage., fish. *verb* fill, .roll, fire, destroy, hit, leak, explode, .contain, attack, replace
17841 | 0.95

1867 range *v*
noun age, scale., price, size, score., .percent, rate., response., estimate., variety., temperature., value., color, sample., length *misc* .from, .between, .low, .strongly, whose., widely
18596 | 0.91 A

1868 significantly *r*
.than, .more, .high, .different, .low, increase, .reduce, differ., group, .relate, score
20101 | 0.84 A

1869 somewhat *r*
.more, .than, .different, .less, .similar, likely, appear., .surprising, .difficult, .better, .limit, .surprised, .differently
17674 | 0.96

1870 attract *v*
noun .attention, people, .student, business, .customer, .investment, .audience, .interest, .visitor, .crowd, .tourist, .support, .capital, .investor, ability. *misc* .more, .new, .young, .large, .foreign, .million, hope., enough, order., likely., .hundred
17755 | 0.95

1871 anywhere *r*
go., can., from, .else, .near, .world, never., almost., .without, anytime, anything, anyone., .earth
17548 | 0.97

1872 regime *n*
adj military, new, communist, authoritarian, political, international, democratic, old, totalitarian, current *noun* .change, control, support, trade., opposition,

legitimacy, sanction., apartheid., inspection.
verb overthrow., topple., impose., oppose.,
force, threaten, .collapse, undermine, survive,
challenge
20101 | 0.84 A

1873 fix *v*
noun .problem, eye, thing, gaze, car, .hair, .dinner,
price, mind, .hole *misc* try., everything, .broken,
.upon, broke., firmly, fast, easily
   up .house, get., home, .old, .building, .apartment,
buy., .property, clean, .neighborhood
17660 | 0.96

1874 entirely *r*
not., .different, almost., .new, something., .possible,
.clear, .sure, else., depend., focus., base, matter,
disappear
17626 | 0.96

1875 afford *v*
noun .opportunity, protection, parent., .care,
.insurance, .view, luxury, .cost, .lawyer, .access,
treatment, .payment, .rent, freedom, pleasure
misc can., .to, not., able., .pay, .buy, simply.
17410 | 0.97

1876 length *n*
adj great, focal, full, short, entire, average, total,
overall, available, extraordinary *noun* .time, arm.,
inch, foot, .cm, .stay, width, hair, .service, clarity
verb run., cut., edit., increase, measure., vary, walk.,
extend., range
18327 | 0.92

1877 secret *n*
adj little, dirty, big, top, dark, best-kept, nuclear, open,
guarded, terrible *noun* .success, family, trade., life,
state., company, beauty, identity. *verb* keep., reveal,
share., hold., learn., discover., hide, unlock., whisper,
expose
17602 | 0.96

1878 pleasure *n*
adj great, simple, sexual, real, guilty, pure, greatest,
sheer, sensual, intense *noun* life, pain, business.,
.boat, source., satisfaction, .principle *verb* take., give.,
.meet, enjoy., experience, derive., .welcome, deny.,
smile, express.
17830 | 0.95

1879 file *v*
noun lawsuit, suit, complaint, charge, .bankruptcy,
report, court, claim, .return, .divorce, year, motion,
company, attorney., lawyer. *misc* .against, .federal,
civil, .away, million, .jointly, .seek, recently.
18095 | 0.93 N

1880 tooth *n*
adj white, front, clenched, sharp, sweet, yellow,
bad, perfect, missing, gritted *noun* lip, mouth, gold.,
hair, smile, .nail, face, .fairy, skin, baby. *verb* brush.,
grit., show, bare, clench, grind., .chatter, sink., flash,
stick
18722 | 0.90 F

1881 confirm *v*
noun study, result, finding, suspicion, report, official.,
research, test., diagnosis, data, hypothesis, .presence,
.existence, police, view *misc* .deny, able., .dead, .nor,
recent, neither., refuse., indeed, independently,
merely., officially.
17740 | 0.95

1882 separate *j*
noun way, group, room, state, entity, issue, area,
analysis, bowl, occasion, identity, unit *misc* two,
three, each, four, create, distinct, equal, maintain
17780 | 0.95 A

1883 golden *j*
noun gate, age, state, globe, bridge, year, retriever,
hair, rule, light, eagle, girl *misc* until, brown, bake,
remove, stir, cook, delicious, yellow
18070 | 0.93

1884 photograph *v*
noun .page, camera, detail, image, scene, galaxy,
telescope, photographer, sky, flower, planet, comet,
bear, landscape, visitor *misc* .above, .opposite,
.below, fingerprint, bright
20866 | 0.81 M

1885 meanwhile *r*
.continue, minute., .prepare, heat, oven, aside.,
.combine, .preheat, boil.
17860 | 0.94

1886 except *c*
.for, all., .when, no., nothing., everything., anything.,
.few, .perhaps, every., .where, .maybe, everyone.
17602 | 0.96 F

1887 now *c*
(now that) .that, right., no, especially., realize., clear.,
.mention, .cold, .Saddam, .retire, dollar., 90s.
17711 | 0.95 S

1888 channel *n*
adj clear, local, narrow, main, digital, available, official,
diplomatic, normal, multiple *noun* news, cable., TV,
television, discovery., communication., island,
weather., water, .catfish *verb* change., watch, open,
switch., carry, flip., check., cross., broadcast, air
17759 | 0.94

1889 bedroom *n*
adj spare, single-family, empty, extra, front, closed,
darkened, square, two-story, rear *noun* .door, .night,
master., .window, room, house, floor, wall, bathroom,
kitchen *verb* walk, open, close, enter, sleep, share,
hang, disappear., paint, burst.
18897 | 0.89 F

1890 requirement *n*
adj minimum, federal, legal, specific, basic,
general, environmental, certain, academic,
financial *noun* state, course, education, student,
law, graduation, disclosure., standard, information,
eligibility. *verb* meet., satisfy., impose, comply.,
set, complete., reduce, fulfill., report, apply
19138 | 0.87 A

1891 ancient *j*
noun time, history, world, city, tradition, art, culture,
civilization, site, forest, tree *misc* modern, Greek,
Chinese, Roman, Egyptian, Indian, medieval, study,
contemporary, royal, eastern
18219 | 0.92

1892 coverage *n*
adj universal, live, special, full, medical, extensive,
continuing, complete *noun* media., news.,
health., insurance., press., care, television., drug.
verb provide., continue, offer., receive., watch.,
expand., buy., increase, lack, direct.
18111 | 0.92

1893 trail *n*
adj steep, narrow, easy, scenic, historic, rough, main, cross-country, groomed, marked *noun* campaign., mile, paper., mountain, road, .blazer, map, blood, nature., base. *verb* follow, leave., hike., .lead, walk., blaze., hit., pick, cross, .wind
20886 | 0.8 M

1894 bear *n*
adj black, polar, grizzly, brown, stuffed, golden, defensive, super, still, gummi *noun* .market, .paw, .hug, mountain, season, yard, baby., defense, animal, tree *verb* kill, watch, shoot, hunt, feed, beat, chase, photograph, .roam, load.
18831 | 0.89

1895 host *n*
adj talk-show, whole, conservative, syndicated, annual, popular, gracious, potential, consecrated, live *noun* show., talk., radio., .country, guest, .plant, city, .family *verb* play., feed, infect., solve., offend., interact, .greet, consume, spawn.
17619 | 0.95

1896 his *p*
hand, .own, .head, .wife, .eye, father, face, arm, .mother, shake., .son, .brother, .career, .shoulder
17952 | 0.93 F

1897 check *n*
adj blank, bad, quick, monthly, final, instant, double, internal, constitutional, certified *noun* background., reality., security., system, welfare., manipulation., traveler. *verb* write., keep., send., cash, hold., pay, receive., bounce, sign, cut
17265 | 0.97

1898 stand *n*
adj one-night, strong, tough, thick, firm, principled, courageous, empty *noun* witness., .minute, tree, concession., night., music., roadside. *verb* take., let., sit, hit., .testify, climb., .accuse, hang., .guard, approach.
17576 | 0.95

1899 surgery *n*
adj cosmetic, major, reconstructive, arthroscopic, open-heart, cardiac, orthopedic *noun* plastic., knee, patient, heart., bypass., brain., hospital, cancer, doctor, week *verb* undergo., perform, need, recover., .remove, require, follow., .repair, treat, .correct
18730 | 0.89

1900 perception *n*
adj negative, different, general, visual, physical, common, personal, popular, widespread, environmental *noun* risk, people, child, difference., .reality, study., other, public, depth., value *verb* change, influence, base, affect., assess., examine., create., alter., shape, reinforce.
19254 | 0.87 A

1901 rare *j*
noun case, occasion, species, disease, opportunity, moment, book, event, exception, plant, cancer, bird *misc* very, extremely, such, relatively, medium, quite, increasingly, indeed
17356 | 0.96

1902 struggle *n*
adj political, long, armed, civil, internal, constant, ongoing, daily, ideological, violent *noun* power, class., year, liberation, .independence, freedom, .survival

verb face, engage., .survive, end, wage, lock., reflect., reveal., intensify, resolve
17713 | 0.94 A

1903 era *n*
adj new, modern, early, colonial, bygone, postwar, progressive *noun* war., end., beginning., record, reform, .peace, depression., apartheid., .globalization, swing. *verb* usher., enter., define, .mark, launch., emerge, inaugurate., belong., evoke.
17747 | 0.94

1904 grant *v*
noun right, state, government, permission, court., .status, .interview, .access, authority, .immunity, judge., God., Congress, option, .amnesty *misc* federal, refuse., special, willing.
17409 | 0.96

1905 file *n*
adj single, digital, personal, audio, secret, hard, open, electronic, available, thick *noun* computer, .folder, .cabinet, data, rank., case, name, system, image., program *verb* keep, contain, read, download, send, save, create, store, review., remove
19301 | 0.86 M

1906 ocean *n*
adj deep, open, blue, vast, warm, Indian, gray, living, nearby *noun* .floor, water, view, beach, mile, world, wave, bottom, sea, surface *verb* cross., overlook., swim., sail, protect, form, fly, explore, float., blow
17642 | 0.94

1907 seriously *r*
take., very., more., .consider, too., .injure, .ill, .hurt, .wound, .damage, threat., .enough, .wrong, doubt
16984 | 0.98

1908 clear *v*
noun .throat, .way, head, .name, air, table, .mind, area, .path, smoke., hurdle, sky., road, tree, dust. *misc* .away, once, increasingly., finally., quickly, immediately., abundantly., entirely., equally., completely, fairly.
   up problem, .confusion, try., .misconception, matter, infection, mystery, .misunderstanding, mess, quickly
17424 | 0.95 F

1909 confidence *n*
adj public, great, full, complete, increased, total, growing *noun* consumer., level, .ability, .interval, vote., lot., investor., sense. *verb* give., lose., gain., build., express., restore., inspire., lack., undermine., share
17287 | 0.96

1910 aside *r*
set., put., push., step., brush., pull., leave., toss., money, move., cast., stand., bowl., shove.
17482 | 0.95

1911 tear *n*
adj hot, single, close, silent, sudden, near, unshed, bitter, angry, salty *noun* eye, .gas, .cheek, wear., .joy, verge., trail., sweat., voice, crocodile. *verb* burst., wipe., fill, shed, .stream, .run, feel., .well, break., .roll
18249 | 0.91 F

1912 judgment *n*
adj moral, good, bad, better, poor, final, best, professional *noun* value, summary., day, court, error.,

.call, rush., matter, motion _verb_ make., base, pass., trust., exercise., sit., concur., form., apply, depend
18020 | 0.92 A

1913 industrial _j_
noun revolution, policy, average, country, sector, development, production, park, city, nation, society, area _misc_ commercial, large, agricultural, major, military, modern, urban, economic
18373 | 0.90 A

1914 expectation _n_
adj high, great, low, unrealistic, reasonable, social, realistic, different, future, cultural _noun_ student, people, teacher, performance, role, behavior, level, .success, standard, set. _verb_ meet., exceed., raise., live., create, base, lower., fall., fulfill., establish
18000 | 0.92 A

1915 resolution _n_
adj high, peaceful, spatial, continuing, final, joint, angular _noun_ council., security., conflict, dispute, nation., year., .trust, budget. _verb_ pass, adopt, support, vote., .authorize, approve, require, introduce, .condemn, seek
18030 | 0.92 S A

1916 copy _n_
adj hard, free, original, multiple, single, available, exact, signed, additional, perfect _noun_ .book, transcript., .report, .letter, paper, .editor, .magazine, carbon., .machine, record _verb_ sell., make., send., give., buy., receive., obtain, pick., provide.
17183 | 0.96

1917 wing _n_
adj right, left, white, military, conservative, liberal, broken, blue, huge, tiny _noun_ west., bird, air, chicken., angel., butterfly., .chair, tip, east., leg _verb_ flap, spread, wait., fly, beat, fold, flutter, stretch, extend, sprout
17429 | 0.95

1918 doubt _n_
adj reasonable, serious, lingering, guilty, slight, growing, nagging, considerable, initial, substantial _noun_ .mind, benefit., shadow., fear, guilt, lot, moment., room., outcome, proof. _verb_ cast., leave., raise., express., prove., throw, remove., .exist, .arise, resolve
17122 | 0.96

1919 fun _n_
adj great, little, serious, clean, exciting, plain, pure, sheer _noun_ lot., people, family, kid, game, kind, bit., sun _verb_ have., make., poke., sound., join., miss., .last, spoil.
17380 | 0.95

1920 totally _r_
.different, .out, almost., agree, .wrong, .control, .destroy, .ignore, .dependent, .unacceptable, completely, .disagree, .unexpected
17273 | 0.95 S

1921 pour _v_
noun water, .glass, .mixture, .cup, coffee, money, bowl, wine, oil, pan, .tea, .batter, milk, sauce, blood. _misc_ .into, .over, .through, .himself, hot, until., .onto, billion
out blood., water, .heart, smoke., word., story, .onto, .coffee, .feeling **in** money., water, .through, begin., light., start., sunlight., order., donation. **down** rain., .face, sweat., tear., water., blood., .cheek, .throat
17756 | 0.93 F

1922 gender _n_
adj sexual, social, racial, ethnic, male, female, opposite, masculine, feminine _noun_ .difference, race, age, .role, class, ethnicity, effect, issue, .identity, .gap _verb_ base., examine., indicate, relate, suggest, reveal, differ, influence, exist, perform
19678 | 0.84 A

1923 surprised _j_
noun reaction, expression, smile, glance, observer, joy, onlooker, demonstrator _misc_ I, not, if, see, when, find, how, look
17447 | 0.94 F

1924 beer _n_
adj cold, empty, light, cheap, warm, green, stale _noun_ bottle, wine, can, root., glass, drink, bar, cigarette, case. _verb_ buy., sip., sell, open, order., finish., serve, taste, lift., guzzle.
17755 | 0.93 F

1925 clean _v_
noun .house, room, .air, tooth, street, bathroom, .wound, .toilet, blood, .plate, window, hour _misc_ .after, cook, .off, wash, remove, thoroughly, wipe, properly, feed, easily, dirty, carefully, .contaminated, regularly, paint
up .mess, .after, .act, site, help, .try., .waste, .environment, kitchen, .pollution **out** .closet, .desk, .locker, .garage, .refrigerator, .attic, .barn, .gutter
17226 | 0.96

1926 score _v_
noun run, .touchdown, .goal, student, .team, .victory, player., .hit, average, second, participant., record, measure, .success, play _misc_ .high, .low, each, .significantly, lead, .above, .point, .twice
18663 | 0.88 N

1927 bond _n_
adj municipal, strong, corporate, common, social, short-term, special, emotional, foreign _noun_ .fund, stock., .market, junk., treasury., government., .issue _verb_ buy., sell, form, hold, break, create, .yield, forge, strengthen., .mature
18437 | 0.89 N

1928 plus _i_
cup., year, tablespoon, hour, million, cost, minute, per, .shipping, percent, .additional, tax, four, five
17513 | 0.94 M

1929 debt _n_
adj national, foreign, bad, external, federal, long-term, total, public _noun_ credit, card., interest, payment, .relief, .service, .crisis _verb_ pay., owe, reduce., repay., incur, increase, forgive, carry, rise, accumulate
17687 | 0.93

1930 smart _j_
noun people, guy, card, thing, man, kid, woman, move, way, money, girl, bomb _misc_ very, enough, too, funny, pretty, tough, beautiful, figure
17271 | 0.95

1931 English _n_
adj fluent, standard, plain, broken, perfect, accented, limited _noun_ language, professor., school, word, teacher, math, degree. _verb_ speak., learn., teach., write., translate., read, understand., convey
17256 | 0.95

1932 terrible *j*
noun thing, mistake, time, tragedy, day, problem,
situation, accident, pain, idea, loss, crime
misc something, happen, feel, such, suffer,
sound, awful, horrible
17473 | 0.94 S

1933 witness *n*
adj key, potential, credible, hostile, Christian, silent,
live, independent *noun* .stand, expert., prosecution,
testimony, star., list, evidence, .protection, .program
verb call, .testify, bear., hear, interview, describe,
present, question, identify, tamper
17726 | 0.92 S

1934 reference *n*
adj specific, explicit, historical, direct, future,
particular, personal, sexual, numerous, passing
noun point, frame., .book, .material, .group,
.image(s), case, letter, library *verb* make, include,
provide, contain., check, cite, incorporate.,
define
18000 | 0.91 A

1935 account *v*
noun factor., .difference, variance, model., change,
variable, effect, industry., data, amount, cost,
population., theory., practice, behavior *misc* .for,
which., .about, .more, .only, .nearly, billion
18009 | 0.91 A

1936 separate *v*
noun .entity, parent, wall., line., wife, husband,
distance, fence., space, glass, twin, difference.,
month, .birth, layer *misc* .from, two, each, .himself,
.themselves, difficult.
   out .from, can., .those, difficult., .effect, .fact,
.different, .any
16925 | 0.97

1937 mean *j*
noun score, age, difference, time, value, rating,
number, response, street, length *misc* I, between,
standard, yeah, low, significant, total, significantly
18386 | 0.89 S A

1938 vice *j*
noun president, chairman, candidate, director,
presidency, chair, nominee, principal, chancellor,
minister, debate, president-elect *misc* senior,
presidential, former, general, corporate, serve,
assistant, chief
18027 | 0.91 N

1939 black *n*
adj young, poor, free, southern, African, likely, racial,
middle-class, civil, urban *noun* white, .Hispanics, .sea,
percent, woman, south, number., minority, .Asian,
pitch. *verb* .vote, .move, .represent, exclude, hire,
compare, .tend, admit, treat, register
17531 | 0.93

16. The vocabulary of spoken English

The nearly 80 million words of spoken English in the Corpus of Contemporary American English come
from transcripts of unscripted conversation on radio and television programs such as *Oprah, Geraldo,
The Today Show, 20/20, All Things Considered*, and so on. Searches for phrases such as *I guess that, how
do you, do you think, I mean, ... you know ..., ... well ...*, and *... sure ...* do show that the frequency of
these phrases in the spoken portion of Corpus of Contemporary American English is much higher than
in the other genres, and so these transcripts do reflect spoken English quite well. However, as can be
seen in the following lists, there is still an orientation toward the vocabulary of "media English," which
is not perfectly representative of everyday, informal, conversational English.

The following tables show the most frequent words (grouped by part of speech) that are at least three
times as common (per million words) in the transcripts of spoken English as in the other four genres,
along with the frequency of each lemma (or headword).

[noun] lot $_{82640}$, news $_{53355}$, thanks $_{27123}$, vote $_{17955}$, bit $_{16994}$, troop $_{14793}$, jury $_{13266}$, murder $_{12079}$, poll $_{11787}$,
witness $_{7808}$, terrorism $_{5840}$

[verb] think $_{375655}$, know $_{372469}$, talk $_{107174}$, mean $_{105485}$, happen $_{78171}$, thank $_{62590}$, join $_{34746}$, guess $_{22431}$,
vote $_{16394}$, testify $_{4943}$, convict $_{3432}$, excuse $_{3393}$, tune $_{3156}$, campaign $_{2256}$, rape $_{2084}$, bomb $_{2053}$, prosecute $_{1998}$,
jail $_{1533}$, indict $_{1422}$, veto $_{1376}$

[adjective] interesting $_{15884}$, Iraqi $_{11738}$, correct $_{8920}$, guilty $_{7452}$, OK $_{5501}$, rigid $_{3103}$, terrific $_{2885}$, unbelievable $_{1637}$,
partisan $_{1505}$, undercover $_{1307}$, convicted $_{1044}$, pro-life $_{644}$, teen-age $_{539}$, anti-war $_{463}$

[adverb] well $_{223269}$, very $_{192068}$, here $_{174650}$, really $_{130202}$, right $_{106598}$, today $_{79677}$, all $_{74992}$, actually $_{48585}$, OK $_{45211}$,
tonight $_{30209}$, certainly $_{26699}$, absolutely $_{23671}$, pretty $_{21702}$, ahead $_{17819}$, obviously $_{15837}$, basically $_{14907}$,
tomorrow $_{14593}$, yesterday $_{13648}$, like $_{8675}$, frankly $_{5338}$,

1940 rest v
noun hand, head, arm, eye, minute, .peace, chin,
back, elbow, .second, table, side, body, soul, floor
misc .against, put., .upon, .assured
up while, before, week., need., .tomorrow
17411 | 0.94 F

1941 hero n
adj national, local, unsung, super, tragic, unlikely,
greatest, romantic, genuine, revolutionary
noun war, action., sport., folk., .heroine, role,
.journey, .worship, status _verb_ become., honor, hail.,
celebrate, welcome, regard., rescue, depict., cheer.,
.stride
16967 | 0.96

1942 bomb n
adj atomic, nuclear, dirty, smart, homemade, terrorist,
German, British, guided, thermonuclear _noun_ car.,
time., roadside., .attack, .threat, atom., hydrogen.
verb drop, .explode, kill, use, build., .fall, detonate,
plant, set, hit
17461 | 0.93 S

1943 below i
just., .level, .surface, .average, well., .line, fall., foot.,
far., .poverty, above., percent., price, rate
17037 | 0.95

1944 rating n
adj high, low, mean, overall, favorable, negative,
significant, top, individual, sexual _noun_ approval.,
star, .scale, teacher., percent, .system, credit., TV,
president., parent _verb_ base, receive., determine.,
indicate, compare, average., assign, .drop, earn.,
peer.
18241 | 0.89 A

1945 busy j
noun day, street, schedule, life, man, work,
week, night, season, road, weekend, intersection
misc too, keep, so, very, stay, pretty, extremely,
working
16991 | 0.96

1946 cite v
noun example, study, reason, case, report, evidence,
source, article, .concern, court, official., research,
.lack, author, figure _misc_ .as, often., frequently.,
.above, among, widely.
17602 | 0.92 A

1947 corporation n
adj major, big, multinational, American,
international, private, public, federal, nonprofit,
giant _noun_ government, development., business,
broadcasting, individual, tax, service, insurance.,
money, trust. _verb_ own, .pay, control, operate, form,
benefit, .invest, sue, acquire, .announce
17680 | 0.92

1948 representative n
adj elected, local, national, democratic, congressional,
special, various, federal, official, sole _noun_ house.,
state, US., trade., industry, senator, group, sales.,
service. _verb_ meet, include., send., elect, .vote, pass,
serve, attend, contact., act
17245 | 0.94

1949 everywhere r
there, look, .else, seem, almost., blood., fly., sign.,
everything, .except, note., nowhere, scatter., available.
16825 | 0.96

1950 soil n
adj organic, rich, fertile, moist, poor, well-drained,
foreign _noun_ water, .erosion, plant, surface, moisture,
.conservation, nutrient, .sample, .scientist, type
verb grow, improve, cover, reduce, .contain, increase,
till, enrich, .dry, fill
18942 | 0.86 M A

1951 highway n
adj national, interstate, federal, main, two-lane, busy,
four-lane, coastal _noun_ .safety, road, .traffic, state.,
.administration, .system, .patrol, car, mile, side.
verb drive, build, head, cross, travel, connect, hit.,
block, roll, .link
17290 | 0.94 N

1952 frame n
adj wooden, single, cold, internal, main, lanky, slight
noun time., .reference, .mind, door., window.,
picture., aluminum, .house _verb_ build, enter., fill.,
freeze., hang, fit, lean., exit., feature, extend
18616 | 0.87 M

1953 stretch v
noun arm, leg, hand, .mile, muscle, back, line,
.limit, neck, body, bed, minute, field, exercise, floor
misc .across, .far, .over, .thin, long, .before, .toward,
.beyond
out his, her, arm, .hand, leg, long, .before
17420 | 0.93 F

1954 oppose v
noun .war, group., .abortion, government, president,
.bill, .plan, Republican, .idea, policy, right, Democrat.,
.tax, party, administration _misc_ to, .any, strongly.,
adamantly., vigorously.
17311 | 0.93

1955 Catholic j
noun church, school, bishop, priest, university,
teaching, faith, tradition, charity, community,
theology, family
19014 | 0.85

1956 cloud n
adj dark, white, black, low, thick, gray, red, huge,
heavy, molecular _noun_ dust, sky, .smoke, gas, storm.,
rain, .cover, mushroom., light _verb_ move, form, rise,
.hang, .gather, break, watch., drift, .roll, blow
17792 | 0.91 F

1957 initial j
noun offering, stage, reaction, investment, study,
response, phase, cost, report, step, result, analysis
misc after, during, public, follow, despite, beyond,
minimum
17637 | 0.91 A

1958 variable n
adj dependent, independent, other, demographic,
significant, social, dummy, continuous, key,
environmental _noun_ study, analysis, predictor.,
.table, outcome, number, control., result, criterion.,
set. _verb_ include, relate, measure, examine, affect,
identify, explain, determine
20585 | 0.78 A

1959 essential j
noun part, element, component, oil, service,
ingredient, skill, acid, role, information, feature,
nature _misc_ absolutely, provide, consider, understand,
human, fatty, successful
17651 | 0.91 A

1960 travel *n*
adj international, foreign, corporate, domestic, interstellar, online, independent *noun* .agent, time, air., .office, .agency, business, space. *verb* .highlight, reduce., involve, .cost, specialize, limit, arrange, restrict, facilitate, ease.
17297 | 0.93

1961 improvement *n*
adj significant, continuous, dramatic, environmental, substantial, marked, vast, recent, educational, overall *noun* home., quality, school, performance, program, efficiency, room., system, capital., plan *verb* make, show., need, lead., report., result, suggest., produce., demonstrate., represent.
17645 | 0.91 A

1962 opening *n*
adj grand, narrow, official, tiny, rough, arched, vaginal *noun* .statement, .ceremony, day, door, .night, .line, .scene, .weekend, job., .act *verb* create, attend., celebrate., fill, mark., announce., delay, deliver., block, widen
16605 | 0.97

1963 necessarily *r*
not., do., .mean, .bad, though., .reflect, .involve, .imply, .better, .agree, nor., .order, .represent, .translate
17001 | 0.94 A

1964 nurse *n*
adj registered, social, wet, male, professional, visiting, practical, clinical, licensed, female *noun* doctor., hospital, physician, .practitioner, patient, health, care, school., .aide, association *verb* train, hire, employ, treat, .administer, attend, assist, dress, .rush, recruit
18312 | 0.88

1965 incident *n*
adj isolated, critical, involved, terrorist, whole, particular, alleged, international, single, unfortunate *noun* year, number., report, police, .place, shooting., kind, investigation, fire., response *verb* .occur, .happen, .involve, describe, remember., recall., investigate, relate, .result, discuss.
16741 | 0.96

1966 abortion *n*
adj legal, partial-birth, illegal, surgical, poor, spontaneous, legalized, forced, botched, planned *noun* right, issue, woman, .clinic, law, birth, doctor, ban, decision, debate *verb* perform, oppose., support, choose., legalize., restrict., reduce., prevent, fund., approve
17908 | 0.89 S

1967 divide *v*
noun .group, .number, country, .category, .section, .part, class, cell., .dough, area, community, party, nation, .team, .mixture *misc* .into, by, .between, .among, evenly
up .into, .among, how., all, country, world, money, .task, work, .responsibility
16889 | 0.95 A

1968 aim *v*
noun program., gun, policy., project., study., strategy., research., target, law., camera, weapon, rifle, .audience, pistol, missile *misc* .at, .toward, .directly, primarily, specifically
16671 | 0.96

1969 tired *j*
noun eye, voice, face, leg, muscle, smile, excuse, joke *misc* get, so, too, look, feel, sick, very
17190 | 0.93 F

1970 careful *j*
noun attention, analysis, planning, consideration, study, examination, reading, observation, look, research, scrutiny, monitoring *misc* not, very, about, more, must, need, require, avoid
16476 | 0.97

1971 question *v*
noun police, authority, .value, .wisdom, .motive, critic., .ability, .assumption, other., .decision, official, .validity, expert., .need, analyst. *misc* .whether, .about, one, .why, begin., no., never.
16508 | 0.97

1972 cheap *j*
noun labor, price, shot, stock, oil, land, wine, hotel, energy, plastic, good, import *misc* buy, easy, relatively, sell, expensive, plentiful, abundant, quick
16829 | 0.95

1973 beside *i*
.her, sit., stand., .me, down., bed, kneel., seat., .point, chair, lay., table, walk., lie.
18442 | 0.86 F

1974 apart *r*
fall., tear., foot., far., set., break., inch., pull., rip., year, keep., about., mile., shoulder-width.
16543 | 0.96

1975 criminal *j*
noun justice, case, system, charge, court, investigation, law, activity, record, trial, defense, attorney *misc* against, international, civil, face, federal, file, involve, possible
17007 | 0.93

1976 employ *v*
noun people, worker, strategy, method, technique, study, company, number, measure, technology, industry, firm, force, research, term *misc* .by, .full-time, currently., frequently., gainfully.
17446 | 0.91 A

1977 rush *v*
noun yard, .hospital, door, .room, air, touchdown, .judgment, car, season, .scene, record, .window, ambulance, .passer, .print *misc* .into, .out, .through, .back, .over, .toward, .off, .past, .forward
17217 | 0.92 F

1978 user *n*
adj heavy, current, potential, available, registered, active, likely, average, experienced, industrial *noun* drug., Internet., computer., .fee, .interface, service, site, end. *verb* allow., provide, enable., require, .choose, .access, .download, design, compare, select
18828 | 0.84 A

1979 upper *j*
noun body, side, class, lip, arm, hand, deck, level, limit, back, floor, part *misc* low, left, middle, right, gain, respiratory, along, elementary
16937 | 0.94

1980 winner *n*
adj big, clear, two-time, Grammy, three-time, past, open, annual, semifinal, eventual *noun* game, award.,

prize., year, match, Oscar., trophy. _verb_ pick.,
announce, declare., choose, .receive, produce.,
determine, emerge, finish, .advance
17495 | 0.91 N

1981 fashion n
adj similar, timely, typical, orderly, dramatic, linear,
Italian _noun_ .show, .designer, .magazine .editor,
.model, .statement, .industry _verb_ wear, dress,
behave., respond., proceed., feature, influence,
dictate, unfold., sacrifice.
17011 | 0.93

1982 tip n
adj southern, quick, northern, anonymous, following,
very, helpful, sharp, simple, eastern _noun_ .finger,
.iceberg, .tongue, .nose, news., rod., .island, .tail,
wing, .knife _verb_ offer., follow., touch, share., receive.,
act., press, .ensure
17070 | 0.93 M

1983 apple n
adj big, red, bad, green, golden, fresh, wild, sliced,
chopped, warm _noun_ .computer, .tree, .pie, .juice,
.cider, .orchard, cup, slice, crab. _verb_ eat., add, peel,
pick, compare., buy, cut, place, combine, fill
17098 | 0.93 M

1984 rise n
adj rapid, sharp, dramatic, sea-level, meteoric, recent,
steady _noun_ .fall, price, .power, level, percent, rate,
temperature, sea, crime _verb_ give., let., cause,
contribute., explain., witness., experience.
16718 | 0.95

1985 vast j
noun majority, amount, number, array, area, expanse,
network, space, land, resource, quantity, difference
misc across, empty, right-wing, surround, stretch,
complex, untapped, underground
16519 | 0.96

1986 specifically r
more., design, ask, United States, study, .address,
focus, target, mention, refer, develop, relate, deal, use
17270 | 0.91 A

1987 limited j
noun number, resource, time, amount, government,
use, partnership, access, space, success, edition, range
misc very, only, available, because, offer, within,
remain, due, English
17161 | 0.92 A

1988 enormous j
noun amount, pressure, power, problem, number,
cost, impact, money, potential, energy, change,
success _misc_ create, face, economic, despite, under,
financial, generate
16339 | 0.97

1989 holiday n
adj happy, national, special, Jewish, annual, favorite,
Roman _noun_ .season, weekend, Christmas, .gift,
.shopping, .party, celebration, spirit, sales, card
verb celebrate, spend., enjoy, decorate., observe.,
plan, honor, mark, wish, feature
16928 | 0.93

1990 e-mail n
adj unsolicited, internal, commercial, daily, angry,
incoming, web-based, unwanted _noun_ .address,
.message, phone, call, letter, question, site, .account

verb send., receive., write, read., use, check., answer.,
reach., delete, download
17458 | 0.90

1991 emphasize v
noun .importance, .need, .role, program., point,
approach, study, .aspect, value, skill, development,
teacher, .difference, .relationship, model. _misc_ also.,
shall., tend., strongly, repeatedly, critical, historical,
increasingly.
17548 | 0.90 A

1992 merely r
not., rather., than., instead., .matter, .reflect, beyond.,
.nod, content., .shrug, .means, object, .curious,
.decorative
16881 | 0.93 A

1993 dance v
noun music, night, girl, eye, ballet, .street, light, .tune,
party, couple, rhythm, concert, wedding, .circle, stage
misc .around, sing, .together, .across, drink, naked,
.wildly
16866 | 0.93 F

1994 core n
adj hard, very, expanded, central, inner, common,
urban, solid _noun_ .curriculum, .value, .group,
.business, .area, .issue, .course, .subject, .belief
verb form., lie, focus., identify, remove., surround,
consist, constitute., shake., define
17022 | 0.92 A

1995 match v
noun color, .description, level, performance, age, size,
.need, pattern, speed, sample, profile, shoe, type,
.offer, blood _misc_ .against, mix., closely., perfectly,
exactly, evenly.
   up .with, .well, .against, can., how., quite.,
.perfectly, exactly, DNA., size.
16353 | 0.96

1996 landscape n
adj political, American, cultural, urban, natural, vast,
rural, beautiful, surrounding, changing _noun_ painting,
.architect, .painter, feature, .architecture, change,
.designer, artist, element, desert _verb_ paint, create,
dot, dominate, transform, alter., design, surround,
reveal, define
18274 | 0.86 M

1997 overall j
noun rate, effect, performance, health, score,
rating, quality, level, satisfaction, result, cost, market
misc improve, reduce, increase, low, significant,
economic, contribute
17249 | 0.91 A

1998 golf n
adj miniature, professional, junior, pro, competitive,
amateur, ultimate, virtual _noun_ .course, .club,
.ball, .tournament, game, .cart, tennis, .magazine
verb play., hit., build, swing, enjoy, overlook., rank,
host.
19153 | 0.82 M N

1999 lack v
noun .skill, .power, .resource, .experience, .knowledge,
.ability, .confidence, .motivation, .information,
.awareness, .imagination, .capacity, .understanding,
education, .access _misc_ because., .any, often., due.,
.sufficient, .basic
16748 | 0.94 A

2000 virtually *r*
.all, .every, .no, .impossible, .any, .nothing, .same, .identical, .everything, .everyone, .entire, .eliminate, .unknown
16602 | 0.95

2001 route *n*
adj different, direct, short, main, best, easy, circuitous, scenic *noun* escape., trade., road, bus., mile, map, paper., parade., migration., supply. *verb* take, follow, choose, travel, drive, plan, retrace., head, link, .connect
16850 | 0.93

2002 flow *n*
adj free, steady, natural, constant, current, international, financial, normal, continuous, future *noun* cash., blood., water, information, .rate, traffic, air, ebb. *verb* increase, control., stop., reduce, improve., stem., regulate., slow, produce, .occur
17281 | 0.91 A

2003 fewer *d*
.than, there., .people, far., percent, year, mean., less, minute., .half, .per, five, job, .employee
16711 | 0.94

2004 cable *n*
adj local, fiber-optic, basic, digital, coaxial, regional, optical, premium, live, thin *noun* .network, .TV, .television, .company, .channel, .news, .guy, .system *verb* connect, carry, attach, own, install, broadcast, lay, plug, .snap, hook
17391 | 0.90 N

2005 gate *n*
adj golden, front, main, wooden, wrought-iron, locked, pearly, rear *noun* iron., city, guard, security., heaven, starting., garden, fence, entrance, street *verb* open, close, walk, stand, pass., swing, lock, enter, reach., shut
16808 | 0.93 F

2006 tie *n*
adj close, strong, black, economic, political, social, diplomatic, red, closer, blue *noun* shirt., suit., family, bow., jacket, silk., coat. *verb* wear., maintain., break., sever., cut., loosen, strengthen., straighten., knot, match
16447 | 0.95

2007 proud *j*
noun man, father, parent, mother, moment, son, accomplishment, owner, heritage, achievement, dad, daughter *misc* very, so, feel, too, myself, happy, extremely
16359 | 0.96

2008 promise *n*
adj great, broken, full, empty, future, unfulfilled, greatest, solemn, considerable *noun* campaign., .keeper, president, government, land, lot., hope, exchange., kind, politician *verb* make, keep, hold., show., break., deliver., offer., fulfill, live., .help
16078 | 0.97

2009 dish *n*
adj main, shallow, favorite, dirty, vegetarian, Chinese, covered, deep, individual, light *noun* baking., side., satellite., serving., table, pasta., petri., .towel, casserole., food *verb* wash., serve, bake, cook, prepare, place, cover, eat, set, clear
17295 | 0.90 N

2010 beneath *i*
her, .surface, .foot, .tree, lie., water, skin, eye, ground., hide., floor, bury., lay., earth
17434 | 0.90 F

2011 increased *j*
noun risk, use, demand, level, cost, pressure, rate, number, competition, activity, production, tax *misc* lead, associate, result, because, due, economic, cause
17505 | 0.89 A

2012 succeed *v*
noun president, strategy., candidate., attempt, extent, .chairman, experiment., negotiation., coup., determination., revolution., .expectation, .throne, motivation., perestroika. *misc* if., fail, help., likely., finally., eventually.
16269 | 0.96

2013 barely *r*
can., .enough, year, .hear, .visible, .able, .speak, .move, .notice, .audible, .touch, .above, word, .breathe
16771 | 0.93 F

2014 narrow *j*
noun street, road, eye, path, range, strip, window, room, focus, gap, face, view *misc* through, very, long, down, too, between, along, lead
16485 | 0.94 F

2015 solid *j*
noun waste, ground, foundation, line, evidence, rock, management, wall, wood, base, food, gold *misc* municipal, build, freeze, form, represent, pretty, liquid, hazardous
16453 | 0.94

2016 contemporary *j*
noun art, artist, culture, museum, music, life, society, world, issue, theory, history, center *misc* American, African, political, historical, social, traditional, modern, cultural, native, Christian
17619 | 0.88 A

2017 accuse *v*
noun man., .crime, president, government, .murder, police, official, other, officer., Republican, critic., Democrat, .rape, leader, lawsuit. *misc* .of, .kill, falsely., .sexual, wrongly.
16588 | 0.94 S

2018 unfortunately *r*
.many, .most, fortunately, .none, .neither, documentation
16201 | 0.96

2019 useful *j*
noun information, tool, way, purpose, life, data, thing, model, feature, product, knowledge, work *misc* may, very, more, provide, find, most, prove, might
16963 | 0.91 A

2020 noise *n*
adj loud, white, strange, deafening, joyful, ambient, internal *noun* .level, background., crowd, traffic, engine, sound, .pollution, vibration, wind, street *verb* make., hear., reduce., listen., shout, complain., wake, block., startle, minimize.
16655 | 0.93 F

2021 expose *v*
noun .level, risk, .air, body, .sun, breast, .radiation, .sunlight, .element, material, .weakness, .violence,

.corruption, .virus, condition *misc* .himself, directly, potentially, threaten., completely.
16106 | 0.96

2022 mass *n*
adj critical, solar, dark, total, Catholic, solid, Arab, huddled, daily, poor *noun* body., bone., muscle., .index, land., center., star, sun, air *verb* attend., celebrate, reach., increase, reveal, form, determine, contain, exceed, decrease
16780 | 0.92 A

2023 multiple *j*
noun line, regression, equation, sclerosis, analysis, time, source, choice, intelligence, level, partner, test *misc* use, including, across, involve, require, single, perform, simultaneously
17345 | 0.89 A

2024 vegetable *n*
adj fresh, tender, grilled, whole, organic, roasted, steamed, canned, hot, dark *noun* fruit., .oil, cup, .garden, tablespoon, chicken, .broth, .soup, root., food *verb* eat., grow, add, cook, stir, cut, sell, plant., toss, place
17615 | 0.88 M

2025 seed *n*
adj top, tiny, toasted, whole, dried, green, dry, future, native, hybrid *noun* teaspoon, sesame., mustard., .company, .money, pumpkin., sunflower., poppy., cup *verb* plant, sow, grow, remove, produce, contain, .germinate, add, sell, sprinkle.
17442 | 0.89 M

2026 reject *v*
noun .idea, court., .proposal, .offer, .notion, .argument, .claim, .request, voter., Senate, judge., Congress, .suggestion, view, model *misc* accept., Supreme, explicitly., ultimately., flatly.
16559 | 0.93 A

2027 decline *v*
noun .percent, year, rate, population, number, .request, price., official., company., .offer, stock, level, .invitation, spokesman., .age *misc* .comment, .interview, .discuss, continue., begin.
16709 | 0.93 N

2028 experiment *n*
adj social, human, scientific, early, recent, medical, successful, present, agricultural, controlled *noun* result, laboratory., subject, series., science., animal, .station, field., participant, data *verb* conduct, .show, perform, design, .involve, .test, suggest, .demonstrate, describe, participate.
17293 | 0.89 A

2029 legislation *n*
adj federal, new, proposed, national, environmental, civil, major, similar, pending, recent *noun* piece., Congress, state, year, reform., right, law, passage., crime. *verb* pass, introduce, enact, .require, support, .allow, propose, sign, consider, push.
16795 | 0.92

2030 hat *n*
adj black, top, white, hard, red, wide-brimmed, floppy *noun* straw., cowboy., coat, .head, brim, glove, boot, suit., jacket, fur. *verb* wear., take., put., tip., pull, remove., hang., throw., dress, tie
16700 | 0.92 F

2031 either *d*
.side, .way, one, .case, .party, .end, .direction, candidate, .sex, .alone, .gender, .option, .scenario, mile.
15856 | 0.97

2032 secret *j*
noun service, agent, police, life, weapon, society, place, meeting, code, garden, information *misc* keep, top, reveal, hide, share, Soviet, nuclear, uniformed
16032 | 0.96

2033 massive *j*
noun star, amount, effort, attack, project, program, force, campaign, change, scale, tax, number *misc* cause, military, launch, suffer, despite, result, huge, nuclear, concrete
16126 | 0.96

2034 grass *n*
adj green, tall, long, dry, wet, thick, blue, ornamental, sweet *noun* .root, tree, leaf, blade., field, .clipping, patch., sea., lemon. *verb* .grow, cut., sit, eat., lie., mow, cover, plant, fall, rise
16840 | 0.91 F

2035 definitely *r*
I, .not, most., yes, oh., yeah, something, .worth, .wrong, .interested, trend, weird, sexy, .savor
16443 | 0.94 S

2036 closer *r*
.to, get., move., come., than, step., bring., draw., .home, .together
16441 | 0.94 F

2037 liberal *j*
noun art, Democrat, democracy, party, education, college, group, state, media, policy, view, society *misc* more, democratic, conservative, most, political, social, economic, traditional
16897 | 0.91 A

2038 stir *v*
noun mixture, bowl., sugar, flour, water, ingredient, salt, pepper, .tomato, juice, pot, vanilla, .controversy, memory, breeze *misc* until, .occasionally, add, .constantly, .together, .often, .frequently
up .trouble, .controversy, dust, .more, .memory, feeling, emotion, .hornet, .interest, fear **over** .heat, .medium, .high, .low, cook., pan.
18009 | 0.85 M

2039 captain *n*
adj assistant, marine, retired, veteran, defensive, Dutch, experienced *noun* team, ship, sea., army, police., boat, crew, navy., .cook, .industry *verb* name, .order, nod, shout, reply, promote., .sail, command, retire, appoint
17024 | 0.90 F

2040 revolution *n*
adj American, industrial, cultural, French, sexual, green, social *noun* war, information., world, technology, Republican., computer., communication, .minute *verb* .begin, lead, .occur, fight, .transform, launch, .sweep, undergo., spark., export.
16576 | 0.93 A

2041 typically *r*
.include, .less, cost, .require, .involve, .occur, .associate, .range, .last, charge, month, hour, .contain, .consist
16714 | 0.92 A

2042 sector n
adj private, public, industrial, financial, agricultural, economic, informal, commercial, social, various _noun_ .economy, service., manufacturing., state, government, business, energy., industry, job, growth _verb_ employ, expand, .account, dominate, affect, encourage, divide., operate, organize, .decline
17801 | 0.86 A

2043 hand v
noun .card, paper, .glass, money, .phone, .key, .envelope, bag, .cup, box, .letter, bill, .bottle, .note, .piece _misc_ .him, .her, .me, .down, .them, .back, off, empty, .pink, .joint
   over .power, .money, .control, .key, .weapon, .check, document, simply. **out** .free, .card, award, money, .condom, .flyer, .leaflet, .copy
16723 | 0.92 F

2044 approve v
noun plan, Congress, FDA, drug, voter, board, state, Senate, .use, committee, bill, council, president, city, resolution _misc_ .by, .million, .billion, already., recently., unanimously, .disapprove, overwhelmingly.
16261 | 0.94 N

2045 uncle n
adj young, favorite, rich, maternal, dear, beloved, paternal _noun_ aunt, father, cousin, brother, mother, house, grandfather, sister _verb_ .die, remember., visit, cry, own, nod, marry, belong., yell, inherit
17464 | 0.88 F

2046 volume n
adj high, large, low, sheer, total, huge, full, slim _noun_ water, sales, traffic, trade, .material, space, increase, .control, page, trading. _verb_ turn., speak., publish, reduce., include, produce, contain, handle., fill, rise
16379 | 0.93 A

2047 explanation n
adj possible, simple, alternative, plausible, only, likely, scientific, detailed _noun_ .finding, .difference, error., .phenomenon, number, word, kind, .event, sense, description _verb_ offer, give, provide., require, suggest, accept., demand., .lie, .account, satisfy
16551 | 0.92 A

2048 sentence n
adj mandatory, maximum, single, light, minimum, suspended, 10-year, final, tough, complex _noun_ death., life., prison., year, word, jail., judge, length, murder, .structure _verb_ serve., finish., receive., read, write, impose, carry, face., commute, complete.
16034 | 0.95

2049 escape v
noun .notice, .prison, .death, heat, .attention, air, .poverty, .lip, trap, steam., .fate, .punishment, slave, .reality, gas. _misc_ .from, try., manage., allow., able.
15869 | 0.96

2050 unusual j
noun punishment, case, thing, way, circumstance, situation, step, behavior, name, event, feature, combination _misc_ not, very, most, cruel, nothing, something, highly
15728 | 0.97

2051 distribution n
adj rigid, normal, spatial, equitable, unequal, equal, geographic, mass _noun_ .transmission, .deadline,

.system, income, power, .center, production., food, table., resource _verb_ control., determine., affect, compare, reflect, assume., influence., examine., result, gain.
17174 | 0.89 A

2052 rural j
noun area, community, school, town, population, county, people, life, development, setting, district, village _misc_ urban, small, poor, live, suburban, especially, southern, particularly
17189 | 0.89 A

2053 cast v
noun shadow, vote, .ballot, light, eye, .doubt, .glance, .spell, .net, .role, voter. _misc_ .over, .aside, long, .across, .upon
   out demon, .line, .spirit, .net, .devil, .fear, Jesus. **off** .line, before., boat, ready.
15844 | 0.96

2054 drink n
adj soft, cold, free, long, hot, alcoholic, cool, favorite, tall _noun_ food., .water, bar, beer, coffee, table, sport., sip., glass, couple. _verb_ take., buy., pour., order., offer, finish., sell, .contain
16649 | 0.92 F

2055 sleep n
adj good, deep, obstructive, dreamless, restless, restful, fitful, cold _noun_ night, hour., .apnea, .disorder, lack., eye, .deprivation, .pattern, bed _verb_ go., get., need, lose., wake, let., die., fall.
16548 | 0.92 F

2056 household n
adj American, average, median, poor, common, typical, total, urban, female-headed, nuclear _noun_ .income, .name, head, family, child, member, .chore, .waste, .product, .item _verb_ become., live, .own, .receive, represent, maintain, .earn, manage, contribute, consist
17180 | 0.89 A

2057 celebrate v
noun .anniversary, .birthday, year, holiday, .Christmas, .victory, family, mass, .wedding, party, event, festival, .diversity, .birth, church _misc_ recently., gather., .centennial, cultural, tonight
15879 | 0.96

2058 taste n
adj good, bad, sweet, bitter, personal, poor, acquired _noun_ .mouth, food, smell, texture, matter., .test, .seasoning, sense., .salt _verb_ get., like, develop., suit., .adjust, acquire., reflect., share.
16025 | 0.95

2059 characteristic n
adj physical, personal, certain, important, social, different, common, specific, similar, defining _noun_ student, personality., study, sample, family, teacher, relationship, participant, performance, population _verb_ identify, share., describe, examine., base, exhibit., possess., consider, affect, influence
18003 | 0.84 A

2060 outside j
noun world, force, door, help, wall, expert, influence, observer, pressure, source, air, edge _misc_ from, hire, rely, inside, independent, in-house, dependent
15652 | 0.97

2061 addition *i*
(in addition to) .to, .provide, .regular, .traditional, .standard, benefit, .usual, .duty, .basic, function, above, .contribution, .obvious, teaching
16315 | 0.93 A

2062 acquire *v*
noun skill, knowledge, company, year, information, .weapon, land, student, property, power, right, experience, data, museum, .trade *misc* .new, .through, .nuclear, recently, necessary, billion
16383 | 0.93 A

2063 closely *r*
more, work, look, watch, very, follow, .relate, .resemble, most, monitor
15867 | 0.96

2064 proper *j*
noun place, way, name, use, care, role, procedure, behavior, technique, training, balance, perspective *misc* without, ensure, maintain, necessary, teach, lack, determine, medical
15880 | 0.96

2065 tone *n*
adj soft, light, neutral, emotional, serious, rich, moral, harsh, muted, deep *noun* .voice, skin, color, muscle, dial, earth, flesh, .quality *verb* set, speak, change, sound, adopt, strike, listen, soften, match, sing
16367 | 0.93 F

2066 topic *n*
adj similar, hot, important, specific, major, particular, main, controversial, favorite, sensitive *noun* .concept, document, discussion, research, interest, .conversation, variety, range, book, article *verb* find, discuss, cover, include, address, relate, choose, focus, explore
16982 | 0.89 A

2067 towards *i*
move, attitude, walk, head, turn, step, .end, .door, policy, point, direct, lean, trend, push.
17140 | 0.88 F

2068 waste *n*
adj hazardous, solid, toxic, nuclear, radioactive, municipal, industrial, medical, human *noun* .time, .management, disposal, .site, .stream, .facility, .money, ton, amount, household. *verb* reduce, generate, dispose, recycle, lay, store, clean, contain, collect, contaminate
18240 | 0.83 A

2069 wheel *n*
adj rear, front, big, asleep, hot, spinning, squeaky, huge, back, tubeless *noun* steering, hand, car, .fortune, wagon, spoke, bicycle, drive, rim, training. *verb* turn, spin, sit, grip, reinvent, steer, roll, climb, grab, lock
17020 | 0.89 F M

---

17. The vocabulary of fiction texts

In the Corpus of Contemporary American English, the fiction texts come from nearly 75 million words in novels, short stories, plays, and movie scripts. Notice the high degree of concrete nouns, the verbs denoting physical movement and appearance, and the descriptive adjectives and adverbs—all of which are an important part of narration.

The following tables show the most frequent words (grouped by part of speech) that are at least three times as common (per million words) in fiction as in the other four genres, along with the frequency of each lemma (or headword).

[noun] hand 114904, eye 103343, head 80920, room 79276, door 77861, face 74067, mother 73338, father 61551, voice 48768, girl 46151, boy 45513, arm 44069, hair 39458, light 38758, window 37514, bed 32997, wall 30797, floor 28759, finger 25502, shoulder 25386

[verb] look 206546, sit 70921, stand 65788, walk 55092, pull 45033, wait 44021, smile 31790, stare 31593, shake 29573, laugh 28586, close 25973, nod 23062, wonder 21782, hang 20956, lay 19814, lean 18584, notice 17968, step 17506, sleep 17349, touch 16890

[adjective] dead 24327, dark 21706, sorry 18709, empty 12890, tall 11777, quiet 11446, strange 10645, thin 10006, alone 9897, thick 9705, silent 9438, gray 9427, brown 9427, yellow 9388, tired 8004, pale 7454, asleep 6837, glad 6523, stupid 6505, wet 6492

[adverb] away 60710, maybe 45211, suddenly 23941, slowly 17663, inside 15466, please 15106, okay 13662, anyway 13263, outside 10418, somewhere 9846, straight 9730, barely 8109, closer 7400, quietly 7152, gently 6185, softly 5710, besides 4697, upstairs 3859, o'clock 3776, silently 3542

2070 athlete *n*
adj female, high, professional, male, young, Olympic, great, black, best, competitive *noun* sport, coach, student, school, college, team, elite., woman, study, level *verb* .compete, indicate, .participate, train, .receive, .perform, identify, examine, influence., reveal
21786 | 0.69 A

2071 convince *v*
noun .people, .jury, .public, .voter, .American, .judge, .Congress, official, evidence, doctor, administration, campaign., .juror, .reader, argument *misc* try., .myself, .himself, able.
15555 | 0.97

2072 alternative *n*
adj other, only, viable, traditional, better, best, attractive, effective, cheap, healthy *noun* program, policy, education, energy, treatment, response., transportation., .violence, .prison *verb* offer., provide., consider, suggest, develop., choose, present, propose, .exist, discuss
16159 | 0.93 A

2073 pepper *n*
adj red, black, green, hot, white, cracked, grilled, stuffed, Italian, tender *noun* salt., teaspoon, bell., cup, onion, ground., garlic, cayenne, sauce, tablespoon *verb* .taste, add, chop, dice, sprinkle, roast, crush., grind., peel, drain
17923 | 0.84 M N

2074 cream *n*
adj sour, whipped, heavy, light, cold, shaving, whipping *noun* ice., cup, .cheese, vanilla, butter, chocolate, sugar, tablespoon, sauce, milk *verb* whip., add, serve, eat., beat, stir, shave., .soften, fill, melt
16688 | 0.90 M

2075 land *v*
noun .job, plane, .airport, helicopter, .role, troop, .Mars, fish, aircraft, floor, .contract, .jail, flight., ball, ground *misc* .on, before., .near, .safely, fly., .softly, crash
15787 | 0.95

2076 technical *j*
noun assistance, support, skill, problem, information, difficulty, college, expertise, school, training, issue, term *misc* provide, scientific, financial, economic, require, highly, professional, legal
16572 | 0.91 A

2077 square *n*
adj public, central, main, downtown, ordinary, tiny, mean, wide, gray, framing *noun* time., .garden, town., city, market., street, red., park, center, village. *verb* cut., fill, place, form, gather., overlook., cross., surround, locate, frame
15750 | 0.95

2078 plenty *p*
(plenty of) .of, there., .time, .room, still., leave, .water, .money, .opportunity, sure., offer., .space, food, drink.
15886 | 0.94 M

2079 behind *r*
leave., from., far., fall., stay., close., child., lag., follow., remain., trail., grab., step., .payment
15824 | 0.95 F

2080 invest *v*
noun money, company, fund, .stock, dollar, business, capital, .technology, energy, .future, amount, resource, firm, .education, saving *misc* .million, .heavily, much, billion, mutual, willing., save., fully., private, .wisely
16521 | 0.91 M

2081 mind *v*
noun .business, .asking, .store, .manner, joke, .saying, .cold *misc* do., you, never., if, come., bring., .own, seem., immediately., spring., nobody.
16021 | 0.93 F

2082 potential *n*
adj great, full, human, economic, enormous, greatest, tremendous, future, commercial, significant *noun* growth, .conflict, development, technology, market, energy, profit, .abuse, .violence, .success *verb* realize., reach., develop, recognize., offer., create, reduce, increase, .exist, maximize.
16267 | 0.92 A

2083 regard *v*
noun American., .suspicion, expert, .threat, critic, being, .expression, .skepticism, observer., colleague, scholar, historian, .symbol, .hero, tendency. *misc* .as, highly., widely., generally., .themselves, tend.
15856 | 0.94 A

2084 intervention *n*
adj military, early, effective, divine, direct, human, medical, humanitarian, surgical, foreign *noun* .program, government., group, .strategy, state, US., child, prevention, effect, assessment. *verb* design, require, implement, develop, support, suggest, focus, .reduce, target, .address
18820 | 0.79 A

2085 illegal *j*
noun drug, immigration, alien, activity, use, abortion, law, worker, act, trade, border, weapon *misc* legal, nothing, anything, hire, declare, engage, immoral, immigrant
15912 | 0.94

2086 lower *v*
noun .rate, head, .voice, .cost, .price, .level, eye, .risk, tax, .cholesterol, .pressure, .interest, .standard, hand, .temperature *misc* .your, raise., slowly, .himself, .onto, .until
15816 | 0.94

2087 compete *v*
noun team, company, athlete., player, game, .attention, chance., firm, economy, .marketplace, .space, .championship, .tournament, competition, .prize *misc* .with, .against, .each, .other, able., must., allow., successfully
15941 | 0.93 N

2088 talent *n*
adj great, young, special, musical, artistic, natural, top, local, raw *noun* .development, ability, .show, pool, .search, lot., .scout, interest, .agency *verb* develop, recognize, discover., display., possess, attract., lack., hide, acquire, encourage
16183 | 0.92

2089 guilty *j*
noun jury, charge, murder, plea, verdict, crime, defendant, party, court, pleasure, manslaughter, fraud *misc* not, plead, feel, find, innocent, until, proven, on-line
16221 | 0.91 S

2090 living *j*
noun thing, condition, space, room, quarter, will, area, organism, creature, expense *misc* every, dead,

breathing, only, independent, southern, greatest,
improve, assisted
15457 | 0.96

2091 milk *n*
adj soy, whole, powdered, evaporated, hot, condensed
noun cup, egg, cow, breast., glass., chocolate, sugar,
coconut., cream, carton *verb* drink., add, stir, pour,
produce, buy., combine, contain, consume, flow
16044 | 0.92 M

2092 height *n*
adj new, full, average, medium, afraid, tall, maximum,
commanding, varying, mean *noun* inch, foot, weight,
.width, age., shoulder., .season, neighborhood, length,
seat. *verb* reach., rise., measure, adjust., scale., soar.,
vary, achieve, climb, range
15948 | 0.93 M

2093 list *v*
noun table, name, book, site, company, species, .order,
page, item, category, report, information, ingredient,
event, source *misc* .as, .below, .above, .under, among
15771 | 0.94

2094 live *j*
noun music, oak, coverage, show, performance,
television, picture, TV, entertainment, birth, bait,
news *misc* real, report, broadcast, watch, perform,
feature, dead, tonight
15884 | 0.93 S

2095 assistance *n*
adj technical, financial, public, economic, federal,
military, foreign, humanitarian, international, legal
noun .program, government, development., US,
family, research., support, training, food, security.
verb provide., need, receive., offer., seek., require,
request., state, promise, extend
16182 | 0.91 A

2096 personality *n*
adj strong, multiple, individual, human, split, certain,
antisocial, similar *noun* .disorder, .trait, type,
.characteristic, factor, radio., character, style, change,
aspect. *verb* develop, reflect, fit, relate, reveal,
.emerge, express, affect, alter., tend
15819 | 0.93

2097 Israeli *j*
noun minister, government, soldier, force, official,
army, troop, occupation, leader, security, defense,
settlement
16892 | 0.87 S

2098 gay *j*
noun man, right, marriage, people, community,
couple, group, issue, activist, bar, movement, person
misc lesbian, openly, bisexual, among, straight, male,
ban, civil
15943 | 0.92

2099 forever *r*
will., go., change, live., last., life., stay., seem., lose.,
remain., .ever, disappear., alter, memory
15531 | 0.95 F

2100 assess *v*
noun student, study., item., .impact, .effect, .risk,
scale., .performance, need, measure., .damage,
.situation, teacher, ability, skill *misc* how, .whether,
design., difficult.
17456 | 0.84 A

2101 weak *j*
noun economy, spot, point, link, government, dollar,
force, knee, voice, argument, muscle, leg *misc* too,
strong, very, feel, relatively, remain, poor, extremely
15276 | 0.96

2102 female *n*
adj black, likely, unidentified, African-American,
mean, pregnant, African, similar, average, adult
noun male, percent, egg, number., study, gender,
athlete, minority, sample, percentage. *verb* report,
compare, .lay, .tend, mate, indicate, produce,
.participate, .appear, attract.
17329 | 0.85 A

2103 cigarette *n*
adj burning, unlit, cheap, dangerous, safer, safe,
unfiltered, expensive, fire-safe, half-smoked
noun .smoke, pack, .smoking, tax, .butt, .lighter,
.company *verb* light., put, drag., hold, buy., pull,
stub., burn, roll, .dangle
16189 | 0.91 F

2104 permit *v*
noun state, law, use, government, weather., rule.,
court, .access, agency, space., activity, regulation,
technology., construction, parking *misc* not., shall.,
require, obtain, refuse, operate, concealed., grant.,
legally, .direct
15848 | 0.93 A

2105 passenger *n*
adj front, fellow, rear, front-seat, female, male,
stranded, scheduled *noun* .seat, .car, .side, .door,
airline, crew, train, .window *verb* carry., open, fly, kill,
board, arrive, pick., .travel, check, ride
15524 | 0.94

2106 criticism *n*
adj literary, public, social, harsh, ethical, constructive,
recent, cultural, international, sharp *noun* art.,
lot., theory, history, kind., administration, media,
target., film., barrage. *verb* draw., respond., face.,
receive, accept., deflect., dismiss., mount, aim,
prompt
16049 | 0.91 A

2107 twenty *m*
.year, .minute, .ago, than., about., more, .foot, .later,
over., after, .dollar, .percent, .thousand, .thirty
16118 | 0.91 F

2108 honor *n*
adj high, great, national, top, military, dubious,
greatest, numerous, civilian, selected *noun* medal.,
.student, .society, .roll, guest., place., code, badge.
verb receive., name., win., graduate., earn., bestow,
award, defend., accept, restore.
15246 | 0.96

2109 creative *j*
noun process, thinking, way, writing, people, director,
work, activity, artist, idea, art, energy *misc* more,
most, teach, develop, critical, highly, innovative,
productive
15994 | 0.91 A

2110 offer *n*
adj better, final, special, generous, tender, initial,
multiple, attractive, online, formal *noun* job.,
company, opportunity, scholarship., contract.,
buyout., card, settlement. *verb* make, accept.,
reject., turn., refuse, receive., decline.
15360 | 0.95 N

2111 knock v
noun .door, head, wall, .ground, wind, floor, window, ball, tooth, back, guy, .wood, knee, .glass, chair *misc* .on, .off, .him, again, .unconscious, around **out** power, tooth, storm., .opponent, .cold, .tank, .electricity, missile **down** .wall, .door, tree, building, .barrier, .pass, .shot
15747 | 0.93 F

2112 display v
noun screen, image, behavior, art, museum, firework., data, computer, figure, wall, color, sign, information, monitor, picture *misc* prominently, proudly., .throughout, publicly, standard, graphically
15596 | 0.93 A

2113 campus n
adj main, sprawling, entire, corporate, diverse, virtual, leafy *noun* college., university, student, school, community, center, life, .police, building *verb* walk., live., arrive., visit., locate, attend, shut, welcome, participate, surround
15923 | 0.91

2114 definition n
adj broad, different, clear, operational, legal, very, precise *noun* .term, problem, .success, dictionary., art, concept, .identity, .marriage, consensus. *verb* include, provide, fit., meet., change, offer, expand., .constitute, broaden., depend
16354 | 0.89 A

2115 gray j
noun hair, eye, suit, sky, area, shade, cloud, face, day, color, beard, stone *misc* black, white, wear, dark, blue, long, brown, light
16215 | 0.90 F

2116 signal n
adj digital, clear, strong, electrical, wrong, busy, weak, direct, nonverbal, verbal *noun* radio., hand., traffic., warning., .processing, distress. *verb* send., give., use, receive, transmit, pick., detect, carry, produce, .indicate
15637 | 0.93

2117 warning n
adj early, fair, repeated, final, verbal, prior, issuing, urgent, sufficient *noun* .sign, .system, .label, .light, .shot, .signal, .danger, letter, advance., .effect *verb* give., issue., ignore., heed., receive., send, sound, fire., flash, require
15020 | 0.97

2118 physician n
adj primary, medical, American, primary-care, personal, responsible, individual, willing, Greek, practicing *noun* patient, hospital, family., nurse, emergency., .assistant, team. *verb* treat, prescribe, consult., refer, train, perform, practice, .recommend, examine, diagnose
16735 | 0.87

2119 column n
adj weekly, recent, syndicated, white, spinal, regular, monthly, vertebral, huge, tall *noun* newspaper, water., week, row., steering., magazine, page, post, gossip., advice. *verb* write., read., .appear, .replace, publish, discuss, form, mention, feature, intend
15507 | 0.93

2120 interaction n
adj social, significant, human, complex, positive, personal, strong, direct, economic, face-to-face

noun effect, student, group, gender, peer, pattern, type, .term *verb* .occur, involve, indicate, examine., facilitate., result, promote., base, study., encourage
17462 | 0.83 A

2121 dramatic j
noun change, increase, effect, way, result, story, shift, improvement, event, moment, impact, difference *misc* most, more, less, produce, undergo, quite, occur, pretty
15118 | 0.96

2122 review v
noun case, study, article, court, literature, book, research, record, data, policy, committee., program, board, information, paper *misc* after., carefully, briefly., .determine, regularly, periodically
15573 | 0.93 A

2123 republic n
adj new, other, democratic, independent, socialist, breakaway, nuclear, Slavic *noun* people., president, union, independence, leader, federal., parliament, capital, relation., commonwealth *verb* declare, recognize, .secede, proclaim, found, overthrow, invade, bind, station., .ratify
16126 | 0.89

2124 primarily r
.because, focus., use, base, concerned, due, consist., design, serve, .responsible, rely., interested
15882 | 0.91 A

2125 priority n
adj high, top, low, national, administrative, clear, main, educational, legislative, urgent *noun* list, policy, education, budget., number, research, issue, goal, administration, .mail *verb* give, set., become., place, remain, shift, reflect, assign, receive., identify
15342 | 0.94 A

2126 achievement n
adj academic, high, individual, low, greatest, significant, educational, personal, standardized, crowning *noun* student, .test, level, award, school, goal, score, motivation, lifetime. *verb* measure, improve, relate, recognize., affect., assess, promote., represent, focus, examine
17190 | 0.83 A

2127 fun j
noun thing, game, time, lot, stuff, kid, day, activity, place, fact, night, factor *misc* it, more, really, most, watch, always
15365 | 0.93

2128 request n
adj available, formal, written, reasonable, simple, unusual, urgent, numerous, associated, strange *noun* interview, information, president, budget., price., administration., freedom., .proposal, .assistance, data *verb* respond., deny, refuse., decline., receive, send, grant, reject., turn., reprint.
15107 | 0.95

2129 wrap v
noun arm, .paper, .plastic, .blanket, hand, towel, head, leg, .foil, body, finger, gift, box, hair, foot *misc* .around, her, tightly, .herself, .himself, carefully, .inside, quickly, individually **up** all., get., so., week, case, .series, today, .nomination, .special, investigation
15429 | 0.93 F

2130 engineer n
adj mechanical, electrical, chief, civil, chemical, senior, structural, agricultural, retired, aeronautical _noun_ scientist, design, software, computer, project, society., architect, flight., aerospace., technology _verb_ work, .build, .develop, hire, train, enable., .test, employ, .estimate, consult
16899 | 0.85

2131 rice n
adj brown, white, wild, cooked, fried, steamed, sticky _noun_ cup, bean, state., .vinegar, .field, bowl, .paddy, grain, chicken, vegetable _verb_ serve, cook, add, eat., stir, combine., prepare, cover, absorb
15687 | 0.91 N

2132 scholar n
adj other, legal, young, national, literary, international, visiting, biblical, religious, constitutional _noun_ study, student, research, number., .field, association., art, generation., history, .enterprise _verb_ .argue, write, .believe, .agree, .suggest, .point, .debate, publish, cite, address
16268 | 0.88 A

2133 airline n
adj American, major, big, commercial, eastern, regional, international, domestic, foreign, low-cost _noun_ .flight, .industry, pilot, .ticket, passenger, year, business, employee, security, air _verb_ fly, .offer, buy, operate, check, own, .cancel, cost, force, .announce
16048 | 0.89 N

2134 expense n
adj other, living, annual, public, administrative, low, total, personal, extra, major _noun_ year, .ratio, time, business, operating., .account, travel., taxpayer, company, money _verb_ pay, cover., incur, reduce, spare, include, operate., save, deduct, justify.
15331 | 0.93

2135 observation n
adj direct, personal, systematic, early, close, general, recent, careful, scientific, clinical _noun_ interview, classroom, data, participant., field, study, .deck, .post, period, .room _verb_ make, base., .suggest, record, confirm, conduct, support, offer, .indicate, .reveal
16340 | 0.87 A

2136 gap n
adj rich, poor, huge, widening, wide, growing, audio, cultural, unbridgeable _noun_ gender., achievement., knowledge, generation., income., wage., store, budget., bridge., trade. _verb_ fill., close., help., widen, narrow, .exist, reduce., address., remain, .separate
14888 | 0.96

2137 agenda n
adj political, national, domestic, American, social, hidden, economic, legislative, conservative _noun_ research., president, policy., item, issue, reform, top., Republican, meeting, security _verb_ set., push., .include, pursue., promote., advance., dominate, control, outline, establish
15344 | 0.93

2138 creation n
adj human, economic, divine, artistic, collective, literary, biblical, artificial, poetic, musical _noun_ job., story, process, wealth, .myth, act, .science, knowledge, growth, doctrine. _verb_ lead., allow., support., announce., result., propose., contribute., inspire, enable.
15736 | 0.90 A

2139 drag v
noun foot, body, street, chair, ground, floor, bag, month, hair, dog, .heel, chain, net, truck, soldier _misc_ .out, .into, .through, .away, .across
on long, war., .month, case., .until, process., negotiation., talk., conflict., trial.
15352 | 0.93 F

2140 suspect v
noun reason, police., scientist., official., researcher., doctor., murder, crime, investigator., terrorism, play, expert., disease, .involvement, agent _misc_ might, begin., strongly., highly., immediately.
14746 | 0.96

2141 fishing n
adj commercial, bass, recreational, offshore, favorite, deep-sea, bottom _noun_ .boat, hunting, .trip, .village, .line, .industry, trout., water, .gear, .rod _verb_ enjoy., limit, permit, prohibit, regulate., decline, restrict, concentrate
16861 | 0.84 M

2142 bread n
adj white, fresh, French, crusty, homemade, daily, stale _noun_ loaf, slice, .crumb, .butter, cheese, corn., piece., cup, wheat., .wine _verb_ bake, eat, serve, buy., cut, break., toast, .rise, taste
15361 | 0.92 M

2143 hi u
.how, hello., there, will, good, welcome, yes, oh., new., .everybody, .name
17579 | 0.81 S

2144 unable j
noun patient, debt, frustration, gaze, investigator, curiosity, consensus, employee _misc_ find, unwilling, speak, move, seem, themselves, stop, himself, reach, anything, sleep, resist
14757 | 0.96

2145 scream v
noun woman., mother, girl, head, face, .pain, kid, voice, .help, sound, mouth., .top, baby, .murder, headline _misc_ hear., start., run, yell, kick., again
out .name, want., .window, .pain, .help, every, word, night, someone.
15978 | 0.89 F

2146 journalist n
adj American, foreign, British, investigative, veteran, Russian, prominent, prize-winning, award-winning, liberal _noun_ author, politician, television, group, story, writer, freelance., news, media, association _verb_ .write, .cover, .report, protect., interview, visit, .publish, kidnap, invite, pose
15773 | 0.90 S

2147 constitution n
adj new, federal, proposed, original, interim, Soviet, written _noun_ state, US., law, right, article, power, provision, country, clause, Congress _verb_ amend., write, require, protect, violate., .provide, change., interpret., .allow, defend.
15745 | 0.90 A

2148 lucky j
noun one, man, day, guy, break, number, strike, star, girl, charm, boy, person _misc_ get, if, enough, very, feel, consider, alive, guess
15134 | 0.94 F

2149 excellent *j*
noun job, star, example, source, way, choice, point, opportunity, quality, book, work, performance *misc* good, provide, offer, extraordinary, produce, rate, otherwise
14878 | 0.95

2150 mass *j*
noun destruction, media, transit, culture, production, murder, grave, communication, market, movement, murderer, audience *misc* produce, develop, critical, popular, modern, attend, nuclear, Iraqi
15047 | 0.94

2151 payment *n*
adj monthly, down, low, social, federal, due, annual, minimum, final, third-party *noun* mortgage., interest., year, debt, cash., .system, balance., government, welfare., percent *verb* make, receive., require, pay, reduce., demand., miss., accept., cut, save
15296 | 0.92 N

2152 deep *r*
.into, down, .inside, .within, .enough, run., as., too., dig., .heart, water, bury., .pocket, voice
14949 | 0.94 F

2153 selection *n*
adj natural, wide, random, final, sexual, careful, appropriate, preferential *noun* .process, jury., criterion, .committee, group, method, site, .procedure, theory, .bias *verb* include, offer., base, choose, .favor, involve, influence., announce, feature, reflect
15437 | 0.91 A

2154 lab *n*
adj national, creative, mobile, private, yellow, independent, forensic, corporate, chemical, living *noun* research., .test, computer., crime., .coat, work, .technician, scientist, animal, media. *verb* wear., conduct, analyze, visit., process, operate, confirm, equip, house, .experiment
15141 | 0.93

2155 arrest *v*
noun police., people, suspect, officer, authority, .murder, week, drug, agent, member, .crime, leader, month, official, .possession *misc* .him, .charge, after, before, later, detain, .convicted, anyone
14999 | 0.94 S

2156 deeply *r*
more., .into, breathe., feel, .involved, .root, care., .concerned, .religious, inhale., .move, affect, love, .personal
14542 | 0.97

2157 sad *j*
noun thing, day, story, eye, face, song, part, smile, fact, state, truth, news *misc* very, so, feel, really, happy, little, angry
14990 | 0.94 F

2158 childhood *n*
adj early, happy, normal, middle, troubled, unhappy, entire *noun* memory, .education, .friend, .abuse, .adolescence, .program, .development *verb* spend, remember., recall., describe, experience, remind., survive., suffer, mark, overcome.
14880 | 0.95

2159 suppose *v*
noun reason., universe, .sake, fantasy *misc* I., .shall, might, let., yes., example
15482 | 0.91 F

2160 fairly *r*
.well, treat., .easy, .large, .common, seem., .simple, .quickly, .small, .certain, .low, remain., .typical
14647 | 0.96

2161 prosecutor *n*
adj special, federal, chief, criminal, independent, assistant, top, tough, guilty, veteran *noun* case, county., police, .office, defense, attorney, trial, lawyer, jury, department *verb* say, .charge, .argue, .seek, appoint, .investigate, .decide, .file, accuse, cooperate.
15758 | 0.89 S N

2162 violent *j*
noun crime, behavior, act, conflict, death, criminal, man, offender, action, incident, protest, attack *misc* more, most, become, commit, against, often, less, sometimes
14729 | 0.95

2163 recover *v*
noun body, .surgery, economy., .cost, .injury, fumble, patient, .loss, .damage, .memory, market., stock., police, heart, victim *misc* .from, never., fully, still., help., quickly
14463 | 0.97

2164 roof *n*
adj red, thatched, green, flat, leaky, retractable, sloping, red-tiled *noun* house, building, wall, tin., car, tile, window, .mouth, rain., edge *verb* fall, climb., .leak, cover, blow, .collapse, support, hit, install, jump.
15230 | 0.92 F

2165 amendment *n*
adj constitutional, proposed, clean, balanced-budget, subsequent, organic, flag-burning, substitute, anti-abortion *noun* right, budget., .protection, clause, marriage, court, issue, freedom, speech, case *verb* pass, protect, violate., .require, support., offer, .ban, .allow, vote., propose
15833 | 0.89 A

2166 emotion *n*
adj negative, human, strong, raw, intense, powerful, personal, deep, basic, overcome *noun* feeling, thought, voice, range., lot., expression., control, kind, behavior, display. *verb* show., express., experience, mix., stir, evoke, deal., convey, affect, betray.
14777 | 0.95

2167 existing *j*
noun system, law, program, home, structure, research, state, sales, data, technology, literature, service *misc* new, already, under, within, social, replace, improve, international
15500 | 0.90 A

2168 far *c*
(as far as) as, .can, .concerned, go, .know, .tell, .eye, least., stretch., .anyone, .mile, .aware, extend., without
14883 | 0.94 S

2169 graduate *n*
adj recent, young, female, high-school, foreign, top, fellow, advanced, prospective, four-year *noun* school, .student, university, college, program, education,

.degree, .study, percent _verb_ teach, attend, earn, prepare, receive, produce., hire., recruit, survey, staff
15338 | 0.91 A

2170 factory n
adj small, chemical, abandoned, nearby, Russian, German, rubber, pharmaceutical, converted
noun .worker, job, .floor, farm, company, .owner, garment., chocolate. _verb_ work, build, .produce, close, run, open, own, visit., shut, operate
15055 | 0.93

2171 schedule n
adj busy, daily, regular, flexible, full, hectic, tough, tight _noun_ work., time, year, school, class, week, flight., month, fall., interview. _verb_ keep, .include, set, .allow, change, fit., maintain., start, check., begin
14795 | 0.94 N

2172 avenue n
adj main, broad, wide, promising, tree-lined, fruitful, metropolitan _noun_ street, fifth., west, north, south, store, building, block, end., apartment _verb_ walk., open, provide., drive, close, cross., line, pursue, intersect
14963 | 0.93 N

2173 spiritual j
noun life, leader, experience, practice, power, value, world, belief, tradition, journey, dimension, need
misc physical, religious, moral, emotional, social, cultural, personal, psychological
15640 | 0.89 A

2174 ride n
adj long, free, smooth, wild, short, bumpy, rough, comfortable _noun_ bike., bus., car, train., boat., roller-coaster., hour, plane., carriage., cab. _verb_ take., give., hitch., offer., enjoy., catch., accept., .last
16154 | 0.86 M

2175 wash v
noun .hand, .dish, .face, water, .clothes, .hair, car, .machine, sink, body, rain, wave., soap, .window, beach _misc_ .away, .over, .off, .dry, thoroughly, hot, carefully, finish., .onto
   up .shore, .beach, body., bathroom, .along, .dinner, dish, debris. **out** road, .sea, color, rain, bridge, mouth, .soap
14987 | 0.93 F

2176 planning n
adj strategic, financial, urban, central, careful, regional, economic, local, involved _noun_ family., .process, program, .commission, development, city., .stage, service, management, .effort _verb_ require, involve, focus, engage., participate., relate, promote, assist, guide
15430 | 0.90 A

2177 self n
adj old, inner, usual, physical, whole, authentic
noun sense., .other, .esteem, image, .defense, concept, identity, .confidence, control, .interest
verb define, reveal, note., construct, relate, constitute, hide, express, .emerge, view
15668 | 0.89 A

2178 later j
noun year, life, date, stage, moment, work, period, generation, use, age, study, hour _misc_ than, sooner, early, save, welcome, store, till, schedule
14740 | 0.94 A

2179 shout v
noun man, voice, .name, crowd, door, word, boy, .order, .slogan, driver, ear, .noise, .joy, .encouragement, .warning _misc_ hear, .back, someone., stop, wave, hey, everyone, suddenly, point
   out .name, .answer, .window, question, .loud, somebody., audience., .comment, .hey
15857 | 0.88 F

2180 silent j
noun moment, room, auction, night, film, prayer, majority, movie, spring, minute, partner, crowd
misc fall, remain, keep, stand, sit, long, stay, everyone
15450 | 0.90 F

2181 brief j
noun moment, time, period, history, description, statement, discussion, message, summary, visit, overview, conversation _misc_ during, after, provide, follow, file, relatively, commercial
14475 | 0.96

2182 error n
adj standard, human, serious, medical, fatal, fundamental, typographical, significant, grave, periodic _noun_ margin., trial., type., .rate, measurement, source., .correction, .explanation, room., pilot. _verb_ make, contain., correct, commit., .occur, cause, reduce., avoid., result, report
15180 | 0.91 A

2183 widely r
.use, .as, most., vary., .available, more., .used, .accept, .hold, become., .recognize, .report, .regard, among
14924 | 0.93 A

2184 description n
adj detailed, brief, accurate, physical, following, complete, general, apt _noun_ job., program, employee., photo, .file, cover., analysis, .process, image(s)., .experience _verb_ provide, give, fit., include, read., write, match., offer, defy., apply
15280 | 0.91 A

2185 dark n
adj afraid, quiet, growing, still, near, moonless, endless, utter _noun_ light, night, eye, room, hair, face, sky, street, cup, hour _verb_ sit., hang, grow., glow., lay, surround, lie., stare, fall, hide
15528 | 0.89 F

2186 immediate j
noun family, future, need, response, problem, action, threat, impact, effect, concern, attention, aftermath
misc more, no, most, beyond, provide, require, demand
14610 | 0.95 A

2187 purchase v
noun ticket, land, home, company, equipment, product, .insurance, property, money, service, item, share, good, .acre, car _misc_ recently., million, able., .additional, .separately, afford.
14784 | 0.94

2188 leading j
noun cause, role, edge, man, candidate, scorer, nation, expert, company, figure, country, lady _misc_ one, become, play, among, economic, all-time, democratic, industrial
14620 | 0.95

2189 funding *n*
adj federal, public, additional, private, increased, available, adequate, full *noun* research, state, program, source, government., school, education, project, agency, level *verb* provide, receive., cut, increase, support, seek., secure., obtain., address, propose
15010 | 0.92 A

2190 settlement *n*
adj Jewish, negotiated, political, final, peaceful, human, out-of-court, comprehensive *noun* dispute, peace., pattern, .house, tobacco, .agreement, divorce. *verb* reach, negotiate., agree, build, establish, receive, accept., approve
15348 | 0.90 A

2191 prayer *n*
adj public, silent, little, daily, religious, common, quick, brief, unanswered, answered *noun* school, book, .service, time, morning., group, .meeting, meditation, night *verb* answer, offer, lead., recite., pray, kneel., attend., repeat, heal, invoke
14952 | 0.92

2192 initiative *n*
adj major, strategic, local, faith-based, private, individual, global, public, diplomatic, recent *noun* ballot, policy., education, peace., health., defense., reform *verb* take., support, launch, announce, .aim, pass, promote, undertake, seize., .improve
15018 | 0.92 A

2193 coalition *n*
adj national, international, broad, ruling, provisional, conservative, environmental, governing *noun* .force, .government, group, member, .partner, party, director., .authority, rainbow., leader *verb* form, build., lead, join., support, .include, organize, forge., oppose, seek
14976 | 0.92

2194 comparison *n*
adj social, direct, multiple, mean, statistical, international, difficult, interesting, planned, constant *noun* group, student, data, test, figure, purpose, basis., price, method *verb* allow., draw., pale., base, .reveal, .indicate, conduct, invite., facilitate., perform
15489 | 0.89 A

2195 portion *n*
adj large, small, significant, good, substantial, major, low, upper *noun* .population, .size, food, tax, .cost, .budget, .income, .proceed, .test, county *verb* eat, spend., serve, pay., represent., cut., cover., devote, insert., control.
14566 | 0.95

2196 opponent *n*
adj political, democratic, formidable, tough, vocal, potential, primary, outspoken, staunch, conservative *noun* Republican., abortion, supporter, war, death, group, penalty, .reform, plan, action *verb* hold., .argue, face., attack, beat., outscore., .claim, accuse, defeat., force
14689 | 0.94 N

---

18. The vocabulary of popular magazines

In the Corpus of Contemporary American English, the texts from popular magazines come from more than 80 million words in magazines representing a wide range of domains—politics, religion, parenting, foods and nutrition, gardening, sports, and so on. Notice the vocabulary related to specific domains, such as foods, sports and fitness, and arts and crafts.

The following tables show the most frequent words (grouped by part of speech) that are at least three times as common (per million words) in popular magazines as in the other four genres, along with the frequency of each lemma (or headword).

[noun] photograph 30939, artist 24024, cup 23992, painting 20185, weight 17251, heat 16475, garden 16121, inch 15418, fat 13470, sugar 10621, salt 10616, trail 10484, bike 10064, pepper 9866, fruit 9573, vegetable 9559, muscle 9483, teaspoon 8986, diet 8279, tablespoon 8013

[verb] paint 9765, stir 9335, bake 5985, install 5871, chop 3669, hunt 3320, hike 3306, drain 3214, boost 3152, blend 3084, slice 3038, sprinkle 2768, ski 2569, boast 2263, simmer 1747, coat 1717, cruise 1462, whisk 1455, rotate 1402, rinse 1354

[adjective] digital 6098, solar 5414, medium 4676, organic 4431, olive 3268, immune 3056, chopped 2991, tender 2901, rear 2839, dried 2700, soy 2585, optional 2221, excess 1708, inexpensive 1671, planetary 1599, dietary 1578, decorative 1576, saturated 1535, handy 1512, nutritional 1509

[adverb] evenly 1900, finely 1781, thinly 1281, outdoors 1175, clockwise 1110, coarsely 734, lengthwise 498, solo 493, opposite 488, ultra 477, uphill 404, chemically 383, diagonally 269, snugly 238, seamlessly 234, electrically 222, downwind 189, counterclockwise 143, nutritionally 122, refreshingly 108

2197 tension *n*
adj racial, high, ethnic, social, sexual, growing, inherent, constant, religious, creative *noun* muscle, source., lot., conflict, surface., stress, level, .headache *verb* create, feel, ease, reduce., cause, rise, increase, build, relieve., .exist
14566 | 0.94 A

2198 chapter *n*
adj new, local, final, late, entire, short, concluding, sad, regional *noun* book, .history, .bankruptcy, .protection, .verse, state, society, club, opening, title *verb* write, read., file., include, devote, open, .entitle, close, present, summarize
15171 | 0.91 A

2199 bother *v*
noun thing., conscience, injury, .folk, fly, cold., headache., makeup, .knocking, arthritis, .answering *misc* do., .me, why., even., never., really., seem.
14643 | 0.94 F

2200 curriculum *n*
adj national, general, academic, regular, integrated, existing, hidden *noun* school, education., student, .development, teacher, study, core., music, part., art *verb* develop, teach, include, design, integrate., focus, implement, emphasize, plan, support
17881 | 0.77 A

2201 consist *v*
noun group., .item, sample., .student, system., study., part, team., scale., program., series, set, participant, section, subject *misc* .of, .mostly, .primarily, .mainly, largely
15440 | 0.89 A

2202 immigrant *n*
adj illegal, new, legal, Mexican, recent, undocumented, European, American, Russian, German *noun* child, number., group, wave., nation, influx., generation, citizen, worker, benefit *verb* arrive, .live, settle, .enter, hire., .seek, deny, welcome., deport, absorb.
16336 | 0.84 A

2203 enable *v*
noun .student, system., technology., program., teacher, .user, information, .researcher, skill., software., .individual, process., development, .scientist, tool. *misc* will., .us, develop, design., thus.
15117 | 0.91 A

2204 faculty *n*
adj part-time, full-time, academic, senior, junior, tenured, diverse, mental, elementary, essential *noun* .member, student, university, college, .staff, community, administrator, school, education, program *verb* teach, join., hire, involve, encourage, participate, evaluate, engage, recruit, conduct
18307 | 0.75 A

2205 steel *n*
adj stainless, heavy, cold, structural, galvanized, corrugated, welded *noun* .mill, .industry, .door, iron., glass, aluminum, US., .frame, concrete, .plate *verb* produce, reinforce, protect, bend, replace, attach, construct, feature., cast, surround
14797 | 0.93 M

2206 desert *n*
adj high, vast, dry, Saudi, hot, open, empty
noun .storm, operation., .shield, mountain, .island,

sand, night, middle., .floor, .sun *verb* drive., cross., wander., rise, surround, survive, stretch, strand., bloom
14610 | 0.94

2207 asset *n*
adj net, valuable, real, greatest, personal, foreign, military, economic, current, natural *noun* fund, value, .management, company, stock, .allocation *verb* sell, freeze, buy., protect., manage, seize, acquire, hide., exceed, .total
15403 | 0.89

2208 slow *v*
noun growth, economy, rate, pace, car, .process, heart, breathing, progress, development, .progression, population *misc* .stop, economic, speed, .bit, .considerably, dramatically, significantly, eventually
   down economy, stop, .process, even, start, growth, sign.
14319 | 0.95

2209 housing *n*
adj public, affordable, new, urban, federal, low-income, fair, permanent, subsidized *noun* .development, .project, .market, .authority, unit, city, program, job, .complex, community *verb* build, provide, live., construct, afford, subsidize, improve
14840 | 0.92 N

2210 transform *v*
noun life, world, society, process, experience, .economy, landscape, image, space, energy, technology., culture, industry, .relationship, nature *misc* .into, .itself, .themselves, radically., human, completely., gradually., cultural
14609 | 0.93 A

2211 regarding *i*
information., question., issue, decision., policy., .use, student, concern., provide., teacher, data., research., knowledge, finding.
15672 | 0.87 A

2212 perceive *v*
noun student, teacher, .threat, individual., other, ability, parent, athlete., risk, participant., need, level, public, relationship, role *misc* .as, .themselves, may., social, often.
15677 | 0.87 A

2213 depression *n*
adj great, major, clinical, severe, economic, deep, manic, tropical, mental *noun* anxiety, symptom, disorder, level, war, stress, postpartum., .score, treatment., risk. *verb* suffer., treat., cause, experience, associate, relate, predict., indicate, affect, result
15349 | 0.89 A

2214 inform *v*
noun public, student, parent, .decision, patient, .reader, policy, participant, research, teacher, consumer, Congress, .risk, agency, theory *misc* .about, keep., fully., fail., regret., properly., adequately.
14424 | 0.95 A

2215 formal *j*
noun education, training, room, program, structure, garden, system, dining, process, schooling, rule, complaint *misc* no, more, informal, less, without, receive, file, legal
14977 | 0.91 A

2216 abandon *v*
noun mother, plan, .idea, father, .ship, .effort, car, .hope, policy, project, baby, .position, building, husband, practice *misc* force., completely, .altogether, .traditional, quickly.
14171 | 0.96

2217 release *n*
adj early, recent, late, upward, immediate, quick, theatrical, current, limited *noun* press., hostage, news., year, prisoner, .date, time, .prison, album, week *verb* issue, schedule., secure., sign., demand., send., negotiate., gain., promote, coincide.
14426 | 0.94

2218 chip *n*
adj blue, single, hot, baked, integrated, sweet, fried, Japanese, crushed, crisp *noun* potato., chocolate., computer., wood., .cookie, tortilla., memory. *verb* use, .fall, eat., serve, sell, contain, place, implant, toss, replace
15079 | 0.90 M

2219 double *j*
noun standard, door, occupancy, life, digit, play, bed, figure, jeopardy, duty, murder, whammy *misc* per, lead, white, revised, single, base, nearly
14134 | 0.96

2220 remaining *j*
noun ingredient, percent, moment, mixture, oil, salt, sugar, butter, cheese, dough, item, question *misc* add, few, repeat, last, sprinkle, only, stir, four, serve
14631 | 0.93

2221 existence *n*
adj very, human, continued, mere, independent, daily, physical, aware, everyday, earthly *noun* year, evidence., reason., condition., reality, nature, meaning, proof., threat., level *verb* deny., acknowledge., prove., threaten, justify., confirm., owe., recognize., reveal., depend
14971 | 0.91 A

2222 cheese *n*
adj Parmesan, blue, fresh, Swiss, grilled, grated, melted *noun* cup, cream., goat., cheddar., macaroni., bread, ounce., .sandwich, cottage., slice *verb* grate., .melt, sprinkle., serve, add, shred, stir, eat., .soften, beat
15480 | 0.88 M

2223 link *n*
adj direct, strong, missing, weak, possible, causal, weakest, economic, vital *noun* chain, web, cuff., .fence, evidence., information, .past, cancer, communication., .topic *verb* find., provide., establish., create., suggest., click., forge., maintain., break, .connect
14432 | 0.94 A

2224 joint *j*
noun venture, chief, staff, chairman, committee, effort, project, force, commission, statement, implementation, session *misc* between, several, form, former, military, economic, international, issue
14612 | 0.93 A

2225 savings (PL) *n*
adj medical, federal, personal, significant, private, annual, potential, substantial, low, long-term *noun* .loan, cost., . account, bank, retirement., rate, life., energy. *verb* achieve, invest, spend, offer, increase, realize, result, pass, dip., accumulate
14884 | 0.91

2226 rule *v*
noun court., judge., world, country, case, law, death, .favor, justice., decision, official., jury., commission., doctor, .roost *misc* Supreme., federal., .against, state, refuse., .unanimously, ultimately.
   out not., can., .possibility, do., .any, .other, .option, .anything
14241 | 0.95

2227 preserve *v*
noun forest, effort., nature, .culture, .integrity, space, land, .tradition, .environment, .status, history, memory, .peace, record, site *misc* help., while, national, protect, order., seek.
14487 | 0.94

2228 diet *n*
adj healthy, low-fat, total, vegetarian, balanced, rich, steady, daily, high-fat, regular *noun* fat, exercise, food, value., .pill, weight, health, protein, change, book *verb* eat, base., follow., include, add, feed., supplement., .reduce, .contain, .consist
15688 | 0.86 M

2229 territory *n*
adj occupied, new, Palestinian, Indian, uncharted, familiar, vast, disputed, hostile, foreign *noun* state, enemy., control, country, home., claim., mile., nation, lot., male *verb* occupy, defend., enter., cover, mark., explore., settle., gain, acquire, belong
14680 | 0.92 A

2230 tea *n*
adj iced, green, hot, herbal, black, sweet, mint *noun* cup., coffee, .party, .bag, glass, afternoon., .leaf, water, .room, table *verb* drink., serve, pour., bring, brew, offer, .contain, fix, cool
14785 | 0.91 F

2231 bend *v*
noun knee, head, elbow, leg, arm, foot, hand, .rule, .waist, body, hip, side, .shape, light, .angle *misc* .forward, slightly, .toward, left
   down .pick, .kiss, head, .touch, .retrieve, .whisper, .grab, .examine, .tie **over** .backwards, .backward, .pick, head, .kiss, .desk, .touch, knee
15037 | 0.90 F

2232 gain *n*
adj big, net, political, economic, personal, financial, average, short-term, long-term, annual *noun* weight., loss, tax, percent, year, efficiency, cut, productivity *verb* make, show., achieve, produce., realize, report, offset, result, post., cause
14861 | 0.91

2233 arrange *v*
noun .meeting, slice, marriage, flower, plate, .order, platter, table, .visit, trip, interview, dish, .transportation, hair, tomato *misc* .around, .meet, carefully., .themselves, neatly
14137 | 0.95

2234 resolve *v*
noun problem, issue, .conflict, .dispute, question, .difference, crisis, matter, case *misc* try., help., must., quickly
14278 | 0.94 A

2235 walk *n*
adj long, short, brisk, front, random, easy, five-minute *noun* .life, day, space., .street, beach, morning, river,

minute, nature., .wood _verb_ take., go., draw., enjoy.,
slow., resume.
14368 | 0.94 F

2236 passage _n_
adj safe, following, narrow, final, middle, certain,
inside, famous, descriptive, above _noun_ .time, rite.,
book, year, .law, .legislation, .act, reading, air,
.proposition _verb_ read, quote, allow., mark, describe,
contain, cite, block., win., illustrate
14613 | 0.92 A

2237 lock _v_
noun door, eye, room, .place, car, arm, bathroom, gate,
office, cell, knee, gaze, elbow, wheel, prison _misc_ .away,
.down, .behind, keep., .inside, .together, .onto
  up keep., prison, .tight, criminal, brake, everything,
wheel, stay.
14381 | 0.93 F

2238 tear _v_
noun .piece, heart, page, paper, .ligament, clothes,
building, .hair, .shred, throat, .hole, .limb, wind., flesh,
arm _misc_ .apart, .off, .out, .away, .through, .open
  up eye., start., street, .knee, .paper, grass, .letter,
garden **down** .wall, house, building, old, .barrier,
.fence, .replace, .rebuild
14376 | 0.93 F

2239 resistance _n_
adj rolling, armed, strong, Kuwaiti, cultural, Iraqi,
passive, Islamic _noun_ disease, .movement, .training,
drug, antibiotic, insulin., form., force, gene, path.
verb meet., develop, encounter., offer., overcome.,
increase, face., cause, test, measure
14703 | 0.91 A

2240 present _n_
adj historical, perfect, immediate, eternal, expensive,
going-away, wrapped, perpetual _noun_ past., .future,
Christmas., birthday., wedding., tree, attorney.,
graduation., anniversary., memory _verb_ buy., open,
bring., focus, live., wrap, include, unwrap., survive.
14270 | 0.94 A

2241 stream _n_
adj steady, constant, endless, thin, nearby,
continuous, main, light, deep _noun_ water, river, lake,
revenue., field., data, jet. _verb_ .flow, run, cross., feed,
pour, enter, blow., spit., trickle, dry
14371 | 0.93

2242 slide _v_
noun door, hand, foot, .floor, side, arm, car, finger,
wall, chair, glass, bed, table, body, window _misc_ .into,
.out, .off, .back, .open, .across, .under, .over, let.,
.away, .around
  down her, tear., .slope, hand., .cheek, .face, .throat,
window
15108 | 0.89 F

2243 green _n_
adj dark, bright, pale, deep, light, mixed, olive, brilliant,
wild, sweet _noun_ .leaf, salad., .mountain, color, red,
.fee, shade., bowling., baby., lime. _verb_ mix., hit, add,
dress, cook, toss, reach., wear, place
14934 | 0.90 M

2244 sharp _j_
noun knife, contrast, edge, eye, pain, tooth, turn,
increase, decline, drop, focus _misc_ cut, draw, clear,
short, bright, quick, pretty, thin
14284 | 0.94 F

2245 display _n_
adj public, digital, visual, full, spectacular, permanent,
impressive, prominent, dazzling _noun_ .case, museum,
screen, window, art, video., color, computer, object,
glass _verb_ put., .show, feature, arrange, view, mount,
accompany, witness., flash, admire.
14313 | 0.94

2246 cycle _n_
adj vicious, menstrual, natural, economic, solar,
complete, endless, normal, entire, annual _noun_ life.,
time, business., election., .violence, .poverty, stage.,
phase., news., carbon. _verb_ break., repeat, end,
perpetuate., ride., execute, generate, .last, correspond,
resume
14809 | 0.90 A

2247 pose _v_
noun threat, question, problem, risk, challenge,
danger, .picture, .hazard, photo, dilemma, model,
difficulty, security, .obstacle, camera _misc_ .by, .serious,
.great, .significant, .major
14092 | 0.95 A

2248 phase _n_
adj new, early, initial, final, various, transitional,
distinct, acute, sentencing _noun_ study, transition,
trial, development, moon, project, treatment,
penalty., stance., baseline _verb_ enter., complete,
occur, involve, consist, .last, identify, represent,
conduct, undergo.
15185 | 0.88 A

2249 transition _n_
adj democratic, smooth, political, difficult, successful,
economic, easy, peaceful, seamless _noun_ period,
.democracy, phase, .team, time, process, economy,
program, .market _verb_ make., ease., .occur, mark.,
undergo., facilitate., experience., complete., plan,
coincide
14786 | 0.90 A

2250 reduction _n_
adj significant, substantial, large, dramatic, overall,
federal, drastic, sharp, gradual, future _noun_ deficit.,
percent., emission, tax, cost, risk, rate, arm., poverty,
stress. _verb_ achieve, result, lead., show., require,
cause, produce, experience., reduce, .occur
15004 | 0.89 A

2251 negotiation _n_
adj involved, international, direct, political, ongoing,
serious, final, future, difficult, successful _noun_ peace.,
trade., process, year, contract., government, issue,
party, budget., week _verb_ lead, continue, enter.,
resume, break, conduct, involve, engage., agree, .fail
14814 | 0.90 A

2252 manufacturer _n_
adj American, national, pharmaceutical, leading,
foreign, retail, domestic, chemical, European,
various _noun_ product, equipment, car, company,
drug, computer., automobile., auto., .instruction
verb .offer, .produce, .sell, provide, follow.,
recommend, .claim, represent, .design,
contact.
14868 | 0.90 M

2253 interview _v_
noun people, .story, student, .article, .job,
police, witness, official, week, member, teacher,
reporter, candidate, officer, worker _misc_ decline.,
several, recently, .dozen, personally, individually
14582 | 0.92 S

2254 quote *v*
noun article, official, source, passage, report,
newspaper, book, word, statement, agency., paper,
.scripture, .Bible, magazine, expert *misc* say, .above,
often., .unquote, directly, frequently
14312 | 0.93 S

2255 deserve *v*
noun .credit, attention, respect, .chance, recognition,
.support, .consideration, .treatment, punishment,
.mention, .protection, .praise, .blame, honor,
reputation *misc* they., .better, .die, believe., .special,
certainly., .serious, probably.
13784 | 0.97

2256 trust *n*
adj public, national, mutual, charitable, fiduciary,
blind, living, sacred *noun* .fund, land, investment.,
security., estate., bank, resolution., .doctrine, level.,
relationship *verb* build., put., establish, hold, place,
gain., earn., betray., win.
14111 | 0.95

2257 sale *n*
adj available, proposed, average, retail, potential,
illegal, quick, initial *noun* .price, home, garage., yard.,
.sign, stock, item, product, ticket, property *verb* offer.,
approve., ban., prohibit., close, announce, restrict.,
generate, .benefit
14192 | 0.94 N

2258 layer *n*
adj thin, single, outer, thick, multiple, extra,
protective *noun* ozone., cake, skin, .paint, surface,
top, boundary., paper, ice, soil *verb* add., cover,
apply., build., place, spread, peel., form, create,
remove.
14878 | 0.89 M

2259 wedding *n*
adj royal, beautiful, traditional, perfect, golden,
upcoming, double, gay, indoor, same-sex
noun day, .ring, .dress, .party, .anniversary, .cake,
night, .reception, .band *verb* plan, attend.,
celebrate., perform., invite., dance, postpone,
cry, feature
14259 | 0.93

2260 discovery *n*
adj scientific, recent, startling, significant, surprising,
medical, remarkable, greatest, accidental, initial
noun .channel, process, shuttle., space, science,
drug., oil, voyage., research, planet *verb* make, lead,
announce., report., share, await., confirm, prompt,
revolutionize, spark
14411 | 0.92

2261 mine *p*
friend., hand., eye., yours, face., next., close.,
colleague., favorite., lip., dear., dream., buddy., fault.
14499 | 0.92 F

2262 academy *n*
adj national, American, military, naval, royal,
Christian, annual *noun* .award, .science, .art, air.,
force., member, US., police., .pediatrics, .music
verb attend., graduate, enter., establish, .recommend,
sponsor, enroll., host, issue, honor
14244 | 0.93 N

2263 sand *n*
adj white, wet, fine, hot, dry, soft, coarse *noun* .dune,
beach, water, grain, line., gravel, head., foot, rock,

desert *verb* fill, blow, bury., cover, build, throw, kick,
stretch, shift, spread
14293 | 0.93 F

2264 hit *n*
adj big, direct, huge, major, current, instant, top,
immediate *noun* .man, show, .innings, song, movie,
.list, record, .TV, .series, game *verb* take., get., allow.,
become., score., include, produce.
14506 | 0.92 N

2265 missile *n*
adj ballistic, nuclear, Iraqi, surface-to-air, long-range,
guided, anti-ballistic, military *noun* .defense, cruise.,
.system, .attack, .crisis, patriot. *verb* fire, launch, hit,
destroy, deploy, build., develop., .strike, carry, send
14643 | 0.91 S

2266 elect *v*
noun .president, .governor, year, Congress, member,
state, Republican, .leader, .mayor, .official, .Senate,
house, parliament, Democrat, representative
misc first, newly., democratically., directly, recently.
14209 | 0.93 S

2267 climate *n*
adj global, political, current, economic, social,
motivational, positive, changing, harsh, favorable
noun .change, school., effect., .system, impact,
model, earth., business., .control, panel. *verb* create.,
affect, address., .warm, improve, adapt., contribute.,
influence, alter, establish
15004 | 0.88 A

2268 participation *n*
adj political, active, public, full, social, voluntary,
athletic, female, popular, civic *noun* sport, student,
activity, level, woman, program, .rate, study,
community, process *verb* encourage., increase,
require, promote., exclude., ensure., facilitate.,
enhance, indicate, influence
15756 | 0.84 A

2269 knife *n*
adj sharp, paring, serrated, bloody, thin, dull, tiny,
quick, X-acto *noun* hand, fork, blade, kitchen., edge,
pocket, butcher., army., .throat, palette. *verb* use.,
cut, hold, pull., put., carry., stick, pick, draw, .slice
14518 | 0.91 F

2270 benefit *v*
noun student, program, company, proceed.,
community, patient, consumer, economy, society,
.intervention, charity, environment, corporation,
population, shareholder *misc* .from, will., can., may.,
also., most, might., both, greatly, million
14150 | 0.94 A

2271 atmosphere *n*
adj upper, political, low, thin, thick, Martian, relaxed,
warm, outer, friendly *noun* earth., star, carbon,
dioxide., gas., planet, family, kind., ocean, surface
verb create., enter., release., charge, foster, absorb,
.surround, contribute, form, study.
14373 | 0.92

2272 joke *n*
adj old, practical, bad, little, funny, cruel, private,
running *noun* kind., butt., lot., sort., family, .expense,
book, comment, standing., conversation *verb* make.,
tell., laugh, play, hear, crack., share, smile, enjoy.,
remind
14110 | 0.94 F

2273 urge *v*
noun president, Congress, government, parent, member, leader, official, letter., .American, .court, .caution, .reader, nation, department, board
misc .him, .them, her, strongly., .stay, .join, .accept, .avoid, .attend, repeatedly., Iraqi, gently, hurry, issue., .contact
13859 | 0.96

2274 ordinary *j*
noun people, life, citizen, man, American, thing, person, matter, folk, language, experience, income
misc out, extraordinary, nothing, human, universal, beyond, everyday
13795 | 0.96

2275 visual *j*
noun impairment, art, image, field, effect, acuity, information, artist, culture, representation, cue, experience *misc* provide, auditory, verbal, create, tactile, basic, well, aural
15313 | 0.86 A

2276 numerous *j*
noun study, time, occasion, award, book, example, article, group, way, problem, case, report *misc* other, including, receive, include, among, despite, contain, well
14296 | 0.92 A

2277 occasion *n*
adj special, rare, numerous, different, separate, social, certain, festive, various, solemn *noun* number., couple., event, .anniversary, .birthday, experience, celebration, sense, honor., gift *verb* rise., mark., dress., celebrate, recall, visit, .arise, refer, .demand, drink
13741 | 0.96

2278 philosophy *n*
adj political, moral, public, different, natural, educational, personal, western, modern, judicial
noun history, science, professor, education, life, religion, art, literature, theology, music *verb* teach, base, study., share, develop, reflect, adopt., embrace, argue, emphasize
14826 | 0.89 A

2279 suicide *n*
adj assisted, physician-assisted, attempted, mass, political, apparent, altruistic *noun* .bomber, .bombing, .attempt, .attack, rate, .note, death, .bomb, .prevention *verb* commit., assist., consider., contemplate., die., prevent., threaten., prompt
13982 | 0.94

2280 shall *v*
noun congress, law, truth, constitution, commandment *misc* we, thou, overcome, administrative, upon, forget, ye, thy, nor, thee, respecting, tomorrow, forever
14281 | 0.92

2281 glad *j*
noun boy, chance, opportunity, thanks, tiding, dad, sir, folk, excuse, pleasure *misc* I, you, see, so, here, very, hear, finally
14369 | 0.92 F

2282 goods (PL) *n*
adj other, sporting, baked, manufactured, public, canned, imported, dry, durable, foreign
noun consumer., trade., material., capital, household., export, demand., import, worth., product *verb* sell,

produce, buy, deliver., provide, purchase, .store, carry., damage.
14223 | 0.93 A

2283 moreover *r*
.although, .suggest, .argue, analysis, .despite, .unlike
15161 | 0.87 A

2284 coat *n*
adj white, black, long, heavy, red, blue, fresh
noun pocket, fur., lab., trench., hat, .paint, winter., .arm, sport., suit. *verb* wear., take., put., hang, pull, apply., grab., cover, drape, drop
14653 | 0.90 F

2285 consistent *j*
noun finding, result, research, pattern, policy, data, manner, use, behavior, view, approach, theory
misc with, more, most, previous, across, remain, fairly, internally
14958 | 0.88 A

2286 alcohol *n*
adj heavy, excessive, moderate, pure, excess
noun drug, use, .abuse, tobacco, .consumption, problem, .firearm, cigarette, level, marijuana
verb drink., consume, rub., serve, avoid., reduce, measure, burn, convert., eliminate.
14226 | 0.93

2287 opposite *j*
noun page, direction, side, end, sex, effect, wall, way, corner, view, bank, shore *misc* just, quite, exactly, sit, below, exact, photograph, above
14483 | 0.91 M

2288 cop *n*
adj bad, undercover, uniformed, top, local, tough, corrupt, racist, crooked, retired *noun* car, street, traffic., city, .killer, beat, .show, guy, police, .robber *verb* call., play., kill, shoot, .arrive, .arrest, .bust, .rush, fire, hire
15065 | 0.87 F

2289 universe *n*
adj early, entire, whole, parallel, expanding, physical, observable, dark, moral, known *noun* center., expansion, age., matter, galaxy, structure., view., energy, star, miss. *verb* .expand, create, exist, understand, fill, .evolve, .contain, explore., discover., observe
15350 | 0.86 M

2290 breathe *v*
noun air, .life, .sigh, .relief, mouth, room, breath, nose, .neck, oxygen, lung, .fire, heart, .difficulty, .smoke
misc .hard, .deeply, .through, .heavily, .again, barely.
14500 | 0.91 F

2291 practical *j*
noun matter, purpose, application, way, reason, problem, experience, term, joke, use, implication, solution *misc* more, theoretical, provide, both, offer, well, moral, rather, ethical
14221 | 0.92 A

2292 therapy *n*
adj physical, occupational, cognitive, effective, medical, behavioral, complementary, natural, available, marital *noun* gene., drug., hormone., group, patient, replacement., radiation., .session *verb* .help, receive., undergo., treat, develop, respond., seek., recommend, .involve, .reduce
15194 | 0.86 M

2293 shift *n*
adj major, dramatic, significant, fundamental, cultural, subtle, sudden, radical, seismic, gradual *noun* night•, policy, day, power, paradigm•, •attitude, •emphasis, •focus *verb* work•, •occur, represent•, reflect, cause, mark•, require, signal•, •end, result
13972 | 0.94 A

2294 racial *j*
noun group, discrimination, minority, preference, difference, identity, issue, tension, profiling, line, diversity, equality *misc* ethnic, cultural, religious, against, sexual, across, social, economic
14579 | 0.90 A

2295 elsewhere *r*
•world, United States, Europe, America, Africa, attention•, seek•, argue, region, Asia, similar, China, lie•
13910 | 0.94

2296 rarely *r*
•see, only•, very•, •ever, such, •speak, though•, •mention, •anything, occur, •discuss, •visit, •used, •anyone
13690 | 0.96

2297 essentially *r*
•same, remain•, •unchanged, •nature, argument, •identical, •flat, consist, •correct, •meaningless, •conservative, •equivalent, •irrelevant, •equal
13913 | 0.94

2298 discipline *n*
adj other, academic, different, various, social, scientific, fiscal, military, strict, spiritual *noun* •problem, art, student, school, child, order, lack• *verb* teach, learn, require, impose, maintain•, develop, enforce•, relate, incorporate, introduce
14702 | 0.89 A

2299 reply *v*
noun voice, •smile, •letter, •tone, lady, hesitation, •grin, general, •shrug, uncle, •unison *misc* yes, quickly, •softly, •quietly, •calmly
14793 | 0.88 F

2300 Mexican *j*
noun government, border, American, immigrant, state, food, official, worker, president, restaurant
14284 | 0.91 A

2301 passion *n*
adj real, sexual, lifelong, intense, shared, consuming, wild, secret *noun* life, love, music, •fruit, •play, crime•, energy, emotion, •commitment *verb* share•, pursue•, stir, develop•, indulge•, arouse, inflame•, discover•, inspire, reflect•
13588 | 0.96

2302 tale *n*
adj cautionary, tall, old, classic, strange, sad, similar, ancient, dark, moral *noun* fairy•, story, folk•, •love, wife•, •woe, morality•, version•, winter•, collection• *verb* tell, hear•, spin•, read, listen•, recount•, share•, relate•, entertain•, unfold
13818 | 0.94

2303 dust *n*
adj fine, thick, red, interstellar, cosmic, yellow, gray, Martian *noun* cloud, gas, particle, •storm, air, •bowl, •mite, dirt, wind, grain *verb* •settle, cover, blow, kick, gather•, •rise, collect, swirl, remove•, bite•
14328 | 0.91 F

2304 kiss *v*
noun •cheek, hand, lip, •forehead, neck, •goodbye, girl, night, mother, head, •ass, wife, •top, boy *misc* her, him•, •me, lean•, bend•, gently, •passionately
15030 | 0.86 F

2305 iron *n*
adj cast, wrought, hot, black, heavy, long, flat, short, corrugated *noun* calcium•, •steel, •curtain, •gate, •bar, wood, •fist, •fence *verb* pump•, contain•, hang, swing, surround, bind, burn, absorb, cook, press
13853 | 0.94

2306 independence *n*
adj political, economic, national, financial, Baltic, full, judicial, total *noun* declaration•, •day, war•, •movement, energy•, freedom, struggle• *verb* declare•, gain•, achieve•, fight•, recognize•, win•, maintain•
14216 | 0.91 A

2307 contact *v*
noun •office, company, •police, member, official, lawyer, attorney, agency, media, dealer, •author, •authority, •manufacturer, visitor, participant *misc* please•, far•, more•, •national, •local, •directly, immediately
14217 | 0.91 M

2308 Spanish *j*
noun language, war, word, moss, government, conquest, explorer, class, speaker, inquisition
14320 | 0.91

2309 advance *n*
adj technological, sexual, medical, recent, scientific, major, important, significant, late, rapid *noun* •technology, day, month•, year•, week•, •directive, ticket, •science, •notice, hour• *verb* make, pay•, plan•, prepare•, represent•, receive•, agree•, reject•, enable, mark•
13655 | 0.95

2310 pot *n*
adj large, boiling, medium, heavy, fresh, steaming, ceramic, hanging, glazed, wooden *noun* •water, coffee, melting•, clay•, •roast, soup, tea, chicken, •pie, oil *verb* bring, cook, fill, stir, smoke•, cover, place, set, grow, remove
14130 | 0.92

2311 potato *n*
adj sweet, mashed, baked, small, large, hot, red, fried, white, boiled *noun* •chip, •salad, couch•, pound•, meat•, mixture, water, •pie, bag•, gravy *verb* peel, add, cook, serve, eat•, mash, bake, grow, taste, stuff
14326 | 0.91 M

2312 motor *n*
adj electric, outboard, brushless, sensory, trolling, used, joint, molecular, superconducting, cochlear *noun* •vehicle, •skill, •company, car, •development, •oil, performance, boat, control, drive *verb* develop, power, shut, perform, install, replace, own, combine, gun•, engage
14695 | 0.88

2313 pack *v*
noun bag, box, •lunch, suitcase, car, •belongings, •gear, clothes, food, •leaf, •punch, stuff, equipment, hour, crowd *misc* •into, •leave, firmly•, •away, •light, •fresh, tightly, loosely•
    up •his, •leave, •their, go, her, •move, my, family
13839 | 0.94 M

2314 dominate v
noun market, world, industry, politics, .news, area, party, business, game, landscape, economy, culture, issue, policy, .debate _misc_ .by, still., political, continue., increasingly.
13813 | 0.94 A

2315 marketing n
adj direct, international, aggressive, mass, corporate, global, green _noun_ director, president., sales, company, .strategy .manager, product, .campaign, advertising, .executive _verb_ develop., focus, target, handle., .promote, hire, launch, .aim, oversee, approve.
14330 | 0.90 N

2316 disaster n
adj natural, environmental, major, economic, ecological, federal, financial, humanitarian, potential, impending _noun_ .relief, .area, response, .recovery, recipe., .assistance, .plan, victim, .management _verb_ .strike, .happen, avoid., lead., declare., .occur, cause, avert, prevent., respond.
13582 | 0.95

2317 exposure n
adj northern, environmental, human, possible, toxic, chronic, prolonged, UV, public, repeated _noun_ time, level, risk, sun, effect., radiation, .violence, film, media, community _verb_ reduce., cause, increase, limit, result, occur, require, avoid., die., receive
14547 | 0.89 A

2318 complaint n
adj common, formal, only, criminal, similar, somatic, legitimate, civilian, frequent, main _noun_ consumer., number., customer, citizen, discrimination, office, patient, letter, lot., official _verb_ file, hear, receive., investigate., respond., lodge, dismiss, voice, deal, answer.
13631 | 0.95 N

2319 cap n
adj white, polar, red, blue, peaked, knitted, flat, bathing _noun_ baseball., salary., ice., bottle, .head, market., jacket, ball., hair, price _verb_ wear., put., pull, remove., set, lift., raise., unscrew., melt, fit
13569 | 0.95

2320 congressional j
noun committee, office, district, budget, hearing, leader, caucus, Democrat, election, delegation, campaign, investigation _misc_ black, before, democratic, former, presidential, according, recent, Republican
13996 | 0.92

2321 jacket n
adj black, white, yellow, green, red, blue, brown, light, smoking _noun_ leather., pocket, pant, life., suit., shirt, tie, sport., tweed., denim. _verb_ wear., put, pull, reach., hang, remove., grab, drape
14358 | 0.90 F

2322 intense j
noun pressure, competition, heat, scrutiny, interest, eye, pain, debate, period, experience, color, light _misc_ more, so, most, very, become, under, less
13315 | 0.97

2323 touch n
adj finishing, nice, personal, light, final, soft, human, warm, close _noun_ sense., .screen, .button, .football,

finger, taste, sight, healing., .reality, style _verb_ lose., add., keep., put., stay., feel, apply, lend., promise, .linger
13609 | 0.94

2324 for c
.year, reason, wait., need., while, support, .month, .minute, .hour, search., responsible., account., .second, prepare.
13566 | 0.95 F

2325 impose v
noun sanction, state, restriction, tax, government, law, limit, cost, penalty, rule, burden, order, standard, .will, court _misc_ .on, .by, .upon, try., economic
14094 | 0.91 A

2326 electric j
noun power, mixer, utility, motor, car, gas, company, chair, light, guitar, bill, vehicle _misc_ general, use, until, medium, current, beat, magnetic
13981 | 0.92 M

2327 implement v
noun program, policy, plan, strategy, reform, school, change, teacher., intervention, measure, government, law, procedure, agreement, regulation _misc_ develop., design, fully., require, successfully, difficult.
14891 | 0.86 A

2328 enforcement n
adj local, federal, environmental, strict, tough, effective, international, criminal, lax, selective _noun_ law., .agency, .official, .officer, drug., .administration, state, .authority, .action _verb_ involve, monitor, step., assist., strengthen., rely, permit., block., favor.
14138 | 0.91

2329 analyze v
noun data, study, student, result, sample, information, article., process, .effect, researcher., .situation, computer, research, test, .relationship _misc_ use, collect., each, .determine, describe, identify
14399 | 0.89 A

2330 sure r
for., I, know., .how, .hell, .hope, nobody., .sound, .appreciate, .wish, .heck
13616 | 0.94

2331 retire v
noun year, age, .season, general, boomer., force, month, officer, career, debt, chairman, worker., executive, editor, decade _misc_ .from, after, who., when., before., now, until.
13943 | 0.92 N

2332 deficit n
adj federal, social, huge, current, fiscal, annual, academic, projected, long-term, significant _noun_ budget., trade., .reduction, attention., year, .disorder, US., .spending _verb_ reduce., cut., run., increase, bring, overcome., eliminate., rise, shrink, .soar
14197 | 0.90 S

2333 emphasis n
adj great, strong, special, particular, original, heavy, increased, current, increasing, primary _noun_ education, program, shift., skill, area, development, family, difference, culture, lot. _verb_ place, put., .add, reflect., receive., lay, differ, repeat., combine
14371 | 0.89 A

2334 concentrate *v*
noun effort, ₌area, power, work, attention, mind, ₌task, ability, ₌region, population, production, thought, inability, ₌painting, wealth *misc* ₌on, try, instead, hard, tend, able, highly, heavily
13310 | 0.96

2335 accomplish *v*
noun ₌goal, mission, thing, ₌task, ₌objective, feat, work, ₌purpose, ₌aim, method, learning, function, tool, achievement, sanction *misc* can, ₌through, ₌something, try, ₌anything, able, hope, order, easily
13404 | 0.95

2336 previously *r*
than, ₌report, mention, ₌unknown, describe, note, United States, discuss, ₌publish, identify, ₌serve, material
13937 | 0.92 A

2337 symbol *n*
adj religious, national, powerful, cultural, potent, visible, universal, ultimate, very, key *noun* ticker, status, sex, system, sign, set, flag, culture, ₌hope, peace *verb* become, use, represent, ₌transcribe, serve, remain, recognize, display, interpret, employ
13701 | 0.93 A

2338 bureau *n*
adj federal, Indian, national, central, assistant, statistical, Australian *noun* census, ₌chief, US, ₌statistics, ₌investigation, new, visitor, ₌land, ₌management, ₌labor *verb* ₌report, contact, establish, ₌estimate, head, ₌welcome, cite, oversee, administer, ₌project
13678 | 0.93

2339 laboratory *n*
adj national, clinical, marine, biological, scientific, educational, industrial, living, planetary, academic *noun* research, study, ₌test, ₌experiment, propulsion, jet, science, ₌animal, scientist, school *verb* conduct, produce, perform, establish, analyze, measure, design, demonstrate, confirm, investigate
14305 | 0.89 A

2340 attach *v*
noun importance, wire, end, side, cable, body, ₌wall, meaning, line, condition, back, rope, arm, significance, piece *misc* still, ₌themselves, emotionally, firmly, securely.
13460 | 0.95 M

2341 fundamental *j*
noun change, right, question, problem, principle, issue, difference, value, nature, skill, law, shift *misc* most, more, between, human, basic, economic, raise, address
14131 | 0.90 A

2342 whenever *r*
₌possible, ₌want, ₌feel, wherever, ₌someone, ready, visit, ₌anyone, occur, ₌choose, avoid, ₌mention, ₌wish, whatever.
13320 | 0.96

2343 arrangement *n*
adj new, living, institutional, political, social, floral, economic, cooperative, complex, contractual *noun* security, flower, funeral, kind, business, seating, travel. *verb* make, ₌allow, create, involve, discuss, negotiate, enter, establish, handle, accept.
13558 | 0.94 A

2344 investigator *n*
adj private, federal, principal, chief, criminal, senior, medical, independent, primary, British *noun* police, evidence, department, government, team, report, information, research, lawyer, homicide. *verb* tell, ₌find, ₌believe, hire, lead, ₌determine, ₌conclude, ₌examine, ₌discover, send.
13778 | 0.92

2345 mark *n*
adj high, German, high-water, low, top, indelible, short, distinguishing, blue, dark *noun* question, quotation, face, punctuation, stretch. *verb* say, make, leave, give, ₌shield, hit, miss, set, receive, bear.
13373 | 0.95

2346 another *p*
one, yet, ₌person, ₌reason, ₌example, ₌minute, month, ₌hour, ₌factor, ₌round, ₌option, ₌edition, ₌aspect
13310 | 0.96

2347 shock *n*
adj electric, initial, total, economic, sudden, electrical, complete, septic *noun* ₌wave, state, culture, oil, ₌absorber, ₌therapy, ₌treatment, ₌value *verb* send, absorb, cause, stare, ₌wear, receive, express, experience, react, recall
13452 | 0.94

2348 adjust *v*
noun eye, ₌inflation, ₌seasoning, rate, ₌position, body, taste, ₌height, control, mirror, ₌glass, ₌heat, color, temperature, setting *misc* ₌accordingly, must, quickly, automatically.
13387 | 0.95

2349 employer *n*
adj large, private, prospective, potential, current, previous, willing, medical, legal, future *noun* employee, worker, insurance, plan, ₌mandate, health, company, contribution, benefit, ₌sanction *verb* ₌pay, require, ₌hire, ₌provide, offer, allow, sue, ₌match, force, ₌contribute
13745 | 0.92

2350 visible *j*
noun light, eye, sign, star, world, window, part, wavelength, surface, spectrum, sky, presence *misc* most, more, become, no, highly, through, barely, clearly
13665 | 0.93

2351 pass *n*
adj free, short, single, perfect, incomplete, backstage, light, deep, narrow, forward *noun* touchdown, mountain, day, ₌rush, ₌rusher, season, ₌defense, play, run *verb* catch, throw, complete, require, let, intercept, drop, cross, ₌fail, allow
14195 | 0.89 N

2352 priest *n*
adj Catholic, high, Jesuit, Episcopal, local, religious, orthodox, abusive, Anglican, active *noun* parish, church, bishop, woman, father, abuse, minister, number, shortage *verb* become, ordain, ₌accuse, marry, ₌molest, perform, bless, remove, confess, pray
13996 | 0.91

2353 volunteer *n*
adj local, healthy, active, trained, medical, male, unpaid, willing, female, global *noun* ₌work, group, program, community, student, organization, corps,

.fire, member _verb_ .help, recruit, train, serve, organize, seek, staff., teach, participate, involve.
13570 | 0.94

2354 interpretation n
adj historical, open, constitutional, biblical, broad, literal, alternative, correct, multiple, various
noun data, .law, result, analysis, text, court, history, .event, .finding, theory _verb_ offer, base, support., present, argue, involve, influence, accept., differ, affect.
14818 | 0.86 A

2355 entertainment n
adj live, popular, mass, interactive, musical, digital, pure _noun_ .industry, news, company, sport, .center, business, home., art., television, form. _verb_ provide, offer, feature, combine, specialize., host., devote., disguise
13722 | 0.92 N

2356 habit n
adj bad, old, good, healthy, personal, poor, smoking, nasty, hard, sexual _noun_ eating., work., drug., study., .mind, health., spending., reading., change., attitude _verb_ develop., become, break, kick., support., learn, form, .die, acquire
13294 | 0.95

2357 illustrate v
noun figure, .point, example, case, story, book, table, problem, study, article, issue, .importance, process, concept, effect _misc_ by, .how, following, clearly., vividly.
14085 | 0.90 A

2358 equally r
.important, both, treat., divide, apply., share, .among, .effective, almost., distribute, .strong, .likely, .powerful, .impressive
13460 | 0.94 A

2359 prospect n
adj economic, top, long-term, political, better, democratic, financial, poor, dim, bright _noun_ job, growth, .war, company, college, .democracy, employment, career., economy, marriage _verb_ face., improve, raise., offer., excite., enhance., discuss., thrill., relish., worry
13409 | 0.94

2360 enhance v
noun student, performance, .ability, learning, .life, .quality, skill, experience, .understanding, program, .security, development, .value, .image, opportunity
misc .by, may., far., greatly., design.
14178 | 0.89 A

2361 severe j
noun problem, pain, case, injury, disability, damage, depression, weather, patient, shortage, illness, loss
misc more, suffer, most, cause, less, mental, economic, moderate
13615 | 0.93 A

2362 other i
(other than) each., .than, look., talk., against., love., anything., something., face, no., none., any., stare., fight.
13030 | 0.97

---

19. The vocabulary of newspapers

In the Corpus of Contemporary American English, the texts from popular magazines come from more than 76 million words in newspapers, containing domestic and international news, sports, lifestyle, business, and so on. Notice the vocabulary related to specific domains, such as sports, business, current events, and government.

The following tables show the most frequent words (grouped by part of speech) that are at least three times as common (per million words) in newspapers as in the other four genres, along with the frequency of each lemma (or headword).

[noun] game $_{71585}$, team $_{63228}$, season $_{46980}$, player $_{42599}$, official $_{38149}$, county $_{35356}$, director $_{33725}$, executive $_{23146}$, district $_{22233}$, coach $_{22203}$, league $_{19703}$, manager $_{19311}$, editor $_{19094}$, restaurant $_{15076}$, sales $_{14924}$, resident $_{14819}$, fan $_{13498}$, baseball $_{13286}$, football $_{12782}$, chairman $_{12165}$

[verb] win $_{46159}$, coach $_{10395}$, score $_{9616}$, retire $_{6085}$, pitch $_{4018}$, host $_{3734}$, average $_{3679}$, oversee $_{2432}$, staff $_{1994}$, total $_{1507}$, commute $_{1249}$, e-mail $_{1172}$, bat $_{1150}$, rebound $_{1077}$, single $_{936}$, preheat $_{898}$, lease $_{850}$, sauté $_{795}$, renovate $_{784}$, refrigerate $_{760}$

[adjective] chief $_{10848}$, Olympic $_{7287}$, defensive $_{5720}$, downtown $_{5091}$, offensive $_{4730}$, longtime $_{3830}$, retail $_{3675}$, retired $_{3505}$, consecutive $_{3476}$, associated $_{3241}$, all-star $_{2852}$, pro $_{2732}$, nonprofit $_{2636}$, select $_{2521}$, veteran $_{2485}$, head $_{2212}$, managing $_{2143}$, winning $_{2084}$, saturated $_{1782}$, statewide $_{1473}$

[adverb] PM $_{42287}$, AM $_{18195}$, downtown $_{2497}$, defensively $_{407}$, offensively $_{327}$, nightly $_{317}$, upfront $_{191}$, athletically $_{82}$

2363 monitor *v*
noun .progress, system, .activity, program, student, group, computer, .performance, .situation, .behavior, agency, level, .condition, .change, .quality *misc* closely, carefully, continue., constantly., continuously
13456 | 0.94 A

2364 amazing *j*
noun thing, story, grace, experience, amount, ability, number, feat, race, discovery, stuff, sight *misc* it, how, most, really, pretty, truly, absolutely
13578 | 0.93 S

2365 poverty *n*
adj social, extreme, rural, poor, economic, urban, federal, abject, absolute, grinding *noun* .line, .level, child, .rate, war., family, problem, percent, crime, reduction *verb* live., reduce., fight., escape., rise, alleviate., .increase, grow, born., experience
13858 | 0.91 A

2366 increasing *j*
noun number, pressure, demand, rate, level, use, amount, population, cost, frequency, tax, interest *misc* among, ever, rapidly, economic, face, despite, because
13873 | 0.91 A

2367 boss *n*
adj female, male, corporate, immediate, reputed, ultimate, abusive, demanding *noun* .man, party., .tweed, mob., office, union., crime., worker, mafia., pit. *verb* tell, fire, complain., impress, hire, please., convince., persuade., sue., resign
13347 | 0.94

2368 inspire *v*
noun .confidence, work, other, story, book, artist, .generation, idea, art, movie, painting, music, film, .fear, design *misc* .by, young, part, motivate, partly., divinely., directly., truly.
13326 | 0.94 M

2369 anger *n*
adj public, righteous, sudden, growing, intense, popular, pent-up *noun* frustration, lot., fear, voice, feeling, .resentment, face, pain, .management, expression *verb* feel, express., direct, rise, vent., control., deal., cause, flare, experience
13241 | 0.95

2370 heavily *r*
rely., more., invest., weigh., most., breathe., .armed, depend., area, .influence, lean., .involved
12960 | 0.97

2371 parking *n*
adj free, empty, underground, handicapped, downtown, nearby, deserted *noun* .lot, .space, .garage, car, .area, street, .ticket, valet., .spot *verb* pull., walk, drive, accept., cross., fill, recommend., permit, surround, locate
13718 | 0.91 N

2372 print *n*
adj fine, large, small, environmental, electronic, floral, bold, commercial, final, botanical *noun* .media, color, .ad, shoe., television, Braille, .shop, .job, .dress, photograph *verb* read., appear., produce, publish, check, match, rush., select, process, .depict
14315 | 0.88

2373 maker *n*
adj big, American, leading, major, foreign, key, independent, chemical, pharmaceutical, European *noun* policy., decision., film., computer, auto., car., furniture. *verb* meet, force, sue., .announce, enable., .scramble, .risk, .underestimate
13741 | 0.91

2374 involvement *n*
adj parental, active, military, great, American, political, direct, personal, social, professional *noun* parent., community, level, student, family, government, activity, sport, process, teacher *verb* deny., increase., require., report., encourage., promote., limit, reflect, examine, measure
14129 | 0.89 A

2375 queen *n*
adj homecoming, African, reigning, evil, undisputed, wicked *noun* king., .mother, beauty., .bee., .soul, prom., majesty., .conch *verb* save., crown, name, knight., reign, celebrate, honor, feature, greet, hail.
13343 | 0.94

2376 gene *n*
adj human, single, different, specific, particular, defective, certain, individual, similar, common *noun* .therapy, cell, .pool, protein, mutation, sequence, expression, cancer, disease, number *verb* find, carry., identify, turn, cause, insert, pass, discover, contain., determine
14028 | 0.89 M

2377 vary *v*
noun .state, price., size, rate., .country, level, .region, group, type, cost., age, degree, individual, .function, length *misc* .from, .widely, may., .depending, .greatly, .considerably
13853 | 0.90 A

2378 approximately *r*
.percent, .million, year, .minute, .per, each, .hour, .half, .billion, .same, .mile
14076 | 0.89 A

2379 gallery *n*
adj national, African, commercial, main, online, upper, downtown, exclusive *noun* art, museum, courtesy., city, .owner, exhibition, photo, artist, portrait., painting *verb* represent., open, exhibit, feature, display, visit, own, hang, enter., .devote
15261 | 0.82 M

2380 evaluate *v*
noun student, study., .performance, program, .effectiveness, teacher, .effect, information, method, .impact, ability, .quality, test, research, outcome *misc* use, .whether, must., carefully, develop., .base, critically.
14523 | 0.86 A

2381 fat *j*
noun man, woman, lady, people, content, cat, guy, intake, cell, body, boy, chance *misc* big, sit, too, low, saturated, little, less, eat
13623 | 0.91 F M

2382 trade *v*
noun stock, company, share., market, .place, player, team, good, security, commodity, price, bond, firm, investor, season *misc* publicly., recently., .away, willing., actively., freely
13565 | 0.92 N

2383 transfer v
noun student, money, .plate, .mixture, power, technology, .platter, .university, data, fund, information, pan, image, .hospital, skill _misc_ .from, .large, .onto, .wire, easily, .prepared, immediately, drain.
13410 | 0.93

2384 exercise v
noun power, .right, .control, .option, .authority, .influence, caution, .judgment, .leadership, muscle, .discretion, body, .restraint, freedom, .responsibility _misc_ .over, eat, .regularly, must., able.
13752 | 0.91 M A

2385 usual j
noun suspect, place, self, sense, routine, stuff, practice, pattern, manner, hour, response, spot _misc_ more, instead, beyond, little, early, than, rather
13119 | 0.95 F

2386 mystery n
adj great, unsolved, medical, divine, enduring, complete _noun_ murder., life, man, .novel, .writer, woman, hour, sense, death _verb_ solve, remain., .surround, unravel., read., .continue, explain, unlock., shroud., explore.
13065 | 0.95

2387 entry n
adj forced, late, winning, illegal, limited, easy, temporary, correct _noun_ journal., point, data., .level, diary., .form _verb_ gain., receive, write, send., read, allow, deny., refuse.
13270 | 0.94 A

2388 ring v
noun phone., bell, doorbell, telephone., ear, voice., shot., word., alarm, morning, .hollow, sound, minute, buzzer, hour _misc_ .again, .true, .off, hear., answer, loud, .twice, suddenly., constantly
out shot., voice., bell., gunshot., suddenly., loud, .across, cry., shout., laughter. **up** .sales, .sale, .purchase, clerk.
13543 | 0.92 F

2389 mood n
adj good, bad, negative, depressed, positive, public, somber, foul, festive _noun_ .swing, .state, change, .disorder, music, depression, profile, anxiety, shift, .induction _verb_ set., improve, create., reflect., affect, lighten, capture., experience., express, brighten
13140 | 0.94

2390 bean n
adj green, black, white, fresh, drained, whole, sweet, tender, hot, refried _noun_ rice, coffee., Lima., .soup, vanilla., kidney., fava., .sprout, water, pound. _verb_ add, drain, cook, eat., stir, spill., cut, cover, fill., snap.
13818 | 0.90 M

2391 still j
noun life, other, time, water, air, image, camera, photograph, picture, leaf, photo, video _misc_ there, stand, sit, I, while, paint, perfectly, digital
13186 | 0.94

2392 objective n
adj primary, main, major, environmental, strategic, economic, stated, foreign, ultimate, overall _noun_ goal., policy, program, student, activity, learning., course, strategy, teacher, project _verb_ achieve., meet, accomplish., pursue, learn, define, reach, attain, relate
14363 | 0.86 A

2393 capable j
noun student, force, person, missile, hand, machine, individual, murder, leader, understanding, speed, lawyer _misc_ produce, quite, less, anything, perfectly, only, handle
12953 | 0.96

2394 constant j
noun reminder, threat, change, pressure, companion, stream, fear, contact, motion, struggle, source, attention _misc_ remain, require, hold, maintain, almost, relatively, fairly, cosmological
13029 | 0.95

2395 light v
noun .cigarette, .candle, .fire, eye., face, room, lamp, night, match, window, .cigar, fuse, street, tree, screen _misc_ dimly., brightly., .another, .within, poorly.
up eye., face., sky., .cigarette, night, room, smile, screen, window, .cigar
13617 | 0.91 F

2396 substance n
adj other, toxic, hazardous, controlled, illicit, illegal, natural, banned, chemical, various _noun_ .abuse, treatment, problem, health, .abuser, style, disorder, body _verb_ use, contain, release, relate, identify, .cause, occur, reduce, lack., form
13828 | 0.89 A

2397 total n
adj grand, combined, annual, final, cumulative, overall, estimated, equal _noun_ percent, year, point, sum, vote, season, participant, .score, career., fund _verb_ bring., include, spend, receive., raise., increase, reach, exceed, contain., result.
13346 | 0.93

2398 strongly r
feel., very., agree, disagree, believe, more., .support, .suggest, .influence, .oppose, most., .against, .associate, .recommend
13325 | 0.93 A

2399 exception n
adj notable, possible, only, rare, major, single, sole, certain _noun_ .rule, norm, .trend, health, couple, data, industry, .rape, handful, abortion _verb_ take., allow, prove, .exist, grant, carve., justify, constitute., regulate., qualify.
13219 | 0.93 A

2400 commander n
adj military, top, senior, Supreme, allied, chief, regimental, naval, overall _noun_ US, force, army, field, general, company., battalion., police, lieutenant., air _verb_ order, name, appoint, warn, replace, retire, advise, .complain, inform, urge
13460 | 0.92

2401 spending n
adj federal, military, social, public, increased, domestic, discretionary, total _noun_ government., .money, defense., tax, cut, consumer., .bill, .program, increase, percent _verb_ reduce., .rise, limit, .grow, control., slash., slow, boost., .decline, vote
13449 | 0.92

2402 crucial j
noun role, question, issue, point, part, time, moment, element, factor, difference, information, step _misc_ play, most, understand, consider, prove, determine, absolutely, miss
13255 | 0.93 A

2403 acre *n*
adj green, skiable, additional, prime, wooded, vertical, rolling, western, northern, remaining *noun* .land, forest, park, area, farm, .wetland, .farmland, tree, .wilderness, .corn *verb* cover., buy., burn, plant, purchase., sell, surround, protect, encompass., acquire.
13614 | 0.91

2404 wire *n*
adj barbed, electrical, thin, electric, live, woven, twisted, invisible, overhead, tangled *noun* .rack, fence, .service, .mesh, pan, copper., telephone., razor., chicken. *verb* cool, attach, connect, hang, string, pull, place, wear., cover, stretch
13348 | 0.92 M

2405 command *n*
adj central, military, high, strategic, unified, simple, joint, single, overall, low-probability *noun* chain., .center, .control, .post, force, .structure, second., .economy *verb* take., obey., send, issue, assume., respond., enter, relieve., execute, .oversee
13102 | 0.94

2406 nervous *j*
noun system, breakdown, energy, wreck, laugh, laughter, smile, investor, glance, disorder, tension, habit *misc* about, make, get, very, little, central, feel
13041 | 0.95 F

2407 cross *n*
adj red, southern, wooden, burning, Christian, double, northern *noun* .section, .country, .shield, .hair, gold., .street, .fire, .hospital, silver, star *verb* burn, bear, hang, carry, wear, die., mark, nail., dangle, .line
12864 | 0.96

2408 so-called *j*
noun state, war, world, group, life, tax, expert, program, right, issue, art, drug *misc* these, soft, smart, normal, partial-birth, golden, scientific, dirty
12985 | 0.95

2409 competitive *j*
noun market, advantage, sport, world, edge, environment, price, industry, company, business, pressure, athlete *misc* more, very, highly, become, most, remain, less, stay
13943 | 0.88 A

2410 Asian *j*
noun country, American, woman, market, nation, crisis, student, art, immigrant, economy
13672 | 0.90 A

2411 tower *n*
adj tall, cooling, residential, round, wooden, empty, midsize *noun* office., water., trade, world, ivory., bell., control., building, top., clock. *verb* build, stand, climb., .collapse, rise, hit, fall, crash., fly, .loom
13039 | 0.94

2412 veteran *n*
adj American, medical, disabled, seasoned, decorated, foreign, Indian, 20-year, 10-year, swift *noun* war, .affair, .administration, department., .memorial, army, .center, woman., combat., service *verb* .serve, honor., .suffer, treat, .retire, discharge, decorate., recruit, .deserve, enroll
13360 | 0.92 N

2413 creature *n*
adj other, living, small, little, strange, poor, wild, tiny, beautiful, heavenly *noun* sea., .comfort, earth, kind., night, .habit, animal, being, sort, bird *verb* .live, inhabit, evolve, .emerge, .crawl, encounter, .stir, transform, .survive, belong
13679 | 0.90 F

2414 smoke *n*
adj black, thick, secondhand, white, blue, gray, acrid *noun* cigarette., cloud., fire, tobacco., air, .detector, puff., plume., flame, smell *verb* blow., .rise, fill, billow, .clear, .drift, .pour, watch, .hang, .curl
13350 | 0.92 F

2415 Arab *j*
noun world, country, state, leader, nation, league, government, society, nationalism
15912 | 0.77 A

2416 prince *n*
adj young, Saudi, royal, handsome, evil, ruling, crowned *noun* crown., princess, king, son, queen, father, brother, .peace, frog. *verb* marry, direct, bet., rescue, separate., divorce., .gaze
13246 | 0.93

2417 alliance *n*
adj northern, national, military, strategic, western, global, unholy, uneasy, close, shifting *noun* member, party, business, force, director, security, organization, system, opposition, coalition *verb* form., forge., create, build., join., enter, maintain, establish, seek, shift
13475 | 0.91 A

2418 transportation *n*
adj public, regional, federal, local, mass, alternative, personal *noun* department, .system, .board, .safety, secretary, service, US., cost, communication, mode. *verb* provide, arrange., improve, operate, rely., supply, lack, facilitate
13413 | 0.91 N

2419 stop *n*
adj full, quick, final, sudden, complete, dead, four-way *noun* bus., .sign, truck., car., tour, rest., pit., campaign, traffic *verb* make., come., put., pull., skid., include, roll., slow.
12942 | 0.95

2420 luck *n*
adj good, bad, best, better, little, dumb, hard, tough, sheer, pure *noun* stroke., lady, bit., .draw, lot., skill, kind, run., .charm, .club *verb* wish., try., bring., believe., push., curse., press., bless, .intervene, .befall
12943 | 0.95 F

2421 symptom *n*
adj physical, common, severe, similar, menopausal, mild, clinical, early, respiratory, significant *noun* patient, disease, sign., problem, level., onset, treatment, score, withdrawal., stress *verb* report, .include, experience, cause, show., treat., relieve., suffer., .appear, .occur
14365 | 0.85 M A

2422 bury *v*
noun .face, head, body, .ground, father, .grave, .foot, treasure, .rubble, son, husband, nose, baby, earth, .sea *misc* .under, dead, there, .deep, .beneath, .alive, .within, die.
12914 | 0.95 F

2423 clinic *n*
adj medical, free, public, dental, pediatric, psychiatric, veterinary, legal, primary *noun* abortion., health., hospital, woman, doctor, patient, care, outpatient., fertility., director *verb* run, open, .provide, visit., attend., operate, treat, perform, establish, enter.
13040 | 0.94

2424 illness *n*
adj mental, chronic, serious, terminal, foodborne, severe, physical, long, life-threatening *noun* death, injury, disease, child, treatment, patient, health, symptom, risk., cause. *verb* suffer., treat., die, diagnose, prevent, deal., affect, result, .occur, reduce
13408 | 0.91

2425 championship *n*
adj national, major, open, consecutive, European, amateur, back-to-back, regional, outdoor, annual *noun* world., .game, team, state., year, series, league., season, conference. *verb* win., play, .finish, compete., host., earn, capture., claim, defend., contend.
14729 | 0.83 N

2426 prisoner *n*
adj political, Iraqi, American, fellow, federal, Palestinian, female, Arab, condemned, male *noun* .war, release, abuse, .dilemma, treatment., prison, camp, woman, exchange *verb* take, hold, free, treat, kill, torture, execute, .escape, beat, visit.
12896 | 0.95

2427 reputation *n*
adj good, bad, national, international, academic, professional, solid, growing *noun* company, .quality, name, career, .integrity, .reliability *verb* earn., build., gain., develop., establish., damage, ruin, enjoy., enhance., acquire.
12705 | 0.96

2428 edition *n*
adj special, new, late, limited, revised, final, weekly *noun* weekend., morning., .news, week., book, focus., paperback., print, anniversary., teacher. *verb* publish, listen, welcome., produce., .contain, issue, illustrate, .feature, launch, .omit
14348 | 0.85 S

2429 juice *n*
adj fresh, olive, clear, remaining, frozen, creative, natural, reserved, fresh-squeezed, digestive *noun* lemon., orange., cup, lime., tablespoon, fruit., teaspoon, apple., .salt, glass *verb* add, squeeze., drink., stir, combine., pour, .run, mix, taste, .flow
13763 | 0.89 M

2430 sauce *n*
adj soy, hot, red, chili, dipping, spicy, remaining, creamy, orange, tartar *noun* tomato., cup, tablespoon, pepper, teaspoon, pasta, fish, cream, barbecue., cheese *verb* serve, add, stir, pour, combine, thicken, taste, prepare., spoon, simmer
14269 | 0.85 M N

2431 peak *n*
adj high, stiff, soft, jagged, tall, central, sharp, snowy, electric, craggy *noun* mountain, year, .season, .period, .hour, .demand, .performance *verb* reach., .form, .occur, rise, hit., climb., scale., mark, exceed, .vary
13455 | 0.91 M

2432 confront *v*
noun problem, issue, challenge, .reality, situation, dilemma, .threat, force, tear, police, choice, .past,

society, difficulty, enemy *misc* .with, when., must., directly, rather., afraid.
12794 | 0.95

2433 breakfast *n*
adj continental, full, free, hearty, quick, light, healthy, English *noun* .lunch, morning, bed, .dinner, .table, room, day, .cereal, egg, kitchen *verb* eat., serve, include, cook., sit, finish., skip., gather, clean, .consist
13129 | 0.93 F

2434 recognition *n*
adj international, national, diplomatic, growing, public, official, federal, mutual *noun* name., speech., voice., word., system, need, .test, award, pattern., .role *verb* receive., gain., deserve, win., achieve., seek., earn., demonstrate, struggle., nod.
13343 | 0.91 A

2435 smell *v*
noun air, .smoke, breath, room., .perfume, .sweat, .rose, flower, .blood, .odor, .scent, hair, .coffee, food, fish *misc* .like, can., .good, .bad, something
13891 | 0.87 F

2436 ally *n*
adj European, political, close, closest, western, key, military, strong, powerful, natural *noun* friend, war, enemy, .region, force, coalition, American, Congress, partner, union *verb* support, seek, attack, consult., gain, alienate., defend, abandon, persuade., urge
13150 | 0.92

2437 pure *j*
noun form, water, color, joy, pleasure, gold, vanilla, love, heart, extract, science, loss *misc* simple, white, economic, clean, than, smooth, unadulterated, innocent
12663 | 0.96

2438 toy *n*
adj new, favorite, stuffed, wooden, expensive, plush, electronic, broken, tiny, popular *noun* child, .store, .gun, game, .company, .car, plastic., clothes, .soldier, food *verb* play, buy., sell, pick., fill., collect, own, toss., scatter, hand.
13084 | 0.93

2439 salary *n*
adj annual, monthly, minimum, six-figure, median, modest, decent, corporate, equal, competitive *noun* .cap, year, player, teacher, .bonus, base., increase, month *verb* pay, earn., receive., raise, cut, offer, draw., rise, double, reduce
13068 | 0.93 N

2440 electronic *j*
noun system, device, media, equipment, mail, data, computer, communication, information, control, commerce, music *misc* use, such, send, digital, available, via, mechanical
13174 | 0.92

2441 bathroom *n*
adj tiny, tiled, closed, adjoining, steamy, communal, locked *noun* .door, kitchen, .mirror, floor, room, bedroom, .night, .sink, .window, shower *verb* go., use., walk., run., open, lock, clean, close, head., emerge.
13608 | 0.89 F

2442 surely *r*
will, must, as., slowly., almost., .deserve, .aware, .worth, .ought, .coincidence, .jest, .goodness, swiftly, .mercy
12853 | 0.94 F

2443 psychological *j*
noun distress, problem, well-being, effect, health, factor, state, service, adjustment, impact, test, need *misc* physical, social, American, emotional, physiological, medical, such, cultural, spiritual
13987 | 0.86 A

2444 evaluation *n*
adj negative, critical, formative, clinical, psychological, initial, psychiatric *noun* program, student, teacher, process, performance, system, research, assessment, result, .form *verb* include, conduct, base, require, complete, receive, undergo., determine, develop, indicate
15040 | 0.8 A

2445 dimension *n*
adj new, human, political, different, important, spiritual, moral, religious, various, physical *noun* relationship, personality, image, satisfaction, scale, change, number., behavior, temperament, conflict *verb* add., suggest, represent, examine, focus, indicate, exist, consist, differ, calculate
13754 | 0.88 A

2446 block *v*
noun way, .view, road, .path, .access, door, .shot, .light, effort, .sun, street, attempt, court., .entrance, car *misc* try., completely, federal, effectively.
  out .sun, .light, .sound, .noise, sky, .sunlight, .everything, ear., .distraction, .view **off** street, road, completely.
12583 | 0.96

2447 race *v*
noun car, heart., horse., mind., auto., team, road, bike, street, door, pulse., season, truck, speed, mountain *misc* .through, .down, .toward, .around, .across, .off, .past, .ahead
13055 | 0.92

2448 personnel *n*
adj military, medical, armored, trained, key, qualified, administrative *noun* school., service, .carrier, security., director, office, management, emergency., .decision, force *verb* train, enlist., armor., support, hire, prepare, assist, protect, maintain, employ
13328 | 0.90 A

2449 belt *n*
adj black, wide, equatorial, main, dark, thick, brown, automatic, explosive, tribal *noun* seat., conveyor., .buckle, asteroid., leather., sun., safety., Bible. *verb* wear., tighten., fasten., hang, pull, reach, tuck., cinch, .fit, replace
12785 | 0.94

2450 accompany *v*
noun text, change, story, wife, .article, sound, .increase, .husband, photograph, image, growth, exhibition, loss, letter, picture *misc* .by, often., must., each, usually.
12674 | 0.95 A

2451 implication *n*
adj important, political, social, practical, profound, significant, economic, clear, serious, broad *noun* policy, study, finding, .work, .education, health, conclusion, development, change, discussion. *verb* understand., discuss, consider., explore., carry., suggest, examine., realize., resent., .arise
13642 | 0.88 A

2452 album *n*
adj new, late, live, recent, double, entire, upcoming *noun* photo., year, song, debut., solo., .cover, record, family., band, music *verb* sell, produce, .feature, buy., promote., finish, .contain, .chronicle
14520 | 0.83 M

2453 perfectly *r*
.well, fit., .good, .normal, .still, .clear, seem., .fine, .legal, .safe, suit, .happy, understand.
12588 | 0.95

2454 strike *n*
adj military, general, preemptive, nuclear, lucky, pre-emptive, joint, terrorist, surgical *noun* air., .zone, hunger., worker., force, lightning., baseball., missile., player. *verb* call, begin, launch., end, throw., kill, break, .occur, support, .protest
12931 | 0.93

2455 jet *n*
adj private, jumbo, corporate, commercial, regional, military, chartered, defensive *noun* fighter, .engine, .fuel, .propulsion, .laboratory, .lag, .plane, .stream, .ski *verb* fly, .crash, land, board., blow, .bomb, travel, beat, charter., replace
13127 | 0.91 N

2456 hello *u*
say., .hi, yes, .welcome, there, new, phone., oh
15715 | 0.76 S

2457 shape *v*
noun life, policy, force., world, event, experience, culture, factor., history, process, identity, attitude, perception, society, view *misc* .by, .like, help., human, economic, .future, largely, form, perfectly., moral, .western, define, .fit, significantly.
  up .as, how., what., thing., race., better, battle., .ship, summer, fast
12769 | 0.94 A

2458 relative *n*
adj other, close, distant, closest, male, living, female, dead, elderly, visiting *noun* friend, family, victim, parent, neighbor, blood., mother, group, patient, sister *verb* live, visit, .die, stay., send, care, .gather, interview., attend, locate.
12547 | 0.96

2459 tourist *n*
adj American, foreign, popular, major, German, international, western, European, main, female *noun* .attraction, .destination, .industry, town, city, .office, hotel, .season, business, .trade *verb* .visit, attract., draw, arrive, .flock, travel, cater., crowd, pose, .line
12753 | 0.94

2460 phenomenon *n*
adj new, natural, social, cultural, complex, recent, interesting, common, global, similar *noun* explanation., understanding., example., culture, weather., theory, analysis, researcher, investigation, media *verb* explain., .occur, describe, understand, study, observe, examine., .exist, represent, cause
13234 | 0.90 A

2461 fellow *j*
noun student, member, citizen, man, officer, traveler, soldier, worker, being, teacher, passenger, countryman *misc* his, their, my, human, among, join, urge, respect
12389 | 0.97

2462 toss v
noun salad, head, bowl., .ball, mixture, pasta, bag, .hair, pepper., coin, oil, .air, paper, vegetable, ingredient *misc* .into, .out, .back, .aside, .coat, over, .onto, .away, gently
13104 | 0.91 F

2463 publication n
adj other, recent, original, available, scientific, major, official, numerous, scholarly, various *noun* book, year, article, trade., journal, research, magazine, date, number, editor *verb* include, write, accept., follow, consider., submit., consult., produce, receive, cease.
13124 | 0.91 A

2464 nearby j
noun town, school, village, star, park, city, tree, table, building, hospital, area, island *misc* where, visit, locate, relatively, elementary, lots, distant, rural
12703 | 0.94

2465 consideration n
adj important, other, political, serious, economic, special, careful, social, major, financial *noun* factor, policy, cost, security, design, decision, health, interest, .role, race *verb* take., give, require., base., deserve., include, receive., suggest, involve, withdraw.
13262 | 0.90 A

2466 rather c
(rather than) .than, one, individual, focus, .later, sooner., .simply, rule, rely, specific, exception, .risk
12598 | 0.95 A

2467 holy j
noun spirit, land, grail, war, place, church, cross, city, day, man, shit, site *misc* Muslim, Roman, Christian, Islamic, Catholic, Shiite, Jewish, sacred
12949 | 0.92

2468 enterprise n
adj free, private, black, small, commercial, large, whole, criminal, human, entire *noun* business, .system, .zone, company, resource, development, scholar., starship., .planning, firm *verb* create, own, state., operate, promote, privatize, establish, manage, engage, launch
12933 | 0.92 A

2469 due j
noun process, respect, date, course, time, diligence, credit, month, tax, payment, clause, baby *misc* all, in, part, next, lack, large, before, without
12315 | 0.96

2470 inner j
noun city, circle, life, ear, working, tube, self, voice, thigh, system, strength, door *misc* outer, own, solar, reveal, spiritual, touch, explore, rural
12571 | 0.94

2471 watch n
adj close, digital, expensive, Swiss, terrorist, careful, constant *noun* pocket, gold., .list, night., neighborhood., wrist, group, .minute, hour, .program *verb* look., keep., check., glance., stand., wear., set, turn, work, consult.
12888 | 0.92 F

2472 Indian n
adj American, native, wild, Cherokee, hostile, ancient, tribal, Sioux, Hopi, drunken *noun* plain., group, tribe, cowboy., Pueblo., number., mission *verb* .live,

.remain, trade, attack, claim, convert, portray, inhabit, .occupy, .lack
13874 | 0.86 A

2473 pray v
noun .God, night, prayer, father, church, .peace, knee., Jesus, .miracle, .rain, .soul, hour, Muslim., mosque, Christian. *misc* .for, hope., together, .hard, sing, kneel., silently
12696 | 0.93 F

2474 creek n
adj clear, dry, deep, nearby, narrow, muddy, tidal, frozen *noun* rock., park, river, road, water, mill., willow., spring, trail, .bed *verb* cross., .flow, feed, visit, wind, overlook., hike, splash, swim., border
13410 | 0.88 N

2475 supply v
noun water, information, food, company, power, energy, .percent, oil, data, service, material, contract, electricity, .answer, plant *misc* .by, demand, enough, local, necessary, natural, .missing
12505 | 0.95

2476 boot n
adj black, rubber, red, knee-high, brown, muddy, blue, stiff, left, wet *noun* .camp, cowboy., pair., leather., ski, heel, work., toe, coat, jacket *verb* wear., put, pull., fit, kick, buy, lace, remove., crunch, ride.
13793 | 0.86 F M

2477 whisper v
noun .ear, voice, word, .name, mother, girl, boy, breath, prayer, wind, secret, sister, mom, mouth, dad *misc* .something, lean., hear., over, softly, smile, .urgently, .hoarsely, stare
14002 | 0.84 F

2478 resist v
noun .temptation, .urge, .pressure, .effort, .change, .attempt, .arrest, .impulse, .disease, .pull, .occupation, .desire, tendency, .proposal, .peer *misc* can., hard., able., long, unable., first, continue., initially.
12383 | 0.95

2479 journey n
adj long, spiritual, personal, difficult, arduous, final, incredible, safe *noun* end, life, night, leg., hero., train, step., return., mile, faith *verb* make., begin, start, continue, embark., complete., resume., .last, progress, .span
12316 | 0.96

2480 flag n
adj American, red, white, national, yellow, green, blue, checkered, waving *noun* Confederate., state, battle., .football, symbol, .pole, allegiance., prayer., .pin, .imagery *verb* fly, wave, raise., burn, carry., hang, plant, drape, .flutter, wrap.
12486 | 0.95

2481 disorder n
adj mental, bipolar, other, psychiatric, genetic, neurological, obsessive-compulsive, rare, affective, statistical *noun* eating., personality., attention., deficit., stress, anxiety., child, sleep. *verb* suffer., treat., cause, diagnose., develop, .affect, associate, prevent, relate, identify
13466 | 0.88 A

2482 designer n
adj interior, graphic, young, industrial, chief, floral, leading, expensive, professional, European

noun fashion**,** architect, costume**,** **.**clothes, landscape**,** clothing, system**,** garden**.** *verb* **.**create, wear, hire, feature, inspire, enable**,** credit, borrow, **.**experiment, consult
13028 | 0.91 M

2483 literally *r*
mean, quite**,** **.**hundred, **.**thousand, **.**figuratively, almost, **.**million, hour, **.**apart, **.**dozen, metaphorically
12378 | 0.95 S

2484 apparent *j*
noun reason, heir, difference, lack, contradiction, effect, size, effort, success, suicide, trend, conflict *misc* become, no, more, readily, immediately, without, despite, soon
12620 | 0.93 A

2485 permanent *j*
noun collection, member, damage, resident, home, job, status, residence, change, housing, loss, base *misc* become, five, temporary, establish, create, cause, build, legal
12356 | 0.95

2486 angle *n*
adj different, right, new, low, wide, 45-degree, 90-degree, various *noun* degree, camera**,** head, sun, face, knee, shot, floor, seat, wall *verb* change, measure, cut, form, bend**,** tilt**,** shoot, view**,** **.**reveal, adjust**.**
14342 | 0.82 F

2487 smooth *j*
noun skin, surface, transition, ride, mixture, face, voice, stone, hair, motion, muscle, sailing *misc* until, add, as, stir, process, blend, white, pour
12833 | 0.92 M

2488 unlike *i*
.other, **.**most, **.**many, **.**any, however, **.**early, **.**counterpart, **.**predecessor, **.**previous, **.**rest, **.**traditional, **.**sister, **.**majority, **.**colleague
12235 | 0.96

2489 tablespoon *n*
adj fresh, chopped, minced, remaining, scant, rounded, generous *noun* **.**oil, **.**butter, cup, teaspoon, sugar, juice, lemon, salt, water, **.**olive *verb* chop, add**,** mince, melt, taste**,** stir, slice**.**
14802 | 0.79 M N

2490 smoke *v*
noun **.**cigarette, **.**cigar, **.**pipe, **.**marijuana, **.**pot, drug, kid, **.**pack, **.**crack, **.**dope, tobacco, adult, **.**weed, restaurant, bar *misc* drink, never**,** **.**joint, likely**,** hot
12596 | 0.93 F

2491 consultant *n*
adj political, democratic, financial, independent, senior, private, environmental, educational *noun* management**,** business, news, industry, marketing**,** media**,** computer**.** *verb* hire, serve**,** **.**advise, **.**specialize, act**,** **.**recommend, employ, **.**study, **.**review, inform
12864 | 0.91 N

20. The vocabulary of academic journals

In the Corpus of Contemporary American English, the texts from academic journals come from more than 76 million words in journals representing a wide range of domains—education, history, technology, medicine, law, and so on. Notice the vocabulary that is related to these specific domains, as well as the more abstract vocabulary (as opposed to fiction, for example) that deals with ideas and processes.

The following tables show the most frequent words (grouped by part of speech) that are at least three times as common (per million words) in academic journals as in the other four genres, along with the frequency of each lemma (or headword).

[noun] student $_{163046}$, study $_{108068}$, teacher $_{73873}$, education $_{67286}$, level $_{61510}$, research $_{61043}$, community $_{56722}$, result $_{55682}$, process $_{53533}$, development $_{51798}$, use $_{51365}$, policy $_{48208}$, data $_{48070}$, effect $_{45702}$, experience $_{44830}$, activity $_{44133}$, model $_{42673}$, analysis $_{40610}$, behavior $_{40419}$, difference $_{40129}$

[verb] provide $_{73643}$, suggest $_{40118}$, develop $_{39775}$, require $_{37581}$, base $_{33053}$, indicate $_{31471}$, describe $_{30752}$, identify $_{29310}$, represent $_{26974}$, increase $_{26032}$, present $_{24867}$, note $_{24542}$, determine $_{24423}$, occur $_{23936}$, relate $_{23803}$, establish $_{22807}$, examine $_{21117}$, state $_{20879}$, compare $_{20499}$, reflect $_{19508}$

[adjective] social $_{80721}$, political $_{63690}$, economic $_{43584}$, significant $_{37691}$, cultural $_{30243}$, environmental $_{29711}$, physical $_{27783}$, specific $_{23780}$, similar $_{23717}$, individual $_{23127}$, various $_{21850}$, religious $_{21673}$, positive $_{20001}$, traditional $_{19861}$, academic $_{19351}$, African $_{19323}$, sexual $_{19305}$, particular $_{18709}$, present $_{18065}$, effective $_{17667}$

[adverb] however $_{70754}$, thus $_{39524}$, (for) example $_{36060}$, therefore $_{21538}$, e.g. $_{18417}$, significantly $_{15657}$, generally $_{14601}$, highly $_{12450}$, (in) addition $_{12087}$, relatively $_{12025}$, i.e. $_{11234}$, moreover $_{10350}$, frequently $_{9231}$, specifically $_{9077}$, primarily $_{8981}$, approximately $_{8787}$, furthermore $_{7452}$, similarly $_{7159}$, previously $_{6989}$, effectively $_{6415}$

2492 twin *n*
adj identical, fraternal, Siamese, conjoined, evil, single, pregnant, male, living, surviving *noun* .sister, .brother, .tower, .city, .peak, birth, .bed, set, .boy, .daughter *verb* .born, separate, .share, deliver, adopt., dress, conceive, collapse, mistake., adore
12749 | 0.92

2493 favor *v*
noun policy, government, group, party, approach, tax, Republican, Democrat, American., majority., selection., .abortion, .use, candidate, reform *misc* .by, .over, tend., strongly., heavily.
12408 | 0.95

2494 throat *n*
adj sore, dry, parched, tight, scratchy, burning, bare *noun* back., hand, nose., lump., mouth, heart., knife., ear, .cancer, finger. *verb* clear., cut, slit, catch., grab., rise., stick., close, burn, .tighten
13305 | 0.88 F

2495 construct *v*
noun building, model, .validity, identity, system, knowledge, meaning, image, facility, wall, narrative, theory, material, space, plant *misc* new, socially., carefully., newly., poorly.
13132 | 0.89 A

2496 birthday *n*
adj happy, annual, upcoming, belated, actual, memorable *noun* .party, .cake, day, year, .present, .celebration, child, .card, week, mother *verb* celebrate., sing, remember, mark., approach, reach., share., plan, near, commemorate.
12421 | 0.94

2497 soon *c*
(as soon as) as, .get, start, leave, begin, almost., .hear, .finish, home, .arrive, .hit, .open, .walk, stop
12456 | 0.94 F

2498 swing *v*
noun door, arm, leg, pendulum., .bat, side, .club, foot, head, hand, ball, gate, .action, tree, .sword *misc* .open, .around, .into, .down, .over, .toward, again, .onto, .wide, .wildly, .off
13073 | 0.90 F

2499 supporter *n*
adj strong, staunch, political, ardent, longtime, early, democratic, enthusiastic, loyal, major *noun* president, right, party, friend., group, abortion, candidate, Congress, leader, action *verb* .argue, .hope, .claim, rally, .gather, .vote, urge, .point, greet., encourage
12564 | 0.93 N

2500 testing *n*
adj genetic, nuclear, mandatory, standardized, educational, random, extensive, psychological, clinical *noun* drug., .program, DNA., result, .service, .procedure, .ground, laboratory, policy, lab *verb* require, conduct, undergo., perform, indicate, .reveal, prove, submit., participate, resume.
12964 | 0.90 A

2501 reasonable *j*
noun doubt, price, person, expectation, cost, amount, standard, rate, chance, explanation, suspicion, degree *misc* seem, beyond, any, assume, expect, within, sound, perfectly
12328 | 0.95

2502 mail *n*
adj electronic, direct, daily, regular, certified, overnight, first-class *noun* voice., .order, junk., service, phone, letter, piece., .fraud, message, hate. *verb* get, send, receive, deliver, arrive, read., open., pick., contact., pile
12206 | 0.96

2503 silver *n*
adj Olympic, heavy, bright, gleaming, pure, gilded, polished *noun* gold, .medal, hair, .bronze, .bullet, .lining, .star, .medalist, .screen *verb* win, wear, .line, hang, carry, flash, shine, earn., polish, gleam
12645 | 0.92 F

2504 retirement *n*
adj early, individual, mandatory, personal, comfortable, phased, normal *noun* .plan, .age, .account, year, .saving, .benefit, .income, .fund, .community, security *verb* announce., save., reach., near., force., approach., increase, contribute, .last, .loom
12911 | 0.90 N

2505 sensitive *j*
noun issue, area, information, skin, need, man, subject, topic, material, data, technology, matter *misc* more, very, most, highly, environmentally, particularly, politically
12238 | 0.95

2506 gentleman *n*
adj good, old, elderly, southern, perfect, fine, English, distinguished, sorry, merry *noun* lady., .agreement, .jury, .club, officer., country., .caller, .farmer, .suit, audience *verb* thank, welcome, remain., .name, .appreciate, .prefer, .expire, behave, oblige.
13681 | 0.85 S

2507 navy *n*
adj royal, retired, British, Japanese, Russian, Soviet, Finnish, German, imperial, French *noun* US., army., force., .ship, .officer, .seal, .pilot, war, man, .pier *verb* serve, join., enlist, retire, order, train, discharge, station, .assign, .deploy
12466 | 0.93

2508 terrorism *n*
adj international, global, domestic, nuclear, Islamic, state-sponsored *noun* war., act., threat, state, fight., .expert, issue, violence, security, force *verb* combat., stop, deal., end, prevent., promote, threaten, pose, handle., defend
13014 | 0.89 S

2509 occasionally *r*
stir., .until, only., minute, turn, cook., heat, though, .add, simmer., visit, tender, .remove, bowl
12306 | 0.94 M

2510 glance *v*
noun .watch, .shoulder, .window, room, .clock, door, eye, .mirror, .direction, .side *misc* .at, she., .over, .around, .back, .down, him, then, .toward, away, quickly, .across, behind
up .at, down, smile, .toward, .briefly, nurse, barely., occasionally
14127 | 0.82 F

2511 observer *n*
adj political, international, outside, casual, independent, foreign, military, northern, longtime,

keen *noun* industry., participant, group, election, .mission, team, behavior, view, position, data
verb .believe, .note, .agree, .expect, .report, .record, train, .notice, .assume, .count
12984 | 0.89 A

2512 constantly *r*
stir., change, .until, heat, must., cook., minute, .remind, whisk., .changing, monitor, .evolve
12084 | 0.96

2513 bind *v*
noun hand, foot, law, wrist, leather, rule, receptor, protein, molecule, arm, tape, ankle, agreement, .wound, contract *misc* .to, .by, .together, not., them
12159 | 0.95

2514 wet *j*
noun hair, grass, weather, eye, clothes, suit, snow, bar, towel, face, season, sand *misc* dry, cold, soak, warm, hot, cool, dripping, heavy
12779 | 0.91 F

2515 line *v*
noun wall, street, .side, tree, road, shelf, .pocket, car, paper, shop, baking, bottom, pan, building, cell *misc* .with, .behind, .along, narrow, main, down, tall, neatly, dark, deep, .outside, tiny, neat, .next, deeply.
  up people., .behind, .against, .outside, .along, .front, job, already., .buy
12216 | 0.95

2516 dig *v*
noun hole, .grave, .trench, .heel, .dirt, hand, finger, pit, tunnel, .ditch, well, soil, root, shovel, nail *misc* .into, .out, .in, .through, .deep, .deeper, .around, .deeply
  up .dirt, bone, plant, .grave, garden, .information, body, .root, ground, .bulb
12368 | 0.94 F

2517 quit *v*
noun .job, .school, .drinking, smoker., .turkey, .post, .race, .teaching, engine., .crying, winner., adviser, chef. *misc* when, after, call., never., decide., smoke, before, ready., force., .smoking, threaten., .altogether
12150 | 0.95

2518 digital *j*
noun camera, technology, video, image, system, computer, signal, music, equipment, photo, imaging, age *misc* use, personal, audio, create, convert, electronic, available
13375 | 0.87 M

2519 straight *j*
noun line, game, year, hair, face, man, back, talk, victory, answer *misc* win, second, three, third, four, keep, fourth, five
12349 | 0.94

2520 vs *i*
winner, game, no, next., United States, match, Roe., Friday., central
14285 | 0.81 N

2521 assist *v*
noun .student, teacher, program, .game, .development, .suicide, government, team, member, patient, organization, .client, educator, individual,

computer. *misc* develop, design, local, prepare, available.
12626 | 0.91 A

2522 employment *n*
adj equal, full, federal, full-time, gainful, future, temporary, paid, permanent *noun* .opportunity, education, .commission, .status, service, discrimination, program, growth, job, .law
verb find., seek., provide, create, obtain., offer, maintain., .rise, decline, limit
12827 | 0.90 A

2523 suggestion *n*
adj helpful, following, specific, future, open, useful, valuable, additional, constructive, simple
noun comment., research, teacher, idea, question, .improvement, power., article, list., reader
verb make, offer., provide, follow., reject., send., dismiss., accept., discuss, bristle.
12235 | 0.94 A

2524 rapidly *r*
grow., more., change, move, very., .growing, .become, expand, rise, as., increase, .changing
12279 | 0.94

2525 estimate *n*
adj conservative, high, best, current, rough, accurate, total, early, official, late *noun* cost, year, intelligence., population, percent, size, risk, table, government., analyst. *verb* base, provide, .suggest, .range, .indicate, .vary, obtain, produce., compare, yield.
12789 | 0.90 A

2526 embrace *v*
noun .idea, .concept, .technology, .change, community, arm., policy, view, .notion, .role, leader, model, .democracy, .cause, philosophy *misc* fully., democratic, enthusiastically, wholeheartedly, willing., quickly
11978 | 0.96

2527 junior *j*
noun year, college, student, officer, team, guard, varsity, league, member, class, championship, player
misc senior, national, elementary, win, attend, secondary, middle
12634 | 0.91 N

2528 stomach *n*
adj sick, empty, full, upset, flat, queasy, weak, nervous, bare *noun* hand., pit., .cancer, pain, acid, knot, muscle, chest, .problem, .ulcer *verb* feel, turn, lie., hold, .churn, cause, .hurt, .growl, lay., tighten
12723 | 0.91 F

2529 extreme *j*
noun case, condition, example, right, sport, poverty, measure, position, view, event, situation, weather
misc most, more, such, less, left, represent, because
12129 | 0.95

2530 pretty *j*
noun girl, woman, face, picture, thing, boy, sight, dress, hair, lady, baby, flower *misc* she, look, very, little, young, much, nice, pink
12509 | 0.92 F

2531 mine *n*
adj abandoned, open-pit, lost, underground, proposed, nearby, dangerous, anti-tank *noun* land.,

gold., coal., .worker, .shaft, .field, copper. _verb_ work.,
close, step., hit., operate, lay, explode, clear, own, .shut
12033 | 0.96

2532 recovery *n*
adj economic, full, complete, remarkable, speedy,
miraculous, jobless _noun_ .plan, time, .program,
.effort, process, rate, road., .period _verb_ speed.,
promote., facilitate., aid., slow, assist., achieve,
experience., wish., boost
12410 | 0.93

2533 negotiate *v*
noun agreement, .contract, .deal, government,
.settlement, treaty, .price, .peace, company, trade,
.term, .identity, union, leader, administration
misc .with, try., .between, able., willing., refuse.,
.directly, successfully.
12206 | 0.94

2534 impression *n*
adj lasting, strong, wrong, general, overall, initial,
favorable, distinct _noun_ .management, .formation,
artist, task, seal., sense., cost _verb_ give., make., get.,
leave., create., convey., form, confirm, reinforce,
correct.
11915 | 0.96

2535 wage *n*
adj minimum, low, real, living, hourly, decent,
prevailing, lost, better, poor _noun_ worker, job,
increase, .earner, labor, price, hour, .rate, condition
verb pay, raise., earn, rise, receive, fall, cut, drive,
demand., push
12461 | 0.92

2536 fifth *m*
.grade, fourth., .amendment, .year, .sixth, .day,
.floor, .grader, finish., .century, third., .season,
game, win
12083 | 0.95 N

2537 false *j*
noun statement, alarm, sense, claim, information,
hope, security, memory, start, positive _misc_ tooth,
impression
11912 | 0.96

2538 count *n*
adj guilty, high, accurate, total, final, official, wrong,
complete, sexual, manual _noun_ hand., vote, body.,
blood., head., cell., felony. _verb_ charge., lose., keep.,
convict., face., indict., drop, order, .range, .repeat
11990 | 0.96

2539 pink *j*
noun flower, dress, slip, rose, color, face, shirt, house,
shade, skin, cheek, lip _misc_ her, white, blue, wear,
yellow, red, pale, turn
12576 | 0.91 F

2540 absence *n*
adj complete, conspicuous, total, clear, significant,
physical, effective, relative, specific, notable
noun presence., leave., .evidence, father, .data,
.government, .leadership, .light, .threat, .regulation
verb note., explain., notice, indicate, occur., reflect.,
result, compensate., signify, stem
12531 | 0.91 A

2541 aggressive *j*
noun behavior, program, policy, campaign, child,
action, growth, approach, treatment, fund, effort,

style _misc_ more, very, most, become, less, sexually,
toward
12158 | 0.94

2542 corn *n*
adj sweet, fresh, frozen, dried, yellow, blue, creamed
noun .syrup, bean, .bread, field, cup, soybean, ear.,
kernel, wheat, crop _verb_ grow, add., eat., plant, cut,
cook, pop, produce, stir
12440 | 0.92

2543 mixture *n*
adj remaining, smooth, hot, complex, liquid, strange,
cool, odd, pure, cooked _noun_ flour., egg, minute,
spoon., bowl, butter., cheese, cup, milk, oil _verb_ add,
stir, pour., beat, spread., sprinkle, transfer., .thicken,
bring, .resemble
13413 | 0.85 M

2544 substantial *j*
noun number, amount, change, increase, evidence,
portion, difference, investment, effect, reduction,
cost, benefit _misc_ there, require, provide, economic,
receive, result, financial, quite, fairly
12469 | 0.91 A

2545 grandmother *n*
adj maternal, paternal, dead, dear, beloved, elderly,
dying, doting _noun_ mother, .house, aunt, grandfather,
father, sister, death, daughter, .kitchen, mom _verb_ live,
.die, remember, visit, .teach, belong., inherit., cook,
born, cry
12486 | 0.91 F

2546 quietly *r*
say., sit., speak., stand., move, door, talk., slip, walk,
watch, listen, close, .behind, wait
12553 | 0.91 F

2547 jail *n*
adj Israeli, overcrowded, crowded, juvenile, Mexican,
makeshift, Saudi _noun_ county., time, year, day,
month, .cell, .sentence _verb_ put., spend., serve.,
throw., release., face., sit., end., land., .await
12235 | 0.93 S

2548 specialist *n*
adj medical, public, clinical, certified, educational,
technical, ritual, foreign, top, religious _noun_ health.,
education, music., school, computer., team, resource.,
media., cancer. _verb_ train, hire, refer., consult,
.recommend, contact, educate, .diagnose, recruit,
.prescribe
12182 | 0.93

2549 dealer *n*
adj local, national, convicted, independent, primary,
illegal, reputable, used-car, authorized, Chevy
noun drug., car., art., arm., gun., antique., auto.
verb sell, contact, visit, .operate, .specialize, rob,
negotiate, bust, supply, ship
12304 | 0.92 M

2550 poem *n*
adj long, short, epic, selected, famous, favorite,
collected, lyric, autobiographical, complete
noun book, story, line, love, collection, song, prose.,
title, tone., subject _verb_ write, read., recite., publish,
compose, .entitle, quote, illustrate, inspire, collect
12986 | 0.88 M

2551 butter *n*
adj unsalted, melted, brown, softened, cold, sweet,
clarified _noun_ tablespoon., peanut., cup, sugar,

.margarine, bread., cream, stick., oil, salt _verb_ melt,
add, cut, .soften, beat., stir, combine., brush.
13120 | 0.87 M N

2552 conventional _j_
noun wisdom, force, weapon, treatment, method,
system, war, way, medicine, therapy, approach, arm
misc than, more, use, military, nuclear, compare,
challenge, beyond
12386 | 0.92 A

2553 pace _n_
adj slower, rapid, fast, steady, faster, brisk, leisurely,
moderate, easy, comfortable _noun_ change, .life,
.reform, .growth, snail., .inflation, .development,
minute, record _verb_ keep., slow, pick, set., quicken,
accelerate, increase, maintain., match, rise
11912 | 0.95

2554 intention _n_
adj good, best, original, stated, serious, sexual,
authorial, Soviet, evil, actual _noun_ implementation.,
behavior, author, attitude., goal, turnover., desire,
continuance., motive, purpose _verb_ announce.,
declare., state., express, indicate., form, .quit,
.terminate, signal.
12114 | 0.94 A

2555 peer _n_
adj male, likely, deviant, sighted, similar, sexual,
female, professional, scientific _noun_ .group, .pressure,
teacher, .review, relationship, interaction, child, school,
support, influence _verb_ compare., interact., accept,
perceive, indicate, reject., associate, involve., engage,
examine
13335 | 0.85 A

2556 restore _v_
noun power, .confidence, .balance, democracy, effort.,
peace, .sense, .hope, operation., .faith, plan.,
.credibility, .trust, .dignity, attempt. _misc_ help.,
.natural, fully., seek., maintain, order.
11884 | 0.95

2557 wooden _j_
noun box, spoon, chair, table, door, floor, bench,
house _misc_ small, sit, old, large, until, long, carved,
heavy
12401 | 0.91 F

2558 criticize _v_
noun president, government, administration, policy,
Republican, right, report, other, official, leader,
Democrat, .plan, .decision, action, press _misc_ .for,
sharply., publicly, widely., harshly.
12041 | 0.94

2559 nevertheless _r_
.remain, .continue, .despite, finding, substantial,
limitation, .useful, considerable, apparent, .spite,
theoretical, optimistic, caution, .sufficient
12429 | 0.91 A

2560 approval _n_
adj final, congressional, federal, public, regulatory, full,
prior _noun_ .rating, president, percent, drug, .process,
seal., government, job., stamp., board _verb_ get., win.,
give., require., seek., receive., need., gain., nod., obtain.
11954 | 0.95

2561 historic _j_
noun site, preservation, district, building, place,
city, home, house, landmark, moment, park, event

misc national, preserve, cultural, near, restore,
downtown, scenic
12338 | 0.92 N

2562 secure _v_
noun .border, .right, .position, effort., job, loan,
.support, .future, .release, area, .funding, .peace,
.supply, interest, .victory _misc_ help., order., safe.,
enough, able., necessary, financially., fail.
11898 | 0.95

2563 preparation _n_
adj professional, academic, mental, adequate,
educational, careful, psychological _noun_ teacher,
.time, .program, .minute, food., education, college,
course, personnel., training _verb_ make., begin,
require, receive, involve, complete, improve, assist.,
emphasize, entail
12663 | 0.89 A

2564 Latin _j_
noun country, American, study, nation, word, music,
government, name, market, leader, player
13016 | 0.87 A

2565 lord _n_
adj good, dear, feudal, English, sweet, risen, precious
noun God, drug., .prayer, name, .mercy, .lady, king,
.savior, war, .chancellor _verb_ thank, praise., pray, bless,
forgive, trust, accept., grant, .command, belong
12348 | 0.92 F

2566 teaspoon _n_
adj fresh, dried, ground, chopped, remaining, divided,
rounded, measuring, level _noun_ salt, pepper, cup,
tablespoon, powder, sugar, oil, .vanilla, cinnamon,
garlic _verb_ chop, grate, mince, add., crush, divide,
sprinkle., mix, slice.
14603 | 0.77 M N

2567 musical _j_
noun instrument, student, performance, experience,
theater, style, music, skill, idea, score, sound, comedy
misc play, sing, perform, cultural, creative, best,
traditional, artistic
15631 | 0.72 A

2568 weigh _v_
noun .pound, .ton, .ounce, .option, .risk, factor,
.benefit, .evidence, .mind, scale, fish, baby., .pro,
month, bike. _misc_ .than, .more, .about, .less, much,
.heavily, .against, .hundred
   in .on, also., president, .about, court., expert.
11860 | 0.95

2569 comment _v_
noun official., .report, .article, teacher., .matter,
investigation, spokesman, participant, .professor,
.aspect, .allegation, .detail, .lawsuit, critic., .specific
misc .on, decline., like., refuse., .upon
11934 | 0.95 N

2570 pan _n_
adj large, roasting, prepared, hot, medium, shallow,
tart, heavy, square _noun_ .heat, frying., baking., pot.,
cake., rack, bottom, water, oil, side _verb_ remove.,
place, cover, .cook, pour, set, cool, shake
12794 | 0.88 M

2571 assure _v_
noun .safety, public, success, .quality, doctor., security,
.reader, .access, victory, .survival, stability, minister,
.continuity, .compliance, .equality _misc_ .me, best.,

.accurately, .himself, order., virtually., .continued, .adequate, repeatedly
11681 | 0.97

2572 viewer n
adj young, average, regular, male, familiar, female, live, casual, contemporary, online *noun* TV., television., .eye, reader, show, .attention, painting, video, week, network *verb* .watch, draw., allow., remind., invite, .tune, attract., welcome., engage., share
12550 | 0.90

2573 arise v
noun problem., question., issue., conflict., need., situation., opportunity., difficulty., dispute., result, complication., controversy., action, .context, tension. *misc* .from, when, .out, may., such, might., often
12518 | 0.90 A

2574 administrator n
adj public, senior, academic, athletic, local, top, assistant, chief, educational, colonial *noun* school., teacher, faculty, college., program, university, hospital., staff, board, coach *verb* state, support, hire, train, assist, appoint, select, survey, evaluate, interview
13145 | 0.86 A

2575 immigration n
adj illegal, legal, Chinese, federal, Mexican, European, Jewish *noun* .law, .policy, .reform, .service, .naturalization, US., issue, .official, history, state *verb* stop, control, reduce., deal, restrict, encourage, affect, curb.
13267 | 0.85 A

2576 plant v
noun tree, seed, garden, foot, crop, year, flower, bomb, corn, farmer., soil, bulb, .vegetable, ground, land *misc* firmly, .harvest, .along, newly., .tall, weed, .water, wet, deliberately., plow
12458 | 0.90 M

2577 honest j
noun man, people, answer, work, broker, person, truth, mistake, opinion, guy, living, discussion *misc* about, very, let, keep, open, perfectly, completely
11761 | 0.96

2578 origin n
adj national, ethnic, common, historical, social, European, African, unknown, modern, specific *noun* country., family., .species, place., .life, point., theory., myth, religion, culture *verb* trace., explain., understand., identify., determine., explore., owe., reflect, .date
12662 | 0.89 A

2579 giant j
noun planet, step, company, slalom, tree, leap, screen, star, squid, corporation, panda, hand *misc* like, red, forward, form, resemble, green, elliptical, pharmaceutical
11950 | 0.94

2580 diversity n
adj cultural, biological, ethnic, great, genetic, racial, religious, human, rich, increasing *noun* species, plant, issue, community, program, life, culture, population, unity, .opinion *verb* reflect., promote., represent, celebrate., increase, .exist, value, appreciate., respect., characterize
12850 | 0.87 A

2581 tomato n
adj fresh, green, ripe, red, chopped, sun-dried, medium, small, diced, roasted *noun* .sauce, cup, cherry., .juice, .paste, slice, lettuce, plum., .plant *verb* add., dice, chop, stir., cut, combine., place, pick, taste, cover
13017 | 0.86 M

2582 advise v
noun .president, .client, student, doctor, expert., government, lawyer, parent, patient, firm, attorney, official, consultant., reader, department *misc* .against, .avoid, strongly., .seek, instead, financial, best, ill.
11711 | 0.96

2583 biological j
noun diversity, parent, science, agent, father, control, mother, system, warfare, research, clock *misc* chemical, nuclear, physical, social, human, cultural, natural, environmental
12445 | 0.90 A

2584 shell n
adj outer, empty, hard, tart, soft, hollow, protective, heavy, crushed, nuclear *noun* artillery., oyster., .casing, .game, pie, mortar., pastry. *verb* fill, fire, .explode, hit, remove, .fall, crack., form, .land, hide
12018 | 0.93 M

2585 essay n
adj short, recent, famous, personal, brief, present, introductory, seminal, interesting, numerous *noun* collection., book, section., photo., review, question, .contest, series., catalogue., art *verb* write, publish, read., include, .appear, argue, .examine, .entitle, .focus, .explore
12894 | 0.87 A

2586 roll n
adj sweet, fresh, French, fat, warm, crusty, slow, whole-grain, tight, forward *noun* rock., .call, paper, welfare., .film, honor., egg., jelly., spring. *verb* cut, shoot., reduce., bake, grab., slice, tear., arrange
11993 | 0.94

2587 historian n
adj military, political, presidential, architectural, cultural, public, British, local, future, academic *noun* art., author, critic, history, immigration, science, church., film., artist, attention *verb* write, note, .argue, .believe, .describe, .agree, .observe, cite, .record, ignore
12673 | 0.88 A

2588 deputy n
adj foreign, national, top, federal, senior, Iraqi, principal, associate *noun* .director, .secretary, sheriff, .minister, .chief, .attorney, .state, .assistant, .editor *verb* serve., name, appoint., arrive, act, .arrest, elect, assign, promote., hire.
12098 | 0.93 N

2589 date v
noun .year, man, woman, guy, letter., girl, .month, friend, history., relationship, tradition., .period, site, season, origin *misc* .from, .early, start., ancient, sexual, married, .last, seriously, briefly, .teenage, consecutive.
   back .year, .century, .least, tradition., history., .far, .decade, ancient, origin., record.
11953 | 0.94

2590 effectively *r*
more., use, work., most., deal, communicate,
function., manage, ability., able., teach, efficiently
12264 | 0.91 A

2591 fast *j*
noun food, track, lane, fact, car, pace, break,
restaurant, friend, start, growth, speed *misc* too, real,
furious, slow, hard, eat, easy, drive
11754 | 0.95

2592 schedule *v*
noun meeting, day, hearing, election., week, trial,
month, .appointment, .release, event, .may, hour,
class, launch, .fall *misc* .begin, originally., .later,
tentatively., .early
12002 | 0.93 N

2593 buck *n*
adj big, young, mature, extra, quick, fast, dominant,
eight-point, almighty *noun* couple., thousand., bang.,
deer, .hour, .month, trophy., season *verb* make, pay.,
.stop, spend, cost., pass., save., spot., .travel, rattle
12781 | 0.87 M

2594 tube *n*
adj inner, feeding, top, fallopian, Eustachian,
rubber, optical, neural *noun* test., plastic., end, seat.,
vacuum., aluminum., glass, toothpaste., .throat,
.assembly *verb* feed, insert, remove, place, attach,
connect, pull, contain, squeeze, form
12533 | 0.89 M

2595 refugee *n*
adj Palestinian, high, political, Haitian, Cuban,
Afghan, international, Jewish, Vietnamese, economic
noun .camp, thousand., problem, number., country,
nation., status, .crisis *verb* .flee, return, live, arrive,
resettle, settle, accept., protect., .cross, .pour
12377 | 0.90

2596 depth *n*
adj great, maximum, emotional, psychological, dark,
various, murky, average, historical, strategic *noun* .inch,
.foot, width., water, breadth, .field, ocean, surface,
.perception, .chart *verb* add., reach., understand,
plumb., explore., reveal., emerge., vary, extend, descend.
12037 | 0.93

2597 flat *j*
noun tax, surface, rock, land, side, voice, back, fee,
face, rate, stone, ground *misc* fall, lay, large, relatively,
lie, across, wide, broad
11943 | 0.93 M

2598 precisely *r*
.what, .because, more., .same, .why, .where, .kind,
.point, .reason, yet., .moment, .opposite, define,
measure
12042 | 0.93 A

2599 mad *j*
noun cow, dog, scientist, hell, dash, magazine, rush,
mom, dad, scene, doctor, king *misc* at, get, me,
make, because, really, drive, enough
11933 | 0.93 F

2600 alternative *j*
noun energy, medicine, source, fuel, school, program,
way, approach, method, strategy, explanation, model
misc provide, offer, develop, such, create, suggest,
minimum
12309 | 0.90 A

2601 disability *n*
adj physical, developmental, severe, mental, social,
visual, multiple, specific, low, special *noun* student.,
child., people., learning., individual., .act, .insurance
verb serve, identify, cause, suffer, relate, affect,
diagnose., accommodate., define, overcome.
13359 | 0.83 A

2602 destruction *n*
adj mass, environmental, human, total, assured,
nuclear, personal, natural, creative, massive
noun weapon., death., habitat, property, forest,
document, ozone, evidence, politics., violence.
verb cause, lead., result, prevent., threaten, involve.,
.occur, witness., wreak, possess.
11840 | 0.94

2603 dream *v*
noun girl, sleep., future, .success, career, .competition,
nightmare, athlete., butterfly, astronomer., dreamer,
.flying, rat, escape, .dragon *misc* .about, never.,
always.
   up can., .by, who., .new, .way, .idea, something,
never, scheme, might.
11959 | 0.93 F

2604 drop *n*
adj big, vertical, sharp, steep, single, significant,
dramatic *noun* .blood, percent, water, foot, .oil, price,
.bucket, rate, pressure, temperature *verb* .fall, add.,
cause, .hit, experience., spill, squeeze., drink, place.,
shake.
11703 | 0.95

2605 assumption *n*
adj basic, underlying, different, fundamental, implicit,
common, certain, economic, general, reasonable
noun set., value, question, .nature, belief, .power,
data, method, homogeneity, behavior *verb* make,
base., .underlie, operate., rest., support, proceed.,
predicate., imply, undermine.
12571 | 0.88 A

2606 normally *r*
will, .associate, function., .distribute, .require,
.difficult, eat, cell, .reserve, breathe., .occur, his.,
hour, behave.
11458 | 0.97

2607 angel *n*
adj blue, fallen, avenging, dark, littl, bright, holy,
dirty, destroying *noun* guardian., .wing, .food, .cake,
.death, .hair, .fire, voice, .pasta *verb* sing, fall, fly,
dance, .descend, hover, .fear, wrestle, summon,
rescue
11791 | 0.94 F

2608 pop *v*
noun head, eye., question, .pill, .mind, cork, top,
bubble, ear, trunk, ball, window, summer, .oven,
button *misc* .out, .into, .open, .off, suddenly., .onto,
tiny, tire
   up .all, .over, keep., name., .everywhere, .around,
head, .again
11901 | 0.93 F

2609 criteria (PL) *n*
adj following, important, specific, different, objective,
certain, primary, major, multiple, main *noun* selection,
performance, inclusion, .variable, study, student,
.measure, set., .validity, eligibility. *verb* meet., base,
include, determine, develop, satisfy., fit.
13159 | 0.84 A

2610 minor *j*
noun league, injury, change, problem, role, baseball, player, child, planet, party, leaguer, difference
misc only, major, relatively, play, few, such, compare, suffer
11535 | 0.96

2611 crop *n*
adj new, other, current, bumper, agricultural, modified, annual, alternative, native, green
noun year, food., farmer, corn, cash., production, .yield, plant, loss, water *verb* grow, produce, harvest, sell, .fail, cover, reduce, protect., feed, tend
12693 | 0.87 A

2612 barrier *n*
adj great, cultural, physical, significant, social, concrete, major, effective, legal, economic
noun trade., language., .island, .reef, color., sound., use, .investment, communication, vapor. *verb* break., overcome, remove., create., cross., erect, reduce., .prevent, form., act.
11885 | 0.93 A

2613 assign *v*
noun student, group, task, value, case, number, role, teacher, participant, officer, .responsibility, subject, team, duty, grade *misc* randomly., .different, .specific, special, .base
11992 | 0.92 A

2614 elementary *j*
noun school, teacher, student, education, child, level, grade, program, music, principal, classroom, class *misc* secondary, high, middle, teach, public, physical
12861 | 0.86 A

2615 valuable *j*
noun information, player, resource, lesson, time, tool, experience, asset, insight, contribution, service
misc most, more, provide, very, become, learn, prove, extremely
11702 | 0.94 A

2616 testimony *n*
adj congressional, sworn, personal, videotaped, oral, written *noun* jury, expert., court, trial, day., case, evidence, week, eyewitness., committee *verb* give, hear., provide, present, base., offer, listen., contradict, convict, confirm
11909 | 0.92 S

2617 stake *n*
adj high, financial, personal, huge, wooden, enormous, controlling, vital, direct *noun* percent., .company, issue., interest., money., equity., ownership., future, delegate, .outcome *verb* raise., sell., buy., drive, burn., pull., own., win, anchor, .outline
11695 | 0.94

21. New words in American English

The following lists show the most frequent words in the Corpus of Contemporary American English that are at least three times as common (per million words) in the texts from the 2000s (2000–2008; 180+ million words) as in the 200+ million words from the 1990s. Each table shows the lemmas (grouped by part of speech), along with the frequency of each lemma. Notice how nicely these reflect changes in society itself—politically, technologically, and so on.

[noun] e-mail 14326, terrorism 10360, terrorist 8889, affiliation 8713, adolescent 7212, homeland 4157, website 3909, Sunni 3637, wireless 3492, prep 3362, Taliban 3006, insurgent 2433, globalization 2354, SUV 2068, RPG 1970, anthrax 1954, steroid 1898, genome 1867, blog 1765, detainee 1733, militant 1610, ethanol 1601, insurgency 1561, yoga 1533, recount 1491, cleric 1466, coping 1380, tsunami 1310, cellphone 1149

[verb] host 5535, click 4094, e-mail 2139, download 1851, preheat 1364, bully 916, makeover 853, freak 649, partner 638, mentor 587, morph 349, vaccinate 286, restart 258, reconnect 257, sauté 251, hijack 245, co-write 236, ditch 183, reference 148, swipe 142, outsource 141, transition 136, upload 127, refuel 126, profile 122, encrypt 117, workout 117, prep 115, splurge 114, snack 106

[adjective] online 9219, terrorist 7908, Afghan 2776, Taliban 2095, Shiite 2052, Pakistani 1967, same-sex 1397, sectarian 1138, upscale 1057, embryonic 1036, Islamist 929, iconic 765, faith-based 754, broadband 738, handheld 734, pandemic 719, web-based 711, nonstick 689, steroid 655, insurgent 586, avian 553, dot-com 532, Chechen 396, old-school 360, clueless 356, performance-enhancing 350, high-stakes 337, Al-Qaida 331, 21st-century 331, gated 326

[adverb] online 6034, famously 1173, postoperatively 226, offline 158, wirelessly 141, healthfully 72, preemptively 66, intraoperatively 58, triply 33, day-ahead 30, forensically 28, inferiorly 26, pre-emptively 25, multiculturally 22, counterintuitively 21, synchronically 21

2618 concert *n*
adj free, live, outdoor, annual, classical, special, final, sold-out *noun* .hall, music, rock., series, year, .tour, ticket, band, .pianist, benefit. *verb* play, attend., perform, .feature, act., sell, organize., conduct, host, .celebrate
12230 | 0.90 N

2619 label *n*
adj major, independent, private, organic, ethnic, liberal, negative, familiar, fancy *noun* record., food, warning., product, direction, music, bottle, name, designer., consumer *verb* read., use, check., apply, list, sign, carry, require, attach, identify
11664 | 0.94 M

2620 routine *n*
adj daily, normal, regular, usual, everyday, familiar, stand-up, basic *noun* part, exercise., morning, work, activity, .maintenance, matter, practice, .procedure, .use *verb* become., follow, perform, change, establish., settle., maintain., break., vary, consist
11546 | 0.95

2621 wealth *n*
adj great, personal, national, vast, enormous, private, inherited *noun* power, .information, nation, distribution., material, source., oil., status, creation *verb* create, share., accumulate, bring, redistribute., provide., increase, generate, display, influence
11864 | 0.92

2622 professional *n*
adj other, medical, young, black, social, public, military, trained, local, skilled *noun* health., care., student, school, education, .field, service, healthcare., teacher, worker *verb* work, help, provide, train, hire, .develop, teach, require, account., involve
12262 | 0.89 A

2623 gang *n*
adj rival, criminal, violent, whole, armed, Russian, fellow, hard-core *noun* .member, capital., drug, street., .violence, youth, leader, .activity *verb* join., shoot, deal, attack, hang, form, .rape, control, organize, operate
11900 | 0.92

2624 incorporate *v*
noun .element, system, technology, program, design, model, idea, information, teacher., material, .feature, research, strategy, process, music *misc* .into, .both, until., environmental, fully.
12247 | 0.89 A

2625 brand *n*
adj new, different, popular, particular, major, luxury, favorite, global, unique, available *noun* .name, product, store, .loyalty, consumer, house, image, .manager, market, price *verb* sell, buy, build., include, create, carry, choose, vary, develop., advertise
11958 | 0.91 M

2626 recipe *n*
adj favorite, simple, basic, healthy, secret, original, perfect, tasty, French, vegetarian *noun* .page, book, sauce., family, cake, food, chicken, .disaster, ingredient, cup *verb* follow, serve, adapt, share., test, create, prepare, add, send, offer
12416 | 0.88 M N

2627 vacation *n*
adj paid, annual, two-week, favorite, extended, popular, working *noun* summer., family., time, week, day, .home, .spot *verb* take., go., spend., plan, return, enjoy, fly, afford.
11501 | 0.95

2628 utility *n*
adj electric, public, local, municipal, private, clinical, practical, potential *noun* sport., .vehicle, .company, power, .bill, water, .industry, .district *verb* pay, require, own, demonstrate., regulate, reduce, save, state, examine., limit
12335 | 0.89

2629 satellite *n*
adj small, global, Soviet, commercial, digital, military, Galilean, live, artificial, astronomical *noun* .dish, system, .radio, communication, TV, cable, .image, .phone, television *verb* use, launch, orbit, build, beam, detect, track, join., broadcast, transmit
11836 | 0.92 M

2630 extraordinary *j*
noun thing, star, event, power, story, circumstance, woman, effort, amount, measure, experience, step *misc* most, something, ordinary, such, four, quite, excellent
11459 | 0.95

2631 wave *v*
noun .hand, .arm, flag, .finger, .gun, car, crowd, .wand, air, door, banner, hair, .paper, .goodbye, camera *misc* .at, her, him, .back, .away, .off, .toward, .over, .front, stand., .through, frantically
12447 | 0.88 F

2632 ultimate *j*
noun goal, end, test, question, power, reality, authority, responsibility, success, decision, source, purpose *misc* human, perhaps, achieve, divine, retain, spiritual, universal, driving
11453 | 0.95

2633 chemical *n*
adj toxic, other, hazardous, synthetic, certain, natural, dangerous, agricultural, heavy, various *noun* .weapon, brain, use., company, water, plant, body, industry, food, level *verb* produce, contain., .cause, expose., mix, spray, treat, test, reduce, control
11897 | 0.91 M

2634 advocate *n*
adj strong, public, leading, human, civil, effective, patient, outspoken, free, poor *noun* right, consumer., child, health, devil., policy, privacy., victim, community *verb* become., .argue, .point, .claim, serve., act., .fear, .worry, .contend, .warn
11697 | 0.93

2635 wonder *n*
adj natural, small, one-hit, ancient, modern, technological, wide-eyed, gutless, childlike *noun* world, sense., boy, .drug, head., awe, kind, science, beauty, joy *verb* make., fill., stare., experience, discover., explore, witness., .cease
11371 | 0.96

2636 educator *n*
adj physical, special, environmental, professional, social, early, important, public, future, effective *noun* music., teacher, parent, art., school, education, study, program, health, community *verb* .need, .teach, help, .develop, .consider, .recognize, suggest, assist, encourage, train
14430 | 0.75 A

2637 cake n
adj round, yellow, remaining, moist, red, fried, cooled, light, miniature, iced *noun* chocolate., piece., .pan, birthday., wedding., layer, crab., pound. *verb* bake, eat, serve, cut, place, ice., prepare, cool, cook, order.
12089 | 0.90 M

2638 phrase n
adj familiar, key, common, two-word, famous, short, single, certain, favorite, musical *noun* word., catch., meaning, turn., sentence, book, noun., language, sound, list *verb* use, hear, coin, repeat, borrow., .describe, contain, sing, utter, .refer
11653 | 0.93

2639 yell v
noun voice, father., kid, boy, .name, guy, mom, dad, .help, crowd, coach, fire, phone, fan., .obscenity *misc* .at, .out, scream, .back, hear., start., stop
12091 | 0.90 F

2640 personally r
take., me., feel, .believe, like, professionally, .responsible, .involved, both., experience, involve, affect, attack, myself
11357 | 0.95 S

2641 respondent n
adj female, male, white, significant, likely, sexual, Hispanic, potential, environmental, total *noun* percent., survey, majority., table, number., group, percentage., poll, information, level *verb* ask, .indicate, .report, .believe, .identify, .agree, .answer, assess, compare, suggest
13806 | 0.79 A

2642 Palestinian j
noun authority, state, leader, people, refugee, territory, official, minister, land, uprising
13253 | 0.82 S

2643 classic j
noun example, case, movie, story, style, book, study, film, rock, car, period, tale *misc* American, French, modern, Italian, contemporary, western, southern
11514 | 0.94 M

2644 snap v
noun .finger, .picture, head, .photo, eye, .attention, neck, light, jaw, twig, .shot, ball, camera, photographer., tree *misc* .out, .off, .shut, .open, suddenly
up .by, head., company, investor., buyer., .stock, quickly, .share, .copy, bargain **back** head., .into, .place, .forth
12078 | 0.90 F

2645 via i
.e-mail, .Internet, .satellite, computer, .phone, send., .telephone, .web, information, .mail, service, .cable, reach., connect.
11772 | 0.92 A

2646 lawsuit n
adj federal, civil, class-action, frivolous, pending, similar, environmental, potential, separate, expensive *noun* court, action., shareholder., plaintiff, settlement, class., harassment., discrimination., malpractice., industry *verb* file, bring, settle., .claim, face., win., .seek, .accuse, dismiss, .challenge
11939 | 0.91 N

2647 install v
noun system, software, equipment, computer, company., government, program, window, camera, device, panel, line, door, wall, air *misc* new, easy., newly., recently., .solar, plan., properly, expensive, permanently., existing, .operate, square.
12490 | 0.87 M

2648 sweep v
noun .floor, wave., eye., .room, arm, hand, .country, wind., hair, area, .rug, street, .office, fire., .nation *misc* .away, .through, .into, .across, .over, .past
11476 | 0.94 F

2649 festival n
adj annual, international, cultural, local, religious, Olympic, major, outdoor, musical, traditional *noun* film., music., art, year, jazz., summer, event, folk. *verb* .feature, celebrate, attend., present, organize, sponsor, perform, .honor, host., dance
12198 | 0.89 N

2650 draft n
adj early, final, rough, composite, military, top, second-round, original *noun* .choice, pick, year, first-round., player, .report, round., .constitution, .board *verb* write, enter., avoid., read., prepare, dodge, review., circulate, present, comment.
11736 | 0.92 N

2651 heaven n
adj blue, dear, pure, culinary, literal, hillbilly *noun* .earth, .sake, .hell, gate, kingdom., angel, name, star, stairway., manna. *verb* go., thank., .forbid, die, reach., create., ascend., enter., rise., sing
11462 | 0.94 F

2652 switch v
noun .light, .side, .party, .gear, .leg, .lamp, position, .channel, .mode, Republican, phone, television, computer, focus, machine *misc* .from, .off, .back, repeat, quickly, .complete, suddenly., recently., automatically.
on .light, .lamp, .radio, .TV, .off, .flashlight, .television, power, .computer **off** .light, .lamp, television, .radio, .engine, .TV, .machine, .ignition, .flashlight
11379 | 0.95

2653 activist n
adj political, environmental, gay, social, conservative, democratic, black, longtime, liberal, young *noun* right., group, community., woman, AIDS., animal., peace., leader *verb* organize, support, .seek, .claim, .oppose, .argue, .protest, arrest, .complain, urge
11776 | 0.92

2654 ceiling n
adj high, low, vaulted, wooden, arched, domed, soaring *noun* wall, floor, room, .fan, glass, light, window, .tile, beam, foot *verb* stare., hang, fall, reach., suspend., hit., dangle., collapse, bounce., climb
11717 | 0.92 F

2655 clock n
adj biological, digital, internal, atomic, antique, astronomical, giant *noun* alarm., time, wall, ticking, .radio, grandfather., hour, tick, .tower *verb* look., turn., run, work., set, glance., stop, .read, .strike, watch.
11496 | 0.94 F

2656 graduate v
noun .school, student, college, .degree, senior, .honor, June, spring, .top, .May, institute, .tech, athlete, engineer, alumni *misc* .from, after., .cum, .laude, recently.
11447 | 0.94 N

2657 aunt *n*
adj young, favorite, crazy, elderly, maternal, dear, distant, beloved *noun* uncle, mother, cousin, house, sister, grandmother, grandparent *verb* live, die, visit., stay, smile, kiss, nod, belong., remind, whisper
12584 | 0.86 F

2658 darkness *n*
adj total, complete, cold, utter, cool, outer, growing, near *noun* light, night, eye, cover., hour, shadow, silence, window, prince., .fall *verb* disappear., stare., plunge., wait, emerge., .close, lay, descend, peer., surround
12295 | 0.88 F

2659 daddy *n*
adj big, dear, sorry, mad, proud, angry, drunk, loving *noun* mommy., mama, girl, mother, sugar., baby, mummy., mom *verb* love, .die, cry, .stare, hate, sleep, marry, kiss, scream, grab
12358 | 0.87 F

2660 royal *j*
noun family, society, palace, court, college, highness, oak, commission, museum, crown, police, hospital *misc* British, blue, Saudi, Dutch, Canadian, Caribbean, astronomical, mounted, ancient
11663 | 0.92

2661 advertising *n*
adj national, outdoor, political, negative, online, commercial *noun* .campaign, .agency, company, .revenue, marketing, television, .executive, product, .promotion, sales *verb* sell, spend, ban., increase, accept., promote, restrict, target, regulate., feature
11845 | 0.91 N

2662 rough *j*
noun time, edge, terrain, sea, surface, hand, water, spot, road, day, estimate, diamond *misc* little, pretty, tough, hit, tumble, smooth, wooden
11344 | 0.95

2663 pregnant *j*
noun woman, month, child, wife, mother, girl, daughter, teen, female, teenager, sister, girlfriend *misc* she, get, become, while, again, when, eight
11415 | 0.94

2664 penalty *n*
adj civil, stiff, severe, maximum, tough, financial, anti-death, heavy, ultimate, serious *noun* death., .case, tax, marriage., law, .phase, opponent, .kick *verb* pay., face., impose, seek., carry., support., oppose., apply, abolish., commit
11647 | 0.92

2665 distant *j*
noun galaxy, past, relative, cousin, future, star, place, voice, light, mountain, memory, object *misc* more, seem, hear, most, toward, grow, third, sound
11624 | 0.92 F

2666 developing *j*
noun country, world, nation, program, cancer, skill, child, technology, story, economy, strategy, relationship *misc* many, developed, especially, such, economic, particularly, reduce, rapidly
12184 | 0.88 A

2667 yield *v*
noun .result, .serving, .information, .percent, analysis., .effect, data, score, bond., study., .insight, .benefit,

.difference, fund., rate *misc* .about, .significant, .different, .better, .similar, desire.
11858 | 0.90 M A

2668 wind *v*
noun .way, road, path., head, trail., river, street, mile, arm, season., hair, clock, mountain, .hill, hour *misc* .through, .around, tightly, narrow, .along, .tight
   up may., might., .pay, eventually., often., .dead, .spend, probably., .jail, .cost **down** season., career, clock., cold
11151 | 0.96

2669 armed *j*
noun force, service, conflict, robbery, guard, man, group, member, struggle, police, soldier, officer *misc* heavily, against, serve, military, Soviet, Iraqi, dangerous, Islamic
12367 | 0.86 A

2670 mechanism *n*
adj different, social, effective, psychological, possible, international, various, complex, responsible, formal *noun* control, defense., market., coping., enforcement., dispute., .change, body, funding., policy *verb* use, provide, create, understand., develop, establish, .allow, suggest., cope, .ensure
12174 | 0.88 A

2671 rank *n*
adj high, mean, front, growing, professional, senior, upper, academic, democratic, middle *noun* .file, .order, school, table, officer, name., class, .top, nation, score *verb* join., rise., break., swell, close., fill., promote., enlist., enter., result
11350 | 0.94

2672 killer *n*
adj serial, natural, real, convicted, born, cold-blooded, accused, leading, silent *noun* .whale, child, cop., victim, .cell, .instinct, disease, pain., .bee *verb* find., catch, identify., confess, track., .strike, .stalk, claim, murder, search.
11451 | 0.93

2673 fence *n*
adj chain-link, white, barbed, wooden, barbed-wire, electric, tall, wrought-iron, split-rail *noun* wire, picket., side., .post, .line, border, iron., yard, link., chain. *verb* build, surround, climb., jump., mend., stand, sit., lean., .separate, enclose
11545 | 0.92 F

2674 ahead *i*
(ahead of) .of, .time, .him, .them, .me, .her, year., step, far., .schedule, stay., put., game, .curve
11130 | 0.96

2675 universal *j*
noun coverage, health, care, right, studio, declaration, access, language, principle, value, education, law *misc* human, almost, provide, nearly, ordinary, particular, basic, achieve
11550 | 0.92 A

2676 terror *n*
adj global, sheer, nuclear, pure, holy, absolute, abject *noun* war., .attack, reign., act., .group, .network, threat, campaign, .suspect *verb* fight., strike, scream., flee., fill., experience, freeze., grip, inflict, seize
11471 | 0.93 S

2677 wolf *n*
adj gray, lone, howling, hungry, northern, Canadian, ravenous *noun* medicine., pack, man, bear, dog, boy, sheep, .hunt, animal, correspondent. *verb* kill, cry., howl, catch, reintroduce, shoot, .roam, trap, .attack, chase
11795 | 0.90 F

2678 house *v*
noun building., center, museum, office, collection, program, service, city, facility, area, department, art, .worker, inmate, structure *misc* build., feed, .homeless, .poor, multifamily., currently., .elderly, temporarily., subsidize., .armed, random., formerly.
11226 | 0.95 N

2679 anxiety *n*
adj high, cognitive, somatic, social, competitive, low, general, increased, severe, extreme *noun* depression, level, state., .disorder, trait., fear, stress, performance *verb* reduce., cause, experience, suffer., create, express., increase, relieve., decrease, produce
12628 | 0.84 A

2680 chemical *j*
noun weapon, reaction, plant, company, agent, industry, composition, warfare, attack, process, fertilizer, engineer *misc* biological, use, nuclear, against, physical, produce, cause, toxic
11490 | 0.92

2681 found *v*
noun company, year, organization, school, .employee, city, center, business, Institute, .principle, community, art, century, bank, colony *misc* .by, who., .ago, since., .upon
11565 | 0.92

2682 protein *n*
adj soy, lean, human, dietary, complete, high-quality, viral, low-fat, adequate *noun* .carbohydrate, fat, gram, .vitamin, sugar., fiber, sodium, source, gene, animal. *verb* produce, contain, eat., bind, encode, form, identify, consume, combine, discover
12691 | 0.83 M

2683 engineering *n*
adj mechanical, genetic, electrical, social, civil, environmental, chemical *noun* science, professor, design, degree, student, department, technology, .firm, computer, research *verb* study., teach., apply, graduate, major., solve, combine, hire, integrate, pursue.
13436 | 0.79 A

2684 clothing *n*
adj protective, warm, used, expensive, casual, outdoor, civilian *noun* food., .store, woman, line, man., shelter, piece., article., item, designer *verb* wear, dress., buy., sell, remove., cover, own, hang, tear, sew
11057 | 0.96

2685 proceed *v*
noun court, .caution, process, trial, development, project, analysis, negotiation., .assumption, .manner, investigation, direction, stage, .recipe, impeachment *misc* then., how., shall., allow., .slowly, decide.
11054 | 0.96

2686 fiber *n*
adj dietary, optical, soluble, natural, moral, synthetic, insoluble, thin, soft, elastic *noun* .mg, sodium, .sugar, carbo., grain, carbohydrate., .cholesterol, carbon.,

protein, .optic *verb* contain, eat., increase, weave, pack., connect, consume, load., absorb, boost.
12431 | 0.85 M

2687 react *v*
noun people., body., .situation, .news, market., .shock, public., .horror, official., audience., .crisis, American., .surprise, oxygen, .anger *misc* how., .when, .differently, .quickly, .against
11074 | 0.95

2688 bottom *j*
noun line, half, bracket, edge, lip, drawer, end, side, row, corner, shelf, panel *misc* left, hit, top, affect, bite, hurt, bet, boost
11278 | 0.94 M

2689 spin *v*
noun wheel, head., .control, .tale, .web, story, air, .circle, mind., .yarn, .heel, star, .chair, light, arm *misc* .around, .away, start., .faster, .toward
off .its, company, plan., firm, sell, .subsidiary, cable **out** story, .tale, .onto, .scenario
11623 | 0.91 F

2690 roughly *r*
.percent, .million, .same, year, .half, .billion, .size, .equal, .equivalent, .mile
11200 | 0.94 M

2691 drama *n*
adj high, human, political, creative, modern, real-life, historical *noun* music, .series, school, comedy, family, TV., television, art, actor., courtroom. *verb* unfold, create, add., watch., star, direct, .surround, capture, feature, act
11364 | 0.93

2692 liberty *n*
adj civil, American, religious, individual, human, personal, negative, positive *noun* right, statue., life., freedom, .justice, .pursuit, equality, .property, .media, .group *verb* take., protect, enjoy, secure, defend., preserve, violate, guarantee, infringe., deny
11554 | 0.91 A

2693 ingredient *n*
adj remaining, active, dry, key, essential, main, fresh, large, natural, important *noun* bowl, food, list, cup, oil, product, dish, mixture, sauce, salad *verb* combine., add, stir, mix, use, contain., blend, place, buy
12083 | 0.87 M

2694 hip *n*
adj right, left, low, wide, narrow, artificial, broken, broad, slim, wider *noun* hand., knee, shoulder, leg, .hop, .fracture, .replacement, bone, .pocket *verb* keep, bend, lift, move, break., sway, swing, raise, join., rotate
11730 | 0.90 F M

2695 provision *n*
adj constitutional, key, environmental, general, basic, statutory, certain, adequate, educational, various *noun* service, law, act, care, health, tax, enforcement., citizen, court, convention *verb* include., contain., .allow, .require, apply, add, violate., enforce., .protect, implement
12538 | 0.84 A

2696 burden *n*
adj heavy, financial, economic, additional, undue, huge, terrible *noun* .proof, tax., debt, care,

responsibility, cost, caregiver, taxpayer, share•, beast•
verb bear•, carry, place, put•, impose, shift, ease•, reduce•, shoulder•, •fall
11264 | 0.93

2697 teen *n*
adj early, late, black, pregnant, troubled, gay, likely, active, typical, online *noun* •pregnancy, •year, parent, child, •mother, girl, kid, rate, age *verb* teach, enter, smell•, •smoke, attend, encourage, aim•, target•, charge, hire
11434 | 0.92 N

2698 survival *n*
adj long-term, economic, political, human, very, cultural, essential, necessary, basic, overall *noun* •rate, chance•, •skill, species, strategy, struggle•, matter•, instinct, patient, •guide *verb* ensure•, •depend, threaten•, fight•, improve•, increase•, assure•, decrease, •vary, •hinge
11382 | 0.92 A

2699 unlikely *j*
noun place, event, source, candidate, hero, scenario, ally, pair, possibility, coalition, friendship, combination *misc* it, seem, highly, very, most, any, such
10998 | 0.95

2700 Italian *j*
noun restaurant, immigrant, food, renaissance, parsley, family, sausage, bread, woman, government, city, wine
11539 | 0.91

2701 chamber *n*
adj local, main, upper, inner, sleeping, dark *noun* •commerce, •music, gas•, president, •orchestra, torture•, •pot, combustion•, •deputy *verb* enter•, fill, •contain, form, echo, house, install, empty, pace, illuminate
11178 | 0.94

2702 lost *j*
noun time, cause, child, world, revenue, soul, city, tribe, love, boy, opportunity *misc* get, replace, regain, recover, restore, reclaim, search
10871 | 0.96

2703 communicate *v*
noun ability•, information, message, parent, idea, language, teacher, •public, need, computer, •feeling, •audience, •vision, cell, •value *misc* •with, able•, •each, •other, effectively, •another, learn•, •directly, clearly
11123 | 0.94 A

2704 stupid *j*
noun thing, question, man, kid, idea, girl, mistake, stuff, bitch, joke, boy, game *misc* so, something, too, really, feel, enough, sound, anything
11498 | 0.91 F

2705 bet *v*
noun •dollar, stock, •horse, •farm, investor•, •baseball, race, future, •buck, •ranch, casino, gambler•, trader•, •rent, Microsoft• *misc* I•, you, will, •against, best•, willing•, •heavily
on •game, want•, when, just, own, because, any, thing, •whether, about
11178 | 0.93 F

2706 advance *v*
noun technology, •interest, •cause, argument, •career, •agenda, theory, •understanding, team•, idea, goal,

•round, •knowledge, research, level *misc* far, •toward, political, •beyond, order•
11114 | 0.94 A

2707 Muslim *j*
noun world, country, woman, community, leader, group, population, man, nation, brother
11783 | 0.89 A

2708 bell *n*
adj closing, final, distant, diving, faint, tardy *noun* •pepper, church•, ring, •whistle, •tower, alarm•, •curve, door, ringing, warning• *verb* hear•, sound, •toll, set•, jingle, answer, •chime, hang, clang, strike
11089 | 0.94 F

2709 onion *n*
adj green, red, medium, chopped, large, small, yellow *noun* garlic, cup, pepper, oil, heat•, tomato, celery, tablespoon, carrot, potato *verb* add•, chop, cook, stir, sauté, dice, •soften, brown, fry
12255 | 0.85 M N

2710 disagree *v*
noun people•, •statement, percent, other•, expert•, court, judge, Republican, scientist•, •conclusion, American•, scholar•, pornography *misc* •with, strongly, agree•, whether, respectfully•
11255 | 0.93 S

2711 encounter *v*
noun problem, difficulty, student, •resistance, obstacle, experience, •opposition, type, individual, culture, •variety, •hostility, visitor•, environment, barrier *misc* when, first, may•, never•, ever•
11117 | 0.94 A

2712 constitutional *j*
noun right, amendment, law, court, state, issue, government, protection, reform, convention, principle, provision *misc* violate, ban, federal, legal, pass, political, protect, require
11838 | 0.88 A

2713 cabinet *n*
adj wooden, locked, entire, upper, antique, dark, presidential, inner, diverse *noun* member, •minister, kitchen•, medicine•, file•, president, •secretary, •door *verb* open, •meet, build, appoint•, approve, form, name, install, lock, contain
10966 | 0.95

2714 remarkable *j*
noun thing, story, woman, success, achievement, ability, life, change, career, performance, job, feat *misc* most, really, quite, show, truly, perhaps, pretty, rather
10859 | 0.96

2715 broken *j*
noun glass, bone, heart, leg, window, promise, piece, arm, home, branch, rib, nose *misc* suffer, fix, left, repair, mend, replace, litter, lay
11086 | 0.94 F

2716 latter *d*
•part, •case, •half, •group, while•, former, during•, •category, choose•, although•, especially, •stage, example, •being
11713 | 0.89 A

2717 overcome *v*
noun obstacle, problem, •fear, barrier, challenge, difficulty, •resistance, •limitation, hurdle, •deficit,

.adversity, effort., .feeling, .opposition, weakness
misc help., must., able., difficult.
10913 | 0.95 A

2718 virus *n*
adj human, deadly, cold, positive, live, lethal,
specific, known *noun* AIDS., bacteria, computer.,
flu., influenza., infection, hepatitis., cell,
immunodeficiency., disease *verb* cause,
infect, spread, carry, kill, contract., transmit,
attack, .mutate
11441 | 0.91

2719 stranger *n*
adj total, complete, perfect, mysterious, handsome,
tall, intimate, familiar, gentle, passing *noun* friend,
kindness., eye, street, face, group, .town, sex,
.controversy, .train *verb* talk., meet, stare,
approach, share, welcome, trust., sleep,
introduce, touch
11232 | 0.93 F

2720 retain *v*
noun .control, .power, .right, student, ability, .water,
.moisture, .information, .identity, .employee, .heat,
interest, memory, .status, .title *misc* while., still.,
attract., .original, able.
11187 | 0.93 A

2721 match *n*
adj perfect, good, shouting, better, exact, final, close,
waterproof *noun* winner, wrestling., soccer., .play,
tennis., boxing., cup., box., championship *verb* win.,
find, light, strike., lose, meet., prove, .burn, .last,
touch
11140 | 0.93

2722 prize *n*
adj grand, big, top, international, prestigious,
ultimate, literary, coveted, nifty *noun* .winner, peace.,
.money, year, award, .physics, cash., .literature,
consolation., .chemistry *verb* win., receive., offer,
share., earn., claim., honor, .total, .elude
10944 | 0.95

2723 string *n*
adj long, consecutive, thin, endless, broken, knotted,
unbroken *noun* .quartet, .theory, .bean, purse., bead,
.pearl, guitar, piece., instrument, band *verb* pull.,
.attach, tie, hold, hang, cut, pluck., stretch, vibrate,
control.
10986 | 0.95

2724 exhibition *n*
adj international, major, recent, annual, traveling,
current, retrospective *noun* art, museum, .game,
gallery, work, .space, works, solo., artist, painting
verb include, organize, open, present, feature, mount,
.entitle, enter, accompany, represent
12767 | 0.81 M

2725 expansion *n*
adj economic, rapid, major, far, international, future,
global, existing, industrial, urban *noun* .team,
universe, plan, program, rate, .franchise, market,
trade, growth, period. *verb* support., cause, oppose.,
finance., slow, limit., increase, prevent., halt.,
accelerate
11351 | 0.91 A

2726 tremendous *j*
noun amount, pressure, impact, opportunity, power,
growth, number, change, energy, problem, success,

support *misc* there, create, under, cause, because,
economic, generate, financial
11013 | 0.94 S

2727 bunch *n*
adj whole, wild, fresh, diverse, rowdy, lively, friendly
noun .people, .guy, .kid, .thing, .stuff, .grape, .flower,
.money *verb* buy., hang, throw, gather, sound., score.,
hand., hire.
11109 | 0.93

2728 assistant *n*
adj special, personal, administrative, digital, editorial,
medical, top, dental, legislative *noun* research.,
deputy., .secretary, .president, teaching., graduate.,
executive., physician. *verb* serve., hire., employ, train,
.handle, assign, .administer, .hand, appoint., instruct
10976 | 0.94

2729 initially *r*
least, at, although., appear, .refuse, .focus, .oppose,
.skeptical, .resist, .identify, .reluctant, .intend, .attract,
design
11106 | 0.93 A

2730 accurate *j*
noun information, description, picture, assessment,
data, count, prediction, measurement, estimate, way,
diagnosis, representation *misc* more, most, provide,
less, fair, complete, highly
11036 | 0.94 A

2731 cheek *n*
adj left, pink, right, pale, round, hot, sunken, smooth,
full, flushed *noun* tear., hand, eye, lip, kiss., hair,
nose, color, tongue., forehead *verb* touch., turn, run.,
feel, roll., press, brush., stroke., rub., puff
12061 | 0.86 F

2732 index *n*
adj composite, fit, right, economic, major, leading,
body-mass, various *noun* .finger, .fund, price., stock,
consumer., body., mass., .card *verb* .rise, measure, .fall,
provide, calculate, .close, track, .drop, .indicate, .gain
11540 | 0.90 A

2733 occupy *v*
noun .position, space, place, land, territory, house,
building, room, mind, country, office, center, Iraq,
troop, force *misc* .by, .same, once., .central, .entire
10952 | 0.95

2734 gear *n*
adj high, low, protective, full, outdoor, electronic,
shifting, high-tech, switching, running *noun* fishing.,
landing., .photography, car, camping., rain., bag, type,
.ratio, riot. *verb* shift., put., switch., wear., carry, kick.,
pack., change., grind, haul.
11907 | 0.87 M

2735 guarantee *v*
noun right, loan, .accuracy, security, constitution,
.success, .safety, law, government, freedom, job,
amendment, protection, .access, health *misc* will,
can., virtually., million, .equal, order., necessarily.,
practically.
10833 | 0.95

2736 chocolate *n*
adj hot, dark, white, bittersweet, rich, melted,
unsweetened *noun* .cake, .chip, milk, .cookie, cream,
.bar, cup, butter, ice, .mousse *verb* melt, eat., stir, add,
pour, buy, drink, contain, taste, spread
11324 | 0.91 M

22. American vs. British English

The Corpus of Contemporary American English (COCA: http://www.americancorpus.org) is the largest balanced corpus of American English, and the British National Corpus (BNC; http://www.natcorp.ox.ac.uk/) is the largest, balanced corpus of British English. This list shows the difference in vocabulary in these two corpora, and is based on the implementation of the BNC found at http://corpus.byu.edu/bnc.

Some of the differences in vocabulary in the two dialects are related to culture, society, politics, or current events (e.g. Am *Republican, congressional, baseball, Iraqi*; Br *Tory, parliamentary, Victorian*), some are just different words for the "same" concept (e.g. *store/shop, attorney/solicitor, apartment/flat, mom/mum*), and some words in COCA (1990–2008) refer to things that are too new to have made it into the pre-1993 BNC (e.g. *web, Internet, high-tech, online*).

+American (COCA) / –British (BNC)
The following are just a sampling of the words that are much more common in COCA than in the BNC. In all cases, the word is at least twice as far down the list in the BNC wordlist as in COCA (e.g. #2000 in COCA, #5000 in BNC).

Verb: call, report, focus, guess, sign, step, figure, roll, fire, hire, file, oppose, wrap, interview, accomplish, testify, bake, track, evolve, violate, target, pitch, flip, ruin, hike, invade

Noun: student, president, percent, kid, guy, nation, photo, arm, American, Republican, phone, movie, store, lawyer, Democrat, professor, expert, senator, break, camera, coach, item, mom, dream, attorney, scientist, web, camp, truck, apartment, bowl, baseball, internet, basketball

Adjective: American, federal, tough, native, Iraqi, crazy, smart, Israeli, Mexican, congressional, elementary, online, gifted, athletic, ongoing, African-American, suburban, Hispanic, scary, high-tech, cute, nonprofit, immigrant, skeptical, aging, low-income, interstate

+British (BNC) / –American (COCA)
The following are just a sampling of the words that are much more common in the BNC than in COCA. In all cases, the word is at least twice as far down the list in the COCA wordlist as in the BNC (e.g. #2000 in the BNC, #5000 in COCA).

Verb: ensure, suppose, regard, voice, bind, retain, undertake, phone, wan, allocate, knit, book, abolish, envisage, incur, fancy, commence, enclose, enquire, sack, adjourn, tidy, query, retort, queue, nick, remand, smelt

Noun: council, minister, union, pound, scheme, shop, principle, village, provision, sector, appeal, parliament, mum, tea, lord, cabinet, pension, flat, expenditure, solicitor, coal, crown, castle, pub, parish, tenant, councillor, countryside, plaintiff, autumn, cottage

Adjective: British, European, English, royal, French, industrial, Scottish, lovely, working, bloody, parliamentary, alright, statutory, keen, Welsh, Tory, socialist, unemployed, delighted, Victorian, liable, superb, working-class, compulsory, splendid, post-war, dreadful, redundant, inland, wee

2737 ceremony *n*
adj religious, closing, traditional, annual, private, formal, civil, brief, solemn, ribbon-cutting *noun* opening•, award•, wedding•, graduation•, day, master•, marriage•, white, signing• *verb* hold, attend•, perform, open•, conduct, honor, follow, •mark, participate•, •celebrate
11008 | 0.94

2738 button *n*
adj hot, red, mute, wrong, blue, off, left, nuclear *noun* belly•, shirt, push•, elevator, finger•, door, touch•, •mushroom, call•, panic• *verb* hit•, punch•, click•, wear•, release, pop, fasten
11353 | 0.91 F

2739 shopping *n*
adj one-stop, online, suburban, busy, downtown, electronic, regional *noun* .center, .mall, .bag, .cart, .list, home, grocery, .trip, holiday, .guide *verb* build, buy, carry, fill, push, finish, .cook, enjoy.
11047 | 0.94 N

2740 pay *n*
adj low, equal, high, take-home, better, average, extra, annual *noun* .phone, percent, year, .cut, .benefit, worker, work, teacher, increase, executive. *verb* .raise, receive, earn, suspend, keep, accept.
11015 | 0.94 N

2741 dispute *n*
adj legal, political, territorial, domestic, bitter, involved, alternative, major, ongoing, long-running *noun* resolution, settlement, labor, .trade, border, contract, .mechanism *verb* resolve, settle, involve, .arise, mediate, end, solve, deal, adjudicate, avoid
11586 | 0.89 A

2742 like *r*
just, guy, mean, really, .oh, kind, sort
12092 | 0.85 S

2743 furniture *n*
adj American, antique, fine, painted, outdoor, upholstered, wooden, used *noun* piece, room, .store, .maker, office, wall, art, design, wood, floor *verb* move, buy, sell, rearrange, fill, arrange
11674 | 0.88 M

2744 marine *j*
noun mammal, US, fishery, life, biologist, division, resource, environment, ecosystem, officer, unit, species *misc* national, former, service, retired, expeditionary, coastal, terrestrial, environmental, freshwater
11351 | 0.91

2745 statistics *n*
adj descriptive, national, vital, available, official, recent, economic, federal, educational *noun* bureau, labor, table, health, education, crime, number, government, data, analysis *verb* .show, .indicate, keep, compile, .suggest, report, cite, base, collect, present
11123 | 0.93 A

2746 Olympic *j*
noun game, committee, team, gold, medal, park, trial, athlete, medalist, champion, sport, stadium
12067 | 0.85 N

2747 balance *v*
noun .budget, need, .work, .interest, .checkbook, book, .demand, body, .career, weight, cost, .leg, attempt, account, .edge *misc* try, .against, must, .federal, precariously
   out will, all, thing, kind, .life, .over
10690 | 0.96

2748 wipe *v*
noun hand, .eye, .tear, .face, .mouth, .sweat, .nose, .forehead, table, finger *misc* .off, .away, .clean, down, .across, .dry, whole, quickly, carefully, nearly, virtually, gently
   out can, .by, entire, whole, disease, saving, virtually, species, nearly, .dinosaur
11338 | 0.91 F

2749 spokesman *n*
adj national, foreign, chief, military, official, presidential, leading, corporate, eloquent

noun house, department, state, company, US, president, government, police, ministry, army, *verb* say, .decline, .deny, comment, .confirm, quote, .insist, .acknowledge, press, concede
11775 | 0.87 N

2750 super *j*
noun bowl, team, delegate, champion, power, victory, game, season, hero, coach, model, star *misc* win, play, four, rich, superconducting, Austrian, host, straight
11323 | 0.91 N

2751 Islamic *j*
noun group, world, jihad, law, republic, movement, state, revolution, fundamentalism, militant, country, fundamentalist
12011 | 0.86 A

2752 track *v*
noun .progress, .movement, system, computer, .change, police, .trend, firm, stock, camera, .activity, satellite, ability, .sales, storm *misc* try, able, closely, .across, easy, difficult, easily
   down try, help, able, finally, .killer, investigator, .terrorist, .source, .suspect, effort.
10711 | 0.96

2753 translate *v*
noun language, .English, word, book, .action, .French, text, .practice, .Arabic, .German, computer, success, .document, knowledge, article *misc* .into, .Spanish, roughly, necessarily, directly
10827 | 0.95 A

2754 interpret *v*
noun way, result, court, data, law, .constitution, finding, .caution, .information, .meaning *misc* .as, how, .mean, difficult, .differently, correctly, analyze, broadly, thus, widely, .literally
11472 | 0.89 A

2755 testify *v*
noun witness, .Congress, .trial, court, .jury, .hearing, expert, .committee, case, .oath, officer, week, police, official, agent. *misc* .before, .against, .grand, .under, refuse.
11147 | 0.92 S

2756 cooperation *n*
adj economic, international, regional, military, great, full, mutual, environmental, close *noun* security, .development, organization, state, government, agreement, level, competition, lack, conference. *verb* require, promote, seek, facilitate, encourage, enhance, foster, gain, establish, emphasize
11716 | 0.87 A

2757 friendly *j*
noun fire, way, face, relation, smile, country, service, place, voice, relationship, government, manner *misc* environmentally, very, warm, helpful, nice, everyone, outgoing, familiar
10562 | 0.97

2758 profile *n*
adj high, low, psychological, demographic, similar, public, typical, unique, genetic, lipid *noun* type, student, personality, core, case, .courage, DNA, mood, face, risk. *verb* keep, fit, raise, maintain, create, match, develop, reveal, indicate, contain
11096 | 0.92 A

2759 pants (PL) *n*
adj black, white, baggy, long, blue, short, hot, red, gray, green *noun* shirt, .leg, pair., jacket, pocket, leather., hand., shoe, boot, sweater *verb* wear., pull, put, drop, wet., roll, unzip., hang, fit, pee.
11379 | 0.90 F

2760 whereas *c*
.other, percent, male, female, .tend, score, past, participant, .latter, .previous, traditional, positive, sexual., negative
11629 | 0.88 A

2761 honor *v*
noun .memory, .commitment, .father, member, .request, tradition, .veteran, .ancestor, contract, .promise, .agreement, player, .obligation, .soldier, individual *misc* respect, .thy, recently., choose., refuse., deeply., .fallen, gather., truly.
10658 | 0.96

2762 elite *n*
adj political, ruling, military, economic, cultural, urban, intellectual, educated, popular, administrative *noun* group, .athlete, member., power, .school, business., .team, media, country, .unit *verb* join., control, .seek, dominate, train, .maintain, belong., compete, favor, educate
11543 | 0.88 A

2763 decline *n*
adj economic, steady, sharp, steep, significant, rapid, gradual, dramatic, general *noun* percent, rate, year, .number, population, price, market, stock, reason., .value *verb* show., lead., cause., experience., contribute., suffer., reverse., .occur, appear, reveal.
11161 | 0.91 A

2764 port *n*
adj serial, southern, busy, parallel, main, foreign, various, Irish, Mediterranean, eastern *noun* .authority, .city, ship, .side, .call, .facility, town, sea., security, home. *verb* leave., arrive., open, connect, reach., close, sail., enter., return., .handle
10964 | 0.93

2765 complicated *j*
noun issue, thing, system, process, life, situation, problem, case, story, question, relationship, matter *misc* more, than, very, too, become, much, little
10468 | 0.97

2766 cousin *n*
adj distant, close, female, wild, male, favorite, chemical, European, dear, long-lost *noun* uncle, aunt, brother, friend, sister, father, marriage, wedding *verb* marry, visit, kiss., resemble., murder, free., .drown
11039 | 0.92 F

2767 strategic *j*
noun planning, study, plan, interest, defense, alliance, decision, importance, initiative, weapon, arm, force *misc* international, nuclear, political, economic, develop, military, tactical, major
11450 | 0.89 A

2768 terrorist *n*
adj suspected, international, foreign, potential, nuclear, known, alleged, religious, wanted, domestic *noun* attack, country, group, weapon, war, hand, target, criminal, terrorism, drug *verb* kill, fight., .strike, stop., capture, negotiate., deal., support, .operate, defeat
11282 | 0.90 S

2769 chart *n*
adj organizational, electronic, following, accompanying, periodic, astrological, genealogical *noun* .page, billboard., table, week, pop., star., .position, number, pg., depth. *verb* see., .show, top., list, read, .compare, .omit, check., indicate, hit
11100 | 0.92 M

2770 drawing *n*
adj detailed, preliminary, original, schematic, initial, finished, accurate, composite, complete, black-and-white *noun* painting, .board, .room, line., child, figure, paper, charcoal, graphite, color *verb* create, include, produce, .depict, study, enter., transfer, finish, feature, illustrate
12599 | 0.81 M

2771 though *r*
.mean, .yeah, OK, nice., pretty., fun., interesting., thanks, stuff., okay, funny., matter.
11030 | 0.92 S

2772 gently *r*
her, hand, down, pull, push, .until, touch, stir, toss, press, arm, shoulder, finger, head
11261 | 0.90 F

2773 pack *n*
adj heavy, light, whole, empty, crumpled, loaded *noun* cigarette, ice, rat, wolf, battery., day, back, dog, leader, .animal *verb* lead., carry, pull, buy., smoke., drop., open., .contain, .weigh
12050 | 0.84 M

2774 odd *j*
noun thing, job, way, couple, man, angle, moment, place, hour, behavior, number, feeling *misc* seem, very, something, feel, sound, little
10854 | 0.93 F

2775 incentive *n*
adj financial, economic, strong, powerful, private, added, additional, federal, long-term, special *noun* tax., program, government, policy, plan, structure, package, care, use, price *verb* provide., give., offer., create., reduce, .encourage, increase, change, remove., .attract
11247 | 0.90 A

2776 innocent *j*
noun people, man, child, life, civilian, victim, person, bystander, woman, death, charge, girl *misc* kill, guilty, until, proven, prove, believe, young
10717 | 0.95 S

2777 imply *v*
noun name., term., word., result., change, finding., relationship, article., sex, model, .existence, approach, .endorsement, nature, meaning *misc* seem., such, necessarily., .certain, strongly., clearly.
11355 | 0.89 A

2778 taste *v*
noun pepper., salt, food, wine, sauce, mouth, water, sugar, .blood, juice, fruit, air, chicken, lip, tongue *misc* .like, .good, .better, .serve, freshly, add, .sweet, smell, ever., fresh, hot, eat
11213 | 0.90 N

2779 stadium *n*
adj new, Olympic, domed, empty, municipal, indoor *noun* football., game, baseball., mile., field, giant., team, fan, home, sport. *verb* build, play, fill, finance., name, enter., arrive., .cost, .host, .seat
11745 | 0.86 N

2780 scenario *n*
adj worst-case, bad, possible, likely, best-case, whole, hypothetical, alternative, similar, various *noun* case., nightmare., kind., price, doomsday., war, climate, participant, analysis, range *verb* describe, imagine., create, present, consider, .involve, assume, envision, .occur, .unfold
10902 | 0.93 A

2781 shooting *n*
adj drive-by, final, fatal, three-point, deadly, outside, free-throw, mass, foul *noun* school, police, percent, .guard, .death, .star, .script, .war, .range, .incident *verb* start, .occur, stop, kill, investigate, witness., improve, charge., accuse., injure.
10851 | 0.93 N

2782 blind *j*
noun man, eye, student, people, child, date, spot, person, faith, boy, vision, woman *misc* who, visually, turn, deaf, impaired, impair, legally, low, nearly
10868 | 0.93

2783 assembly *n*
adj general, national, legislative, final, entire, constitutional, provincial *noun* .line, state., .plant, member, speaker, nation, constituent., election, school, seat *verb* elect, pass, require, adopt, approve, .vote, address, convene, attend, organize
11055 | 0.91 A

2784 withdraw *v*
noun troop, .Kuwait, Iraq, money, hand, Israel., .support, fund, nomination, decision., Saddam., Hussein., .name, army, .race *misc* .from, force, agree., completely, decide.
10584 | 0.95

2785 strip *n*
adj comic, thin, narrow, commercial, white, wide, green, magnetic, coastal, blue *noun* bank., .mall, .club, .land, center, sunset., landing., shopping, .joint, .search *verb* cut., place, slice., lay, tear., wrap, glue, remove., attach, apply
10639 | 0.94

2786 market *v*
noun product, company, farmer., .force, fish., drug, service, price, .research, food *misc* bring., plan., .themselves, aggressively, .itself, directly, design
10868 | 0.92

2787 lover *n*
adj male, secret, married, jealous, female, lesbian, longtime, Latin, star-crossed *noun* friend, music., wife, husband, art., animal., nature. *verb* become., kiss, sing, abandon, murder., embrace, betray, reunite, dump., .quarrel
10760 | 0.93 F

2788 process *v*
noun .information, data, food, material, appeal., system, product, claim, application, image, brain., computer, admission., transaction, blender. *misc* .until, .smooth, collect., quickly, .blend
11095 | 0.91 A

2789 mainly *r*
.because, focus, consist., base, .due, occur., rely., concerned, compose., aim, .interested
10662 | 0.94 A

2790 aircraft *n*
adj military, commercial, civilian, unmanned, allied, tactical, light, flying *noun* .carrier, air, fighter., .engine, missile, part, ship, pilot, .industry, jet. *verb* fly, shoot, land, build, carry, send, drop, operate, involve
10991 | 0.91

2791 newly *r*
.form, .create, .elect, .arrive, .discover, .independent, .acquire, .establish, .open, .appoint
10598 | 0.95

2792 ideal *j*
noun condition, place, situation, body, weight, world, person, woman, type, candidate, image, model *misc* for, provide, less, describe, current, female, male
10840 | 0.93 M A

2793 dirt *n*
adj red, loose, soft, bare, brown, packed, fresh *noun* .road, .floor, .track, .path, dust, rock, foot, pay., .bike, grass *verb* dig., hit., cover, remove., kick, brush., throw, eat., pull, wash
10950 | 0.92 F

2794 flow *v*
noun water., river, blood., stream., fluid, tear., juice., current., hair, body, .lake, .north, sea, fund, electron *misc* .from, .into, .through, .out, .freely
10478 | 0.96

2795 boundary *n*
adj national, political, social, international, cultural, traditional, maritime, clear, disciplinary, professional *noun* state, line, park., area, .condition, .layer, community, land, .dispute, space *verb* cross., set, define, push., mark., establish, transcend., blur., create, .separate
11156 | 0.90 A

2796 resort *n*
adj luxury, popular, all-inclusive, exclusive, Caribbean, western, coastal, contemporary *noun* ski., hotel, beach., mountain., .town, spa, golf, island, area *verb* .offer, own, visit, .feature, .cater, .attract, lodge., .boast, .overlook, rent
11365 | 0.88 M

2797 genetic *j*
noun engineering, material, code, disease, testing, information, diversity, test, research, disorder, makeup, variation *misc* human, environmental, cause, identify, carry, develop, rare, biological
11172 | 0.89 M

2798 stick *n*
adj big, long, little, short, wooden, measuring, sharp, digging, crooked, green *noun* .butter, walking., cinnamon., carrot., end., .figure, .stone, hockey., needle. *verb* use, hold, carry., throw, pick., poke, grab., shake., soften, swing.
10718 | 0.93 F

2799 concentration *n*
adj high, low, large, atmospheric, intense, heavy, total, greatest, increased, average *noun* .camp, power, level, blood, serum., carbon, water, ozone, memory, air *verb* increase, contain., require, reduce., measure, lose., break, exceed, decrease, cause
11290 | 0.88 A

2800 naturally *r*
occur, come., quite., body, produce, grow, hair,
.assume, plant, substance, tend, flow, arise, bacteria
10506 | 0.95 M

2801 ministry *n*
adj foreign, public, international, Christian, pastoral,
various, ordained, active, lay *noun* defense,
.education, official, finance, health, .affair,
government., church, .culture, .spokesman
verb enter., support, .announce, establish, head,
.issue, found, .confirm, engage, sponsor
11105 | 0.90

2802 surprising *j*
noun number, result, thing, finding, way, fact,
amount, news, answer, discovery, strength, degree
misc it, not, that, most, find, hardly, perhaps, shall
10406 | 0.96

2803 adviser *n*
adj national, senior, economic, financial, top, political,
chief, foreign, legal, presidential *noun* security.,
president, policy., investment., council., campaign,
science., friend., deputy *verb* serve., .recommend,
.urge, hire., consult., act., resign, .warn, .insist,
.convince
10991 | 0.91 N

2804 recommendation *n*
adj following, future, final, strong, current,
dietary, consistent, key, appropriate, practical
noun commission, report, policy., committee,
letter., conclusion., finding., health, change, practice
verb make, base, follow., include, provide, offer,
implement, accept, present, consider
10915 | 0.91 A

2805 similarly *r*
.situate, price, .size, .equip, treat, affect, dress,
behave., respectively., .configure, .dramatic
11215 | 0.89 A

2806 justify *v*
noun .action, .means, war, end., cost, .existence,
.decision, .policy, .ground, evidence, violence,
argument., force, intervention, claim *misc* use,
enough., such, order., difficult., hard., morally, fully.,
sufficient.
10761 | 0.93 A

2807 wildlife *n*
adj endangered, local, native, abundant, marine,
threatened, exotic *noun* fish., .refuge, .service,
US., .habitat, park, area, .biologist, .management,
.conservation *verb* protect., preserve, manage,
view, affect., attract, harm., .depend, thrive,
abound
11235 | 0.89 M

2808 bench *n*
adj wooden, federal, front, flat, rear, concrete, green,
padded *noun* park., .press, seat, foot, judge, player,
stone., piano., coach, lab. *verb* sit., stand, lie, face,
rest, approach., step, appoint., legislate., lay
10781 | 0.92 F

2809 bullet *n*
adj magic, stray, single, rubber, speeding, fatal,
.38-caliber *noun* .hole, head, silver., gun, .wound,
chest, lead, .train, body, .fragment *verb* hit, fire,
dodge., put., shoot, bite., kill, strike, .fly, riddle.
10816 | 0.92

2810 mode *n*
adj different, various, narrative, dominant, primary,
preferred, normal, automatic, particular, manual
noun .transportation, .production, .thought,
.expression, .communication, .operation,
transmission, .thinking, .presentation, survival.
verb use, switch., operate., shift., select, adopt.,
define, correspond, .enable, slip.
11285 | 0.88 A

2811 square *j*
noun foot, mile, inch, kilometer, area, meter, footage,
root, building, block, yard, face *misc* per, than, about,
million, more, cover, every, small, over
10604 | 0.94

2812 champion *n*
adj national, Olympic, two-time, three-time, reigning,
four-time, eventual, junior, grand, past *noun* world.,
defending., heavyweight., state., cup., .record, league,
bowl., boxing., class. *verb* defend., become., .win,
beat, repeat., defeat, crown, knock, reign, .struggle
11360 | 0.87 N

2813 dismiss *v*
noun case, charge, .idea, motion., .notion, claim,
.possibility, .concern, .suggestion, class, evidence,
officer *misc* .as, against, easily., simply, easy., quickly
10401 | 0.95

2814 deck *n*
adj upper, low, top, main, wooden, rear, front,
continuous *noun* .card, flight., .chair, ship, tape., boat,
observation., back., pool, sun *verb* stand., sit., stack,
hit., build, clear., .overlook, fall, shuffle., step.
10983 | 0.90 F

2815 lifetime *n*
adj whole, entire, average, honorary, limited, virtual,
brief *noun* .achievement, .award, .partner, experience,
.use, number, .employment, activity, opportunity, course.
verb last., spend., receive., face., honor, earn, achieve
10284 | 0.96

2816 extensive *j*
noun research, use, experience, study, program,
damage, network, system, collection, training, work,
review *misc* more, most, require, conduct, provide,
include, after
10821 | 0.92 A

2817 attractive *j*
noun woman, man, alternative, option, place, girl,
feature, price, investment, stock, investor, target
misc more, make, very, find, most, less, young
10306 | 0.96

2818 politically *r*
.correct, more., .incorrect, economically, .active,
become., socially, .charge, .motivate, .sensitive,
.motivated, both., .powerful
10676 | 0.93

2819 regularly *r*
who., use, meet., attend, exercise., .scheduled, visit,
appear, eat, check, church, meeting
10482 | 0.94 M

2820 raw *j*
noun material, data, meat, score, sewage, power, food,
deal, vegetable, umber, sienna, egg *misc* eat, cooked,
rub, red, fresh, burnt, contain, yellow
10392 | 0.95

2821 fault *n*
adj comparative, electrical, relative, geologic, double, grievous, geological, deepest *noun* .line, earthquake, .zone, Congress, media, ground., .divorce, .approach *verb* find., .lie, admit, correct, expose, rupture, trigger, forgive, compensate, injure
10376 | 0.95

2822 clinical *j*
noun trial, study, psychologist, research, professor, practice, patient, experience, depression, psychology, setting, data *misc* social, assistant, conduct, base, medical, associate, experimental, randomized
12508 | 0.79 A

2823 detect *v*
noun .change, cancer, test., difference, system., sensor., .presence, problem, signal, ability., virus, disease, planet, level, .sign *misc* can., .any, able., .early, difficult., significant, easy.
10953 | 0.90 A

2824 considerable *j*
noun time, amount, attention, effort, number, power, research, evidence, interest, influence, debate, support *misc* there, spend, require, receive, among, political, cause, although
10852 | 0.91 A

2825 working *j*
noun class, group, relationship, condition, mother, woman, people, man, day, family, environment, parent *misc* poor, establish, environmental, single, middle, develop, close, ordinary
10386 | 0.95

2826 partly *r*
.because, least., due, only., .result, .responsible, .blame, .explain, base, .response, reason, .cloudy, .reflect
10367 | 0.95

2827 platform *n*
adj democratic, wooden, raised, stable, elevated, wide, floating, solid *noun* party., Republican., swim., train, .shoe, oil., station, edge., plank, subway. *verb* stand, provide, run, build, step, serve, share, campaign., rest, endorse
10384 | 0.95

2828 remote *j*
noun control, area, village, location, place, island, region, sensing, site, corner, possibility, mountain *misc* most, seem, rural, pick, grab, near, northern, via
10408 | 0.95

2829 blue *n*
adj deep, dark, ultramarine, pale, bright, light, better, cerulean, traditional, soft *noun* rhythm., sky, jazz, red, .singer, color, navy., baby. *verb* play, sing., wear., paint., mix, range., chase.
10700 | 0.92

2830 respect *v*
noun right, need, .law, .privacy, .decision, opinion, .wish, rule, belief, .authority, .freedom, .elder, dignity, .boundary, .integrity *misc* must., .each, .other, love., highly., learn., .human, teach., widely.
10181 | 0.97

2831 top *i*
(on top of) .of, on., her, .other, sit., place., .head, stay., .each, pile, put., .another, lay., .everything
10423 | 0.95 F

2832 fortune *n*
adj good, small, personal, political, vast, considerable, ill, entire, changing *noun* .company, fame., family., wheel., .cookie, .teller, reversal., soldier., editor, executive *verb* make., cost., spend., seek., build, amass., lose, .estimate, accumulate, own
10872 | 0.91

2833 slave *n*
adj African, black, freed, runaway, female, escaped, male, British, civil, domestic *noun* .trade, .labor, .owner, master, descendant., .ship, sex., .trader *verb* free, become, own., sell, buy, born, escape, treat., descend., .obey
10729 | 0.92

2834 delivery *n*
adj special, effective, instructional, vaginal, overnight, premature, immediate *noun* service, .system, care, .truck, health, .room, model, .man *verb* improve., ensure., speed., facilitate., affect, arrange., order, resume
10529 | 0.94

2835 worth *n*
adj net, personal, intrinsic, moral, equal, inherent, relative *noun* dollar., year., day., money., week. *verb* sell., buy., prove., estimate, determine., steal, purchase.
10406 | 0.95

2836 reflection *n*
adj theological, critical, personal, accurate, far, moral, quiet, philosophical, pale, direct *noun* mirror, time, window, .glass, student, experience, moment., water, light, process *verb* see., catch., stare., check., cast, study., encourage., scatter, float
10807 | 0.91 A

2837 relevant *j*
noun information, question, issue, data, study, factor, research, literature, experience, knowledge, variable, material *misc* more, most, particularly, provide, less, culturally, especially
11245 | 0.87 A

2838 unknown *j*
noun reason, number, cause, man, artist, world, person, woman, word, source, origin, quantity *misc* remain, still, previously, virtually, largely, relatively, yet
10284 | 0.96

2839 pause *v*
noun .moment, .breath, .second, .effect, minute, step, .thought, .top, .beat, foot, smile, finger, .gaze, corner, entrance *misc* .look, .before, again, .long, let
11326 | 0.87 F

2840 likely *r*
will., most., more, very., .result, .continue, .increase, .remain, less, .cause, .contribute, impact, .benefit, increased
10379 | 0.95

2841 tissue *n*
adj soft, connective, human, fetal, normal, surrounding, healthy, fibrous, various *noun* cell, .paper, muscle, scar., brain., bone, sample, damage, breast. *verb* remove, cause, grow, wrap., form, surround, produce, destroy., reduce, hand.
11005 | 0.04 A

2842 sink *v*
noun heart., ship, .tooth, sun., foot, boat, .ground, .floor, head, .putt, .seat, stock., submarine, .root, .earth *misc* .into, .down, .low, .deep, .deeper, slowly, .onto **in** let., begin, really, word, start, slowly, reality, finally, message, realization. **back** .into, .down, .onto, .against **down** .into, .onto, slowly
10578 | 0.93 F

2843 counter *n*
adj front, wooden, retail, stainless-steel, cosmetic, fast-food, floured *noun* kitchen, lunch, ticket, bean, checkout, girl, store, glass, sink, stool *verb* sit, stand, lean, walk, reach, set, sell, wipe, head, cross
10788 | 0.91 F

2844 Bible *n*
adj holy, English, Catholic, favorite, weekly, illustrated, leather-bound *noun* .study, story, .school, .belt, verse, reading, .class *verb* read, teach, believe, open, quote, carry, contain, .forbid, inspire, .condemn
10737 | 0.91

2845 license *n*
adj medical, commercial, valid, suspended, artistic, personal, poetic, nonresident, professional, issuing *noun* driver, .plate, .number, marriage, .fee, car, pilot, liquor. *verb* get, give, lose, obtain, revoke, drive, suspend, require, renew, apply
10303 | 0.95

2846 tragedy *n*
adj terrible, great, personal, human, real, national, horrible *noun* family, death, comedy, triumph, kind, history, week, victim, sense, loss *verb* .happen, .strike, .occur, prevent, end, .unfold, cause, suffer, deal, .befall
10374 | 0.94 S

2847 assistant *j*
noun professor, coach, secretary, director, attorney, manager, editor, principal, chief, superintendent, administrator, commissioner *misc* general, former, managing, clinical, serve, vice, head
10586 | 0.92 N

2848 dialogue *n*
adj national, political, interreligious, intergroup, ongoing, constructive, genuine, internal *noun* kind, scene, policy, .race, line, character, religion, conversation, partner, cooperation *verb* engage, open, continue, create, promote, enter, encourage, establish, facilitate, resume
10821 | 0.90 A

2849 mutual *j*
noun fund, respect, stock, friend, company, understanding, interest, trust, benefit, support, aid, insurance *misc* between, invest, among, buy, base, other, each, manage
10850 | 0.90

2850 loose *j*
noun end, hair, cannon, ball, change, skin, woman, rock, soil, shirt, confederation, powder *misc* break, let, cut, turn, hang, wear, shake, pull
10467 | 0.93 F

2851 external *j*
noun factor, force, pressure, control, threat, source, environment, affair, canal, debt, validity, influence *misc* internal, such, auditory, both, economic, require, domestic
11557 | 0.85 A

2852 pride *n*
adj great, national, gay, civic, ethnic, cultural, personal, certain, racial *noun* sense, source, .joy, .place, lot, point, .prejudice, matter, .parade *verb* take, feel, swallow, swell, beam, express, shine, .blind
10161 | 0.96

2853 awareness *n*
adj public, environmental, great, growing, increased, heightened, global, cultural, social *noun* level, student, program, .issue, knowledge, need, education, lack, .campaign, skill *verb* raise, increase, develop, create, heighten, promote, bring, focus, foster, contribute
10936 | 0.89 A

2854 electricity *n*
adj running, static, solar, cheap, renewable, reliable, retail, wind-generated *noun* water, price, gas, power, percent, cost, fuel, generation, market, energy *verb* generate, produce, provide, sell, convert, restore, .flow
10896 | 0.90

2855 diverse *j*
noun group, student, population, community, background, culture, need, school, society, country, interest, sample *misc* more, as, culturally, most, ethnically, such, among, cultural
10953 | 0.89 A

2856 advanced *j*
noun technology, system, degree, study, student, research, placement, course, program, class, country, age *misc* more, most, technologically, such, develop, industrial, international, require
10766 | 0.91 A

2857 free *v*
noun slave, hostage, prisoner, .mind, .prison, .fund, soldier, .bail, capital, task, .bond, soul, .shackle, .foreigner *misc* .from, .himself, last, set, .themselves, .herself, struggle, .itself, finally, **up** .money, .more, .space, .time, .resource, .fund, .cash, .capital, .dollar, .land
10074 | 0.97

2858 faster *r*
.than, much, move, grow, time, run, even, little, walk, far, lot, rise, heart, beat.
10388 | 0.94 M

2859 conservative *n*
adj Christian, fiscal, black, political, compassionate, economic, strong, southern, staunch, mainstream *noun* liberal, Republican, party, .tank, lot, issue, moderate, Congress, movement, voter *verb* .believe, win, support, .oppose, .argue, vote, .agree, criticize, attack, appeal.
10826 | 0.90 S

2860 online *j*
noun service, course, site, discussion, company, information, group, resource, magazine, business, music, community *misc* available, offer, such, provide, free, visit, commercial
10845 | 0.90 M

2861 assault *n*
adj sexual, aggravated, physical, deadly, frontal, amphibious, military, final *noun* .weapon, .rifle, charge, ban, robbery, rape, victim, air, .battery, murder *verb* launch, report, lead, convict, aggravate, .occur
10297 | 0.95

23. Frequency of synonyms

One of the challenges for language learners is knowing how to use synonyms. A typical thesaurus will list several synonyms for a word, but it doesn't give any indication of which are more common, or in which genres they are used (including formal / informal). With the Corpus of Contemporary American English, however, this is quite easy.

For example, the following table is the output from the simple, one-word query **[=strong]** in the web interface. This table shows the frequency of each synonym of *strong* in the five main genres of the corpus, as well as the overall frequency for each word. Note that on the web, one would see all 53 synonyms, and that in the web interface they are color-coded for normalized frequency (frequency per million words), so it is very easy to compare the frequency across genres.

	Synonym	Total	Spok	Fic	Mag	News	Acad
8	effective	34579	4277	814	7641	4172	17675
9	powerful	32042	5339	3688	8736	5905	8374
13	sharp	16000	1184	6154	3978	2700	1984
14	intense	13864	2042	2060	3842	2910	3010
18	compelling	5782	1006	360	1463	1114	1839
20	fierce	4870	571	1567	1118	1084	530
21	passionate	4290	847	763	1172	939	569
23	convincing	3882	730	565	862	697	1028
26	robust	3010	305	243	768	645	1049
28	sturdy	2695	97	742	1314	382	160
29	muscular	2685	164	955	709	359	498
30	spicy	2171	154	283	872	838	24
32	biting	2027	213	899	486	318	111
34	persuasive	1839	296	181	369	264	729
36	stout	1336	57	514	468	207	90
38	ardent	1191	93	173	354	311	260
40	pungent	845	18	325	260	205	37
41	burly	832	13	427	217	162	13
42	staunch	829	164	89	176	231	169
44	fervent	697	57	139	185	169	147
47	beefy	482	9	201	183	89	0
48	deep-seated	420	48	10	96	79	187
49	stalwart	395	19	82	135	125	34
50	strapping	346	32	145	96	67	6
51	brawny	247	10	96	95	41	5

Finally, note that in the web interface it is also possible—with just 2–3 clicks of the mouse—to directly query to see which synonyms occur much more in one genre than in another. For example, by comparing the synonyms of *strong* in Fiction and Academic, one sees that Fiction prefers *beefy, burly, strapping, spicy, brawny, pungent*, and *biting*. Academic, on the other hand, prefers *effective, deep-seated, compelling, clear-cut, durable, robust*, and *persuasive*.

2862 shortly *r*
.after, .before, .thereafter, die, begin, .afterward, leave, arrive, .death, return, .midnight
10083 | 0.97

2863 finance *n*
adj personal, international, public, corporate, global, shaky, external, behavioral *noun* campaign., .reform, .committee, .minister, ministry, chairman, company, .law, family., director *verb* help., manage., handle., pass, investigate.
10502 | 0.93 N

2864 originally *r*
.plan, .design, .intend, .develop, .publish, .write, .build, .schedule, .propose, .conceive, .present, .appear
10189 | 0.96

2865 founder *n*
adj American, chief, original, legendary, charismatic, retired, visionary, firm *noun* president, company, .director, CEO, chairman, .executive, .editor, coalition *verb* .intend, name., envision, honor., regard., .anticipate, embody
10653 | 0.91 M

2866 lie *n*
adj big, white, outright, future, total, absolute, casual, bald-faced, obvious, secret *noun* .detector, .test, truth, sex., kind., pack. *verb* tell, believe, live., catch., pass., cover, expose, spread, repeat, detect
10290 | 0.95

2867 characterize *v*
noun relationship, period, .level, condition, culture, pattern, process, relation, style, approach, situation, conflict, environment, activity, feature *misc* .by, .as, often., best., generally.
11037 | 0.88 A

2868 protest *n*
adj political, violent, public, social, peaceful, mass, popular, recent, nonviolent *noun* student., .movement, street., .march, government, form., .vote, letter, week *verb* organize., lead, stage., join., spark., resign., file., plan, erupt, lodge.
10347 | 0.94

2869 pole *n*
adj long, celestial, light, magnetic, opposite, wooden, top, Irish, 10-foot *noun* north., south., telephone., totem., .vault, fishing., ski. *verb* hold, win., reach, hang, plant, carry, support, climb., fly, attach
10617 | 0.92 M

2870 intellectual *j*
noun property, life, right, development, ability, history, challenge, capital, tradition, curiosity, capacity, level *misc* moral, social, political, emotional, cultural, academic, physical
11157 | 0.87 A

2871 communist *j*
noun party, regime, government, leader, country, China, rule, member, state, world, system, power *misc* former, Chinese, Soviet, under, eastern, central, join, socialist
10938 | 0.89

2872 infection *n*
adj bacterial, viral, respiratory, chronic, fungal, common, serious, parasitic, frequent, hospital-acquired *noun* ear., risk., rate, tract., patient, disease, virus,

yeast., sinus., sign. *verb* cause, prevent., treat, fight., develop, .occur, spread, associate, die., result
11576 | 0.84 M A

2873 controversy *n*
adj political, public, current, recent, considerable, major, whole, growing *noun* year, center., lot., subject., source., debate, matter., quarterback., storm., kind. *verb* .surround, stir., create., cause., generate, spark., .erupt, .involve, .continue, .arise
10308 | 0.94

2874 double *v*
noun number, .size, population, price, rate, .amount, sales, percent, .money, revenue, tax, .value, stock., hour, space *misc* more., nearly., almost., .since, expect., roughly., easily., per, approximately.
  over .pain, .laughter, gasp, almost., .clutch, .laugh, .agony, .fall, cough **up** .laughter, .fist, .relative
10312 | 0.94

2875 freeze *v*
noun .death, face, .place, asset, ice, water, hand, moment, ground, winter, account, .fear, image, bank, smile *misc* until, before, .solid, suddenly.
  over hell., until., lake., before, .winter, bay., river., water., .ice, pond.
10613 | 0.91 F

2876 portrait *n*
adj famous, double, photographic, formal, intimate, official, detailed, individual, female, African *noun* artist, family, .gallery, painting, .painter, oil, group *verb* paint, hang, draw, create., include, present, commission, depict, display, line
11331 | 0.86 M

2877 proof *n*
adj living, scientific, positive, clear, conclusive, final, reasonable, definitive *noun* burden., standard., .pudding, evidence, .existence, kind., .citizenship, claim, offer., burglar. *verb* need, provide., require, show, .exist, demand., shift, cite., bear., rest
10047 | 0.96

2878 satisfaction *n*
adj high, great, overall, sexual, patient, personal, marital, low, grim *noun* job., life, level, customer., student., body., relationship, work, measure, sense. *verb* give., relate, express., report., derive, indicate, increase, influence, examine., gain
11179 | 0.87 A

2879 insight *n*
adj valuable, great, additional, unique, special, deeper, spiritual, better, sudden, cultural *noun* .nature, student, experience, information, perspective, knowledge, understanding, offer., character, kind *verb* provide., give., gain., share., might, yield., lead, appreciate, develop, achieve
10669 | 0.91 A

2880 headquarters *n*
adj corporate, national, military, central, regional, global, temporary *noun* company., police., new, party., world., building, office, campaign., city, news. *verb* move., send, serve., build, visit., establish., arrive., house, occupy, .overlook
10414 | 0.93 N

2881 stair *n*
adj narrow, front, steep, wooden, dark, main, spiral, carpeted, concrete, wide *noun* flight., bottom., room,

door, foot., back., head., basement, set., footstep.
verb climb., come., walk., run., lead, start., descend.,
fall., carry, reach
11251 | 0.86 F

2882 crash *n*
adj fatal, loud, fiery, frontal, deadly, terrible,
spectacular, rear-end *noun* plane., car., .site, .course,
market., stock., .flight, .test *verb* die., kill, cause,
hear., survive., .involve, .occur, injure., reduce.,
investigate.
10376 | 0.93

2883 constitute *v*
noun .percent, .threat, .part, .majority, definition.,
element, community, .endorsement, .violation,
act, experience, .approval, .basis, journal.,
relationship *misc* .large, .important, .major,
social, .significant
11177 | 0.87 A

2884 thirty *m*
.year, .ago, .minute, about., than., more, .second,
.foot, twenty., over., .day, .percent, .later, after
10595 | 0.91 F

2885 alter *v*
noun way, .course, life, .behavior, .structure,
.pattern, .nature, .perception, .landscape,
.balance, .relationship, ability, color, image,
activity *misc* radically., significantly.,
fundamentally., dramatically., slightly
10362 | 0.93 A

2886 sudden *j*
noun death, change, loss, movement, silence,
appearance, infant, wind, burst, interest, pain, shift
misc feel, cardiac, cause, unexpected, experience,
violent, sharp, severe
10487 | 0.92 F

2887 not *c*
(whether or not) .only, .enough, .yet, .sure, or.,
whether., simply, certainly., .necessarily, .mention,
.anymore, .proofread, .surprising, .merely
10588 | 0.91 S

2888 potentially *r*
.dangerous, .fatal, .harmful, .important, .effect,
.serious, .situation, .deadly, .hazardous, .significant,
.lethal, .explosive
10362 | 0.93 A

2889 dirty *j*
noun work, secret, trick, word, water, laundry, clothes,
bomb, dish, hand, look *misc* little, old, wear, clean,
dangerous, quick, brown, yellow
10251 | 0.94 F

2890 evolve *v*
noun system, year, species, technology, process,
society, relationship, century, organism, role, strategy,
model, industry, star, decade *misc* .into, .from, how.,
.over, continue., rapidly
10554 | 0.91 A

2891 teenager *n*
adj American, pregnant, typical, normal, sexual,
troubled, active, rebellious, innocent, gangly
noun child, parent, adult, group., mother, kid,
drug, baby, couple., summer *verb* act, dress, attend,
smoke, .engage, hire., aim., abuse, .dance, behave
10260 | 0.94

2892 violation *n*
adj human, federal, international, serious, alleged,
clear, constitutional, gross, flagrant, major *noun* right.,
.law, code, traffic., safety., ethics *verb* commit., .occur,
constitute., involve., cite, allege., charge., investigate.,
report, result
10588 | 0.91

2893 joy *n*
adj great, pure, sheer, greatest, full, tremendous,
absolute, utter *noun* life, pride., tear., sorrow, love,
pain, moment, peace, happiness, sense. *verb* bring.,
feel., share., experience., fill., jump., discover, radiate,
overflow, comfort
10144 | 0.95

2894 smell *n*
adj sweet, strong, bad, fresh, burning, faint, sour, sharp,
musty, thick *noun* sense., air, taste, sound, smoke,
sight., .sweat, .blood, .coffee, .oil *verb* fill, like., .waft,
love., remember., breathe., .rise, .hang, notice., burn
11066 | 0.87 F

2895 possess *v*
noun power, knowledge, skill, .weapon, quality, .ability,
individual., .characteristic, .degree, person., .level,
teacher., talent, .trait, .capacity *misc* must., already.,
.nuclear, .certain, human, .strong
10453 | 0.92 A

2896 hurricane *n*
adj major, devastating, powerful, natural, severe,
deadly, fierce, dangerous *noun* .season, .center, storm,
category., victim, wind, aftermath, damage., .relief,
force *verb* hit., .strike, cause, follow., destroy,
devastate, affect., survive., displace.
10665 | 0.90 S

2897 offense *n*
adj impeachable, total, serious, criminal, federal,
passing, similar, nonviolent, balanced *noun* defense,
yard, drug., team, season, rank, player, .quarterback,
capital., starter. *verb* take., commit, run, .rush, lead,
play, charge, score, struggle, .average
10984 | 0.88 N

2898 relax *v*
noun muscle, body, shoulder, face., .grip, rule,
minute, second, standard, restriction, .bit, pressure,
tension, finger, breathing *misc* just., .enjoy, let, feel,
help., sit
10304 | 0.93 F

2899 appeal *v*
noun .court, .decision, case, .ruling, .audience, .voter,
.conviction, .judge, idea, lawyer., .sentence, .verdict,
.taste, attorney, .public *misc* particularly., .directly,
design., especially, plan., .broad, immediately
10044 | 0.96

2900 mount *v*
noun .campaign, evidence, pressure, .wall, .attack,
.horse, .defense, .challenge, .step, tension, exhibition,
operation, loss, show, .stair *misc* .against, continue.,
.above, .effective
up .ride, then., .behind, begin, .over
10187 | 0.94 M

2901 treaty *n*
adj international, nuclear, comprehensive, strategic,
bilateral, formal, binding, environmental, legal,
multilateral *noun* peace., right, union, test., ban.,
arm., nonproliferation., missile, .organization, nation

verb sign, ratify, negotiate, establish, conclude, violate., .end, support., .reduce, guarantee
10998 | 0.87 A

2902 prior _i_
(prior to) .to, year., week., month., .war, during, study, period., .election, interview, immediately., .start, exist., hour.
10836 | 0.88 A

2903 memorial _n_
adj national, makeshift, living, fitting, permanent, outdoor _noun_ .day, .service, .hospital, war., .weekend, .center, veteran., .church, .stadium, .award _verb_ attend., build, dedicate, plan, .honor, visit., erect, establish, .mark, gather.
10472 | 0.92 N

2904 establishment _n_
adj military, political, medical, national, religious, educational, foreign, liberal, scientific, diplomatic _noun_ .clause, state, food., .religion, party, defense., law, education., Republican, policy. _verb_ lead., violate., support, require, prohibit, prevent., announce., propose., result., facilitate.
10685 | 0.90 A

2905 hold _n_
adj firm, strong, powerful, tight, tenuous, indefinite, precarious _noun_ hand, .arm, life, cargo., .power, ship, edge., choke., .minute, career. _verb_ take., get., put., grab., keep., catch., let, break., release., tighten.
10079 | 0.95 F

2906 tap _v_
noun .shoulder, foot, finger, phone, door, .window, .glass, resource, power, .key, toe, arm, wall, .floor, potential _misc_ .into, .against, lightly, able., gently, nervously
   out .message, .rhythm, .excess, .code, .beat, consumer., .cigarette, computer, fund.
10190 | 0.94 F

2907 swim _v_
noun fish., pool, river, .lap, head, sea, lake, shark, .ocean, eye, beach, dolphin, mile, boy., shore
misc .through, .away, .toward, learn., .across, teach., underwater, .upstream
10355 | 0.92 F

2908 properly _r_
use, work., function., .understand, train, handle, fail., manage, treat, prepare, fit, .design
9961 | 0.96

2909 gulf _n_
adj Persian, northern, eastern, Arabian, oil-rich, widening, unbridgeable _noun_ .war, .coast, .crisis, .state, .region, oil, force., country, water, troop. _verb_ serve., head., .separate, enter., rebuild., cross., bridge., employ.
10783 | 0.89

2910 tongue _n_
adj native, pink, sharp, thick, red, forked, foreign, wet
noun mouth, lip, mother., tip., tooth, .cheek, slip., throat, ear, base _verb_ stick., speak., bite., hold., run., roll., touch, cluck., flick., click.
10729 | 0.89 F

2911 salad _n_
adj fresh, mixed, simple, chopped, Italian, Greek, marinated, cooked, Thai, French _noun_ chicken,

potato., .green, fruit., .dressing, tomato, vegetable, bowl, pasta, cup _verb_ serve, toss, eat., add, order., prepare, .top, pour., pick.
10948 | 0.87 M

2912 practice _v_
noun .law, .medicine, year, skill, art, week, religion, form, technique, physician, team, lawyer, doctor, psychologist, .yoga _misc_ widely., currently., regularly, commonly., routinely
10033 | 0.95

2913 favorite _n_
adj personal, perennial, local, all-time, current, sentimental, overwhelming, heavy, traditional
noun family, fan., crowd, .staff, mother, father, cult., holiday. _verb_ become., include, .win, remain., pick., consider., feature, vote., select.
10245 | 0.93 M

2914 shelter _n_
adj homeless, temporary, safe, makeshift, underground, adequate, permanent, abusive
noun food., woman, tax., animal., bomb., clothing, emergency., home _verb_ provide., take., find., seek., live., build., offer, feed, house, operate
10067 | 0.95

2915 correspondent _n_
adj national, senior, chief, foreign, medical, political, special, congressional _noun_ news., house., war., new, security., affair., business., science., consumer., .dinner _verb_ .report, .join, .cover, .contribute, name., .examine, .visit, interview, appoint.
11272 | 0.85 S

2916 introduction _n_
adj new, brief, recent, general, formal, excellent, gentle, gradual _noun_ .page, technology, letter., species, product, section, reference., article, disease, .edition _verb_ write., provide., include., follow., note, mention., present, delay., precede, allude
10750 | 0.89 A

2917 funeral _n_
adj proper, prepaid, elaborate, mock, mass, double
noun .service, .home, .director, .procession, father, mother, .parlor, .arrangement _verb_ attend., hold, plan, announce, arrange, prepare., conduct, preach., handle, honor
10339 | 0.92

2918 literary _j_
noun criticism, critic, theory, study, history, text, work, works, tradition, world, magazine, character
misc American, cultural, artistic, historical, contemporary, traditional, critical, well
12179 | 0.78 A

2919 convert _v_
noun .text, .ASCII, character., .PDF, energy, .Christianity, .Islam, .electricity, .Catholicism, gas, .use, fuel, plant, .signal, body _misc_ .into, easily., directly, recently.
10214 | 0.93

2920 violate _v_
noun .law, right, .rule, .principle, .constitution, .agreement, privacy, .standard, .clause, act, .regulation, trust, .term, .spirit, .norm _misc_ .federal, .constitutional, civil, human, .international
10177 | 0.94

2921 rub *v*
noun hand, .eye, back, .shoulder, .face, head,
finger, .nose, skin, .chin, leg, .elbow, .neck, side,
body *misc* .against, .over, .together, .across, .wrong
off .on, .me, .him, skin, attitude.
10672 | 0.89 F

2922 entrance *n*
adj main, front, grand, early, rear, narrow, dramatic
noun park, .hall, building, .fee, .exam, side, .college,
door, room, cave *verb* stand, .block, .walk, pass,
guard, mark, gain, head, .loom
10246 | 0.93 F

2923 episode *n*
adj whole, final, recent, entire, early, psychotic,
major, single, particular *noun* star, show, season,
series, TV, week, depressive, pilot, .violence,
treatment, *verb* watch, .occur, shoot, end, direct,
feature, experience, air, describe, illustrate
10169 | 0.94

2924 tournament *n*
adj national, major, annual, regional, consecutive,
qualifying, professional, past, Invitational, Olympic
noun golf, year, state, team, game, conference,
basketball, tennis, round, week *verb* win, play, enter,
host, compete, reach, finish, miss, attend, .feature
11533 | 0.82 N

2925 vital *j*
noun interest, role, part, sign, information, organ,
statistics, issue, importance, security, force,
component *misc* play, most, national, provide,
remain, consider, economic, protect
10119 | 0.94 A

2926 stable *j*
noun condition, environment, family, government,
relationship, price, system, life, democracy,
population, rate, economy *misc* more, remain,
relatively, less, provide, enough, create, fairly
10204 | 0.93 A

2927 split *v*
noun party, vote, .difference, .hair, .middle, wood,
stock, .cost, .atom, .faction, pair, profit, sample, voter,
lip *misc* .into, .two, .between, evenly, .off, .apart,
.open, .down, .half, .among, .along, equally, .wide
up when, parent, after, .into, family, then, couple,
good, recently, .search
9792 | 0.97

2928 representation *n*
adj visual, proportional, political, legal, accurate,
social, graphic, equal, adequate *noun* woman, minority,
form, system, .transcription, reality, space, mode,
taxation, politics *verb* provide, create, increase, ensure,
construct, achieve, relate, obtain, entitle, constitute
11289 | 0.84 A

2929 stress *v*
noun .importance, .need, point, .role, .value,
education, teacher, official, relationship, .nature,
theme, expert, .quality, .character, author,
misc also, shall, repeatedly, rather, highly,
.individual, contribute, due, careful, heavily.
out so, get, .about, all, feel, really, .over, little,
parent, totally.
10264 | 0.93 A

2930 fiction *n*
adj short, American, historical, contemporary,
literary, popular, narrative *noun* science, fact, writer,

pulp, book, work, section, poetry, story, .nonfiction
verb write, read, .appear, publish, separate,
maintain, distinguish, sound, explore, portray
10992 | 0.86 A

2931 lane *n*
adj fast, narrow, left, right, dark, passing, slow, single
noun traffic, bike, car, road, memory, country,
shipping, sea, victory, *verb* drive, add, change,
open, walk, close, cross, block, swerve, head
10226 | 0.93 N

2932 distinction *n*
adj important, clear, dubious, sharp, crucial, legal,
fundamental, key, basic, critical *noun* class, .art,
gender, kind, .public, .type, award, honor, concept
verb make, draw, blur, serve, maintain, recognize,
earn, .belong, exist, argue
10691 | 0.89 A

2933 segment *n*
adj large, small, different, certain, growing,
fastest-growing, following, various, particular,
final *noun* .population, .society, market, industry,
.morning, video, news, .public, body, minute
verb include, represent, divide, identify, air,
feature, contain, tape, appeal, target.
10238 | 0.93

2934 transfer *n*
adj reverse, nuclear, electronic, international, peaceful,
financial, illicit, direct, massive, orderly *noun* technology,
heat, student, .power, .rate, information, .station,
knowledge *verb* allow, .occur, involve, facilitate,
receive, promote, request, approve.
10922 | 0.87 A

2935 comprehensive *j*
noun program, plan, study, approach, health,
education, system, care, reform, assessment, service,
test *misc* more, most, provide, develop, offer, include,
environmental, require
10688 | 0.89 A

2936 confident *j*
noun ability, subject, voice, smile, victory, person,
tone, manner, prediction, stride, demeanor, attitude
misc that, feel, more, very, enough, seem, less, pretty
9802 | 0.97

2937 easy *r*
make, how, life, .enough, little, job, breathe,
cheap, faster, task.
9906 | 0.95

2938 prominent *j*
noun role, family, leader, member, figure, place,
feature, lawyer, people, Democrat, politician,
woman *misc* most, more, become, among, play,
several, including, political
10055 | 0.94 A

2939 presentation *n*
adj oral, visual, clinical, formal, dramatic, initial,
brief, various, professional, annual *noun* information,
slide, video, .news, multimedia, data, order, mode,
.channel, art *verb* make, give, follow, prepare,
attend, feature, deliver, vary, highlight, .differ
10476 | 0.90 A

2940 net *n*
adj wide, neural, wider, broad, commercial, huge,
estimated *noun* safety, fishing, fish, mosquito,

butterfly., ball., pound., income, sport., cargo.
verb cast., catch, surf., set, pull, fall, drag, throw,
drop, connect
10235 | 0.92

2941 squeeze _v_
noun hand, eye, .juice, .shoulder, arm, .trigger,
.lemon, finger, water, .blade, profit, .lime, heart,
.drop, .shot _misc_ .into, .through, .between, .shut
out as, water, .excess, .much, juice, liquid, .last,
.every, tear., .drop
10257 | 0.92 F

2942 tobacco _n_
adj big, major, smokeless, environmental, smoking,
chewing, stale _noun_ .company, .industry, alcohol, use,
.firearm, .product, .smoke _verb_ chew., grow, sell,
regulate., spit, smell.
10108 | 0.93

2943 significance _n_
adj statistical, great, historical, special, political, social,
religious, cultural, particular, practical _noun_ level, test,
difference, meaning, event, value, finding, effect,
task., .testing _verb_ reach., understand., approach.,
determine, attach, explain., recognize., grasp.,
demonstrate., examine.
10756 | 0.88 A

2944 imagination _n_
adj popular, human, wild, creative, vivid, literary,
active, historical, moral, collective _noun_ stretch.,
child, figment., memory, power., creativity, lack.,
public, product., reality _verb_ capture., use., let., .run,
fire., limit., catch., fill, encourage, .soar
10158 | 0.93

2945 pretend _v_
noun actor., .indifference, cop, .innocence,
.ignorance, actress, .nonchalance, neighbor, cow,
affection, thief _misc_ not, like, try., .notice, .hear, let.,
.read
10384 | 0.91 F

2946 mere _j_
noun fact, year, percent, presence, mortal, word,
existence, mention, month, thought, foot, hour
misc than, more, beyond, million, rather, reduce,
transcend, compare
10041 | 0.94

2947 mix _n_
adj right, eclectic, ethnic, odd, racial, diverse,
interesting, volatile, rich, complex _noun_ cake.,
product, .tape, trail., package, soup., salad., energy,
pancake., pudding. _verb_ add., combine, include,
blend, offer., contain, stir, throw., .incorporate
10127 | 0.93 M

2948 spot _v_
noun car, .sign, bird, police, trouble, .buck, binoculars,
camera, .trend, officer, window, plane, truck, corner,
target _misc_ easy., able., easily., hard., suddenly., .near
10182 | 0.93 F

2949 fade _v_
noun memory, face, .background, .view, darkness,
mind, picture, screen, flower., summer, shadow,
.silence, .obscurity, afternoon., wind _misc_ .away, .into,
.out, then, .black, begin., quickly, slowly
out slowly., gradually., instrument., .approximately,
.entirely **in** out, black., music.
10482 | 0.90 F

2950 steady _j_
noun stream, growth, hand, job, flow, decline, voice,
supply, increase, pace, income, work _misc_ hold, slow,
keep, remain, maintain, strong, fairly, relatively
9856 | 0.95

2951 neither _d_
.them, .side, .one, .any, .party, .ever, .speak, .anything,
though., .parent, yet, although., .candidate, .whom
9729 | 0.97

2952 target _v_
noun program, area, group, company, intervention,
effort, .civilian, market, population, service, police,
species, .audience, force, campaign. _misc_ .specific,
specifically., directly, unfairly., deliberately.,
particularly, carefully.
10008 | 0.94

2953 nowhere _r_
go, out., .near, .else, come., middle., find, appear.,
.sight, lead., everywhere, .evident
9827 | 0.96

2954 variation _n_
adj genetic, wide, slight, considerable, different,
regional, significant, individual, cultural, natural
noun theme, temperature, pattern, color, number,
population, range., coefficient., model, difference
verb show., explain, reflect, account, .exist, .occur,
produce, indicate, represent, determine.
10594 | 0.89 A

2955 radical _j_
noun change, group, reform, Islam, idea, movement,
departure, transformation, cleric, party, feminist, right
misc more, most, Islamic, political, social, economic,
free, undergo
10227 | 0.92 A

2956 adventure _n_
adj new, great, outdoor, exciting, military, excellent,
wild, grand, romantic, foreign _noun_ story, travel,
sense., space, game, camp, series, tale, spirit., trip
verb offer, seek, share, embark., enjoy., experience,
recount., chronicle, .await, boast
10037 | 0.94 M

2957 profession _n_
adj medical, legal, historical, chosen, entire, various,
honorable, specific, allied, noble _noun_ teaching.,
education, health., work, teacher, member.,
accounting., music, business _verb_ enter., leave.,
choose, teach, establish, pursue., recognize, promote,
practice, define
10631 | 0.88 A

2958 exciting _j_
noun thing, time, life, way, part, opportunity,
place, game, story, development, event, experience
misc most, very, more, new, really, as, something
9827 | 0.95

2959 fate _n_
adj similar, ultimate, cruel, terrible, tragic, uncertain,
common, eventual _noun_ hand, twist., destiny, luck,
quirk., turn., fortune _verb_ decide., suffer., determine.,
seal, meet., avoid., await, accept., share., escape.
9733 | 0.96

2960 regardless _r_
.of, .their, .whether, .how, .race, .age, .where, .level,
.status, .gender, .happen, .size, political, .type
10040 | 0.93 A

2961 load v
noun truck, base, item., gun, bag, food, back, weapon, data, gear, film, pack, machine, .ambulance, stuff
misc .into, .onto, fully., heavily, ready
   up car, .truck, .stock, .wagon, .plate, .debt, cart, bus, gun, grocery
9901 | 0.95

2962 singer n
adj popular, famous, female, favorite, professional, legendary, talented, choral *noun* country., lead., opera., jazz., blues., gospel., .songwriter, folk.
verb .sing, .perform, feature., record, train., accompany, .entertain, .croon, honor, imitate
10300 | 0.91

2963 distribute v
noun .information, food, company, money, product, material, fund, weight, .news, service, film, copy, power, .picture, data *misc* evenly, .among, widely., .throughout, .across, million
9996 | 0.94 A

2964 ton n
adj metric, estimated, solid, dry, nuclear, hazardous, radioactive, toxic, additional, chemical
noun .waste, .money, .food, .carbon, .material, .dioxide, .oil, .coal, .steel, .brick *verb* weigh., produce, carry., generate, dump., emit, haul, import., contain., bury.
10302 | 0.91

24. Comparing words

One of the challenges for a language learner is to acquire a sense of the nuances between two related words—where one would be used, but not the other. With the Corpus of Contemporary American English, this is quite easy. Users simply enter the two words, and then the corpus shows which collocates (nearby words) occur with one word but not the other, and vice versa. For example, the following table shows just a fragment of the output for *small* versus *little*. We will not explain all of the numbers here, though that explanation is available online. For our purposes, we see that *small* occurs with *business* and *amount*, for example, while *little* occurs with *league* and *secret*.

Word 1 (W1): **small** (35.5%)				Word 2 (W2): **little** (64.5%)			
1 amounts	828	7	0.99	2.80	1 while	2115	10	1.00	1.54
2 fraction	517	5	0.99	2.79	2 bit	15677	94	0.99	1.54
3 percentage	902	10	0.99	2.79	3 league	1045	7	0.99	1.54
4 firms	422	5	0.99	2.79	4 brother	1062	10	0.99	1.54
5 businesses	2199	32	0.99	2.78	5 sister	908	11	0.99	1.53
6 telescopes	119	2	0.98	2.77	6 sympathy	142	2	0.99	1.53
7 fee	175	3	0.98	2.77	7 secret	367	6	0.98	1.52

With the web interface, users can compare any set of words, to see semantic (meaning) differences, as well as cultural differences in the use of two related words. The following table gives just a small sampling of some of these searches.

[A]	[B]	Collocate POS	Collocates with [A]	Collocates with [B]
1 [boy]	[girl]	[j*]	growing, rude	sexy, working
2 Democrats	Republicans	[j*]	open-minded, fun	mean-spirited, greedy
3 Clinton	Bush	[v*]	confessed, groped, inhale	assure, deploying, stumbles
4 utter.[j*]	sheer	[nn*]	silence, despair	beauty, joy
5 ground.[n*]	floor.[n*]	[j*]	common, solid	concrete, dirty
6 [rob].[v*]	[steal].[v*]	[nn*]	bank, store	cars, money

2965 instance *n*
adj other, particular, rare, specific, certain, single, numerous, isolated, individual, mild *noun* violence, .innuendo, drug, number., .abuse, behavior, type, sex, couple., document *verb* cite, .occur, involve, recall, identify., reveal, record, suggest, require, witness.
10285 | 0.91 A

2966 affiliation *n*
adj religious, political, ethnic, cultural, tribal, institutional, denominational *noun* author., party., .editor, .writer, group, feedback, e-mail, church, university, peer *verb* .contribute, .teach, switch., correlate., retain., misstate.
10765 | 0.87 M

2967 hunting *n*
adj public, happy, traditional, favorite, illegal, excellent, recreational *noun* fishing, deer, .season, .dog, .ground, area, .rifle, .knife *verb* go., allow, offer, enjoy., ban., prohibit, bargain.
11196 | 0.83 M

2968 pale *j*
noun face, eye, skin, hair, light, color, man, hand, sky, wall, lip, moon *misc* her, blue, look, yellow, green, pink, white, beyond
10681 | 0.87 F

2969 paint *n*
adj white, lead-based, fresh, acrylic, black, red, thick, blue, yellow, green *noun* oil., .job, coat., brush, lead., layer., color, wall, can, spray. *verb* use, apply, peel, mix, cover, .dry, remove, match, contain
11730 | 0.79 M

2970 poet *n*
adj romantic, famous, greatest, female, favorite, fellow, prize-winning, lyric, Chinese *noun* .laureate, writer, woman, novelist, artist, critic, poem, author, playwright, .essayist *verb* write, read, name, describe, publish, .sing, quote, inspire, praise, feature
10275 | 0.90 A

2971 gradually *r*
.into, .become, .add, .increase, until, .over, begin, change, move, .sugar, .lose, .beat, build, grow
9884 | 0.94

2972 partnership *n*
adj limited, private, public-private, domestic, strategic, public, global, professional, successful, equal *noun* program, community, business, school, education, development, .peace, .agreement, industry *verb* form., develop, create, build, establish, forge., enter., require, promote, seek
10157 | 0.92 A

2973 capability *n*
adj military, nuclear, human, offensive, technological, technical, chemical, full, limited, biological *noun* weapon, missile, intelligence., defense., technology, communication, performance, production., data, development *verb* develop., provide, build, increase, enhance., improve., include, add, acquire, demonstrate.
10301 | 0.90 A

2974 Canadian *j*
noun government, company, border, law, province, policy, minister, society, team, official, industry, culture
12104 | 0.77 A

2975 tech *n*
adj high, low, urban, digital, electrical, forensic *noun* .stock, .support, .company, .university, .center, .coach *verb* beat, graduate., attend., invest, specialize, .soar, .rebound, massacre.
10567 | 0.88 N

2976 commerce *n*
adj interstate, electronic, international, foreign, global, online, maritime *noun* chamber., department, secretary, US., .committee, .clause, energy., state, house., trade *verb* regulate., engage., affect., promote, violate., discriminate., disrupt., .flow
10229 | 0.90

2977 grandfather *n*
adj great, maternal, paternal, great-great, blind, beloved, doting, aging *noun* father, grandmother, .clock, house, mother, uncle, brother, .farm, .great-grandfather, .clause *verb* .die, remember, belong., .teach, found, born, .own, name., visit., sing
10231 | 0.90 F

2978 bake *v*
noun .minute, pan., oven, cookie, cake, bread, pie, hour, potato, loaf, cornmeal., biscuit, stone, bowl, parchment *misc* .until, prepared., .golden, brown, together, uncover, .preheat, covered
11009 | 0.84 M

2979 shelf *n*
adj continental, top, long, low, bottom, open, short, outer, bare, middle *noun* book, .life, .space, product, supermarket., room, closet, ice., grocery, food *verb* sit., line, fill, .hold, pull, hit., reach, fly., place, display
9905 | 0.93 F

2980 honey *n*
adj sweet, sorry, Africanized, fresh, warm, wild, golden, European, pure *noun* .bee, cup, tablespoon, teaspoon, milk., sugar, vinegar, butter, oil, juice *verb* love, add, mix, combine., stir, taste, pour, sweeten., drink, melt
10110 | 0.91 F

2981 round *j*
noun table, face, trip, eye, window, rock, head, hole, top, pan, glass, cake *misc* small, big, large, little, each, perfectly, white, smooth
9863 | 0.93 F

2982 flee *v*
noun .country, people., refugee., family., .home, .city, thousand., .war, .south, other., .scene, police, resident., .fighting, village *misc* after, before, force., .across, fight, .avoid, attempt., .hide, eventually, immediately, scream, Jewish., fear, apparently
9705 | 0.95

2983 adapt *v*
noun change, need, .environment, recipe, .book, technology, .use, style, .circumstance, species., .climate, technique, material, model, method *misc* .from, .changing, learn., quickly, easily, able., successfully.
10022 | 0.92 A

2984 buyer *n*
adj potential, first-time, prospective, young, willing, foreign, private, would-be, likely, average *noun* home., .seller, car., market, .guide, product, agent, stock, ticket., interest *verb* find, .pay, .beware, sell, attract., represent., .purchase, offer, lure., .choose
10202 | 0.90 N

2985 divorce *n*
adj no-fault, final, bitter, messy, painful, nasty, parental, ugly, impending, expensive *noun* marriage., .rate, child, year, .case, .law, parent, .lawyer, wife, separation *verb* get., end., file., seek., grant, sue., handle., settle, .proceed
9670 | 0.95

2986 defensive *j*
noun end, back, coordinator, player, line, lineman, position, team, posture, linebacker, strategy, system *misc* offensive, best, play, former, tackle, top, coach, senior
10473 | 0.87 N

2987 bombing *n*
adj terrorist, allied, deadly, massive, heavy, strategic, accidental, African *noun* suicide., city, embassy, .campaign, center., attack, .raid, week, car., suspect *verb* kill, stop, carry, condemn., destroy, .occur, survive., order, investigate., blame
10170 | 0.90 S

2988 scared *j*
noun death, kid, boy, hell, wit, dog, look, height, cat, animal, rabbit, ghost *misc* I, get, so, too, because, really, feel
9944 | 0.92 F

2989 gesture *n*
adj symbolic, grand, obscene, dramatic, simple, sweeping, nice, empty, humanitarian, final *noun* hand, word, arm, expression, head, kind., goodwill, face, movement, body *verb* make., appreciate., return, .indicate, repeat, interpret, communicate, nod, .invite, .convey
9979 | 0.92 F

2990 poetry *n*
adj American, lyric, contemporary, modern, romantic, English, Arabic *noun* book, .reading, music, prose, fiction, art, collection, volume., writing, song *verb* write., read, publish, recite., teach, study, sing, express, .evoke
10130 | 0.90 A

2991 reserve *n*
adj federal, national, foreign, large, strategic, marine, injured, huge, international, short-term *noun* oil., army., world, gas, biosphere., nature., petroleum., cash., .interest, .rate *verb* hold, .raise, increase, create, build, establish, join., protect, maintain, .cover
10022 | 0.91

2992 satisfy *v*
noun .need, .requirement, .demand, .desire, .curiosity, .criterion, customer, .appetite, .hunger, .craving, .standard, .concern, answer, .urge, explanation *misc* .with, enough., .both, must., order., until, completely.
9543 | 0.96

2993 pollution *n*
adj environmental, industrial, light, marine, toxic, global, chemical, atmospheric *noun* air., water., .control, .prevention, source, problem, level, .act, oil., noise. *verb* reduce., cause, prevent., cut., contribute, clean., affect, result, monitor, relate
10895 | 0.84 A

2994 lawn *n*
adj front, green, manicured, wide, broad, sloping, healthy, rolling, flat *noun* .mower, .chair, house,

garden, oak., south., tree, .care, grass, water *verb* mow., sit., cut, walk., cross., surround, push, park, spread, stretch
9944 | 0.92 F

2995 depending *i*
(depending on) .on, or., .how, vary., .your, .size, .whether, .where, different., .type, .level, .condition, per., .circumstance
9654 | 0.94

2996 wisdom *n*
adj conventional, common, human, ancient, prevailing, received, practical, collective, popular, divine *noun* word., knowledge, experience, age, .tradition, .tooth, folk., strength, bit., wit. *verb* question., .hold, share, offer, challenge., seek., defy., possess., guide, discern
9700 | 0.94

2997 since *r*
have., ever., long., .become, year, before, .return, .retire, .expand, .recover, .replace, .adopt, decade., .remarry
9509 | 0.96

2998 comfort *n*
adj great, cold, close, relative, personal, physical, patient, modern, maximum *noun* level, .zone, .food, creature., safety, woman, sense., convenience, security, source. *verb* take., find., give., provide., offer., bring., seek., ease, reassure
9685 | 0.94 M

2999 plot *n*
adj small, alleged, terrorist, involved, experimental, main, basic, individual, communist, crucial *noun* .land, .line, character, family., garden, terror., .twist, assassination. *verb* .involve, .blow, .thicken, uncover, foil, hatch, plant, tend, disrupt, .unfold
9735 | 0.94

3000 vulnerable *j*
noun people, child, population, group, attack, area, position, society, pressure, member, disease, point *misc* more, most, make, leave, feel, particularly, very
9521 | 0.96

3001 explosion *n*
adj nuclear, huge, massive, loud, powerful, sudden, recent, tremendous, atomic, enormous *noun* population., supernova., fire, bomb, sound, .place, series., gas, information, challenger *verb* hear, cause, .occur, kill, .rock, set, create, die., rip, blow
9616 | 0.95

3002 tail *n*
adj long, red, bushy, blue, top, stiff, fluffy, forked, muscular *noun* .end, head., leg, dog, tip., comet, .feather, fin, lobster., wing *verb* wag, turn, hang, chase., twitch, grab., curl, lift, thump, flick
9941 | 0.92 F

3003 differ *v*
noun group, study, result, approach, opinion., view, individual, culture, .degree, gender, sample., age, female, attitude, size *misc* .from, .significantly, .those, may., .between, .greatly
10455 | 0.87 A

3004 fellow *n*
adj senior, young, old, little, poor, visiting, postdoctoral, fine, nice, honorary *noun* .institute,

research., .institution, .center, .name, .enterprise, foundation, craft, kind, sort. *verb* elect., pray, marry., found, .gather, vote, .applaud, hail, nominate
9601 | 0.95

3005 sustain v
noun life, injury, .growth, damage, relationship, loss, interest, ability., effort, support, resource, economy, .population, force, environment *misc* can., help., enough., able., .itself, create., difficult., necessary.
9770 | 0.93 A

3006 doubt v
noun reason., .ability, expert., .sincerity, analyst., scientist., .existence, .claim, .wisdom, .intention, observer., .veracity, critic, .accuracy, .efficacy *misc* I., .that, .will, there, little., one., ever, never., .whether, begin.
9487 | 0.96

3007 stability n
adj political, economic, social, financial, regional, long-term, relative, international, emotional *noun* peace., security, .region, price., .control, threat., growth, .ball, order, prosperity *verb* provide., maintain., bring., ensure., threaten., promote., achieve., enhance., depend, determine
10132 | 0.90 A

3008 fantasy n
adj sexual, male, romantic, pure, erotic, ultimate, female, secret, paranoid *noun* world, reality, life, man, child, fiction, science, play, .novel, .land *verb* live., indulge., act, fulfill., share, .involve, feed., engage, inspire
9755 | 0.93

3009 obligation n
adj moral, legal, ethical, contractual, religious, general, special, constitutional, certain, military *noun* right., family, state, sense., responsibility, duty, law, treaty, debt., community *verb* meet., feel., fulfill., .provide, .protect, impose, accept, assume, comply, .ensure
9864 | 0.92 A

3010 God n
adj dear, almighty, loving, Greek, triune, merciful, Hindu *noun* love, Lord, work, heaven, war, sun, fire *verb* thank., know, .bless, believe., think, see, pray., create, ask, .forbid
9972 | 0.91 F

3011 damage v
noun liver., brain, reputation, kidney, system, cell, .credibility, fire, car, lung, .relationship, .environment, relation, tissue, vessel *misc* .by, badly., severely., seriously., heavily.
9454 | 0.96

3012 bike n
adj stationary, available, complete, light, cross-country, racing, recumbent, yellow, expensive, folding *noun* mountain., road., .ride, .path, .shop, race, trail, .lane *verb* buy., build, pedal, sell, push, jump., park, lock., .cost, roll
15763 | 0.57 M

3013 dining n
adj fine, formal, private, outdoor, elegant, casual *noun* .room, .table, .area, .hall, kitchen, living, chair, hotel, night, restaurant *verb* sit., eat, enter., seat., feature, gather.
9984 | 0.91

3014 guide v
noun student, principle, policy, .development, .decision, research, question, hand, teacher, action, .behavior, team, media, .tour, framework. *misc* .by, .through, .us, help., .toward, .future
9634 | 0.94 A

3015 custom n
adj local, social, traditional, religious, ancient, common, tribal, cultural, native, strange *noun* law, .official, .agent, immigration, .service, border, .officer, design, .union *verb* build, follow., create., .fit, adopt, maintain, adapt., .dictate, specialize., differ
9695 | 0.93

3016 ill j
noun patient, people, child, health, effect, will, ease, mother, person, care, feeling, treatment *misc* mentally, become, terminally, seriously, fall, very, feel, chronically
9559 | 0.95

3017 celebrity n
adj local, minor, favorite, famous, international, instant, hot, overnight, newfound *noun* .status, .news, culture, .chef, media, sport, magazine, .guest, .justice, .golf *verb* become., feature, enjoy, treat, attract, achieve., .line, endorse, attain., pitch
9785 | 0.92

3018 leather n
adj black, brown, red, soft, white, thick, worn *noun* .jacket, .chair, shoe, .boot, .glove, .seat, .bag, .belt *verb* wear., sit, bind, carry, dress., hang, smell, lean., settle., stretch
10051 | 0.90 F

3019 given j
noun time, day, moment, year, name, situation, area, period, level, point, night, individual *misc* any, at, within, determine, particular, depend, specific, associate
9890 | 0.91 A

3020 framework n
adj conceptual, theoretical, legal, institutional, political, social, agreed, general, broad, basic *noun* .convention, policy, .change, model, development, .agreement, analysis, theory, assessment, education *verb* provide., develop, establish, create., .understand, offer., base, present, build, .guide
10674 | 0.84 A

3021 beat n
adj long, steady, sure, silent, awkward, bass, hip-hop, Latin, tense *noun* heart, .minute, drum, cop, music, rhythm, silence, .generation, reporter, drummer *verb* miss., skip., walk, wait, cover, march., combine, pause., sing
12543 | 0.72 F

3022 owe v
noun money, debt, tax, .life, .apology, government, .existence, duty, dollar, .success, .allegiance, bank, .origin *misc* you, .me, much, .something, .anything, .nothing
9289 | 0.97

3023 slight j
noun smile, increase, difference, movement, change, breeze, variation, edge, chance, angle, accent, improvement *misc* only, cause, notice, detect, experience, except, due, moderate
9577 | 0.94 F

3024 witness v
noun year, event, .death, change, scene, .violence, .murder, .execution, century., decade., .rise, period, .birth, performance, .increase *misc* .firsthand, experience, recent, personally., .dramatic, past.
9293 | 0.97

3025 tendency n
adj natural, strong, general, human, political, central, suicidal, growing, violent, increased *noun* action, society, measure., participant, approach., characteristic, depression, response, .violence, procrastination. *verb* show., reflect, .view, avoid, .focus, reinforce, exhibit, demonstrate., associate, .treat
10031 | 0.90 A

3026 load n
adj heavy, full, high, light, viral, total, maximum, cognitive, huge, average *noun* debt., .cell, fund, course., case, work., teaching., .capacity *verb* carry., reduce, lighten., handle., haul., increase, apply, drop., dump., teach.
10204 | 0.88 M

3027 crack n
adj sharp, loud, tiny, deep, narrow, slight, sickening *noun* .cocaine, door, .house, wall, .dawn, .addict, .dealer, .baby, window, rock *verb* open, fall., hear., slip., sell., smoke., .appear, fill, cause, .form
9552 | 0.94 F

3028 briefly r
then, very., only., describe, let., eye., speak., discuss, .consider, .before, mention, meet, pause., explain
9335 | 0.96

3029 derive v
noun benefit, study, .source, satisfaction, pleasure, fact, meaning, theory, experience, income, analysis, authority, research, sense, .plant *misc* .from, part, .directly, largely, .primarily
10228 | 0.88 A

3030 speaker n
adj native, public, motivational, democratic, featured, Spanish, Arabic, non-English, inspirational *noun* house, guest., .word, keynote, .court, assembly, system, phone, parliament, sound *verb* thank, listen, elect., .address, feature., blare, invite., introduce, blast, resign
15714 | 0.57

3031 scandal n
adj corporate, political, financial, sexual, major, growing, huge, past, steroid, cheating *noun* sex., abuse., corruption., house, campaign., accounting., loan. *verb* .involve, .break, cause, create, rock, .hit, .surround, .erupt, implicate., investigate.
9732 | 0.92 S

3032 fifteen m
.year, .minute, about., .ago, ten., after, .later, .foot, .twenty, hundred, .hour, .old, .percent, .mile
9823 | 0.91 F

3033 scheme n
adj grand, broad, different, regulatory, various, elaborate, whole, overall, conceptual, defensive *noun* color., .thing, pyramid., classification., .doctrine, tax, management. *verb* devise, fit., .involve, propose, implement, hatch., participate., introduce, .defraud, .aim
9741 | 0.92 A

3034 jazz n
adj classical, modern, live, Latin, traditional, contemporary, cool, smooth, classic *noun* music, .musician, .band, .festival, blue, .club, .singer, rock *verb* play, listen., perform, sing, feature, record, invent., .mingle, .waft
10032 | 0.89 N

3035 in c
(in that) which, year, new, way, place, .world, life, school, country, case, .area, city, .United States, .fact
9200 | 0.97

3036 elderly j
noun people, woman, man, patient, care, population, person, couple, home, program, resident, health *misc* who, among, disabled, poor, frail, young, especially
10381 | 0.86

3037 celebration n
adj annual, centennial, religious, traditional, cultural, joyous, musical, bicentennial, inaugural *noun* day, anniversary, birthday., Christmas, holiday, family, cause., victory *verb* hold, join., plan, .mark, attend, .feature, organize, honor, host, gather.
9454 | 0.95

3038 can n
adj empty, rinsed, drained, full, soft, heavy, light, 12-ounce, fresh, rusty *noun* beer, garbage., tomato, trash., soda, .bean, tin., aluminum., .opener *verb* open., hold, drain, throw, pick., buy., kick., recycle
9554 | 0.93 F

3039 evolution n
adj human, natural, cultural, social, stellar, biological, Darwinian *noun* theory, year., life, process, stage., teaching., galaxy, species, origin., selection *verb* teach, understand., trace., explain, study., .occur, describe., reflect., .proceed, shape
10152 | 0.88 A

3040 fighter n
adj foreign, tactical, advanced, northern, Arab, Kurdish, armed, Islamic, fierce, marine *noun* jet, .pilot, .plane, freedom., .aircraft, stealth., fire. *verb* fly, kill, shoot, train, fight, capture, .attack, scramble, .cross, battle
9600 | 0.93

3041 publicly r
.trade, .company, speak., United States, .own, .hold, .available, never., president, announce, privately, .funded, acknowledge, criticize
9459 | 0.94

3042 store v
noun data, information, memory, energy, food, water, file, waste, good., bag, body, fat, record, sample, plant *misc* them, .away, .airtight, dry, .inside, safely, properly, enough, collect.
up energy, memory, enough, .food, extra
9629 | 0.93 M

3043 trace v
noun finger, .line, .history, .root, .origin, .path, .development, pattern, .evolution, .outline, .ancestry, .lineage, police., gun, paper *misc* able., .along, .across, directly, .onto, difficult., modern, easily.
9336 | 0.95

3044 rid *v*
noun .Saddam, body, .weapon, .stuff, desire, .debt, .dirt, .wrinkle, .cellulite, .corruption, .racism, .steroid *misc* .of, get., .them, want., try., .himself, .themselves, .itself, .myself, .ourselves, .herself, glad., .yourself, .nuclear, .excess
9349 | 0.95 S

3045 detective *n*
adj private, retired, female, undercover, amateur, famous, burly *noun* police., homicide., .work, .story, .novel, .agency, .fiction *verb* tell, play, .investigate, hire, .assign, question, .testify, .arrive, .search, .track
10021 | 0.89 F

3046 closer *j*
noun look, inspection, examination, tie, relationship, attention, scrutiny, home, truth, cooperation, relation, view *misc* to, than, take, any, much, move, bring, pay, reveal
9160 | 0.97

3047 limitation *n*
adj functional, inherent, important, present, certain, major, possible, future, human, potential *noun* study, statute., term., space, strength, power, use, result, approach *verb* impose, overcome., recognize., include, understand., accept., address., consider, .apply, face
10211 | 0.87 A

3048 besides *r*
.add, else, anyway., tired, anymore., hardly, fun, reason, plenty, reply., perfectly, .doubt
9648 | 0.92 F

3049 soup *n*
adj hot, thick, cold, homemade, canned, delicious, grilled, primordial, Italian *noun* chicken., bowl, .kitchen, salad, vegetable., bean., cream, tomato., pot, can *verb* serve, eat., add, ladle., stir, cook, pour, simmer, taste, boil
9736 | 0.91 M

3050 oven *n*
adj Dutch, preheated, hot, electric, conventional, wood-burning, double, wood-fired, outdoor, clean *noun* .degree, heat, minute, microwave., pan., .temperature, rack, .door, convection., toaster. *verb* preheat., bake, remove., place, cook, turn, roast, reduce, return., warm
10238 | 0.87 M N

3051 rapid *j*
noun growth, change, development, rate, expansion, increase, population, pace, response, succession, rise, progress *misc* more, economic, lead, technological, experience, cause, undergo, because
9724 | 0.91 A

3052 chase *v*
noun car, dog, .dream, police., .ball, guy, girl, storm, boy, cat, kid, street, .tail, .shadow, .rabbit *misc* .after, .away, out, .around, off
   down .lead, try., .every, .ball, car
9409 | 0.94 F

3053 sophisticated *j*
noun system, technology, equipment, computer, technique, way, weapon, software, program, analysis, tool, model *misc* more, most, very, become, use, increasingly, highly, develop
9317 | 0.95

3054 tribe *n*
adj other, American, native, lost, different, local, various, federal, ancient, Sioux *noun* member, nation, Indian, treaty, plain, reservation, chief, hill., clan, language *verb* live, recognize, belong, .operate, form, force, .inhabit, divide, unite, settle
10119 | 0.88 A

3055 pipe *n*
adj long, broken, concrete, exposed, perforated, hot, rusty, galvanized *noun* water, organ, .bomb, .dream, sewer., plastic., .cleaner, length, system *verb* smoke., lay, light., carry, .burst, install, pass, puff., fill, connect
9721 | 0.91

3056 deer *n*
adj white-tailed, red, wild, dead, fallow, antlerless, lame *noun* mule., hunter, hunting, elk, .season, .population, herd, bear, buck, antelope *verb* hunt, shoot, kill, feed, eat, hit, .graze, spook., hide, spot.
10826 | 0.82 M

3057 illustration *n*
adj medical, narrative, perfect, graphic, vivid, black-and-white, original, detailed, striking, dramatic *noun* photo, color, author., page, .picture, book, figure, .courtesy, magazine, .board *verb* .omit, provide, .depict, accompany, reproduce, .highlight, .convey, .clarify
10284 | 0.86 M

3058 ok *j*
noun dad, honey, mom, mommy, daddy *misc* it, that, everything, guess, sure, no, hey, yeah, oh, perfectly, glad
10027 | 0.88 S

3059 arrest *n*
adj cardiac, sudden, arbitrary, respiratory, cardiopulmonary, immediate, mandatory *noun* house., warrant, police, drug, record, month, .conviction, case, charge, officer *verb* make, lead., issue, resist., follow, result., place., announce., report, .occur
9445 | 0.94

3060 mm-hmm *u*
.so, right, yeah, OK, yes
12918 | 0.68 S

3061 uniform *n*
adj white, blue, military, green, gray, dark, khaki, brown, official, standard *noun* man., school., woman., army, soldier., police., dress. *verb* wear., put., change., hang, press, fit, adopt., wash., .bear, .consist
9422 | 0.94 F

3062 transmission *n*
adj automatic, manual, five-speed, cultural, four-speed, sexual, heterosexual, mother-to-child, light *noun* distribution., .deadline, .line, engine, power, data, radio., disease, system, risk. *verb* prevent., reduce., shift, control., .operate, affect., facilitate., block., monitor., leak
10010 | 0.88 S

3063 storage *n*
adj cold, long-term, underground, temporary, additional, extra, liquid *noun* .space, .tank, .area, .room, .facility, .system, data., .capacity, water. *verb* provide, build, offer, process, rent, design, leak, transfer, double, exceed
9881 | 0.89 M

3064 pile n
adj small, big, huge, neat, whole, growing, thick, separate, tall *noun* compost., .paper, rock, .rubble, .book, .clothes, .stone, wood, leaf, body *verb* lay, stack, pick, lie, sort., place, point., throw, bury., surround.
9759 | 0.90 F

3065 survivor n
adj only, sole, long-term, immediate, lone, breast-cancer, Jewish, ultimate, adult *noun* .wife, cancer., child, victim, family, .son, breast., .benefit, .husband, .daughter *verb* .include, die., search., interview, rescue, .abuse, .flee, treat, .struggle, dig.
9664 | 0.91

3066 resemble v
noun mixture., figure, pattern, shape, structure, form, .meal, model, hair., scene, star, flower, .crumb, animal, leaf *misc* closely., something, .other, .each, remotely., vaguely., increasingly.
9382 | 0.94

3067 incredible j
noun story, thing, amount, hulk, experience, number, power, speed, job, sense, opportunity, ability *misc* just, most, such, absolutely, pretty, shrinking, truly
9486 | 0.93 S

3068 impress v
noun friend, .girl, .coach, .ability, .performance, audience, client, visitor, judge, boss, .scout, colleague, .neighbor *misc* .with, .by, so., .me, try., .upon, really., particularly.
9151 | 0.96

3069 economist n
adj chief, senior, political, international, private, agricultural, regional, mainstream, conservative, neoclassical *noun* university, bank, business, government, policy, health., labor., economy, lawyer, home *verb* .call, .argue, .believe, .predict, .expect, .agree, .estimate, .question, .refer, advocate
9731 | 0.91 N

3070 efficient j
noun way, energy, use, system, market, fuel, government, method, service, technology, manner, resource *misc* more, most, than, effective, less, become, highly
9590 | 0.92 A

3071 fifty m
.year, hundred., .dollar, than., more, about., .percent, .ago, .thousand, .foot, over., .mile, .yard, .cent
9705 | 0.91 F

3072 shade n
adj gray, blue, dark, different, green, pink, black, deep, partial, various *noun* .tree, sun, window., lamp, light, .red, evening, hair, plant, skin *verb* sit., provide., pull, wear., paint., grow, choose, match, fade, cool
9713 | 0.91 F M

3073 opera n
adj metropolitan, grand, lyric, royal, Italian, civic, comic, light *noun* soap., .house, .singer, .company, music, city., theater, ballet, production, .star *verb* sing, watch., perform, present, produce, listen., attend., compose, feature, study.
10016 | 0.88 N

3074 calculate v
noun rate, .cost, .number, value, percentage, formula, risk, .distance, model, amount, computer., variable,

price, tax, response *misc* use, average, total, .base, .divide, carefully.
9741 | 0.90 A

3075 preference n
adj racial, personal, sexual, strong, individual, different, political, clear, religious, special *noun* student, style, policy, consumer., matter., gender., learning, food, difference., music *verb* give, express., show., indicate., base, reflect, learn, state., influence, determine
9993 | 0.88 A

3076 guideline n
adj new, federal, general, national, specific, strict, dietary, clear, following, current *noun* set., practice, policy, state, treatment, safety, research, agency, procedure, association. *verb* follow., provide, use, develop, establish, meet., issue, recommend, suggest, require
9707 | 0.91 A

3077 consume v
noun food, amount, percent, energy, alcohol, water, fire, American., product, resource, quantity, fat, flame, animal, process *misc* .by, .less, nearly, .approximately, billion, quickly
9412 | 0.93 M

3078 maintenance n
adj low, regular, preventive, proper, deferred, poor, scheduled *noun* health., .organization, cost, operation, repair, .worker, .program, system, service, building *verb* require, perform, reduce., contribute., ensure, defer
9559 | 0.92 A

3079 formation n
adj spiritual, planetary, tight, geologic, close, perfect *noun* rock., star., identity, process, state, galaxy, planet, capital. *verb* lead., prevent., announce., fly., contribute., result., encourage., occur, break, inhibit.
9797 | 0.90 A

3080 glove n
adj rubber, black, bloody, golden, surgical, heavy, yellow, red, left, thin *noun* hand, pair., .compartment, leather., hat, .box, latex., boxing. *verb* wear., put., pull, fit, remove., plant., open, lay, drop, pick
9452 | 0.93 F

3081 scholarship n
adj full, athletic, recent, academic, historical, feminist, modern, legal, biblical, private *noun* college, student, .program, .fund, year, money, football, teaching, art, research *verb* win., offer., receive., award, provide, earn., establish, accept., .focus, grant
9623 | 0.91 A

3082 educate v
noun child, people, .student, .public, parent, .kid, .other, .consumer, university, health, girl *misc* .about, well, need., highly., help., .themselves, .yourself, inform, raise, poorly.
9357 | 0.94 A

3083 proportion n
adj high, large, small, great, significant, total, low, direct, substantial, increasing *noun* .population, .student, .woman, .child, epidemic., sense., .patient, .variance, .minority, increase. *verb* reach., blow., grow, represent., indicate, rise, assume., contain., decline, occur
9862 | 0.89 A

3084 appointment *n*
adj judicial, political, special, presidential, federal, scheduled, follow-up, dental, academic, joint
noun doctor, court, president, book, .counsel, judge, faculty., cabinet, recess., .process
verb make., announce, keep., schedule., set., cancel., miss., accept., arrive, attend
9184 | 0.96

3085 fund *v*
noun program, project, research, government, study, money, school, grant, tax, foundation, education, company, group, department, organization *misc* .by, .through, fully., federally., publicly.
9359 | 0.94

3086 conviction *n*
adj religious, criminal, strong, moral, political, deep, firm, absolute *noun* court, murder, felony., courage., arrest., .rate, case, sentence, appeal, drug
verb overturn, lead., base, share., win., uphold, reverse, result., express., strengthen
9178 | 0.95

3087 myth *n*
adj Greek, ancient, popular, urban, modern, racial, religious, Christian, African, classical *noun* legend, .reality, history, creation., origin, culture, ritual, version, rape. *verb* dispel., perpetuate., debunk., base, .surround, explode., shatter., destroy., promote, relate
9506 | 0.92 A

3088 solar *j*
noun system, wind, energy, power, panel, cell, planet, eclipse, radiation, mass, flare, technology *misc* our, inner, outer, total, thermal, such, install, electric
10617 | 0.82 M

3089 vessel *n*
adj naval, broken, ceramic, Japanese, empty, foreign, tiny, coronary, French, British *noun* blood., pressure., fishing, .wall, research., heart, ship, water, size, nerve
verb .carry, cause, constrict, sail, operate, dilate, contain, sink, damage, board.
10204 | 0.86 A

3090 wealthy *j*
noun family, people, man, tax, country, nation, woman, individual, businessman, class, corporation, suburb *misc* very, powerful, poor, cut, enough, fabulously, extremely, independently, relatively
9223 | 0.95

3091 friendship *n*
adj close, cross-sex, personal, social, emotional, civic, lifelong, unlikely, beautiful *noun* relationship, love, family, .network, quality, group, closeness, treaty, bond., respect *verb* develop, form, maintain., forge, establish, build, strike., renew., share, .last
9343 | 0.94

3092 membership *n*
adj full, annual, cultural, honorary, total, general, permanent *noun* group, organization, club, union, .fee, church, party, society, community, .due
verb include, .grow, increase, apply., offer, claim., seek., expand, maintain., .cost
9654 | 0.91 A

3093 craft *n*
adj small, contemporary, traditional, local, Indian, alien, native, handmade, ancient, unmanned

noun art., museum, .store, .movement, .show, landing., food, .shop, college. *verb* learn., land, sell, teach, practice, feature., hone., master., .orbit
10725 | 0.82 M

3094 qualify *v*
noun student., job, team, .loan, .Medicaid, .benefit, .car, .aid, teacher, person, candidate, background., credit, income, position *misc* .for, .as, who., enough., highly., must, order., fail., uniquely.
9268 | 0.94 N

3095 French *n*
adj fluent, classic, excellent, broken, passable, impeccable, high-school *noun* English, German, Italian, .subtitle, word, century., .toast *verb* speak, learn., translate., teach., study., fight, open, publish., lead, attack
9242 | 0.95

3096 earnings (PL) *n*
adj annual, high, corporate, future, strong, average, quarterly, net, projected *noun* .growth, company, year, percent, time., .share, quarter, stock, rate, analyst *verb* report, increase, estimate, expect, .grow, .rise, .fall, boost., base., .decline
10946 | 0.8 M N

3097 waste *v*
noun .time, money, energy, life, water, resource, hour, minute, effort, .breath, tax, space *misc* .away, .precious, .little, .valuable, lay., afford.
9136 | 0.96

3098 asleep *j*
noun bed, night, wheel, couch, chair, baby, morning, minute, right, class, dinner, dawn *misc* fall, she, when, still, while, sound, fast, until
9935 | 0.88 F

3099 porch *n*
adj front, screened, wooden, wide, screened-in, covered, sleeping, enclosed *noun* back., step, house, .light, door, .swing, chair, floor, side, roof *verb* sit., stand., walk, wait, lean, climb, .overlook, hang, cross, paint
10067 | 0.87 F

3100 controversial *j*
noun issue, decision, figure, program, topic, book, case, subject, plan, proposal, film, policy *misc* most, more, very, become, highly, remain, less, somewhat
9267 | 0.94

3101 painful *j*
noun experience, memory, process, thing, death, lesson, decision, reminder, past, moment, procedure, period *misc* very, more, too, most, less, long, often, difficult
9118 | 0.96

3102 congressman *n*
adj democratic, conservative, veteran, influential, disgraced, distinguished, incumbent *noun* Republican., senator, new, office, committee, question, .thanks, freshman. *verb* let, thank, agree, vote, introduce, welcome, elect, sponsor, chair, excuse
10614 | 0.82 S

3103 mama *n*
adj big, hot, happy, dear, sick, sweet, red-hot
noun daddy, .Papa, .boy, baby, day, .bear, kitchen,

25. Irregular plurals

The following are the major categories of irregular plural forms in English, along with the most frequent lemmas for each category. Note that most of the Latin forms are limited primarily to formal, academic writing, and that many irregular forms also have a newer, regular variant (e.g. *oxen/oxes, fish/fishes, syllabi/syllabuses*).

f > v [spelling]	lives 51475, leaves 16644, wives 7066, shelves 4778, wolves 3673, knives 2694, thieves 2198, calves 1669, selves 1396, halves 1294, hooves 1013, scarves 952, housewives 884, elves 840, loaves 803, bookshelves 599, sheaves 136
o > oe [spelling]	potatoes 9051, tomatoes 8258, heroes 6045, mosquitoes 2026, echoes 1425, volcanoes 1083, negroes 821, frescoes 483, dominoes 332, torpedoes 324, embargoes 159, cargoes 147
only singular form (top 35 forms)	people 657689, police 82960, staff 41009, fish 34722, personnel 13744, aircraft 11164, deer 11094, salmon 8271, cattle 7618, sheep 6128, trout 4866, tuna 3507, militia 3494, livestock 3388, spacecraft 3213, clergy 3152, offspring 3005, infantry 2944, sperm 2796, poultry 2365, moose 2173, cavalry 2046, catfish 1961, dice 1823, gentry 1325, herring 1298, bison 1297, pike 1283, squid 1186, cod 1126, flora 999, fauna 925, caribou 922, shellfish 907, reindeer 894
only plural form (top 35 forms)	series 52396, thanks 44064, species 34302, sales 33544, clothes 25951, means 22489, works 18458, statistics 11616, earnings 11096, headquarters 10773, corps 9378, ethics 9161, odds 8722, Olympics 7829, dynamics 5705, graphics 5383, remains 4109, surroundings 3156, credentials 2735, binoculars 2445, sneakers 2134, humanities 2126, grassroots 2015, outskirts 1880, scissors 1783, barracks 1714, belongings 1637, riches 1511, pajamas 1448, demographics 1220, fundamentals 1212, residuals 1186, whereabouts 1127, essentials 1053, auspices 878
us/um > i (Latin)	alumni 2175, stimuli 2018, fungi 1305, nuclei 1069, cacti 365, foci 293, pylori 281, syllabi 264, radii 151, loci 150, cognoscenti 145, literati 140
a > ae (Latin)	larvae 1599, algae 1547, nebulae 752, vertebrae 554, supernovae 488, antennae 483, minutiae 327, formulae 220, personae 172, vitae 163, pneumoniae 141, hyphae 130, sequelae 147
um > a (Latin)	data 74049, media 49780, bacteria 7225, curricula 2458, memorabilia 1282, spectra 921, strata 772, maxima 261, consortia 198, fora 195, memoranda 167, ova 130, referenda 107
ix > ces (Latin)	matrices 496, appendices 115, interstices 114
sis > ses	analyses 8649, crises 3170, hypotheses 2651, diagnoses 1015, parentheses 520, theses 396, emphases 329, oases 150, neuroses 131
other Latin (on > a, us > era, a > ata)	criteria 10482, phenomena 3887, genera 399, schemata 189, stigmata 117
eau > eaux (French)	tableaux 256
-men and related forms (top 20 forms)	women 205388, men 151710, gentlemen 8983, fishermen 4128, businessmen 2868, freshmen 2073, policemen 2050, congressmen 1654, gunmen 1233, servicemen 927, firemen 904, craftsmen 846, countrymen 821, linemen 811, salesmen 745, spokesmen 725, horsemen 632, sportsmen 630, workmen 611, chairmen 582
child > children	children 214008, grandchildren 4843, schoolchildren 1125, great-grandchildren 323
other Old English forms	teeth (tooth) 16645, mice (mouse) 3434, geese (goose) 1627, brethren (brother) 1010, lice (louse) 510, oxen (ox) 430. (Note that most of these words have regular plurals as well.)

face _verb_ tell, love, die, cry, .smile, whisper, nod, wake, yell, kiss
10348 | 0.84 F

3104 monitor _n_
adj international, heart-rate, 17-inch, independent, cardiac, portable, external _noun_ science., computer., video., TV., heart., screen, color, television., image _verb_ .show, watch, display, evaluate, stare., .ensure, check, regulate, attach, flash
10967 | 0.8 N

3105 surprise _v_
noun .people, .lot, answer, .me, reaction, .reader, success, .observer, .audience, finding., analyst, .bear, tone, earnings, move. _misc_ you, .by, .him, may., might., .everyone, anyone, .quickly, .everybody
9232 | 0.94

3106 infant _n_
adj young, newborn, human, maternal, premature, tiny, visual, blind, sighted, normal _noun_ .mortality, child, rate, .death, mother, .son, .daughter, .formula _verb_ .born, die, hold., feed, carry, .sleep, care., adopt., cry, nurse
9448 | 0.92

3107 cow _n_
adj mad, sacred, holy, dead, fat, sick, brown, grazing _noun_ milk, .disease, cash., horse, .pasture, dairy., .manure, field, .dung _verb_ feed, .graze, eat, kill, produce, sell, drink, .chew, slaughter, wander
9336 | 0.93 F

3108 proposed _j_
noun change, rule, amendment, legislation, project, tax, regulation, budget, law, solution, cut, model _misc_ under, federal, include, support, environmental, constitutional, discuss, approve
9754 | 0.89 N A

3109 sufficient _j_
noun time, number, evidence, reason, information, condition, power, resource, data, quantity, amount, force _misc_ not, provide, necessary, lack, without, allow, alone
9626 | 0.90 A

3110 oak _n_
adj white, live, red, old, black, royal _noun_ .tree, forest, pine, leaf, .lawn, grove, .table, maple, post., .door _verb_ shade, hang, line, surround, plant, age, dominate, climb, construct., .arch
9618 | 0.90 N

3111 terrorist _j_
noun attack, group, organization, threat, act, activity, network, bombing, cell, target, incident, plot _misc_ against, after, since, prevent, possible, international, bin Laden, major, potential
9649 | 0.90 S

3112 mall _n_
adj national, local, suburban, downtown, regional, antique, nearby _noun_ shopping., strip., store, street, center, lot, .parking, outlet., office, town _verb_ walk, build, visit., head., house, own, line., wander., .cater, .host
9462 | 0.92 N

3113 punishment _n_
adj corporal, cruel, unusual, severe, harsh, physical, appropriate, collective, just _noun_ capital., crime, reward., form., law, attitude., kind., death, use., sin

verb receive, inflict, .fit, impose, deserve, escape., face., accept., .violate, .deter
9348 | 0.93 A

3114 helpful _j_
noun comment, information, suggestion, hint, tip, advice, reviewer, tool, resource, discussion, staff, article _misc_ very, may, also, find, might, most, especially, particularly
9308 | 0.93 A

3115 ongoing _j_
noun process, investigation, part, debate, effort, study, program, research, project, war, relationship, problem _misc_ between, provide, require, because, professional, despite, involve
9394 | 0.92 A

3116 admission _n_
adj free, general, affirmative, financial, selective, special, regular, legal, racial, tacit _noun_ college, .policy, hospital, price, standard, director, museum, .office _verb_ include, gain., require, deny., pay., charge., offer., vary, discriminate
9599 | 0.90 N

3117 frequency _n_
adj high, low, great, increasing, different, increased, relative, resonant, various, descriptive _noun_ radio., table, .response, use, .distribution, range, behavior, intensity, .percentage, duration _verb_ increase, report, occur., reduce., determine, measure, indicate, shift, vary, decrease
10415 | 0.83 A

3118 ratio _n_
adj high, low, signal-to-noise, average, focal, total, student-teacher, energy-output, female, financial _noun_ odds., expense., aspect., percent, sex., compression., stock, table, debt, gear. _verb_ increase, calculate, indicate, compare, measure, determine, reduce, decrease, vary, improve.
9919 | 0.87 A

3119 delay _n_
adj long, developmental, significant, average, slight, brief _noun_ time, house, year, leader., flight, cost, month, rain., hour, traffic. _verb_ cause, result, avoid, experience, .occur, blame, face., explain., prevent, contribute.
9330 | 0.93

3120 privacy _n_
adj personal, electronic, medical, individual, online, financial, complete _noun_ right, invasion., issue, .law, .home, information, protection, .policy, security, concern _verb_ protect., invade., violate, respect., provide., maintain., ensure., guarantee, .prevail
9278 | 0.93

3121 trick _n_
adj old, dirty, magic, little, cheap, simple, neat, real, favorite, stupid _noun_ bag., .question, hat., kind., dog., card., parlor. _verb_ play, use, learn, try, turn, pull, perform., teach, fool, .lure
9198 | 0.94

3122 etc _r_
computer., equipment., box., rhythm., sex., B
9477 | 0.91 A

3123 circuit _n_
adj integrated, short, federal, electrical, closed, judicial, printed, complex _noun_ .court, .judge,

.board, county., .breaker, decision, lecture., .training *verb* .rule, complete., hit., ride, travel., race., connect, control, repeat., blow
9668 | 0.89 A

3124 musician *n*
adj professional, great, local, classical, black, popular, fellow, famous, talented, fine *noun* jazz., music, artist, rock., group, street., blue., teacher, performance., union *verb* .play, become, perform, train, feature., record, listen, hire, invite, .gather
9821 | 0.88

3125 sue *v*
noun company, state, right., government, court, lawyer, city, group., parent, .damage, department, attorney, patient., law, .employer *misc* .over, .federal, threaten., .under, successfully.
9315 | 0.93 N

3126 purchase *n*
adj available, recent, original, online, foreign, initial, future, minimum, total, outright *noun* .price, home, stock, land, .order, museum., money *verb* make, finance., pay, complete., negotiate., increase, approve., plan, arrange., boost
9305 | 0.93 A

3127 aide *n*
adj top, senior, congressional, presidential, chief, close, military, longtime, legislative *noun* house., president, teacher., nurse., home., campaign., health. *verb* say, .describe, hire, .insist, .acknowledge, .concede, recall, .admit, assign, quote
9687 | 0.89 N

3128 modest *j*
noun house, home, increase, amount, means, success, proposal, goal, price, gain, growth, apartment *misc* more, even, very, only, relatively, compare, quite, fairly
9068 | 0.95

3129 helicopter *n*
adj Apache, military, Israeli, marine, heavy, fixed-wing, presidential, flying, light, waiting *noun* .pilot, army., attack, .gunship, police., .crash, cobra. *verb* fly, use, shoot, land, .hover, drop, send., arrive, .carry, destroy
9391 | 0.92 S

3130 empire *n*
adj Roman, Ottoman, British, Soviet, evil, Russian, vast, financial, inland *noun* .state, media., fall., collapse., business., century, .builder, estate., publishing., .style *verb* build., create, expand, .strike, rule, control, extend, .stretch, establish, .crumble
9274 | 0.93

3131 detailed *j*
noun information, description, analysis, study, account, plan, map, report, discussion, data, instruction, explanation *misc* more, provide, give, most, offer, include, require, highly
9362 | 0.92 A

3132 efficiency *n*
adj high, great, economic, improved, low, increased, maximum, improving, thermal *noun* energy., fuel., improvement, gain, cost, percent, .standard, effectiveness, use, speed *verb* improve., reduce, achieve, enhance., promote., boost., result, save, decrease, .vary
9789 | 0.88 A

3133 humor *n*
adj good, black, wry, dry, dark, self-deprecating, wicked, wonderful, sly, gentle *noun* sense., use., wit, attempt., bit., intelligence, .magazine, gallows., joke, irony *verb* enjoy, appreciate, cope, inject., rely., combine., defuse, restore, .deflect, .ease
8951 | 0.96

3134 sanctions (PL) *n*
adj economic, international, tough, military, legal, effective, severe, possible, imposing, official *noun* trade., .regime, country, employer., threat., government, security, policy, imposition., pressure *verb* impose, lift, .work, enforce., apply, support., face., continue, maintain, ease.
9835 | 0.87 S

3135 badly *r*
so., need, want, how., very., hurt, feel., .damage, behave., too., treat, as., beat, burn
8916 | 0.96

3136 tennis *n*
adj professional, junior, international, pro, indoor, Olympic, competitive *noun* court, .player, .shoe, .ball, golf, .club, table., .racket, .tournament, game *verb* play., wear., enjoy, throw, squeeze., quit., retire.
9347 | 0.92 N

3137 emission *n*
adj low, global, total, toxic, greenhouse-gas, industrial, spontaneous, future, significant, current *noun* carbon., gas, greenhouse., reduction, dioxide, .standard, percent, vehicle, country, plant *verb* reduce., cut., control, limit, increase, meet., produce, set, cause, result
10826 | 0.79 A

3138 desperate *j*
noun need, people, housewife, attempt, situation, time, measure, effort, search, help, act, hope *misc* become, increasingly, sound, escape, save, poor, pretty, final
8960 | 0.96

3139 garlic *n*
adj minced, large, fresh, chopped, roasted, green, crushed *noun* clove, onion, oil, teaspoon, pepper, salt, tablespoon, .powder, cup, sauce *verb* .mince, add., chop, stir, cook, .peel, sauté, slice, combine., taste
10247 | 0.84 M N

3140 contest *n*
adj annual, presidential, democratic, athletic, primary, close, staring *noun* beauty., winner, essay., popularity., prize, week, entry, costume., photo., recipe. *verb* win., enter., plead., sponsor, judge, compete., participate., feature, conduct, announce
9070 | 0.94

3141 strengthen *v*
noun .muscle, position, .family, .hand, .security, .tie, .relationship, effort, .bond, economy, government, .institution, education, exercise, .hamstring *misc* help., far., order, greatly.
9425 | 0.91 A

3142 demonstration *n*
adj public, mass, large, peaceful, massive, hands-on, live, recent, clear, civil *noun* .project, student, street, .program, protest, research, week, .site, technology, police *verb* organize, hold, provide, include, stage., lead, participate., follow, break, conduct
9156 | 0.93 A

3143 restriction *n*
adj new, legal, severe, federal, foreign, political, environmental, certain, dietary, tough *noun* trade, state, government, import, immigration, law, access, right, activity, .movement *verb* impose, place, put, lift, ease., .apply, include, .limit, face, loosen.
9297 | 0.92 A

3144 Irish *j*
noun Catholic, immigrant, people, woman, American, government, music, pub, family, republic, community, sea
10247 | 0.83

3145 hunter *n*
adj professional, avid, experienced, native, fellow, lonely, veteran, ethical *noun* deer, bounty., turkey., treasure., duck., season, crocodile. *verb* shoot, hunt, allow, bargain., .pursue, discover, .stalk, .prefer, attract., spot
9814 | 0.87 M

3146 standing *n*
adj good, social, long, legal, political, international, final, moral, academic *noun* .ovation, .committee, .position, .room, member., point, .doorway, figure, .order, class. *verb* see., remain., receive., improve., maintain., notice., enhance., .qualify
8897 | 0.96

3147 handful *n*
adj small, tiny, relative, mere, double, select, scant *noun* .people, .company, .state, .woman, .case, .country, .player, .other, .seed *verb* grab., throw., pick., pull., scoop., toss., eat.
8944 | 0.95

3148 explode *v*
noun bomb, car., star, head, shell., flame, population, air, supernova, door, face, tank, wall, firework, scene *misc* .into, about, when, .around, suddenly., .kill, ready.
9187 | 0.93 F

3149 prompt *v*
noun question, change, .call, concern, action, .official, decision, attack, move, death., .Congress, .speculation, complaint, behavior, incident. *misc* part, .federal, .seek, growing, likely., .renewed
8988 | 0.95

3150 absorb *v*
noun water, body, energy, liquid, light, .shock, .heat, .cost, .moisture, ability., skin, radiation, .impact, nutrient, .loss *misc* .into, completely., able., easily, quickly
9045 | 0.94 M

3151 suspect *n*
adj prime, possible, potential, criminal, likely, chief, main, primary, British *noun* police, murder, terror., bombing, .custody, list, crime, arrest, terrorism., victim *verb* identify, become., consider., name., shoot, track., question, kill, .flee, .confess
9302 | 0.91 S

3152 eager *j*
noun hand, face, audience, scientist, anticipation, politician, customer, investor, crowd, fan, buyer, smile *misc* seem, too, young, learn, please, share, willing
8897 | 0.96

3153 temporary *j*
noun worker, job, order, shelter, program, home, work, measure, housing, relief, visa, basis *misc* only, permanent, provide, restraining, cause, issue, grant, part-time
8839 | 0.96

3154 commissioner *n*
adj high, assistant, associate, acting, regional, interim, agricultural *noun* county., police., state, insurance., baseball, city, deputy., new, board., office *verb* appoint, act., .vote, .decide, .approve, .announce, elect, name, hire, .order
9596 | 0.88 N

3155 diamond *n*
adj black, rough, white, blue, tiny, yellow, double, industrial, pink, African *noun* .ring, gold, baseball., .earring, .necklace, .mine, blood. *verb* buy., wear, sell, cut, discover, flash, steal, sparkle, glitter, own.
9097 | 0.93

3156 curious *j*
noun way, eye, look, fact, crowd, mind, onlooker, person, phenomenon, glance, visitor, tourist *misc* about, just, why, kind, merely, rather, naturally, intellectually
8958 | 0.95 F

3157 differently *r*
.than, thing., see., treat., think, very., little., feel., different, might., may., quite., behave., respond.
8811 | 0.96

3158 across *r*
.from, come., sit., get., .him, foot., .her, message., mile., down, point., about., inch., reach.
9079 | 0.93 F

3159 reservation *n*
adj Indian, full, serious, free, major, military, available, tribal, nuclear, on-site *noun* card, .credit, dinner., .system, Navajo., hotel, land, information, .parking, beer. *verb* make., .accept, .require, express., live., cancel, book, voice., reside.
9396 | 0.90 N

3160 downtown *j*
noun area, street, office, building, hotel, city, district, center, business, restaurant, store, park *misc* where, near, historic, commercial, locate, busy, beautiful, high-rise
9453 | 0.89 N

3161 adjustment *n*
adj structural, social, psychological, emotional, economic, psychosocial, poor, academic, difficult, personal *noun* .program, .problem, policy, period, process, school, difficulty, range *verb* make, require, need, allow, relate, associate, experience, result, force, predict.
9645 | 0.88 A

3162 composition *n*
adj chemical, musical, racial, ethnic, original, overall, similar, demographic *noun* student, body., species., change., color, music, size., class, structure, improvisation *verb* create, determine., reflect, teach., alter., vary, analyze., relate, improve, paint
10400 | 0.81 A

3163 relative *j*
noun importance, risk, power, value, humidity, position, size, price, strength, ease, term, lack

misc each, determine, compare, absolute, economic, assess, indicate, various
9616 | 0.88 A

3164 tiger n
adj white, Bengal, saber-toothed, Siberian, Sumatran, hungry, stuffed, caged *noun* lion, •shark, paper•, •bone, skin, •stripe, •tail, •mosquito *verb* •win, crouch•, beat, ride, fight, shoot, leap, •roar, hunt, chase
9454 | 0.89 N

3165 fabric n
adj social, very, soft, synthetic, thin, woven, space-time, natural, urban, luxurious *noun* piece•, part•, color, •society, cotton, design, silk, •store, pattern, thread *verb* weave•, cover, cut, create, choose, tear, buy, pull, stretch, drape
9494 | 0.89 M

3166 assert v
noun •right, •authority, •control, claim, power, •identity, •independence, •privilege, interest, official•, value, report•, •leadership, need, •jurisdiction
misc •itself, •themselves, simply, repeatedly•, merely, confidently•, boldly
9415 | 0.90 A

3167 discrimination n
adj racial, sexual, religious, reverse, past, ethnic, intentional *noun* sex, law, •woman, form•, employment, case, race, age•, gender•, price• *verb* •base, prohibit•, face, end•, suffer•, experience•, file, fight•, •exist, result
9290 | 0.91 A

3168 float v
noun body, idea, •river, cloud, head, •space, boat, •sea, balloon, •top, proposal, face, voice•, rumor, mind
misc •around, •through, •above, •away, seem•, •past
9214 | 0.92 F

3169 request v
noun information, •anonymity, •assistance, •permission, government, letter•, service, •meeting, •copy, •help, administration•, court, teacher, member, report *misc* million, •additional, send, free, specifically•, formally•, •complete, deny, repeatedly•
8841 | 0.95

3170 math n
adj basic, simple, advanced, remedial, fuzzy, eighth-grade, applied *noun* science, •teacher, student, reading, •class, school, •problem, •skill, •test, •score *verb* read, teach•, learn•, write, study•, solve, improve•, pass•, fail•, •account
9359 | 0.90

3171 overlook v
noun window•, •river, •fact, hill•, room•, •lake, balcony•, park, house•, •bay, bluff•, •ocean, •garden, •city, office•
misc often•, easy•, tend•, largely•, easily•, willing•, frequently•
8786 | 0.96

3172 corps n
adj marine, conservation, medical, diplomatic, civilian, professional, receiving, airborne *noun* army•, •engineer, peace•, press•, US•, officer•, air•, member, volunteer, service• *verb* join•, serve, train, retire, command, •issue, •recruit, order, bugle•, •drill
9123 | 0.92

3173 sequence n
adj main, entire, correct, specific, following, logical, short, historical, chronological *noun* •event, DNA,

gene, genome, action, image, scope•, opening•, step, learning *verb* follow, repeat, occur, determine, omit, present, compare, identify, end, complete•
9417 | 0.89 A

3174 complex n
adj military-industrial, industrial, military, sprawling, huge, whole, vast, entire, retail, nuclear *noun* apartment•, office•, housing•, sport•, building, center, inferiority•, art•, entertainment• *verb* build, •include, house, form, •contain, own, surround, •consist, construct, face
8960 | 0.94 N

3175 heel n
adj right, black, left, low, hot, red, three-inch, narrow, snug, short *noun* toe, boot, shoe, head•, foot, ankle, dress, back, pocket, skirt *verb* come, wear•, turn•, dig•, kick•, click, follow•, sit•, lift, cool•
9321 | 0.90 F

3176 successfully r
use, •complete, student, treat, •defend, able•, implement, manage, compete, argue, •sue
9055 | 0.93 A

3177 examination n
adj physical, closer, close, medical, careful, thorough, clinical, detailed, comprehensive, direct *noun* •room, student, •table, history, •data, patient, entrance•, finding, record, college *verb* •reveal, require, include, pass•, perform, conduct, allow•, undergo•, •identify, test
9862 | 0.85 A

3178 horizon n
adj new, western, eastern, distant, far, blue, southern, northern *noun* event•, time•, sun, line, cloud•, sky, light, star, sunset, •expectation *verb* expand•, stretch•, appear, broaden•, loom•, scan•, rise, open, disappear•, glow
9152 | 0.92 F

3179 German n
adj European, fluent, Nazi, Jewish, ordinary, average, decent, flawless *noun* French, east•, Italian, Japanese, English, Jew *verb* speak•, translate•, fight, capture, force, attack, •remain, •invade, arrive, publish•
9133 | 0.92

3180 absolute j
noun power, value, truth, term, right, number, certainty, difference, necessity, zero, control, authority
misc best, relative, above, total, than, moral, rather
8947 | 0.94 A

3181 anticipate v
noun •problem, change, •need, market, event, consequence, effect, •outcome, •growth, •arrival, •reaction, failure, •attack, challenge, •impact
misc eagerly•, fail•, •future, difficult•, originally•, fully•
8731 | 0.96

3182 yours p
like•, friend•, mine•, •truly, his, fan•, choice•, sincerely, similar•, ours, forever, pretty, fault•, girlfriend•
9177 | 0.91 F

3183 dominant j
noun culture, group, force, role, power, position, society, class, party, theme, player, ideology
misc become, most, political, remain, social, within, cultural, ethnic
9406 | 0.89 A

3184 bull *n*
adj young, raging, huge, papal, mature, mechanical, charging, bucking, enraged *noun* .market, pit., .horn, .eye, .elk, .rider, .moose, .session *verb* ride, play, lead, rage., beat, shoot, charge, hunt., grab, spot.
9286 | 0.90 N

3185 prevention *n*
adj effective, primary, secondary, school-based, tertiary, healthy, universal, clinical, smoking *noun* disease., control., .program, pollution., treatment, education, intervention, .effort, cancer., .strategy *verb* focus, implement, conduct, emphasize., aim, address, promote
9705 | 0.86 A

3186 meter *n*
adj cubic, square, high, long, tall, wide, light, electric, deep, triple *noun* water, parking., .reading, level, flow., .sea, thousand., ground *verb* win., measure, install, rise, feed., locate., spin, range.
9325 | 0.90

3187 legitimate *j*
noun concern, government, question, business, interest, reason, power, claim, right, authority, purpose, issue *misc* political, perfectly, only, consider, recognize, raise, accept, illegitimate
8939 | 0.93 A

3188 mask *n*
adj surgical, wooden, rubber, facial, female, ceremonial, hydrating, diving *noun* gas., oxygen., ski., man., glove, eye, helmet, death., type, figure *verb* wear., put., pull., cover, remove., hide, apply, carry, face., .represent
10296 | 0.81 F

3189 bite *v*
noun .lip, .tongue, nail, dog, .bullet, head, hand, mosquito, snake, bug, .dust, tooth., mouth., .fingernail, .piece *misc* .into, .off, .down, back, .low, .hard, tender., scratch
9134 | 0.91 F

3190 suit *v*
noun .need, .purpose, style, .taste, .task, .interest, environment, type, action, product., personality, size, .situation, variety, approach *misc* well., better., perfectly, ideally., .yourself, .against
   up .for, get., player., before, .again, night, astronaut, .head, already., ready
8763 | 0.95

3191 stroke *n*
adj single, different, bold, short, massive, minor, mild, slow, thick, powerful *noun* attack, brush., risk, disease, .luck, patient, .pen, color, pedal. *verb* suffer., die., cause, prevent., finish., reduce, recover., apply, paralyze, .render
9241 | 0.90 M

3192 assignment *n*
adj random, special, tough, specific, difficult, general, daily, individual, overseas, temporary *noun* student, homework., class, work, writing., committee., teaching. *verb* give, include, read, accept., receive., require, choose, prepare, hand, determine
9133 | 0.91 A

3193 lion *n*
adj red, male, golden, cowardly, wild, African, green, literary, hungry, famous *noun* sea., mountain., .share,

head, .den, .population, .tamer *verb* kill, roar, receive., hunt, shoot, attack, .sleep, account., stalk, .roam
8922 | 0.93

3194 sense *v*
noun .presence, .change, .danger, .tension, .opportunity, moment, .movement, .mood, .fear, .trouble, ability., animal., thought, crowd, .excitement *misc* can., .something, seem., begin., somehow, .behind, immediately
8926 | 0.93 F

3195 rifle *n*
adj automatic, high-powered, semiautomatic, semi-automatic, bolt-action, .22-caliber, rocket-propelled, scoped, British, light *noun* assault., hunting., barrel, .fire, .shot, sniper., .shoulder, butt, scope, air. *verb* shoot, carry., hold, raise., arm., aim, grab., point, lean, rest
9405 | 0.88 F M

3196 brilliant *j*
noun color, light, idea, career, sky, star, mind, sun, student, scientist, performance, flash *misc* most, blue, young, white, red, absolutely, yellow, beautiful
8735 | 0.95

3197 appoint *v*
noun president, court, judge, commission, committee, member, counsel, .director, board, justice, government, .position, .head, lawyer, force *misc* special, newly., .chief, independent, recently.
8846 | 0.94

3198 boom *n*
adj economic, sonic, recent, dot-com, postwar, current, loud *noun* baby., year, .box, oil., .generation, .time, building. *verb* hear, click., fuel, hit, experience., enjoy., cause, ride., .last, .transform
8819 | 0.94

3199 naked *j*
noun eye, body, woman, man, bed, girl, picture, truth, child, waist, skin, aggression *misc* her, see, stand, lie, run, strip, sit, visible
9175 | 0.90 F

3200 hungry *j*
noun people, child, food, man, eye, kid, dog, mouth, baby, meal, bed, animal *misc* feed, eat, feel, tired, always, cold, thirsty, poor
8875 | 0.93 F

3201 tight *j*
noun end, budget, control, race, market, jeans, security, circle, spot, space, labor, line *misc* keep, very, wear, hold, little, under, black, abs
8758 | 0.95

3202 flame *n*
adj blue, open, orange, low, eternal, bright, Olympic, tiny, medium, medium-high *noun* fire, smoke, candle, wall., gas, tongue., .retardant, keeper., ball., sky *verb* burst., burn, fan., .shoot, engulf, light, .lick, .rise, watch., explode
9054 | 0.92 F

3203 Palestinian *n*
adj displaced, wanted *noun* Israeli, Arab, thousand., Jew, number. *verb* kill, .live, .agree, accept, represent, claim, negotiate, .remain, insist, deny
9926 | 0.84 S

3204 economics n
adj international, supply-side, trickle-down, neoclassical, agricultural, applied, ecological
noun professor, politics, law., school., science, business, home., degree., market., history
verb teach, study., major., apply, specialize, .dictate, dominate, revolutionize., concern
9083 | 0.91 A

3205 cabin n
adj main, small, tiny, forward, aft, one-room, first-class
noun log., door, night, wood, room, passenger, mountain, .fever, window, light _verb_ build, stay, fill, enter., share, rent, hide, .feature, emerge., .accommodate
9195 | 0.90 F

3206 print v
noun paper, newspaper, name, letter, .money, page, copy, book, story, color, image, article, .ad, photograph, form _misc_ fit., .recycled, save, electronic, .directly, privately., neatly, original, publish
8827 | 0.94

3207 orange j
noun peel, bowl, zest, light, rind, grove, tree, slice, glow, blossom, jumpsuit _misc_ bright, yellow, grate, wear, red, blue, black
8881 | 0.93

3208 wander v
noun mind., .street, eye., .house, night, .hall, attention., .road, .desert, .town, gaze., thought., dog., park, .aisle _misc_ .around, .through, .into, .off, .away, let., .about, .among, .far, .aimlessly
9021 | 0.92 F

3209 taxpayer n
adj American, local, wealthy, average, individual, common, middle-income, middle-class, middle, huge _noun_ .money, .dollar, cost., expense, year, government, .fund _verb_ pay, spend, save., subsidize, protect., waste., support, allow, .foot, require
9140 | 0.90 N

3210 romantic j
noun comedy, relationship, love, partner, life, notion, interest, poet, dinner, image, music, movie
misc most, sexual, less, French, beautiful, English, classical, hopeless
8831 | 0.93

3211 devote v
noun time, .life, attention, resource, .energy, year, effort, .hour, issue, chapter, study, section, site., research, organization. _misc_ .to, .more, .himself, .entire, .themselves, .exclusively, .entirely
8760 | 0.94

3212 inflation n
adj low, high, economic, annual, double-digit, general, runaway, rampant _noun_ rate, percent, year, unemployment, price, interest, growth, economy, wage, cost _verb_ adjust., keep., rise, fall, reduce, .remain, cause, control., fight., index.
9214 | 0.89

3213 furthermore r
study, research, .although, process, .suggest, data
9594 | 0.86 A

3214 pine n
adj white, tall, green, yellow, lone, towering, knotty _noun_ .tree, .forest, .nut, .needle, oak, .cone,

mountain, fir, stand., wood _verb_ grow, cut, smell., cover, plant, surround, whisper., line, sprinkle., dominate
9014 | 0.91 M

3215 agriculture n
adj sustainable, American, urban, commercial, intensive, organic, irrigated _noun_ department, US., food, industry, secretary, state., ministry, water, .organization, land _verb_ support., affect, promote., engage., employ, clear., relate, destroy, decline, .account
9320 | 0.88 A

3216 legacy n
adj historical, enduring, colonial, political, cultural, lasting, greatest, rich _noun_ part., family., life, .slavery, father, apartheid, system, generation, .carrier _verb_ leave, continue, carry., create, build, pass, preserve., inherit, overcome., reflect.
8693 | 0.95

3217 extension n
adj cooperative, natural, logical, agricultural, full, two-year, one-year, five-year, direct, indefinite
noun contract., .service, .cord, life, leg, program, .agent, hip., research, knee _verb_ sign., grant, file., support., seek., represent., oppose., .expire, strengthen
8972 | 0.92 A

3218 barrel n
adj wooden, double, huge, rifled, golden, fluted, octagonal, adjusting _noun_ .oil, .day, gun, pork., rifle, price, stock, bottom., shotgun, .chest _verb_ produce., point, stare., fill, sell, drop, rise, fire, stick, place
8935 | 0.92

3219 arrival n
adj new, recent, late, dead, imminent, international, unexpected, impending, expected, scheduled
noun time, departure, month., age, hour., immigrant, spring, .troop, minute., .European _verb_ await., announce., wait., greet., prepare., celebrate., signal., coincide, anticipate., .prompt
8571 | 0.96

3220 register v
noun voter, face, .degree, car, thermometer., offender, mind, .complaint, .surprise, gun, .Republican, .course, poll, citizen, Democrat _misc_ .vote, require., barely., million, fail., insert., officially.
8524 | 0.96

3221 flavor n
adj rich, sweet, strong, fresh, mild, intense, full, nutty, subtle, smoky _noun_ texture, color, food, dish, fruit, aroma, tomato, ice, chocolate, chicken _verb_ add, blend, bring., enhance, develop, retain., taste, impart., enjoy., .meld
9335 | 0.88 M N

3222 versus i
percent, issue, low, per, debate, continued., Roe., male, difference, nature, private, poor, benefit
9136 | 0.90 A

3223 risk v
noun .life, perception, reduction, consequence, .death, .limb, .injury, .loss, .career, .damage, .wrath, .confrontation, .reputation, .neck, exposure _misc_ .lose, willing., rather., .everything, decide., worth.
8483 | 0.97

3224 flesh *n*
adj human, soft, white, dead, sweet, pink, bare, burning, tender, rotting *noun* .blood, bone, skin, word., .tone, spirit, body, color, bit., piece. *verb* eat., cut., tear, press., rip, touch, .hang, burn, scoop., pierce.
9151 | 0.90 F

3225 submit *v*
noun report, proposal, application, plan, budget, question, bill, bid, work, court *misc* to, must., require., written, invite., refuse., force., voluntarily.
8707 | 0.94 A

3226 garage *n*
adj two-car, underground, three-car, 2-car, attached, converted, detached *noun* parking., .door, car, .sale, house, basement, .night, .sales, floor, back *verb* open, pull, park, build, close, attach, clean., enter
8878 | 0.92 F

3227 cotton *n*
adj white, blue, black, organic, thin, soft, Egyptian, printed *noun* .shirt, .field, .candy, .ball, .dress, .bowl, wool, silk, .club, crop *verb* wear., pick., grow, plant, stuff, produce, wrap., soak, .absorb, stretch
8990 | 0.91

3228 operator *n*
adj small, independent, local, human, private, smooth, heavy, commercial, skilled, cellular *noun* cable., tour., owner., system., radio., telephone., boat. *verb* allow., require, .answer, dial, .handle, charge, enable., hire, .monitor, permit
8768 | 0.93

3229 nut *n*
adj chopped, dried, tough, whole, roasted, hard, fresh, hot, mixed, remaining *noun* pine., .bolt, fruit, cup, tree, .case, butter, wing., food, guy *verb* crack, add, eat., stir, toast, sprinkle., tighten., spread, loosen, gather
8825 | 0.93 M

3230 rate *v*
noun .director, item, student, participant., teacher, subject., respondent., performance, minute, behavior, parent, peer, .level, .star, quality *misc* .as, high, highly, low, .significantly
9371 | 0.87 A

3231 blade *n*
adj sharp, thin, curved, dull, electric, flat, double-edged, gleaming *noun* shoulder., razor., knife, .grass, metal., steel, edge, rotor., sword, processor. *verb* cut, pull, fit., squeeze., draw, .slice, spin, lift, attach, swing
9604 | 0.85 F

3232 girlfriend *n*
adj new, old, pregnant, longtime, steady, beautiful, current, serious *noun* wife, boyfriend, house, son, father, brother, live-in., college, apartment, actress *verb* meet, kill, break, marry, visit, dump, propose., beat., kiss, murder
8909 | 0.92

3233 fly *n*
adj dry, black, tiny, dead, male, Spanish, stable, wet, light *noun* .rod, .ball, fruit., fishing, sacrifice., line, .ash *verb* .buzz, catch, hit., swat., drop., kill, cast, unzip., .land
9095 | 0.90 M

3234 dependent *j*
noun variable, child, measure, aid, family, economy, oil, government, other, relationship, analysis, care *misc* on, upon, become, more, heavily, less, highly, each
9288 | 0.88 A

3235 carbon *n*
adj organic, atmospheric, activated, total, pure, excess, stiff, radioactive *noun* .dioxide, .emission, .monoxide, .fiber, atmosphere, .tax, level, water, nitrogen, oxygen *verb* reduce., produce, release, emit, absorb, cut., contain., form, rise, burn
9499 | 0.86 M A

3236 heritage *n*
adj cultural, American, national, rich, African, common, ethnic, natural, proud, religious *noun* .foundation, world., part., .site, culture, history, .center, museum, family, language *verb* preserve., celebrate., share, protect., reflect, maintain., reclaim., promote, .date, embody
8886 | 0.92 A

3237 organic *j*
noun matter, food, material, compound, soil, farm, farmer, product, carbon, farming, molecule, waste *misc* volatile, grow, such, buy, natural, certified, produce, inorganic
9407 | 0.87 M

3238 ambassador *n*
adj American, Iraqi, Soviet, French, Israeli, Saudi, British *noun* US., .nation, state, goodwill., residence, south, deputy, conference, federation, council. *verb* thank, serve., send., appoint., name., agree, recall, welcome, nominate., complain
9207 | 0.89 S

3239 invasion *n*
adj Iraqi, Soviet, American, military, British, Israeli, US-led *noun* .privacy, .force, .occupation, land, home., ground., squatter. *verb* follow., launch., support., condemn., justify., oppose., prevent., .occur, protect., defend.
8879 | 0.92

3240 summit *n*
adj economic, European, annual, two-day, successful, presidential *noun* .meeting, president, leader, week, world, budget., mountain, .conference, .mount, foot *verb* hold, reach., attend., host., convene, climb., sign, sponsor, arrange., .collapse
8998 | 0.91 S

3241 lifestyle *n*
adj healthy, active, sedentary, alternative, lavish, gay, traditional, simple, homosexual, urban *noun* change, .choice, diet, .factor, family, kind., activity, habit, section *verb* live., maintain., lead, adopt., promote., enjoy., support., fit., encourage, suit
8767 | 0.93 M

3242 agricultural *j*
noun research, land, production, product, service, sector, area, development, use, practice, system, center *misc* industrial, such, rural, urban, reduce, increase, environmental, traditional
9827 | 0.83 A

26. Variation in past tense forms

English has variation with forms of the simple past (*he dived/dove into the pool*) and past participle (*he had proved/proven his point*). The variant A in the following tables is the most frequent form in these pairs, and the rightmost column (A+B) shows the total number of tokens for both A and B in the corpus. Note that in some cases, the raw frequency masks semantic differences between the two forms, such as *he shined the shoes* (transitive) / *the sun shone brightly* (intransitive).

Simple past (*he dove/dived into the pool*)

A	B	%A	A+B
learned	learnt	1.00	22105
drank	drunk	1.00	5522
sank	sunk	0.99	3315
forbade	forbad	0.99	544
spilled	spilt	0.98	1213
hung	hanged	0.97	8514
burned	burnt	0.95	3970
lit	lighted	0.94	3896
thrived	throve	0.93	708
knelt	kneeled	0.91	1917
dreamed	dreamt	0.86	2759
strove	strived	0.85	317
shone	shined	0.83	1954
sprang	sprung	0.81	2303
wove	weaved	0.75	683
bade	bid	0.74	338
spat	spit	0.67	863
dove	dived	0.65	832
shrank	shrunk	0.62	904
knitted	knit	0.59	121
leaped	leapt	0.57	2942
stunk	stank	0.55	472
sneaked	snuck	0.54	1086

3243 shrug *v*
noun .shoulder, head, .coat, .jacket, .apology, .resignation *misc* ask., again, .guess, merely., simply., .helplessly
   off .question, .any, .jacket, easily, .threat, .comment, .suggestion, .responsibility, .talk
9737 | 0.84 F

3244 counsel *n*
adj special, legal, chief, outside, senior, corporate *noun* office., house., president, defense., .law, independent., deputy., general., investigation, committee *verb* appoint, seek., .investigate, serve., represent, offer, name, hire., advise, act
9055 | 0.90 S

3245 associate *n*
adj senior, close, closest, longtime, consulting, financial, junior, regional, postdoctoral, long-time *noun* research., business., friend., .degree, family., president., company, consultant, .professor, survey *verb* earn., engage, hire, cope, conduct, complete, design, consult, .clean, contact.
8772 | 0.93 N

3246 major *n*
adj English, double, open, professional, retired, liberal, female, declared, prospective, triple *noun* .league, education., .general, player, college, minister., science, sergeant., undergraduate., music. *verb* win, involve, play, lead., report, command, offer, retire., face, pitch.
8758 | 0.93 N

Past participle (*he had proved / proven his point*)

A	B	%A	A+B
swelled	swollen	1.00	783
thrived	thriven	1.00	286
learned	learnt	0.99	21522
forgotten	forgot	0.99	9965
woven	weaved	0.99	1525
struck	stricken	0.99	7257
shrunk	shrunken	0.98	1043
spilled	spilt	0.98	1166
shown	showed	0.97	31298
forbidden	forbade	0.97	2209
shaved	shaven	0.97	755
sown	sowed	0.95	364
dreamed	dreamt	0.93	2373
lit	lighted	0.91	3999
woken	waked	0.89	604
burned	burnt	0.89	6606
beaten	beat	0.89	5643
hung	hanged	0.88	5912
lied	lay	0.88	1367
mowed	mown	0.88	148
knelt	kneeled	0.87	76
bitten	bit	0.86	1398
got	gotten	0.85	144451
bid	bidden	0.84	232
sheared	shorn	0.81	469
shone	shined	0.79	189
spit	spat	0.74	473
sewn	sewed	0.73	1000
sawed	sawn	0.71	124
knit	knitted	0.68	320
striven	strived	0.66	146
sneaked	snuck	0.57	301
laid	lain	0.56	9191
leaped	leapt	0.55	328
proved	proven	0.51	9516

3247 distinguish *v*
noun .type, group, ability., difference, characteristic, feature, .form, .reality, .species, factor., .object, quality, attempt., behavior, approach *misc* .from, .between, .other, .themselves, able., difficult., clearly
9045 | 0.90 A

3248 menu *n*
adj regular, tasting, full, vegetarian, main, extensive *noun* item, restaurant, dinner, dish, option, start., food, lunch., choice, bar
verb .include, offer, feature, serve, choose, create, plan., order, read, list
9251 | 0.88 N

3249 awful *j*
noun lot, thing, time, day, place, truth,
moment, night, feeling, noise, news, stuff
misc there, feel, something, happen, sound,
pretty, spend
8718 | 0.93 S F

3250 wound *n*
adj old, self-inflicted, deep, gaping, bleeding, multiple,
surgical, fatal, mortal, emotional *noun* gunshot.,
head, healing, war, blood, bullet., stab., puncture.,
body *verb* heal, inflict, die., suffer, open, lick., treat,
clean., close, cause
8617 | 0.94 F

3251 manufacturing *n*
adj light, computer-aided, Japanese, advanced,
chemical, high-tech, traditional *noun* company, .job,
.process, .sector, .plant, industry, design, technology,
.facility, service *verb* lose, develop, employ, decline,
improve, .rise, outsource, .account, own, eliminate
9280 | 0.88 A

3252 consumption *n*
adj high, human, low, conspicuous, domestic, total,
public, increased, mass, personal *noun* energy.,
alcohol., production, fuel., food, level, oil, pattern,
percent, water *verb* reduce., increase, cut., rise, limit.,
encourage, relate, .decline, decrease, lower
9339 | 0.87 A

3253 permission *n*
adj written, prior, special, parental, official, following,
express, explicit *noun* .information, parent, government,
.publisher, request., .slip, court, author, department,
form *verb* give., ask., get., reprint., use, grant, obtain.,
need., receive., seek.
8552 | 0.95

3254 twelve *m*
.year, .hour, ten., .old, .month, .day, about., .ago, .foot,
age., .hundred, .later, .thousand, .thirteen
8836 | 0.92 F

3255 offensive *j*
noun line, coordinator, lineman, tackle, player,
coach, weapon, team, force, game, operation, action
misc find, defensive, against, launch, military, former,
patently, deeply
9105 | 0.89 N

3256 shower *n*
adj hot, cold, separate, quick, warm, outdoor, bridal,
heavy *noun* meteor., .curtain, room, water, head,
bathroom, .stall, baby., bath, tub. *verb* take., turn,
step., sing, hit, throw, wet., finish, .last, .rinse
8828 | 0.92 F

3257 collapse *v*
noun building., system., union., economy., tower.,
.bed, roof., .chair, market., ground, regime., lung, arm,
.exhaustion, category *misc* .into, after, before, .under,
.onto, Soviet., .die
   back .into, .onto, .itself
8414 | 0.96

3258 undergo *v*
noun .surgery, .change, patient., .treatment,
.transformation, .procedure, .test, woman, year,
.training, .therapy, .testing, .operation, .evaluation,
experience *misc* .major, must., .extensive, .significant,
.radical, .dramatic
9071 | 0.89 A

3259 function *v*
noun system, family., ability., society, brain., market,
context, community, capacity, role, environment,
organization, democracy, language, structure *misc* .as,
how., .well, .properly, still., .without, .effectively, able.
8882 | 0.91 A

3260 consciousness *n*
adj human, national, public, social, political,
collective, altered, historical *noun* state., level.,
class., stream., loss., form, mind, change, evolution.
verb lose., raise., regain., develop, enter., fade, reflect,
exist, transform, penetrate.
9190 | 0.88 A

3261 correct *v*
noun problem, error, mistake, .record, .situation,
.imbalance, .deficiency, surgery., .impression, vision,
step., digit., .injustice, failure, violation *misc* try.,
attempt., immediately, quickly, politically., order.,
easily., necessary.
8359 | 0.97

3262 dry *v*
noun hand, sun, hair, water, towel, skin, tear,
paint., eye, clothes, dish, face, blood, ink.,
ground *misc* .off, .quickly, hang., allow.,
thoroughly, completely
   up money., source, .blow, funding., supply, river,
fund., lake., well, spring **out** soil., .quickly, prevent.,
skin, plant, hair, .completely, meat.
8855 | 0.91 M

3263 frustration *n*
adj growing, sexual, deep, pent-up, enormous,
increasing, mounting, intense *noun* anger, sense.,
level, feeling., source., lot., disappointment, rage,
confusion *verb* express., feel, vent., experience, lead,
understand., deal, cause, .build, shake.
8351 | 0.97

3264 operating *n*
adj chief, standard, annual, total, normal, joint,
net, basic, maximum *noun* .system, .officer, .room,
.budget, .table, .procedure, company, .expense
verb .cost, reduce., cover., increase, wheel., install,
license, lower, generate.
8941 | 0.90

3265 ease *v*
noun .pain, tension, .burden, .transition, pressure,
.restriction, .fear, door, .concern, .mind, .strain, car,
.sanction, .anxiety, .traffic *misc* .into, .out, help.,
.back, .down, try., .onto
   up .little, .bit, might., .enough
8501 | 0.95

3266 carrier *n*
adj armored, big, long-distance, American,
low-cost, regional, local, foreign, international,
common *noun* aircraft., personnel., air, insurance.,
mail., .group, tank., letter. *verb* fly, .offer, land,
operate, launch, .deliver, switch., sink, .charge,
attack
8710 | 0.93

3267 scope *n*
adj large, broad, limited, full, narrow, global, wider,
geographic *noun* .article, size., .study, power, project,
rifle, scale, .paper, nature, .sequence *verb* limit.,
expand, broaden., define, determine., extend.,
.reveal, widen., fall., aim
9427 | 0.86 A

3268 grain *n*
adj whole, small, fine, fresh, refined, rich, basic, low-fat, coarse, individual *noun* vegetable, sand, rice, .salt, cereal, .elevator, dust, price, wood *verb* eat, feed, produce, cut., contain, buy., store
8766 | 0.92 M

3269 distinct *j*
noun group, advantage, identity, type, possibility, culture, difference, pattern, community, way, impression, population *misc* from, two, three, each, separate, four, quite, yet
8971 | 0.90 A

3270 ranch *n*
adj large, working, sprawling, modest, three-bedroom, wild, neighboring, suburban, four-bedroom *noun* .house, cattle., farm, family, .hand, dude., guest *verb* buy., live., own, visit., manage., purchase., bet., surround, hunt, .border
8980 | 0.90 N

3271 workshop *n*
adj professional, educational, free, special, hands-on, various, two-day, three-day, one-day, numerous *noun* teacher, participant, conference, training, summer., writer., course, writing., lecture, center *verb* attend., hold, conduct., offer, teach, lead, provide, participate., .focus, develop
8999 | 0.90 A

3272 auto *n*
adj American, Japanese, average, European, German, used, antique, Italian, ordinary *noun* .industry, .part, .insurance, .worker, .company, .maker, .accident *verb* .race, sell, reduce, own, force., purchase.
8903 | 0.91 N

3273 publisher *n*
adj associate, commercial, academic, traditional, leading, assistant, retired, wealthy, longtime, respected *noun* editor, book, newspaper, magazine, president., news, software., textbook. *verb* name., publish, sell, announce, reject, .print, contact, market, appoint., sue
9536 | 0.84 N

3274 narrator *n*
adj first-person, omniscient, unreliable, female, authorial, Irish, third-person, nameless *noun* scene., character, boy, story, reader, voice, author, protagonist, mind, .comment *verb* .describe, .recount, .inform, .remark, undermine, overhear, .allude, underscore.
13504 | 0.6 F

3275 brush *v*
noun hair, .tooth, hand, .oil, side, finger, face, lip, .cheek, .top, .butter, water, arm, .egg, .mixture *misc* her, his, .against, .aside, .away, .back, lightly **off** .dirt, .hand, .concern, .question, .knee, .pant **up** .on, .against, .your, .skill, need.
8933 | 0.90 F

3276 ban *v*
noun law., weapon, state, .use, .abortion, government, amendment., .marriage, bill., gun, .sale, legislation., book, party, .import *misc* .from, constitutional., .gay, federal, .smoke, vote., .altogether
8613 | 0.93 N

3277 portray *v*
noun woman, character, media, image, movie, film, actor., figure, picture, television, culture, attempt., event, animal, screen *misc* .as, .himself, often., try., .themselves, accurately., seek., usually.
8623 | 0.93 A

3278 fighting *n*
adj heavy, fierce, intense, ultimate, recent, ethnic, bitter, factional *noun* .force, .man, day, war, .chance, .vehicle, week, .spirit, street., month *verb* stop, continue, end, .begin, .break, kill, die, flee., .erupt
8723 | 0.92

3279 borrow *v*
noun .money, .phrase, .car, bank, .friend, book, government., idea, term, dollar, fund, loan, cost, interest, rate *misc* .from, .against, .heavily, beg., .steal, .directly, freely
8378 | 0.96

3280 seize *v*
noun .opportunity, .power, .control, .moment, government, property, hand, asset, police., force, chance, troop., .initiative, agent., authority *misc* .by, .upon, suddenly., immediately, quickly **up** heart, market, muscle., after, leg.
8472 | 0.95

3281 psychology *n*
adj social, educational, clinical, introductory, cognitive, human, evolutionary, transpersonal *noun* school., professor, student, sport., department, course, .program, education *verb* study., teach, enroll., relate, publish, major., earn., derive., concern, embrace
10162 | 0.79 A

3282 subsequent *j*
noun year, analysis, study, event, development, research, performance, generation, work, behavior, change, decision *misc* during, each, influence, affect, reveal, confirm, initial, therefore
9128 | 0.88 A

3283 exceed *v*
noun .expectation, .percent, .limit, cost, .standard, level, rate, number, value, income, benefit, demand, .supply, sales., .goal *misc* far., .million, .billion, meet., often., expect, already., greatly.
8776 | 0.92 A

3284 crack *v*
noun voice., door, .joke, egg, .code, .case, .smile, nut, .whip, .top, .knuckle, ice, wall, bone, face *misc* .open, hard, .under, break, tough., dry., .apart, .wise **down** government., .illegal, police., try., effort., .crime, .militant, .hard, authority., .terrorism
8492 | 0.95 F

3285 killing *n*
adj mass, innocent, brutal, involved, serial, responsible, recent, indiscriminate, senseless, intentional *noun* .field, .spree, .machine, .civilian, mercy., .ground, contract., death *verb* stop, .occur, charge., end, order., condemn., accuse., investigate., convict., link
8528 | 0.94

3286 deadline *n*
adj rigid, tight, statutory, self-imposed, looming, artificial, firm, 48-hour *noun* distribution.,

week, trade., entry, trading., application, midnight, hour, filing., .submission *verb* meet., set, miss., extend., .pass, face., .approach, impose, .loom, near
9319 | 0.86 S

3287 athletic *j*
noun director, ability, association, department, performance, program, role, conference, coach, team, model, club *misc* high, national, academic, collegiate, western, intercollegiate, female, physical
10058 | 0.8 N

3288 wise *j*
noun man, use, decision, choice, guy, word, investment, policy, movement, person, move, advice *misc* old, enough, beyond, foolish, smart, crack, prudent, politically
8389 | 0.96

3289 medication *n*
adj over-the-counter, prescribed, certain, psychotropic, oral, antidepressant, available, common, medical, stimulant *noun* pain., prescription., patient, use, doctor, effect, treatment, blood, side, therapy *verb* take, prescribe, need, treat, .help, stop, receive., control, administer, reduce
9017 | 0.89 M

3290 repeatedly *r*
tell, ask, United States, show, official., warn, .deny, himself, fail, refer, demonstrate, rape, insist, lie
8371 | 0.96

3291 frequent *j*
noun contributor, use, flier, visitor, guest, visit, contact, trip, flyer, traveler, change, reference *misc* more, most, less, become, among, require, report, increasingly
8597 | 0.93 A

3292 rocket *n*
adj solid, multiple, chemical, conventional, southern, homemade, expendable, anti-tank *noun* .scientist, .launcher, .attack, .science, .engine, game, .ship, booster *verb* fire, launch, hit, build, shoot, carry, .fall, explode, .figure, .propel
9729 | 0.82 N

3293 fame *n*
adj national, international, greatest, sudden, newfound, instant, worldwide, growing *noun* hall., .fortune, money, minute., walk., wealth, .career *verb* win, gain., bring, achieve., claim., earn, enjoy., seek., .spread, .eclipse
8670 | 0.92 N

3294 lung *n*
adj black, right, left, normal, full, collapsed, punctured, healthy, artificial *noun* .cancer, heart, .disease, air, blood, .function, .tissue, breath, risk, patient *verb* fill, cause, breathe, burn, develop, collapse, puncture, damage., affect, .ache
8578 | 0.93

3295 depict *v*
noun figure, scene, painting, woman, life, image, film, artist, table, event, mural., art, character, subject, landscape *misc* as, often., female, accurately, various, sexual, graphically
8995 | 0.89 A

3296 persuade *v*
noun .Congress, .other, effort., leader, court, .judge, official, .voter, .jury, .public, campaign., attempt., argument, .colleague, ability. *misc* try., help., able., hope., finally.
8412 | 0.95

3297 tent *n*
adj big, huge, two-person, makeshift, light, heavy, nearby, inner, freestanding *noun* .city, .pole, camp, bag, canvas., flap, food, wall, circus., pup. *verb* pitch., set, live., sleep, erect, fold., enter., fill, share, house
9326 | 0.86 M

3298 ah *u*
.yes, .well, no, .ha, oh, .yeah, OK, .hell, ooh
9025 | 0.89 F

3299 motivation *n*
adj intrinsic, high, academic, political, primary, strong, personal, extrinsic, human, internal *noun* student, achievement, level, sport, lack., theory, goal, behavior, skill, factor *verb* learn, provide, understand., increase., relate, enhance., affect., identify, focus, predict
9463 | 0.84 A

3300 odds (PL) *n*
adj long, better, overwhelming, impossible, enormous, incredible, insurmountable *noun* .ratio, .end, .success, survival, .favor, .arrest, log., marriage *verb* beat., increase., improve., put., defy., face, overcome., .stack, calculate., reduce.
8316 | 0.96

3301 worried *j*
noun parent, face, official, expression, sick, mom, investor, voice, glance, frown, consumer, smile *misc* about, so, very, more, look, too, might, really
8453 | 0.94 F

3302 principal *j*
noun investigator, component, analysis, factor, owner, reason, source, sponsor, author, cause, concern, goal *misc* whose, serve, assistant, elementary, exploratory, analyze, yield, strategic
8659 | 0.92 A

3303 firm *j*
noun grip, hand, believer, voice, commitment, belief, ground, control, conclusion, foundation, handshake, evidence *misc* until, hold, yet, enough, soft, tender, slightly
8373 | 0.95

3304 ugly *j*
noun thing, head, face, duckling, word, side, truth, building, scene, dog, place, scar *misc* turn, bad, rear, little, beautiful, pretty, fat
8503 | 0.94 F

3305 adequate *j*
noun care, supply, time, resource, support, protection, health, water, level, food, progress, information *misc* provide, without, ensure, receive, lack, meet, maintain
8842 | 0.90 A

3306 nonetheless *r*
but., remain, significant, manage, .insist, powerful, substantial, impressive, considerable, useful, distinct, discourse, .crucial, valuable
8590 | 0.92 A

3307 criminal *n*
adj violent, convicted, common, dangerous, hardened, petty, international, tough, habitual, serious *noun* war., crime, career., justice, law, street, police, master., adult., officer *verb* treat., catch, violate, prosecute., .commit, arrest, .proceed, act, execute, identify.
8349 | 0.95

3308 widespread *j*
noun use, support, problem, belief, practice, acceptance, concern, corruption, abuse, attention, adoption, perception *misc* there, more, among, become, most, despite, cause, lead
8669 | 0.92 A

3309 transformation *n*
adj social, political, economic, radical, personal, cultural, major, dramatic, profound, structural *noun* process, .society, change, economy, conflict., data, market, strategy *verb* undergo., .occur, involve, lead, require, describe, experience, witness., achieve., perform
8925 | 0.89 A

3310 physically *r*
mentally, emotionally, .active, .abuse, .fit, both., feel, psychologically, .demand, sexually, .disabled, spiritually
8325 | 0.95

3311 provider *n*
adj other, large, medical, private, primary, social, leading, preferred, financial, content *noun* service., care., health., Internet., healthcare., abortion., family, child, company, cable. *verb* .offer, require, pay, choose, check, .charge, compete, .assess, link, assist
9407 | 0.84 A

3312 admire *v*
noun work, man, .view, .courage, artist, .beauty, .ability, quality, writer, .handiwork, .scenery, .honesty, critic, politician, visitor. *misc* .her, .him, much, most, always., greatly, really.
8330 | 0.95

3313 headline *n*
adj late, big, national, front-page, tabloid, front, international, quick, sensational, top *noun* news, newspaper., story, day, week, morning, health., banner., page, look. *verb* make., read, grab., run, scream, dominate., .announce, hit, blare, proclaim
8577 | 0.92 S

3314 miracle *n*
adj economic, medical, modern, minor, alive, near, greatest, absolute *noun* .worker, .cure, .drug, .boy, kind., .baby *verb* .happen, work., perform., believe., expect., hope., pray., .occur, witness., produce
8357 | 0.95

3315 institutional *j*
noun investor, change, structure, board, review, arrangement, effectiveness, support, framework, policy, church, reform *misc* political, social, revolutionary, such, within, personal, individual, economic, cultural
9630 | 0.82 A

3316 homeless *j*
noun people, shelter, man, child, woman, family, person, youth, city, population, street, program *misc* help, leave, live, poor, among, million, mentally, ill, house
8625 | 0.92 N

3317 impressive *j*
noun result, number, record, list, array, performance, collection, victory, figure, display, gain, achievement *misc* most, more, very, even, as, pretty, less
8322 | 0.95 M

3318 chef *n*
adj top, head, French, personal, local, award-winning *noun* executive., pastry., restaurant, food, owner, kitchen, recipe, celebrity., .knife, master. *verb* cook, prepare, teach, hire., train, name, feature, .whip, inspire, .mix
8977 | 0.88 N

3319 tactic *n*
adj new, political, military, aggressive, effective, diversionary, strong-arm, similar, legal, common *noun* strategy, scare., campaign, guerrilla., war, pressure, sales., use *verb* employ, .work, change, adopt, switch., engage., resort., defend, .fail, apply
8345 | 0.95

3320 measurement *n*
adj accurate, precise, direct, curriculum-based, standard, objective, actual, quantitative, physical, recent *noun* error, system, instrument, data, method, model, performance, .technique, study, .period *verb* make, take, base, include, obtain, compare, allow, determine, .indicate, perform
9490 | 0.83 A

3321 identification *n*
adj early, positive, ethnic, personal, strong, religious, specific, organizational *noun* .number, process, .card, problem, system, .procedure, level., team, form. *verb* require, lead., include, base, allow, indicate, carry., facilitate., obtain, correlate
9163 | 0.86 A

3322 province *n*
adj southern, northern, Canadian, eastern, central, Serbian, maritime, sole, exclusive, various *noun* state, capital, governor., area, home., frontier., village., Sunni, renegade., authority *verb* visit., locate, .border, divide, populate., administer, govern, tour., .secede
8664 | 0.91 A

3323 moderate *j*
noun Republican, Democrat, level, exercise, activity, amount, heat, correlation, leader, party, intensity, risk *misc* more, high, severe, low, conservative, expensive, under, liberal
8487 | 0.93

3324 consensus *n*
adj general, national, broad, political, scientific, international, growing *noun* building, group, lack., issue, policy, decision, .view, .conference, panel, .builder *verb* reach, build., .emerge, achieve, develop, .exist, reflect., base, seek., support
8695 | 0.91 A

3325 lovely *j*
noun woman, lady, girl, wife, day, face, eye, place, man, house, home, garden *misc* young, little, such, oh, beautiful, quite, blue, sweet
8548 | 0.92 F

3326 comedy *n*
adj romantic, musical, stand-up, black, best, dark, divine *noun* .series, show, .club, drama, situation., film, TV, music, tragedy, .writer *verb* direct, feature, perform, mix., air, .ensue, .concern, .depict
8742 | 0.90 N

3327 shore *n*
adj eastern, far, western, opposite, southern, distant *noun* lake, island, mile., sea, water, .drive, wave., river, boat, .excursion *verb* reach., stand., walk., line., hit., approach.
8347 | 0.94

3328 photographer *n*
adj professional, amateur, famous, official, free-lance, underwater, chief *noun* reporter., .picture, writer, press., news., nature., fashion., staff. *verb* .shoot, .capture, .snap, photograph, .cover, pose, .document, hire, .record, feature
8959 | 0.88

3329 venture *n*
adj joint, new, commercial, successful, cooperative, foreign, late, risky, golden, profitable *noun* .capital, .capitalist, business., .firm, company, partner, .fund *verb* form., invest, launch, finance, involve, .fail, enter., announce, pursue., succeed
8781 | 0.90 N

3330 competitor *n*
adj foreign, major, big, fierce, tough, main, closest, direct, nearest, Japanese *noun* market, company, business, customer, price, advantage., industry, product, sport, technology *verb* buy, beat., sell, face, compare., eliminate., .enter, force, gain, match
8858 | 0.89 N

3331 nomination *n*
adj democratic, presidential, judicial, Emmy, Grammy, gubernatorial, negative *noun* Republican., Oscar., party, president, court, award., academy., .process *verb* win., get., receive., seek., accept., earn., withdraw, oppose., support
8695 | 0.90 S

3332 confusion *n*
adj considerable, total, moral, general, apparent, utter, mass *noun* lot., circle., state., fear, source., anger, chaos, frustration, identity, pain *verb* cause., create., add., lead., avoid., result, .surround, arise, clear., .reign
8189 | 0.96

3333 attribute *v*
noun success, problem, difference, fact, failure, change, .factor, .cause, increase, effect, performance, outcome, .responsibility, influence, expert. *misc* .to, often., directly, largely, usually.
8662 | 0.91 A

3334 horror *n*
adj full, unspeakable, mock, absolute, sheer, growing, utter *noun* .story, .movie, .film, .show, face, look., shock. *verb* watch., hear., stare., realize, fill., react., imagine, recoil., freeze., .unfold
8308 | 0.94 F

3335 orientation *n*
adj sexual, religious, political, different, competitive, strong, moral, theoretical, homosexual *noun* goal., task., .mobility, ego., value., gender., sport, achievement. *verb* include, relate, base, change, reflect, indicate, assess, develop, receive., influence
9716 | 0.81 A

3336 weekly *j*
noun standard, newspaper, editor, magazine, basis, news, meeting, show, session, column, program,
report *misc* meet, daily, write, publish, monthly, twice, attend, average
8349 | 0.94

3337 legislature *n*
adj national, democratic, local, federal, Soviet, elected, Republican-controlled, provincial, provisional, bicameral *noun* state., law, year, governor, court, member, session, Republican, executive, seat. *verb* pass, approve, elect, enact, .consider, create, require, .decide, allow, lobby.
8570 | 0.92 N

3338 basket *n*
adj hanging, full, woven, empty, easy, wooden, winning, game-winning, round *noun* egg., .case, picnic., fruit, wicker., laundry., bread, ball, gift., wire. *verb* fill, carry., hold, weave, set, place, hang, lift., .contain, line
8495 | 0.92 F

3339 crash *v*
noun plane., car, wave., wall, flight., .ground, market., jet., .party, helicopter., vehicle, .earth, airline., .window, airplane. *misc* .into, .down, .through, come., before., .against, .onto
8423 | 0.93 F

3340 continued *j*
noun growth, existence, use, presence, development, success, effort, research, need, interest, participation, expansion *misc* ensure, continue, economic, versus, despite, military, support, because
8843 | 0.89 A

3341 blanket *n*
adj electric, warm, heavy, thick, wet, soft, thin, blue, extra, woolen *noun* pillow, bed, sheet, wool., security., baby, .shoulder, beach., snow, .chest *verb* wrap., cover, pull, lay, spread, throw, sit, drape
8610 | 0.91 F

3342 orange *n*
adj fresh, bright, brilliant, frozen, burnt, sliced, calcium-fortified, fresh-squeezed *noun* .juice, cup, apple., red, lemon, agent., tablespoon, glass., cadmium, color *verb* add, mix, combine., compare., paint., glow., pick, hang
8444 | 0.93 M

3343 eagle *n*
adj bald, golden, American, black, double, legal, giant, blue, defensive, wild *noun* .scout, .nest, .feather, eye, wing, .river, rock, .forum, talon, .pass *verb* .soar, fly, .land, earn., .perch, spot, capture, carve
8727 | 0.90 N

3344 changing *j*
noun time, world, environment, condition, role, nature, pattern, need, attitude, circumstance, face, society *misc* rapidly, constantly, keep, adapt, reflect, political, meet, economic
8401 | 0.93 A

3345 mouse *n*
adj little, white, dead, transgenic, blind, mighty, normal, female, optical, gray *noun* cat., click, rat, keyboard, computer., field., house, .pad *verb* use, catch, feed, inject, .scurry, chase., test., .scamper, .pause
8711 | 0.90

3346 ethics *n*
adj medical, Christian, professional, social, environmental, public, legal, biomedical, sexual *noun* .committee, code., house., .rule, law, business., professor, Senate., center, issue *verb* teach, violate., question., deal, discuss, address, conduct, compromise., .prohibit, integrate
8601 | 0.91 A

3347 high *r*
up, .than, .enough, rate, .above, too., score, price, level, rank.
8079 | 0.97

3348 ghost *n*
adj holy, friendly, pale, hungry, gray, scary, mere, resident *noun* .town, .story, .dance, .past, father, .ship, image, .present, sage., .writer *verb* see., haunt, believe., chase., visit, wander, exorcise., disappear, vanish, hover
8677 | 0.90 F

3349 everyday *j*
noun life, experience, activity, practice, world, object, reality, use, language, problem, routine, situation *misc* our, normal, ordinary, common, such, practical, simple, deal
8332 | 0.94 A

3350 rope *n*
adj jumping, thick, heavy, knotted, tight, braided, coiled *noun* end., hand, jump., .neck, velvet., foot, .ladder, length., piece., nylon. *verb* tie, pull, hold, hang, climb, attach, grab., throw, skip., bind
8581 | 0.91 F

3351 formula *n*
adj simple, mathematical, magic, secret, following, winning, basic, complex, standard, successful *noun* baby, infant., .success, funding., milk, bottle, driver, product, diet *verb* use, base, calculate, apply, follow., determine, develop, change, feed, .contain
8370 | 0.93 M

3352 exhibit *v*
noun behavior, work, level, painting, .characteristic, pattern, .symptom, .sign, skill, individual., .trait, show, rate, type, collection *misc* .great, .significant, .similar, likely., tend., African, frequently., generally., female
8781 | 0.89 A

3353 nerve *n*
adj facial, cranial, raw, peripheral, cochlear, pinched, laryngeal *noun* .cell, .gas, .damage, .ending, optic., .center, .fiber, .agent *verb* get., touch., lose., strike., hit, calm, cause, control, jangle, connect
9182 | 0.85

3354 cope *v*
noun .strategy, stress, .problem, family, child, ability., .situation, resource, .demand, .loss, challenge, athlete, individual, .illness, effect *misc* .with, how., help., try., learn., able., better, must., struggle., unable., effectively
8950 | 0.87 A

3355 running *j*
noun mate, water, back, game, shoe, time, electricity, board, commentary, start, play, ad *misc* no, cold, without, rinse, presidential, under, vice
8287 | 0.94

3356 psychologist *n*
adj clinical, social, developmental, cognitive, educational, forensic, licensed, organizational, female,

doctoral *noun* school., university, child., psychiatrist, sport., .author, role, research, association. *verb* .study, .specialize, train, develop, argue, note, practice, conduct, .agree, assist
10027 | 0.78 A

3357 acid *n*
adj fatty, folic, sulfuric, lactic, salicylic, nitric, hydrochloric *noun* amino., .rain, stomach, vitamin, level, .test, alpha., effect, oil, soil *verb* contain., produce, cause, reduce, form, drop., neutralize., prevent, burn, dissolve
9188 | 0.85 M

3358 principal *n*
adj assistant, elementary, vice, professional, retired, female, effective, male, high-school, reactive *noun* school, teacher, .office, student, counselor, superintendent, interest, role, behavior, relationship. *verb* report, pay., perceive, hire, interview, .select, .analyze, evaluate, influence, guarantee
9048 | 0.86 A

3359 pet *n*
adj healthy, exotic, beloved, wild, favorite, virtual, lost, cute *noun* .owner, .store, .food, dog, .project, family, .shop, .peeve *verb* keep, allow, feed, sell, treat, care., own., adopt, protect., .wander
8368 | 0.93

3360 pitch *n*
adj high, perfect, wild, slow, final, fast, tinnitus *noun* sales., fever., .black, voice, rhythm, ball, tone, .angle, pine, .count *verb* make., throw., hit, reach., hear., sing, swing, rise., match, listen.
8770 | 0.89

3361 occupation *n*
adj military, foreign, Nazi, professional, continued, certain, full-time, traditional, various, primary *noun* age., .force, education, war, invasion., land, .authority, .bank, army, status *verb* end, list, resist., oppose., employ, fight., engage., .last, .cease
8532 | 0.91 A

3362 courage *n*
adj great, moral, political, personal, extraordinary, tremendous, physical *noun* strength, .conviction, lot., act., profile., .determination, integrity, badge., wisdom, .fire *verb* have., take, give., find., show, gather., muster., summon., lack., .speak
8081 | 0.96

3363 defeat *v*
noun .enemy, bill, force, army, team, effort, .purpose, vote, candidate, proposal, week, election, .insurgency, Senate, party *misc* help., easily., soundly., narrowly., order., decisively
8380 | 0.93 N

3364 pregnancy *n*
adj teenage, unwanted, unintended, early, unplanned, adolescent, teen-age *noun* teen., woman, month., rate, .test, week., .birth, drug, risk, disease *verb* prevent., terminate., end, reduce, avoid., carry, result, occur, experience., face.
8338 | 0.93

3365 actress *n*
adj best, supporting, young, black, famous, aspiring, French, award-winning, Oscar-winning *noun* actor., movie, wife, film, Oscar, award, role, model, singer,

27. Creating nouns

The following table shows the most common suffixes for creating nouns, and the organization
and meanings are based on Biber et al. (1998) *Longman Grammar of Spoken and Written English*
(pp. 321–22). The most frequent words for each meaning (rightmost column) come from the Corpus
of Contemporary American English, and the frequency column shows the combined frequency of those
words.

Suffix	Meaning	Freq	Most frequent words
-age	a collection of N	5928	baggage, lineage, entourage, assemblage, plumage
	action/result of V	3948	drainage, leakage, blockage, slippage, stoppage, postage
	cost of N/V-ing	2548	brokerage, postage
	measure of N-s	4626	mileage, voltage, acreage, yardage, shrinkage
	place for N	1659	orphanage, hermitage, parsonage,
-al	action/instance of V-ing	42518	approval, survival, arrival, withdrawal, removal
-an, -ian	person who lives in N	13888	American, German, Italian, European, Indian
	language of N	6935	German, Italian, Egyptian, Russian
	person associated with N	20578	historian, politician, musician, guardian, technician
-ance, -ence	action or state of V-ing	101370	performance, appearance, existence, resistance, emergence
	state of being A	61168	importance, silence, confidence, significance, compliance
-ant, -ent	person who V-s	311880	president, student, consultant, assistant, opponent
	something used for V-ing	1750	lubricant, pollutant, disinfectant, stimulant, coolant
-cy	state or quality of being A/N	39241	privacy, efficiency, presidency, accuracy, consistency
-dom	state of being A/N	44922	freedom, wisdom, boredom, stardom, martyrdom
-ee	person who has been or is to be V-ed	12557	employee, appointee, detainee, trainee, interviewee
	person to whom something has been or is to be V-ed	7542	nominee, trustee, referee, amputee, addressee
	person who V-s or has V-ed	975	retiree, narratee, escapee, returnee
	person who is A	1344	absentee, devotee
-er, -or	person who V-s	221791	director, teacher, professor, leader, manager
	something used for V-ing	58945	computer, monitor
	person concerned with N	28670	lawyer, philosopher, astronomer
	person living in N	2767	New Yorker, Londoner, cottager
-ery,	action/instance of V-ing	38196	recovery, discovery, delivery, robbery, bribery

Suffix	Meaning	Freq	Most frequent words
-ry	place of V-ing	9976	fishery, nursery, bakery, winery, brewery
	art/practice involving N	7502	imagery, pottery
-ese	person living in N	9746	Japanese, Chinese, Portuguese, Vietnamese, Timorese
	language in the style of N	120	legalese, bureaucratese, vocalese, computerese, lawyerese
-ess	female N	20725	actress, princess, waitress, mistress, hostess
	wife of N	8646	princess, duchess, empress, countess
-ette	small N	11309	cigarette, dinette, kitchenette, rosette, statuette
-ful	amount that fills N	10761	handful, mouthful, spoonful, roomful, fistful
-hood	state of being A/N	49942	neighborhood, childhood, likelihood, adulthood, motherhood
-ician	person concerned with N	21128	physician, politician, musician, technician, pediatrician
-ie, -y	diminutive or pet name for N	4166	sweetie, auntie, birdie, junkie, veggie
-ing	action/instance of V-ing	143376	meeting, understanding, beginning, learning, feeling
	something that one V-s or has V-ed	85490	building, painting, recording
	place for V-ing	9347	landing, crossing, dwelling
	material for V-ing	2472	lining, coloring, binding
	material for making N	2576	coating, fencing, shirting
-ism	doctrine of N	2769	Buddhism, Marxism, Nazism, Hinduism
	movement characterized by A/N	41410	criticism, terrorism, capitalism, nationalism, communism
-ist	person believing in or following N/A-ism	6320	leftist, Baptist, racist, feminist, realist
	person concerned with N	55468	artist, scientist, journalist, tourist, psychologist
-ite	person from N	134	muscovite, Israelite
	person following N	563	Shiite, Mennonite, suburbanite, Luddite, urbanite
-ity	state or quality of being A	215692	security, ability, activity, reality, responsibility
-let	small N	2679	booklet, tablet, starlet, leaflet, coverlet
-ment	action/instance of V-ing	220214	development, treatment, movement, agreement, argument
-ness	state or quality of being A	54037	darkness, awareness, illness, consciousness, fitness
-ship	state of being N	38037	membership, ownership, friendship, partnership, citizenship
	skill as N	1981	craftsmanship, sportsmanship, workmanship, musicianship, showmanship
-tion	action/instance of V-ing	155261	production, election, collection, investigation, competition
-ure	action/instance of V-ing	75257	pressure, failure, departure, closure, seizure

.series *verb* .play, win, become, nominate, name, star, marry, date, portray, feature.
8671 | 0.89

3366 patch *n*
adj small, rough, dark, little, blue, tiny, open, bald, fuzzy, isolated *noun* eye, .grass, skin, .ground, .sky, cabbage., pumpkin., oil., nicotine. *verb* wear., hit., lie, contain, install., notice., remove, reveal., step, clear.
8432 | 0.92 F

3367 margin *n*
adj large, high, wide, small, gross, slim, net, huge, average, comfortable *noun* profit., .error, victory, percent, safety, operating., vote, .society, .call *verb* win., operate., increase, provide., maintain., push., .shrink, relegate., narrow, .decline
8346 | 0.93

3368 reinforce *v*
noun behavior, .idea, .notion, .belief, view, image, message, value, .point, .stereotype, .concept, .sense, skill, impression, identity *misc* .by, far., mutually., social, serve.
8591 | 0.90 A

3369 collective *j*
noun bargaining, action, identity, security, agreement, memory, right, farm, effort, consciousness, responsibility, experience *misc* our, individual, personal, unconscious, social, cultural, rather, engage
8692 | 0.89 A

3370 brick *n*
adj red, old, yellow, exposed, solid, brown, crumbling *noun* .wall, .building, .house, stone, home, .road, floor, street, window, ton. *verb* build, throw., lay, hit., surround, line, construct., pave, crumble
8367 | 0.92 F

3371 script *n*
adj final, original, feminine, female, cursive, prepared, written, Gothic, funny *noun* movie., shooting., film, screening., writer, page, actor, copy., show, sequence. *verb* write, read., follow., send., rewrite, develop, stick., omit., contain, co-write
8262 | 0.94

3372 cooking *n*
adj French, southern, Italian, Chinese, Mexican, vegetarian, slow *noun* .spray, .time, water, .class, .school, vegetable., oil, food, minute, home *verb* stop., continue., enjoy., teach., finish., require, smell., .vary
8575 | 0.90 M N

3373 tunnel *n*
adj dark, long, underground, narrow, main, concrete, deep, secret, dank *noun* end., wind., bridge, wall, .syndrome, .vision, subway., light, entrance, train *verb* .lead, dig, build, enter., walk., emerge., connect, fill, disappear, link
8496 | 0.91 F

3374 document *v*
noun study, case, research, report., history, .change, effect, record, photograph, evidence, process, researcher., data., experience, activity *misc* able., carefully., thoroughly., clearly., previously.
8506 | 0.91 A

3375 concrete *j*
noun floor, wall, block, step, slab, building, evidence, example, way, action, barrier, experience *misc* build, pour, specific, onto, abstract, historical, gray, precast
8199 | 0.94

3376 recruit *v*
noun student, participant, .member, school, woman, player, volunteer, effort., group, study, teacher, college, worker, university, .minority *misc* try., .train, .retain, actively., highly, difficult., heavily, aggressively
8270 | 0.93

3377 grocery *n*
adj small, local, Asian, Korean, retail, online, weekly, nearby, Indian *noun* .store, bag, .shopping, .chain, food, .list, restaurant, .cart, shop, shelf *verb* buy, carry., sell, pick, pay, own, order, unpack., .scatter
8183 | 0.94

3378 lemon *n*
adj fresh, grated, little, dried, medium, minced, preserved, light, sweet, warm *noun* .juice, tablespoon, teaspoon, cup, zest, oil, salt, .peel, sugar, slice *verb* add., grate, squeeze., stir, serve, combine., taste, garnish., cook, .prevent
8897 | 0.87 M

3379 dare *v*
noun look, .glance, politician., resistance, novelist., fool., stranger., outsider., journalist., Christian. *misc* how., never., anyone, .hope, .challenge, hardly.
8318 | 0.93 F

3380 exact *j*
noun number, word, time, location, moment, date, nature, amount, science, spot, test, position *misc* same, opposite, remember, determine, although, almost, pinpoint, difficult
7932 | 0.97

3381 battery *n*
adj rechargeable, dead, electric, lithium-ion, sexual, aggravated, standard, alkaline, simple, heavy *noun* power, .life .pack, car, charge, assault., system, lithium. *verb* recharge, run, replace, .last, require, operate, .die, buy, check., remove.
8688 | 0.89 M

3382 surprisingly *r*
not., .little, perhaps, .large, .strong, .easy, voice, somewhat., .light, .simple, .similar, prove., .effective, .common
8093 | 0.95 M

3383 artistic *j*
noun director, expression, talent, value, form, production, tradition, life, vision, creation, freedom, merit *misc* literary, cultural, political, social, scientific, creative, musical, aesthetic
8681 | 0.88 A

3384 shit *n*
adj holy, little, full, deep, fucking, crazy, stupid, sick, sorry, dumb *noun* piece., dog., pile, .fan, hell, chicken, dude, piss *verb* give., beat., scare., fuck, eat., pull, .hit, smell., kick, shoot
10121 | 0.76 F

3385 indication *n*
adj clear, good, early, strong, only, positive, slight
noun .surgery, .trouble, sort, .Congress, .progress,
.tonsillectomy, advance *verb* give., provide., .intend,
interpret., constitute., yield.
8143 | 0.94

3386 cookie *n*
adj chocolate-chip, tough, baked, ungreased, hot,
fresh, favorite, warm, basic, remaining *noun* .sheet,
chocolate., chip., dough, .cutter, .jar, fortune.
verb make, bake, eat., place, cut, buy., sell., cool,
press, crumble
8549 | 0.90 M

3387 intensity *n*
adj high, low, emotional, great, light, moderate,
physical, increasing, negative, equal *noun* level,
energy., exercise, frequency, duration, color, activity,
pain, .feeling, anxiety *verb* increase, vary, reduce.,
measure, reach, determine, decrease, indicate, focus,
adjust
8517 | 0.90 A

3388 dramatically *r*
change, increase, improve, .reduce, .different, rise.,
drop., .year, .over, most., number, grow., .since, .past
8084 | 0.95

3389 piano *n*
adj grand, upright, classical, electric, acoustic, digital,
live *noun* .lesson, player, music, .concerto, key,
.teacher, .bench *verb* play, sit., sing, study., teach,
perform, practice., sound, .tinkle
8434 | 0.91

3390 concerning *i*
question., information., issue, article, decision., .use,
law, research., correspondence., policy, matter, data.,
debate., knowledge.
8766 | 0.87 A

3391 lap *n*
adj last, first, final, fastest, fast, ample, bony
noun hand., head., mother., .pool, book., victory.,
dog, .belt, .money, napkin. *verb* sit., hold, run, fall.,
rest., fold., lead, lay, drop., climb.
8490 | 0.90 F

3392 inquiry *n*
adj scientific, critical, historical, spiritual, free,
technical, congressional, intellectual, formal,
international *noun* line., impeachment., information.,
process, area., field., commission., method, form.,
research *verb* begin, conduct., receive, respond.,
focus, pursue, answer., launch, engage., .involve
8558 | 0.89 A

3393 Catholic *n*
adj Roman, Irish, devout, conservative, practicing,
faithful, lapsed *noun* Protestant, church, Jew, percent,
evangelical, number. *verb* raise., believe, .attend,
.support, marry, claim, teach, .oppose, divide, born.
9115 | 0.84 M

3394 discourse *n*
adj public, political, social, dominant, cultural,
academic, critical, narrative, religious, scientific
noun .analysis, community, level, practice, form,
language, text, function, mode., theory *verb* engage.,
dominate, argue, shape, construct, enter., define,
constitute, participate., express
9970 | 0.76 A

3395 laughter *n*
adj nervous, loud, raucous, hysterical, silent, mocking,
muffled *noun* sound., tear, room, music, burst.,
audience, voice, applause, peal, love *verb* hear., roar.,
break., fill, erupt, howl., .die, shake, join, .echo
8418 | 0.90 F

3396 anniversary *n*
adj happy, one-year, golden, upcoming, centennial,
approaching, tragic *noun* year, wedding., celebration,
.death, day, .birth, week, birthday, .party, .edition
verb celebrate., mark., commemorate., approach,
observe., honor., forget.
8021 | 0.95

3397 telescope *n*
adj large, small, optical, ground-based, infrared,
amateur, binocular, modern, space-based
noun space., radio., sky., mirror, image, .science,
astronomer, star, mount, optics *verb* use, build,
.show, point, observe, .reveal, operate, .detect, aim,
discover
12101 | 0.63 M

3398 swear *v*
noun .God, oath, president, .secrecy, .allegiance,
.truth, .testimony, .breath, office, witness, officer,
.loyalty, affidavit, governor, .constitution *misc* I, .off,
solemnly., .under, .uphold, .softly, touch
8277 | 0.92 F

3399 park *v*
noun car, truck, van., .side, vehicle, pickup, .curb,
.block, building, space, .corner, bike, yard, town, drive
misc .front, where., .outside, .near, .behind
8289 | 0.92 F

3400 charity *n*
adj local, private, favorite, annual, religious,
various, faith-based, nonprofit, financial, individual
noun money, .work, .event, .care, child, hospital,
health., act., service *verb* give, donate., raise, support,
benefit, contribute., accept, sponsor, fund, operate
8115 | 0.94

3401 clue *n*
adj important, only, visual, tantalizing, obvious, vital,
slight, crucial *noun* .nature, search., police, .past,
context., puzzle, trail., .cause, .meaning, .character
verb have., give., provide., look., find, offer., leave,
.lead, reveal, pick
7968 | 0.95

3402 grave *n*
adj mass, shallow, unmarked, open, fresh, common,
native, watery, empty *noun* mother, cemetery,
father, cradle., flower, foot., stone, parent, husband,
.repatriation *verb* dig., visit., bury., stand, mark,
walk., lay, lie, fill, rise.
8146 | 0.93 F

3403 narrative *n*
adj historical, personal, biblical, traditional, grand,
literary, fictional, first-person, dominant, visual
noun story, history, master., captivity., event, form,
character, experience, analysis, text *verb* write, create,
construct, describe, present, suggest, reveal, reflect,
.emphasize, shape
9845 | 0.77 A

3404 hypothesis *n*
adj null, following, consistent, alternative, working,
general, initial, original, theoretical, competing

noun study, support., result, test, research, testing, evidence, analysis, method, set *verb* .predict, suggest, reject, examine, confirm, base, develop, formulate, .state, .explain
9282 | 0.82 A

3405 upset *v*
noun .balance, stomach, .cart, order, fan, .status, .equilibrium, .stability, .ecosystem *misc* so, .because, her, really., little., .over, extremely., terribly., visibly., bit., particularly., .delicate, clearly., deeply., easily.
7946 | 0.95

3406 acceptable *j*
noun level, behavior, way, risk, standard, reliability, solution, limit, range, form, alternative, result *misc* more, socially, find, consider, become, perfectly, within
8189 | 0.93 A

3407 favor *n*
adj sexual, special, big, political, personal, huge, divine, enormous, royal *noun* party., curry., percent, odds., champagne, vote., argument., gift, toast, scale. *verb* do., ask, return., fall., work., find., gain., rule.
7811 | 0.97

3408 couch *n*
adj asleep, comfortable, living-room, comfy, overstuffed, lumpy, sagging, upholstered *noun* room, .potato, chair, living, leather., back, arm, cushion, .TV, bed *verb* sit., sleep., lie., lay., fall., settle., lean, seat., .face, sprawl.
8484 | 0.89 F

3409 defendant *n*
adj guilty, criminal, black, federal, corporate, individual, potential, particular, indigent, attractive *noun* case, court, right, trial, jury., plaintiff, lawyer, evidence., judge, action *verb* find., convict, represent, allow, name., .plead, claim, prove, deny, .face
8764 | 0.86 A

3410 compose *v*
noun music, group, student, song, letter, piece, poem, team., committee., .member, image, force., melody, picture, element *misc* .herself, .entirely, .mostly, primarily, largely, .mainly
8321 | 0.91 A

3411 cool *v*
noun minute, rack, water, pan, air, heat, hour, .heel, cake, cookie, engine, skin, cup, .degree, planet *misc* .down, .completely, .slightly, allow., .before, aside., until, let.
off after, .bit, weather
8243 | 0.92 M

3412 ballot *n*
adj military, secret, disputed, presidential, provisional, statewide, primary, confusing, questionable, manual *noun* absentee., .box, initiative, voter, state, measure, election, name., paper., issue *verb* cast., count, vote, appear., recount, place., stuff., .arrive
8610 | 0.88 S N

3413 related *j*
noun issue, problem, service, article, activity, group, study, question, species, field, research, health *misc* other, closely, such, including, special, well, separate, involve
8540 | 0.88 A

3414 cluster *n*
adj globular, open, large, dense, distant, double, tight, individual, similar, blue *noun* star, galaxy, .analysis, flower, .bomb, member, .office, .building, core, peer. *verb* form, .contain, lie, identify, produce, surround, consist, gather, group, observe
9229 | 0.82 M

3415 pie *n*
adj homemade, economic, baked, perfect, humble, favorite, prepared *noun* apple., pumpkin., piece., .crust, pecan., .plate, cream, .pan, slice., pot. *verb* bake, eat., serve, fill, cook, place, cover, throw, prepare, .cool
8177 | 0.92

3416 concern *v*
noun issue., question., problem., safety, .relationship, research., .effect, data., debate., aspect, .nature, quality, article., factor, attitude *misc* .about, most, .itself, .themselves, especially., .ourselves, .yourself, particularly., environmental, deep., specific, directly
8100 | 0.93 A

3417 recording *n*
adj audio, live, digital, original, early, magnetic, available, electronic, cast, professional *noun* .studio, tape., .industry, .artist, video., sound, .session, .contract *verb* make, play, listen., hear, release, sing, produce, feature, obtain, review
8312 | 0.91

3418 rail *n*
adj light, high-speed, top, bottom, front, wooden, heavy *noun* .line, .system, .car, commuter., road, side., bus, .service, .yard, .station *verb* lean., ride., stand, build, cut, connect, grab., .link, climb., grip.
8257 | 0.91

3419 decrease *v*
noun .percent, number, rate, level, .risk, .amount, cost, behavior, size, pressure, activity, .chance, .likelihood, population, body *misc* significantly, .during, actually., slightly, dramatically
8579 | 0.88 A

3420 rape *n*
adj sexual, attempted, statutory, alleged, brutal, marital, mass, forcible *noun* victim, murder, case, date., woman, .incest, charge, crime, assault, .trial *verb* report, commit, accuse., convict., .occur, involve, deal, arrest., prevent.
8301 | 0.91 S

3421 interrupt *v*
noun thought, moment, conversation, voice, girl., .flow, phone, sound, call, sleep, reverie, career, cycle, silence, dinner *misc* .by, let., sorry., hate., suddenly., rudely., frequently, briefly
8116 | 0.93 F

3422 architect *n*
adj chief, local, principal, famous, renowned, naval, Italian, French *noun* landscape., designer, engineer, building, design, artist, project, course., golf., generation *verb* build, hire, train, commission, select, renovate, practice, .specialize, collaborate, .sketch
8345 | 0.90 M N

3423 sigh *v*
noun .relief, shoulder, .pleasure, forehead, .resignation, .exasperation, .frustration, .satisfaction,

.contentment *misc* .deeply, .heavily, .loudly, .herself,
.wish, smile, .happily, .contentedly, .suppose
9048 | 0.83 F

3424 remark n
adj racist, introductory, recent, closing, sarcastic,
prepared, offhand, personal, negative, sexist
noun president, opening., kind, senator, .reporter,
transcript., comment, .speech, .conference, chance.
verb make, hear., deliver, suggest, ignore., quote,
apologize., recall, respond., .intend
7860 | 0.96

3425 Christian n
adj evangelical, conservative, orthodox,
fundamentalist, born-again, devout, faithful,
Lutheran, practicing *noun* Jew, Muslim, faith,
number., community., majority, persecution.
verb .believe, .live, find, .pray, claim, .seek,
.support, persecute, attack, profess.
8855 | 0.85

3426 invent v
noun game, story, device, technology, character,
tradition, term, product, form, concept, .future,
guy., century, language, computer *misc* imagine,
practically., newly., virtually., independently,
.entirely
7908 | 0.95

3427 prescription n
adj nonmedical, available, over-the-counter,
lethal, cheap, expensive, affordable, valid, leftover,
high-priced *noun* .drug, .medication, doctor,
.benefit, use, coverage, .medicine, cost, plan, policy.
verb write, fill, provide., pay., buy, offer., cover, refuse.,
.cure, .relieve
8071 | 0.93

3428 reward n
adj financial, great, extrinsic, monetary, economic,
potential, personal, greatest, just, rich *noun* system,
.punishment, risk, .information, work, power,
.structure *verb* offer, reap., receive., provide., bring,
earn, deserve, encourage, collect., increase
8010 | 0.94 A

3429 sacred j
noun place, heart, site, space, text, cow, ground,
object, land, church, mountain, thing
misc most, nothing, secular, consider, religious,
profane, native
8305 | 0.90 A

3430 organ n
adj other, internal, vital, reproductive, sexual, major,
sensory, various, female, light *noun* .transplant,
body, pipe, tissue, .donation, donor, system, .music
verb play, donate, remove, grow, affect, receive,
function, fail, damage, contain
8063 | 0.93

3431 abroad r
home., American., travel., study., here., live., both.,
year, send., trip., sell.
8096 | 0.92

3432 devil n
adj red, little, poor, incarnate, very, handsome, evil,
sly *noun* dust., .advocate, work, angel, soul, deal.,
pact., .tower, .dress, .cauldron *verb* play, .wear, speak,
kill., beat, dance, possess, chase., tempt, .lurk
7929 | 0.94

3433 dear j
noun friend, God, life, mother, boy, Lord, heart, child,
wife, father, dad, sister *misc* my, old, hold, oh, write,
thank, please
8293 | 0.90 F

3434 rank v
noun team, state, year, world, .nation, .number,
student, country, list, defense, .order, fund,
importance, respondent., value *misc* .among,
.high, .top, .second, last, .third, .behind, .near,
.best, consistently.
8197 | 0.91 N

3435 superior j
noun court, judge, performance, force, officer,
quality, power, ability, product, position, system, skill
misc far, morally, inferior, vastly, produce, clearly,
prove, equal
7986 | 0.93 A

3436 military n
adj American, Israeli, Iraqi, civilian, Soviet, Russian,
Chinese, professional, involved, Indonesian *noun* US.,
role, control, policy, gay., mission, operation, soldier,
use, institution *verb* say, remain, .take, .become, give,
.begin, .announce, .prepare, argue, accuse
8861 | 0.84 S

3437 greatly r
.reduce, .increase, vary., .improve, .influence, .expand,
benefit, .enhance, .affect, differ.
8057 | 0.93 A

3438 airplane n
adj small, commercial, hijacked, conventional,
chartered, giant, ultralight, crippled *noun* model.,
flight, .crash, engine, pilot, part, .ticket, wing, .hangar,
seat *verb* fly, build, jump., land, buy., .carry, hijack.,
board.
7959 | 0.94

3439 host v
noun show, party, .game, event, conference, dinner,
city, year, meeting, tournament, club, play., lady.,
.guest, television *misc* .annual, .Olympic,
.international, special, recently.
8586 | 0.87 N

3440 habitat n
adj natural, critical, native, aquatic, endangered,
different, suitable, prime, riparian, tropical
noun wildlife., species, loss, .humanity, destruction,
animal, area, fish, bird, forest *verb* provide., protect.,
destroy, create, build, preserve., restore., .support,
occupy, occur
8817 | 0.85 M A

3441 coal n
adj hot, clean, burning, black, solid, glowing,
medium-hot, dirty, domestic, brown *noun* .mine,
.miner, oil, gas, .plant, .mining, .company, .industry,
fuel, power *verb* burn, produce, generate, carry.,
convert., rake., cook, shovel., heat, .account
8049 | 0.93

3442 soccer n
adj national, professional, international, indoor, pro,
European, competitive *noun* .team, .game, .player,
.field, .ball, league, boy, basketball, girl., woman.
verb play., watch., coach., attend., participate,
practice, .unite
8502 | 0.88 N

3443 entitle *v*
noun .opinion, right, .benefit, law, .protection, defense, painting., share, jury, .compensation, individual., defendant, .hearing, .privilege, .immunity *misc* feel., legally., certainly., .legal, .vote
7931 | 0.94 A

3444 delay *v*
noun year, flight, decision, .vote, .action, .release, .onset, week, plan, trial, court, .start, justice, .payment, launch *misc* .until, .because, may., long, prevent, deny, indefinitely
7790 | 0.95

3445 instructor *n*
adj part-time, certified, clinical, English, personal, female, effective, male, individual, driving *noun* student, course, college, class, ski., flight., education, program, drill., teacher *verb* teach, learn, train, hire, encourage, assign, present, indicate, conduct, discuss
8784 | 0.85 A

3446 integrity *n*
adj territorial, public, structural, personal, ecological, moral, academic, bodily, cultural *noun* honesty, man., system, character, treatment., sovereignty., .process, data, person, honor *verb* maintain., preserve., protect., ensure., compromise., question., undermine.
7985 | 0.93 A

3447 shine *v*
noun light, sun., eye, star., flashlight, face, moon., shoe, window, spotlight, hair, morning, beam, gold, glass *misc* .through, .like, .brightly, .down, .brighter, .brilliantly
8249 | 0.90 F

3448 mess *n*
adj whole, big, bloody, real, tangled, terrible, huge, sorry, financial, complete *noun* .hall, hair., .floor, .tent, kind., .kit, kitchen, budget., officer., loan. *verb* make, clean., leave, create, sort, straighten, fix., clear, stink, drip
7917 | 0.94 F

3449 norm *n*
adj social, cultural, subjective, moral, traditional, political, human, local, sexual, societal *noun* value, group, rule, attitude, culture, peer., exception, gender., practice, set. *verb* become., establish, violate., base, conform., compare., .govern, reflect., .favor, promote
8470 | 0.88 A

3450 allegation *n*
adj sexual, serious, specific, recent, unsubstantiated, similar, widespread, credible, improper, unfair *noun* abuse, president, corruption, investigation., fraud, harassment, police, evidence., official, kind. *verb* deny., investigate., involve, support., respond., report, base, dismiss., contain, .surface
8207 | 0.91 S

3451 pill *n*
adj birth-control, bitter, morning-after, white, magic, blue, contraceptive, purple, chewable *noun* control., birth., bottle, diet., .day, sleeping., abortion., poison. *verb* take., give, swallow, pop., prescribe, stop, contain, sell, sleep, hand
7938 | 0.94

3452 tight *r*
hold., .end, too., pull., .around, very., her, .against, eye, sit., hand, keep., shut., arm
8218 | 0.90 F

3453 cry *n*
adj far, shrill, sharp, loud, muffled, anguished, plaintive, soft, strangled, piercing *noun* .help, rallying., battle., baby, war., .pain, boy., .freedom *verb* hear., give., listen., utter., stop, rally., respond., ignore., .fill, answer
8048 | 0.92 F

3454 okay *j*
noun guy, baby, Mom, honey, dad, sweetie *misc* be, it, that, everything, nod, sure, no, guess, fine, cry, assure
8561 | 0.87 F

3455 pleased *j*
noun result, progress, performance, smile, surprise, expression, glance *misc* with, very, see, look, seem, himself, meet, hear
7947 | 0.93 F

3456 plain *n*
adj great, coastal, high, white, vast, Indian, open, flat, dry, western *noun* flood., mountain, north, cup., river, .state, .yogurt, .dealer, desert, tribe *verb* stretch, cross., rise, roam., stake., sweep., surround, settle, overlook., wander
8087 | 0.92

3457 inspector *n*
adj chief, postal, international, Iraqi, female, resident, atomic, electrical, veteran, agricultural *noun* .general, weapon., office, building., report, police., .field, health., city., custom. *verb* .find, allow, send, .check, .visit, .arrive, cooperate., .discover, hire., .examine
8021 | 0.92 S

3458 forum *n*
adj open, public, economic, national, international, online, global, regional *noun* world., news., discussion, policy., freedom., candidate, section., .article, channel. *verb* provide., hold, create, discuss, serve., sponsor, attend., address, express, monitor.
8049 | 0.92 A

3459 powder *n*
adj white, black, packed, fine, fresh, loose, deep *noun* teaspoon, .salt, baking, flour., chili., garlic., curry., .soda, tablespoon, sugar *verb* bake., add, stir, sprinkle, contain, dust., taste, pour, ski., .explode
8757 | 0.84 M

3460 sin *n*
adj original, mortal, deadly, human, greatest, grave *noun* .city, .tax, .father, death, forgiveness., .pride, punishment, homosexuality., doctrine., redemption *verb* commit, confess., forgive, die, atone., repent., hate., .manifest
8305 | 0.89

3461 evident *j*
noun change, difference, effect, pattern, trend, influence, concern, lack, style, success, pride, tension *misc* become, more, also, most, particularly, clearly, especially, already
8178 | 0.90 A

3462 sponsor *v*
noun program, bill, conference, group, event, state, company, school, legislation, government, university, center, research, team, department *misc* .by, annual, international, jointly, cultural, regional, professional, participate, locally, .briefly, currently.
7946 | 0.93 N

3463 acceptance *n*
adj social, public, widespread, great, general, growing, wide, broad *noun* .speech, peer, woman, rejection, level, exhibition, .rate, letter, .responsibility, understanding *verb* gain., receive., win., achieve., promote., increase, seek., note, judge., correlate
8241 | 0.90 A

3464 prosecution *n*
adj criminal, federal, successful, key, selective, malicious, aggressive, vigorous *noun* .case, witness, defense, evidence, .team, immunity., crime, investigation., trial, jury *verb* .prove, argue, face., testify, avoid., .present, .rest, claim, escape., grant.
8358 | 0.88 S

3465 cognitive *j*
noun development, process, ability, skill, anxiety, theory, student, level, strategy, function, therapy, style *misc* behavioral, affective, social, emotional, somatic, physical, such, suggest
9267 | 0.8 A

3466 presidency *n*
adj vice, modern, successful, collective, failed, entire, powerful *noun* year, office., candidate., run., power., campaign., Congress, election, Republican, college *verb* win., assume., seek., lose., resign., define, weaken, rotate, .unravel
8057 | 0.91 S

3467 finance *v*
noun project, company, government, money., bank, tax, campaign, business, development, fund, .education, .construction, .purchase, loan, capital *misc* .by, help., .through, privately., publicly.
8015 | 0.92 N

3468 favor *i*
(in favor of) .of, vote., argument., rule., argue., bias., abandon., speak., court., reject., tax, strong, strongly., decision.
7850 | 0.94 A

3469 magic *j*
noun word, wand, number, bullet, trick, marker, kingdom, show, carpet, moment, flute, formula *misc* wave, perform, industrial, light, practical, attic, invisible, sooner
7787 | 0.95

3470 northwest *n*
adj rural, upper, inland, fabled, rainy, remote, near *noun* mile., .airline, .coast, .corner, .territory, .side, north, .passage, area, region *verb* locate., head., travel, stretch., sail., situate., relocate.
7942 | 0.93 N

3471 regulate *v*
noun state, government., law., industry, power., activity, authority., .use, Congress., system, drug, agency., .behavior, .commerce, business *misc* .by, .under, highly., strictly., heavily.
8215 | 0.90 A

3472 exclude *v*
noun woman, .analysis, group, study, .possibility, .other, patient, policy., .participation, black, data, person, activity, reason, category *misc* .from, specifically., military, largely., tend., explicitly., previously.
8236 | 0.89 A

3473 colonial *j*
noun period, rule, power, government, history, era, time, state, administration, society, policy, authority *misc* British, during, Spanish, French, early, former, European, postcolonial, indigenous, native, throughout, imperial
8800 | 0.84 A

3474 rent *v*
noun house, .apartment, .car, .room, .space, movie, place, video, tenant, truck, .boat, bike, property, cottage, store *misc* buy, sell, .drive, private, cheap, .near, afford.
   out .room, .house, who., .space, home, .apartment, .two, property, unit, owner.
7758 | 0.95

3475 peer *v*
noun .window, eye, face, room, head., wall, .corner, .hole, .screen, top, .windshield, mirror, tree, telescope, astronomer. *misc* .at, .into, .through, .out, .over, .around, .inside
8221 | 0.89 F

3476 civilian *j*
noun control, casualty, population, government, life, leader, authority, force, clothes, employee, death, rule *misc* military, nuclear, conservation, democratic, armed, avoid, Iraqi, elected, Israeli
9227 | 0.8 A

3477 harbor *n*
adj safe, cold, inner, natural, busy, protected, crowded *noun* bar., island, ship, .seal, boat, town, view, spring, city, sea *verb* attack, sail., overlook., enter., dock., visit., head, anchor., clean., spill
7827 | 0.94

3478 estimated *j*
noun people, percent, value, time, number, population, rate, price, life *misc* million, billion, cost, worth, spend, per, kill, annual, total
7980 | 0.92 N

3479 rhythm *n*
adj natural, circadian, steady, normal, slow, regular, cardiac, familiar, traditional, complex *noun* .blue, heart, music, pattern, melody, .life, .section, pitch, song, harmony *verb* play, beat, sing, break, establish., tap., listen, clap., form, maintain
8412 | 0.87

3480 midnight *n*
adj past, round, dark, awake, asleep *noun* hour, night, minute., .mass, .basketball, deadline, stroke., .sun, clock., bed. *verb* stay., strike., arrive, approach, return, end., rise, close, finish, expire.
7798 | 0.94 F

3481 counselor *n*
adj professional, high, important, mental, genetic, certified, effective, academic, ethical, financial *noun* school., teacher, guidance., role, educator, college., marriage., parent, study, rehabilitation. *verb* help, talk, meet, suggest, train, serve, recommend, indicate, focus, address
10514 | 0.7 A

3482 highlight *v*
noun .importance, .difference, issue, study, .need, problem, map., .role, .fact, area, article., case., research, .aspect, report. *misc* .between, important, .significant, yellow, order., above, below, previous
8112 | 0.90 A

28. Creating adjectives

The following are the most frequent suffixes that are used to create adjectives. For each suffix, it shows the number of different types (distinct word forms) that occur at least 20 times in the Corpus of Contemporary American English—which gives a good indication of the "productivity" of that suffix—as well as the 15 most frequent words ending in that suffix (in order of frequency). Note that the words in parentheses end in the indicated sequence of letters, but are not derived from other words.

-al	1744	national, political, social, real, local, federal, international, special, general, personal, medical, natural, central, environmental, physical
-ive	546	positive, effective, native, negative, active, alive, expensive, conservative, massive, creative, competitive, alternative, aggressive, sensitive, extensive
-ous	530	serious, various, religious, previous, dangerous, famous, obvious, enormous, numerous, nervous, tremendous, curious, continuous, indigenous, conscious
-ent	413	different, recent, current, independent, present, ancient, silent, consistent, excellent, violent, apparent, permanent, innocent, prominent, confident
-less	246	homeless, endless, countless, useless, helpless, relentless, restless, harmless, hopeless, meaningless, stainless, reckless, worthless, motionless, powerless
-ate	189	private, (late), appropriate, corporate, separate, immediate, ultimate, accurate, desperate, legitimate, adequate, moderate, delicate, intimate, associate
-like	141	(like), (unlike), (alike), childlike, businesslike, dreamlike, lifelike, warlike, godlike, ladylike, birdlike, catlike, flu-like, humanlike, earthlike
-ful	138	beautiful, successful, powerful, wonderful, useful, careful, helpful, painful, awful, peaceful, meaningful, grateful, colorful, faithful, hopeful

3483 palace *n*
adj presidential, royal, imperial, national, grand, golden, ruined *noun* crystal•, •hotel •art, king, •guard, wall, garden, gate, summer•, governor *verb* build, return•, enter•, arrive•, visit•, house, burn, storm•, overlook
8001 | 0.92

3484 trading *n*
adj international, major, heavy, global, online, electronic, multilateral *noun* •partner, day, •system, insider•, •company, stock, •post *verb* establish, engage•, promote•, account, resume, limit, charge•, permit•, extend• dominate
8290 | 0.88

3485 compound *n*
adj organic, chemical, related, active, annual, walled, main, complex, various, similar *noun* branch•, family•, sulfur•, plant, embassy•, •interest, effect, •rate, •eye, metal *verb* contain, produce, enter, test, form, identify, surround, •cause, discover, •derive
7998 | 0.92

3486 bare *j*
noun foot, hand, leg, arm, tree, skin, floor, wall, shoulder, room, chest, ground *misc* her, lay, against, strip, across, touch, except, cold
8170 | 0.90 F

3487 echo *v*
noun sentiment, voice•, word, sound•, view, •head, footstep•, theme, room, concern, comment, •ear,
other, thought, •mind *misc* •across, hear•, •throughout, similar, empty, •inside
down •hall, •hallway, •long
7757 | 0.94 F

3488 integrate *v*
noun system, technology, school, information, program, •curriculum, •society, community, effort•, education, teacher•, study, service, •knowledge, activity *misc* •into, fully•, •within, successfully•, seek•, effectively•
8313 | 0.88 A

3489 slice *n*
adj thin, thick, small, diagonal, single, narrow, tiny, extra, fat *noun* bread, tomato, cheese, lemon, bacon, apple, onion, pizza, •pie *verb* cut•, place, serve, arrange, add, eat•, garnish
8253 | 0.89 M

3490 combat *n*
adj major, military, hand-to-hand, direct, close, actual, mortal, urban *noun* woman•, troop, •unit, force, soldier, •operation, •zone, •mission, •experience, •veteran *verb* fly•, serve•, engage•, kill•, die•, send•, lock•, avoid•, face, •cease
8128 | 0.90

3491 shop *v*
noun store, grocery, home, mall, clothes, consumer•, supermarket, Christmas, car, customer•, town, dinner, month, •bargain, shoe *misc* •for, go•, when•, where•, while•, •online, downtown, •carefully, instead
around •for, •price, •find, consumer•, pay•
7808 | 0.94 M

3492 medium *n*
adj new, interstellar, different, happy, acrylic, mass, intergalactic, electronic, perfect *noun* heat., communication, spirit., television, painting, art, .message, artist, light, yellow. *verb* use, reduce., mix., increase., explore, employ, master
8663 | 0.84 M A

3493 log *n*
adj fallen, daily, hollow, heavy, split, rotting, raw, rotten, rustic *noun* .cabin, web, .home, house, fire, .book, wall, phone., .text, computer *verb* keep, build, sit, cut, roll, lay, fall, burn, pull, check.
8027 | 0.91 M

3494 surgeon *n*
adj orthopedic, American, cosmetic, medical, chief, cardiac, oral, vascular, retired *noun* .general, plastic., heart., physician., brain., hospital, patient, office, army, transplant. *verb* .perform, .remove, .operate, allow., recommend, .specialize, refer, .implant, .insert, consult
7978 | 0.91

3495 excuse *v*
noun .behavior, lady, .expression, .pun, .French, .conduct, .mess *misc* .me, .himself, please, .herself, .myself, .interrupt, .themselves
8134 | 0.90 S F

3496 ritual *n*
adj religious, daily, ancient, sacred, social, public, annual, mating, elaborate, certain *noun* part., ceremony, family, morning., belief, myth, initiation., bedtime., church, culture *verb* perform, involve, create, participate., conduct, observe, practice, repeat, celebrate, .surround
8286 | 0.88 A

3497 resign *v*
noun president, year, .post, week, .position, minister, .office, .fact, .job, .protest, member, secretary, director, .commission, party *misc* he, .from, who., after, shall., force., today
7874 | 0.93 N

3498 net *j*
noun income, worth, loss, effect, asset, gain, result, profit, benefit, percent, value, revenue *misc* million, report, total, estimate, per, increase, rise, positive, restrict
8154 | 0.89

3499 excited *j*
noun state, voice, kid, prospect, crowd, possibility, atom, shout, audience, smile, tone, conversation *misc* I, about, get, so, very, too, really, feel
7714 | 0.94

3500 lightly *r*
until., .brown, take., .surface, .floured, touch, egg, hand, .greased, .beat, brush, coat, dough., oil
8144 | 0.89 M

3501 evil *n*
adj necessary, lesser, great, moral, pure, absolute, radical *noun* axis., force., battle., problem., kind, touch., struggle., face., word, garden. *verb* fight., confront, .exist, deliver., overcome, fear., triumph, defeat., .lurk, .threaten
7908 | 0.92

3502 bitter *j*
noun end, battle, fight, dispute, war, experience, debate, pill, memory, enemy, winter, wind
misc over, between, sweet, angry, cold, taste, sound, slightly
7597 | 0.96

3503 export *n*
adj American, total, Chinese, agricultural, major, strong, economic, primary, main, Mexican *noun* market, US, .control, percent, import, oil, .earnings, .sector, subsidy, job *verb* increase, promote., grow, .rise, produce, expand, .decline, restrict., reduce, .account
8585 | 0.85 A

3504 swing *n*
adj full, western, key, smooth, perfect, wooden, extreme, huge, powerful, violent *noun* ., .voter, .state, .vote, porch., golf., .set *verb* take., sit., .hit, hang, .miss, cause, control, .shift, improve, finish.
8255 | 0.88 M

3505 clay *n*
adj red, white, heavy, wet, hard, fired, soft, baked *noun* .pot, soil, .model, .court, foot, wood, .figure, sand, glass, .pipe *verb* mold, shoot., mix, dig, fill, paint, sculpt., .dry, .absorb
8231 | 0.88 F

3506 logic *n*
adj simple, internal, certain, economic, fuzzy, cultural, formal, pro, inner *noun* reason, .argument, design, kind., control, language, science, circuit, .controller *verb* use, follow., defy., apply, understand., base, .suggest, question., .dictate, operate
8131 | 0.89 A

3507 virtue *n*
adj moral, civic, public, traditional, intellectual, heroic, feminine, greatest, individual, particular *noun* vice, value, patience, book., courage, justice, character, necessity, society, prudence *verb* extol., embody., promote., preach., celebrate., tout., praise., constitute, .transcend
8228 | 0.88 A

3508 container *n*
adj airtight, large, empty, sealed, covered, clear, closed, huge *noun* plastic., store, water, food, glass., .ship, storage., cargo., shipping. *verb* use, fill, place, hold, cover, open, serve, pack, remove, label
8070 | 0.90 M

3509 quarterback *n*
adj best, young, senior, junior, veteran, second-year, third-string *noun* starting., team, season, game, rookie., backup., receiver, football, coach, school *verb* play, start, .throw, lead, win, .complete, sack, sign, protect., score
9107 | 0.8 N

3510 beg *v*
noun .pardon, .question, .forgiveness, .mercy, mother, .money, .food, .help, God, street, father, husband, sister, dad, .indulgence *misc* .for, .your, .differ, please, .let, .off, plead, cry., practically.
7779 | 0.93 F

3511 salmon *n*
adj smoked, wild, grilled, fresh, pink, farmed, commercial *noun* river, fish, farm, trout, .fillet, fishing, run, .steelhead, .farming, species *verb* catch, spawn, eat, serve, .return, place., raise, .swim, save., migrate
8280 | 0.88 M

3512 greet *v*
noun .visitor, .guest, friend, morning, crowd, news, .name, silence, .arrival, .customer, applause, cheer, fan, airport, arm *misc* warmly, .other, .each, enter, rush., rise., enthusiastically, smile, step, .politely
7681 | 0.94 F

3513 curve *n*
adj steep, light, smooth, gentle, normal, low, sharp, flat, graceful, blind *noun* learning., bell., .ball, figure, road, growth., yield., demand., body, supply. *verb* show, follow., throw., round., learn., represent, trace., fit, hit., form
7797 | 0.93

3514 mill *n*
adj old, abandoned, grinding, rolling, historic, converted, olive *noun* steel, paper., .road, water., textile., .town, .worker, grist., lumber., sugar. *verb* build, close, operate, own, shut, .grind, visit, .employ, supply, process
7922 | 0.91 N

3515 closet *n*
adj full, open, dark, front, empty, closed, built-in, electrical, mirrored *noun* .door, walk-in., bedroom, clothes, room, back., hall., broom., shelf, linen. *verb* hang., hide., clean., close, rummage., shut, stay, store, step, .smell
7898 | 0.92 F

3516 interior *n*
adj dark, roomy, domestic, spacious, dim, quiet, deep, soft, vast *noun* department., secretary., ministry., minister., car, exterior, building, leather., sun, island *verb* design, paint, reveal, feature, decorate, light, probe., .contain, expose
7793 | 0.93 M

3517 rod *n*
adj hot, light, spinning, connecting, nuclear, threaded, short, spent, wooden, divining *noun* lightning., fishing., steel., .tip, metal., fuel. *verb* become., bend, pull, carry, grab., spin, connect, spare., fly, drop.
8335 | 0.87 M

3518 candy *n*
adj hard, favorite, crushed, delicious, homemade, handmade, stale *noun* .bar, .store, cotton., .cane, piece., kid, .wrapper, chocolate, box, eye. *verb* eat., sell., buy., steal., place, throw, suck, melt, chew, taste
7882 | 0.92 F

3519 restrict *v*
noun .access, .use, law., state, right, .ability, government, .activity, .abortion, movement, .freedom, .number, area, policy., rule. *misc* severely., .certain, prohibit, largely., permanently.
7876 | 0.92 A

3520 initiate *v*
noun program, process, .action, project, change, .discussion, .contact, study, .conversation, war, policy *misc* .by, environmental, .sustain, prior, newly., rarely.
8076 | 0.89 A

3521 reverse *v*
noun .trend, court, decision, .course, process, .policy, role, .direction, position, order, situation, .decline, effect, .damage, effort. *misc* toward, completely., quickly, prevent., easily., eventually.
7557 | 0.95

3522 ethical *j*
noun issue, standard, question, dilemma, problem, behavior, concern, principle, value, decision, treatment, consideration *misc* moral, legal, raise, social, political, religious, professional
8273 | 0.87 A

3523 secondary *j*
noun school, education, student, level, market, study, program, source, mirror, role, importance, analysis *misc* elementary, primary, public, social, such, teach, physical, junior
8400 | 0.86 A

3524 administrative *j*
noun cost, region, assistant, law, position, office, support, staff, procedure, service, agency, judge *misc* special, political, judicial, chief, legal, federal, academic
8448 | 0.85 A

3525 confuse *v*
noun people, .issue, public, .matter, consumer, reader, voter, audience, jury, .enemy, tendency., .symptom, ballot, .opponent, observer *misc* .about, often., seem., sometimes., totally., easily.
7512 | 0.96

3526 deadly *j*
noun disease, weapon, force, attack, virus, sin, assault, cancer, gas, bombing, fire, violence *misc* serious, most, potentially, seven, prove, dangerous, cause, terrorist
7566 | 0.95

3527 pig *n*
adj little, wild, fat, pink, blind, stuck, roasted *noun* chicken, cow, .farm, .iron, farmer, cattle, horse *verb* eat, feed, raise, kill, buy., slaughter, squeal, .fly, roast, grunt
7673 | 0.94 F

3528 suburban *j*
noun school, area, house, district, city, community, street, sprawl, county, neighborhood, development, mall *misc* urban, rural, live, white, grow, central, home, middle-class
7890 | 0.91 N

3529 medal *n*
adj Olympic, congressional, presidential, total, shiny, coveted, miraculous, first-place *noun* gold., .honor, silver., bronze., .winner, game, team, .freedom, service, .event *verb* win., receive., earn., deserve., wear, present, finish, .hang, .drape, .dangle
8201 | 0.88 N

3530 receiver *n*
adj wide, top, leading, digital, handheld, running, deep, intended, favorite *noun* phone., radio., .ear, quarterback, telephone., transmitter., satellite., game, season, line *verb* pick., run, hold., .catch, lift., replace., slam., cover., grab., place
8171 | 0.88 N

3531 gaze *n*
adj steady, male, intense, piercing, blue, steely *noun* eye, face, .window, moment, mother, viewer, visitor, tourist, spectator *verb* meet., turn, follow., fix, shift, hold., return, avert., .fall, drop
8422 | 0.85 F

3532 collapse *n*
adj Soviet, economic, financial, total, near, sudden, imminent, complete *noun* .union, .communism,

economy, state, verge., regime, .empire, market, price,
building *verb* lead., follow., cause, prevent., result,
avoid., suffer., .occur, trigger., crush
7726 | 0.93

3533 snake *n*
adj poisonous, venomous, brown, deadly, red, giant,
live, coiled *noun* head, .oil, water, eye, .charmer,
garter., skin, .pit, coral. *verb* bite, kill, .slither, eat,
catch, coil, .crawl, writhe, hiss, .shed
7850 | 0.92 F

3534 march *v*
noun army., parade, .Washington, soldier., thousand.,
troop., line, .mile, .step, road, king, protester.,
demonstrator., .town, saint. *misc* .into, .through, .up,
.toward, .across, .off
7630 | 0.94

3535 experimental *j*
noun group, condition, study, design, control, drug,
treatment, research, result, procedure, program,
subject *misc* theoretical, receive, conduct, test,
clinical, assign, significant
8391 | 0.85 A

3536 civilization *n*
adj western, American, ancient, human, modern,
European, advanced, early, Islamic *noun* clash.,
history, world, culture, society, cradle., end, course,
progress, decline *verb* build, destroy, create, renew.,
save., .exist, threaten, advance, .depend, .survive
7863 | 0.91 A

3537 classical *j*
noun music, jazz, tradition, art, theory, world, style,
ballet, musician, form, model, concert *misc* play,
modern, contemporary, listen, western, Greek,
Chinese, traditional
7961 | 0.90 A

3538 fold *v*
noun arm, hand, paper, .chest, mixture, leg, chair,
edge, egg, seat, .lap, clothes, wing, table, .tent
misc .into, .over, .across, .back, neatly, gently.
   down top, rear, back
7902 | 0.91 F

3539 weakness *n*
adj human, major, economic, relative, greatest, inherent,
potential, physical, individual, moral *noun* strength.,
sign., muscle, system, area, moment., control, economy,
.lack, pain *verb* show., identify, exploit, expose., reveal.,
overcome, point., discuss, demonstrate, .spread
7584 | 0.94 A

3540 corridor *n*
adj long, narrow, main, dark, empty, central, short
noun room, end., door, .night, hospital., .power, wall,
floor, street., hotel. *verb* walk., lead, move, connect,
enter, line, light, fill, echo., .stretch
8303 | 0.86 F

3541 harsh *j*
noun reality, word, condition, light, voice, drug,
environment, critic, winter, expression, criticism,
punishment *misc* too, under, little, sound, face,
particularly, pretty
7428 | 0.96

3542 retail *j*
noun store, price, sales, outlet, business, space,
market, food, chain, industry, shop, office *misc* sell,

suggest, wholesale, national, suggested, square,
commercial, residential
7929 | 0.90 N

3543 mortgage *n*
adj adjustable-rate, low, fixed-rate, monthly, reverse,
fixed, residential *noun* rate, .payment, home, loan,
interest, .lender, .company, .broker *verb* pay,
refinance, buy, rise, qualify., afford, apply., cover.,
.average
8137 | 0.88 N

3544 harder *j*
noun time, line, job, question, drug, edge, look, task,
worker, wood, sell, surface *misc* it, make, than, get,
much, work, find
7430 | 0.96

3545 developer *n*
adj private, local, real-estate, financial, urban,
prominent, independent, leading, nonprofit, principal
noun estate., software., land, property, city, project,
builder, curriculum., home, game *verb* .build, sell,
require, .create, .buy, allow., plan, seek, .agree, own
8121 | 0.88 N

3546 legend *n*
adj urban, living, local, ancient, Indian, golden,
Arthurian, famous, medieval *noun* myth, stuff.,
history, music., rock, blue., baseball., jazz.
verb become., .grow, .surround, inspire, bear.,
replace., print, feature., .persist, .circulate
7623 | 0.93

3547 excitement *n*
adj sexual, full, growing, initial, tremendous, nervous,
sheer, intellectual *noun* lot., sense., eye, voice, kind.,
energy, air, level, fear, fun *verb* feel, generate, create.,
add., bring., contain., share., fill, experience,
.surround
7483 | 0.95

3548 enforce *v*
noun .law, rule, .regulation, state, right, standard,
policy, government., court, power., .agreement, order,
police., .sanction, authority. *misc* .environmental,
federal, strictly., .existing, difficult., fail., responsible.,
vigorously, rarely.
7746 | 0.92 A

3549 murder *v*
noun people, man, wife, child, woman, father,
husband, mother, daughter, son, brother, girl, parent,
police, night *misc* brutally., accuse., kill, torture,
attempt., whose., allegedly.
7726 | 0.92 S

3550 occasional *j*
noun series, use, visit, article, call, problem, piece,
trip, tree, appearance, sound, visitor *misc* only, even,
except, despite, well, punctuate, than
7485 | 0.95

3551 cowboy *n*
adj black, urban, gay, wild, authentic, lonesome, lone,
pointy-toed, aging *noun* .hat, .boot, movie, .Indian,
jeans, shirt, rodeo., bowl, season, team *verb* wear., .win,
.ride, watch., sing, beat, dress., feature., marry., .rank
7917 | 0.90 N

3552 minimum *j*
noun wage, standard, requirement, level, size, age,
investment, number, amount, increase, tax, sentence

misc raise, require, pay, meet, set, alternative, mandatory, maximum
7647 | 0.93

3553 flash *v*
noun light, eye, .smile, screen, .mind, lightning., .grin, sign, tooth, image, camera, look, warning, head, .badge *misc* her, .through, red, .across, .before, .past, suddenly., .forward
back mind., .forth
8058 | 0.88 F

3554 reliable *j*
noun source, information, data, measure, system, way, instrument, test, indicator, result, estimate, method *misc* more, most, valid, provide, welcome, less, accurate, safe
7734 | 0.92 A

3555 suburb *n*
adj northern, southern, affluent, western, wealthy, middle-class, quiet, outer, growing, surrounding
noun city, north, south, town, area, county, west, northwest., .mile, resident *verb* live., move., build, drive, locate, flee., surround, spread, commute., house
7714 | 0.92 N

3556 melt *v*
noun butter, snow, ice, cheese., chocolate, heat, margarine, glacier, heart *misc* .into, .away, over, enough., .together, .cool, .remove, completely, .smooth, quickly
down .into, gold, .little, .something, system.
7713 | 0.92 M

3557 fit *j*
noun index, model, finish, subject, body, person, kid, test, individual, parent, duty, statistics *misc* see, good, perfect, stay, throw, physically, natural, better
7694 | 0.92 M

3558 contend *v*
noun critic., official., other., expert., defense., lawyer., court, prosecutor., researcher., opponent., advocate., agency, theory., administration, plaintiff. *misc* must., seriously., illegal., furthermore., nonetheless., .potentially
7760 | 0.92 N

3559 plead *v*
noun .charge, .case, .contest, eye, .misdemeanor, .help, voice, defendant., .manslaughter, .ignorance, .mercy, official, officer., executive., .cause *misc* .guilty, .innocent, beg, later., agree., .lesser, .fifth, cry, .sentence, silently
7503 | 0.95

3560 written *j*
noun permission, word, statement, language, record, text, report, form, material, response, question, test
misc without, in, prior, far, part, provide, oral, submit
7928 | 0.89 A

3561 flood *n*
adj flash, great, devastating, major, catastrophic, massive, annual, sudden *noun* .insurance, water, .plain, river, .damage, .victim, .stage, .protection
verb cause, bring., destroy, sweep, wash, .recede, unleash., control., trigger., release.
7527 | 0.94

3562 unlike *j*
noun war, study, animal, American, business, adult, drug, car, human *misc* other, which, most, anything, however, traditional, previous, quite
7473 | 0.95

3563 stem *n*
adj human, tough, tall, main, neural, fresh, existing
noun .cell, .research, leaf, brain., adult., .line, .end
verb cut, remove, grow, discard, trim, create, produce, derive, break, contain
8085 | 0.88 M

3564 inevitable *j*
noun war, result, change, question, consequence, conflict, death, outcome, comparison, end, conclusion, process *misc* seem, almost, perhaps, accept, probably, natural, delay, but
7385 | 0.96

3565 essence *n*
adj very, spiritual, divine, pure, distilled, vital
noun .magazine, editor, writer, .art, soul, .culture, spirit, .award, .democracy, flower *verb* capture., represent, define., express., .contribute, reveal., grasp., embody., reside
7840 | 0.90 A

3566 pitcher *n*
adj best, young, left-handed, right-handed, winning, veteran, senior, losing *noun* starting, league, baseball, water, relief., .plant, .mound *verb* .throw, win, hit, pitch, sign, fill, pour, trade, strike, order.
8190 | 0.86 N

3567 tip *v*
noun head, .hat, .scale, .balance, hand, chair, .side, .cap, police, .edge, boat, ball, box, mouth, cup
misc .over, .back, .toward, .forward, .favor, .onto, .slightly
off police, FBI, play, .authority, reporter, official, basketball.
7560 | 0.93 M

3568 subtle *j*
noun way, change, difference, color, form, effect, shift, flavor, variation, message, detail, sign *misc* more, very, between, often, yet, complex, sometimes, much
7480 | 0.94 M

3569 stretch *n*
adj long, final, short, lonely, narrow, particular, desolate, dark *noun* .road, .river, .highway, .imagination, .beach, .water, .land, .mark, hour, .sand
verb hold, drive., strengthen, enter., relax, repeat., cross., disappear., fade.
7620 | 0.93 M

3570 slam *v*
noun door, car, .brake, .wall, .phone, .fist, head, hand, back, .face, .ground, side, .trunk, floor *misc* .into, .shut, .down, .against, him, .behind, her, open, again
8407 | 0.84 F

3571 unemployment *n*
adj high, low, economic, massive, official, growing, chronic, mass *noun* .rate, percent, .benefit, inflation, .insurance, poverty, problem, level, job, economy
verb rise, .fall, reduce., .remain, increase, extend., .drop, cause, collect., experience.
7716 | 0.92

3572 trunk *n*
adj full, white, thick, main, dead, dark, wooden, green, hollow, isometric *noun* tree, car, branch, steamer., foot, .lid, bag., back, elephant., arm
verb open, pop, close, slam., lean., carry, load., hide, shut, throw
7762 | 0.91 F

3573 privilege *n*
adj special, attorney-client, social, certain, male, rare, secret, lawyer-client, legal, constitutional *noun* right, executive., power, honor, claim, wealth., .citizen, position, .clause, client *verb* give, enjoy, grant, pay., lose., invoke., protect, assert., deny, waive.
7484 | 0.94 A

3574 burst *v*
noun .tear, door, .flame, bubble, .laughter, .scene, heart., .applause, pipe., air, .song, .flavor, tree, cloud, crowd. *misc* .into, .through, .open, .forth
out .laugh, .cry, suddenly., .laughter, .tear, threaten., crowd.
7800 | 0.90 F

3575 pitch *v*
noun .innings, .tent, game, .idea, .no-hitter, voice, ball, team, guy, pitcher, .product, .camp, series *misc* .against, .forward, .inside, steeply., .strike, everybody., .onto, roll
in .help, all, everyone., everybody., need, volunteer, neighbor., offer, .too, sleeve.
7877 | 0.89 N

3576 architecture *n*
adj modern, traditional, urban, contemporary, Gothic, classical, colonial, religious, domestic *noun* art, design, landscape., school, history, .firm, .critic, engineering, example. *verb* study., describe, feature, admire, inspire, emphasize, integrate, .evolve, analyze, .date
7919 | 0.89 A

3577 monthly *j*
noun payment, fee, meeting, bill, income, magazine, newsletter, check, mortgage, salary, charge, basis *misc* pay, average, meet, weekly, receive, publish, low, regular
7656 | 0.92 M N

3578 render *v*
noun service, decision, judgment, verdict, image, fat, opinion, figure, court, form, .assistance, subject, animal *misc* .more, .useless, .obsolete, .invisible, .vulnerable, .speechless
7717 | 0.91 A

3579 mainstream *j*
noun media, culture, press, society, group, party, value, audience, organization, school, movie, music *misc* into, American, become, outside, political, within, enter, cultural
7497 | 0.94

3580 frankly *r*
quite., think, because, very, speak, .surprised, admit, pretty, .tired, .prefer, bit, .dear, .doubt, .sick
7987 | 0.88 S

3581 obstacle *n*
adj major, big, political, serious, formidable, main, greatest, insurmountable, only, economic *noun* .course, way, .peace, .path, number., opportunity, effort, lot., road, barrier *verb* overcome, face, remove., present., create, encounter, pose., remain, confront, .prevent
7517 | 0.93 A

3582 motivate *v*
noun student, people, behavior, action, individual, employee, other, force, person, interest, need, .greed, player, effort, activity *misc* .by, highly., politically., primarily
7652 | 0.92 A

3583 trap *v*
noun air, .heat, body, water, .car, particle, animal, .building, ice, .rubble, foot, fire, wall, hour, moisture *misc* .inside, feel., .between, become., .under, .within, .beneath
7349 | 0.96

3584 drinking *n*
adj heavy, safe, underage, excessive, clean, moderate, serious *noun* .water, problem, scene, smoking, drug, binge., .age, beer, .use, .act *verb* stop., quit., start, provide., report., reduce, promote, lower
7596 | 0.92

3585 elbow *n*
adj right, left, sore, bony, broken, bruised, inner *noun* knee, arm, hand, shoulder, .surgery, wrist, .room, body, injury, .grease *verb* bend, lean., rest, prop, keep, hold, touch, lock, throw, sit.
7833 | 0.90 F

3586 rumor *n*
adj persistent, unsubstantiated, spreading, rampant, impending, ugly, widespread, distant, mere *noun* .mill, lot., fact, speculation, war, trade., week, truth., innuendo, town *verb* hear., spread, .circulate, start, .fly, deny., .swirl, .persist, .abound, dispel.
7362 | 0.95

3587 swallow *v*
noun pill, water, mouth., .pride, difficulty, throat, food, darkness, air, .lump, .mouthful, tongue, fish, bite, .rest *misc* hard, .whole, chew., enough., easy., bitter, tough., difficult., quickly
up .by, get., .darkness, hole, .everything, again, .small, .much, sound, ground.
7813 | 0.90 F

3588 legislative *j*
noun branch, history, executive, session, process, council, action, body, power, election, agenda, proposal *misc* judicial, during, federal, regulatory, administrative, special, congressional
7877 | 0.89 A

3589 lecture *n*
adj traditional, brief, stern, inaugural, conventional, distinguished, boring, standard *noun* .hall, series, class, note, course, tour, .circuit, book *verb* give, deliver, attend., present, hear., listen., write, teach, offer, feature
7674 | 0.91 A

3590 daily *r*
dinner., lunch., open., almost., hour, .commute, twice., .reservation, breakfast, .living, activity, meal., .physical, serving.
7646 | 0.92 M N

3591 jeans (PL) *n*
adj blue, black, white, faded, old, tight, baggy, skinny, red, dark *noun* T-shirt, shirt, pair., jacket, pocket, denim, leather, shoe, cowboy, designer. *verb* wear., dress., pull, buy, fit, hang, tuck, fade, clad., tear
7542 | 0.93 F

3592 duck *n*
adj lame, wild, unlimited, black, rubber, dead, odd, roasted, diving *noun* goose, wood., .hunting, pond, chicken, .breast, .hunter, .season, head, .egg *verb* sit., shoot, hunt, quack, walk, feed, .fly, .dodge, .waddle, .swim
7721 | 0.91

3593 slope *n*
adj steep, slippery, western, gentle, grassy, downward
noun mountain, north., ski., park., top, forest, west, bottom, valley, road *verb* climb., hit., slide., cover, fall, rise, descend, intercept, head., step
7812 | 0.90 M

3594 t-shirt *n*
adj white, black, blue, red, baggy, faded, gray, green, tight, yellow *noun* jeans, short, pant, cap, cotton., hat, jacket, shirt, .shop, sneakers *verb* wear., sell., .read, pull, buy., dress., print, .bear, .hang, feature
7533 | 0.93 F

3595 inspection *n*
adj closer, visual, nuclear, close, international, on-site, full, final, environmental, previous *noun* .team, weapon., .service, system, safety., health., food., .regime *verb* allow., conduct, pass., .reveal, require, perform, permit., carry, fail, resume
7524 | 0.93

3596 speed *v*
noun .process, car., .development, road, .street, .recovery, truck, driver., rate, police, vehicle, train., .healing, heart, metabolism *misc* .through, .away, .off, .along, .toward, .past
   up .process, way., development, .metabolism, heart, .pace, .production, greatly., .recovery, .considerably
7364 | 0.95

3597 strict *j*
noun rule, standard, law, control, regulation, liability, limit, scrutiny, policy, sense, requirement, code
misc very, under, impose, follow, meet, set, maintain, adhere
7459 | 0.94

3598 overwhelming *j*
noun majority, evidence, support, number, force, sense, response, power, feeling, odds, problem, desire
misc seem, become, against, almost, despite, face, military
7248 | 0.97

3599 assemble *v*
noun team, group, collection, part, force, piece, panel, component, .list, data, crowd., worker., .salad, ingredient, army *misc* easy., quickly, fully., easily, hastily.
7407 | 0.94 M

3600 missing *j*
noun person, child, link, piece, case, data, part, girl, tooth, search, information, soldier *misc* find, report, still, dead, fill, replace, locate
7307 | 0.96

3601 seemingly *r*
.endless, .simple, .impossible, .unrelated, .contradictory, .random, .innocuous, .oblivious, .innocent, his., .minor, .nowhere, .intractable, event
7337 | 0.95

3602 label *v*
noun food, behavior, critic., category, column, consumer, standard, plastic, .failure, sample, .criminal, .racist, .terrorist *misc* .as, each, clearly, often., simply, properly, neatly.
7443 | 0.94 A

3603 fraud *n*
adj corporate, guilty, financial, criminal, widespread, outright, electoral, academic *noun* charge, security., case, .abuse, mail., conspiracy, bank., tax, count., waste *verb* commit, involve, convict., investigate., accuse., allege, expose., .occur, face, claim
7554 | 0.93 N

3604 reach *n*
adj upper, easy, global, long, low, outer, northern, broad, statutory, vast *noun* arm., goal, stream, sight, scope, depth, influence, cable *verb* extend., expand., remain., limit., lie., place., broaden., escape.
7326 | 0.95

3605 plain *j*
noun sight, yogurt, view, language, paper, fact, clothes, face, folk, text, truth, bread *misc* just, old, white, simple, wrong, hide, black, wear
7352 | 0.95

3606 protest *v*
noun .war, government, student., group., .policy, .decision, .action, strike., .innocence, demonstrator., letter, police, activist., worker, resident. *misc* .against, outside, loudly, strongly, publicly
7332 | 0.95

3607 implementation *n*
adj joint, successful, effective, full, actual, initial, practical, proper, existing *noun* program, policy, development., plan, design., system, strategy, project, process, .intention *verb* require, support., follow., ensure., monitor., delay., facilitate., increase, focus, enhance
8657 | 0.81 A

3608 hunt *v*
noun deer, animal, game, dog, bird, hunter, elk, .food, duck, season, .prey, bear, wolf, buffalo, caribou
misc fish, wild, .together, .gather, prefer., heavily, actively., legally
   down .kill, .terrorist, .criminal, .enemy, mission., agent., .cancer, capture
8115 | 0.86 M

3609 boyfriend *n*
adj new, old, current, abusive, serious, longtime, jealous, steady *noun* husband, mother., girlfriend, friend, daughter, sister., relationship, sex, mom, live-in. *verb* meet, break, marry., steal., dump, date, beat, kiss, abuse, murder
7738 | 0.90

3610 integration *n*
adj economic, social, political, regional, academic, global, vertical, racial, full, cultural *noun* process, system, school, technology, level., community, .economy, market, policy, development *verb* achieve, promote., require, support., involve, facilitate., .occur, encourage, reflect, improve
8196 | 0.85 A

3611 rat *n*
adj dead, male, giant, normal, dirty, fat, cornered, drowned *noun* pack, mouse, mole., .race, lab., .hole, .poison, kangaroo., .ass *verb* eat, feed, smell., .scurry, catch, kill, cause, crawl, jump, gnaw
7586 | 0.92 F

3612 wish *n*
adj true, best, dying, fond, secret, fervent, dear, greatest, deepest, ardent *noun* .list, death., father,

mother, parent, Christmas, patient., .fulfillment
verb make., grant, express., respect., carry, follow,
honor., fulfill., keep
7239 | 0.96

3613 broadcast n
adj original, live, audio, official, local, major, special,
direct, televised *noun* radio., news, .network,
television, tape, record, TV, station, cable, .text
verb watch., listen., own, .feature, air, monitor, delay.,
schedule, .beam, originate
7732 | 0.90 S

3614 Korean j
noun war, peninsula, government, official, leader,
president, people, woman, veteran, regime, missile,
company
7965 | 0.87

3615 nail n
adj long, red, tough, short, pink, rusty, galvanized,
manicured, clean, brittle *noun* .polish, .head, hair,
tooth., hand, .coffin, hammer., .hole, bed, .file
verb bite, drive, hit., paint, hang., dig, .stick, bend,
fasten, buff
7650 | 0.91 F M

3616 pen n
adj red, felt-tip, holding, electronic, straight, sharp
noun paper, ink, fountain., pencil, hand, .pal, .name,
ballpoint., pad, pocket *verb* use, write, put., hold,
pick., pull., grab., draw, .sign, .poise
7485 | 0.93 F

3617 consult v
noun .doctor, expert, .physician, president, .Congress,
book, teacher, .lawyer, .professional, .attorney, .map,
.publication, service, leader, source *misc* .with,
without., .before, after., .original, regularly
7254 | 0.96

3618 companion n
adj constant, traveling, longtime, female, senior, male,
faithful, perfect, faint *noun* .animal, star, friend, book,
.piece, dinner., .program, prairie. *verb* travel., choose.,
introduce, glance, accompany, evaporate, remark,
nudge., .shrug, murder.
7523 | 0.92

3619 encounter n
adj sexual, close, brief, personal, casual, initial, recent,
previous, violent, face-to-face *noun* chance., kind,
.death, animal, nature, detail., memory., sort, series.,
UFO *verb* describe., .occur, recall., involve, survive.,
result, experience, avoid, record, engage
7526 | 0.92 A

3620 monster n
adj green, huge, scary, terrible, ugly, alien, two-
headed, green-eyed, hideous *noun* sea., movie, kind.,
.truck, cookie., .storm, .bed, .buck, bone., .mask
verb create., kill, fight., .eat, .lurk, destroy, chase,
.devour, slay., .threaten
7551 | 0.92 F

3621 nightmare n
adj bad, logistical, recurring, true, terrible, horrible,
bureaucratic, living, ultimate, environmental
noun dream., .scenario, night, parent, relation.,
childhood, traffic, stuff., .vision, .reality *verb* become.,
turn., wake, live, .begin, end, face, haunt, relive.,
plague
7328 | 0.95

3622 beef n
adj roast, corned, lean, grass-fed, grilled, dried, shredded
noun ground., chicken, pork, pound., .stew, .broth,
.tenderloin, .cattle, lamb, .steak *verb* eat., add, cook,
serve, raise, buy., combine, contain, grill, crumble
7623 | 0.91 N

3623 win n
adj big, consecutive, straight, easy, huge, impressive,
upset, worldwide *noun* .loss, team, season, week,
game, record., career, touchdown., streak, victory
verb help., snap, earn, mean, seal., end, celebrate.,
finish, post., secure.
8324 | 0.83 N

3624 serving n
adj large, total, individual, fresh, dairy-free, daily,
whole, single, hot, 1-tablespoon *noun* .time, cup,
.bowl, yield., .dish, vegetable, .plate, .platter, .table,
.pound *verb* eat., transfer., place, arrange, .contain,
pour, consume., .cook, recommend
8609 | 0.81 M

3625 globe n
adj golden, entire, terrestrial, celestial, green, blue,
shattered *noun* part., snow., corner., .award,
.nomination, columnist, reporter, editor, map, glass.
verb travel., circle., span., spread., .report, publish,
circumnavigate., spin, sweep., scour.
7309 | 0.95

3626 cholesterol n
adj saturated, high, total, low, bad, elevated, normal,
dietary *noun* .sodium, milligram, fat., .level, blood,
carbohydrate, fiber., pressure, gram., protein.
verb lower., reduce, raise., improve, .drop, decrease,
control., elevate, boost
8524 | 0.81 M

3627 parliament n
adj Russian, new, European, Soviet, British, national,
federal, elected *noun* member., .building, house.,
seat., president, party, speaker, election, government,
majority. *verb* elect, pass, approve, dissolve, .declare,
adopt, represent, .reject, address., storm.
7921 | 0.88

3628 suite n
adj luxury, presidential, royal, two-room, bridal, surgical
noun hotel, room, office, master., executive., night,
bedroom., guest., door *verb* include, offer, enter.,
feature, share, occupy, .overlook, rent., book, house
7660 | 0.91 M N

3629 continuing j
noun education, problem, program, effort, coverage,
development, resolution, debate, operation,
investigation, series, need *misc* despite, economic,
because, professional, reflect, forever, due, amid
7437 | 0.93 A

3630 pop n
adj American, loud, contemporary, mainstream,
traditional, famous, pure *noun* .culture, star, .art,
.singer, .chart, soda., .quiz *verb* hear., sing, drink,
sound, feature, range., influence, sip.
7604 | 0.91

3631 hence r
.name, .need, .title, .importance, decade., identity,
.nickname, relatively, creation, .emphasis, moral,
capacity, selection, fewer
7999 | 0.87 A

29. Collective nouns

In English, there are a class of quantifying, collective, and unit nouns that are used to refer to groups of things or people. The following table provides information on which nouns go together most frequently. The list of categories (*batch, bunch*, etc.) is taken from Biber et al. (1998) *Longman Grammar of Spoken and Written English* (pp. 248–54), but the most frequent collocates (rightmost column) are from the Corpus of Contemporary American English. The number represents the combined frequency of these top five collocates, and it provides some indication of the frequency of the particular quantifying, collective, or unit noun.

batch	45	cookies, letters, eggs, biscuits, chocolate
bunch	990	people, guys, kids, things, stuff
clump	171	grass, hair, trees, bushes, brush
crowd	483	people, reporters, men, onlookers, students
flock	238	birds, sheep, geese, pigeons, crows
gang	101	thugs, men, boys, thieves, kids
group	4578	people, students, men, women, friends
herd	230	cattle, buffalo, cows, elephants, deer
host	288	others, problems, issues, reasons, things
pack	603	cigarettes, wolves, lies, dogs, cards
series	1274	events, questions, articles, meetings, studies
set	1364	rules, circumstances, values, questions, problems
shoal	7	fish, time, wind, torment
swarm	104	bees, people, mosquitoes, locusts, flies
troop	27	boy scouts, soldiers, horsemen, monkeys, baboons
act	1429	violence, terrorism, war, congress, love
bit	1031	information, time, money, luck, history
chip	25	stone, wood, paint, mica, glass
chunk	280	ice, money, change, meat, time
game	512	baseball, golf, basketball, chess, life
grain	627	sand, salt, rice, truth, dust
item	167	clothing, evidence, interest, information, gossip
loaf	518	bread, wonder, rye, wheat, sourdough
lump	137	coal, clay, sugar, meat, ice
piece	3614	paper, evidence, legislation, equipment, cake
scrap	510	paper, information, food, fabric, wood
sheet	1245	paper, plastic, ice, rain, glass
slice	472	bread, pizza, life, cheese, lemon
sliver	146	light, moon, land, glass, silicon
speck	144	dust, blood, light, dirt, land
sprinkling	31	freckles, stars, salt, sugar, lights
strip	284	land, paper, bacon, cloth, sand
trace	159	blood, irony, fat, fear, cholesterol
barrel	546	oil, water, gasoline, monkeys, petroleum
basket	113	food, fruit, goods, bread, stocks
box	347	chocolates, tissues, matches, cereal, candy
crate	29	ammunition, food, wrenches, fruit, equipment
cup	3714	coffee, tea, water, sugar, milk

keg	53	beer, dynamite, gunpowder, bolts, powder
packet	111	information, cigarettes, seeds, sugar, data
sack	226	flour, potatoes, rice, groceries, grain
heap	96	trouble, history, rubble, clothes, garbage
pile	443	rubble, papers, books, rocks, clothes
stick	227	dynamite, butter, gum, furniture, wood
wedge	79	cheese, lime, lemon, light, land
dozens	878	people, times, others, interviews, companies
score(s)	317	people, students, others, children, interviews
load(s)	176	laundry, money, crap, fun, wood
mass(es)	286	people, humanity, earth, material, hair
armful	31	books, wood, papers, clothes, flowers
fistful	42	dollars, cash, hair, bills, coins
handful	512	people, states, companies, others, men
mouthful	71	food, water, air, smoke, blood
spoonful	82	sugar, soup, rice, oatmeal, food
pair	1368	shoes, jeans, scissors, pants, binoculars
couple	13466	years, weeks, days, months, times

3632 lend *v*
noun .support, .money, .hand, bank., .credence, .name, .credibility, institution, .voice, .legitimacy, finding., .sense, .ear, fund, .strength *misc* .itself, .themselves, .million, willing., agree., certain, easily, readily
7261 | 0.95

3633 project *v*
noun image, year, .screen, .power, .future, .wall, population, budget, ability., earnings, slide, deficit, cost, light, film *misc* .onto, million, .increase, .grow, billion, .forward, upon, .beyond
7333 | 0.94

3634 sixth *m*
.grade, fifth., .year, .sense, .grader, .floor, .seventh, finish., .season, .century, .inning, .street, win, game
7429 | 0.93 N

3635 mud *n*
adj black, thick, dried, soft, red, deep, frozen *noun* water, .flat, .hut, foot, .puddle, sand, rain, rock, wall, face *verb* cover., throw., stick, cake, drag., sink., bury., suck, .dry, splatter
7502 | 0.92 F

3636 pump *n*
adj electric, submersible, black, centrifugal, dry, hydraulic, available, efficient, mechanical, double *noun* water, gas., heat., price., air, fuel., station, vacuum. *verb* operate, prime., install, wear, .feature, replace, .deliver, .suck, remove, connect.
8018 | 0.86

3637 flour *n*
adj all-purpose, white, unbleached, remaining, self-rising, excess, sifted, enriched *noun* cup, .mixture, sugar, .salt, .teaspoon, tablespoon, .powder, bowl., butter, wheat *verb* add., combine., stir, sift., mix, blend, grind.
8193 | 0.84 M N

3638 hostage *n*
adj American, western, Iranian, British, foreign, freed, fellow, chief, Filipino, virtual *noun* release, .crisis, .situation, .taker, arm., .issue, .rescue, .negotiator *verb* hold., take, free, kill, kidnap, .surrender, .plead
8325 | 0.83 S

3639 ownership *n*
adj private, public, foreign, local, corporate, full, collective *noun* land, home., gun., property, sense., right, .group, form., company, employee. *verb* claim., retain., transfer., increase, base., encourage, restrict, promote, assume., imply
7608 | 0.91 A

3640 facilitate *v*
noun process, .student, .development, .learning, .communication, change, group, program, .use, .discussion, .access, .understanding, teacher, activity, .movement *misc* help., order., .among, greatly., effective, encourage, necessary, intend.
8161 | 0.85 A

3641 basement *n*
adj full, finished, dark, unfinished, damp, dank, tiny, cramped *noun* room, church, house, door, .apartment, garage, floor, office, stair, .window *verb* live., finish., hide., fill, flood, store., clean., locate., enter, hang
7459 | 0.92 F

3642 correlation *n*
adj significant, positive, high, strong, negative, low, direct, canonical *noun* table., .coefficient, variable, analysis, score, .matrix, result, test, group, pattern *verb* find, show, use, indicate, calculate, report, reveal, examine, .exist, .range
8807 | 0.78 A

3643 hurry *v*
noun door, .room, .street, car, .kitchen, .hall, .step, foot, window, crowd, hallway, footstep, daddy
misc .out, .off, .toward, .away, .through, .over, .past, .across, better., please
up .wait, better., .finish, please
8055 | 0.86 F

3644 insect *n*
adj other, beneficial, small, aquatic, tiny, flying, dead, certain, native, giant *noun* plant, bird, .pest, disease, species, .repellent, scale., fish, .bite, food *verb* eat, kill., feed, attract, control., catch, .fly, .crawl, collect, swarm
8282 | 0.83 M

3645 arena *n*
adj political, new, public, international, main, global, downtown, electoral *noun* sport., .stage, policy, stadium, .football, center, league, basketball., ice., hockey. *verb* enter., build, fill, step., compete, pack, dominate, house, finance, constitute.
7444 | 0.92 A

3646 drift *v*
noun eye., cloud, mind., smoke., thought., boat, snow, water, .room, air, .sleep, window, .current, sea, music. *misc* .into, .away, .through, .toward, let., .across
off .sleep, .into, .again, voice., thought, last., .wake, herself., slowly., .somewhere **back** .sleep, mind., thought., .toward
7667 | 0.90 F

3647 notice *n*
adj short, public, written, special, prior, advanced *noun* moment., day, advance., hour., week, eviction., month., .appeal *verb* take., give., put., receive., escape., send, serve., post, issue, attract.
7199 | 0.96

3648 domain *n*
adj public, eminent, private, specific, different, affective, academic, cognitive, exclusive, various *noun* .name, knowledge, life, decision, policy., score, development, sport, loss., source. *verb* enter., relate, define, exercise, register, extend, expand, address, establish, assess
8023 | 0.86 A

3649 cave *n*
adj dark, mammoth, deep, nearby, underwater, prehistoric, shallow, secret *noun* wall, mouth, entrance, .painting, mountain, bat, snow., floor, rock, wind *verb* live., hide, explore, enter., discover, crawl., visit., sleep, .belong, occupy
7657 | 0.90 F

3650 African-American *j*
noun community, student, history, study, culture, voter, people, population, experience, art, artist
7978 | 0.86

3651 consistently *r*
.high, show, .low, report, .support, study., level, apply, research., .rank, poll., produce, fail, .demonstrate
7461 | 0.92 A

3652 leap *v*
noun heart., .air, flame., car, water, tree, door, arm, dog., window, mind, fire, wall, .conclusion, cat. *misc* .from, .into, .out, .over, .onto, .forward, .ahead, toward, .grab
7813 | 0.88 F

3653 final *n*
adj regional, national, open, sectional, consecutive, 100-meter, all-American *noun* game, conference., year, cup., team, .minute, .week, tournament., point *verb* reach., win, play, lose, advance., contain, .consist, score, miss., include
8072 | 0.85 N

3654 effectiveness *n*
adj institutional, instructional, overall, relative, organizational, long-term, perceived *noun* program, study, teacher, intervention, safety, cost., research, measure, treatment, strategy *verb* evaluate., determine., assess., improve., increase., demonstrate., enhance., examine., reduce, depend
8204 | 0.84 A

3655 maximum *j*
noun rate, amount, number, security, speed, level, sentence, benefit, value, prison, score, efficiency *misc* possible, reach, provide, achieve, allow, minimum, set, allowable
7567 | 0.91 A

3656 array *n*
adj wide, vast, broad, large, impressive, diverse, dizzying *noun* .service, .program, .option, .product, .color, telescope, sensor, .choice, .material *verb* offer., provide, include., produce., contain, face., feature., consist, .range, .measure
7537 | 0.91 A

3657 unexpected *j*
noun way, place, event, result, finding, turn, death, change, problem, twist, effect, development *misc* something, most, happen, totally, expect, sudden, completely
7084 | 0.97

3658 curtain *n*
adj heavy, final, sheer, thick, thin, gauzy, yellow, beaded, front, light *noun* window, iron., shower., lace., side, velvet., .call, .rod, door *verb* draw, pull, open, close, hang, .fall, part, lift, .rise, watch
7590 | 0.90 F

3659 sandwich *n*
adj grilled, cold, fresh, favorite, peanut-butter, half-eaten, green, toasted, delicious, tasty *noun* cheese., salad, butter., peanut., chicken., turkey., ham., tuna., .shop *verb* make, eat., serve, order., bring., buy, finish., munch., sell., place
7441 | 0.92 F

3660 peaceful *j*
noun solution, resolution, world, means, settlement, coexistence, way, life, place, transition, change, protest *misc* more, nuclear, quiet, democratic, relatively, political, stable, seek
7279 | 0.94

3661 humanity *n*
adj common, full, shared, basic, very, essential, modern, suffering *noun* crime., habitat., nature, rest., future, history, whole, sense, genocide, piece. *verb* commit, deny, save, face, recognize, benefit., destroy., .survive, unite, diminish
7533 | 0.91 A

3662 prediction *n*
adj dire, accurate, true, early, future, theoretical, significant, correct, optimistic, general *noun* model, result, accuracy, climate, weather., .outcome, analysis,

variable, data, test _verb_ make., base, support, confirm, contribute., .prove, improve., match, derive, differ
7442 | 0.92 A

3663 Roman _j_
noun empire, emperor, law, numeral, soldier, God, ruin, authority, army, nose
7669 | 0.89 A

3664 ideology _n_
adj political, dominant, social, religious, cultural, nationalist, economic, western, liberal, racial _noun_ gender, party, politics, state, practice, culture, religion, nationalism, end., critique _verb_ base, promote, reflect, share, support, adopt, represent, embrace, impose, argue
7968 | 0.86 A

3665 railroad _n_
adj old, southern, transcontinental, central, federal, abandoned, historic _noun_ .track, .car, .station, underground., .line, .bridge, .company, .worker, .yard _verb_ build, work., run, cross, ride, own, connect, operate, .link, construct
7367 | 0.93

3666 possession _n_
adj personal, prized, illegal, worldly, sole, precious, demonic, full, guilty _noun_ drug, weapon, marijuana, cocaine, spirit., material., charge, gun, .firearm, use _verb_ take., arrest., sell, gain., carry, convict., retain., bust., .belong, pile
7230 | 0.94

3667 horn _n_
adj big, French, golden, loud, English, blaring, principal, muted _noun_ car., bull., head, sound, .player, rhino., blast, saddle., air, animal _verb_ honk, blow, blare, play, hear., toot., lean., beep, lock.
7324 | 0.93 F

3668 replacement _n_
adj total, permanent, joint, possible, potential, temporary, suitable, gradual _noun_ .therapy, hormone., hip., .part, .player, .cost, .surgery, .worker _verb_ find., need, require., hire, buy., name, choose., .arrive, order
7249 | 0.94

3669 announcement _n_
adj public, official, recent, formal, dramatic, stunning, brief _noun_ service., day, president, week, surprise., job., month, morning, hour, policy _verb_ make, .come, follow, hear., expect, read, delay., issue, .mark, post
7254 | 0.94

3670 pond _n_
adj small, little, frozen, shallow, nearby, tiny, muddy _noun_ water, lake, fish, duck, stream, edge., surface, farm., area, tree _verb_ build, swim, dig, stock, overlook., surround, drop., drain, .freeze, dry
7408 | 0.92 M

3671 conduct _n_
adj professional, sexual, disorderly, criminal, personal, homosexual, moral, ethical, human, improper _noun_ code., rule., .war, standard., .disorder, .problem, president, policy, kind., law _verb_ engage., govern., involve, regulate., violate, charge., condemn., prohibit, establish., determine
7427 | 0.92 A

3672 forgive _v_
noun God., father, debt, sin, loan, Lord, Jesus, sir, .sinner, .enemy, .pun, Christ _misc_ .me, .him, never., .her, .us, forget, please., .myself, ever., able., hope., .yourself, .everything
7334 | 0.93 F

3673 past _r_
.present, year., walk., between., drive., .future, car., both., rush., fly., century., decade., roar., slide.
7291 | 0.93 F

3674 Muslim _n_
adj Bosnian, Shiite, religious, moderate, holy, devout, radical, fundamentalist, Pakistani, observant _noun_ Christian, Jew, Croat, Arab., Sunni., Hindu, majority _verb_ .live, believe, kill, fight, .pray, consider, join, attack, arm, target
7636 | 0.89

3675 bishop _n_
adj national, American, local, auxiliary, gay, religious, presiding, Latin, conservative, French _noun_ conference, church, priest, letter, pope, diocese, office, committee, meeting, teaching _verb_ appoint, elect, name, ordain, .issue, address, adopt, .approve, .resign, .declare
7982 | 0.85

3676 aim _n_
adj ultimate, primary, political, main, social, present, stated, careful, dead, principal _noun_ .study, war., article, movement, method, goal, objective, purpose, rifle, strategy _verb_ take., achieve., accomplish., pursue., .improve, state., shift., adjust.
7416 | 0.92 A

3677 top _v_
noun .list, mixture, year, .chart, slice, sales., salad., plate., bowl, .wire, glass, ice, .mark, record, tree _misc_ .each, .million, expect., .evenly, easily.
off .by, .tank, .glass, meal, .coffee **out** .about, .over, .around, price., temperature.
7374 | 0.92 M N

3678 uncomfortable _j_
noun silence, position, situation, feeling, question, moment, chair, talking, truth, fact, seat, conversation _misc_ make, feel, very, look, little, seem, bit
7078 | 0.96

3679 subject _i_
(subject to) .to, .change, .law, .same, .tax, .review, .regulation, .rule, .approval, .control, .scrutiny, federal, therefore., .pressure
7630 | 0.89 A

3680 laugh _n_
adj good, big, little, short, hearty, nervous, throaty, bitter, loud, deep _noun_ .line, lot., smile, .track, belly., .riot, .cry, barrel. _verb_ make., get., give., hear, add., share., stifle., force., feel, bark.
7419 | 0.91 F

3681 rip _v_
noun heart, clothes, shirt, .piece, head, page, door, wall, .shred, bullet., explosion., paper, wind., arm, body _misc_ .out, .through, .apart, .open, .away, .across
off get., clothes, shirt, .mask, roof, taxpayer, head, .piece, someone, .coat
7481 | 0.91 F

3682 random *j*
noun sample, number, sampling, assignment, testing, violence, order, selection, act, event, walk, search
misc stratified, seemingly, publish, select, present, conduct, test, apparently
7209 | 0.94 A

3683 herb *n*
adj fresh, medicinal, dried, Chinese, culinary, wild, natural, fragrant, traditional, perennial
noun .garden, spice, vegetable, flower, garlic, .tea, medicine, mixture, food, supplement
verb use, grow, add, contain, mix, sell, dry, chop., sprinkle., combine.
7680 | 0.88 M

3684 and/or *c*
use, teacher, social, drug, physical, parent, education, behavior, either., activity, specific, skill, professional, treatment
7839 | 0.86 A

3685 dump *v*
noun body, waste, water, truck, garbage, .river, .stock, trash, .ton, bag, .load, .content, storm., material, oil *misc* .into, .onto, simply., unceremoniously, illegally
7089 | 0.95

3686 online *r*
find, buy., post., shop., information., sell., order., service, meet., chat, site, offer, visit, news
7407 | 0.91 M

3687 warm *v*
noun sun, hand, .heart, water, fire, air, heat, earth, climate., foot, room, .idea, oven, planet, face
misc keep., .enough, cool, .before, quickly, slowly, inside, gradually., .bit
  up before, minute, start., stretch, begin, weather., engine, crowd, muscle, .audience
7258 | 0.93 M

3688 guilt *n*
adj sexual, collective, terrible, liberal, tremendous, intense *noun* feeling, .innocence, shame, sense., fear, .association, admission, doubt, survivor. *verb* feel, admit., prove., carry., experience, deny., determine., .wash, overwhelm, motivate
7196 | 0.94

3689 cattle *n*
adj wild, grazing, domestic, spotted, working, live, diseased *noun* sheep, .ranch, herd, rancher, horse, head., beef, land, .ranching *verb* raise, graze, feed, drive, kill, sell, .prod., .roam
7409 | 0.91

3690 strain *n*
adj resistant, different, financial, virulent, severe, deadly, emotional, physical, various, certain
noun .bacteria, stress, virus, flu, muscle, .gauge, sign., .injury, .music, disease *verb* put., show, cause, place, ease., reduce., relieve., .emerge
7240 | 0.93

3691 sheriff *n*
adj local, retired, assistant, corrupt, off-duty, small-town, interim, elected *noun* county., deputy, .department, .office, police, car, officer, town, .station, .detective *verb* call, shoot, arrest, arrive, elect., .park, complain, sue., .seize, alert
7542 | 0.89 F

3692 behave *v*
noun way, people., child, .manner, kid, person, adult, animal, individual., cell, gentleman, atom, .dignity, .estrogen *misc* .like, how., .badly, .differently, better, .toward, expect, .yourself, .themselves, .properly
7006 | 0.96

3693 response *i*
(in response to) .to, .question, change, write., .pressure, letter, .demand, .concern, .need, .request, action, .criticism, .threat, editor.
7335 | 0.92 A

3694 crystal *n*
adj clear, liquid, single, tiny, photonic, fine, delicate, cut *noun* .ball, ice., .chandelier, glass, .palace, water, .spirit, snow., cruise, .meth *verb* form, hang, place, contain, shatter, shine, consist, gaze, dangle, tap
7370 | 0.91

3695 execute *v*
noun instruction, search, law, order, warrant, person, painting, prisoner, .strategy, trade, ability., command, crime, .mission, murder *misc* plan, faithfully., properly, summarily., perfectly
7155 | 0.94

3696 wrist *n*
adj left, right, broken, thin, sore, sprained, bare
noun hand, arm, ankle, finger, watch, elbow, slap., shoulder, flick., bracelet *verb* grab., hold, break, bind, .pull, cut, slit., wear, catch., bend
7514 | 0.90 F

3697 motive *n*
adj ulterior, political, possible, social, primary, strong, real, sexual, main, competitive *noun* profit., .murder, participation, question, .opportunity, reason, behavior, .force, difference., intention *verb* .kill, understand, suggest, explain, drive, suspect., examine., establish., act, reveal
7413 | 0.91 A

3698 painter *n*
adj French, abstract, modern, famous, contemporary, greatest, impressionist, fine, acrylic, figurative
noun .sculptor, landscape, portrait., oil., writer, artist, house., air. *verb* become, .paint, train., admire, inspire, .depict, .contribute, .render, .capture, marry
8502 | 0.79 M

3699 convict *v*
noun .murder, .crime, jury., man, year, court, person., defendant, .rape, .fraud, evidence, officer, .drug, .conspiracy, .manslaughter
misc .sentence, later., wrongly., arrest., wrongfully., someone
7383 | 0.91 S

3700 simultaneously *r*
while., almost., both, several, different, occur., multiple, exist., operate., thus, present, variable., identity, direction
7370 | 0.91 A

3701 recession *n*
adj economic, bad, deep, severe, mild, current, global, recent *noun* economy., year, end, unemployment, war, inflation, rate, .depression, growth, nation. *verb* hit, cause, head., slip., suffer., affect, avoid., hurt, mire., .last
7595 | 0.88 S

3702 await *v*
noun .trial, .arrival, .return, fate, .approval, .word,
.result, death, .court, .sentencing, .charge, .discovery,
.outcome, .execution, .instruction *misc* while.,
eagerly., still., anxiously., long.
6964 | 0.96

3703 hallway *n*
adj long, dark, narrow, empty, front, short, main
noun door, room, .day, floor, school, end., house,
office, light, apartment *verb* stand, lead, run, step.,
line, enter, fill, push, pace., cross.
8103 | 0.83 F

3704 dose *n*
adj high, low, daily, healthy, lethal, heavy, single
noun radiation, drug, vaccine, patient, .vitamin,
study, .medication, .reality, .medicine, distribution
verb take., give., receive., need, administer, deliver,
increase, reduce, .cause, exceed
7707 | 0.87 M

3705 brush *n*
adj thick, broad, sable, round, soft, dry, stiff, wet,
synthetic, dense *noun* paint, .stroke, bristle., hair,
tree, .fire, .death, scrub., pile, .law *verb* use.,
apply, clean, dip, pick, clear, hide, .remove,
disappear., lay
8217 | 0.82 M

3706 endure *v*
noun year, pain, hardship, suffering, .hour, abuse,
.month, .season, century, loss, .period, humiliation,
love, ability., indignity *misc* long, must., force., able.,
willing., .physical
6952 | 0.96

3707 counseling *n*
adj individual, psychological, professional,
comprehensive, genetic, pastoral, premarital,
online *noun* school., .program, .service, student,
group, .center, family, career., .session, guidance
verb provide., need, offer, seek., receive., support,
attend., undergo., focus, teach
8247 | 0.81 A

3708 civilian *n*
adj Iraqi, innocent, Israeli, American, unarmed,
Palestinian, Lebanese, dead, Afghan, Muslim
noun soldier, attack., war, officer, killing., number.,
troop, army, official, military *verb* kill, .die, target.,
protect., shoot, .flee, hit, .catch, murder, fire.
7427 | 0.90 S

3709 suck *v*
noun .air, .breath, life, thumb, water, .blood,
mouth., .finger, lip, baby, wind, .juice, cigarette,
energy, mud *misc* .up, .out, .into, .down, .off,
.away, .dry
7419 | 0.90 F

3710 accommodate *v*
noun .need, .student, change, .demand, schedule,
.growth, room., space., .difference, .interest, .guest,
.range, .request, .passenger, desire *misc* can., enough.,
large, design., must., easily., order.
7145 | 0.94 A

3711 traditionally *r*
woman, .male, .consider, area, .associate, .view, .serve,
.focus, .democratic, .female, .define, role, institution,
value
7241 | 0.92 A

3712 spill *v*
noun oil., blood, water, light., coffee, .bean, .gut, tear.,
.street, content, .drink, gallon, hair., .secret, table
misc .over, .out, .into, .onto, .across
7194 | 0.93 F

3713 fiscal *j*
noun year, policy, budget, responsibility, crisis, quarter,
conservative, discipline, deficit, problem, stimulus,
restraint *misc* end, its, million, monetary, during, last,
current, next, federal
7348 | 0.91 N

3714 welcome *j*
noun mat, home, change, news, back, relief, addition,
sign, guest, sight, visitor, wagon *misc* you, very, thank,
most, quite, join, please, everyone
7209 | 0.93 S

3715 retired *j*
noun general, officer, army, teacher, person, colonel,
worker, professor, executive, police, employee,
engineer *misc* who, American, military, recently,
marine, live, former, senior
7285 | 0.92 N

3716 closed *j*
noun door, eye, system, session, room, window,
society, meeting, season, area, sign, fist *misc* behind,
remain, through, open, stay, PM, tightly, normally,
front
6912 | 0.97

3717 gentle *j*
noun voice, man, hand, breeze, way, slope, eye, giant,
face, smile, touch, hill *misc* very, sweet, soft, warm,
kind, quiet, slow, firm
7202 | 0.92 F

3718 separation *n*
adj constitutional, physical, church-state, racial,
emotional, legal, strict, complete, clear, religious
noun .church, .state, .power, .anxiety, divorce,
degree., wall., principle., .religion, parent
verb violate., maintain., require, cause, .occur,
announce., suffer., accept., establish, justify
7274 | 0.91 A

3719 guard *v*
noun door, soldier, police, .entrance, gate, coast.,
troop, border, .privacy, officer, building, secret, .tower,
.prisoner, army *misc* .against, jealously, closely,
carefully, heavily.
7151 | 0.93

3720 warrior *n*
adj great, cold, young, holy, fierce, wounded, happy,
reluctant, dead, native *noun* road., weekend., woman,
.society, battle, war, king, rainbow., culture, spirit
verb .fight, lead, .ride, .attack, defeat, depict, .guard,
portray., transform., bind
7284 | 0.91

3721 convinced *j*
noun official, need, scientist, guilt, expert, investor,
prosecutor, importance, voter, innocence, owner,
judge *misc* that, I, become, absolutely, remain,
everyone, firmly, finally
6883 | 0.97

3722 southwest *n*
adj American, rural, arid, far, ancient, dry, extreme
noun mile., .airline, .conference, state, .corner, center,

city, .side, area, desert. _verb_ locate., fly, lie., head, travel., situate., shift.
7344 | 0.90 N

3723 drunk _j_
noun driver, guy, bar, kid, wine, beer, tank, alcohol, accident, arrest, charge, uncle _misc_ get, driving, too, drive, little, against, home
7330 | 0.91 F

3724 outdoor _j_
noun activity, life, recreation, pool, area, sport, space, room, advertising, cafe, market, concert _misc_ indoor, living, enjoy, prepare, hot, hike, environmental
7331 | 0.91 M

3725 tune _v_
noun .news, radio, viewer., panel., instrument, week, television, ear, music, .look, frequency, .report, guitar, set, piano _misc_ stay., .into, finely., right., please., watch, fine.
in people., .see, viewer., .next, million., radio, .watch, .tomorrow, American. **out** .message, voter., viewer., ad **up** orchestra., band., musician.
7380 | 0.90 S

3726 patient _j_
noun satisfaction, handling, safety, population, information, group, record, outcome, education, advocate _misc_ wait, medical, improve, per, safe, associate, manual
7970 | 0.83 A

3727 harm _n_
adj physical, great, serious, bodily, irreparable, environmental, real _noun_ .way, .reduction, risk., .other, troop., threat., potential., lot., use _verb_ do, cause, mean., put., inflict, suffer, protect., prevent., result, .occur
7116 | 0.93

3728 cloth _n_
adj white, black, damp, red, blue, soft, wet, whole, clean _noun_ piece., paper, table, cotton., .bag, strip., .napkin, .diaper, bolt. _verb_ cover, wrap, cut., wear, weave, drape, pull, hang, soak, bind
7674 | 0.86 F

3729 wherever _r_
.go, .want, find, .possible, .may, whenever, follow., live, .lead, whatever, travel, .choose, .occur, .else
6839 | 0.97

3730 administer _v_
noun questionnaire, program, student, survey, drug, state, group, dose, medication, service, government, teacher, patient, justice, law _misc_ .during, each, individually, easy., .intravenously, properly, test, easily.
7517 | 0.88 A

3731 short _r_
cut., .order, hair, .enough, catch., .burst, breath, .visit, .vacation, sentence, .sight, .blond, .gasp, skirt
7003 | 0.94 A

3732 supervisor _n_
adj immediate, clinical, male, direct, postal, female, nursing _noun_ board., county., teacher, university., music., student, election, district, program, service _verb_ speak., report, approve, complain, train, cooperate, .fire, promote, .vote, act
7418 | 0.89 N

3733 compromise _n_
adj political, possible, reasonable, territorial, acceptable, grand, bipartisan _noun_ .bill, kind., room., .plan, sort., negotiation, .solution, budget _verb_ make, reach, accept., offer., negotiate., agree, .allow, strike, seek., represent.
7067 | 0.94

3734 grateful _j_
noun author, opportunity, support, help, chance, nation, fan, smile, acknowledgment, look, patient, gift _misc_ I, for, very, so, dead, shall, feel, always
6937 | 0.95 F

3735 Hispanic _j_
noun student, population, community, group, voter, culture, family, immigrant, resident, worker
7405 | 0.89 N

3736 Japanese _n_
adj fluent, average, contemporary, ordinary, fellow, elderly, loyal _noun_ German, American, European, Korean, bride., Italian, English _verb_ speak, buy, .attack, .begin, fight, sell, build, translate., compete., capture
7219 | 0.91

3737 mandate _n_
adj federal, unfunded, British, clear, broad, congressional, individual, local, constitutional, popular _noun_ state, employer., government, law, nation, .change, agency, legislation, .coverage, election _verb_ require, provide, carry, impose, comply., receive, .protect, enforce, .reduce, fulfill.
7237 | 0.91 A

3738 average _v_
noun .point, game, .percent, .yard, .minute, rate., .rating, week, team., .mile, player., growth, price., figure, temperature. _misc_ .about, .million, .over, .less, .across, .nearly, .carry, annual, .least
7510 | 0.88 N

3739 alarm _n_
adj silent, growing, audible, sudden, electronic, internal _noun_ .clock, .system, fire., .bell, car., burglar., smoke., cause. _verb_ sound, set., raise., ring, hear, trigger, install, wake, .blare, .warn
7036 | 0.94 F

3740 cruise _n_
adj Caribbean, seven-day, luxury, short, European, Alaskan, chartered, typical _noun_ .ship, .missile, .line, .control, day., sea, passenger, boat, dinner., .industry _verb_ offer, launch, sail, book., carry, .depart, plan, enjoy, feature, embark
7266 | 0.91 N

3741 injure _v_
noun other, .knee, .attack, car, police, civilian, .crash, fire, blast, season, leg, bomb, shoulder, animal, .fall _misc_ kill, seriously., badly., severely., critically., hundred, dozen
7089 | 0.93 N

3742 sculpture _n_
adj public, abstract, contemporary, figurative, ceramic, outdoor, modern, classical, primitive, fine _noun_ painting., art, .garden, bronze., piece., museum, drawing, glass, ice., wood _verb_ create, represent, depict, feature, display, draw, exhibit, commission, study., present
8040 | 0.82 M

3743 award *v*
noun prize, contract, medal, grant, jury., damage, year, Nobel, court., honor, government, .custody, university, .star, money *misc* .million, recently., federal, .honorary, billion, annually, posthumously
7101 | 0.93 N

3744 drain *v*
noun water, cup, bean, paper, towel, blood, .pasta, face, package., .glass, color, .liquid, oil, .resource, colander *misc* .well, rinse, until., .out, rinsed., .away, .off, emotionally., cool
7374 | 0.89 M

3745 temple *n*
adj Buddhist, Hindu, ancient, gray, left, holy, golden, Jewish, Greek, Mormon *noun* church, finger, stone., eye, wall, site, building, mosque, hair., palace *verb* build, rub., stand, visit., enter., rebuild, massage., tap., .honor
7180 | 0.92 F

3746 dancer *n*
adj exotic, young, professional, male, best, principal, topless, go-go, traditional, masked *noun* ballet., singer, musician, choreographer, belly., company, tap., stage, music, artist *verb* .perform, watch, dance, .wear, train, feature., hire, clad, .spin
7099 | 0.93

3747 towel *n*
adj clean, wet, damp, white, hot, folded, cold, cool *noun* paper., hand, dish., kitchen., head, bath., face, beach., .rack, hair *verb* wrap, throw., place, dry, cover., hang, .wipe, grab., drape, drop.
7303 | 0.90 F

3748 Islam *n*
adj radical, political, militant, fundamentalist, Shiite, moderate, orthodox *noun* Christianity, religion, Judaism, war., interpretation., .leader, democracy *verb* convert., embrace., defend., promote, forbid, study., associate, destroy, justify, .condone
7625 | 0.86 A

3749 continuous *j*
noun action, improvement, variable, process, night, monitoring, quality, auditing, learning, stream, flow, use *misc* provide, enter, require, nearly, than, positive, rather
8624 | 0.76 F A

3750 govern *v*
noun rule., law, regulation., country, state, principle., policy, system, behavior, nation, .use, body, ability., .relationship, party *misc* .themselves, federal, .itself, .human, international, effectively, strict
7125 | 0.92 A

3751 crown *n*
adj triple, royal, British, Spanish, golden, English *noun* .prince, .jewel, .head, .height, .book, .thorn, hair, gold, .land, .winner *verb* wear., win., claim., place, capture., steal., kiss., resemble., .adorn, relinquish.
6976 | 0.94

3752 contractor *n*
adj independent, private, general, military, civilian, large, prime, federal, major, associated *noun* defense., government, building., construction, work, company, city, minority., business, labor *verb* hire, pay, .build, require, employ, .perform, .bid, .install, select., rely
7168 | 0.92 N

3753 adolescent *n*
adj young, American, early, sexual, high, old, African, social, Hispanic, Asian *noun* child., .adult, parent, study, behavior, group, family, school, problem, research *verb* .report, .experience, indicate, suggest, develop, .engage, compare, .participate, .perceive, examine
8849 | 0.74 A

3754 skirt *n*
adj short, long, black, full, pleated, blue, red, matching *noun* blouse, jacket, dress, woman., sweater, top, leg, shirt, silk, hem *verb* wear., pull, lift., smooth., hike, hide, .cover, gather, tug., billow
7451 | 0.88 F

3755 abuse *v*
noun child, woman, .power, .drug, priest, father, .alcohol, system, parent, kid, mother, girl, boy, prisoner, authority *misc* sexually., physically., neglect, verbally., emotionally
7045 | 0.93 S

3756 bacteria (PL) *n*
adj resistant, harmful, beneficial, fecal, common, deadly, pathogenic, intestinal, friendly, anaerobic *noun* virus, fungus, strain., water, growth, type., soil, plant, level, resistance *verb* cause, kill., produce, .grow, contain., .live, carry, allow, prevent, form
7584 | 0.86 M

3757 adoption *n*
adj international, open, widespread, private, transracial, available, foster, domestic, legal, gay *noun* child, .agency, baby, intercountry., law, .process, technology, program, policy, birth *verb* lead., place., consider, promote, facilitate., encourage., choose, finalize, prevent, state
7263 | 0.90 A

3758 intelligent *j*
noun design, life, man, woman, system, person, eye, being, way, decision, species, machine *misc* very, more, highly, most, enough, young, less
6862 | 0.95

3759 praise *v*
noun .God, president, .Lord, work, critic, .effort, teacher, leader, official., .performance, tester., .ability, .beauty, .skill, author *misc* widely., highly., lavishly, quick, publicly.
6852 | 0.96

3760 outer *j*
noun space, edge, layer, bank, wall, limit, world, cell, office, door, planet, shell *misc* inner, solar, remove, open, along, reach, tough, beyond
7103 | 0.92 M

3761 nearby *r*
live., stand., sit., another, park., somewhere., watch, hover., lie., wait, building., tree., town, lay
6991 | 0.94 F

3762 glance *n*
adj quick, backward, sidelong, sideways, furtive, single, cursory, nervous, brief, sharp *noun* .shoulder, .direction, exchange., .back, warning., surprise, viewer, .recognition, .pity *verb* give., cast., shoot., steal., appear, throw., sneak., catch., spare., risk.
7348 | 0.89 F

30. Phrasal verbs

Phrasal verbs present a problem for non-native speakers in English because these verbs are often so idiomatic. For example, in the following phrases the phrasal verb (bold) does not literally mean *out, up,* or *over*: *the play turned **out** well, I didn't make **up** the answer, they took **over** the city.* The following is a list of the 100 most frequent phrasal verbs in the Corpus of Contemporary American English.

Note that the part of speech tagger does not attempt to separate more literal and more figurative meanings (*he looked up the ladder / he looked up several words; she went on a boat / she went on and on*), and so the following frequencies include both types of meanings. Note also that these frequencies do not include separated phrasal verbs (pick it up, wake the children up). Finally, note that these are grouped by lemma, so *come back = come / comes / came / coming back,* etc.

Frequency	Phrasal verb	Frequency	Phrasal verb	Frequency	Phrasal verb
56638	go on	11233	be back	5489	come over
40285	come back	10733	wake up	5446	hold on
37168	come up	10698	look back	5274	line up
35719	go back	10328	go away	5254	hang on
33613	pick up	10038	take off	5251	go through
28067	find out	9841	carry out	5222	turn up
26705	come out	9092	look down	5214	pay off
26094	go out	8851	take up	5194	bring in
25268	grow up	8736	look out	5182	turn back
23949	point out	8266	take over	5156	hang up
23563	come in	8033	pull out	5039	put out
23284	turn out	7932	hold up	4998	break up
21711	set up	7619	move on	4992	lay out
19900	end up	7511	go in	4958	hang out
18558	give up	7458	catch up	4944	welcome back
18207	make up	7457	open up	4874	build up
17658	be about	7381	reach out	4853	start out
17375	sit down	7342	turn around	4822	slow down
17356	look up	7237	look around	4817	sit up
16116	come on	7056	take out	4792	get away
15388	get up	6846	go off	4719	move in
14697	take on	6693	put up	4513	look over
14609	go down	6378	set out	4481	pull up
14505	figure out	6376	break down	4472	walk away
14368	show up	5981	keep up	4413	call out
13668	get back	5915	bring up	4346	hold out
12733	come down	5891	check out	4193	cut off
12618	go up	5736	wind up	4164	take away
12600	get out	5690	clean up	4017	bring about
12559	stand up	5557	shut down	3981	come along
3952	run out	5491	go over	3826	sign up
3935	bring out	3901	stand out	3804	back up
11512	work out	3827	set off		

3763 grip n
adj firm, strong, tight, overhand, better, powerful, underhand _noun_ hand, arm, .power, death., edge., bar, iron., strength, finger, pistol. _verb_ come., get., lose., tighten, loosen., keep., release., hold, relax., break.
7104 | 0.92 F

3764 profound j
noun effect, change, impact, implication, sense, difference, influence, consequence, experience, question, loss, transformation _misc_ more, most, such, social, human, express, economic, undergo
6967 | 0.94 A

3765 trigger v
noun .reaction, .response, event, .memory, attack, change, war, alarm, action, .release, crisis, stress, explosion, process, death _misc_ likely., nuclear, immune, certain, automatically.
6987 | 0.94 M

3766 stuff v
noun pocket, mouth, hand, envelope, turkey, chicken, .face, bill, .cheese, food, clothes, tomato, rice, meat, ball _misc_ .into, .them, .inside, .under, .full, .themselves
7042 | 0.93 F

3767 uncertainty n
adj great, economic, political, scientific, future, strict, considerable, verbal _noun_ risk, .principle, fear, level., lot., condition., period., sense, situation, degree.
verb create, reduce., .surround, face, add., remain, cause, .exist, remove., express
7155 | 0.91 A

3768 driving j
noun force, range, rain, record, distance, school, tour, test, experience, condition, skill, habit _misc_ behind, drunk, drunken, keep, reckless, within, arrest, intoxicate
6834 | 0.95

3769 enthusiasm n
adj great, full, infectious, initial, contagious, youthful, renewed, unbridled, popular _noun_ energy, lack., student, lot., interest, level, excitement, project, passion _verb_ share., show., dampen., generate, lose., express., curb., greet., .wane, inspire
6781 | 0.96

3770 complexity n
adj great, increasing, social, human, cognitive, political, cultural, growing, increased, full _noun_ system, level., .life, issue, size., task, .relationship, diversity, depth, cost _verb_ understand., add., increase, reduce., reveal., recognize., capture., illustrate., .arise, ignore.
7279 | 0.90 A

3771 excuse n
adj good, lame, poor, perfect, convenient, sorry, valid, legitimate _noun_ explanation, .failure, sort., justification, abuse, list., .inaction _verb_ make., use., give., find., provide., .avoid, stop, accept., .ignore, invent.
6793 | 0.96

3772 cafe n
adj outdoor, grand, downtown, nearby, crowded, favorite, open-air _noun_ restaurant, street, .standard,

bar, sidewalk., table, Internet., coffee, owner, .society _verb_ sit, open, .serve, eat, own, drink, hang, line, enter., .host
7226 | 0.90 N

3773 survey v
noun student, .scene, study, area, .room, group, teacher, .damage, American., university., .landscape, analyst., land, field, researcher _misc_ .report, recently., .determine, .indicate, nearly, .regarding, conduct, briefly
6937 | 0.94 A

3774 virtual j
noun reality, world, community, tour, environment, space, monopoly, computer, network, technology, machine, library _misc_ create, become, real, unknown, actual, electronic, interactive, digital
7123 | 0.91

3775 undermine v
noun effort, .credibility, .authority, .confidence, system, .ability, policy, .support, .legitimacy, democracy, .stability, regime, attempt, .integrity, .claim _misc_ try., far., threaten., public, economic, seriously., .traditional, seek., tend., military, severely.
7174 | 0.91 A

3776 unity n
adj national, political, Christian, cultural, racial, visible, thematic _noun_ government, church, sense., party, diversity, organization., family, .purpose, peace, principle _verb_ maintain., achieve, promote., create., form., preserve., seek, depend, .prevail
7378 | 0.88 A

3777 chaos n
adj economic, total, political, social, complete, civil, utter, controlled _noun_ order, .theory, war, confusion, violence, anarchy, kind., midst., disorder _verb_ create., bring, cause, lead, .follow, .reign, descend., throw., result, .ensue
6748 | 0.96

3778 commonly r
most., .use, more., .used, .call, .find, .refer, .associate, .hold, .report
7287 | 0.89 A

3779 endless j
noun possibility, stream, hour, supply, series, list, cycle, line, variety, war, summer, number _misc_ seemingly, seem, almost, spend, blue, gray, virtually
6845 | 0.95

3780 rhetoric n
adj political, classical, inflammatory, harsh, nationalist, religious, empty, common, fiery, official _noun_ kind., campaign, .reality, war, action, lot., policy, art, politics, gap. _verb_ use, .suggest, match, employ, .surround, .sound, avoid, soften., .emphasize, combine
7284 | 0.89 A

3781 trait n
adj common, certain, positive, human, cultural, genetic, personal, different, specific, desirable _noun_ personality., .anxiety, character., gene, measure, value, scale, behavior, individual, plant _verb_ share, associate, possess., exhibit., identify, inherit, develop, pass, define, reflect
7450 | 0.87 A

3782 pension n
adj private, public, traditional, corporate, old-age, monthly, annual *noun* .fund, .plan, .benefit, .system, company, employee., security, state., health, insurance *verb* receive., pay, provide, offer, collect., increase, reduce, qualify., guarantee, grant
7254 | 0.90 N

3783 genuine j
noun concern, interest, article, love, feeling, desire, smile, sense, effort, hero, peace, fear *misc* seem, real, than, rather, reflect, moral, religious, Christian
6835 | 0.95

3784 sweat n
adj cold, stale, light, clammy, nervous, dried, honest *noun* face, .forehead, bead., .brow, night., shirt, blood, body, .eye, smell. *verb* break, wipe., feel, .run, drip, work., soak., drench., glisten, .pour
7281 | 0.89 F

3785 European n
adj eastern, western, southern, northern, contemporary, classic *noun* American, Japanese, African, century, Indian, arrival., contact. *verb* .arrive, become, bring, .begin, agree, dominate, encounter, meet, favor, regard
7167 | 0.91 A

3786 innovation n
adj technological, technical, recent, major, late, scientific, educational, successful, radical, medical *noun* technology, product, policy, creativity, research, market, change, industry, invention, competition *verb* encourage., lead, promote., stifle., foster., .occur, .improve, spur., discourage., finance.
7373 | 0.88 A

3787 no d
(no matter what) there., .one, .idea, .reason, .question, .matter, .what, need, .evidence, .doubt, oh., .know, .difference, .sign
6761 | 0.96

3788 matter d
(no matter what) no., .what, .happen, .kind, .age, .else, .cost, love., .choose, .type, .circumstance, .size, .weather, anyone
6761 | 0.96

3789 currency n
adj hard, foreign, common, single, European, local, national, convertible *noun* market, dollar, US, exchange, value, rate, .crisis, devaluation, comptroller., bank *verb* gain., devalue, issue, stabilize., earn, convert., introduce, float, .appreciate, circulate
7385 | 0.88

3790 forty m
.year, .percent, about., .ago, than., more, .minute, over., thirty., .mile, after, .foot, .later, .thousand
7094 | 0.91 F

3791 lobby n
adj powerful, main, sub, front, environmental, empty, Israeli *noun* hotel, building, gun., door, group, elevator, floor, business., bank, tobacco. *verb* walk., enter, wait, sit., stand, cross., fill, hang., .oppose, block
7036 | 0.92 F

3792 theoretical j
noun framework, model, perspective, approach, study, work, physics, research, basis, foundation, analysis, issue *misc* practical, empirical, provide, develop, base, both, methodological, within
7830 | 0.83 A

3793 bat n
adj brown, wooden, corked, rabid, broken, autographed, potent *noun* baseball., ball, .house, .boy, aluminum., wing, vampire., fruit., crack., .mitzvah *verb* swing., hit, .fly, hold., pick., grab., carry, break, drop, .swoop
6993 | 0.92

3794 makeup n
adj ethnic, genetic, racial, heavy, chemical, psychological, physical *noun* .artist, hair, eye, face, clothes, skin, mirror, .bag, costume, jewelry *verb* wear., put., apply, change, remove., touch, reflect., smear, alter, blend
7134 | 0.91 M

3795 pleasant j
noun surprise, place, experience, voice, day, road, face, way, memory, thing, man, valley *misc* very, more, enough, less, unpleasant, quite, rather, particularly
6903 | 0.94 F

3796 rebuild v
noun .life, .country, city, house, home, .infrastructure, community, effort, .economy, system *misc* help., .after, try., plan., repair, .shattered, completely., quickly
6890 | 0.94

3797 horrible j
noun thing, crime, death, way, story, tragedy, day, place, situation, mistake, experience, feeling *misc* happen, something, feel, most, die, commit, absolutely, terrible
6918 | 0.93 S

3798 pad n
adj legal, yellow, sleeping, concrete, thick, soft, blank *noun* launch., shoulder., launching., .paper, note., brake., sketch. *verb* write, put, wear, scribble., place, replace., attach, touch, adjust, hand.
7287 | 0.89 M

3799 suspend v
noun .game, license, school, year, .air, .ceiling, .pay, .water, .operation, .week, player, .disbelief, season, law, decision. *misc* .from, .above, .between, temporarily., .without, .indefinitely
6738 | 0.96

3800 relieve v
noun .pain, .pressure, .stress, .symptom, .tension, .burden, .duty, .suffering, .congestion, .anxiety, .traffic, .depression, .boredom, muscle, surgery. *misc* help., .finally, greatly., secretly., clearly.
6834 | 0.94

3801 resume v
noun talk, .work, negotiation, .career, play, .activity, search, operation, conversation, flight, .seat, trial., production, class, .position *misc* .normal, .today, later, expect., .nuclear, ready., .native, return.
6794 | 0.95

3802 respectively *r*
percent., female, per., .indicate, .compare, .thus, minute.
7573 | 0.85 A

3803 promotion *n*
adj social, special, aggressive, active, on-air, rapid, overall, continued *noun* health., tenure, advertising., .program, marketing, sales, opportunity, trade, prevention, democracy *verb* pass., deny., offer, receive., end, earn., gain., deserve, aim, .merit
6919 | 0.93 A

3804 technological *j*
noun change, advance, innovation, development, progress, literacy, advancement, breakthrough, revolution, world, society, improvement
misc economic, scientific, social, rapid, such, modern, major, financial
7245 | 0.89 A

3805 galaxy *n*
adj spiral, distant, elliptical, nearby, small, bright, active, entire, individual, brightest *noun* star, cluster, center, distance, formation, dwarf., group, disk, arm, core *verb* form, .appear, .lie, contain, observe, study, discover, collide, photograph, exist
10456 | 0.61 M

3806 altogether *r*
different, stop., avoid., another., out., something., eliminate., disappear., abandon., lose., ignore., else., drop., miss.
6696 | 0.96

3807 apologize *v*
noun need., mistake, .remark, letter, statement, .advance, .slavery, .delay, Japan, sir, pope., minister., ABC., gentleman, .sin *misc* .for, I, shall., later., again, publicly, .profusely
6822 | 0.94

3808 research *v*
noun .book, student., .issue, .history, .topic, .article, information, .subject, .effect, approach, .scientist., role, organization, technology, outcome. *misc* .write, thoroughly, carefully., .indicate, extensively, teach, meticulously., study
6904 | 0.93 A

3809 infrastructure *n*
adj public, economic, social, critical, national, basic, necessary, physical *noun* investment, development, .project, country, transportation., education, information., improvement, water, service *verb* build., need, provide, rebuild., support, destroy, create, develop, improve., maintain
7085 | 0.91 A

3810 shuttle *n*
adj free, regular, flying, future, electric, interplanetary, complimentary *noun* space., .bus, .mission, .flight, .service, .discovery, launch, astronaut, .program, crew *verb* fly, return, land, ride, catch., board., .dock, .explode, arrive, operate
7089 | 0.91

3811 thumb *n*
adj right, left, green, sore, opposable, broken, greasy *noun* rule., finger, .forefinger, index, hand, nose, .mouth, .shoulder, .drive, .print *verb* give., suck, hold, press, put., jerk., stick, rub, hook, run.
6991 | 0.92 F

3812 questionnaire *n*
adj demographic, completed, self-report, self-administered, detailed, original, usable, annual, individual, specific *noun* item, participant, student, response, survey, data, study, question, result, information *verb* complete., use, administer, return, ask, fill., include, develop, send, .assess
8346 | 0.77 A

3813 sidewalk *n*
adj crowded, empty, narrow, concrete, front, cracked, busy, opposite *noun* street, .cafe, city, crack, table, step, park, brick, square, vendor *verb* walk, stand., sit., line, pass, stroll., reach
7080 | 0.91 F

3814 businessman *n*
adj successful, wealthy, small, local, prominent, foreign, retired, private, shrewd, western *noun* politician, group., lawyer, Republican, leader, banker, doctor, millionaire., billionaire., worker *verb* .name, own, .travel, .invest, pose., supply, .fear, .complain, murder, kidnap
6832 | 0.94

3815 weird *j*
noun thing, way, stuff, guy, sort, kid, feeling, place, idea, sound, noise, science *misc* really, feel, something, too, little, kind
6912 | 0.93 F

3816 radiation *n*
adj solar, ultraviolet, infrared, cosmic, electromagnetic, nuclear, intense, gravitational *noun* .therapy, chemotherapy, .treatment, dose, exposure, background., level *verb* emit, cause, expose., absorb, detect, receive, undergo., produce, treat, .reach
7376 | 0.87 M

3817 format *n*
adj digital, traditional, large, standard, packed, instructional, similar, electronic, binary, current *noun* file., response., data, video, group, item, lecture., presentation, interview., content *verb* follow, change, present, .allow, offer, choose, .require, support, adopt, save
7301 | 0.88 A

3818 scare *v*
noun .people, .death, .me, kid, .daylight, .investor, .bird, .bit, .voter, gun., .fish, noise., daddy, anger., mask. *misc* .out, .him, .away, try., really., little, enough
  off investor, .potential, enough., .foreign, .bird, .predator
6825 | 0.94 F

3819 bounce *v*
noun ball, check, head, light., floor, bed, car, .idea, road, ground, seat, rock, basketball, signal, knee *misc* .around, .along, .against, .across, hit
  back .from, after, try., .quickly, always., ability., stock., market., economy., .strong **off** .wall, light., ball., object
6878 | 0.93 F

3820 doll *n*
adj little, tiny, wooden, favorite, beautiful, broken, living, rubber, sleeping *noun* rag., baby., .house, girl, paper., head, plastic., porcelain, hair *verb* play., hold, dress, buy., throw, clutch., stare, lay, dance, resemble
6912 | 0.93 F

3821 attraction *n*
adj main, sexual, big, popular, fatal, major, same-sex, physical, mutual, gravitational *noun* tourist., park, star., roadside., area, sex, visitor, vector., repulsion, restaurant *verb* become., include, offer, must-see., explain., .draw, feature, acknowledge., express., diminish
6800 | 0.94

3822 needle *n*
adj hypodermic, clean, fine, sharp, tiny, thin, used, dead, safer, dry *noun* pine., pin., .arm., .exchange, eye, .haystack, thread, .stick, .program, .aspiration *verb* use, insert, inject, place, drop, pull, pierce, jab, pass, sew
6889 | 0.93 F

3823 Israeli *n*
noun Palestinian, Arab, attack., American, violence., majority., thousand. *verb* say, kill, believe, .live, .withdraw, continue, .pull
7287 | 0.88 S

3824 lock *n*
adj dark, curly, remote-control, electronic, remote, double, outer, virtual, stray, biometric *noun* door, key, .hair, eye, trigger., .stock, air., safety., .box, .step *verb* open, change, turn, pick, break, check., click, push, close, release
6996 | 0.91 F

3825 counterpart *n*
adj male, American, white, European, female, young, western, democratic, likely, Russian *noun* Republican, Senate, .finding, contrast, adult., TV, coast., negotiating., antimatter., marketing. *verb* compare., meet., differ., outnumber., resemble., outperform., .engage, possess, emulate.
6977 | 0.92 A

3826 convey *v*
noun message, .sense, information, .idea, .impression, .meaning, image, word, .feeling, emotion, language, painting., ability., experience, value *misc* try., intend., manage., clearly, seek., effectively, order., accurately
6948 | 0.92 A

3827 compensation *n*
adj financial, just, deferred, monetary, fair, adequate *noun* worker., executive, .committee, system, .package, unemployment., victim, insurance, .benefit, employee *verb* receive., pay, provide, offer, seek., include, require, demand., increase, accept.
7087 | 0.90 N

3828 ship *v*
noun company, product, good, box, order, oil, food, material, weapon, .north, computer, month, truck, arm, .customer *misc* .back, .overseas, million, before., .across, .directly, ready., .abroad
   out before., .Iraq, about, .again, soon, soldier.
   off before., .war, .camp
6799 | 0.94 M

3829 exclusive *j*
noun interview, right, club, use, zone, contract, access, look, domain, report, focus, control *misc* mutually, most, tonight, economic, private, grant, no
6770 | 0.94

3830 twist *v*
noun arm, face, head, hand, mouth., body, hair, neck, .ankle, lip, side, back, .seat, .knob, smile *misc* his, her, .into, .around, turn, off, .together
   up face, back, .inside
7155 | 0.89 F

3831 precise *j*
noun moment, measurement, location, definition, nature, number, detail, control, meaning, word, information, movement *misc* more, very, provide, require, determine, less, although, allow
6767 | 0.94 A

3832 suspicion *n*
adj reasonable, deep, mutual, strong, growing, sneaking, clinical *noun* fear, cloud., hostility, umbrella., index., .murder, distrust, mistrust, evidence, hatred *verb* confirm, raise., arouse., view., fall, regard., report., arrest., cast., avoid.
6615 | 0.96

3833 southeast *n*
adj rural, tropical, sprawling, maritime, booming, extreme, humid *noun* country, .nation, state, .corner, region, city, center, .coast *verb* locate., lie., head., travel., miss., spread., import.
7034 | 0.91

3834 walking *n*
adj easy, brisk, comfortable, normal, guided, fast, continued, level *noun* .stick, .tour, .shoe, exercise, activity., street, .program, .distance, .speed, mile *verb* keep., start., stop., continue., begin, resume., enjoy, pace, practice.
7156 | 0.89

3835 boost *v*
noun .sales, .economy, price, .production, rate, .profit, company, .morale, .energy, .confidence, .performance, .earnings, .revenue, .productivity, .self-esteem *misc* .your, help., .immune, significantly., dramatically, substantially, greatly.
7137 | 0.89 M N

3836 scatter *v*
noun ash, light, .country, ground, wind, piece, room, seed, table, paper, tree, electron, body, field, dust *misc* .across, .around, .over, .throughout, .through, .about
6916 | 0.92 F

3837 rebel *n*
adj military, armed, Iraqi, Islamic, Russian, Shiite, separatist, main, suspected, Marxist *noun* .group, .leader, force, army, troop, soldier, .movement, war, .commander *verb* fight, kill, support., attack, lead, control, claim, capture, join, drive
7081 | 0.90 N

3838 van *n*
adj white, moving, 15-passenger, mobile, yellow, unmarked, Chevy, rented, postal *noun* back., .horn, car, police, news, truck, bus, pool, delivery., pickup *verb* drive, .pull, .park, buy, climb, ride, fill, rent, hit, .pick
6727 | 0.94 F

3839 identical *j*
noun twin, transcription, house, pair, result, set, item, pattern, form, copy, condition, gene *misc* almost, nearly, two, virtually, those, one, original, each
6764 | 0.94 A

3840 shame *n*
adj real, sexual, damn, menstrual, deep, terrible, dirty, secret, awful *noun* guilt, sense., feeling., fear, body, embarrassment, head., anger, crying. *verb* feel, bring., burn, fill, hide, experience., suffer., .accompany, .belong
6737 | 0.94 F

3841 blow *n*
adj big, final, devastating, serious, fatal, major, low, severe, crushing *noun* body., death., hammer., .dryer, knockout., sand., .hole, sound. *verb* deal., strike., deliver., soften., suffer., land, receive
6718 | 0.94 F

3842 delicate *j*
noun balance, hand, skin, situation, flower, feature, act, balancing, finger, face, issue, task *misc* very, between, most, small, white, thin, pink, extremely
6755 | 0.94 F

3843 Olympics (PL) *n*
adj special, junior, previous, modern, consecutive, senior, future *noun* winter., summer., year, gold, month, coverage, .committee *verb* compete., host., watch., qualify., participate., train., attend., prompt, .boost
7286 | 0.87 N

3844 wider *j*
noun range, audience, world, community, variety, context, society, door, part, war, eye, foot *misc* than, much, open, grow, social, slightly, little
6757 | 0.94 A

3845 corruption *n*
adj political, public, rampant, widespread, military, economic, official, corporate *noun* government, charge, .scandal, police, crime, allegation, investigation, case, mismanagement, violence *verb* fight., expose., investigate., accuse., involve, root., end., face., .threaten, undermine
6909 | 0.92

3846 hook *n*
adj left, red, right, grappling, treble, single, baited, barbless *noun* line, fish, phone., .sinker, coat., meat., metal., dough., .back, .shot *verb* let., hang, set, ring., bait, catch, attach, remove, dangle, push
6806 | 0.93 M

3847 lieutenant *n*
adj young, top, retired, marine, French, chief, senior *noun* .governor, .colonel, .general, .commander, army, police., force., officer, .dial *verb* promote., command, commission., order, .shout, .assign, inform, appoint., photograph.
6872 | 0.92 F

3848 firmly *r*
.believe, .establish, hand, place, hold, .pack, plant, .brown, root, press, keep., .against
6660 | 0.95

3849 structural *j*
noun adjustment, change, problem, reform, program, damage, model, analysis, integrity, engineer, equation, element *misc* economic, major, such, social, functional, cultural, address, basic
7361 | 0.86 A

3850 pause *n*
adj long, brief, awkward, short, slight, dramatic, pregnant *noun* moment, .button, second, floor., voice, breath, silence, bombing, thought *verb* give., add, let, continue, hit., answer, press, reply, punctuate., sense
7607 | 0.83 F

3851 invisible *j*
noun hand, man, eye, line, force, wall, air, barrier, presence, spirit, enemy, object *misc* almost, become, nearly, visible, remain, render, virtually
6789 | 0.93 F

3852 forehead *n*
adj high, broad, damp, pale, smooth, wide, sweaty *noun* hand, hair., sweat., eye, cheek, nose, face, line, lip, glass *verb* kiss., wipe., touch, rub., press, fall., wrinkle, lean., crease, place.
7353 | 0.86 F

3853 traveler *n*
adj fellow, frequent, international, foreign, weary, European, registered, seasoned, experienced, popular *noun* business., time., world, .check, air., thousand., space., hotel *verb* offer, .arrive, cater., .visit, fly, attract., .seek, lure., .cross, aim.
6803 | 0.93 N

3854 meaningful *j*
noun way, life, relationship, experience, work, change, learning, activity, reform, information, role, difference *misc* more, any, provide, most, something, between, create, social
7008 | 0.90 A

3855 provided *c*
(provided that) .information, .support, .opportunity, .data, study., service, .evidence, teacher, .insight, .basis, .enough, .additional, model, .protection
6905 | 0.91 A

3856 colony *n*
adj British, American, French, penal, Portuguese, European, whole, southern, original, lost *noun* artist., ant, bee, art., space., crown., .ship, population, leper. *verb* establish, form, found, settle, arrive., destroy, declare, defend., .revert, .persist
7049 | 0.89 A

3857 signature *n*
adj key, digital, unique, chemical, valid, electronic, distinctive, characteristic *noun* .style, .member, .line, .dish, .song, .piece, .issue, .hole, .tune *verb* collect., become., gather., require, forge., bear., carry., sign, match, verify
6673 | 0.94

3858 database *n*
adj national, relational, online, searchable, computerized, conceptual, central, medical, various *noun* information, computer., system, data, software, search, program, .management, record, application *verb* use, create, include, .contain, provide, maintain, develop, build., store, enter.
7449 | 0.84 A

3859 clerk *n*
adj chief, postal, female, friendly, convenience-store, front-desk, junior *noun* law., store., desk., court, office, sales., county. *verb* ask, hire, hand, stare, nod, employ, wave, inform, ring, .reply
6852 | 0.92 F

3860 dedicate *v*
noun .life, book, memorial, art, .memory, resource, service, education, career, park, song, project, monument, hour, page *misc* nonprofit., .solely, exclusively, .fight, totally.
6606 | 0.95

3861 determination *n*
adj final, grim, dogged, fierce, sheer, accurate, preliminary, initial *noun* courage., court, eligibility., strength., sex, self., will, energy, factor, drive.
verb make, require, allow., demonstrate., .succeed, reflect., involve, express., .prove
6762 | 0.93 A

3862 signal *v*
noun .end, .change, .beginning, .shift, presence, .start, .willingness, .arrival, cell, light., .return, .interest, administration, bell., event. *misc* clearly., usually., intend, .potential, .fundamental
6566 | 0.96

3863 anxious *j*
noun parent, face, moment, eye, mother, voice, patient, look, glance, individual, thought, subject *misc* about, get, feel, more, very, depressed, become, seem
6553 | 0.96

3864 sum *n*
adj large, huge, small, substantial, undisclosed, considerable, total, individual, equal, tidy
noun .money, lump., .part, score, payment, dollar, .square, .rule, item, tax *verb* pay, spend, invest, receive, raise., offer, divide, earn., exceed, average
6713 | 0.93 A

3865 frozen *j*
noun yogurt, food, pea, lake, dinner, corn, water, vegetable, ground, fruit, river, pizza *misc* fresh, thaw, cup, stand, across, canned, chopped, solid
6791 | 0.92 M

3866 juror *n*
adj potential, prospective, grand, black, unidentified, white, criminal, female, dismissed, ideal *noun* case, trial, question, jury, court, number, defense, evidence, mind, witness *verb* tell, .hear, believe, .decide, dismiss, convince., serve, allow, .convict., .agree
7181 | 0.87 S

3867 timing *n*
adj bad, perfect, right, critical, sexual, precise, static, impeccable, exact, comic *noun* .analysis, question., sense., .device, market., matter., .closure, .event, condition, .belt *verb* determine., affect, depend, control., vary, adjust, improve, .coincide, ensure, .favor
6817 | 0.92

3868 punish *v*
noun God., law, crime, criminal, offender, parent, .death, act, perpetrator, .enemy, individual, voter., violation, authority., .mistake *misc* severely, reward, deserve, responsible, harshly, refuse, unfairly.
6532 | 0.96

3869 crawl *v*
noun .bed, hand, knee, skin, car, door, wall, ground, baby., foot, ant., belly, leg, body, cover *misc* .into, .out, .through, .over, .under, .back, .inside, .away
up .leg, .back, .onto
7005 | 0.89 F

3870 conscious *j*
noun decision, effort, mind, choice, thought, awareness, experience, level, state, health, attempt, memory *misc* make, more, become, very, unconscious, socially, environmentally, without
6674 | 0.94 A

3871 colonel *n*
adj retired, marine, full, commanding, imaginary, reserve *noun* lieutenant., army, force., air, general, commander, officer., sir, rank, command *verb* thank, promote., order, interview, .assign, salute., brief, appoint.
6934 | 0.90 F

3872 fitness *n*
adj physical, aerobic, health-related, personal, cardiovascular, mental, overall, cardiorespiratory
noun health., level, .center, activity, sport, .program, .test *verb* improve., teach, maintain., promote., develop., achieve., increase, measure, decrease
8530 | 0.73 M A

3873 landing *n*
adj soft, commercial, amphibious, total, hard, safe, lunar, annual, main, perfect *noun* .site, .gear, .area, moon., .zone, .craft, .strip *verb* reach., decline, survive., abort., .average, clear, exceed, glide., stick., approach.
7120 | 0.88

3874 doctrine *n*
adj Christian, religious, military, Catholic, legal, comprehensive, moral, traditional, modern
noun church, trust., .faith, congregation., scheme., court, war, power, .creation, .practice *verb* apply, teach, base, develop, argue, preach, reject., violate., maintain, impose
7567 | 0.83 A

3875 belly *n*
adj bad, big, full, flat, round, swollen, pregnant, soft, huge *noun* .button, hand., fire., breast, .dancer, fat, chest, leg, pot., pork. *verb* fill, rub., laugh, crawl, .swell, lie., pat., scratch, touch, rise
7073 | 0.88 F

3876 pope *n*
adj new, Catholic, Polish, present, holy, spiritual, frail, secular, beloved *noun* visit, church, bishop, death, century., body, holiness., king *verb* meet, elect, choose, .issue, celebrate, condemn, .declare, name, attend., greet
7007 | 0.89

3877 thereby *r*
.reduce, .increase, .create, .provide, .allow, .avoid, .eliminate, .prevent, .enhance, .increasing
7132 | 0.88 A

3878 historically *r*
.black, .college, .significant, .accurate, .low, important, .specific, institution, culturally, rate, culture, .contingent, .associate, .correct
6804 | 0.92 A

3879 playoff *n*
adj divisional, final, consecutive, straight, sudden-death, past, home-field, wild, semifinal, memorable
noun .game, team, season, .spot, .series, .victory, .loss, state., .appearance, .race *verb* make., win, miss., lose, play, reach., clinch., force., end, finish
7898 | 0.79 N

31. Word length (Zipf's Law)

Zipf's Law refers to the natural tendency for common words in the language (e.g. *time, get, good*) to be shorter than less common words (e.g. *reverberation, industrialize, mechanistic*). The following table shows this to hold true for our data from the Corpus of Contemporary American English. For example, there are about 77.5 million tokens (occurrences) in the 385+ million word corpus that have three letters. This decreases to about 20 million tokens for eight-letter words, and just about 0.7 million tokens for 17-letter words. The table also lists the number of distinct word forms ("types") and the most common words for each word length.

No. of Letters	Types	Tokens	Most frequent types
1	26	13,425,201	a, I, p, s
2	604	60,443,376	of, to, in, it
3	5487	77,556,336	the, and, for, you
4	9317	63,720,951	that, with, this, they
5	15822	41,692,974	there, their, about, would
6	21672	31,143,865	people, before, should, little
7	23851	28,254,505	because, through, between, another
8	22100	19,554,520	children, American, students, national
9	18896	13,731,570	something, president, different, political
10	15177	9,032,758	government, university, Washington, everything
11	11427	5,032,380	information, development, significant, performance
12	8262	2,730,687	relationship, particularly, organization, professional
13	5981	1,591,947	international, environmental, understanding, organizations
14	3897	685,142	administration, responsibility, transportation, representative
15	2580	276,937	characteristics, representatives, recommendations, interpretations
16	1645	124,206	African-American, responsibilities, unconstitutional, state-of-the-art

3880 poster *n*
adj wanted, large, framed, missing, huge, colorful, giant, official, promotional *noun* .child, .boy, wall, movie., .board, campaign, .girl, book, film, image *verb* hang, put, read, plaster, cover, .advertise, create, display, feature, decorate
6511 | 0.96

3881 harder *r*
.than, work., make., get, try., even., little., much., become., hit., lot., push.
6520 | 0.96

3882 acquisition *n*
adj recent, proposed, initial, safe, original, territorial, aggressive *noun* merger., skill, data., knowledge, land, language., system *verb* complete., grow, finance., involve, facilitate., focus., promote., expand, enhance, pursue.
6927 | 0.90 A

3883 rescue *v*
noun effort, helicopter, police, force, guard, firefighter, plan, son, baby, officer *misc* .from, try., attempt., wait., .trap, eventually, safely.
6508 | 0.96

3884 departure *n*
adj radical, early, significant, major, abrupt, imminent, sudden, dramatic, daily *noun* point., arrival, date, .gate, minute., month, flight, hour., .board, .lounge *verb* represent., mark., announce., follow., delay., signal., prepare., near
6537 | 0.95

3885 summary *n*
adj brief, following, detailed, excellent, quick, one-page, fair *noun* news, table., .judgment, right., detail., .result, conclusion, report, study, .finding *verb* provide, follow., present, include, offer., contain., prepare., .analyze
7696 | 0.81 A

3886 wrong *r*
go., do., what., something., can., thing., if., how, anything., nothing., everything., when., prove., case
6502 | 0.96

3887 medium *j*
noun heat, onion, bowl, skillet, saucepan, speed, pan, garlic, tomato, carrot, height, potato *misc* add, until, large, over, cook, stir, chop
7601 | 0.82 M

3888 chronic *j*
noun disease, pain, illness, condition, fatigue, problem, patient, syndrome, health, infection, stress, treatment *misc* suffer, acute, such, cause, treat, medical, obstructive, pulmonary
7390 | 0.84 A

3889 evil *j*
noun spirit, man, empire, eye, people, thing, force, person, act, scientist, twin, power *misc* good, off, inherently, truly, intrinsically, dead, Soviet
6545 | 0.95

3890 handsome *j*
noun man, face, woman, boy, guy, feature, prince, building, son, hair, husband, couple *misc* young, very, tall, strong, dark, rich, charming, quite
6878 | 0.90 F

3891 finish *n*
adj best, second-place, third-place, strong, smooth, predicted, fourth-place, top, original, fifth-place *noun* .line, start., race, matte., photo., point, season, place, surface., color *verb* let., cross., apply, paint, reach., fight.
6801 | 0.91 M N

3892 hug *v*
noun arm, mother, .knee, father, mom, body, .tree, girl, .ground, .wall, boy, .wife .coast, baby, dad *misc* .her, .him, she, .me, kiss, .other, .each, around, .tightly, hold, .hard
6873 | 0.90 F

3893 wow *u*
oh., really, yeah, bow., OK, yes, .thank
7202 | 0.86 S

3894 pursuit *n*
adj hot, trivial, relentless, intellectual, academic, individual, active, common, aggressive, single-minded *noun* .happiness, liberty, .truth, goal, .knowledge, .justice, leisure., .excellence, team, .pleasure *verb* continue., follow, engage., abandon., encourage., facilitate., devote., justify.
6566 | 0.94 A

3895 residence *n*
adj private, permanent, primary, official, current, principal, temporary, legal *noun* .hall, place., age., year, ambassador, artist., home, length., location, occupation. *verb* take., enter, maintain., establish., occupy, secure, search., grant., .resemble
6620 | 0.94

3896 loud *r*
out., laugh., so., .enough, too., .clear, hear, as., read., cry., voice, very., talk., music
6843 | 0.90 F

3897 promising *j*
noun result, research, future, approach, career, technology, drug, area, treatment, student, development, sign *misc* most, look, new, more, young, seem, several, appear
6502 | 0.95

3898 disk *n*
adj hard, floppy, compact, herniated, solar, optical, flat *noun* .drive, computer., .space, accretion., file, galaxy, data, .jockey, plastic, surface *verb* form, surround, appear, .contain, store, save., remove, rotate, spin, flatten.
7589 | 0.82 M

3899 doorway *n*
adj open, arched, dark, narrow, empty, front, lighted *noun* room, kitchen, bedroom, window, office, hall, step., bathroom, parlor *verb* stand., appear., watch, stop, walk, lean., .lead, pause., fill
7307 | 0.85 F

3900 diagnosis *n*
adj differential, early, medical, clinical, psychiatric, accurate, initial, definitive, correct *noun* .treatment, cancer, year., patient, disorder, disease, doctor, symptom, age., depression *verb* make, confirm, receive., .base, include, establish, support, accept., obtain, vary
7764 | 0.8 A

3901 scout *n*
adj pro, local, chief, longtime, veteran, lunar, experienced *noun* boy., girl., .troop, eagle., life., .leader, talent. *verb* earn, join, send, .prepare, attend, impress., sue, hire, .ride, recruit
7955 | 0.78 M

3902 cancel *v*
noun flight, .trip, .plan, show, .contract, .order, .appointment, .subscription, service, airline., official, tour, month, concert, performance *misc* after, last, .each, .other, force., delay., decide., threaten., abruptly.
6479 | 0.95

3903 desire *v*
noun information, result, outcome, weight, goal, top, mixture, peace, seed, minute, privacy, unity, reduction, happiness, .grace *misc* leave., whatever., place, .immediately, additional, fresh, truly., sexual
6807 | 0.91 A

3904 amid *i*
stand., .chaos, set., .report, sit., .concern, .growing, resign., .tree, .allegation, .charge, .controversy, .economic, .crowd
6579 | 0.94 N

3905 envelope *n*
adj stamped, self-addressed, white, sealed, brown, thick, outer, business-size *noun* manila., hand, letter, return, back, paper, .pocket, stamp, address, coin. *verb* push., open., .contain, put, send, pull, hold, seal, pick, place
6673 | 0.93 F

3906 sooner *r*
.later, .than, no., .rather, come., much., .better, happen., start, die, expect, lot., maybe, .expected
6437 | 0.96

3907 beam *n*
adj high, wooden, narrow, exposed, low, main, single, powerful, heavy, x-ray *noun* laser., .light, flashlight, electron., ceiling, steel., balance. *verb* use, focus, shine, sweep, .hit, shoot, support, direct, send, produce
7196 | 0.85 F

3908 reluctant *j*
noun official, leader, witness, reader, warrior, hero, decision, smile, acquiescence *misc* very, may, seem, talk, leave, often, accept
6377 | 0.96

3909 spouse *n*
adj male, surviving, military, married, future, supportive, innocent, trailing, working *noun* child, family, parent, friend, partner, .abuse, death, wife *verb* .die, cheat, support, marry, indicate, .earn, care., divorce, interview, .participate
6893 | 0.89

3910 fluid *n*
adj light, amniotic, cerebrospinal, spinal, hydraulic, clear, excess, seminal *noun* body, flow, .dynamics, blood, .motion, .mechanic, heat, movement, pressure, transfer *verb* drink., fill, drain, cause, leak, replace, pump, produce, collect, .drip
6940 | 0.88 A

3911 exit *n*
adj quick, final, rear, graceful, nearest, hasty, main *noun* .poll, .strategy, door, .sign, .ramp, transform., emergency. *verb* head., block, pass, miss., mark, close, rush, race.
6694 | 0.92 F

3912 mild *j*
noun winter, form, drug, climate, expression, case, weather, flavor, depression, symptom, effect, cheese *misc* relatively, severe, suffer, such, moderate, sweet, cause, range
6610 | 0.93 M

3913 electrical *j*
noun power, engineer, system, engineering, stimulation, outlet, equipment, wire, activity, signal, charge, energy *misc* mechanical, current, cause, produce, generate, electronic, convert, generating
6739 | 0.91

3914 bite *n*
adj big, quick, huge, single, tiny, firm, sharp, extra *noun* sound., mosquito., .mark, dog, insect., .apple, .sandwich, .food, tax., snake. *verb* take., eat, grab., chew, savor., swallow., cause, treat.
6507 | 0.94 F

3915 bath *n*
adj hot, private, warm, public, Turkish, shared, boiling-water, ritual *noun* bedroom., water, room, bed, bubble., master., kitchen, shower, .towel, tub *verb* take., give., run, draw., soak, share, feature, relax, .smell, emerge.
6647 | 0.92

3916 decent *j*
noun people, man, job, life, living, guy, wage, society, person, housing, being, chance *misc* good, pretty, human, live, honest, fairly, enough, earn
6389 | 0.96

3917 ankle *n*
adj right, sprained, left, broken, sore, twisted, thick, injured, thin, weak *noun* knee, foot, .injury, leg, wrist, heel, boot, .sprain, .support, weight *verb* break., cross, grab., twist., .swell, wear, fall, suffer, reach., hurt
6810 | 0.90 F

3918 transaction *n*
adj financial, commercial, real, international, economic, involved, electronic, foreign, residential, certain *noun* .cost, business., .processing, company, .place, estate., volume, credit., fee, money *verb* .involve, process, complete, handle., conduct, .occur, report, account, relate, result
6996 | 0.88 A

3919 reporting *n*
adj financial, investigative, additional, international, mandatory, national, fair, environmental *noun* .requirement, credit., news, .system, law, .agency, abuse, .period, data, media *verb* require, base, establish, affect., improve., account, appreciate., facilitate., .disclose
6773 | 0.90

3920 exhibit *n*
adj new, interactive, permanent, special, traveling, popular, educational, main, retrospective *noun* museum, art, .hall, visitor, gallery, space, display, photo, artist, .area *verb* include, feature, open, present, offer, organize, visit, view, explore, .focus
6734 | 0.91

3921 pit *n*
adj open, bottomless, deep, huge, shallow, dark, well *noun* .bull, .stomach, fire., .stop, .crew, gravel., orchestra., mosh. *verb* dig, remove, form, drop, line, dump, spit, escape.
6523 | 0.94 F

3922 practically *r*
.every, .speak, .nothing, .impossible, .everyone, .everything, .anything, .only, .whole, .nonexistent, .beg, .everybody, .entire
6357 | 0.96

3923 oxygen *n*
adj low, dissolved, liquid, pure, maximal, molecular, supplemental *noun* water, level, .mask, .tank, blood, carbon, hydrogen, .atom, air, nitrogen *verb* need, carry., breathe, produce, combine, provide, cause, deliver., form, burn
6582 | 0.93

3924 racism *n*
adj white, institutional, American, black, environmental, blatant, overt, institutionalized *noun* sexism, .discrimination, poverty, issue, charge., form., race., prejudice, anti-semitism, society *verb* .exist, fight., accuse., deal., combat., confront., end., equate., .permeate, .persist
6651 | 0.92

3925 fist *n*
adj clenched, right, closed, left, tiny, tight, gloved *noun* hand., .air, iron., face, table, arm, side, eye, finger, .mouth *verb* clench, raise., shake., slam., close, put., hit, bang., punch, smash
7046 | 0.87 F

3926 garbage *n*
adj full, rotting, green, municipal, regular, burning, residential, just *noun* .bag, .can, .truck, .dump, .collection, .disposal, plastic. *verb* throw., pick, collect, fill, eat., haul, reduce, pile, overflow, line
6495 | 0.94

3927 ban *n*
adj comprehensive, nuclear, federal, smoking, total, outright, proposed, constitutional *noun* test., abortion, weapon, .treaty, assault, .gay, marriage, export, .use, import *verb* lift, support., impose, enforce., pass, end., violate, oppose., uphold., restrict
6572 | 0.93

3928 guitar *n*
adj electric, acoustic, bass, classical, Spanish, battered, six-string *noun* .player, steel., music, drum, song,

string, rock, .case, air., band _verb_ play., sing, strum.,
pick, bring., teach, accompany, tune
7038 | 0.87

3929 expertise _n_
adj technical, professional, special, scientific, particular,
necessary, medical, technological, legal _noun_ area,
knowledge, experience, level., field, technology,
resource, skill, lack., teacher _verb_ need, develop, use,
share., provide, require, bring, combine, .enable
6691 | 0.91 A

3930 parade _n_
adj annual, gay, military, endless, ticker-tape,
inaugural, passing, steady _noun_ day., .ground, street,
.route, pride., Thanksgiving., night., Christmas., float,
victory. _verb_ march, lead., watch., join., feature, .pass,
.celebrate, rain, participate., plan
6465 | 0.94

3931 exploration _n_
adj far, human, scientific, future, personal, planetary,
robotic, initial _noun_ space., oil., gas., .production,
.development, commitment, area, program, career.,
identity _verb_ begin, encourage., allow., continue.,
drill, .reveal, permit., warrant., invite., spur
6691 | 0.91 A

3932 carve _v_
noun stone, wood, .niche, figure, name, .rock,
.turn, face, .turkey, wall, ski, initial, knife, .block, tree
misc .into, wooden, deep, above, ancient, intricately.,
deeply, beautifully., elaborately.
  out .niche, new, .time, .own, .space, .place, .role,
.career, .identity, .exception
6782 | 0.90 M

3933 realm _n_
adj public, political, private, spiritual, human,
economic, cultural, whole, domestic, aesthetic
noun .possibility, spirit, .politics, .art, .science,
culture, theory, idea, reality, religion _verb_ enter.,
exist., lie, belong., extend., explore., expand.,
encompass, constitute
6771 | 0.90 A

3934 recipient _n_
adj social, large, passive, current, intended, foreign,
recent, able-bodied, financial, top _noun_ welfare.,
award, aid, care, security., .country, donor., job,
percent, work _verb_ require, .receive, name., force,
select, hire, .sign, identify., honor., demand.
6687 | 0.91 A

3935 residential _j_
noun area, development, program, neighborhood,
school, street, treatment, building, property, facility,
customer, community _misc_ commercial, real,
industrial, retail, quiet, near, private, single
6770 | 0.90 N A

3936 bias _n_
adj racial, cultural, liberal, political, social, potential,
possible, personal, strong, optimistic _noun_ gender.,
media, study, response., selection., prejudice, result,
source., desirability., evidence. _verb_ show., reflect,
reduce., introduce., .exist, eliminate., avoid., affect,
report, .occur
6895 | 0.88 A

3937 sunlight _n_
adj bright, direct, full, strong, brilliant, harsh, reflected
noun morning., window, water, shaft., afternoon., ray.,

room, shadow, exposure, tree _verb_ reflect, .stream,
.filter, shine, .pour, expose., .fall, .reach, glint, catch
6759 | 0.90 F

3938 lamp _n_
adj fluorescent, single, incandescent, hanging,
electric, used, overhead, compact, dark, shaded
noun table, light, oil., street., desk., kerosene., floor.,
shade, bedside. _verb_ turn., switch., .burn, hang, cast,
illuminate, .glow, .flicker, pick., blow
6768 | 0.90 F

3939 donor _n_
adj international, potential, big, major, living,
anonymous, foreign, western, single, rich _noun_ organ,
egg, sperm, blood, .country, aid, .recipient, cell,
marrow., money _verb_ .contribute, seek., match, sign,
choose, identify., fund, screen, disclose., .pledge
6599 | 0.92

3940 repair _n_
adj major, general, necessary, automotive, expensive,
surgical, simple, extensive, serious, permanent
noun .shop, maintenance, auto., car, .work, cost,
home. _verb_ make, need., pay., perform, require, .fix,
damage., complete, cover, close
6572 | 0.93 M

3941 sharply _r_
rise., contrast., fall., .reduce, increase, turn., cut, drop.,
price, .criticize, decline.
6477 | 0.94

3942 hers _p_
his., she, hand., eye., friend., face., against., mouth.,
next., lip., body., meet., mine, touch.
6980 | 0.87 F

3943 guidance _n_
adj spiritual, parental, comprehensive, little, moral,
clear, divine _noun_ .counselor, school, teacher, .system,
.program, counseling, student, support, classroom.
verb provide., give., need, offer., seek., receive, issue.,
assist
6833 | 0.89 A

3944 diplomatic _j_
noun relation, effort, solution, recognition, mission,
tie, pressure, initiative, correspondent, support, front,
negotiation _misc_ economic, military, political,
establish, full, international, Soviet, formal
6764 | 0.90

3945 classic _n_
adj American, modern, instant, literary, western,
Italian, French, senior, religious, minor _noun_ film,
movie, cult., book, holiday., golf., professor, version.,
department, baseball. _verb_ become., win., consider.,
read, study., perform, picture., feature, range., stick.
6593 | 0.92 N

3946 purple _j_
noun heart, flower, color, sky, face, dress, shade,
mountain, shirt, rain, hair, star _misc_ blue, red, pink,
yellow, green, white, wear, deep
6646 | 0.91 F

3947 princess _n_
adj little, beautiful, late, Indian, grand, pretty,
Egyptian _noun_ prince, .Di, death, fairy, .grace, queen,
ice, love, daughter, crown _verb_ marry, .die, rescue.,
dress, portray., accompany, wed., .flee, bow, await
6745 | 0.90 F

3948 candle *n*
adj votive, white, flickering, burning, single, standard, Roman, lighted, blue *noun* light, table, flame, wax, room, lighting., birthday, .holder, night, .wind *verb* .burn, blow., hold., .flicker, put, place, .glow, illuminate, carry, fill
6650 | 0.91 F

3949 advocate *v*
noun right, policy, group., position, program, government, .violence, education, party, role, other, view, health, leader., organization. *misc* long., strongly., civil, support, publicly., openly., democratic
6628 | 0.91 A

3950 generous *j*
noun people, amount, benefit, man, support, portion, spirit, gift, policy, pension, grant, heart *misc* very, more, most, offer, less, enough, receive, extremely
6300 | 0.96

3951 strip *v*
noun .clothes, tree, leaf, bed, .waist, .bark, .power, .skin, .title, .ball, .underwear, electron, citizenship, .sheet, land *misc* .away, .its, .naked, .bare, .everything, clean
off .her, .clothes, .shirt, .glove, begin., .clothing, .jacket, .coat **down** .bare, .naked
6334 | 0.96

3952 necessity *n*
adj basic, economic, absolute, military, political, medical, practical, moral, bare, historical *noun* life, choice, food, business., virtue, matter., freedom, convenience, belief., argument *verb* become, must, understand, recognize., consider, born., accept., avoid, demonstrate., arise
6588 | 0.92 A

3953 tuck *v*
noun bed, shirt, hand, .corner, hair, head, leg, chin, foot, side, blanket, paper, .end, body, .wing *misc* .into, his, her, .under, .away, .behind, .inside, .back
6708 | 0.90 F

3954 debate *v*
noun issue, Congress, question, .merit, bill, Senate., policy, topic, scientist., week, scholar., expert., candidate., official., reform *misc* .whether, hotly., shall, continue., discuss, widely., openly
6411 | 0.94 S

3955 statue *n*
adj ancient, Greek, famous, wooden, life-size, giant, huge, equestrian, tall, religious *noun* .liberty, bronze., marble., stone., Buddha, base, painting, God, square, building *verb* stand, erect, carve, .depict, topple, represent, honor, remove, stare, destroy
6593 | 0.92

3956 frame *v*
noun face, window, question, issue, picture, hair, debate, view, door, eye, tree, image, policy, discussion, light *misc* .terms, .within, .hang, dark, perfectly
6431 | 0.94

3957 elevator *n*
adj private, empty, slow, crowded, express, waiting, nearest *noun* .door, floor, .shaft, button, grain., bank, lobby, .operator, building, space. *verb* take, .open, ride., step., wait, walk, .stop, .close, .arrive, enter.
6980 | 0.86 F

3958 popularity *n*
adj growing, increasing, enormous, recent, widespread, increased, personal, rising, immense *noun* .contest, president., .rating, poll, sport, reason., height., rise., level., surge. *verb* gain., grow, enjoy., increase, soar, explain., win., lose., decline, wane
6397 | 0.94

3959 indicator *n*
adj economic, good, leading, key, important, social, best, reliable, early, better *noun* performance, health, quality, success, development, index., .light, use, change, data *verb* include, provide, serve., .suggest, develop, .point, base, define., examine, .rise
6901 | 0.87 A

3960 entity *n*
adj other, political, private, single, small, corporate, independent, governmental, large, different *noun* government., state, business., information, interest, relationship, individual, agency, organization, type *verb* create, exist, own, require, control, form, represent, operate, regulate, emerge
6762 | 0.89 A

3961 interior *j*
noun ministry, designer, minister, design, space, wall, decorator, room, official, monologue, light, decoration *misc* former, exterior, announce, install, French, Russian, coastal, vast
6454 | 0.93 M

3962 limb *n*
adj residual, low, prosthetic, upper, artificial, long, broken, short, phantom, heavy *noun* tree, life., .tissue, .amputation, length, .socket, pain, shape, movement, torso *verb* lose., move, tear., risk., cut, stretch, hang, remove, swing, spread
7457 | 0.81 F

3963 bold *j*
noun color, move, step, plan, stroke, action, statement, letter, initiative, idea, pattern, print *misc* new, big, enough, fresh, bright, red, beautiful
6289 | 0.96

3964 hesitate *v*
noun .moment, door, .second, .instant, .doorway, .answering, .fraction, blade *misc* .before, ask, answer, .nod, .briefly
6816 | 0.88 F

3965 magic *n*
adj black, real, powerful, pure, sympathetic, dark, female *noun* kind., .mountain, movie, bit., form, mystery, science, .television, sorcery, sword *verb* work., .happen, perform, possess, experience., capture., .protect, recapture., transform, discover.
6780 | 0.89 F

3966 starting *n*
adj useful, excellent, recommended, defensive, obvious, projected, offensive, logical, solid *noun* .point, .position, .lineup, .quarterback, .job, .pitcher, .line *verb* return., provide., .pitch, .repeat, earn., compete., lower., crack, .tackle, regain.
6599 | 0.91 N

3967 diminish *v*
noun power, value, role, .importance, effect, .ability, number, quality, capacity, threat, chance, influence, age, property, sense *misc* greatly., significantly, gradually., tend., considerably
6388 | 0.94 A

3968 inside *n*
adj deep, soft, beautiful, pink, empty, wet, moist, identical, burning *noun* door, .thigh, .mouth, .cheek, foot, outside, .wrist, box, glass, skin *verb* feel, look, bite., paint., eat., line., lock., fill, chew.
6396 | 0.94 F

3969 readily *r*
.available, can., more., .admit, .apparent, .accept, as., .accessible, most., .agree, .acknowledge, information, .identify, .understand
6545 | 0.92 A

3970 elegant *j*
noun room, woman, man, restaurant, way, house, home, hotel, solution, design, dining, dinner
misc most, very, simple, beautiful, yet, white, tall
6455 | 0.93 M

3971 engagement *n*
adj civic, active, political, social, academic, military, constructive, emotional, productive, critical *noun* .ring, rule., student, school., policy, level., .party, activity, behavior, diamond.
verb break., speak., announce, require, promote, increase, support, .occur, foster., .last
6664 | 0.90 A

3972 rage *n*
adj jealous, full, blind, violent, murderous, late, sudden, impotent, current, pent-up *noun* road., face, fit., frustration, anger, pain, grief, fear, tear, .despair
verb feel, fly., become., fill., express, scream, vent., shake, explode, boil
6415 | 0.94 F

3973 destination *n*
adj popular, final, favorite, ultimate, unknown, major, prime, particular, hot, various *noun* tourist., vacation., .charge, travel, country, resort, journey., mile, route., island *verb* reach., become., arrive., choose, drive., approach., near.
6354 | 0.94

3974 realistic *j*
noun goal, expectation, approach, view, chance, model, assessment, option, plan, picture, situation, fiction *misc* more, most, only, expect, practical, develop, possible, base
6364 | 0.94

3975 intent *n*
adj original, criminal, congressional, clear, legislative, specific, serious, hostile, evil *noun* .purpose, Congress, letter., voter, law, statement, evidence., act, notice., .legislation *verb* seem., determine, prove, sign, express., establish, indicate., announce., reflect.
6418 | 0.93 A

3976 metaphor *n*
adj visual, apt, extended, perfect, powerful, central, linguistic, cultural, particular *noun* use., symbol, language, simile, analogy, metonymy, sport., model, .identification *verb* become., .describe, serve., mix., employ, extend, express, apply, .imply, .capture
7089 | 0.84 A

3977 automobile *n*
adj American, Japanese, luxury, expensive, European, antique, Brazilian *noun* .industry, .accident, .association, .manufacturer, company, .insurance, .dealer *verb* drive, kill., buy., sell, build, produce, die, reduce, own., park
6488 | 0.92

3978 productive *j*
noun life, society, work, way, activity, citizen, member, use, worker, capacity, land, economy
misc more, most, become, less, highly, healthy, lead, creative
6509 | 0.92 A

3979 endorse *v*
noun president, .candidate, plan, .idea, bill, group, Republican, government, party, .product, policy, .view, organization., .use, approach *misc* .by, strongly., refuse., publicly., support, likely., enthusiastically.
6453 | 0.93

3980 isolate *v*
noun .rest, community, .gene, cell, virus, patient, population, society, scientist., researcher., effort., bacteria, attempt., culture, regime *misc* .from, feel., socially., increasingly., completely.
6440 | 0.93 A

3981 confess *v*
noun .crime, .sin, .murder, police, killer, priest, .love, wife, suspect., faith, husband, guilt, .affair, .killing, .fear *misc* must., .kill, finally., force.
6285 | 0.95

3982 wilderness *n*
adj designated, pristine, vast, remote, Alaskan, Canadian *noun* .area, .society, park, acre., mountain, land, .act, forest, .experience, mile *verb* preserve, designate., protect., hike, wander., cry., explore, surround, comprise
7395 | 0.81 M

3983 minimize *v*
noun .risk, .impact, .effect, .cost, .damage, way., .problem, .loss, .chance, effort, .casualty, .amount, .exposure, strategy., .error *misc* try., help., design., maximize, order., .potential, prevent, seek.
6631 | 0.90 A

3984 diagnose *v*
noun .cancer, .disease, problem, patient, doctor., child, case, woman, illness, .age, .syndrome, .heart, physician, .brain, .disability *misc* .with, .treat, .early, recently., difficult., correctly
6612 | 0.90

3985 happiness *n*
adj human, great, personal, greatest, happy, future, eternal *noun* pursuit, life, health., love, joy, money., peace, satisfaction, success, feeling. *verb* find., bring., buy., pursue., achieve, wish., seek., .depend, .consist, .elude
6439 | 0.93

3986 spectrum *n*
adj political, broad, wide, full, electromagnetic, entire, whole, visible *noun* end., part., color, side., star, radio., light, energy, absorption., portion. *verb* cover., represent., span., obtain, range, measure, record, .reveal, study, emit
6799 | 0.88 A

3987 hint *n*
adj slight, helpful, only, subtle, faint, mere, bare *noun* .smile, .color, .trouble, flavor, .irony, .danger, .accent, .humor, .fear, .sarcasm *verb* give., take., drop., offer., show., provide., catch.
6305 | 0.95

3988 eating *n*
adj healthy, disordered, good, emotional, bad,
healthful, poor *noun* •habit, •disorder, food, •pattern,
•behavior, •plan, exercise, weight, drinking *verb* stop•,
finish•, start, keep•, develop•, associate
6515 | 0.91 M

3989 tune *n*
adj little, different, popular, familiar, happy, favorite,
fine, catchy, sweet *noun* song, show•, dance•, pop•,
folk•, signature•, title, •dollar, gospel•, collection•
verb play, sing•, change•, hum•, whistle•, write, carry•,
recognize, feature, sound
6408 | 0.93

3990 volunteer *v*
noun time, student•, •information, •service, school,
corps•, study, organization, teacher, job, parent•,
clinic, participant, class, lawyer *misc* •participate,
willing•, encourage•, contact, eagerly•
6210 | 0.96

3991 abstract *j*
noun painting, concept, art, expressionism,
expressionist, form, idea, principle, design, pattern,
painter, shape *misc* more, such, examine, concrete,
highly, rather, than
6748 | 0.88 A

3992 revolutionary *j*
noun war, party, guard, change, movement, idea,
force, government, leader, period, era, regime
misc institutional, during, armed, truly, Iranian,
democratic, ruling, popular
6444 | 0.92 A

3993 gym *n*
adj local, empty, nearby, high-school, fancy,
cavernous, makeshift *noun* •class, school•, •bag, day,
•teacher, jungle•, home•, room, •night, •shoe *verb* go•,
work, hit•, join•, walk, head•, enter
6544 | 0.91 M

3994 addition *n*
adj new, recent, late, welcome, key, valuable, nice,
later, useful, simple *noun* •subtraction, change,
line, multiplication, •collection, building, nitrogen,
•vanilla, •garden, renovation *verb* beat, blend•,
build, include, require•, mix, provide, help,
announce•, create
6429 | 0.92

3995 Russian *n*
adj ethnic, nuclear, average, wealthy, fluent
noun American, •Ukrainians, French, German,
majority•, generation• *verb* •live, fight, kill, beat•,
•move, •build, •begin, •send, deal, •claim
6438 | 0.92 S

3996 disappointed *j*
noun lack, fan, investor, look, expectation, audience,
crowd, client, expression, glance *misc* I, very, feel,
little, seem, angry, surprised
6192 | 0.96

3997 particle *n*
adj small, charged, elementary, large, subatomic,
fine, microscopic, high-energy, airborne, solar
noun dust, •physics, size, •accelerator, energy,
•physicist, air, soil, matter, field *verb* produce,
•move, form, remove•, contain, trap, cause,
interact, •travel, bind
7352 | 0.81 M A

3998 repair *v*
noun •damage, car, equipment, road, zipper,
shop, •relationship, bridge, leak, ship,
•infrastructure, •relation, crew, •facility,
•hole *misc* replace, •damaged, •broken,
surgically•, •torn
6235 | 0.95

3999 dynamic *j*
noun process, system, duo, range, assessment, nature,
model, economy, relationship, force, environment,
interaction *misc* most, between, change, create,
static, complex, basic, highly
6659 | 0.89 A

4000 pump *v*
noun water, •gas, blood, heart•, •money, oil, air,
•fist, arm, •iron, leg, system, adrenaline, body
misc •through, •full, enough, hard
   up get•, •volume, all•, •price, •stock, tire, crowd,
muscle, •economy, artificially• **out** water, blood•,
amount, •enough, •sea, stomach
6226 | 0.95

4001 kiss *n*
adj big, long, quick, passionate, little, wet, French
noun •cheek, hug•, •death, lip, mouth, •forehead,
face, goodbye, goodnight, chocolate• *verb* give•,
blow•, plant•, break, steal•, throw•, return•, press,
taste, •last
6618 | 0.90 F

4002 value *v*
noun life, family, company, culture, society, education,
work, art, opinion, deal•, diversity, teacher, parent,
relationship, •friendship *misc* highly, •million, •billion,
•less, equally, particularly•, indicate•, greatly•
6474 | 0.92 A

4003 automatically *r*
system•, •assume, •adjust, computer, almost•, shut,
software•, data, generate, update, switch, itself,
•transfer, •qualify
6337 | 0.93

4004 overall *r*
•district, week•, year, result, percent, •however, season,
•star, rate, score, pick, •economic, indicate,
•acceleration
6581 | 0.90 A

4005 dawn *n*
adj new, early, gray, pale, coming, approaching,
lunar *noun* dusk, light, morning, day, hour•,
crack•, night, sky, •age, •century *verb* wake,
•break, begin, rise, arrive, wait, return, awake,
greet•, •creep
6369 | 0.93 F

4006 ruling *n*
adj federal, recent, legal, final, favorable, unanimous,
preliminary, lower-court *noun* court•, judge, case,
appeal, circuit, landmark•, district, decision, justice,
abortion *verb* issue•, uphold, overturn, •allow,
reverse, affect, •require, win•, await•, •apply
6506 | 0.91 N

4007 mechanical *j*
noun engineering, engineer, system, device,
problem, failure, design, property, arm, energy,
part, reproduction *misc* electrical, such, electronic,
cause, chemical, thermal, than, rather
7446 | 0.79 A

4008 feel n
adj better, soft, solid, smooth, modern, airy, casual
noun .home, skin, look, .safe, smell, .texture, .cotton
verb .like, get., love., remember., enjoy., capture.,
prefer.
6316 | 0.94

4009 vitamin n
adj daily, essential, certain, extra, adequate, multiple,
sufficient _noun_ .mineral, calcium, protein.,
supplement, source., acid, deficiency, level,
antioxidant, food _verb_ take., contain., .help, add,
prevent, .reduce, eat, fortify., absorb, pack.
7588 | 0.78 M

4010 silly j
noun thing, question, putty, girl, stuff, game, woman,
song, story, joke, grin, hat _misc_ seem, sound, feel,
little, laugh
6336 | 0.93 F

4011 handle n
adj wooden, long, better, comfortable, curved, broken,
firm _noun_ door., hand, knife, broom., metal, bag,
blade, plastic., ax., finger _verb_ get., pull, grab., turn,
hold, reach., grasp., attach, fly., carry
6466 | 0.91 F M

4012 artificial j
noun intelligence, heart, light, insemination,
turf, sweetener, surface, limb, line, hip, leg, reef
misc create, natural, develop, such, rather, than
6284 | 0.94

4013 outstanding j
noun award, share, job, contribution, performance,
student, debt, service, achievement, issue, warrant,
player _misc_ most, recognize, name, including, truly,
honor, total
6362 | 0.93

4014 age v
noun child., .year, woman., kid., man., adult.,
girl., percent., boy., student., rate, wine, .dignity
misc .old, young, .over, among., .under
6400 | 0.92

4015 peel v
noun potato, skin, paint, onion, carrot, apple, shrimp,
orange _misc_ .cut, .away, .slice, .seed
  off skin, layer, .clothes, then., .bill, .paper, start.,
.glove, .shirt, begin. **back** .layer, .reveal, lip.
6514 | 0.91 M

4016 rescue n
adj international, dramatic, involved, heroic,
daring, massive, failed, emotional _noun_ operation,
.team, .worker, .mission, .effort, search., .squad
verb come., help., .arrive, send., ride., wait., save,
rush., mount
6249 | 0.94

4017 oral j
noun sex, history, tradition, argument, reading,
contraceptive, communication, language,
presentation, fluency, cavity, culture _misc_ written,
perform, write, during, receive, anal, treat
6908 | 0.85 A

4018 o'clock r
at., .morning, ten., nine., five., four., eight., six.,
three., two.
6531 | 0.90 F

4019 undertake v
noun study, project, research, effort, task, action,
activity, government, reform, program, mission
misc major, economic, military, similar, .massive
6607 | 0.89 A

4020 lonely j
noun man, heart, life, people, woman, place, night,
planet, road, child, boy, girl _misc_ feel, very, sad,
sometimes, little, bored, depressed, scared
6317 | 0.93 F

4021 servant n
adj civil, public, domestic, indentured, faithful,
black, loyal, humble, obedient, suffering _noun_ house,
master, .girl, household, slave, hall, politician, worker,
career., employee _verb_ bring, send, .carry, hire, treat.,
employ, act, order., dismiss, .clear
6436 | 0.92 F

4022 indigenous j
noun people, community, culture, knowledge,
population, group, right, land, tradition,
organization, practice, language _misc_ local,
among, cultural, political, African, traditional,
native, ethnic
7819 | 0.75 A

4023 civic j
noun center, education, leader, group, association,
organization, responsibility, duty, engagement,
virtue, community, business _misc_ political,
social, local, religious, cultural, moral, qualify,
active
6683 | 0.88 N A

4024 full-time j
noun job, student, employee, faculty, worker, staff,
year, member, position, teacher, employment, college
misc work, part-time, become, employ, hire, teach,
return, professional
6368 | 0.92

4025 worry n
adj big, real, financial, only, constant, major, main,
sick, greatest _noun_ fear, money, health, .future, line,
lot., parent, cause., mind, measure. _verb_ express.,
share, ease., increase, forget., relate, free., rise,
overcome.
6187 | 0.95

4026 cooperate v
noun .teacher, government, .investigation,
.authority, .police, weather., .prosecutor, agency,
willingness., .investigator, nation, .inspector,
department, refusal., .enforcement _misc_ .with,
fully, refuse., agree., willing.
6252 | 0.94

4027 casual j
noun sex, conversation, observer, clothes, relationship,
look, fan, partner, style, attitude, acquaintance,
encounter _misc_ more, even, engage, wear, sexual,
dress, sound, formal
6410 | 0.92

4028 behavioral j
noun problem, change, disorder, science, child,
student, intervention, pattern, control, response,
consultation, intention _misc_ emotional, cognitive,
social, academic, psychological, such, affective,
parental
7531 | 0.78 A

4029 shortage *n*
adj severe, critical, chronic, serious, nursing, acute, special, future, widespread, foreign *noun* food, water, labor•, teacher, housing, worker, power•, area, priest *verb* face•, cause, create, suffer•, lead, experience•, result, address•, •force, reduce
6300 | 0.93

4030 reception *n*
adj warm, cool, critical, mixed, enthusiastic, chilly, hostile *noun* •area, wedding•, •room, •desk, cocktail•, •dinner, •hall, touchdown• *verb* hold, receive, include•, follow, attend•, host, feature, enter•, honor, •celebrate
6300 | 0.93

4031 offering *n*
adj public, initial, new, late, burnt, secondary, academic, traditional, recent, current *noun* stock, course•, •price, program, share, service, product•, peace•, market, college *verb* •include, expand•, raise, place, •range, complete, accept, improve, enhance, •attract
6350 | 0.92

4032 huh *u*
uh•, •yeah, no, •oh, pretty•, •yes, bad•, cool•, nice•, •OK, stuff•, funny•
7050 | 0.83 S F

4033 credibility *n*
adj instant, scientific, moral, institutional, perceived, academic, added *noun* •problem, issue, witness, lot•, •gap, loss•, •public, source, legitimacy *verb* lose•, give•, undermine•, establish•, lend•, gain•, damage•, restore•, destroy•, lack•
6313 | 0.93 S

4034 chin *n*
adj double, pointed, strong, sharp, cleft, bearded, pointy *noun* hand, nose, eye, •chest, head, cheek, hair, finger, shoulder, lip *verb* lift•, rest, rub•, tuck, raise, scratch•, stroke•, tilt, jut, drop
6760 | 0.87 F

4035 physics *n*
adj nuclear, theoretical, applied, modern, fundamental, atomic, high-energy *noun* law•, chemistry, professor, particle•, quantum•, •department, student, science, biology, prize• *verb* teach, study•, understand, predict, •assume, earn•, defy•, govern•, •dictate, solve
8709 | 0.67 A

4036 vanish *v*
noun •air, face, smile•, light•, moment, month, tree, fear•, sun•, sky, minute, screen, •crowd, grin•, pain• *misc* before, seem•, simply•, •without, quickly
6477 | 0.91 F

4037 blend *v*
noun mixture, egg, color, ingredient, flavor, bowl, flour, sugar, oil, butter, salt, blender•, cream, sound, processor• *misc* •with, until•, •into, well, stir, •together
    in •with, well, •better, almost•, able•, easily, perfectly, ability•, •among, seamlessly
6606 | 0.89 M

4038 noon *n*
adj high, past, hot, bright, following, sunny *noun* day, morning, time, sun, hour, •night, sale• *verb* begin, start•, arrive, sleep•, wake, finish, drink•
6648 | 0.88 N

4039 precious *j*
noun time, metal, life, resource, stone, thing, commodity, moment, gift, child, water, gold *misc* most, few, more, too, something, waste, lose, spend
6130 | 0.96

4040 command *v*
noun •attention, •respect, force, •price, army, general, troop, God•, voice, •support, officer, division, king•, authority, colonel *misc* •high, special•, military, top, naval
6246 | 0.94

4041 wake *n*
adj Irish, immediate, deadly, devastating, turbulent, foaming *noun* •war, •attack, •hurricane, •scandal, boat, •death, •disaster, •tragedy, •bombing, •island *verb* leave•, follow•, trail•, emerge•, attend•, form•, suffer•
6093 | 0.96

4042 flip *v*
noun •switch, •page, •light, •coin, book, hair, hand, head, •channel, car, side, •card, paper, air, radio *misc* •over, •through, •open, then•, •off, •back, down, •onto, •upside, •forward
6510 | 0.90 F

4043 scary *j*
noun thing, movie, part, story, thought, place, stuff, guy, situation, face, feeling, experience *misc* it, very, really, little, pretty, too
6245 | 0.94 S

4044 pizza *n*
adj frozen, local, grilled, fresh, leftover, cold, refrigerated *noun* slice, •crust, •parlor, cheese, •dough, •box, •delivery, pasta, pepperoni•, •place *verb* eat•, order•, deliver, serve, bake, pick, sell, taste
6330 | 0.92

4045 toilet *n*
adj portable, public, composting, chemical, closed, marine *noun* •paper, •seat, water, •bowl, roll, shower, sink, •training, bathroom, •tank *verb* flush, use•, sit•, clean•, throw, scrub, install, •train, fix•, overflow
6336 | 0.92 F

4046 representative *j*
noun sample, government, democracy, group, committee, body, data, institution, example, figure, system, sampling *misc* nationally, truly, select, democratic, broadly, obtain, fairly
6495 | 0.90 A

4047 silk *n*
adj black, white, red, blue, green, fine, yellow, embroidered, pink, raw *noun* •dress, •shirt, •scarf, •tie, •blouse, cotton, •gown, suit, jacket, •robe *verb* wear•, wrap, cover, remove, hang, pull, drape, weave, line
6474 | 0.90 F

4048 bid *n*
adj presidential, low, hostile, winning, Olympic, unsuccessful, successful, failed, automatic *noun* •committee, re-election, city, price, takeover•, reelection *verb* make•, lose•, win, submit, accept, receive, reject•, fail, launch•, solicit•
6525 | 0.90 N

4049 gathering *n*
adj large, social, public, small, annual, informal, recent *noun* .place, family., intelligence., information, .spot, .storm, news, hunting, party *verb* attend., speak., host., organize, address., invite., .feature, ban., aim, arrange.
6107 | 0.96

4050 softly *r*
say., she, speak., ask., her, laugh., sing, door, play., hear, cry., voice, close, smile
6906 | 0.85 F

4051 annually *r*
million., billion., percent., about, spend., dollar., grow., ton., .next, award., .since, average, earn., .according
6489 | 0.90 M

4052 hook *v*
noun fish, computer, thumb, finger, arm, .drug, guy, machine, cable, line, phone, nose, leg, .belt, claw *misc* get., .onto, .together, immediately., instantly., firmly
up get., computer, monitor, .IV, cable, try., hose, phone, .again, someone
6239 | 0.94 M

4053 suffering *n*
adj human, physical, terrible, unnecessary, innocent, emotional, personal, severe, mental, enormous *noun* pain., death, .other, victim, loss, patient, cause., animal, joy, violence *verb* end., alleviate., relieve., endure, inflict, ease., experience, reduce., .occur, arise
6403 | 0.91 A

4054 accuracy *n*
adj great, historical, better, pinpoint, scientific, factual, diagnostic, technical *noun* .speaker, .word, percent, level, degree., speed, data, test, rate, information *verb* guarantee., improve., check., increase., ensure., assess., determine, provide., depend, demonstrate.
6655 | 0.88 A

4055 marine *n*
adj American, young, Iraqi, British, royal, fellow, dead, wounded, decorated *noun* soldier, sailor, army, merchant., navy, air, airman, troop, unit, ground *verb* kill, join., send, .die, .land, .fight, .move, serve, .arrive, enlist.
6445 | 0.91 S

4056 broker *n*
adj honest, online, real-estate, full-service, local, cultural, prime, retail, traditional, independent *noun* estate., power., mortgage., stock, insurance., discount., .deal, company, .peace, ticket. *verb* sell, buy, act., represent, .estimate, .charge, hire, .handle, invest, contact.
6594 | 0.88 N

4057 hopefully *r*
.will, soon, improve, tomorrow, someday, resolve, towards, temporary, .peaceful, momentum
6382 | 0.91 S

4058 descend *v*
noun .stair, .step, .staircase, silence., darkness, plane., line, ladder, .chaos, earth, .level, elevator, floor, .hill, trail *misc* .from, .upon, begin., .toward, slowly, quickly
6329 | 0.92 F

4059 tide *n*
adj high, rising, low, red, incoming, brown, growing, ebbing *noun* .pool, wind, ocean., flood., ebb., wave, .boat, beach, sea, .line *verb* turn, stem., rise, sweep, .lift, .wash, swim., carry, ride., cause
6166 | 0.94

4060 trail *v*
noun voice., powder., point, game, mile, finger, paper., mountain, star., campaign., dog, poll, park, hair, .wake *misc* .behind, after, along, .away, badly
off voice., she, .as, .into, word., .silence, sentence., laughter, .embarrassed
6452 | 0.90 F

4061 stumble *v*
noun door, room, .word, .rock, .stair, .kitchen, horse, path, tree, .bathroom, leg, tongue, bear., .mile, hunter. *misc* .into, .upon, .across, .through, .onto, .back
over .word, .rock, .something, .own, almost.
6418 | 0.91 F

4062 verbal *j*
noun abuse, skill, behavior, ability, communication, score, expression, aggression, interaction, performance, form, instruction *misc* physical, visual, nonverbal, written, such, sexual, negative, emotional
6789 | 0.86 A

4063 spring *v*
noun .life, .action, eye, tear., .leak, trap, .surprise, door, industry., hope., hair., movement., tree, .seat, .chair *misc* .from, .into, .out, .mind, .open, .around, .forward, .across, ready.
up .around, .all, .over, .across, .overnight, industry., .throughout **back** .lightly, .life, until., cake., .shape
6181 | 0.94 F

4064 collector *n*
adj private, American, serious, solar, avid, major, African, popular, commercial, western *noun* art, tax., dealer, .item, data., bill., shell. *verb* buy, sell, seek, own, collect, acquire, purchase, .prefer, appeal., prize
6575 | 0.88 M

4065 judicial *j*
noun system, review, process, court, nominee, activism, decision, branch, power, nomination, judge, philosophy *misc* legislative, supreme, federal, political, administrative, legal, conservative, comparative
6711 | 0.87 A

4066 burning *j*
noun fuel, fossil, building, oil, coal, fire, sensation, smell, desire, house, question, issue *misc* cause, hot, produce, prevent, clean, prescribed, trap
6152 | 0.94 F

4067 inventory *n*
adj large, personal, excess, low, self-report, just-in-time, entire, quick, moral *noun* item, .control, system, personality., style., depression., .management, anxiety., cost, .level *verb* take., keep, complete., reduce, build, maintain, list, .consist, .assess, release.
6600 | 0.88 A

4068 fool *n*
adj old, only, poor, stupid, complete, damned, total, absolute *noun* day, .gold, .errand, kind., .love, .joke, ship., .paradise *verb* make., think, look., feel., play., suffer., .believe, act., .respond, .rush
6419 | 0.90 F

4069 way *r*
under., .too, get., now, already., well., effort., half.,
project., .much, investigation., study., change., plan.
6115 | 0.95

4070 loyalty *n*
adj personal, strong, ethnic, fierce, dual, blind,
familial, deep, conflicting, absolute *noun* party, family,
oath, brand., customer., sense., love, commitment,
value. *verb* show, win., demonstrate., inspire., prove.,
demand., question., owe, develop., .lie
6216 | 0.93 A

4071 performer *n*
adj top, young, great, black, poor, female, all-time,
low, solid, professional *noun* composer, music,
audience, street., circus., stage, star, show, performance,
solo. *verb* include, feature., .sing, .wear, photograph,
record, dance, motivate., reward., drag.
6435 | 0.90

4072 kit *n*
adj first-aid, medical, shaving, whole, free, at-home,
med, hands-free *noun* tool., home, test., survival.,
aid., emergency., starter. *verb* .include, .contain, buy,
sell, carry, build, offer, assemble, order, .cost
6430 | 0.90 M

4073 romance *n*
adj little, historical, medieval, interracial, modern,
budding *noun* .novel, love, sex, office., adventure,
marriage, summer., mystery, friendship, .writer
verb read., .last, blossom, rekindle, pursue., combine,
.bloom, inspire., celebrate, specialize.
6242 | 0.93

4074 quantity *n*
adj large, small, great, sufficient, unknown, known,
commercial, mass, sheer *noun* quality, water, .food,
material, price, type, .money, frequency, .chemical,
.gas *verb* produce., consume, buy., sell, increase.,
eat., contain., determine, reduce., .demand
6398 | 0.91 A

4075 alleged *j*
noun victim, abuse, violation, plot, crime, incident,
rape, investigation, case, affair, attack, assault
misc about, sexual, against, investigate, because,
involve, including
6235 | 0.93

4076 therapist *n*
adj physical, occupational, respiratory, licensed,
professional, certified, marital, qualified, recreational
noun family., sex., massage., marriage., speech.,
patient, music., doctor, .author, relationship.
verb .help, train, .treat, recommend, consult,
.specialize, hire, .encourage, .warn, interview
6803 | 0.85 M

4077 longtime *j*
noun friend, resident, member, activist, partner,
supporter, fan, executive, director, coach, employee,
critic *misc* former, political, democratic, marry, chief,
replace, civil, conservative
6495 | 0.89 N

4078 sink *n*
adj stainless, dirty, full, double, stainless-steel, filthy,
freshwater, integrated *noun* kitchen., water, bathroom.,
dish, hand, toilet, carbon, window, counter, cabinet
verb stand., wash, fill, lean., hang, bend., spit, .dry, fix
6481 | 0.89 F

4079 sentiment *n*
adj public, anti-American, strong, similar, nationalist,
popular, anti-immigrant, growing, religious, common
noun theory., kind., rise, expression., consumer.,
feeling, investor., .Congress, shift., .rationality
verb echo, express, share, reflect, voice, agree.,
fuel, appreciate., capture., .exist
6179 | 0.93 A

4080 sodium *n*
adj dietary, low, excess, liquid, excessive, increased,
reduced *noun* cholesterol., milligram., fiber,
carbohydrate, fat., protein, .gram, potassium,
.channel, .chloride *verb* contain., reduce., lower,
consume, load., detect., .flavor, restrict.
7139 | 0.81 M N

4081 seal *v*
noun fate, .deal, bag, door, plastic, envelope, lip.,
.border, edge, record, window, end, hole, air, .moisture
misc .inside, shut, tightly, close, .place, completely
   off .from, area, window, completely, hermetically.,
room, automatically. **up** .tight, .crack, .hole
6095 | 0.95

4082 trailer *n*
adj double-wide, flatbed, semi, cramped, air-
conditioned, rented, camp *noun* .park, truck,
house, tractor., home, boat., horse., door, back,
.court *verb* live., pull, tow, buy., haul, rent, enter.
6222 | 0.93 F

4083 spread *n*
adj rapid, wide, global, far, upward, two-page,
worldwide *noun* .disease, .AIDS, .weapon, word.,
.virus, .technology, .democracy, cheese., effort.,
.infection *verb* prevent., stop., help., control.,
reduce., slow., halt., limit., cover, lay.
6126 | 0.94

4084 shared *j*
noun experience, value, responsibility, vision, interest,
sense, history, belief, goal, understanding, decision,
community *misc* our, common, among, base, widely,
together, cultural, develop
6364 | 0.91 A

4085 equity *n*
adj private, social, average, global, educational,
environmental, generational *noun* .fund, home,
gender., .market, .firm, investment., .loan, percent,
issue, company *verb* return., build, invest, sell,
achieve., raise, buy, tap., promote., increase
6667 | 0.86

4086 banking *n*
adj commercial, international, online, private,
financial, federal, retail, central *noun* .system,
investment., .industry, .committee, business, house.,
.firm, mitigation. *verb* offer, expand., conduct.,
combine, reform., .collapse, separate, chair
6458 | 0.89 N

4087 ridiculous *j*
noun thing, item, idea, question, notion, story, price,
situation, thought, argument, statement, amount
misc look, most, seem, sound, absolutely, course
6160 | 0.93

4088 processing *n*
adj cognitive, digital, central, visual, parallel,
auditory, mental, emotional *noun* information,
word., .plant, data., food., .system, image., .facility,

signal. *verb* require, involve, occur, handle, increase, facilitate., reduce, engage., .cost, control
6861 | 0.84 A

4089 please v
noun God, .parent, mother, desire., father, other, .audience, .customer, .crowd, .boss, .palate, .voter, eagerness., politician, .constituent *misc* try., want., ask., eager., .everyone, .everybody, hard., .yourself
6089 | 0.95 F

4090 dilemma n
adj ethical, moral, social, real, difficult, common, similar, current, terrible, personal *noun* prisoner., solution., security., policy, answer., design., choice, conflict, .simultaneity, type *verb* face, pose, resolve., present, solve., create, confront, deal, address, involve
6314 | 0.91 A

4091 quest n
adj spiritual, personal, human, epic, scientific, never-ending, endless, eternal *noun* vision., .truth, .power, .knowledge, .justice, .identity, .peace, tribe., .certainty, .freedom *verb* begin, continue, embark., end, join, abandon., pursue., complete., succeed
6139 | 0.94

4092 pillow n
adj soft, extra, embroidered, red, fluffy, inflatable, firm, cervical *noun* head, bed, face, blanket, sheet, .talk, .case, night, hair, .fight *verb* put., prop., lay, pull, throw, sit, sleep, cover, place, lie
6489 | 0.89 F

4093 slice v
noun onion, mushroom, pepper, tomato, knife., potato, bread, .strip, apple, .air, cheese, .top, meat, blade., chicken *misc* thinly., .into, .through, peel., fresh, .thin
6518 | 0.88 M

4094 shock v
noun .world, .nation, heart, .silence, American, .conscience, public, audience, crime., murder, .reader, fan, revelation, .sensibility, tone *misc* .by, really., .learn, .hear, totally.
5990 | 0.96

4095 lately r
have, but, lot., much., seem, though, news., notice, bit., attention., busy., act., pretty., hard
6093 | 0.94

4096 laser n
adj red, powerful, monochrome, chemical, green, airborne, blue, high-energy *noun* .beam, .printer, .surgery, .light, system, .disc, .treatment, .pulse, .show *verb* use, focus, shoot, fire, scan, measure, develop, aim, point, remove
6697 | 0.86 M

4097 rigid j
noun deadline, distribution, body, rule, structure, system, control, arm, frame, schedule, standard, foam *misc* meet, order, in, less, flexible, fixed, overly, narrow
6729 | 0.85 S

4098 ours p
as., like., than., friend., country., such., different., much., society., next., theirs, similar., nation, land.
5971 | 0.96

4099 prohibit v
noun law., state, .use, rule., government, .discrimination, act., amendment., regulation., policy., .sale, abortion, legislation., .exercise, activity *misc* .from, federal, public, specifically., strictly., restrict., .sexual, explicitly.
6328 | 0.91 A

4100 switch n
adj asleep, on-off, electrical, dim, off, electric, quick, sudden, reset *noun* light., power, wall, .hitter, flick., flip., .box, bait., toggle., computer *verb* make., turn, throw., hit., pull., press., control, cause, activate, push
6225 | 0.92

4101 genius n
adj creative, comic, musical, artistic, eccentric, mathematical, evil *noun* stroke., .grant, boy., kind., marketing., artist, computer., .award, myth., talent *verb* .figure, consider., recognize., .lie, .lay, admire, possess, declare., .invent, proclaim
6021 | 0.95

4102 starter n
adj returning, senior, three-year, four-year, key, slow, electric, projected, two-year, full-time *noun* season, game, defense, .kit, fire., .home, player, conversation., motor, .outlook *verb* return, lose, become., replace., name., .throw, .average, pitch, .score, graduate
6787 | 0.84 N

4103 stem v
noun problem., .tide, .fact, charge., .flow, part, effort, loss, violence, lack, difference, fear, difficulty., interest, failure *misc* .from, may., partly, largely., .directly, .primarily
6142 | 0.93 A

4104 primary n
adj democratic, presidential, open, gubernatorial, contested, mayoral *noun* Republican., new., state, caucus, party, voter, week, candidate, election, vote *verb* win., hold, lose, enter., defeat, focus, choose, challenge., .determine, include
6469 | 0.88 S

4105 cart n
adj full, electric, rolling, horse-drawn, wooden, wheeled, two-wheeled, motorized *noun* golf., shopping., horse, grocery., food, wheel, .path, donkey. *verb* push, pull, put., drive, fill, load, ride., roll, walk, carry
6256 | 0.91 F

4106 trap n
adj double, snap, live, blue, abandoned, deadly, magnetic, fat, optical *noun* .door, booby., sand., crab., death., lobster, tourist. *verb* fall, set, catch, use, avoid., lay, escape., spring, shut, haul
6227 | 0.92

4107 Cuban j
noun government, crisis, missile, people, exile, revolution, refugee, community, American, official
6326 | 0.90

4108 inmate n
adj other, fellow, death-row, black, female, federal, male, condemned, Hispanic, mental *noun* prison, death, row., state, jail, percent., number., program, population, camp *verb* house, .serve, allow, .receive, represent, treat, .escape, execute, .commit, .await
6286 | 0.91 N

4109 sacrifice *n*
adj human, great, personal, willing, ultimate, necessary, shared, ritual, financial, Supreme *noun* .fly, animal., blood., war, kind., willingness., lot., courage, .cannibalism, commitment *verb* make, require, offer, involve, demand., perform, honor, entail, prepare, save
6123 | 0.93

4110 officially *r*
.recognize, .begin, .sanction, .open, .declare, .end, government, .name, .announce, though., yet, .designate, season., .dead
5948 | 0.96

4111 slap *v*
noun hand, .face, .back, .knee, arm, water, .thigh, head, palm, foot, .side, .forehead, door, .table, .wrist *misc* .on, his, her, .him, .me, .down, .against, .across
6448 | 0.88 F

4112 credit *v*
noun .success, parent, bank, account, official., .helping, .wife, .invention, coach, historian., analyst., observer., column., .mentor, Reagan *misc* give, widely., often., generally.
6062 | 0.94 N

4113 mysterious *j*
noun way, death, woman, man, world, thing, force, object, figure, disease, power, place *misc* remain, dark, somewhat, beautiful, strange, ancient, powerful, complex
5998 | 0.95

4114 Arab *n*
adj fellow, Shiite, moderate, neighboring *noun* Sunni., Jew, Israeli, .Muslim, Palestinian, Gulf, conflict *verb* .live, kill, fight, .remain, .support, accept, hate, urge., unite, seek
6707 | 0.85 A

4115 specialize *v*
noun company., firm., lawyer., .issue, attorney., .case, art, writer., area, doctor., fund., business, research, .health, service *misc* medical, .treat, highly., .particular, tend., increasingly.
  in company., firm., doctor., artist., architect.
6110 | 0.93 M

4116 fork *n*
adj middle, left, front, carbon-fiber, spading, three-pronged *noun* knife, .river, .road, spoon, carbon, travel, frame., suspension, plate, aluminum. *verb* use., put., hold, pick., mix, stir, fluff., pierce, set, stick.
7239 | 0.79 M

4117 invitation *n*
adj open, formal, engraved, official, coveted, irresistible, seductive *noun* party, dinner, wedding, letter, friend, .tournament, standing., event, list *verb* accept., receive., send, extend, decline., issue, turn., refuse., respond., .arrive
5940 | 0.96

4118 sail *v*
noun ship, boat, sea, .world, ocean, water, .air, vessel, ball., .coast, island, cruise, .England, .river, fleet. *misc* .through, .into, set., .over, .away, .across, .around, .past
6108 | 0.93 F

4119 regulatory *j*
noun agency, commission, state, system, process, policy, authority, energy, requirement, program, action, approval *misc* federal, nuclear, legal, environmental, create, require, legislative
6764 | 0.84 A

4120 cartoon *n*
adj political, editorial, animated, popular, favorite, classic, original *noun* .character, .network, morning., show, .series, .art, .figure, .strip *verb* watch., draw., publish, .depict, run, feature, .appear, print, portray, illustrate
6048 | 0.94

4121 stiff *j*
noun competition, peak, penalty, neck, leg, lip, body, finger, arm, wind, back, breeze *misc* until, too, feel, form, upper, stand, beat
6233 | 0.91 F M

4122 courtroom *n*
adj federal, packed, criminal, empty, crowded, hushed, mock *noun* camera., .day, judge, .drama, trial, jury, lawyer, juror, scene, testimony *verb* sit., leave., walk., enter., allow., testify, .erupt, gather., .explode, .hush
6263 | 0.91 S

4123 import *n*
adj foreign, Japanese, American, total, British, increased, full, dependent, expensive, middle *noun* oil., export, percent, country, restriction, tariff, food, duty, .substitution, car *verb* increase, ban., reduce, rise, restrict., impose., allow, .account, compete, exceed
6552 | 0.87 A

4124 tightly *r*
her, hold., so., wrap, .around, hand, more., cover, .control, arm, together, close, pack, too.
6110 | 0.93 F

4125 flash *n*
adj hot, white, bright, blinding, sudden, red, blue, quick, green, brilliant *noun* .light, lightning, news., eye, camera, night, .pan, .anger, .insight, .fire *verb* see., show., catch, illuminate, fill, explode, cause, reveal, disappear, reduce
6238 | 0.91 F

4126 equation *n*
adj multiple, structural, simple, differential, mathematical, following, significant, general, quadratic, whole *noun* line., regression., part., side., variable, model, solution., factor., .modeling, .state *verb* .represent, use, enter., solve, change, estimate, .describe, include, calculate, .predict
6967 | 0.81 A

4127 treasure *n*
adj national, buried, hidden, real, greatest, lost, archaeological, priceless, secret, historic *noun* .island, .trove, .chest, art., .hunter, house, pirate., .map, blood. *verb* find, bury, hide, discover., search., seek, hunt, protect., guard., .await
6088 | 0.93

4128 jaw *n*
adj low, strong, open, square, broken, upper, powerful, shut, gaping, firm *noun* muscle, tooth, set, .drop, line, face, bone, mouth, nose, neck *verb* clench, break, snap, .tighten, move, rub.
6302 | 0.90 F

4129 scan *v*
noun eye•, •room, •crowd, •sky, •face, image, •horizon, page, •area, system, computer, line, •list, document, wall *misc* quickly, •ahead, •entire, constantly•, carefully
6249 | 0.91 F

4130 condemn *v*
noun •death, resolution•, •attack, •action, government, •violence, •Israel, •act, right, •bombing, council•, statement•, •terrorism, leader, •Iraq *misc* strongly•, human, •die, roundly•, publicly•, widely•
6045 | 0.94

4131 improved *j*
noun performance, quality, health, technology, system, efficiency, relation, service, management, version, communication, condition *misc* new, lead, result, better, provide, increased, include, such
6271 | 0.90 A

4132 pickup *n*
adj old, full-size, red, white, blue, compact, battered, green, four-wheel-drive, stolen *noun* •truck, •game, back•, car, bed, vehicle, utility, •basketball, •line, cab•
verb drive, park, pull, load, climb, ride, jump, •drag, •roll, •haul
6149 | 0.92

4133 dignity *n*
adj human, great, personal, quiet, equal, inherent *noun* sense•, right, person, honor, freedom, death•, worth, grace, value, being *verb* treat•, maintain•, die, restore•, lose, respect, preserve•, uphold•, •constitute
6076 | 0.93

4134 inspiration *n*
adj divine, artistic, original, creative, sudden, spiritual, greatest *noun* source•, artist, moment•, painting, design, information, other, song, flash•, past *verb* find•, draw•, provide•, serve•, seek•, •strike, receive, derive, gain•, motivate
6005 | 0.94 M

4135 automatic *j*
noun transmission, weapon, system, rifle, machine, control, pilot, door, pistol, teller, response, thought *misc* four-speed, five-speed, fully, carry, fire, six-speed, manual
6056 | 0.93

4136 merchant *n*
adj wealthy, rich, online, foreign, downtown, retail, prosperous, prominent, enterprising, traveling *noun* •ship, •marine, association, •class, wine•, arm•, business, •seaman, •vessel *verb* sell, travel, own, trade, dominate, •refuse, sink, haggle, donate, persuade•
6084 | 0.93

4137 Greek *j*
noun word, tragedy, God, mythology, revival, island, church, myth, philosopher, chorus, text, Cypriot
6100 | 0.92

4138 hostile *j*
noun environment, takeover, force, world, work, aggression, bid, territory, action, attitude, act, witness *misc* toward, against, create, often, increasingly, openly, less, towards
5968 | 0.94

4139 extended *j*
noun family, period, time, member, warranty, trip, stay, hour, analysis, care, use, discussion *misc* over, during, immediate, nuclear, dry, due, objective
6027 | 0.93 A

4140 homeland *n*
adj ancestral, Jewish, Palestinian, independent, traditional, adopted, ancient *noun* •security, department•, secretary, defense, director, office•, committee *verb* return•, leave•, create, protect•, flee•, defend•, secure•, fight
6136 | 0.92

4141 gasoline *n*
adj reformulated, unleaded, leaded, regular, cheap, conventional, burning *noun* price, tax, gallon•, oil, •engine, fuel, •station, diesel, car, •pump *verb* sell, run, reduce, burn, buy•, pay, raise, pour, •cost, douse•
6085 | 0.92

4142 gravity *n*
adj low, strong, weak, artificial, light, specific, normal, lunar *noun* center•, force, •wave, earth, law•, theory•, planet, •situation, •field, pull *verb* defy•, understand•, cause, shift, produce, fight•, detect•, •act, form, •exist
6408 | 0.88

4143 defeat *n*
adj military, crushing, humiliating, political, major, electoral, stunning, total, certain *noun* victory, war, election, party, Republican, agony•, •communism, admission•, landslide• *verb* suffer•, concede•, accept•, admit•, follow•, face•, avoid•, weaken•, •eliminate, •haunt
5935 | 0.95

4144 near *j*
noun term, side, death, miss, distance, collapse, end, certainty, tear, monopoly, extinction, silence *misc* very, eastern, least, total, ancient, far, future, perfect
5832 | 0.96

4145 thoroughly *r*
so•, more•, until•, mix, dry, •enjoy, wash, •modern, investigate, as•, •heat, rinse, water, •before
5909 | 0.95 M

4146 exchange *v*
noun •glance, •look, word, information, •idea, gift, prisoner, money, •greeting, letter, •smile, •pleasantry, •data, •message, •e-mail *misc* •few, •vow, •quick, •brief, freely, willing•
5927 | 0.95 F

4147 bow *n*
adj red, little, black, slight, deep, pink, short, final *noun* •tie, •arrow, boat, shot•, string, ship, •stern, hair, line, wave *verb* take•, draw, shoot, wear•, pull•, carry•, bend, hang, •scrape, attach
6268 | 0.90 F M

4148 glory *n*
adj old, great, past, crowning, reflected, full, greatest, personal *noun* •day, morning•, •year, power, moment•, blaze•, path•, dream, fame, honor *verb* bring, bask•, restore•, cover•, seek, recapture•, share•, recall•, fade, shine
5924 | 0.95

4149 reserve *v*
noun right, room, cup, seat, space, .judgment, table, area., power, liquid, spot, juice, land, term, .admission *misc* usually., special, once., normally.
5906 | 0.95

4150 optimistic *j*
noun future, view, reason, bias, scenario, prospect, projection, assumption, note, outlook, estimate, assessment *misc* about, more, very, most, remain, cautiously, overly, less
5939 | 0.94

4151 sergeant *n*
adj retired, technical, mounted *noun* army, staff., drill., police., .major, master., detective., .arm *verb* arrive, shout, promote., command, order, retire, yell, question, salute
6149 | 0.91 F

4152 casualty *n*
adj civilian, American, heavy, high, military, mass, low, only, allied, possible *noun* war, number., property., .rate, percent, report, force, .side, .figure, damage *verb* suffer., inflict., become., cause, avoid., minimize., mount, reduce., result, expect
6130 | 0.91 S

4153 concede *v*
noun official., .point, .defeat, critic., administration, .election, Democrat, aide., supporter., opponent., expert., .error, .legitimacy, .inch *misc* willing., readily., refuse., finally., ready., privately, force.
5910 | 0.95

4154 bloody *j*
noun war, battle, hand, glove, nose, murder, hell, conflict, mess, knife, face, scene *misc* civil, scream, fight, violent, broken, brutal, plant, terrible
6034 | 0.93 F

4155 barn *n*
adj old, red, converted, wooden, weathered, haunted, wobbly *noun* .door, house, horse, night, side, cow, roof, farm, hay, wall *verb* build, walk, sleep, close., head., enter., burn, clean., hang
6188 | 0.90 F

4156 donate *v*
noun .money, .blood, .charity, year, organ, company., land, food, dollar, family, fund, .egg, .kidney, proceed, church *misc* to, .by, willing., agree., sell, pledge.
5957 | 0.94 N

4157 unite *v*
noun country, world, party, nation, community, group, opposition, Republican, issue, American, Europe, force, bond, organization, interest *misc* .behind, .against, .common, .under, stand
5930 | 0.94

4158 pro *n*
adj real, seasoned, assistant, longtime, second-year, head *noun* .con, quid., .forma, golf., tour., college, club, tennis., amateur, PGA. *verb* turn., play, weigh., discuss., hire., .win, debate., compete, argue., ride
6234 | 0.90 M

4159 senior *n*
adj high-school, low-income, disabled, poor, fifth-year, college-bound, 17-year-old *noun* school., junior.,

student, college, drug, child, percent, prescription, group, adult. *verb* say, graduate, offer, .play, .spend, .receive, return, .sign, lead, target
6143 | 0.91 N

4160 feedback *n*
adj positive, negative, specific, immediate, corrective, verbal, visual, constructive *noun* student, performance, teacher, .loop, comment, system, author, affiliation, type, information *verb* provide., give., receive, .send, base., offer., indicate, obtain, seek, suggest
6972 | 0.8 A

4161 grief *n*
adj good, anticipatory, deep, personal, private, profound, shared, terrible *noun* loss, anger, pain, lot., death, .counselor, feeling, shock, rage, depression *verb* feel, cause, deal., share., express., die, experience, fill, overwhelm, compound
6057 | 0.92 F

4162 spite *i*
(in spite of) .of, .fact, .herself, .himself, .effort, .everything, yet., .myself, smile., .difference, .difficulty, .attempt, success, .opposition
5949 | 0.94 A

4163 steep *j*
noun slope, hill, price, trail, mountain, terrain, road, decline, hillside, side, angle, incline *misc* up, climb, too, down, narrow, long
6348 | 0.88 M

4164 productivity *n*
adj high, low, increased, agricultural, economic, lost, increasing, primary *noun* growth, gain, worker, increase, labor., quality, cost, rate, loss, improvement *verb* improve., boost., reduce, raise., rise, enhance., decline, affect., focus, contribute
6290 | 0.89 A

4165 conceive *v*
noun child, idea, project, baby, plan, art, nation, couple., mind, design, son, nature, .term, culture, character *misc* .as, originally., ever., .execute, difficult., .terms, poorly., able., hard.
6077 | 0.92 A

4166 tender *j*
noun vegetable, potato, age, meat, rice, onion, bean, leaf, care, skin, moment, plant *misc* until, or, about, cook, stir, very, add, pierce
6278 | 0.89 M

4167 continent *n*
adj African, American, European, entire, dark, whole, vast, Antarctic *noun* ocean, earth, culture, edge, island, region, rest., ice, interior., wilderness *verb* cross., spread., travel., span., sweep., visit, explore, drift, split
6143 | 0.91

4168 hardware *n*
adj military, available, local, necessary, expensive, additional, electronic, high-tech, specialized *noun* .store, software, computer., system, home, center, piece., company, technology, .problem *verb* sell, buy, require, install, own, purchase, upgrade
6581 | 0.85 M

4169 equip *v*
noun computer, force, kitchen, device, army, .technology, .equipment, .radio, .video, facility, .weapon, engine, .bag, classroom, .knowledge *misc* .with, better., fully., well., train
5985 | 0.93 M

4170 wagon *n*
adj old, covered, red, horse-drawn, welcome, empty, wooden, mule-drawn *noun* station., .train, .wheel, horse, back., road, family, paddy., ride, hay. *verb* pull, drive, circle., load, fall., hitch., .roll, carry, haul, push
6145 | 0.91 F

4171 besides *i*
other., something., one, only, else., .fact, anything., anyone., someone., factor., .obvious, option., .usual, .myself
5729 | 0.97

4172 output *n*
adj total, high, economic, industrial, low, maximum, current, annual, agricultural, cardiac *noun* input., power., percent, level, energy., growth, price, rate, oil., signal *verb* produce, reduce, measure, provide, boost., decline, .fall, .rise, raise, require
6667 | 0.83 A

4173 withdrawal *n*
adj unconditional, immediate, complete, military, social, full, early, total *noun* troop, .force, .symptom, timetable., plan, bank, water., reason, date, sport *verb* call., begin, lead, announce., demand., follow, allow, occur, trigger
6099 | 0.91

4174 elder *n*
adj tribal, young, Asian, traditional, Indian, respected, male, ethnic, chief, rural *noun* village., minority., family, church, community, surgeon, .statesman, council, party., leader *verb* speak, respect., teach, .die, listen, share, interview, gather, honor., .participate
6320 | 0.88 A

4175 cage *n*
adj gilded, empty, wooden, indoor, golden, loose, locked, ornate *noun* rib., bird., wire., door, batting., bar, metal., steel. *verb* open, rattle., place, clean., .contain, hang, lock., build, pull, escape.
6092 | 0.91 F

4176 coastal *j*
noun area, water, city, state, town, region, community, zone, development, wetland, island, forest *misc* along, marine, southern, northern, arctic, inland, protect, plain
6338 | 0.88 A

4177 patience *n*
adj little, thin, infinite, endless, exaggerated, considerable, enormous, incredible *noun* time, lot., virtue, perseverance, persistence, skill, love, practice, understanding, tolerance *verb* lose., require, need., run, try, learn., show., wait, .wear, test.
6050 | 0.92

4178 shallow *j*
noun water, dish, bowl, pan, pool, lake, grave, baking, breathing, end, breath, area *misc* into, large, wide, place, deep, relatively, near, along
5995 | 0.93 M

4179 earthquake *n*
adj major, strong, devastating, powerful, massive, natural, future, huge, deadly *noun* fire, magnitude, flood, hurricane, damage, victim, fault, .insurance *verb* .hit, .strike, cause, .occur, shake, follow, kill, destroy, trigger, survive.
6180 | 0.90 S

4180 voting *n*
adj electronic, early, conservative, congressional, liberal, weighted, computerized *noun* .right, .record, .machine, .booth, .act, .system, .bloc, member, .booth, election *verb* consider., prevent., influence., extend, affect., abstain., lower., restore, .consist
6023 | 0.92

4181 input *n*
adj public, sensory, direct, agricultural, visual, significant, creative, organic, parental *noun* .output, data, student, level, signal, energy, process, community, .device, teacher *verb* provide., use, require, seek., receive, base., include, solicit., .differ, generate
6529 | 0.85 A

4182 canvas *n*
adj large, white, blank, black, stretched, entire, green *noun* oil., .bag, paint, painting, color, paper, .tent, acrylic., panel, artist *verb* cover, stretch, tone, hang, carry, mount, capture, prepare, depict, stare.
7232 | 0.77 M

4183 slide *n*
adj original, downward, electric, downhill, slow, linear, steep *noun* .show, color., water., .film, .presentation, division, .competition, .projector, .rule *verb* use, send, stop., project, present, reverse., prepare, place, view, shoot
7249 | 0.76 A

4184 click *v*
noun .button, site, heel, door, .link, icon, tab, mouse, .tongue, box, camera., file, phone, folder, lock *misc* .off, .on, something, open, .away, .shut, .together, choose, select, online
6609 | 0.84 F M

4185 sword *n*
adj double-edged, two-edged, short, flaming, magic, ceremonial, bloody *noun* hand, blade, hilt, shield, samurai., arm, fire., .fight, .scabbard, .sheath *verb* draw., hold, raise, swing., carry., fall, hang, pull., wield., .cut
6493 | 0.85 F

4186 mate *n*
adj running, potential, perfect, ideal, suitable, prospective, chief *noun* soul., male, choice, female, band., selection, office., cell., .class *verb* find., choose., attract., meet., pick., seek., select., .possess, guard, cheat
5978 | 0.93 M

4187 portfolio *n*
adj diversified, average, entire, professional, overall, electronic, personal, senior, balanced *noun* stock, .manager, investment, fund, assessment, bond, company, loan., growth, .management *verb* include, diversify., build., hold, manage, invest, create., develop, buy, .contain
6975 | 0.79 M

4188 bug n
adj bad, acting, electronic, nasty, super, big-eyed, squashed, entrepreneurial _noun_ lightning., .spray, water, love., computer, millennium., gold., .bite, .repellent _verb_ eat, catch., keep, kill., fix, .cause, .fly, .crawl, squash., pick
6041 | 0.92 F

4189 refrigerator n
adj small, airtight, cold, electric, efficient, tiny, built-in, energy-efficient _noun_ .door, store., freezer, hour, stove, food, kitchen, container., magnet, beer _verb_ open., keep, cover, place, buy, remove, thaw., marinate., cool, .hum
5967 | 0.93

4190 escape n
adj great, only, narrow, possible, daring, easy, quick, attempted _noun_ fire., .route, .hatch, means., .attempt, .plan, .clause _verb_ make., offer., seek., provide., block, prevent.
5807 | 0.95

4191 heat v
noun .oil, water, skillet, oven, .home, pan, house, gas, saucepan, energy, .butter, stove, milk, grill, fire _misc_ until, .through, thoroughly., .remaining, cool, medium-high, slowly, .remove, bake., burn
   up thing., start., begin., again, water, competition., war., debate, battle, race.
6011 | 0.92 M

4192 northeast n
adj far, industrial, rural, upper, Brazilian, impoverished, extreme _noun_ mile., state, .corner, city, region, area, center, .coast, .corridor, river _verb_ locate., head., lie, blow, travel., dominate, stretch
5960 | 0.93

4193 seventh m
.grade, .eighth, .day, .grader, .year, .century, .inning, sixth., .floor, .game, .street, .season, finish., .generation
5903 | 0.94 N

4194 post v
noun sign, message, .record, company., .Internet, year, .loss, information, .gain, notice, .profit, picture, .victory, guard, board _misc_ keep., .online, .million, .outside, .along, recently.
5909 | 0.93 N

4195 combined j
noun effect, company, force, group, effort, score, income, sewer, cycle, record, therapy, rate _misc_ million, billion, total, annual, exceed, Nordic, mean, average, gross, worth, due
6039 | 0.91 A

4196 alien n
adj illegal, resident, undocumented, legal, criminal, evil, non-resident, friendly, slapped, humanoid _noun_ space., .country, enemy., earth, citizen, human, border, .sedition, amnesty., encounter _verb_ hire., abduct., .land, .enter, arrest, attack, invade, wonder, claim, sound
6559 | 0.84 F

4197 willingness n
adj great, apparent, increasing, increased, growing, average, seeming _noun_ ability, .risk, .sacrifice, teacher, court, attitude., individual, public, capacity

verb show., .pay, demonstrate., indicate., .accept, express., .participate, .engage, .share, .consider
6053 | 0.91 A

4198 hidden j
noun camera, agenda, cost, treasure, meaning, videotape, world, place, curriculum, message, video, danger _misc_ from, reveal, discover, behind, OK, uncover, secret, catch, contain
6334 | 0.87

4199 accounting n
adj general, financial, public, full, accepted, corporate, creative _noun_ .office, .firm, .system, .information, company, report, .practice, .standard, .profession, .rule _verb_ use, demand., base, study, implement, enroll, oversee.
7093 | 0.78 A

4200 sexually r
.abuse, .transmitted, .active, .disease, .assault, .explicit, woman, .harass, her, .aggressive, become., .molest, .behavior, .material
6389 | 0.86

4201 chop v
noun cup, onion, tablespoon, garlic, clove, teaspoon, pepper, parsley, tomato, cilantro _misc_ fresh, finely., coarsely., medium, large, small, seed., .off
   up .into, .little, .onion, .piece, small
6672 | 0.83 M

4202 patrol n
adj civil, military, mounted, marine, armed, increased, mobile, coastal _noun_ border., .car, highway., .agent, officer, .boat, state. _verb_ join., conduct, step., .arrive, ambush, fly, ride, spot, .check, guard
5884 | 0.94

4203 symbolic j
noun meaning, gesture, value, form, capital, act, significance, power, importance, representation, language, order _misc_ largely, social, real, highly, both, cultural, represent, economic
6330 | 0.87 A

4204 ruin v
noun life, career, reputation, day, .chance, .economy, season, .relationship, .marriage, plan, credit, road., rain, .sport, .mood _misc_ .everything, whole, nearly., completely, financially
5797 | 0.95 F

4205 rock v
noun boat, world, baby, .side, explosion., head, car, scandal, foot, cradle, ship, earthquake., .vote, motion, seat _misc_ .forth, gently, sit., .sleep, .forward, slowly, ready.
5922 | 0.93 F

4206 drum n
adj bass, red, double, African, rotating, wooden, freshwater, electronic _noun_ oil., beat, steel., .roll, .set, .machine, snare., .major _verb_ play., hear, bang., pound, dance, sound, hit, rattle
5955 | 0.92

4207 opposed i
(as opposed to) .to, as., .just, one, .percent, real, individual, .traditional, .simply, actual, .merely, .mere, .conventional, .purely
5895 | 0.93 A

4208 sheer *j*
noun number, size, volume, force, cliff, joy, wall, power, will, pleasure, rock, luck *misc* through, out, because, terms, physical, overwhelm, wear, but
5755 | 0.95

4209 ideological *j*
noun difference, position, line, conflict, struggle, party, reason, commitment, battle, issue, agenda, spectrum *misc* political, between, cultural, social, religious, economic, within
6424 | 0.85 A

4210 discourage *v*
noun .use, .investment, government, policy., effort, practice, behavior, worker, .development, .growth, tax., .participation, price., rule., attempt *misc* try, actively., seek, strongly., tend.
5742 | 0.96

4211 canal *n*
adj auditory, external, grand, spinal, industrial, anal, fallopian, vaginal *noun* ear., street, water, root., .zone, birth., irrigation., love., river, system *verb* build, dig, pass, cross., enter., connect, flow, divert, operate, .link
6114 | 0.90

4212 prior *j*
noun permission, experience, research, knowledge, year, study, approval, history, record, conviction, use, finding *misc* or, without, in, written, part, no, base, consistent
6242 | 0.88 A

4213 haul *v*
noun truck, water, .ass, .load, car, wood, .gear, boat, bag, .court, rope, wagon, body, freight, trailer *misc* .out, .up, .away, .back, .himself, before, .onto, home, .aboard, .myself
  off .jail, .hit, .slap, .punch, .slug, .smack, handcuff, .kick
5935 | 0.92 F

4214 protective *j*
noun service, child, factor, effect, gear, measure, custody, clothing, layer, order, suit, equipment *misc* wear, very, against, around, provide, such, form, fiercely
5829 | 0.94

4215 regard *i*
(in/with regard(s) to) .to, with., particularly., especially., issue, policy, question, .use, difference, gender, behavior, position., differ., role
6176 | 0.89 A

4216 conspiracy *n*
adj vast, right-wing, criminal, guilty, international, federal, grand, involved, alleged, communist *noun* .theory, charge, part., .theorist, fraud, count, government, .silence *verb* .commit, convict., .involve, .kill, .murder, plead., engage., prove., allege, join.
5863 | 0.93 S

4217 steam *n*
adj full, hot, superheated, fragrant, excess, flash, rising *noun* .engine, water, .turbine, .room, cloud., .locomotive, minute, heat, power, head. *verb* .rise, let., run, blow., pick., lose., .escape, produce, gather., hiss
5951 | 0.92

4218 embassy *n*
adj American, Chinese, British, Soviet, Israeli, French, German *noun* US., bombing, official, attack., .staff, spokesman, officer, .compound, east, .suite *verb* bomb, close, contact, seize, surround, arrive, .issue, protect., .warn, .advise
6032 | 0.91 S

4219 tackle *v*
noun .problem, .issue, .question, .subject, team., .challenge, .project, game, .task, .interception, .topic, .fumble, player., .ground, effort. *misc* .tough, ready., .difficult, serious, willing.
5960 | 0.92 N

4220 tropical *j*
noun forest, storm, rain, fruit, plant, fish, island, depression, tree, species, region, rainforest *misc* subtropical, lush, temperate, such, warm, eastern, exotic, botanical
6102 | 0.90 M

4221 instantly *r*
almost., kill., become, recognize, die., .recognizable, fall, .transform, realize, .regret, voice, respond., love, asleep
5904 | 0.92 F

4222 bubble *n*
adj tiny, speculative, dot-com, pink, real-estate, high-tech, acrylic *noun* .gum, air., .bath, .burst, soap., .economy, .wrap, gas, plastic., stock *verb* blow., pop, form, create., fill, .appear, remove., float, prick., .expand
5860 | 0.93

4223 calm *v*
noun .nerve, .fear, voice, .mind, breath., situation, traffic, effort., sea, .anxiety, attempt., crowd, breathing, horse, wind. *misc* try., him, her, help, .himself, .herself, .myself, .yourself, relatively.
  down she, just, try., now, need., after, .little, let, until., .bit
5944 | 0.92 F

4224 sheep *n*
adj black, wild, grazing, lost, domestic, cloned, mad *noun* goat, cattle, cow, bighorn, flock., horse, mountain, dog, wolf, pig *verb* graze, raise, kill, count., shear, feed, eat, clone, .wander, bleat
5974 | 0.91

4225 rent *n*
adj low, monthly, free, available, cheap, due, annual, average, median *noun* month, money, apartment, .control, food, .payment, .utility, increase, tenant, income *verb* pay., collect., raise., cover, rise, afford., charge., receive, .range, reduce.
5895 | 0.93 N

4226 accent *n*
adj southern, thick, heavy, foreign, strong, slight, soft, funny, fake, strange *noun* voice, color, trace., pillow, plant, gold, .piece, wood, east. *verb* speak., add, lose., .sound, imitate., affect., recognize, acquire., betray, highlight
5849 | 0.93 F

4227 grasp *v*
noun hand, .concept, arm, .handle, .straw, .meaning, .significance, .idea, finger, truth, mind., .bar, .nature, .opportunity, .importance *misc* fully., fail., seem., hard., difficult., able., both
5830 | 0.93 F

4228 modify v
noun .search, interest., .behavior, .rule, system, design, .policy, law, .environment, structure, .use, model, curriculum, .litigation, contract. *misc* .your, genetically., slightly, .existing, allow, easily., significantly
6431 | 0.85 A

4229 grin v
noun .ear, .camera, smile, .delight, .pride, .relief, .triumph, .anticipation *misc* .at, him, back, .broadly, nod, suddenly, .sheepishly
6547 | 0.83 F

4230 toxic j
noun waste, substance, effect, material, metal, release, site, gas, exposure, air, dump, pollution *misc* highly, less, contain, chemical, reduce, produce, such, potentially
6100 | 0.89 M

4231 mixed j
noun result, message, bag, blessing, review, feeling, signal, emotion, waste, race, salad, group *misc* send, receive, produce, draw, despite, green, best, martial
5845 | 0.93 A

4232 magnitude n
adj faint, absolute, bright, visual, similar, sheer, relative, apparent, full *noun* order., star, .problem, earthquake, change, .effect, difference, quake, event, brightness *verb* reach., understand., determine., vary, estimate, brighten., indicate, fade., realize., range
6741 | 0.81 M A

4233 afterward r
soon., shortly., long., year., immediately., week., month., hour., .lay, reporter., minute., dinner., recall, wash
5837 | 0.93

4234 root v
noun .tradition, culture, .history, .experience, terrorism, .spot, .corruption, ground, tree, fan., identity, sense, .nature, .past, value *misc* deeply., firmly., .around, deep, remain.
  out .corruption, .terrorist, try., .insurgent, effort., terrorism, .fraud, evil, Taliban, .cause
5720 | 0.95

4235 progressive j
noun party, movement, era, tax, policy, disease, politics, education, school, change, idea, group *misc* more, most, social, democratic, political, liberal, conservative, politically
5964 | 0.91 A

4236 manipulate v
noun system, ability., image, object, .information, .data, computer, level, .price, media, other, .environment, .public, process, .opinion *misc* by, try., control, easily., able., easy.
5791 | 0.94 A

4237 vaccine n
adj effective, available, pneumococcal, experimental, oral, developing, contaminated, dangerous, engineered *noun* flu., AIDS., polio., dose, smallpox., development, disease, virus, cancer, trial *verb* develop, receive., produce, .prevent, test, .protect, .cause, .contain, create, administer
6415 | 0.85

4238 monument n
adj national, ancient, public, historical, historic, cultural, natural, architectural, dead, funerary *noun* park, museum, building, city, site, stone., memorial, dinosaur., commission, cactus. *verb* build, erect, stand, create, visit., .commemorate, dedicate, .mark, preserve, construct
6066 | 0.90

4239 trace n
adj faint, only, human, slight, visible, lingering, remaining, mere, bare *noun* .element, .metal, .amount, .evidence, .gas, .mineral, .accent, .smile, .irony, .fat *verb* leave., find., show., contain., vanish., disappear., .remain, remove., carry., discover
5818 | 0.93 F

4240 verdict n
adj guilty, unanimous, final, not-guilty, split, just, official *noun* jury., case, trial, court, juror, death, murder, reaction., .form, history *verb* reach., read, return., render., hear., announce, deliver, overturn, wait., appeal.
6025 | 0.90 S

4241 flexible j
noun schedule, work, system, hour, approach, arrangement, spending, scheduling, plastic, plan, policy, benefit *misc* more, enough, allow, less, remain, strong, highly, adaptable
5881 | 0.92 A

4242 declaration n
adj universal, joint, public, formal, unilateral, final, official, congressional *noun* .independence, .war, .right, principle, .love, nation., document, emergency, author. *verb* sign, issue, write, read, adopt, .state, draft., rescind., .reflect, .proclaim
5985 | 0.90 A

4243 costume n
adj elaborate, native, Indian, bathing, cheap, medieval, goofy *noun* .designer, Halloween., .jewelry, set, .design, .party, .contest *verb* wear, dress., sew., feature, fit, clad., .consist, portray
5887 | 0.92

4244 drawer n
adj top, bottom, full, locked, warming, secret, middle *noun* desk, chest., dresser., cabinet, file., kitchen, bureau, table, sock., back *verb* open., pull, rummage., reach., close, .hold, slide, remove, shut, .contain
6158 | 0.88 F

4245 bless v
noun God., .America, .heart, child, Lord, .soul, gift, priest, union, church, baby, marriage, Allah., sir, memory *misc* .with, curse, truly., lucky, incredibly
5686 | 0.95

4246 rack n
adj roasting, middle, bottom, overhead, rear, wooden, cooling *noun* wire., pan, .minute, oven, .lamb, grill, magazine., bike., towel., coat. *verb* cool, place., transfer., remove, set, hang., bake, .hold
6069 | 0.89 M

4247 secure j
noun place, environment, job, area, system, future, border, facility, base, position, attachment, person *misc* more, feel, less, safe, provide, most, help, enough
5612 | 0.96

4248 position *v*
noun side, chair, camera, body, subject, ball, arm, .advantage, boat, rack, bed, screen, .cursor, tank., sensor *misc* .himself, .themselves, well., .itself, better., .yourself, .around, carefully., perfectly., strategically., .along
5737 | 0.94 M

4249 deeper *j*
noun understanding, water, level, meaning, problem, issue, sense, question, cut, insight, appreciation, root *misc* than, into, more, much, even, dig, far, lead, gain
5693 | 0.95

4250 divorce *v*
noun parent., wife, husband, mother, child, father, couple, daughter, son, month, mom, dad, .reality, .politics, spouse *misc* .from, she, when, after, married, twice, recently.
5672 | 0.95

4251 neutral *j*
noun position, color, tone, response, ground, party, state, zone, hydrogen, expression, country, site *misc* remain, keep, negative, positive, stay, morally, toward, politically
5864 | 0.92 A

4252 fascinating *j*
noun story, thing, people, book, history, study, question, subject, case, person, stuff, character *misc* most, find, really, watch, absolutely, endlessly, quite, particularly
5714 | 0.94 S

4253 terrific *j*
noun job, guy, book, movie, idea, story, thing, player, film, performance, opportunity, actor *misc* look, really, thank, oh, absolutely, sound, OK, pretty
5902 | 0.91 S

4254 sympathy *n*
adj great, public, deepest, personal, certain, deep, international, genuine, profound *noun* lot., empathy, .victim, expression., understanding, support, .devil, .card, lack., compassion *verb* feel., express., show., offer., gain., win., extend., elicit., .lie, inspire
5648 | 0.95

4255 draft *v*
noun plan, player, .legislation, constitution, bill, law, team, .army, .letter, committee., document, report, agreement, regulation, proposal *misc* .by, help., military, originally., carefully.
5799 | 0.93 N

4256 spectacular *j*
noun view, success, scenery, display, result, growth, mountain, event, show, image, setting, performance *misc* most, offer, less, produce, truly, quite, pretty, absolutely
5765 | 0.93 M

4257 ounce *n*
adj fresh, dried, chopped, sliced, cream, smoked, frozen, shredded, extra, bittersweet *noun* .cheese, pound., cup, .chocolate, water, tomato, juice, butter, package., .gold *verb* weigh., chop, .shred, drink., dice, slice, grate, contain, taste.
6147 | 0.87 M

4258 rear *j*
noun end, seat, window, door, derailleur, front, view, suspension, leg, car, wall, mirror *misc* behind, left, open, fold, wheel, onto, middle
6433 | 0.83 M

4259 inn *n*
adj historic, bed-and-breakfast, nearby, local, Victorian, faithful, colonial, Japanese, crowded *noun* holiday., room, country., hotel, restaurant, night, breakfast, bed, .spa, street *verb* stay., own., operate, .feature, .overlook, .boast, recommend., .cater, dine., convert.
6008 | 0.89 M N

4260 collaboration *n*
adj interdisciplinary, successful, international, close, professional, effective, creative, active *noun* teacher, community, research, project, communication, process, cooperation, opportunity, agency, partnership *verb* work, develop, require, involve, encourage., promote., facilitate, foster., enhance, support
6227 | 0.86 A

4261 clip *n*
adj little, audio, short, fast, quick, annual, brief, rapid, faster *noun* video., paper., film., movie, show, look., hair, money., news., .art *verb* begin., end., play, watch., listen., pull, empty., check., remove., .depict
6124 | 0.87 S

4262 instruct *v*
noun student, teacher, participant., subject., jury, parent, judge, .staff, class, computer, employee, officer, .secretary, .reader, agent *misc* .return, specifically., .perform, prepare, carefully., properly.
5656 | 0.95 A

4263 sock *n*
adj white, black, dirty, blue, athletic, extra, heavy, wet, clean, brown *noun* shoe, pair., underwear, wool., pant, .drawer, short, knee., tube., sneakers *verb* wear., put, pull., knock., buy, match, change, remove., pick., slip
5889 | 0.91 F

4264 rider *n*
adj low, easy, free, young, rough, experienced, recreational, lone, light, serious *noun* horse, bike, bull., bus, freedom., subway. *verb* pass, carry, attract., attach, compete, .pedal, .climb, .gallop, .dismount, match
6950 | 0.77 M

4265 revelation *n*
adj new, divine, Christian, personal, startling, shocking, biblical, sudden, final *noun* book., moment., reason, truth, faith, .abuse, tradition, meaning., term *verb* follow., receive, experience., shock, .emerge, stun, witness, prompt, cite, constitute
5888 | 0.91

4266 object *v*
noun parent., member., other., .use, design, official., provision, critic., defense., .ground, Democrat., quota, establishment, .donation, .discrimination *misc* .to, strongly, strenuously, vehemently, vigorously
5556 | 0.96

4267 accomplishment *n*
adj great, personal, major, greatest, proud, significant, important, past, individual, impressive *noun* sense., feeling., pride., record., list., goal, level., achievement,

task, .administration _verb_ celebrate., recognize, consider, achieve, acknowledge, highlight., honor., praise.
5645 | 0.94

4268 seal n
adj spotted, green, gray, presidential, official, tight, airtight, imperial _noun_ navy., .approval, harbor., fur., elephant., pressure., monk., water _verb_ break, check., bear., kill, hunt, form, dive, test., obtain., award
6035 | 0.88

4269 faint j
noun star, light, sound, smile, object, voice, galaxy, glow, smell, magnitude, line, scent _misc_ hear, feel, grow, appear, blue, detect, distant, extremely
6348 | 0.84 F

4270 ease n
adj ill, relative, great, practiced, apparent, greatest, equal, natural, surprising _noun_ .use, mind., .access, speed, .movement, comfort, installation, convenience, .pain, tension _verb_ put., feel., seem., help., reflect, demonstrate., accomplish.
5595 | 0.95

4271 spell v
noun name, word, .trouble, .end, .disaster, .doom, .difference, .death, term _misc_ correctly, learn., read, unconventionally., .wrong, .backwards, conventionally, specific
   out letter, clearly, .detail, word, name, .exactly, rule, document, message, term
5520 | 0.96

4272 gospel n
adj social, Christian, contemporary, traditional, Gnostic, synoptic, southern, holy, old-time _noun_ .music, .singer, .choir, song, church, blues, truth, .album, message, group _verb_ preach., sing, spread., read, write, proclaim, record., share., feature, portray
6206 | 0.86 M

4273 whale n
adj blue, gray, large, white, beached, baleen, marine, modern, giant, beaked _noun_ killer., bowhead., humpback., sperm., beluga., .shark, water, pilot. _verb_ watch, save., swim, kill, migrate, eat, feed, spot, touch., count
6532 | 0.81

4274 theatre n
adj national, musical, Jewish, professional, Greek, outdoor, abandoned, interactive _noun_ .company, art, center, dance., alliance., music., .production, stage, night, ballet. _verb_ present, perform, .feature, attend., operate., found., renovate., integrate.
6499 | 0.82 N

4275 coordinator n
adj offensive, defensive, national, regional, assistant, clinical, medical _noun_ program, project., state, education, service, community, coach, office, event., volunteer. _verb_ serve., hire, fire, name., replace, appoint., interview, assist, supervise, .advise
5956 | 0.89 N

4276 talented j
noun student, people, player, team, woman, man, program, child, artist, guy, group, actor _misc_ gifted, who, very, most, young, academically, beautiful, enough
6123 | 0.87

4277 alongside i
work., .other, run., sit., place., stand., fight., road, walk., pull., serve., .each, .river, car
5551 | 0.96

4278 cab n
adj yellow, regular, extended, double, waiting, empty, checkered _noun_ .driver, truck, crew., taxi., night, back., door, .company, window, .pickup _verb_ take, hail., drive, call., .pull, climb., .stop, sit, ride, catch.
6016 | 0.88 F

4279 isolation n
adj social, economic, relative, international, geographic, physical, total, diplomatic, splendid, reproductive _noun_ sense., feeling., loneliness, depression, .cell, .lack, fear, alienation, poverty, .ward _verb_ live., end., experience, break., reduce., exist., consider., result, foster, heighten
5797 | 0.92 A

4280 costly j
noun system, mistake, program, war, service, process, regulation, care, litigation, problem, project, treatment _misc_ more, less, too, very, most, time-consuming, prove, require
5715 | 0.93

4281 tragic j
noun death, event, story, accident, life, loss, situation, consequence, case, result, mistake, figure _misc_ most, happen, die, sad, comic, recent, occur, terrible
5551 | 0.96

4282 loud j
noun voice, noise, music, bang, explosion, door, laughter, speaker, crack, crash, rock, whisper _misc_ hear, too, real, suddenly, sound, laugh, soft
5823 | 0.91 F

4283 instinct n
adj basic, natural, good, maternal, political, human, right, strong, bad, competitive _noun_ gut., survival, killer., animal., .self-preservation, hunting., herd. _verb_ .tell, trust., follow., rely., act., .lead, develop, fight, listen., appeal.
5548 | 0.96

4284 seat v
noun .chair, room, .bench, .row, .side, .couch, floor, .stool, .sofa, dinner, .kitchen, .dining, .cushion _misc_ .next, .behind, .around, .across, dozen
5762 | 0.92 F

4285 intimate j
noun relationship, knowledge, detail, life, connection, moment, way, contact, friend, conversation, experience, relation _misc_ more, most, between, very, personal, share, such
5615 | 0.94

4286 underlying j
noun cause, problem, assumption, structure, principle, issue, factor, value, reason, theme, condition, disease _misc_ address, reflect, understand, reveal, economic, identify, remain
5871 | 0.90 A

4287 respect i
(with respect to) .to, with., issue, particularly., policy, use, position., difference., especially., role, matter, decision, action, .gender
6229 | 0.85 A

4288 influential *j*
noun group, people, member, book, leader, factor, role, figure, man, teacher, family, woman *misc* most, more, become, highly, among, political, powerful
5718 | 0.93 A

4289 pastor *n*
adj senior, Baptist, associate, Lutheran, local, Methodist, black, evangelical, assistant *noun* church, father, parish, congregation, wife, member, priest, youth, leader, role *verb* serve., .preach, pray, .encourage, appoint, ordain, preside, counsel, contact, .baptize
6197 | 0.85

4290 presumably *r*
.because, therefore, .due, .refer, somewhere, .reference, intelligent, latter., .asleep, .response, .loyal
5635 | 0.94 A

4291 cook *n*
adj good, short-order, excellent, serious, southern, busy, Chinese, assistant, avid, amateur *noun* minute, heat., home., prep., pot, camp., ship., gourmet., .helper, waiter *verb* .stir, add., .turn, cover, .whisk, clean, watch, serve, name, eat
5886 | 0.90

4292 skip *v*
noun .school, .beat, .meal, heart., .class, .step, .breakfast, .rope, .lunch, .town, .generation, .stone, .dinner, morning, .dessert *misc* .over, .across, .ahead, .altogether, decide.
  out .early, .bill
5633 | 0.94

4293 eleven *m*
.year, .o'clock, .old, after, ten., .day, .month, about., age., .ago, .twelve, hundred, .later, morning
5746 | 0.92 F

4294 tens *m*
.thousand, .million, .dollar, .people, .billion, year, .hundred, .American, cost., few., spend., kill., worth., .mile
5656 | 0.93

4295 whoever *p*
.want, .win, .might, kill, .else, whatever, .responsible, .control, nominee, .charge, own, .elect, vote, .hell
5643 | 0.94 F

4296 ancestor *n*
adj common, human, early, distant, direct, ancient, dead, African, female, native *noun* spirit, land, name, God, .worship, generation, century, bone., Indian, ritual *verb* .live, honor., share., evolve, represent., .settle, .fight, .survive, inherit., trace
5989 | 0.88 A

4297 safely *r*
can., home, back, return, land., .away, out, until., bring., arrive., drive., tuck, ground, .behind
5490 | 0.96

4298 nominee *n*
adj presidential, judicial, presumptive, likely, general, federal, vice-presidential, top, particular, gubernatorial *noun* court., Republican., president, party, Oscar., year, award., attorney, .governor *verb* become., support., choose, confirm, select, announce, pick., oppose.
6029 | 0.88 S

4299 exotic *j*
noun species, animal, plant, dancer, place, bird, locale, fruit, food, location, material, creature *misc* more, such, foreign, less, native, beautiful, tropical
5602 | 0.94

4300 minimal *j*
noun amount, level, impact, cost, effect, standard, risk, effort, damage, support, requirement, change *misc* require, provide, only, least, receive, environmental
5765 | 0.91 A

4301 uncertain *j*
noun future, term, time, world, outcome, situation, status, environment, prospect, voice, fate, economy *misc* about, whether, remain, no, still, face, economic
5519 | 0.95

4302 Persian *j*
noun Gulf, war, crisis, oil, region, rug, state, carpet, empire, conflict, area
6008 | 0.88

4303 parental *j*
noun involvement, control, right, child, consent, support, education, behavior, family, school, notification, responsibility *misc* between, without, require, behavioral, terminate, relate, low, such
6216 | 0.85 A

4304 orchestra *n*
adj Philharmonic, full, professional, virtual, entire, live, symphonic *noun* symphony., band., music, chamber., chorus, conductor, concert, school., choir, youth. *verb* play, conduct, perform, lead, join, feature, accompany, present, rehearse
6174 | 0.85 N

4305 treasury *n*
adj federal, national, short-term, long-term, public, royal *noun* secretary, .department, US., .bond, .bill, yield, .security, .official, state., .note *verb* buy, cost., sell, invest., issue, .announce, back., finance, loot., borrow
5867 | 0.90

4306 tolerate *v*
noun behavior, society, patient, .presence, ability., soil, .condition, .pain, .abuse, plant., practice, sun, drug, American., .temperature *misc* not., will., can., long, well
5486 | 0.96

4307 gallon *n*
adj regular, average, crude, unleaded, fresh, estimated, raw, extra, liquid, additional *noun* .water, mile., .day, .gas, .gasoline, .fuel, .oil, .minute, .milk, price *verb* produce, cost, spill, drink., carry., buy., dump., save, burn, consume
5671 | 0.93

4308 thigh *n*
adj inner, right, left, upper, low, outer, fat, thin, skinless, front *noun* hand., leg, hip, muscle, knee, chicken., calf, .bone, inside., head *verb* slap., press, touch, rest., rub, spread, stroke., face, cover, place
5963 | 0.88 F

4309 fortunately *r*
.there, .most, unfortunately, .able, .no, .none, .plenty, rare, menu
5552 | 0.95 M

4310 ambitious *j*
noun plan, project, program, goal, effort, man, agenda, woman, undertaking, politician, proposal, campaign
misc most, more, young, too, less, far, overly
5573 | 0.94

4311 actively *r*
.involved, participate, .engage, .seek, student, .involve, work, .support, .promote, .pursue, become.,
encourage
5790 | 0.91 A

4312 flexibility *n*
adj great, regulatory, maximum, increased, local, considerable, financial, operational *noun* strength, state, .analysis, degree., need., freedom, lot., endurance, design, cost *verb* give., allow, provide, offer., increase., show., improve, require, maintain., demonstrate.
5763 | 0.91 A

4313 jar *n*
adj full, empty, little, clean, tight-fitting, sterilized, ceramic, cool, sealed, airtight *noun* glass., water, cookie., lid, Mason., pickle, canning., jelly, butter, food *verb* fill, open., hold, cover, place, set, .contain, store, shake, sterilize.
5778 | 0.91 F M

4314 cocaine *n*
adj powdered, prenatal, pure, alleged, raw, refined
noun crack., heroin, use, marijuana, drug, possession, user, addiction, powder, alcohol *verb* sell., buy., test., snort., deal, flood, .originate
5754 | 0.91

4315 incredibly *r*
.important, .difficult, feel., .powerful, .strong, .beautiful, .hard, .complex, .lucky, .rich
5572 | 0.94 S

4316 consequently *r*
.teacher, behavior, performance, environment., lack, purpose, .tend, participant
6089 | 0.86 A

4317 documentary *n*
adj new, best, short, award-winning, historical, acclaimed, controversial *noun* film, .evidence, .filmmaker, television, .series, TV, history, subject, video, producer *verb* produce., watch., direct, shoot, feature, narrate, capture, .explore, .chronicle, .trace
5667 | 0.92 N

4318 charge *i*
(in charge of) .of, who., put., man., official., .operation, president., agent., .security, special., vice., officer., person., agency.
5488 | 0.95

4319 insert *v*
noun .center, gene, toothpick., thermometer, tube, needle, card, key, knife., catheter, minute., doctor., .end, .portion, .finger *misc* .into, .come, .through, .register, bake., tiny, remove, thin
5635 | 0.93 M

4320 ambition *n*
adj political, personal, territorial, global, regional, modest, driving, secret, blind, stated *noun* dream., goal, desire, drive, lack., career., talent, greed, energy., .tour *verb* .become, realize, harbor., pursue., fulfill., achieve, match, motivate, satisfy., expand
5507 | 0.95

4321 functional *j*
noun assessment, status, analysis, limitation, group, unit, area, impairment, vision, level, capacity, food
misc fully, such, structural, behavioral, highly, decorative, than, beautiful
6208 | 0.84 A

4322 bankruptcy *n*
adj personal, federal, corporate, moral, near, potential, intellectual *noun* .court, .protection, company, chapter., .law, .filing, year, .judge, case, airline *verb* file., declare., force., emerge., seek., face., avoid., sell, rise, .wipe
5868 | 0.89 N

4323 runner *n*
adj front, high, long-distance, cross-country, fast, red, fastest, successful, male, avid *noun* distance., marathon., .position, base, road., blade., group, race, wind., drug. *verb* move, hit, throw, .steal, cross, .compete, advance, .complete, .gain, tag.
5855 | 0.89 N

4324 execution *n*
adj public, mass, scheduled, actual, perfect, poor, extrajudicial, parallel *noun* .unit, stay., method, death, instruction, planning., .chamber, .date *verb* witness., carry, stop., await., order., watch., proceed, deter
5886 | 0.89

4325 crush *v*
noun garlic, skull, car, .press, .death, army, weight, head, .rebellion, leg, bone, cigarette, body, ground, tank *misc* .under, .against, .beneath, nearly., easily, fresh
5525 | 0.95

4326 buddy *n*
adj old, best, sorry, running, longtime, muddy
noun .guy, school, .system, college., army., shot., fishing., drinking., hunting. *verb* drink, hire, cheer, impress, rescue., .swear, chat, assign., .skip, exercise.
5949 | 0.88

4327 workplace *n*
adj safe, changing, drug-free, healthy, modern, flexible, friendly *noun* woman, home, safety, school, discrimination, harassment, problem, violence, employee, issue *verb* create, enter., test, affect, improve, occur., address., succeed., foster
5734 | 0.91

4328 skull *n*
adj human, fractured, thick, full, complete, tiny, soft, bald *noun* bone, base, back., brain, fracture, top., hole., .crossbone, .cowboy, piece *verb* crush, crack., open, smash, fill, suffer., penetrate., grin, belong
5757 | 0.91 F

4329 cord *n*
adj spinal, umbilical, vocal, electrical, long, electric, thin, light *noun* .injury, .blood, extension., power., bungee., phone., cell, end, rip., telephone. *verb* cut., pull., tie, wrap, attach, hang, yank., stretch, connect, strike.
5660 | 0.92

4330 fixed *j*
noun rate, income, price, cost, amount, exchange, mortgage, point, system, position, number, asset
misc remain, pay, than, such, within, rather, monthly, per
5667 | 0.92 A

4331 equivalent *n*
adj moral, modern, political, functional, visual, musical, electronic, rough, literary *noun* cash., energy., oil, .dollar, barrel, ton, .cent, grade, gallon, century. *verb* become., pay., cost., earn., create., receive., produce.
5522 | 0.95

4332 casino *n*
adj Indian, grand, downtown, floating, land-based, lucrative, proposed, legalized *noun* gambling, hotel, city, .night, resort, riverboat., state, .floor, .owner, .operator *verb* open, build, operate, run, own, legalize, enter., generate, attract, .employ
5800 | 0.90 N

4333 reliability *n*
adj internal, high, interrater, acceptable, adequate, low, overall *noun* validity, .coefficient, consistency., alpha, scale, data, system, measure, study, analysis *verb* report, assess, demonstrate., establish, improve., determine, .range
6378 | 0.82 A

4334 expected *j*
noun value, rate, cost, benefit, level, return, result, direction, outcome, behavior, growth, number *misc* than, better, much, low, long, million, base, future, early
5696 | 0.92 A

4335 boil *v*
noun water, .minute, pot, mixture., blood., potato, pasta, kettle, broth., sauce, egg, frustration *misc* until, stir, bring., .reduce, constantly
over heat, .high, water., frustration., anger., tension., rage, temper. **down** all., often., basically., argument, ultimately., largely. **up** anger., cloud., dust.
5619 | 0.93 M

4336 whip *v*
noun .cream, wind., hair, head, egg, .face, .shape, sugar, air, .horse, butter, .frenzy, tail, ass, .gun *misc* .around, .into, .through, .across, .past
up wind., .batch, .dish, dinner, chef., .support, .frenzy, .crowd, .wave **out** .gun, .knife, .cell, .camera, .checkbook, .pistol
5730 | 0.91 F

4337 divine *j*
noun intervention, revelation, nature, power, love, right, Providence, presence, law, grace, creation, will *misc* human, natural, itself, holy, reveal, claim, supernatural, therefore
6485 | 0.8 A

4338 proposition *n*
adj expensive, general, risky, difficult, losing, approved, scary *noun* voter., ballot, business., passage., value., initiative, tax, support., response., measure *verb* pass, vote., test., accept., approve, oppose., dedicate., state, seek, limit
6040 | 0.86 A

4339 census *n*
adj recent, national, federal, official, agricultural, accurate *noun* .bureau, US., .data, .figure, population, .tract, state, .number, source., statistics *verb* .show, .report, count, conduct, .indicate, base., .reveal, release, .estimate, miss
5836 | 0.89 A

4340 correction *n*
adj front-page, minor, surgical, automatic, quick, slight, severe, immediate *noun* department, .officer, .article, error., edition., .official, .story, course., market, .factor *verb* make, require, apply, publish, state, issue, undergo., result., adjust
5712 | 0.91 N

4341 jump *n*
adj long, high, big, triple, vertical, huge, broad, sudden *noun* .shot, percent., .rope, ski., .start, .seat, .price, foot, .suit, .ball *verb* make., get., let., startle, win, hit., land, miss.
5554 | 0.94

4342 diary *n*
adj personal, daily, private, secret, original, detailed, visual *noun* .entry, letter, journal, food., page, video., war., girl, excerpt, note *verb* keep., write, read, record, publish, complete, document, .chronicle
5600 | 0.93

4343 nest *n*
adj empty, underground, cozy, comfortable, communal, sizable, tidy *noun* .egg, bird., cuckoo., eagle., love., .site, rat. *verb* build., find, leave., return., protect, .contain, guard., place, feather.
5980 | 0.87 M

4344 statute *n*
adj federal, environmental, criminal, independent, unconstitutional, general, common, various, relevant, proposed *noun* .limitation, state, law, court, counsel., provision, right, interpretation., language, purpose *verb* .require, .provide, enact, pass, apply, .allow, .prohibit, violate, interpret., protect
6615 | 0.78 A

4345 exam *n*
adj final, physical, medical, rectal, annual, written, pelvic, oral, digital, thorough *noun* student, entrance., school, bar., state., .room, score, college, .year, breast. *verb* take., pass., fail., prepare., study., require, cram., finish., .reveal, .assess
5603 | 0.93

4346 metropolitan *j*
noun area, museum, opera, city, authority, police, district, center, region, transportation, transit, life *misc* major, large, within, statistical, southern, urban, throughout, entire
5715 | 0.91 N

4347 star *v*
noun movie, film, series, actor, .Broadway, hit, picture, video, musical *misc* .as, who., which., also., .opposite, former, currently.
in .movie, .film, direct., produce.
5805 | 0.89 N

4348 nutrition *n*
adj human, good, clinical, poor, proper, better, adequate *noun* .information, health, food, .program, center, .score, .research, professor., .fact *verb* provide., teach., improve., study., check., specialize.
6321 | 0.82 M

4349 breeze *n*
adj cool, warm, light, gentle, slight, soft, stiff, hot, cold *noun* sea., ocean., night., summer, hair, evening., window, face, leaf, tree *verb* .blow, feel, stir, catch, carry, shoot., sway., rustle, flap., flutter
5840 | 0.89 F

4350 illusion *n*
adj optical, aesthetic, grand, visual, three-dimensional, dangerous, mere, theatrical, dramatic *noun* reality, .space, .depth, power, .control, truth, object, nature, .movement, freedom *verb* create., give., shatter, produce., maintain., harbor., sustain., foster, persist, .dissolve
5648 | 0.92

4351 anonymous *j*
noun alcoholic, reviewer, source, letter, call, author, meeting, tip, group, comment, donor, referee *misc* remain, receive, helpful, wish, thank, send, attend
5486 | 0.94

4352 coup *n*
adj military, failed, attempted, successful, bloodless, abortive, bloody *noun* .attempt, .d'état, .leader, .grace, power., .plotter, stage., palace., .plot, .strategy *verb* lead, fail, follow., overthrow, support., score., pull., oust, end, .occur
5986 | 0.86

4353 midst *n*
adj great, economic, civil, very, enormous, ongoing, heated, bitter *noun* .war, .crisis, .chaos, .campaign, .depression, .revolution, .debate, .crowd, .battle, .recession *verb* live., stand., occur., explode., land., pause., situate.
5345 | 0.97

4354 edit *v*
noun letter., .clarity, book, .length, .space, film, collection, volume, story, video, right., file, music, image, essay *misc* .by, write, publish, compile., carefully.
5581 | 0.93

4355 experienced *j*
noun teacher, player, team, people, group, man, user, hand, worker, woman, professional, pilot *misc* more, most, even, less, old, highly, sexually
5585 | 0.93 A

4356 castle *n*
adj white, medieval, royal, magic, enchanted, ancient, haunted *noun* .rock, wall, sand., tower, garden, gate, courtyard, ruin, stone, .pine *verb* build, live, enter, surround, visit., house, arrive, own., overlook, .loom
5692 | 0.91 F

4357 sort *v*
noun .feeling, mail, problem, .pile, claim, data, paper, process, box, .clothes, emotion, material, .laundry, .confusion, .fiction *misc* .through, able., .itself, difficult., .according, .various, quickly, carefully, classify, impossible.
 out try., help., problem, difficult., .feeling, .difference, mess, able., hard., attempt.
5386 | 0.96

4358 exploit *v*
noun resource, opportunity, weakness, company., .advantage, .potential, worker, technology, .situation, .loophole, other, market, .labor, vulnerability, ability *misc* try., fully., able., seek., .natural, attempt., order, poor, abuse, eager.
5541 | 0.93 A

4359 jewelry *n*
adj fine, expensive, antique, contemporary, beautiful, handmade, ethnic *noun* .store, piece., .box, gold., costume., silver., clothing, art, .designer, clothes

verb wear, sell, buy, steal, own, feature, remove., .belong, dangle
5753 | 0.90 M

4360 diabetes *n*
adj juvenile, developing, gestational, adult-onset, insulin-dependent, severe, developed *noun* type., disease, people., blood, risk., cancer, pressure, patient, .association, obesity *verb* diagnose., develop, prevent., treat., control, suffer., cause, increase, .account
6190 | 0.83 M

4361 translation *n*
adj literal, original, simultaneous, foreign, direct, loose, rough, accurate, correct *noun* language, text, Bible, process, address., .service, .program, .software *verb* lose., provide, publish, read, appear, complete, preserve, render, survive., .accommodate
5802 | 0.89 A

4362 Dutch *j*
noun oven, company, government, painting, church, master, society, child, artist, painter, team, art
5627 | 0.92 M

4363 upset *j*
noun stomach, victory, loss, win, mom, winner, fan, bid, coach, Senate *misc* about, get, very, so, because, too, become, really
5498 | 0.94 S

4364 harm *v*
noun child, .other, .environment, .health, patient, .baby, animal, .reputation, consumer, action., American, .wildlife, competition, .fetus, enemy *misc* might., never., anyone, cause, someone, seriously.
5361 | 0.96

4365 irony *n*
adj great, certain, bitter, cruel, ultimate, tragic, sad, final *noun* sense., .situation, humor, trace., bit., hint., paradox, touch. *verb* .lose, note., point., appreciate., laugh., miss, recognize., .escape, enjoy.
5442 | 0.95

4366 associated *j*
noun press, story, service, problem, cost, risk, contractor, health, activity, group, disease, factor *misc* tell, report, according, quote, obtain, contribute, general, distribute
6186 | 0.83 N

4367 utilize *v*
noun study, method, technology, .resource, system, student, technique, strategy, program, teacher, skill, research, data, .service, ability. *misc* fully., develop, better., effectively, able.
6109 | 0.84 A

4368 rabbit *n*
adj white, dead, wild, lucky, live, stuffed, frightened *noun* .ear, .hole, .foot, dog, squirrel, bunny., .fur, hunting, animal *verb* pull, eat, catch, chase., kill, hop, hunt., shoot, feed, cry
5698 | 0.90 F

4369 soap *n*
adj antibacterial, liquid, mild, favorite, insecticidal, scented, real-life *noun* .opera, water, bar., dish, hand, .bubble, shampoo, box, television, .star *verb* use, watch., wash, smell., buy, clean, rinse, scrub, feature
5493 | 0.94

4370 booth n
adj wooden, private, empty, token, tanning, nearby, soundproof, darkened, adjacent *noun* phone., voting., back, ticket, toll., corner, information., telephone., table, broadcast. *verb* sit., slide., set, enter., .sell, vote, feature, line, seat., approach
5637 | 0.91 F

4371 minimum n
adj bare, mandatory, absolute, moral, legal, guaranteed, recommended *noun* .year, .hour, percent, month, maximum, .visit, client., wage, .effort, league. *verb* keep., require, need, base., pay., reduce., raise., cost., range, increase
5503 | 0.93

4372 immune j
noun system, response, cell, body, function, disease, deficiency, disorder, patient, syndrome, effect, reaction *misc* boost, human, suppress, stimulate, attack, weaken, strong, no
6074 | 0.85 M

4373 gut n
adj leaky, fat, sick, empty, tight *noun* .feeling, .instinct, .reaction, blood., heart, guy, beer., .check, pain, bacteria *verb* feel, hate., spill., trust., hit., suck., puke., shoot, tear., wrench
5466 | 0.94 F

4374 appreciation n
adj great, new, deep, aesthetic, better, deeper, full, cultural *noun* understanding, art, music, capital., price., nature, history, .value, .culture, lack. *verb* express., show., gain., develop., enhance., foster., extend, promote.
5552 | 0.93 A

4375 cast n
adj supporting, great, entire, all-star, original, whole, strong, talented, diverse, short *noun* .character, .crew, plaster., member., rest., arm, leg, .thousand, actor, .mind *verb* .include, join., feature., head, wear., draw, perform, assemble, direct, .sing
5510 | 0.93

4376 scramble v
noun egg, company., official., bed, .cover, boy., .ladder, bank, seat, wall, worker, .tree, brain, knee, ground *misc* .out, .find, .back, .away, .over, .onto, .around, mad., across
   up .ladder, .bank, .slope, .down, .onto, .steep, .egg
5588 | 0.92 F

4377 upstairs r
go., room, back., run., bedroom, head., bed, hear, walk., office, live., downstairs, carry.
5796 | 0.89 F

4378 punch v
noun hole, .button, .number, .clock, ticket, fist, .key, card, .dough, wall, .air, guy, .shoulder, .mouth, machine *misc* .into, .through, kick, .hard, hit, somebody, best., left, lightly, repeatedly
   out .number, hole, window, before, wall
5579 | 0.92 F

4379 gross j
noun product, income, revenue, margin, sales, motor, profit, violation, growth, negligence, receipt, abuse *misc* domestic, national, adjusted, million, per, capita, annual, total, human
5429 | 0.95

4380 liability n
adj strict, potential, legal, limited, joint, civil, political, criminal, medical *noun* product., tax., .insurance, asset., company, issue, law, case, .act, compensation *verb* become., limit, impose, avoid., reduce, face, pay, apportion., .arise, .attach
6523 | 0.79 A

4381 accessible j
noun information, wheelchair, public, area, site, technology, material, boat, form, book, care, computer *misc* more, make, easily, only, most, readily, become
5495 | 0.93 A

4382 mechanic n
adj celestial, applied, statistical, computational, classical, solid, orbital, general, chief, structural *noun* auto., car, fluid., body., pilot., physics, shop, relativity, garage, theory *verb* learn, teach, .fix, apply, study, explain, check, train, repair, inspect
5683 | 0.90

4383 ass n
adj fat, sorry, dumb, nice, bare, smart, sweet, fucking, skinny, stupid *noun* pain., rat., kick., piece., horse., tit., .jail, .gear, shit, thigh *verb* get, kiss., save., haul., bust., cover., fuck., laugh, bet.
6196 | 0.83 F

4384 aesthetic j
noun value, experience, quality, education, art, illusion, object, judgment, form, sensibility, sense, appreciation *misc* social, moral, political, cultural, artistic, than, spiritual
6351 | 0.81 A

4385 dessert n
adj sweet, frozen, favorite, rich, light, decadent, fine, elegant *noun* chocolate, fruit, wine, coffee, plate, cake, dinner, cream, pie, dish *verb* serve, eat., order, skip., finish, love, enjoy, prepare, .arrive, feature
5767 | 0.89 N

4386 waist n
adj small, narrow, naked, tiny, thick, thin, slender, slim *noun* arm., hand, hip, belt, leg, shoulder, .level, size, hair, knee *verb* bend., tie., hold, wrap., grab., pull, hang., strip., cinch., paralyze.
5768 | 0.89 F

4387 alike r
look., much., Republican., Democrat., student., adult., friend., critic., teacher., parent., dress.
5344 | 0.96

4388 brave j
noun man, world, woman, people, face, soul, soldier, thing, girl, boy, word, warrior *misc* new, very, enough, young, strong, little, fight, courageous
5444 | 0.94 F

4389 loop n
adj closed, endless, inner, continuous, outer, scenic, double *noun* feedback., belt., trail, road, wire, mile, line, string, tape, rope *verb* throw., close., create, form, unroll, tie, pull, complete., catch, twist
5697 | 0.90

4390 passing j
noun game, yard, car, day, year, grade, leader, interest, lane, reference, motorist *misc* each, every, bear, stare, rush, wave, merely, all-time
5465 | 0.94

4391 partially *r*
.by, only., least., .cover, may., .explain, .support, .responsible, .fund, .fill, result, .successful, .oil, .because
5437 | 0.94 A

4392 statistical *j*
noun analysis, significance, data, test, difference, method, result, study, model, evidence, technique, power *misc* use, between, diagnostic, reach, show, base, social, mental
6054 | 0.84 A

4393 correctly *r*
if., .identify, answer, understand., use., read., remember., hear., point, question, spell, .predict, .classify
5439 | 0.94 A

4394 pin *n*
adj rolling, little, straight, red, Olympic, skeletal, surgical, locking *noun* lapel., safety., edition., number, bowling., .oak *verb* wear, pull., stick, hold, hear., remove, secure, .drop, knock, attach
5564 | 0.92

4395 practitioner *n*
adj general, medical, social, reflective, public, private, rural, early, religious, mental *noun* nurse., health., researcher, family., work., care., solo., student *verb* help, provide, .develop, train, suggest, consult, .agree, .seek, recommend, assist
6083 | 0.84 A

4396 encouraging *j*
noun sign, result, word, news, development, investment, thing, behavior, participation, role, smile, finding *misc* very, positive, supportive, private, despite, promote, foreign, than
5411 | 0.94 A

4397 syndrome *n*
adj respiratory, premenstrual, metabolic, ovarian, post-polio, pulmonary *noun* down., fatigue., tunnel., death., alcohol., bowel., infant., patient, disorder, compartment. *verb* call., suffer., cause, diagnose., born., develop, describe, affect, .occur, result
5793 | 0.88

4398 tribal *j*
noun leader, member, government, council, area, group, land, culture, elder, community, nation, society *misc* local, ethnic, Indian, traditional, religious, political, federal, native
6311 | 0.81 A

4399 persist *v*
noun problem., .year, rumor., .month, pattern., symptom., century, pain., condition., feeling., .effort, species., trend., task, population *misc* if., long, .after, still., .until, .despite, .throughout
5530 | 0.92 A

4400 trash *n*
adj white, full, burning, tabloid, nearby, overflowing, residential, rotting *noun* .bag, .can, .bin, pile, plastic., .heap, piece., street *verb* pick, take., throw., talk, toss., dump, collect, fill, carry, burn
5429 | 0.94 F

4401 teenage *j*
noun girl, boy, daughter, year, pregnancy, son, mother, child, mutant, parent, drug, kid *misc* two, young, among, sexual, unwed, pregnant, unlimited, normal
5427 | 0.94

4402 self-esteem *n*
adj low, high, positive, academic, collective, global, adolescent, poor *noun* level., child, student, .scale, score, depression, sense, girl, relationship, confidence *verb* build., enhance., relate, increase, boost., associate, develop, improve, predict, correlate
6110 | 0.83 A

4403 preliminary *j*
noun hearing, study, result, analysis, finding, data, report, research, investigation, evidence, injunction, work *misc* suggest, indicate, show, provide, conduct, base, according, present
5522 | 0.92 A

4404 stay *n*
adj short, long, average, overnight, brief, extended, automatic, minimum, two-night, temporary *noun* hospital., length., home, .execution, court, night, hotel, nursing, care, cost *verb* let., grant, enjoy., extend., require, issue, .open, reduce, shorten., prolong.
5361 | 0.95

4405 sunset *n*
adj red, beautiful, spectacular, golden, glorious, gorgeous, magnificent, breathtaking *noun* sunrise., hour., .strip, sky, beach, light, .district, color, minute., evening *verb* watch., ride., fade, enjoy, end, rise, catch., admire., near
5611 | 0.91 M

4406 harassment *n*
adj sexual, verbal, racial, environmental, individual, constant, discriminatory *noun* case, woman, charge, policy, issue, discrimination, .suit, workplace, .lawsuit, complaint *verb* report., file, accuse., constitute., define, experience., prevent., .occur, endure., .cease
5726 | 0.89

4407 reportedly *r*
.million, .tell, .pay, .offer, .kill, .plan, .receive, official., police, .sell, military, leader, .cost, .worth
5515 | 0.92 N

4408 quote *n*
adj direct, following, famous, favorite, exact, interesting, wonderful *noun* stock., end., price., news, couple., reporting., source, insurance, dealer *verb* .contain, read., update., attribute, illustrate, refer, state, cite., obtain., paraphrase
5746 | 0.89 S

4409 fever *n*
adj high, yellow, typhoid, scarlet, rheumatic, low-grade, mild *noun* night., .pitch, hay., pain, symptom, jungle., chill, headache, cabin., malaria *verb* run, cause, catch., die., reach., develop., break, include.
5451 | 0.93

4410 panic *n*
adj sudden, financial, widespread, blind, moral, sheer, near *noun* .attack, .disorder, fear, .button, moment., anxiety, state., voice, sense., wave. *verb* feel, cause., set, rise, create., fight., flee, spread, avoid., suffer.
5447 | 0.93 F

4411 charter *n*
adj public, original, illegal, corporate, royal, present, Olympic *noun* .school, .boat, .member, nation, city., .flight, company, .operator, fishing *verb* require, sign, grant, operate, adopt, approve, state, establish, amend., .authorize
5572 | 0.91 N

4412 outlook *n*
adj positive, economic, bleak, political, long-term, optimistic, whole, early, global *noun* life, .express, .article, season., stock, market, e-mail, section, change, economy *verb* improve, share., reflect, shape, alter., maintain., brighten, .deteriorate
5773 | 0.88 N

4413 foster *v*
noun .development, .sense, .growth, environment, .relationship, program., .understanding, policy, attitude, teacher, skill, learning, education, .cooperation, effort. *misc* help., .among, social, economic, design., .positive, .home
5728 | 0.89 A

4414 comprise *v*
noun group, item, sample, student, part, population, team., system, member, study, individual, category, .majority, community, committee. *misc* which., .about, each, .approximately, total, .nearly, .mainly, .hundred
5772 | 0.88 A

4415 known *j*
noun world, fact, species, risk, case, universe, history, terrorist, site, cause, factor, quantity *misc* no, only, any, last, lesser, every, unknown, large
5439 | 0.93 A

4416 Thanksgiving *n*
adj happy, closed, traditional, annual, wonderful, memorable, healthy *noun* day, .dinner, .Christmas, turkey, holiday, .weekend, .parade *verb* spend., celebrate., cook, eat, prepare, close., .feature, shop.
5508 | 0.92

4417 short-term *j*
noun rate, memory, interest, fund, bond, gain, goal, problem, solution, debt, effect, investment *misc* long-term, economic, political, financial, feed, than, raise, rather
5561 | 0.91

4418 shed *v*
noun tear, .pound, blood, .skin, .image, .weight, .clothes, .coat, .layer, .identity, cell *misc* .some, may., might., .light, hope., able.
5269 | 0.96

4419 cooperative *j*
noun learning, program, effort, group, extension, research, agreement, student, activity, relationship, service, development *misc* more, tag, during, between, develop, competitive, less, promote
6030 | 0.84 A

4420 alley *n*
adj dark, blind, right, nearby, deserted, darkened *noun* bowling., back., street, end., .night, tin., building, .cat, .theater, wall *verb* walk, run, lead, pass, disappear., enter., head, duck., park., line
5747 | 0.88 F

4421 subsidy *n*
adj federal, public, large, direct, annual, European, private, poor, Soviet, foreign *noun* government., farm., tax, state, program, export, price, industry, taxpayer, business *verb* provide, receive., cut, reduce, offer., eliminate., pay, end, .entice, .encourage
5722 | 0.89

4422 secular *j*
noun state, society, world, government, religion, culture, purpose, humanism, Jew, life, authority, party *misc* religious, between, sacred, modern, both, political, liberal, spiritual
5993 | 0.85 A

4423 aluminum *n*
adj lightweight, thin, heavy, heavy-duty, shiny, recycled, polished *noun* .foil, frame, steel, .can, plastic, .tube, .fork, glass, pan, sheet *verb* cover., wrap., contain., replace, cast, construct., recycle., .prevent
6060 | 0.84 M

4424 cliff *n*
adj sheer, steep, white, red, towering, rugged, vertical, ancient, overhanging *noun* edge, .face, .dwelling, sea, rock, side, top, base., sandstone., wall *verb* fall, .overlook, jump., climb., rise, drop, drive., throw, perch., tumble
5529 | 0.92 F

4425 gram *n*
adj saturated, total, daily, cubic, dietary, soy, square, whopping, pure, soluble *noun* protein, carbohydrate, .fat, fiber, .percent, sodium., weight, .cocaine, calorie *verb* contain., weigh., trace, consume., save., count., shave., exceed., multiply
6613 | 0.77

4426 outline *v*
noun plan, president, article, step, strategy, program, goal, issue, procedure, speech, proposal, letter, figure, .idea, vision *misc* follow., clearly, briefly., specific, general
5448 | 0.93 A

4427 mentally *r*
.ill, physically, .retarded, people, .disabled, prepare, emotionally, person, severely., both., tough, .handicap, .challenge, .healthy
5348 | 0.95

4428 invade *v*
noun Iraq, .Kuwait, country, .privacy, force., .space, troop, army., home, territory, .body, decision., .neighbor, plan., American *misc* when., after., before., since., Soviet, .occupy, .neighboring
5333 | 0.95

4429 confrontation *n*
adj military, direct, violent, physical, major, nuclear, dramatic, final *noun* kind, conflict, cooperation, violence, strategy, superpower, politics. *verb* avoid., lead, provoke., involve, seek., .occur, force, escalate, risk., erupt
5456 | 0.93

4430 sacrifice *v*
noun .life, .quality, .altar, willingness., God, animal, .health, .principle, .comfort, .safety, .freedom, .goal, benefit, individual, .performance *misc* willing., .themselves, .everything, ready., prepare.
5269 | 0.96

4431 dissolve *v*
noun sugar., water, marriage, heat, parliament, salt, acid, union, .tear, gelatin, cornstarch, yeast, partnership, cup, bowl. *misc* until., stir, completely, slowly, quickly, .through, slow., hot, gradually.
5825 | 0.87 F

4432 shy *j*
noun man, smile, people, girl, child, person, month, boy, kid, guy, student, behavior *misc* about, just, too, very, feel, quiet, little
5350 | 0.94

4433 coin *n*
adj small, rare, Roman, commemorative, silver, common, lucky, lost, two-sided *noun* side., gold., dollar., .toss, flip, hand, note, collection, money, .collector *verb* drop, throw, collect, count., pull, pick, sell, strike
5442 | 0.93 F

4434 speculation *n*
adj pure, wild, rampant, possible, mere, financial, widespread, intense, considerable *noun* lot., rumor, matter., subject., market, land., media, kind., deal., .future *verb* .might, lead., fuel., base, end., prompt., raise, encourage., .surround, .abound
5292 | 0.95

4435 creativity *n*
adj human, individual, artistic, musical, creative, implicit, entrepreneurial, intellectual, spontaneous *noun* student, intelligence, imagination, innovation, theory., art, skill, thinking, teacher, energy *verb* encourage., require, stifle., teach, enhance., foster., develop, promote., describe, inspire
5897 | 0.86 A

4436 custody *n*
adj joint, protective, legal, temporary, federal, physical, sole, full *noun* child, .battle, .case, police, court, divorce., suspect., father, mother, parent *verb* take., lose., give., award., remain., release., fight., seek., grant.
5500 | 0.92 S

4437 interfere *v*
noun .ability, .life, government., .process, activity, .affair, .operation, business, law, .sleep, behavior, .learning, .function, drug., action *misc* .with, not., may., anything., .normal, directly
5312 | 0.95

4438 spoon *n*
adj wooden, greasy, measuring, long-handled, stirring, bent *noun* .mixture, bowl, fork, silver., cup, back., .sauce, .batter, plate, plastic. *verb* use., stir, remove, .transfer, put, hold., drop, pick., dip, .scoop
5638 | 0.90 M

4439 bee *n*
adj Africanized, wild, busy, buzzing, quilting, solitary, golden *noun* honey., spelling., pollen, .sting, queen., worker., killer., swarm. *verb* fly, buzz, attract., pollinate, hum, collect, .hover
5797 | 0.87

4440 rolling *j*
noun stone, hill, pin, resistance, meadow, blackout, field, thunder, boil, rock, terrain, wave *misc* gently, roll, green, across, tire, floured, vast, onto
5582 | 0.90 M

4441 interact *v*
noun student, opportunity., .environment, teacher, factor, .peer, system, individual, ability., particle, matter, person, computer, kid, adult *misc* .with, .other, how., .each, .another, learn, allow., directly, able.
5660 | 0.89 A

4442 damn *j*
noun thing, fool, Yankee, place, shame, business, lie, house, bit, sight *misc* give, about, so, too, whole, pretty, every, worth
5760 | 0.87 F

4443 dam *n*
adj hydroelectric, small, earthen, low, proposed, huge, major, federal, concrete, inflatable *noun* river, water, construction, .project, lake, reservoir, road, .site, building, lock. *verb* build, break, construct, remove, complete, generate, release, destroy, breach, repair.
5561 | 0.91

4444 unfair *j*
noun advantage, practice, trade, competition, tax, treatment, system, burden, labor, law, business, criticism *misc* it, think, seem, very, little, fair, grossly
5332 | 0.94

4445 someday *r*
will, might, hope., may, maybe, .soon, perhaps, .able, marry, someone, return, dream., somebody, somehow
5333 | 0.94 F

4446 liquid *n*
adj clear, hot, reserved, thick, excess, flammable, remaining, cold, natural, boiling *noun* cup, cooking., gas, water, glass, solid, food, bottle, heat, pan *verb* add, absorb, pour, cook, .evaporate, .reduce, drain., stir, drink., discard
5510 | 0.91 M

4447 disclose *v*
noun information, company, term., .detail, name, .status, official, .identity, price, plan, report, .source, failure., firm., client *misc* require., fail., fully., publicly., refuse.
5500 | 0.92 N

4448 mushroom *n*
adj wild, dried, white, large, black, green, red, chopped, hot, edible *noun* onion, portobello., .cloud, .cap, .soup, sauce, pound., stem, chicken, .mixture *verb* add., slice, sauté, stir, grow, remove, eat, stuff, mix, discard
5863 | 0.86 M

4449 disabled *j*
noun people, list, child, student, person, veteran, individual, woman, adult, worker, group, parent *misc* learn, elderly, developmentally, mentally, become, severely, physically, blind
5565 | 0.90 N

4450 counter *v*
noun .threat, .effect, effort, .argument, attempt, charge, .attack, defense, .terrorism, .trend, .influence, Republican, .tendency, .criticism, move *misc* design., .negative, seek., effectively., order., necessary., successfully.
5288 | 0.95

4451 catalog *n*
adj free, online, whole, messy, complete, entire, electronic, comprehensive, full-color *noun* exhibition, seed., company, mail-order., page, card., order, product, library, essay *verb* offer, include, sell, list, publish, .describe, send, .feature, .contain, buy.
5630 | 0.89 M

4452 gaze *v*
noun face, room, star, moment, .sky, .distance, .ceiling, wall, glass, .sea, .awe, .darkness, .wonder, .horror, .surprise *misc* .at, .into, .out, she., .down, .across, .through, .over, .upon, .toward, .off, sit.
5837 | 0.86 F

4453 publicity *n*
adj bad, negative, free, national, pretrial, adverse, positive, favorable *noun* .stunt, lot., .campaign, kind., .director, media, effort, .tour, glare., amount. *verb* get, receive, .surround, generate, seek., avoid., attract, gain.
5290 | 0.95

4454 compel *v*
noun government, force, reason, story, law, court, .compliance, .testimony, .reader, .attention, authority, statement, argument, individual, .conclusion *misc* .act, seek, .testify, .accept
5321 | 0.94 A

4455 cease *v*
noun .fire, .operation, activity, .publication, production, hostility, rain., .movement, conversation., attack, union., noise., .participation *misc* .exist, never., .desist, .amaze
5305 | 0.95

4456 ideal *n*
adj democratic, high, political, cultural, national, classical, lofty, Christian, human, societal *noun* value, .democracy, beauty, .freedom, idea., nation, body, goal, reality, community *verb* live., embody, promote, represent, base, remain, uphold., embrace., express, associate
5599 | 0.90 A

4457 decorate *v*
noun room, wall, house, tree, home, Christmas, office, table, .picture, building, .motif, cookie, pattern, light, .style *misc* .with, beautifully., .colorful, elaborately., .desire, lavishly
5540 | 0.91 M

4458 surrounding *j*
noun area, community, tissue, water, countryside, county, neighborhood, hill, city, region, land, town *misc* above, soft, buzz, Arab, scan, urban, rural, healthy
5381 | 0.93

4459 exclusively *r*
almost., focus., use., rely., devote., .male, deal., primarily., base, concentrate., .heterosexual
5475 | 0.92 A

4460 bonus *n*
adj added, annual, extra, unexpected, nice, huge, generous *noun* signing., salary., .point, cash., company, program, benefit, Christmas. *verb* receive., pay, give, offer., earn, include, award, raise, .total, .range
5534 | 0.91 N

4461 unprecedented *j*
noun level, number, history, opportunity, step, power, rate, scale, growth, access, way, effort *misc* almost, economic, face, win, enjoy, reach, international
5328 | 0.94

4462 oversee *v*
noun .operation, .program, committee., agency, department, state, .project, board., company, .development, government, service, .construction,

.work, security *misc* who., which., federal, charge., national, responsible., .billion, financial, appoint., .day-to-day
5426 | 0.92 N

4463 touchdown *n*
adj winning, rushing, only, offensive, game-winning, fourth-quarter, go-ahead *noun* yard., interception, .run, game, .season, return, .reception, punt, catch, career *verb* score., throw., .pass, lead, rush, allow., .seal
6413 | 0.78 N

4464 federation *n*
adj national, American, international, retail, united, loose, civic *noun* wildlife., president, state, world., .teacher, woman, consumer., director., labor, .business *verb* form, represent, join, .announce, .declare, found, sponsor, suspend
5476 | 0.92 N

4465 aggression *n*
adj physical, relational, sexual, reactive, proactive, verbal, instrumental, hostile, Iraqi, adolescent *noun* act., war., behavior, level., violence, sport, form., life, peer *verb* stop., associate, deter., commit, prevent., observe, resist., .occur, condemn., decrease
5903 | 0.85 A

4466 behalf *i*
(on behalf of) .of, on., speak., work., act., file., .American, United States, government, .client, effort., action., suit., lawsuit.
5293 | 0.95

4467 well-known *j*
noun name, figure, artist, company, fact, writer, author, example, family, actor, book, brand *misc* most, become, less, such, including, among, include, several
5288 | 0.95

4468 donation *n*
adj private, charitable, suggested, corporate, political, small, individual, generous, local, soft *noun* organ., campaign, egg., fund, blood., cash., community, organization, sperm., member *verb* make, accept, receive., send, solicit., raise, request, seek.
5406 | 0.93 N

4469 desperately *r*
.need, try, want, so., .seek, .poor, search, help, hope, fight, .ill, .love
5268 | 0.95

4470 reward *v*
noun effort, behavior, work, system., performance, employee, .team, teacher, player, success, loyalty, investor, society, incentive., patience. *misc* .with, .punish, often., .yourself, handsomely, financially
5233 | 0.96

4471 high-tech *j*
noun company, industry, equipment, firm, job, world, business, system, weapon, computer, worker, stock *misc* new, such, late, medical, expensive, modern, low-tech, electronic
5459 | 0.92 M N

4472 cheat *v*
noun wife, man, student, husband, .test, college, spouse, .death, .exam, .card, opportunity, marriage, .customer, athlete, .investor *misc* .on, lie, feel., steal, admit., someone., likely.
5287 | 0.95

4473 audio *j*
<u>noun</u> track, tape, video, recording, gap, book, broadcast, system, file, clip, cassette, equipment <u>misc</u> against, check, order, in, digital, original, visual
6190 | 0.81 S

4474 sensation *n*
<u>adj</u> burning, physical, strange, overnight, odd, familiar, strong, unpleasant, pleasant, tingling <u>noun</u> pain, feeling, experience, taste., skin, nerve, loss., image, singing., leg <u>verb</u> feel, .seek, create., cause., become., produce., enjoy., sing, accompany, .spread
5372 | 0.93 F

4475 entrepreneur *n*
<u>adj</u> successful, black, small, American, local, private, individual, wealthy, high-tech, would-be <u>noun</u> business, company, Internet., opportunity, market, capital, industry, worker, minority., investment <u>verb</u> become, .build, .sell, .name, own, .seek, attract, .invest, found, .launch
5838 | 0.86 M

4476 proclaim *v*
<u>noun</u> sign., God, .innocence, banner., word, .love, gospel, church, message, .victory, leader, independence, headline, T-shirt., king <u>misc</u> proudly., loudly., publicly., boldly., officially.
5335 | 0.94

4477 supplier *n*
<u>adj</u> large, major, leading, big, foreign, main, available, primary, independent, dominant <u>noun</u> customer, company, part, equipment, water., oil, price, auto, business, employee <u>verb</u> pay, buy, .sell, .offer, choose, require, ship, purchase., link, order
5687 | 0.88

4478 rival *n*
<u>adj</u> chief, political, main, democratic, potential, bitter, longtime, arch, nearest, foreign <u>noun</u> Republican., business, division., market, party, crosstown., cost, competition, league, conference. <u>verb</u> beat., compete, eliminate., fight, face, kill., challenge, defeat., accuse
5449 | 0.92 N

4479 reminder *n*
<u>adj</u> constant, painful, daily, stark, grim, powerful, only, vivid, gentle, quick <u>noun</u> .past, e-mail, .postcard, letter, .mortality, .card, encouragement, medication. <u>verb</u> serve., need, send, provide., offer., issue., fill.
5157 | 0.97

4480 heal *v*
<u>noun</u> wound, time, body, God., scar, injury, heart, pain, .rift, skin, ability., power., nation, .division, spirit <u>misc</u> help., never., try., begin., completely
5302 | 0.94

4481 case *c*
(in case) .you, just., .need, .something, .any, .wonder, .happen, .miss, .forget, .notice, .ever, .anyone, .someone, .decide
5277 | 0.95 F

4482 beast *n*
<u>adj</u> wild, great, little, huge, sexy, mythical, poor, savage, powerful <u>noun</u> man, .burden, nature., bird, .jungle, animal., king., heart, .prey, teen. <u>verb</u> kill, feed, tame., ride, slay, soothe., starve.
5586 | 0.89 F

4483 uncover *v*
<u>noun</u> evidence, investigation., information, .secret, .truth, research., problem, plot, researcher., investigator., archaeologist., effort., fraud, .detail, .clue <u>misc</u> help., .stir, .hidden, attempt., cook, cover, recently., fail.
5251 | 0.95

4484 merit *n*
<u>adj</u> artistic, individual, scientific, literary, academic, technical, various, particular, intrinsic <u>noun</u> .badge, argument, .scholarship, .scholar, .system, .pay, award, basis., legion., .pamphlet <u>verb</u> base., debate., judge., argue., .raise, discuss., consider., earn.
5331 | 0.94 A

4485 momentum *n*
<u>adj</u> angular, political, forward, positive, gathered, tremendous, growing, behavioral <u>noun</u> energy, lot., movement, change, building, kind., loss., .peace, transfer <u>verb</u> gain., lose., build, keep, give., carry, gather., create, maintain., regain.
5353 | 0.93

4486 stimulate *v*
<u>noun</u> .economy, .growth, interest, .production, .development, .student, brain, cell, activity, .discussion, .research, .investment, .thinking, nerve, .demand <u>misc</u> .by, help., .economic, .immune, design.
5462 | 0.91 A

4487 rational *j*
<u>noun</u> decision, choice, basis, thought, people, way, being, explanation, person, mind, process, approach <u>misc</u> more, any, human, economic, logical, base, scientific, irrational
5571 | 0.89 A

4488 columnist *n*
<u>adj</u> syndicated, political, conservative, liberal, financial, longtime, prize-winning <u>noun</u> new, time., newspaper, post, sport., news, editor, author, magazine, gossip. <u>verb</u> .write, syndicate., shield, .note, observe, quote, cite, .resign, .criticize
5501 | 0.90 S

4489 pioneer *n*
<u>adj</u> black, Mormon, feminist, historic, musical, hip-hop <u>noun</u> woman, family, .award, .spirit, west, computer, son., .league <u>verb</u> help, consider., .settle, establish, launch, found, .encounter, inspire, cite., feature.
5334 | 0.93 M

4490 biology *n*
<u>adj</u> molecular, evolutionary, conservation, human, marine, reproductive, basic, introductory, developmental <u>noun</u> professor, chemistry, science, .teacher, physics, cell., .class, student, department, course <u>verb</u> teach., study., learn., understand, major., integrate., combine, dictate
5731 | 0.87 A

4491 photography *n*
<u>adj</u> digital, creative, still, contemporary, underwater, black-and-white, infrared <u>noun</u> color., art, gear., painting, director., film, nature., news., aerial., book <u>verb</u> teach., study., enjoy, .capture, promote., pursue., .exhibit, specialize., concentrate, .convey
6459 | 0.77 A

4492 innovative *j*
noun program, way, approach, technology, idea, product, design, technique, solution, company, practice, method *misc* most, new, develop, create, creative, provide, such
5427 | 0.92 A

4493 purse *n*
adj public, red, tiny, brown, electronic, matching, drawstring *noun* .string, pocket, hand, wallet, bag, key, money, .shoulder, leather., coin *verb* reach., carry., open., hold, grab., pull, pick., snatch, steal, clutch.
5504 | 0.90 F

4494 franchise *n*
adj successful, fast-food, international, storied, exclusive, existing, universal *noun* .history, company, owner, player, expansion., .record, .fee *verb* buy., own, sell, run, set, open, award., operate., purchase., relocate
5897 | 0.84 N

4495 consent *n*
adj informed, parental, written, unanimous, sexual, mutual, governed, presumed, common *noun* .form, .decree, advice., parent, participant, patient, age., procedure, study, .agreement *verb* give., obtain, sign., require, inform., provide, .participate, write., return., allow
5791 | 0.86 A

4496 outfit *n*
adj small, whole, theatrical, blue, nice, complete, sexy, entire, perfect, favorite *noun* leather., pant, ski., designer., cowboy., construction., golf. *verb* wear, buy, dress., pick, choose, match, love, .cost, .consist, .suit
5365 | 0.93 M

4497 eve *n*
adj new, very, annual, historic *noun* year., Christmas., day, .war, .party, night, election, .service, .celebration, .dinner *verb* spend., celebrate, approach, disappear.
5439 | 0.91

4498 spray *n*
adj nasal, fine, no-stick, light, vegetable-based, gentle *noun* cooking., pepper., hair., vegetable., water, pan., .paint, oil, .bottle, sheet. *verb* cook., use, coat., apply, .contain, adjust.
5473 | 0.91 M

4499 shove *v*
noun hand, door, face, car, .pocket, paper, arm, wall, bag, head, chair, .mouth, box, gun, finger *misc* .into, push., .out, .back, .down, .aside, .away
5711 | 0.87 F

4500 fisherman *n*
adj commercial, local, recreational, bass, avid, artisanal, native, individual, Japanese, ardent *noun* .wharf, fish, hunter., sport., farmer, water, salmon, lake, fishery, trout. *verb* catch, sell, .cast, fly., gather, rescue, land, .haul, employ.
5996 | 0.83

4501 sensitivity *n*
adj great, cultural, high, environmental, heightened, increased, interpersonal, extreme *noun* .issue, .specificity, .training, analysis, lack., awareness, level, need, insulin., test *verb* increase., show., develop., demonstrate., require, improve, reduce.
5591 | 0.89 A

4502 courtesy *n*
adj common, professional, utmost, usual, unfailing, unremitting, diplomatic, elaborate *noun* photo., .gallery, photograph., image., .author, .museum, .art, inch., collection, article. *verb* extend, treat., owe., appreciate.
5893 | 0.84 M

4503 stack *n*
adj neat, tall, thick, huge, short, whole, entire, growing *noun* .paper, .book, box, .bill, .magazine, .card, .letter, .newspaper, .mail, .file *verb* carry., pull., hand., blow., pick., drop, lift., sort., slide, lean
5397 | 0.92 F

4504 pork *n*
adj grilled, boneless, fried, barbecued, smoked, pulled *noun* .chop, beef, .tenderloin, chicken, .loin, .barrel, salt, pound., .roast, .sausage *verb* eat., serve, add, cook, cut, place., remove, cover, brown
5529 | 0.90 N

4505 teammate *n*
adj fellow, Olympic, longtime, veteran, injured, one-time *noun* coach, friend, game, team, player, support, season, college., football., field *verb* join, pass, .score, beat, trust, yell, tease, celebrate, cheer, joke
5931 | 0.83 N

4506 instant *j*
noun messaging, message, gratification, coffee, replay, access, e-mail, success, communication, check, rice, result *misc* become, provide, create, offer, add, send, cup
5281 | 0.94 M

4507 pulse *n*
adj short, electromagnetic, steady, faint, rapid, rhythmic, racing *noun* .rate, blood, pressure, processor., light, finger., laser., radio., heart, .width *verb* feel., take., check., .race, quicken, send., .combine, measure, produce, emit.
5444 | 0.91

4508 outsider *n*
adj cultural, ultimate, so-called, complete, classic, lonely, lone *noun* insider, .art, status, perspective, artist, community, view, presence., contact. *verb* feel., might, run, consider, remain., treat., enter, welcome., threaten, rely.
5303 | 0.93

4509 pro *j*
noun bowl, football, player, team, sport, basketball, shop, game, career, athlete, league, season *misc* play, former, bass, sign, defensive, induct, rata, name
5608 | 0.88 N

4510 helmet *n*
adj blue, protective, Kevlar, yellow, golden, mandatory, plumed *noun* head, mask, bike., light, motorcycle., bicycle., visor, football., hair *verb* wear., put., remove., pull, carry, throw., hit, grab.
5586 | 0.88 F

4511 ladder *n*
adj corporate, economic, social, wooden, evolutionary, tall, socioeconomic *noun* rung., career., top., rope., bottom., .truck, fish., company, roof, .success *verb* climb., move., .lead, reach, stand, descend, fall, step., pull, scramble.
5318 | 0.93 F

4512 openly *r*
.about, .gay, talk., discuss, speak., express, .admit,
.acknowledge, .criticize, serve., .hostile
5176 | 0.95

4513 fierce *j*
noun competition, battle, fighting, eye, wind, debate,
competitor, opposition, resistance, struggle, storm,
attack *misc* among, face, engage, fight, despite, lock,
wild, erupt
5184 | 0.95

4514 bet *n*
adj best, good, safe, sure, better, safest, safer, risky,
fair *noun* stock, fund, investor, entertainment, dollar,
sucker., casino, .baseball *verb* make., place., hedge.,
win., lose., pay, lay., accept.
5273 | 0.93

4515 required *j*
noun course, level, reading, education, number,
law, disclosure, class, skill, surgery, work, amount
misc provide, physical, complete, achieve, perform,
fail, reduce, minimum
5510 | 0.89 A

4516 shrink *v*
noun .size, .percent, year, tumor, number, population.,
economy., budget, deficit, market, force, space, gap,
tax, margin. *misc* .from, .away, begin., continue.,
grow, dramatically, rapidly, billion
 back .from, .into, .against, then, .little
5188 | 0.95

4517 cute *j*
noun girl, guy, kid, thing, boy, baby, dog, couple, face,
name, animal, button *misc* so, little, look, very, really,
too, oh
5453 | 0.90 F

4518 dot *n*
adj red, black, white, small, blue, tiny, green,
single, colored *noun* polka., quantum., line,
multiplication, .light, .map, pattern, color, .inch,
.butter *verb* connect., center., show, appear,
.represent, .indicate, cover, mark, place, paint
5358 | 0.92

4519 weaken *v*
noun economy, system, state, power, .position, law,
government, support, .ability, effort, bone, party,
market, muscle, force *misc* .by, far, immune,
strengthen., political, severely.
5244 | 0.94

4520 filter *n*
adj blue, red, solar, light, digital, adaptive, special,
available, polarizing, perceptual *noun* air., water, system,
oil., paper, media, coffee., sand *verb* use, remove,
change, install, allow, replace, clean, reduce, act., trap
5789 | 0.85 M A

4521 worldwide *r*
people., billion., sell., million., copy., .including, species.,
employee., market., scientist., organization., sales
5289 | 0.93

4522 envision *v*
noun plan., scenario, kind, role, project, official.,
Congress, possibility, sort, planner., researcher.,
.scene, founder, solution, .creation *misc* future,
originally., hard., difficult., exactly., easily.
5154 | 0.95

4523 videotape *n*
adj hidden, instructional, edited, grainy, amateur,
exclusive, promotional, undercover, dramatic
noun proofread., camera., .text, book, film, lie.,
hour., interrogation., photograph, piece. *verb* begin.,
end., show, see., watch., view., record, capture.,
release, shoot
5820 | 0.84 S

4524 partial *j*
noun birth, list, support, correlation, shade,
solution, sun, eclipse, payment, credit, privatization,
explanation *misc* only, least, provide, full, complete,
offer, receive
5339 | 0.92 A

4525 patent *n*
adj original, pending, foreign, legal, intellectual,
corporate, exclusive, high-tech *noun* .office, US.,
.leather, .application, .trademark, .law, .protection,
.system, right *verb* file, hold., grant, issue, apply.,
receive., .expire, infringe., obtain., .cover
5666 | 0.87 M

4526 tray *n*
adj full, wooden, empty, round, ice-cube, top,
warming *noun* .table, food, silver., tea, plastic, coffee,
ice., drink, breakfast., metal. *verb* carry., set., hold,
bring., put., place, pick., slide, drop., bear
5502 | 0.89 F

4527 jungle *n*
adj dense, thick, tropical, concrete, urban, remote,
green, central *noun* .gym, .fever, mountain, law.,
animal, .canopy, .floor, tree, trail, island *verb* live,
hide., emerge, climb, welcome., flee., escape, crash
5277 | 0.93 F

4528 classify *v*
noun student, group, .category, .type, individual,
participant, study., information, subject, patient,
record, response, object, drug, .secret *misc* .as, .into,
.according, correctly., .under
5592 | 0.88 A

4529 specialty *n*
adj medical, local, regional, professional, occupational,
academic, high-end *noun* .store, .shop, .food, area,
market, house, care, product *verb* include, sell, offer,
develop., choose., feature., cook, order, .range, pursue.
5285 | 0.93 N

4530 nasty *j*
noun thing, stuff, habit, surprise, fight, campaign,
weather, word, business, divorce, look, war *misc* very,
little, really, turn, something, particularly, pretty,
brutish
5186 | 0.95

4531 aisle *n*
adj narrow, wide, main, central, middle, crowded,
broad *noun* side., seat, store, center., supermarket,
grocery, end., row, church, walk. *verb* stand, move.,
sit, reach., run., stroll., fill
5342 | 0.92 F

4532 graph *n*
adj horizontal, calibrated, financial, top, comparative,
upper, accompanying, bottom *noun* .figure, table.,
line, chart, bar., .paper, data, .percentage, stock,
curve *verb* .show, transcribe, plot., design., .track,
display, present, .compare, represent, illustrate
6122 | 0.8 A

4533 wound *v*
noun people., other, soldier., man, .attack, war, officer, civilian, police, .battle, thousand, .action, shooting, combat, .leg *misc* kill., dead., seriously., mortally., badly., dozen, hundred
5323 | 0.92

4534 sexy *j*
noun woman, man, girl, voice, dress, guy, body, beast, hair, clothes, smile, eye *misc* very, look, feel, wear, beautiful, hot, smart
5594 | 0.88 M

4535 disturb *v*
noun .peace, .sleep, balance, sound, .neighbor, soil, .equilibrium, bird, .sediment *misc* emotionally., deeply., sorry., nothing, mentally., seriously.
5158 | 0.95 F

4536 excessive *j*
noun force, use, amount, drinking, consumption, cost, alcohol, regulation, growth, violence, weight, heat *misc* cause, seem, avoid, without, prevent, lead, because, such
5274 | 0.93 A

4537 banker *n*
adj central, American, commercial, local, financial, retired, prominent, wealthy, top, independent *noun* investment., .association, lawyer, mortgage., business, accountant, economist, businessman, estate, merchant *verb* .lend, .finance, convince., hire., persuade, accuse, dress.
5467 | 0.90 N

4538 aid *v*
noun effort, .student, .development, government, program, .victim, .enemy, .understanding, .recovery, force, .cause, .search, organization, information., .digestion *misc* .by, .abet, design, greatly, .poor
5240 | 0.93 A

4539 installation *n*
adj military, easy, nuclear, permanent, Iraqi, major, professional, temporary, initial, actual *noun* art, video, cost, artist, .view, software, .maintenance, design, sculpture, equipment *verb* require, include, create, complete, attack., supervise., exhibit, incorporate
5569 | 0.88 M

4540 swimming *n*
adj synchronized, indoor, Olympic, public, outdoor, competitive, heated *noun* .pool, water, tennis, .hole, court, .team, .area, beach, .lesson, activity. *verb* go., include., win, enjoy., feature., prefer., prohibit.
5233 | 0.94

4541 placement *n*
adj advanced, private, foster, residential, appropriate, educational, proper, careful *noun* student, child, job., product., education, program, course, service, class, home *verb* determine, indicate, result, affect, relate., ensure., establish., range
5775 | 0.85 A

4542 attendance *n*
adj average, high, religious, low, daily, perfect, poor, total, regular *noun* school, church., student, record, year, college., .rate, game, percent, class *verb* increase, require, .drop, predict., report., expect, improve, encourage., boost., decline
5427 | 0.90 A

4543 informal *j*
noun sector, network, group, economy, survey, support, discussion, interview, meeting, interaction, system, conversation *misc* formal, through, between, social, both, conduct, among
5527 | 0.88 A

4544 sack *n*
adj empty, heavy, brown, sad, gunny, huge, defensive, hacky, bulging *noun* paper., flour, potato, burlap., stuff., .season, grocery, plastic., lunch, .game *verb* carry., allow, hold, fill, lead, drop., hit., throw, open, hang
5419 | 0.90 F

4545 flood *v*
noun water, market, light, area, room, city, river., street, home, face, field, rain., .call, office, body *misc* .with, .into, suddenly., rise, coastal, entire
   in light, come., .through, water., memory., order., offer, sunlight. **back** come., memory., .into
5090 | 0.96

4546 eighth *m*
.grade, .grader, seventh., .amendment, .inning, .century, .year, .street, .ninth, finish., .season, .note, game, .floor
5239 | 0.93 N

4547 premise *n*
adj basic, underlying, simple, central, fundamental, major, whole *noun* conclusion, quality., argument, freedom, assumption, customer, presentation, starting. *verb* base., accept., start., leave., follow, support., agree., rest., operate., reject.
5310 | 0.92 A

4548 grill *n*
adj hot, outdoor, oiled, mixed, electric, indoor, front *noun* gas., bar., heat, lid, charcoal., barbecue., .pan, rack, side, steak *verb* cook, cover, place, preheat, turn, prepare., remove, fire.
5695 | 0.86 M N

4549 model *v*
noun .behavior, process, .clay, technique, form, effect, .relationship, use, value, type, adult, performance *misc* .after, teach, .appropriate
5456 | 0.89 A

4550 dying *j*
noun man, patient, day, people, father, woman, child, mother, person, process, star, light *misc* dead, sick, lay, die, avoid, care, afraid, lie, fight
5144 | 0.95 F

4551 colorful *j*
noun character, flower, history, life, bird, garden, image, fish, design, fruit, painting, dress *misc* more, most, large, wear, bright, create, fill, full
5305 | 0.92 M

4552 hockey *n*
adj professional, junior, Olympic, pro, international, amateur, organized *noun* .league, .team, .player, .game, ice., field., basketball, baseball, football, .stick *verb* play., watch., coach, attend., swing.
5697 | 0.86 N

4553 backyard *n*
adj suburban, urban, sunny, fenced, shady, fenced-in, narrow *noun* pool, .garden, tree, .barbecue,

.telescope, .astronomer, fence, .bird, window,
.gardener _verb_ play, sit, build, bury., dig, overlook,
plant, land
5277 | 0.92 M

4554 collar _n_
adj white, blue, hot, starched, cervical, clerical,
button-down _noun_ shirt, coat, neck, dog., jacket,
.worker, radio., cuff, lace., fur. _verb_ wear., grab., pull,
turn, fit, open, loosen, adjust., unbutton
5362 | 0.91 F

4555 breathing _n_
adj heavy, deep, shallow, labored, normal, slow, rapid,
regular, ragged, steady _noun_ sound., .room, difficulty.,
.space, trouble., .problem, .tube, heart, technique,
.exercise _verb_ stop., hear., .become, listen., keep,
control., focus., .grow, relax, sleep
5325 | 0.91 F

4556 logical _j_
noun step, conclusion, choice, extension, place, way,
explanation, reason, argument, consequence, thing,
question _misc_ seem, next, most, only, assume,
rational, perfectly, than
5289 | 0.92 A

4557 lightning _n_
adj white, blue, distant, dry, greased, nearby, forked
noun bolt, .rod, thunder, flash, .strike, storm, sky,
.speed _verb_ hit, .illuminate, kill, cause, flicker, catch,
watch., .reveal, .occur
5281 | 0.92 F

4558 dried _j_
noun fruit, thyme, oregano, bean, leaf, blood,
cranberry, basil, apricot, salt, flower, pepper _misc_ or,
fresh, chop, red, crush, cup, add, mince
5537 | 0.88 M

4559 discount _n_
adj available, deep, substantial, steep, significant,
corporate, appropriate, traditional _noun_ .rate, .store,
percent, price, .broker, card, .chain, .retailer, drug,
airline _verb_ offer., give., sell., buy, receive., trade., cut,
.reflect, .range, .understate
5454 | 0.89 M N

4560 sole _j_
noun purpose, source, responsibility, owner, survivor,
power, exception, superpower, reason, representative,
criterion, support _misc_ as, whose, become, surviving,
legitimate, remaining, no, legal
5130 | 0.95

4561 boast _v_
noun city., company, .member, room, area., town.,
hotel, park., record, county, list, official., store, course,
mile _misc_ which., .more, .large, million, proudly.
about .how, something., nothing, often.
5270 | 0.92 M

4562 tag _n_
adj high, hefty, red, yellow, electronic, smart,
numbered, fluorescent _noun_ price., name., .line,
dog., number, game., .team, location _verb_ play., put.,
read, carry., .attach, wear., draw., .recapture, hang,
identify
5267 | 0.92

4563 sibling _n_
adj old, young, other, only, close, surviving, eldest,
closest, bitter _noun_ parent, child, .rivalry, family,

mother, relationship, friend, father, .age, cousin
verb share, fight, tend, adopt, .attend, abuse, separate,
cope, bicker, explore
5343 | 0.91

4564 stove _n_
adj hot, wood-burning, electric, cast-iron, potbellied,
portable, backpacking _noun_ wood., gas., pot, kitchen,
water, refrigerator, heat, fuel, burner, fire _verb_ cook,
turn, stand, burn, light, build, stoke., place
5634 | 0.86 F M

4565 trainer _n_
adj personal, athletic, certified, professional, elliptical,
assistant, physical, corporate _noun_ fitness, coach,
horse, team, dog., .tip, owner, animal. _verb_ hire.,
train, certify, consult, ride, employ, photograph, fire,
.contribute, .monitor
5383 | 0.90 M

4566 vertical _j_
noun foot, line, drop, axis, integration, wall,
position, plane, elevation, force, surface, dimension
misc horizontal, between, nearly, almost, skiable,
along, climb, represent
5576 | 0.87 M A

4567 added _j_
noun benefit, cost, bonus, value, weight, sugar,
pressure, advantage, dimension, incentive, security,
protection _misc_ give, provide, without, because, gain,
extra, worth
5185 | 0.94 M

4568 marketplace _n_
adj global, competitive, international, free, online,
changing, electronic, medical, crowded, religious
noun .idea, business., .newsroom, show.,
competition, product, consumer, technology,
demand, reality. _verb_ compete., .produce, .join,
enter., create, dominate, flood., introduce.,
control
5270 | 0.92

4569 cure _v_
noun .disease, .cancer, .problem, patient, illness,
.ill, drug, doctor., medicine., treatment, .ailment,
.diabetes, infection, .heart, .meat _misc_ prevent,
treat., sick, completely, .ail
5135 | 0.94

4570 curiosity _n_
adj intellectual, natural, scientific, insatiable, intense,
morbid, mere, idle, simple, mild _noun_ interest, desire,
object., sense, .seeker, cabinet, matter, fear, .shop,
lack. _verb_ satisfy., pique, arouse, spark., fill., express.,
stimulate., fade
5165 | 0.94 F

4571 organizational _j_
noun structure, commitment, change, skill, culture,
level, behavior, development, system, resource, chart,
form _misc_ provide, social, within, political, such,
develop, individual, personal
5906 | 0.82 A

4572 shrimp _n_
adj large, fresh, grilled, white, fried, cooked,
jumbo _noun_ pound., crab, salad, chicken, fish,
sauce, .boat, .fishery, .cocktail, scallop _verb_ add.,
cook, peel, serve, eat., stir, place, snap., taste,
top
5849 | 0.83

4573 inherit v
noun .mother, gene, family, money, .parent, land, .property, house, .earth, problem, team, .estate, .wealth, fortune, .business _misc_ .from, meek., genetic, clearly., genetically.
5053 | 0.96

4574 color v
noun hair, crayon, .perception, picture, .sky, cheek, shape, blood, plant, design _misc_ brightly., white, red, black, brilliantly.
5263 | 0.92 M

4575 distract v
noun .attention, .thought, mind, driver, sound, noise, .viewer, .public, attempt., presence, audience, .reader, .voter, commotion _misc_ .from, try., seem., easily., .myself, momentarily.
5182 | 0.93 F

4576 isolated j
noun incident, case, area, community, place, event, population, country, village, island, instance, town _misc_ feel, most, small, become, live, rural, than
5156 | 0.94 A

4577 planner n
adj financial, military, urban, local, fee-only, social, senior, strategic, environmental, top _noun_ city., discharge., county., war., event., party., wedding., work. _verb_ advise, hire., consult., anticipate, target, employ, convince.
5400 | 0.90 N

4578 supposedly r
.represent, .independent, his., character, .objective, .neutral, .intelligent, .secret, .scientific, liberal, allegedly, .universal, .civilized
5039 | 0.96

4579 likewise r
.emphasize, interaction, faculty, dramatic, sibling, involvement., .problematic, .evident
5341 | 0.91 A

4580 monkey n
adj red, little, green, wild, giant, stuffed, golden, drunken, trained _noun_ howler., .wrench, .bar, .business, spider., .house _verb_ throw, eat, swing, climb, feed, steal, jump, .chatter, resemble., act.
5323 | 0.91 F

4581 toll n
adj heavy, high, human, emotional, electronic, terrible, personal, physical, economic, civilian _noun_ death., .road, .booth, bridge, .authority, .plaza, highway, lane, .collection _verb_ take., pay., exact., .rise, .reach, raise., .climb, .mount, collect, estimate
5180 | 0.93 N

4582 embarrassed j
noun silence, smile, voice, laugh, laughter, gaze, fuss, expression, grin _misc_ I, by, feel, look, too, little, seem, slightly
5247 | 0.92 F

4583 deliberately r
.set, slowly., .choose, .try, keep, .avoid, .mislead, .target, .ignore, .design, quite., .kill, .seek, fire
5041 | 0.96

4584 bicycle n
adj stationary, red, recumbent, electric, rusty, cross-country, ten-speed _noun_ wheel, .shop, .ride, .helmet, tour, .path, .messenger, club, .coalition _verb_ pedal, race, walk, buy, fall, sell, own., lean, park
5502 | 0.88 M

4585 stance n
adj tough, political, aggressive, strong, public, moral, critical, neutral, wide _noun_ .phase, .issue, church, abortion, policy, ball, administration., swing, leg, batting. _verb_ take., adopt., assume., change, maintain., soften., shift., reflect, imply
5354 | 0.90 A

4586 orbit n
adj low, elliptical, circular, lunar, eccentric, geosynchronous, stable, polar, similar _noun_ earth, planet, sun, satellite., moon, star, comet, space, spacecraft., asteroid _verb_ move, launch., enter., reach., cross, change, place., achieve., .tilt
6046 | 0.8 M

4587 hormone n
adj thyroid, male, female, natural, synthetic, steroid, raging, parathyroid, certain _noun_ growth., .therapy, .replacement, level, stress., woman, estrogen, body, sex., cortisol _verb_ take., produce, release, cause, .increase, affect, secrete, stimulate, contain. treat
5855 | 0.82 M

4588 depressed j
noun people, child, patient, mood, area, price, economy, woman, person, mother, market, stock _misc_ feel, very, become, more, anxious, economically, severely, clinically
5180 | 0.93

4589 organism n
adj other, living, different, human, marine, large, small, aquatic, single, natural _noun_ environment, soil, gene, group., disease, water, cell, plant, animal, food _verb_ .live, evolve, kill, create, identify, .survive, affect, .adapt, contain, .thrive
5797 | 0.83 A

4590 deploy v
noun troop, force, .Iraq, missile, defense, weapon, technology, bag, number, team, resource, .gulf, officer, .border, space _misc_ military, nuclear, .along, develop., fully.
5191 | 0.93

4591 strictly r
.speak, .limit, .business, .enforce, .control, adhere, .forbid, .regulate, matter, define, .political, military, .basis
5056 | 0.95 A

4592 deem v
noun court, behavior., risk, material., society, treatment, .success, .threat, action., value, judge., organization, .failure, individual., .enemy _misc_ .necessary, .appropriate, .important, .worthy, .essential
5192 | 0.93 A

4593 eyebrow n
adj raised, black, dark, white, left, arched, gray, right, heavy, pierced _noun_ hair, eye, lip, nose, face, .pencil, mouth, eyelash, finger, look _verb_ raise., arch, lift, cock., pluck, wiggle., twitch, smooth, singe, lower
5558 | 0.87 F

4594 legally *r*
can, .blind, .binding, .require, .bind, allow, .recognize, .married, .entitle, .illegally, morally, .responsible
5047 | 0.95

4595 puzzle *n*
adj complex, giant, complicated, interesting, intricate, intriguing, wooden *noun* piece, crossword., jigsaw., .master, edition., game, book, .editor, answer, word *verb* solve, play., put, join, fit, present, remain, complete., assemble, finish.
5800 | 0.83 S

4596 icon *n*
adj American, cultural, religious, Byzantine, holy, beloved, pop-culture, feminist *noun* desktop, pop., style., fashion., status, church, art, rock., computer, relief. *verb* become., click, select, double-click., display, hide., touch, celebrate, resemble
5459 | 0.88 M

4597 pat *v*
noun .back, hand, .shoulder, .head, .arm, .pocket, .knee, .hair, face, dough, .neck, chicken., mixture, fish, finger *misc* .on, .her, .his, she., .dry, .my, rinse., gently
5428 | 0.89 F

4598 closest *j*
noun friend, thing, ally, adviser, relative, approach, aide, associate, competitor, point, confidant, neighbor *misc* one, come, ever, probably, perhaps, among, living
5019 | 0.96

4599 sneak *v*
noun .peek, .look, .glance, window, boy, .town, .cigarette, .bed, .attack, movie, bathroom, .apartment, .thief, .smoke, .peak *misc* .into, .out, try., .through, .away, .back, .across
5208 | 0.92 F

4600 fleet *n*
adj large, entire, Japanese, whole, British, foreign, French, Spanish, combined *noun* US., fishing., ship, car, vehicle, truck, sea, aircraft, bus, air *verb* build., operate, .sail, send, join., command, maintain, expand, arrive, .land
5309 | 0.91 M

4601 conservation *n*
adj environmental, marine, biological, tropical, integrated, community-based, ecological *noun* energy., water., wildlife., resource, soil., program, development, biodiversity, habitat., management *verb* promote., encourage, require, focus, support, protect, contribute., .reduce, relate., prioritize.
5638 | 0.85 A

4602 supportive *j*
noun environment, family, relationship, service, parent, role, teacher, community, friend, group, policy, effort *misc* very, more, provide, less, mutually, generally, extremely, each
5191 | 0.93 A

4603 comparable *j*
noun level, size, rate, group, data, result, price, figure, study, period, quality, number *misc* than, those, roughly, offer, report, less, directly
5260 | 0.91 A

4604 texture *n*
adj rich, creamy, smooth, soft, rough, fine, light, firm, crunchy, chewy *noun* color, flavor, taste, shape, surface, skin, hair, form, pattern, size *verb* add., create, change., improve., achieve, lend., retain., vary, resemble, blend
5535 | 0.87 M

4605 access *v*
noun .information, Internet, service, site, student., data, .web, computer, user., .file, resource, record, material, ability., database *misc* can., give., .through, able., allow., .via, easily., deny., easy., .online, difficult., directly, enable.
5280 | 0.91 A

4606 striking *j*
noun feature, difference, example, resemblance, contrast, similarity, thing, worker, woman, image, result, aspect *misc* most, more, between, bear, perhaps, quite, particularly, bore
5162 | 0.93 A

4607 associate *j*
noun professor, editor, director, degree, justice, producer, pastor, program, research, curator, administrator, counsel *misc* senior, former, clinical, serve, general, athletic
5293 | 0.91 M

4608 Christianity *n*
adj early, evangelical, western, orthodox, traditional, Catholic, Protestant *noun* Judaism, Islam, religion, history., conversion., form., attitude. *verb* convert., embrace, accept, reject, adopt., preach, spread, promote, emphasize, .flourish
5807 | 0.83 A

4609 dip *v*
noun water, hand, head, .finger, temperature., .percent, .toe, brush, sun., .egg, .chocolate, .sauce, bread, chip, mixture *misc* .into, .below, .low, .slightly, rise
 down .into, then, road., head., .again, .toward
5151 | 0.93 F

4610 disappointment *n*
adj big, great, bitter, major, only, greatest, crushing, huge, deep, obvious *noun* frustration, face, anger, sense., season, failure, pain, surprise., look., feeling. *verb* express., feel, hide., set, suffer., deal., avoid., imagine.
5027 | 0.95

4611 sleeve *n*
adj short, left, empty, red, wide, rubber, protective *noun* shirt, jacket, arm, coat, face, trick., nose., sweater, heart., plastic. *verb* roll, pull, tug., wear., push, grab., touch., wipe, .reveal
5358 | 0.89 F

4612 socially *r*
.responsible, .acceptable, more., economically, .construct, politically, .conscious, behavior, .desirable, .conservative, become., .prescribed, culturally
5380 | 0.89 A

4613 wheat *n*
adj whole, white, shredded, golden, green, growing, cracked *noun* field, corn, flour, .bread, rice, .germ, barley, crop, grain, cup *verb* grow, plant, separate., harvest, cut, produce, eat.
5350 | 0.90

4614 chunk n
adj big, large, huge, good, sizable, fresh, whole, significant, nice, red *noun* .ice, .meat, .money, .rock, .wood, pineapple, chocolate, .land, .change, potato *verb* cut, break, spend, buy, own, tear, bite, blow, drop
5127 | 0.93 M

4615 two-thirds m
about, than, more, nearly, .vote, .majority, almost, .American, account, require, .population, roughly, approximately, .respondent
5124 | 0.93

4616 pile v
noun snow, table, book, hair, box, plate, .corner, body, debt, paper, rock, food, clothes, floor, bill, *misc* .on, .high, .into, .against, .onto, behind, neatly
  up snow, .debt, keep, begin, body, bill, continue, .yard, loss, .outside
5126 | 0.93 F

4617 refuge n
adj temporary, safe, federal, peaceful, quiet, welcome, spiritual *noun* wildlife, place, .acre, park, island, oil, city, river, .system, .manager *verb* take, seek, find, provide, become, offer, serve.
5190 | 0.92 M

4618 blank j
noun page, check, space, screen, paper, eye, wall, mind, slate, look, expression, sheet *misc* fill, stare, draw, leave, white, face, point, remain
5147 | 0.93 F

4619 unfold v
noun event, story, drama, life, paper, scene, history, tragedy, scenario, map, .television, piece, .sheet, .napkin, arm *misc* watch, .before, begin, continue, slowly
4926 | 0.97

4620 considerably r
.than, .more, .less, vary, .high, .low, change, .small, increase, improve, differ, .since
5147 | 0.93 A

4621 frontier n
adj new, American, electronic, western, final, northern, eastern, wild *noun* .airline, .town, .forest, .foundation, .province, space, .region, science, settlement, area *verb* cross, explore, push, open, settle, expand, extend, spread, .attract, .separate
5289 | 0.90 A

4622 faster j
noun rate, pace, growth, time, speed, way, computer, result, processor, car, recovery, chip *misc* than, grow, more, any, move, much, cheap, ever
5159 | 0.93 M

4623 suspicious j
noun activity, eye, behavior, package, death, circumstance, police, character, fire, car, case, mind *misc* look, become, very, anything, little, grow, deeply
4975 | 0.96

4624 conception n
adj immaculate, human, traditional, popular, modern, original, particular, liberal, common, virginal *noun* .nature, moment, artist, .art, .citizenship,

.history, .knowledge, .justice, birth, teacher *verb* begin, develop, reflect, .occur, prevent, expand, embrace, reveal.
5606 | 0.85 A

4625 feather n
adj white, red, black, long, yellow, ruffled, light, brown, gray, dark *noun* bird, tail, eagle, hat, .duster, .bed, peacock, .boa, head *verb* ruffle, wear, fly, cover, float, .fall, smooth, pick, preen, fluff
5232 | 0.91 F

4626 elephant n
adj white, African, Asian, pink, huge, hairy, dead, female, giant *noun* herd, .trunk, .room, .seal, .ear, tusk, baby, .population, bull, *verb* kill, ride, shoot, save, eat, .name, dance, ignore, trample, feature.
5277 | 0.90

4627 rain v
noun day, night, fire, morning, bomb, week, debris, glass, .cat, .dog, window, .earth, river, hour, bullet *misc* it, when, start, begin, .hard, .pour, .heavily
  down .on, .upon, fire, debris, bomb, glass, missile, .onto, blow, .around
5186 | 0.92 F

4628 cure n
adj only, known, medical, possible, clinical, potential, miraculous, effective *noun* .disease, cancer, miracle, .rate, treatment, .AIDS, cause, search, race. *verb* find, help, seek, discover, lead, offer, hope, .heal
5068 | 0.94

4629 near r
.where, draw, come, .enough, .far, as, live, end, damn, nowhere, anywhere, stand, store, theater.
5029 | 0.95 F

4630 intellectual n
adj American, public, leading, black, western, prominent, conservative, European, African, literary *noun* artist, group, writer, politician, activist, leader, class, .property, party, role *verb* argue, .seek, tend, criticize, assume, associate, attract, characterize, label, undermine.
5471 | 0.87 A

4631 textbook n
adj medical, traditional, introductory, standard, used, available, current, online, classic *noun* school, history, study, .example, .case, science, .publisher, book, education *verb* write, read, publish, learn, present, rely, rewrite, select.
5594 | 0.85 A

4632 joke v
noun friend, .reporter, wife, husband, dad, humor, teammate *misc* .about, .around, laugh, like, always, often.
5058 | 0.94

4633 glimpse n
adj brief, rare, quick, fleeting, only, occasional, fascinating, tantalizing *noun* .future, window, viewer, visitor, offer, .movement, .greatness, .heaven, .hell *verb* catch, get, give, provide, hope, allow.
5058 | 0.94 F

4634 inevitably r
will, lead, almost, must, such, question, .end, result, follow, .draw, .involve, .arise, perhaps, .produce
5099 | 0.93 A

4635 triumph n
adj great, greatest, personal, ultimate, major, final, eventual, diplomatic *noun* moment., tragedy, .spirit, democracy, victory, .will, .capitalism, sense, failure, look. *verb* celebrate., represent., return., score., mark., end, enjoy.
5005 | 0.95

4636 plunge v
noun stock., hand, .percent, price., .darkness, foot, knife, market, .point, .ice, earth, share, rate, .sea, temperature. *misc* .into, .through, .deep, .ahead, .toward
  down .into, .steep, .hill, cliff, .toward, air.
5082 | 0.94 F

4637 sphere n
adj political, private, economic, social, domestic, celestial, different *noun* .influence, .life, activity, music., public., .action, .interest, power, .sovereignty, surface *verb* expand, enter., define, extend., form., enlarge., surround, occupy., .spin, .float
5375 | 0.89 A

4638 hunger n
adj spiritual, cold, physical, extreme, insatiable, severe, widespread, desperate *noun* .strike, poverty, world., disease, food, thirst, pang, homelessness, stomach *verb* die., satisfy., end., suffer., feed., fight., reduce., .gnaw, overcome, consume
5025 | 0.95

4639 density n
adj high, low, current, average, increased, critical, increasing, total *noun* population., bone., energy., mineral., area, temperature, matter, size, electron, increase *verb* measure, reach, reduce, decrease, determine, maintain., vary, support, .exceed, .range
5673 | 0.84 A

4640 cheer v
noun crowd, fan, audience., thousand, street., foot., boy, flag, spectator, teammate, prospect, .hero, .arrival, .rally *misc* .up, .on, stand., .wildly, clap, everyone., .loudly
5026 | 0.95

4641 balanced j
noun budget, diet, approach, fund, life, plan, view, meal, program, attack, agreement, act *misc* more, fair, provide, pass, eat, require, achieve, maintain
5187 | 0.92 S

4642 protocol n
adj standard, international, experimental, strict, additional, clinical, proper, surgical *noun* treatment., Internet., study, research., interview., convention, data, test., testing. *verb* follow, develop, sign, establish, require, .approve, ratify., .allow, implement, agree
5472 | 0.87 A

4643 part i
(on the part of) .of, on., effort., .government, .both, .student, action., .United States, behavior., .public, interest., .teacher, reluctance., .parent
5213 | 0.91 S A

4644 legislator n
adj federal, local, democratic, conservative, elected, effective, key, congressional, fellow, incumbent *noun* state., governor, year, law, .bill, party, official,

member, county, Congress *verb* .vote, .support, .consider, elect, urge, .introduce, lobby., convince., .seek, limit
5205 | 0.91 N

4645 auction n
adj silent, live, online, public, annual, recent, open *noun* .house, .site, art., .block, dinner, eBay, price, Internet., market, item *verb* sell., hold, buy, .raise, feature, bid, attend., conduct., .honor
5262 | 0.90 N

4646 equality n
adj racial, social, economic, political, human, great, full, legal *noun* woman, gender., freedom, .opportunity, justice, right, liberty, .man, principle., .law *verb* achieve., promote., base, establish, fight., guarantee., ensure.
5392 | 0.88 A

4647 risky j
noun behavior, business, investment, stock, move, loan, strategy, venture, sex, decision, thing, situation *misc* too, more, very, less, sexual, engage, consider
5090 | 0.93

4648 cemetery n
adj national, old, military, Catholic, local, historic, ancient, tiny *noun* grave, city, church, burial, memorial, town, plot, road, gate, ground *verb* bury., visit, pass, fill, surround, own, clean, border
5135 | 0.92

4649 builder n
adj national, local, large, residential, associated, professional, experienced, suburban, reputable *noun* home., association, master., boat., developer, house, body., area, bridge. *verb* offer, .construct, hire, .install, select, sue, advise, .estimate, enable.
5356 | 0.89 M N

4650 awake j
noun night, bed, hour, morning, patient, sleep, dawn, midnight *misc* she, stay, keep, lie, lay, wide, still, shake
5386 | 0.88 F

4651 retailer n
adj other, large, online, small, national, traditional, mass, available, outdoor, giant *noun* store, manufacturer, company, discount., year, home, nation., specialty., clothing, food *verb* sell, hurt, shop, locate., supply, compete, bypass.
5410 | 0.88 N

4652 debut n
adj directorial, major, self-titled, professional, major-league, acting, Olympic, big-screen *noun* .album, year, film, .novel, Broadway., solo, will., week, .CD, season *verb* make., release., mark., .grade, schedule., record, associate, delay.
5413 | 0.88 N

4653 tighten v
noun grip, hand, .belt, muscle, security, .screw, face., lip, finger., throat., stomach, skin, noose, mouth., control *misc* his, her, .around, feel., loosen, .abs, slightly, gradually
  up security, muscle, .its, border, .procedure, race., throat., area, around, .immigration
5140 | 0.92 F

4654 spare *v*
noun life, expense, minute, room., effort, .detail, .pain, death, .embarrassment, .rod, hour, .feeling, energy, second, patient *misc* can., .me, few, little, plenty., .yourself, .tire, extra, order., none
4994 | 0.95 F

4655 compromise *v*
noun security, .ability, .integrity, system, .principle, safety, .quality, health, position, interest
misc without., may., willing., might., seriously.
4960 | 0.96

4656 constraint *n*
adj social, economic, political, financial, legal, structural, free, environmental, physical, fiscal
noun time., budget., opportunity, space, design, policy, behavior, development, capacity, process
verb impose, face, give., place, operate, remove., overcome., result, resource.
5562 | 0.85 A

4657 compliance *n*
adj environmental, federal, full, regulatory, voluntary, international, patient, strict, behavioral, complete
noun .law, program, cost, .standard, state, .regulation, .requirement, .rule, rate, .officer *verb* ensure., monitor., bring., achieve., enforce., require, force., report, reduce, vary
5689 | 0.83 A

4658 sponsor *n*
adj corporate, principal, national, Olympic, major, chief, official, potential, primary, local *noun* bill, state., .terrorism, program, team, project, title., money, .legislation, fund *verb* .include, .pay, sign, seek, attract., .encourage, support, line, .donate, photograph.
5212 | 0.91 N

4659 emerging *j*
noun market, technology, economy, world, democracy, trend, artist, nation, growth, disease, issue, field
misc new, newly, global, such, middle, economic, identify
5302 | 0.89 A

4660 this *r*
.far, .little, .much, get., .many, come., never., .really, .close, nowhere., .girl, .guy, before, .evident
5040 | 0.94 S

4661 elaborate *j*
noun system, plan, scheme, design, set, ritual, ceremony, costume, structure, network, display, process *misc* more, most, build, create, require, develop, wear
5018 | 0.94

4662 atop *i*
sit., stand., perch., .head, high, .hill, .mountain, place., tower, set., rest., mount, building, build.
5104 | 0.92 F

4663 chew *v*
noun .gum, .tobacco, .lip, .food, .piece, .cud, .nail, cigar, .fat, .bit, leg *misc* .swallow, slowly, .spit, .off, stop., .thoughtfully
up .spit, get., .more, dog
5219 | 0.90 F

4664 similarity *n*
adj striking, cultural, important, strong, remarkable, structural, significant, perceived, close *noun*

difference, lot., group, study, degree., experience, language, .measure, value, .situation *verb* show., share., bear., note., .end, reveal., base., notice., strike, .exist
5315 | 0.89 A

4665 pencil *n*
adj colored, yellow, red, sharp, pastel, sharpened, mechanical, stubby *noun* paper, pen, pad, .eraser, drawing, .skirt, graphite., .sketch, line, .sharpener
verb use., write, hold., put., sharpen., draw, pick., tap, mark
5486 | 0.86 F M

4666 calculation *n*
adj political, mathematical, simple, quick, careful, cold, rational, detailed, complicated *noun* number, data, computer, method, cost, table, interest, .second, risk, control *verb* make, use, base, perform, .show, include, .indicate, .suggest, determine, involve
5239 | 0.90 A

4667 tolerance *n*
adj high, religious, great, low, political, racial, cultural *noun* zero., level, risk, policy, pain, .ambiguity, respect, diversity, understanding, glucose. *verb* show., promote., develop., teach., require, build., increase, advocate., characterize, extend
5160 | 0.91 A

4668 astronomer *n*
adj amateur, professional, infrared, able, planetary, stellar, distant, Chinese, modern, European *noun* star, radio., year., galaxy, century., team., image, backyard., space, sky *verb* .use, .find, .discover, .observe, .study, .believe, .measure, allow., enable., .predict
7741 | 0.61 M

4669 bulk *n*
adj great, vast, dark, sheer, massive, huge, extra *noun* .work, .money, weight, material, food, tissue, .population, .sales, product, .fund *verb* buy., provide., sell., spend., add., account., carry., constitute., .block
4989 | 0.94

4670 arm *v*
noun .weapon, .rifle, .gun, .information, .knowledge, missile, .knife, .pistol, bomb, .bow, .handgun, .stick, pilot *misc* .with, heavily., .only, .dangerous, better.
4909 | 0.96

4671 interval *n*
adj long, short, brief, irregular, frequent, mean, decent, various, average, silent *noun* time, confidence., .training, day, minute, behavior, table, workout, data, scale *verb* occur, follow, increase, repeat, space., record, measure., .indicate, place, alternate
5369 | 0.88 A

4672 notebook *n*
adj spiral, small, little, top, blue, red, spiral-bound, loose-leaf *noun* .computer, reporter, paper, page, pen, pencil, desktop, pocket, note, entry *verb* write, keep, .appear, open, fill, pull., carry, record, scribble., close.
5352 | 0.88 F

4673 genre *n*
adj other, new, literary, musical, different, popular, specific, various, particular, whole *noun* music, style, film, .painting, .fiction, movie, novel, writing, convention, example. *verb* create, define, belong., transcend., invent, constitute., explore, emerge, .evolve, embrace
5472 | 0.86 A

4674 likelihood n
adj great, high, increased, maximum, strong, low, future, significant, estimated *noun* .success, behavior, use, .sex, .war, .conflict, increase, .event, .ratio, .method *verb* .will, reduce., decrease., assess., enhance., determine., associate., indicate.
5310 | 0.89 A

4675 liberal n
adj white, political, social, democratic, economic, left, religious, traditional, prominent, northern *noun* Democrat, party, word., moderate, Republican, court, .Congress, deal, press, media *verb* .believe, .argue, .agree, oppose, win, blame, criticize, accuse, hate, attack
5348 | 0.88 S

4676 streak n
adj winning, long, losing, blue, consecutive, hot, mean, black, independent *noun* game, four-game., three-game., five-game., .light, season, record, six-game., seven-game., eight-game. *verb* end, extend., snap, break., ride., stretch, paint
5363 | 0.88 N

4677 rib n
adj prime, broken, short, cracked, left, low, braised, tender, hot, sore *noun* .cage, celery, pork, back, beef, side, bone, .eye, hand, heart *verb* break, chop, cut, poke., crack, serve, kick., stick, hurt, eat
5103 | 0.92 F

4678 scent n
adj sweet, faint, fresh, strong, rich, heavy, human, heady, floral, pungent *noun* air, flower, perfume, .rose, pine, dog, wind, lavender, jasmine, .trail *verb* catch., smell., carry., pick., breathe., follow., fill, inhale., .waft, .drift
5336 | 0.88 F

4679 validity n
adj content, internal, external, concurrent, predictive, convergent, discriminant *noun* reliability, evidence, study, construct., test, measure, scale, instrument, criterion., face. *verb* establish, demonstrate, assess, support, provide, examine, .refer, depend, relate
5967 | 0.79 A

4680 grin n
adj big, wide, broad, toothy, sly, huge, mischievous, wry *noun* .face, eye, tooth, head, .ear, cat, nod, idiot., trademark., killer. *verb* give., flash., break., wear., smile, .spread, turn, add, widen, .fade
5410 | 0.87 F

4681 steer v
noun .course, wheel, .car, .boat, .conversation, .ship, .direction, driver, control, truck, .customer, .ski, bike, .contract, captain. *misc* .clear, .toward, .away, .into, .through
4987 | 0.94 M

4682 intact j
noun family, body, class, dignity, forest, structure, group, limb, wall, skin, marriage, memory *misc* remain, keep, still, leave, survive, largely, stay, relatively
4955 | 0.95

4683 shark n
adj white, blue, gray, coastal, basking, hungry, male *noun* .program, .attack, species, whale., tiger., .fin, number, loan. *verb* .tag, swim, catch, feed, eat, jump., bite, circle
5799 | 0.81

4684 uh u
.huh, .no, oh, well, yeah, yes, .sure, okay, .thanks, sorry, hi, um, sir, hello
5753 | 0.82 F

4685 programming n
adj educational, local, original, regular, special, gifted, object-oriented, cultural, religious *noun* .language, television., child, computer., cable, network, TV, hour., news, education *verb* provide, offer, develop, produce, require, broadcast, interrupt., .consist, transmit, block.
5166 | 0.91

4686 dumb j
noun thing, question, luck, guy, idea, kid, animal, jock, mistake, joke, ass, friend *misc* too, play, really, enough, strike, smart, deaf, pretty
5056 | 0.93 F

4687 formerly r
.as, .director, .communist, .own, artist., .occupy, .editor, .homeless, .prince, .assistant, .senior
5004 | 0.94

4688 squad n
adj full, cheerleading, Olympic, whole, paramilitary, traveling, flying, cheering *noun* .car, death., firing., police, bomb., .leader, .room, member, rescue. *verb* fire., lead, send, face, execute, join, form, organize., .finish, track
5025 | 0.93 N

4689 comply v
noun .law, state, .regulation, .requirement, .rule, order, .standard, .request, .resolution, failure., .demand, obligation, effort., .provision, .title *misc* .with, must., fail., fully, refuse., require., force.
5151 | 0.91 A

4690 debris n
adj marine, flying, orbital, floating, burning, cosmic *noun* pile, piece., dust., .field, space, rock, construction., ton., tree, street *verb* fall, remove, clear., pick, litter, clean., scatter, trap., spread, cause
5023 | 0.93

4691 peasant n
adj poor, indigenous, rural, local, landless, Russian, European, Mexican *noun* .farmer, worker, .woman, land, .community, .organization, .girl, .family, .blouse *verb* organize, dress, .flee, depict, fear, transform, disguise., inhabit, .resist, .demand
5373 | 0.87 A

4692 outlet n
adj retail, other, electrical, creative, fast-food, only, available, traditional, electric, mainstream *noun* media., news., store, .mall, factory., .center, wall. *verb* find., provide., open, plug, sell, own, seek., install, shut, .account
5052 | 0.93 M

4693 chase n
adj high-speed, wild, long, fair, slow-speed, merry, desperate *noun* car., police, goose., .scene, paper., driver, speed., freeway *verb* give., cut., join, enjoy., qualify.
5107 | 0.92

4694 neat j
noun row, thing, house, pile, trick, room, line, hair, stack, stuff, idea, package *misc* little, really, clean, pretty, keep, small, tidy
4971 | 0.94 F

4695 valid *j*
noun point, measure, reason, license, test, concern, question, instrument, data, information, argument, way *misc* reliable, as, equally, remain, only, provide, consider, no
5169 | 0.90 A

4696 kingdom *n*
adj magic, wild, middle, ancient, African, peaceable, heavenly *noun* animal., state, .heaven, .earth, plant., desert., oil, vegetable. *verb* enter., establish, build, rule, create, defend., belong, divide, inherit., comprise
5105 | 0.92

4697 solely *r*
not., base., rely., focus., .because, .responsible, .basis, depend., .purpose, almost., .terms, exist., consist., .upon
5044 | 0.93 A

4698 eligible *j*
noun student, child, voter, parole, benefit, service, bachelor, program, patient, man, woman, player *misc* for, become, those, receive, vote, free, most, participate
5046 | 0.93 N

4699 regret *v*
noun .decision, .error, .loss, .word, mistake, .choice, .vote, .lack, .limitation, .inconvenience *misc* that, never., later, deeply, immediately.
4918 | 0.95

4700 municipal *j*
noun bond, waste, government, water, court, election, state, district, service, utility, city, building *misc* solid, industrial, local, provincial, privatize, agricultural, regional
5234 | 0.89 A

4701 strain *v*
noun eye, voice, relation, relationship, muscle, ear, back, resource, face, liquid, neck, mixture, .credulity, body, .leash *misc* .through, .hear, .against, already, forward
4970 | 0.94 F

4702 deposit *n*
adj federal, safe, large, direct, natural, fatty, checkable, vast, money-market, minimum *noun* .insurance, bank, certificate., .box, account, .corporation, oil, security., mineral., fund *verb* pay, insure., leave, require, form, cover, contain, accept., collect., protect.
5056 | 0.92 M

4703 transport *v*
noun material, truck, .hospital, water, .good, ship, body, troop, vehicle., waste, food, bus., gas, cargo, energy *misc* .back, .across, store, easily, easy.
4898 | 0.95

4704 dough *n*
adj remaining, soft, sticky, frozen, fried, stiff, excess *noun* ball, cookie, flour, bread., pizza., piece, surface, bowl, pie, .hook *verb* roll., make, knead, divide., turn, place, form, cut, rise, .fill
5690 | 0.82 M N

4705 lid *n*
adj tight-fitting, heavy, tight, top, upper, hinged, wooden, removable *noun* box, grill, jar, eye, pot, trunk., plastic, .heat, coffin, container *verb* keep., lift., open, close, put., cover., remove, blow, shut, slam.
5118 | 0.91 F M

4706 voluntary *j*
noun program, association, participation, organization, standard, basis, system, agreement, manslaughter, action, service, compliance *misc* national, private, involuntary, mandatory, entirely, encourage, purely, strictly
5181 | 0.90 A

4707 journalism *n*
adj investigative, yellow, tabloid, literary, responsible, daily, explanatory *noun* school, professor, award, career, excellence., degree, .review, broadcast. *verb* teach., study., practice, print., major., graduate.
5242 | 0.89 N

4708 any *r*
.long, than, .more, .far, .good, wait., .ever, stand., .better, hold., stay, anything.
4906 | 0.95 F

4709 impulse *n*
adj natural, sexual, strong, sudden, creative, human, religious, poor, initial, contradictory *noun* .control, nerve., .buying, brain, .purchase, heart, .response, action, .item, .buyer *verb* resist., feel, act., buy, fight., drive, understand., suppress., seize, .arise
4974 | 0.93

4710 policeman *n*
adj military, uniformed, white, armed, retired, off-duty, mounted, undercover, unidentified *noun* world, fireman, soldier, street, gun, traffic, .uniform, guard, firefighter, border. *verb* kill, shoot, walk, wound, .arrive, train, dress, .patrol, notice, murder
5014 | 0.93 F

4711 objection *n*
adj strong, moral, conscientious, serious, main, obvious, irrelevant, initial *noun* .honor, defense, department, Republican, union, administration, prosecutor, critic, .hearsay, .lack *verb* raise, overrule, voice., sustain, state, overcome., override., drop., .arise, .concern
4970 | 0.93

4712 thrive *v*
noun plant., business., company., economy, species., industry., environment, .soil, area, bacteria., community, organism., .climate, .challenge, competition *misc* .on, survive., continue., .under, .without
4982 | 0.93 M

4713 privately *r*
.own, .hold, .company, official, publicly, meet., .funded, talk., fund, speak., .finance, .run, .operate, admit
4902 | 0.95

4714 cling *v*
noun .life, .hope, body, arm, .side, mother, .skin, tree, .belief, .back, .power, .religion, .idea, neck, leaf *misc* .to, her, .tightly, desperately, .tenaciously
5091 | 0.91 F

4715 halfway *r*
.through, .up, .down, .between, .across, .around, .there, about., meet.
5071 | 0.92 F

4716 unhappy *j*
noun people, marriage, man, life, woman, family, customer, childhood, person, result, experience,

couple *misc* with, about, very, happy, increasingly, lonely, extremely, clearly
4818 | 0.96

4717 rally *n*
adj political, big, mass, huge, recent, massive, anti-war *noun* pep., campaign., stock, protest., peace., market, street, city, car *verb* hold, attend., organize, stage., .support, speak., plan, address, .draw, .demand
5045 | 0.92

4718 scratch *v*
noun .head, .surface, back, .ear, face, .chin, itch, door, hand., .nose, eye, leg, .skin, cat, dog *misc* .behind, bite, barely., claw, around, .wonder, left, easily
   out .living, name, word, eye, .existence, pen., .note
5113 | 0.91 F

4719 robot *n*
adj industrial, humanoid, mobile, autonomous, giant, alien, remote-controlled *noun* .arm, machine, killer., computer, .dog, factory, technology, maintenance. *verb* use, build., send, design, create, control, .name, .pick, replace, construct
5594 | 0.83 F

4720 conversion *n*
adj religious, two-point, personal, Christian, forced, mass, spiritual *noun* process, energy, .Christianity, experience, land, .rate, defense., .efficiency *verb* undergo., require, .occur, complete, result., facilitate., encourage., transform, imply
5235 | 0.89 A

4721 supermarket *n*
adj local, available, giant, financial, typical, nearby, average, nearest *noun* chain, store, food, .tabloid, .shelf, section., aisle, product, line, market *verb* find., buy, sell, .offer, shop, open, .carry, stock, purchase., own
4981 | 0.93 M

4722 blink *v*
noun eye, light, .tear, face, .surprise, moment, machine., screen, sunlight, .sun, star., image, sign., glass, second *misc* .at, then, .back, .away, .off, .rapidly, .hard, .twice
5535 | 0.84 F

4723 philosophical *j*
noun question, difference, issue, tradition, problem, society, position, foundation, argument, debate, approach, view *misc* political, religious, theological, American, historical, scientific, moral, social
5334 | 0.87 A

4724 happily *r*
.married, live., .after, .ever, end., smile., together, couple, marry, quite., along, nod., settle, grin.
4943 | 0.94 F

4725 thread *n*
adj common, golden, thin, single, loose, black, metallic, red, strong, narrative *noun* needle, silk., fabric, cotton., spool., silver, gold, end, .count, number *verb* hang, weave, pull, lose., .connect, pick., tie, follow, sew, spin.
5034 | 0.92

4726 allegedly *r*
who., .kill, after., arrest., murder, .steal, .shoot, police, .commit, .rape, assault, .sell, abuse, officer
4993 | 0.93 S

4727 ash *n*
adj volcanic, black, gray, bottom, green, burning, cold *noun* cigarette, white., wood., fire, .tree, fly., coal., dust, smoke, cloud *verb* scatter, rise., turn, fall, burn., cover, flick., spread, tap., blow
5254 | 0.88 F

4728 dynamics *n*
adj general, social, political, internal, computational, complex, nonlinear, cultural, structural, human *noun* group, family, fluid., population., system, power, community, change, relationship, structure *verb* understand., affect, study., examine., capture., influence, explore., shape, .underlie, contribute
5442 | 0.85 A

4729 denial *n*
adj deep, complete, religious, total, official, outright, categorical, flat, systematic *noun* state., .right, .service, care, .attack, form., .access, deception, self, .reality *verb* issue., result, appeal., recommend., repeat., constitute, justify., .stem
4913 | 0.94

4730 riot *n*
adj urban, recent, mock, near, mass, ensuing, full-scale, communal, armed, Israeli *noun* police, race., year, city, .gear, food., prison., .act, .control, .color *verb* .break, start, erupt, cause., lead, .occur, incite., spark., kill, quell.
4964 | 0.93

4731 soar *v*
noun price., .percent, stock., rate., year, sales., eagle., .foot, temperature., air, spirit., popularity, profit., level, .height *misc* .over, .high, .above, .through, .past, .million, continue., .billion, .overhead, .toward
4985 | 0.93 N

4732 mentor *n*
adj young, spiritual, professional, experienced, longtime, wonderful, onetime, beloved *noun* teacher, student, friend, program, role, model, school, relationship, university *verb* serve., become., .help, provide, act., .teach, seek., assign, match, .guide
5311 | 0.87 A

4733 beard *n*
adj white, long, black, gray, red, full, dark, thick, bushy, short *noun* hair, man., eye, mustache, face, growth., glass, hat, stubble, chin *verb* grow, wear, shave., trim, stroke., pull, scratch., cut, hang, .match
5061 | 0.91 F

4734 widow *n*
adj black, young, elderly, grieving, poor, wealthy, rich, beautiful *noun* woman, wife, .husband, .peak, war., .son, daughter, .walk, brother, .rockfish *verb* live, marry, .name, .remarry, comfort, .grieve, mourn, award, .testify, interview
4921 | 0.94

4735 offender *n*
adj violent, juvenile, convicted, bad, young, first-time, sexual, likely, male, alleged *noun* sex., drug., repeat., law, state, treatment, victim, program, case, number. *verb* register, commit, require, punish, treat., identify, deal., prosecute., catch
5041 | 0.92

4736 landmark *n*
adj historic, national, local, historical, famous, major, natural, cultural, architectural *noun* .case, city, .study,

.decision, court, building, .ruling, .legislation, .book
verb pass, designate., build, point., recognize, visit,
preserve, search.
4941 | 0.93 N

4737 apart *i*
(apart from) .from, set., .other, quite., stand., live.,
.rest, .fact, .each, separate., .another, exist., .else,
themselves.
4872 | 0.95 A

4738 instant *n*
adj brief, single, precise, exact, mere, fleeting, given
noun .silence, .creation, .hesitation, surprise, .clarity
verb feel, realize, change, hesitate., freeze, wonder,
pause., disappear, last.
5248 | 0.88 F

4739 routinely *r*
use, test, patient, .ignore, doctor, police, .monitor,
perform, .deny, .check, .beat, worker, .violate,
agency.
4894 | 0.94

4740 butt *n*
adj big, fat, cute, bare, nice, tight, skinny, lazy
noun cigarette., .joke, rifle, gun, pain., head., .end,
leg, thigh, hip *verb* get, work., sit, bust., save., stick,
flick., throw, slide
5027 | 0.92 F

4741 forbid *v*
noun heaven., state, rule., government, .use, practice,
marriage, .contact, .discrimination, regulation,
alcohol, doctor, employee, .sale, entry *misc* .any,
shall, strictly., anything, federal, absolutely.
4778 | 0.96

4742 bomb *v*
noun US, .Iraq, world, .Baghdad, building, .target,
embassy, plane., war, Israel, harbor, site, air, warplane.,
aircraft. *misc* kill, plot., .noisy, military, threaten.,
heavily
4995 | 0.92 S

4743 migration *n*
adj great, mass, international, seasonal, black, urban,
internal, massive, annual, rural *noun* pattern, .route,
history, labor., process, study, bird, population,
period, rate *verb* follow, .occur, lead, facilitate.,
encourage., associate., enable., prevent., contribute,
.flow
5494 | 0.84 A

4744 carrot *n*
adj medium, shredded, chopped, fresh, raw, tender,
hot, grated, wild, diced *noun* onion, celery, potato,
cup, .stick, baby., .cake, .juice, parsnip *verb* add., peel,
slice, chop, eat., dice, offer, dangle
5177 | 0.89 M

4745 harmony *n*
adj racial, perfect, social, natural, inner, close, vocal,
complete, relative *noun* peace., .nature, melody,
rhythm, color, balance, sense., order, unity, crystal.
verb live., sing., create., work., bring., maintain.,
promote., achieve, restore., form
5023 | 0.91 A

4746 downtown *r*
city, street, drive., near, building., walk., .where, office,
head., center, around., hotel, store., historic.
5135 | 0.89 N

4747 brutal *j*
noun murder, war, regime, crime, killing, attack,
dictator, beating, treatment, rape, police, repression
misc most, against, often, civil, particularly, military,
sometimes, violent
4791 | 0.96

4748 prevail *v*
noun justice., condition, sense., .court, end, reason.,
peace., spirit., truth., argument, .century, democracy.,
circumstance., plaintiff, evil *misc* will., .over, still.,
.upon, .against, must.
4873 | 0.94 A

4749 weed *n*
adj noxious, invasive, aquatic, dead, green, biological,
aggressive, poisonous, fast-growing *noun* grass, .seed,
control, plant, .bed, water, .killer, tree, field, growth
verb grow, pull., keep., kill, smoke., overgrow., cut,
eat., suppress., choke
5161 | 0.89

4750 exhaust *v*
noun day, .possibility, night, effort, option, appeal,
resource, supply, hour, fund, patience, energy, .benefit,
.saving, avenue *misc* after, until., physically., .every,
emotionally
4820 | 0.95 F

4751 pasta *n*
adj fresh, cooked, hot, dried, homemade,
whole-wheat, angel-hair, parmesan *noun* sauce,
salad, .dish, rice, water, vegetable, bread, cup,
tomato, cook *verb* add, toss, serve, drain., eat.,
prepare, boil, combine
5391 | 0.85 M N

4752 distinctive *j*
noun feature, style, way, voice, pattern, culture,
flavor, characteristic, character, identity, sound, group
misc its, most, own, each, create, develop, cultural,
produce
5018 | 0.91 A

4753 fraction *n*
adj small, tiny, large, total, significant, mere,
substantial, sizable *noun* .second, .cost, .inch,
.population, .price, ejection, .size, .amount, value,
.energy *verb* represent., pay., account, cover, contain,
constitute., measure., .exceed
4961 | 0.92 A

4754 remark *v*
noun mother., friend, father, voice, critic., interview,
historian, observer. *misc* once., .upon, often., later.,
casually
4961 | 0.92

4755 emotionally *r*
physically, .charge, child, feel., financially, .disturb,
mentally, .drain, become., intellectually, both., involve,
spiritually, .disturbed
4909 | 0.93

4756 poke *v*
noun .head, .fun, .hole, finger, .nose, stick, fire,
face, .back, arm, door, .chest, shoulder, .ground,
foot *misc* .at, .out, .through, .around, .into, .inside
5099 | 0.90 F

4757 guarantee *n*
adj constitutional, federal, equal, best, only, personal,
international, legal, civil, written *noun* loan., security,

.representation, .success, government, amendment.,
money-back., protection, .freedom, program
verb make., offer., provide, violate., receive,
protect, seek., extend, demand., last
4895 | 0.94

4758 dancing _n_
adj dirty, nude, square, slow, traditional, wild, Indian,
aerobic, tribal _noun_ music, ballroom., .girl, .lesson,
folk., dinner., .shoe, tap., ice., belly. _verb_ start., stop.,
love, watch., teach, enjoy., feature, practice.
4842 | 0.95

4759 trouble _v_
noun question, thought, American, dream,
prospect, trend, sleep, conscience, .critic,
nightmare, observer, allegation, perception,
juror _misc_ .by, deeply., something, particularly.,
lead., especially.
4745 | 0.96

4760 freshman _n_
adj incoming, fellow, top, talented, promising, lowly,
high-school _noun_ .year, .class, college, school,
.sophomore, season, student, .guard, point, team
verb play, redshirt., teach., enter, arrive, finish, enroll,
complete., .average
5153 | 0.89 N

4761 suitable _j_
noun use, habitat, place, area, site, application,
condition, environment, material, land, candidate,
location _misc_ for, find, more, most, provide,
consider, less, deem
4965 | 0.92 A

4762 youngster _n_
adj black, gifted, troubled, emotional, stable,
involved, intact, homeless, single-parent, promising
noun school, parent, age, family, group, program,
adult, need, opportunity, generation. _verb_ help.,
teach., .learn, .grow, .attend, .enjoy, .gather,
educate., care., .explore
4919 | 0.93

4763 slavery _n_
adj sexual, African, wrong, legal, modern, domestic,
transatlantic, modern-day, virtual _noun_ history., issue,
abolition., institution., war, freedom, legacy., end.,
form., racism _verb_ abolish, sell., .exist, born., oppose.,
escape., condemn., endure, .thrive
5194 | 0.88 A

4764 balloon _n_
adj hot-air, red, giant, high-altitude, deflated, tiny,
inflated, beautiful _noun_ air, trial., water., helium.,
weather., .ride, flight, .angioplasty, .payment
verb inflate, float, blow, fill, pop, fly, release, burst,
throw.
4848 | 0.94

4765 opt _v_
noun plan, .surgery, approach, consumer., .abortion,
.independence, .convenience, .silence _misc_ .for, .out,
instead, may., increasingly.
4891 | 0.93 M

4766 crowded _j_
noun room, street, city, field, bus, market,
place, area, condition, restaurant, school, train
misc more, too, through, less, become, already,
across, noisy
4786 | 0.95

4767 liver _n_
adj chopped, chronic, severe, healthy, acute, serious,
abnormal _noun_ .disease, kidney, cancer, heart,
.transplant, .damage, .failure, lung, cell _verb_ cause,
die., receive., spread., eat., suffer., detoxify, process,
.enlarge, .regulate
5142 | 0.89 M

4768 listener _n_
adj good, young, male, female, active, average,
sympathetic, casual, regular, long-time _noun_ radio,
speaker, reader, music, viewer, performer, challenge.,
.conversation, song, .line _verb_ tell., hear, remind.,
.understand, draw., invite., urge., encourage.,
.respond, perceive
5220 | 0.87

4769 calm _j_
noun voice, water, sea, day, face, eye, wind, tone,
demeanor, air, night, weather _misc_ very, stay, keep,
remain, seem, as, try, cool
4859 | 0.94 F

4770 ironically _r_
.enough, .though, .however, very, perhaps, although,
somewhat., title, .despite
4874 | 0.93 A

4771 affirmative _j_
noun action, program, policy, debate, plan,
decision, answer, defense, response, vote, duty,
step _misc_ against, support, end, oppose, federal,
eliminate, racial, civil
5195 | 0.88 S

4772 commodity _n_
adj other, precious, hot, valuable, rare, scarce, global,
international, feminist, foreign _noun_ price, market,
.future, exchange, .chain, .trading, production, world
verb become., trade, sell, produce, buy, rise, treat.,
.decline, .soar, .generate
5063 | 0.90 A

4773 fur _n_
adj white, black, thick, soft, fake, brown, gray, dark,
wet _noun_ .coat, .hat, .trade, .seal, animal, .collar,
feather, cat, .trader, rabbit. _verb_ wear., cover, stroke.,
sell, buy., wrap., trim., .fly, stick, dry
5024 | 0.91 F

4774 freely _r_
move., more., flow., speak., .admit, give, allow.,
.choose, talk., .available, express, roam., able.,
.elect
4768 | 0.95

4775 light _i_
(in light of) .of, especially., .fact, .these, .recent,
particularly., .finding, .experience, .event, .current,
consider., interpret., view., .evidence
5025 | 0.91 A

4776 removal _n_
adj surgical, forced, complete, Indian, easy,
immediate, permanent, prompt _noun_ rate, hair.,
.office, .efficiency, asbestos, snow., .barrier, dam,
process, tumor _verb_ require, follow., lead, allow.,
include, involve., order., result., occur, decrease
5090 | 0.89 A

4777 regard _n_
adj high, low, due, positive, special, significant,
particular, scant, enormous _noun_ .party,

.consequence, lack., .truth, respect, .gender, .ethnicity, affection *verb* hold., note, act., demonstrate., pursue., display.
4912 | 0.93 A

4778 round *v*
noun .corner, .bend, .curve, .base, edge, .suspect, .turn, police., thousand, horse *misc* .out, .off, .third, .nearest, quickly, soon., .sharp
4784 | 0.95

4779 goat *n*
adj fresh, wild, soft, crumbled, mild, herbed, curried *noun* .cheese, sheep, mountain., .milk, cow, meat, herd, ounce. *verb* eat, graze, feed, bleat, chase, sacrifice, stuff., smell, .nibble, .roam
5048 | 0.90 M

4780 shareholder *n*
adj large, major, big, institutional, individual, long-term, happy, current, existing, single *noun* company, .value, fund, .lawsuit, .meeting, return, percent, money, board, .activism *verb* approve, pay, own, file, maximize., protect., benefit, deliver., represent, .reject
5378 | 0.85 N

4781 expedition *n*
adj punitive, military, British, scientific, special, Arctic, Antarctic, Spanish *noun* fishing., member, leader, river, hunting., shopping., .planner, ship, research, mountaineering. *verb* lead, join., send, plan, organize, mount, accompany.
5044 | 0.90 M

4782 loyal *j*
noun friend, fan, customer, following, president, force, supporter, opposition, Republican, party, member, troop *misc* remain, most, very, fiercely, stay, extremely, Shiite
4724 | 0.96

4783 conscience *n*
adj good, social, individual, guilty, moral, religious, bad *noun* freedom., matter., religion, reason., nation, liberty., voice., pang., prisoner., crisis. *verb* vote., follow., bother, examine., act, ease., clear., shock., trouble, permit
4885 | 0.93

4784 fragile *j*
noun life, ecosystem, democracy, economy, peace, state, bone, system, thing, body, area, nature *misc* so, very, more, too, already, remain, protect, vulnerable, delicate
4735 | 0.96

4785 calendar *n*
adj social, year-round, traditional, lunar, Gregorian, full, Jewish, Christian, academic, primary *noun* .year, day, event, wall, date, school., month, page, appointment., clock *verb* mark, check., base, hang, list, publish, clear., feature, circle, display
4782 | 0.95

4786 mineral *n*
adj other, essential, rich, certain, valuable, abundant, ionic, inorganic *noun* vitamin., .water, bone., oil, .resource, .density, .deposit *verb* contain, form, extract, mine, absorb, mix, dissolve, exploit., replenish.
5236 | 0.87 M

4787 coming *j*
noun year, week, month, decade, day, season, election, century, winter, war, weekend, generation *misc* over, during, prepare, presidential, fiscal, global, academic, crucial
4748 | 0.95

4788 circle *v*
noun .wagon, .globe, head, .room, .earth, planet, sun, car, .block, .table, tree, foot, hour, .base, park *misc* .around, other, .each, .overhead, .above, begin., slowly
4949 | 0.92 F

4789 fare *n*
adj low, standard, high, round-trip, traditional, best, light, simple, usual, one-way *noun* air., airline, bus., .increase, .war, discount, cab., service, restaurant, cost *verb* pay., offer, include, serve, raise., cut, reduce, feature, sample.
5012 | 0.90 N

4790 blessing *n*
adj mixed, special, greatest, final, huge, wonderful, official *noun* curse, .disguise, .liberty, peace, prayer., ceremony, .protection, .encouragement *verb* give., count., receive., bestow, offer., enjoy., thank, secure., invoke
4749 | 0.95

4791 liberation *n*
adj national, black, sexual, political, social, gay, human, personal, spiritual *noun* front, .theology, .organization, .movement, people., woman, struggle, war., .theologian, animal. *verb* support., seek, achieve., celebrate., embrace., .free, attain., .sweep, commemorate.
5079 | 0.89 A

4792 steak *n*
adj grilled, chicken-fried, thick, fried, rare, juicy, raw, country-fried *noun* .house, flank., dinner, chicken, sauce, .potato, beef., strip, .knife, tuna. *verb* eat., cook, cut, serve, place., grill, order., .sizzle
5037 | 0.90 N

4793 liquid *j*
noun water, nitrogen, crystal, hydrogen, form, fuel, gas, diet, film, asset, display, eye *misc* use, solid, add, until, pour, fill, exist, stir
4943 | 0.92 M

4794 ecological *j*
noun system, process, disaster, knowledge, research, change, impact, crisis, restoration, behavior, problem, integrity *misc* social, economic, environmental, human, cultural, long-term, evolutionary
5765 | 0.79 A

4795 banana *n*
adj ripe, large, yellow, mashed, sliced, fried, frozen, medium *noun* .tree, apple, .bread, .beer, .leaf, .peel, cream, butter, cup, .pudding *verb* eat., grow, add, sell, mash, wrap, slip., feed., grab.
4948 | 0.92 M

4796 catch *n*
adj total, only, commercial, annual, allowable, nice, diving *noun* .rate, .phrase, yard, fish, species, game, touchdown, .right, .effort, fisherman *verb* make., play., release, increase, sell, reduce., report, .drop, clean.
5985 | 0.76

4797 steadily *r*
grow**.**, increase, rise, decline, move, slowly**.**, **.**over, work**.**, fall, climb, **.**since, improve, **.**increasing
4760 | 0.95

4798 blast *n*
adj full, nuclear, hot, cold, powerful, sudden, atomic, initial, huge *noun* bomb**.**, **.**air, shotgun**.**, **.**furnace, **.**wind, **.**wave, horn, site, fire, **.**past *verb* kill, hear, die**.**, cause, survive**.**, injure, **.**occur, destroy, **.**knock
4821 | 0.94

4799 nonprofit *j*
noun organization, group, foundation, agency, center, research, corporation, service, institution, association, community, health *misc* private, work, help, run, provide, national, base, educational
5092 | 0.89 N

4800 mobile *j*
noun home, phone, unit, device, service, missile, park, launcher, source, system, telephone, lab *misc* upwardly, highly, less, increasingly, biological, downwardly, stationary, fixed
4816 | 0.94

4801 straw *n*
adj final, short, fresh, yellow, woven, dirty, chopped *noun* **.**hat, **.**poll, man, **.**bale, **.**mat, pine**.**, plastic, bag, leaf, **.**basket *verb* wear**.**, **.**break, grasp**.**, draw**.**, cover, set, stick, win**.**, blow, stuff**.**
4885 | 0.93 F

4802 projection *n*
adj dual, digital, current, optimistic, financial, low, economic, rear, long-term, recent *noun* year, screen, population, **.**system, power, budget, image, **.**booth, video**.**, cost *verb* base, **.**slide, exceed**.**, represent, display, compare**.**, revise, cite, rely**.**, employ
4882 | 0.93 A

4803 rubber *j*
noun band, glove, boot, spatula, stamp, ball, bullet, tube, hose, sole, mask, raft *misc* wear, use, black, around, tire, pull, red, thick
4850 | 0.93 F

4804 overnight *r*
stay**.**, happen**.**, change**.**, almost**.**, refrigerate**.**, become, soak**.**, refrigerator, **.**before, virtually**.**, **.**serve, cover**.**, disappear**.**, several
4751 | 0.95

4805 neighboring *j*
noun country, state, town, community, village, county, city *misc* from, republic, district, area, island, region, among, Arab, such, invade, flee, similar
4918 | 0.92

4806 enact *v*
noun law, Congress**.**, legislation, state, reform, policy, year, program, statute, government**.**, bill, measure, legislature, rule, health *misc* federal, recently**.**, require, similar, **.**tough
5061 | 0.89 A

4807 favorable *j*
noun review, condition, attitude, rating, treatment, opinion, outcome, term, impression, rate, environment, result *misc* more, than, toward, most, less, very, receive, unfavorable
4969 | 0.91 A

4808 severely *r*
.limit, **.**damage, **.**restrict, **.**affect, **.**injure, **.**ill, punish, **.**disabled, most**.**, beat, **.**depressed
4741 | 0.95

4809 demographic *j*
noun variable, characteristic, information, data, table, change, questionnaire, factor, group, trend, age, participant *misc* economic, social, include, between, such, collect, provide, complete
5394 | 0.84 A

4810 terrain *n*
adj rough, rugged, steep, difficult, flat, mountainous, hilly, rolling *noun* **.**park, mountain, mile, weather, acre, snow, type, desert**.**, feature, map *verb* cover, explore**.**, navigate**.**, study**.**, negotiate**.**, ride**.**, scan**.**, climb, vary
5427 | 0.83 M

4811 explicit *j*
noun instruction, material, reference, goal, language, sex, policy, statement, knowledge, purpose, scene, content *misc* make, sexually, more, implicit, without, contain, sexual
5149 | 0.88 A

4812 integrated *j*
noun system, management, circuit, approach, program, school, curriculum, development, service, company, model, part *misc* more, develop, vertically, provide, fully, create, racially
5122 | 0.88 A

4813 terribly *r*
not**.**, **.**wrong, something**.**, so**.**, **.**important, feel**.**, **.**sorry, miss**.**, seem**.**, **.**difficult, suffer**.**, **.**sad, **.**concerned, **.**disappointed
4805 | 0.94 S

4814 veteran *j*
noun teacher, player, team, journalist, reporter, actor, correspondent, officer, agent, status, observer, pilot *misc* who, political, sign, democratic, whose, defensive, offensive, photograph
4947 | 0.91 N

4815 level *j*
noun field, ground, table, surface, head, position, flight, floor, thinking, spot, gaze *misc* high, low, significant, upper, grade, playing, local
4975 | 0.90 A

4816 sofa *n*
adj asleep, comfortable, sectional, plush, living-room, Victorian, sagging, convertible *noun* chair, room, table, living, **.**cushion, leather**.**, bed, back, arm, pillow *verb* sit**.**, lie**.**, sleep**.**, **.**watch, lay**.**, fall, lean, settle**.**, seat**.**, **.**face
5075 | 0.89 F

4817 screw *v*
noun face, eye, guy, **.**cap, **.**courage, lid, bulb, wall, piece, hole, mouth, **.**top, filter, hat, **.**silencer *misc* up, **.**around, really**.**, everything, **.**together, **.**onto, **.**tight, glue**.**, **.**shut, totally**.**, temporarily**.**
4949 | 0.91 F

4818 shield *n*
adj human, protective, defensive, federal, magnetic, invisible, missile-defense *noun* desert**.**, operation**.**,

cross., .law, missile., heat., sword, defense., rape.,
team. _verb_ .protect, carry, build., act., mark., form.,
hide, penetrate., remove., bore
4885 | 0.92

4819 invention _n_
adj modern, human, greatest, recent, late, pure,
cultural _noun_ mother., patent, innovation, discovery,
century, tradition, ethnicity, .printing, development,
.press _verb_ lead., credit., license, market., steal.,
exploit., .spawn
4874 | 0.92 A

4820 Iraqi _n_
adj governing, interim, Kuwaiti, Kurdish, armed,
chemical _noun_ .Kuwait _verb_ capture, .surrender,
warn, seize, wound, expel.
5263 | 0.85

4821 perceived _j_
noun threat, ability, competence, level, risk, need,
difference, support, exertion, control, value,
importance _misc_ between, high, social, low,
because, relate, assess, actual
5644 | 0.8 A

4822 leave _n_
adj medical, paid, sick, unpaid, parental,
administrative, annual _noun_ family., .absence,
maternity., .act, week., month, job, paternity.,
policy, shore. _verb_ take., let., pay, grant, offer.,
request
4684 | 0.96

4823 cruel _j_
noun punishment, joke, world, man, thing,
hoax, irony, fate, act, death, animal, treatment
misc unusual, seem, against, inhuman, degrade,
inhumane, sometimes, nor
4735 | 0.95

4824 bomber _n_
adj American, long-range, heavy, strategic, allied,
nuclear, alleged, convicted, mad, dirty _noun_ suicide.,
stealth., fighter, .pilot, .jacket, dive., car. _verb_ kill,
.attack, fly, .strike, send, .carry, stop., build,
.detonate, destroy
4896 | 0.92 S

4825 provoke _v_
noun .response, .reaction, .debate, question,
thought, violence, .controversy, crisis, .discussion,
attack, conflict, .outrage, action, .anger,
.confrontation _misc_ might., try., .among,
.strong, .violent
4756 | 0.94 A

4826 autonomy _n_
adj great, political, local, individual, personal, cultural,
relative, institutional, economic, regional _noun_
degree., state, independence, freedom, satisfaction.,
faculty, level., sense., value., need. _verb_ give., grant.,
enjoy., maintain., preserve., seek., achieve, gain.,
support., protect
5371 | 0.83 A

4827 publishing _n_
adj electronic, major, academic, scholarly, scientific,
digital, online _noun_ .company, .house, .society,
science., book, .industry, desktop., .group, business,
world _verb_ print, found, compile, acquire, purchase,
edit, launch, oversee
5079 | 0.88 N

4828 retreat _n_
adj hasty, private, spiritual, presidential, annual,
religious, strategic, tactical _noun_ weekend., mountain,
.center, summer., country, camp, vacation., glacier,
advance, island _verb_ beat., attend, offer, cover., force.,
block., order., signal.
4786 | 0.94 M

4829 theology _n_
adj Christian, moral, systematic, practical, feminist,
political, natural, trinitarian, contemporary, religious
noun liberation., school., professor, philosophy,
church, science, history, study, practice, religion
verb teach, argue, .emerge, express, embrace,
emphasize, construct., reject, .affirm, stress
7012 | 0.64 A

4830 substantially _r_
.than, increase, .reduce, .high, .more, .less,
change, .different, .low, improve, differ.,
contribute.
4996 | 0.90 A

4831 mansion _n_
adj old, Victorian, historic, elegant, sprawling,
colonial, Georgian, haunted, green, presidential
noun governor., house, hill, .night, room, executive.,
playboy., beach, revival., brick. _verb_ build, live.,
buy., own, .overlook, restore, visit., occupy, .belong,
.feature
4805 | 0.93

4832 developmental _j_
noun child, disability, stage, education, level,
student, delay, process, need, course, program,
task _misc_ cognitive, during, social, early, physical,
comprehensive, such, mental
5598 | 0.8 A

4833 one-third _m_
about., than., more., only., nearly., less, .cup, almost.,
fraction., year, approximately., .population, .total,
account.
4871 | 0.92

4834 transmit _v_
noun information, data, disease, signal, virus,
message, image, knowledge _misc_ .through, .via,
.receive, sexually, able.
4821 | 0.93 A

4835 contemplate _v_
noun .suicide, action, .possibility, .future, change,
moment, .move, .career, death, act, .retirement,
.marriage, administration, scenario, viewer.
misc while, sit., .whether, ever., seriously, terrible,
awful., willing., briefly.
4664 | 0.96

4836 authorize _v_
noun Congress, .use, .force, resolution., president,
state, law, council., act., .war, action, bill., program,
department, .payment _misc_ .by, .military, vote.,
federal, .million, specifically.
4857 | 0.92 A

4837 mathematics _n_
adj applied, advanced, basic, effective, pure, mental,
simple _noun_ science, teacher, student, school, course,
achievement, language, .anxiety, physics, professor
verb teach, learn., improve, solve, apply, emphasize,
major., stress, consist
5968 | 0.75 A

4838 battle *v*
noun .cancer, force, firefighter., troop, .disease, .fire, .blaze, .injury, soldier, team., drug, .control, army, .spot, Republican *misc* .over, .against, continue., fight, constantly, ready, .fiercely
4764 | 0.94 N

4839 old-fashioned *j*
noun way, kind, value, idea, word, oats, work, family, sense, glass, method, politics *misc* good, sound, plain, rather, rolled, cup, quaint
4712 | 0.95

4840 lawmaker *n*
adj federal, key, local, Republican, congressional, legislative, top, liberal, veteran, longtime *noun* state, year, bill, .party, group, house, Congress, official, lobbyist, week *verb* urge., .consider, .vote, .approve, lobby., .agree, .debate, push, face, force
5086 | 0.88 N

4841 threshold *n*
adj low, high, certain, critical, minimum, nuclear, acceptable *noun* .level, pain, .value, percent, hearing, difference, size *verb* cross., stand., reach, step., exceed., meet., pass, hear., lower., shift
5112 | 0.87 A

4842 radar *n*
adj military, ground-penetrating, sophisticated, Iraqi, early, advanced, airborne, ground-based, long-range, mobile *noun* .screen, .system, .image, .gun, .station, plane, .detector, blip., .signal, satellite *verb* use., detect, fly., pick, disappear., fall., stay., lock, slip., monitor
4864 | 0.92 M

4843 seldom *r*
.see, very., .use, .ever, though., .speak, .mention, .anything, .visit, .discuss, .venture, .occur, .except, .anyone
4703 | 0.95

4844 low *r*
.enough, keep., high, down, rate, price, among, score, cost, .pay, voice.
4662 | 0.96

4845 headache *n*
adj severe, big, bad, terrible, major, mild, frequent, common, constant, dull *noun* pain, nausea, migraine, dizziness, tension., fever, symptom., problem, eye *verb* get., give., cause., suffer., complain., include., create., .occur, accompany, strike
4846 | 0.92 M

4846 rental *n*
adj cheap, annual, residential, low-income, affordable, monthly, two-bedroom *noun* car, .property, .company, .fee, video., house, .agency, income, .unit *verb* drive, include, own, cost, park, pick, cover, manage., price., arrange.
4908 | 0.91 N

4847 spy *n*
adj Soviet, American, Russian, British, secret, international, German, Israeli *noun* .plane, .satellite, .agency, .novel, war, .case, network, .game, .magazine *verb* send, catch, shoot, .wear, recruit, detect, act., expose., .pose, capture.
4755 | 0.94

4848 patron *n*
adj wealthy, political, rich, private, regular, royal, primary, chief, longtime *noun* .saint, art, bar, artist, restaurant, friend, library, table *verb* serve., name., please., accommodate., honor., cater, worship.
4912 | 0.91

4849 driveway *n*
adj long, front, circular, narrow, concrete, winding, steep *noun* car., house, end., gravel., road, door, truck., dirt., sidewalk, gate *verb* pull., park., turn, walk., back., sit, stand, drive, .lead, cross
4992 | 0.89 F

4850 till *c*
wait., .get, up., .now, .see, morning, .then, .end, day, .after, .next, last, stay.
4983 | 0.89 F

4851 broadcast *v*
noun radio, television, station, news, network, game, show, program, message, media, signal, report, story, interview, video *misc* .live, .over, .around, local, .throughout, nationally
4823 | 0.92 N

4852 overwhelm *v*
noun system, feeling, sense, .number, emotion, fear, grief, .response, .thought, resource, need, .task, smell, demand, size *misc* threaten., completely., simply., quickly., nearly.
4576 | 0.97

4853 coordinate *v*
noun .effort, .activity, program, .policy, service, group, agency, .action, .work, research, center, department, process *misc* help., national, federal, better, must.
4809 | 0.93 A

4854 vendor *n*
adj other, high-quality, local, outside, major, private, various, low-quality, available, third-party *noun* street., food, software., system, customer, dog., price, information, service, fruit *verb* .sell, purchase, buy, market, deal., compete, feature, install, negotiate, evaluate
5158 | 0.86

4855 transport *n*
adj public, military, international, supersonic, easy, interstate, atmospheric *noun* air., .plane, ozone., .system, .aircraft, area, .service, .communication, .ship, energy *verb* .carry, prevent., reduce, arrive, control., arrange., facilitate., await., .crash, deliver
5003 | 0.89 A

4856 fragment *n*
adj small, large, tiny, only, human, melodic, mere, amplified, tattered *noun* bone, DNA, bullet., glass, metal, sentence, memory, body, rock., piece *verb* find, contain, break, remove, explode, shatter., gather., analyze.
4994 | 0.89 A

4857 hammer *n*
adj pneumatic, wooden, rubber, external, framing, giant *noun* .nail, head, .sickle, chisel, sledge., claw., .blow, .throw, gun, .anvil *verb* use., hit, swing., cock, pick, pull, strike, hold, drop, smash
5113 | 0.87 F

4858 seminar *n*
adj educational, senior, professional, special, annual, weekly, week-long, all-day, electronic *noun* workshop, training, conference, graduate., lecture, program, group, .room, participant, book *verb* attend., hold, conduct, teach, offer, give, include, sponsor, present, run
4818 | 0.92 A

4859 availability *n*
adj limited, increased, ready, easy, increasing, widespread, wide *noun* resource, data, water, service, information, food, quality, cost, drug, support *verb* increase., limit., depend., reduce., base., affect, ensure., check.
5096 | 0.87 A

4860 peanut *n*
adj chopped, creamy, salted, unsalted, hot, spicy, allergic, crunchy, green, smooth *noun* .butter, .oil, .sandwich, cup, .sauce, tablespoon, bag., chocolate, cracker, jar *verb* eat., serve, add, spread, buy., sell, combine., sprinkle.
4830 | 0.92 M

4861 fantastic *j*
noun job, story, thing, world, tale, idea, place, experience, voyage, view, creature, opportunity
misc four, really, oh, absolutely, thank, sound, light, wonderful
4773 | 0.93 S

4862 depart *v*
noun flight, train., tour., hour, ship, cruise., airport, .tradition, plane., month, bus., .scene, .precedent, .peace, .earth *misc* .from, before., after, arrive, leave, .early, soon, recently., return
4670 | 0.95

4863 permit *n*
adj special, federal, comprehensive, available, tradable, annual, required, issuing, driving *noun* work., building., application, system, state, number, process, company, learner. *verb* issue, get., require, obtain., need, apply., allow, grant, receive., .continue
5057 | 0.88

4864 cottage *n*
adj small, little, cozy, tiny, English, thatched, rented
noun .cheese, .industry, .garden, summer., guest., door, beach, country, stone., storm. *verb* build, rent, buy., return., surround, enter., spawn.
4902 | 0.91 F

4865 specify *v*
noun model, standard, law, level, condition, .number, contract, .type, rule, date, criterion, requirement, agreement., amount, regulation *misc* clearly, .exactly, .particular, decline., please., precisely
5067 | 0.88 A

4866 frustrate *v*
noun .lack, .effort, .inability, .attempt, process, official, .pace, .failure, American, desire, Congress, reader, fan, expectation, enforcement *misc* .by, angry, become., feel, increasingly.
4577 | 0.97

4867 disturbing *j*
noun trend, thing, story, news, behavior, question, image, report, fact, thought, dream, picture
misc more, very, most, find, even, deeply, perhaps, particularly
4605 | 0.96

4868 artifact *n*
adj cultural, American, ancient, Indian, native, historical, human, religious, African, early
noun collection, museum, art, site, culture, history, photograph, image, thousand., past
verb collect, contain, sell, examine, preserve, date, fill., remove, identify., .belong
5201 | 0.85 A

4869 basin *n*
adj great, Caribbean, upper, Mediterranean, tidal, shallow *noun* river., water, lake, wash., mountain, drainage., powder., impact., ocean. *verb* fill, form, .contain, surround., locate, flow., drain, hike
5009 | 0.89 A

4870 regain *v*
noun .control, .consciousness, .composure, .strength, .balance, .sense, weight, .power, .confidence, .footing, .trust, .momentum, .form, .ground, .ability *misc* .some, try., help., .lost, struggle., quickly., slowly., order., eventually.
4617 | 0.96

4871 grape *n*
adj red, sour, seedless, white, purple, wild, black, growing, fermented *noun* .juice, wine, .leaf, .vine, .tomato, bunch., .seed, .grower *verb* grow, eat., pick, plant, produce, harvest, drink., .hang, feed.
4907 | 0.90 M

4872 ego *n*
adj big, male, bruised, inflated, huge, healthy, enormous *noun* alter., .orientation, task., .trip, .involvement, .identity, .strength, self, development, .boost *verb* stroke, bruise, feed., check., massage, satisfy.
4855 | 0.91

4873 sometime *r*
.after, .next, .during, .later, .between, .before, .around, .soon, .early, .future, until., tomorrow, morning, again.
4637 | 0.96

4874 organized *j*
noun crime, labor, group, religion, sport, activity, opposition, effort, way, movement, force, program
misc against, play, political, participate, Russian, involved, criminal
4709 | 0.94

4875 charm *n*
adj lucky, southern, certain, personal, considerable, good-luck, boyish, rustic, small-town *noun* part., .bracelet, luck., beauty, .offensive, wit, silver., grace, character, style *verb* work., lose., turn, add., lack., possess., resist., radiate, attract, captivate
4703 | 0.94

4876 sweater *n*
adj black, red, white, blue, gray, pink, green, tight, heavy, V-neck *noun* cashmere., jeans, shirt, wool., pant, skirt, jacket, coat, turtleneck., cotton.
verb wear., pull, put, knit, buy, dress., wrap, hang, match, remove.
4990 | 0.89 F

4877 rim *n*
adj outer, inner, southern, blue, northern, western, removable, inside *noun* canyon, .glass, south., crater, north., wheel, pan, trail, brake, .cup *verb* hit., remove, touch., form, wipe., hang., bend, circle, overlook
5294 | 0.84 M

4878 speculate v
noun scientist., researcher.., .future, analyst., expert.,
other., motive, media., astronomer., scholar.,
investigator.., .advance, diabetes *misc* .about, some.,
may, might, one., only.., .whether, possible, difficult.,
refuse., reasonable., publicly
4664 | 0.95

4879 delight n
adj great, earthly, pure, obvious, sheer, aesthetic,
childish, perverse *noun* garden., eye, surprise.,
crowd, audience, joy, wonder, pleasure, squeal., heart.
verb take., laugh., express., scream., smile., gasp.
4709 | 0.94

4880 fatigue n
adj chronic, physical, perceived, military, mental,
extreme, general, severe, green *noun* .syndrome,
muscle, pain, symptom, stress, headache, depression,
loss, weight, battle. *verb* cause, wear., suffer., reduce.,
dress.., experience, include., .set, diminish, .slow
4924 | 0.90

4881 devastating j
noun effect, impact, consequence, loss, war,
blow, disease, attack, result, news, earthquake, fire
misc most, potentially, suffer, absolutely, economic,
cause, face, pretty
4647 | 0.95

4882 instructional j
noun strategy, program, material, teacher, student,
method, practice, time, activity, technique,
curriculum, school *misc* effective, provide,
develop, within, teach, specific, include
6194 | 0.71 A

4883 plea n
adj guilty, impassioned, common, desperate, final,
urgent, personal, silent *noun* .bargain, .agreement,
.help, .deal, court, .bargaining, part.., .charge,
prosecutor, judge *verb* make., enter., ignore., accept.,
hear., reject., agree, negotiate., respond., issue.
4661 | 0.95

4884 tourism n
adj economic, cultural, local, international,
mass, regional, increased, sustainable, Caribbean
noun industry, development, business, travel, office,
trade, space.., .official *verb* promote., increase,
develop, contact., boost., encourage, affect, support
5016 | 0.88

4885 crowd v
noun people, street, table, other, wall, space, tourist,
building, shelf, office, thousand.., field, sidewalk,
reporter, hall *misc* .into, .around, .together, small
4709 | 0.94 F

4886 warmth n
adj human, maternal, parental, extra, personal, genuine,
sudden *noun* sun, body, light, love, fire, comfort,
food, sense, color, skin *verb* feel., add., provide.,
bring., spread, enjoy., radiate, bask., exude.., .flow
4883 | 0.90 F

4887 jurisdiction n
adj other, federal, local, personal, military, different,
criminal, legal, international, civil *noun* court, state,
law, case, matter, area, .country, committee., agency,
crime *verb* exercise., fall., assert., .require, extend,
lack., accept., involve, claim.., .prescribe
5425 | 0.81 A

4888 update v
noun form.., .quote, information, year, system, site,
software, visit., list, computer, file, record, .look, hour,
application *misc* .every, need., keep., continually,
constantly.
4761 | 0.93

4889 accusation n
adj serious, similar, unfounded, unfair, bitter,
groundless, mere *noun* abuse, charge, .racism,
rape, kind., witchcraft, official, .corruption, police,
investigation *verb* make, deny., face., defend.,
respond.., .fly, investigate, dismiss.., .arise,
.surface
4676 | 0.94

4890 diagram n
adj schematic, complex, detailed, simplified,
accompanying, helpful, branching *noun* .figure,
table., page, block., flow., model, sequence, phase.
verb show, see., draw, illustrate, contain., represent,
depict, .omit, trace, sketch
5340 | 0.82 A

4891 middle-class j
noun family, tax, woman, neighborhood, life,
home, parent, value, suburb, kid, community, voter
misc white, black, American, poor, upper, among,
suburban, mostly
4754 | 0.93

4892 graduation n
adj high-school, academic, passing, eighth-grade,
secondary, expected, required, actual, sixth-grade
noun .rate, school., year, college, .ceremony,
requirement, student, day *verb* attend., follow.,
require., celebrate., miss., complete., near,
.violate
4775 | 0.92

4893 mention n
adj honorable, mere, special, brief, only, specific, very,
passing *noun* .name, .service, .product, .trade, award,
.print, T-shirt., winner, .ribbon, .religion *verb* make,
deserve., receive., hear., include., omit., avoid.
4705 | 0.93

4894 beyond r
world., year., above, room., far., century., lie.,
mountain., hill., .compare, perhaps., field.,
space, lay
4595 | 0.96

4895 within r
from.., .about, .outside, .between, both.., .without,
.across, light.., .among, .beyond, enemy., .minute,
lie.
4683 | 0.94 A

4896 spark v
noun .interest, .debate, .controversy, .protest, war, fire,
.imagination, idea, .discussion, .revolution, .outrage,
.movement, .investigation, light, death. *misc* .by,
.among, .renewed, .intense, .heated
4625 | 0.95

4897 convenience n
adj modern, local, marginal, early, added, all-night,
increased, automated, ultimate *noun* .store, .sample,
.food, .yield, marriage., comfort, station, sake, safety
verb offer., provide, enjoy., prefer., appreciate.,
improve., lack.
4637 | 0.95

4898 chill *n*
adj big, cold, sudden, damp, icy, deep, slight, bitter
noun wind, .hour, .air, .spine, fever, night, winter,
morning, .factor *verb* feel., send., give., shiver.,
shake, catch.
5067 | 0.87 F M

4899 economically *r*
politically, socially, more., .disadvantaged, .viable,
.feasible, most., become., both., culturally, .depressed,
area, environmentally, militarily
4846 | 0.91 A

4900 undergraduate *n*
adj female, male, full-time, advanced, four-year,
upper-level, first-year *noun* .student, .education,
.degree, .program, course, college, .major, study,
graduate, year *verb* teach, enroll, complete, receive,
offer., earn., include, prepare
5247 | 0.84 A

4901 dictate *v*
noun policy, .term, law, government, rule, choice,
.behavior, sense., condition, action, change, price,
letter, circumstance., logic. *misc* shall, let., allow.,
often., .otherwise, than, largely., increasingly.
4612 | 0.95

4902 regulator *n*
adj federal, environmental, financial, top, European,
tough, chief, lax *noun* state., government., bank,
security., company, banking., pressure., insurance.
verb approve, require, allow, .investigate, seize, file,
complain, urge, push, close
4964 | 0.88 N

4903 defender *n*
adj staunch, strong, chief, Japanese, fierce, ardent,
outspoken *noun* .office, .wildlife, president, public.,
county, .faith, deputy., action, position, association
verb represent, .argue, .claim, appoint, .contend,
.surrender, pose., shield., leap, .counter
4764 | 0.92 N

4904 workout *n*
adj good, aerobic, daily, full, cardiovascular, short,
better, total-body, total, upper-body *noun* day, cardio.,
weight, exercise, .schedule, morning., body, .routine,
muscle, .clothes *verb* miss., follow, finish., design,
skip., increase, wear, improve, complete., plan
5827 | 0.75 M

4905 accurately *r*
more., .reflect, describe, .predict, measure, assure.,
transcript., report, .represent, assess, .identify,
.portray
4785 | 0.92 A

4906 tile *n*
adj ceramic, white, red, blue, green, black, mosaic,
cold, decorative, Mexican *noun* floor, roof, wall,
ceiling., glass, kitchen, bathroom, color, marble
verb lay, cover, replace, design, install, remove,
.depict, line, decorate, hit.
4867 | 0.90 M

4907 foreigner *n*
adj Chinese, Japanese, rich, wealthy, illegal,
suspicious, visiting *noun* country, American, number.,
attack., land, citizen, presence., contact., treatment.,
hatred. *verb* own, sell, kill, marry., release, .travel,
.flee, order, grant, cater.
4733 | 0.93

4908 importantly *r*
more., most., but., perhaps., even., .however, purpose,
contribute., equally., secondly.
4725 | 0.93 A

4909 citizenship *n*
adj American, democratic, good, dual, full, global,
national, social, political, liberal *noun* right, .education,
US., law, status, immigration, immigrant, path.,
notion., responsibility *verb* grant., apply., renounce.,
obtain., deny, hold., develop, gain., guarantee, entitle
5265 | 0.83 A

4910 plaza *n*
adj central, grand, main, downtown, historic, concrete,
broad *noun* .hotel, center, city, street, shopping,
building, new, town., market, toll. *verb* walk.,
surround, fill, overlook, gather., cross., crowd.
4843 | 0.90 N

4911 devise *v*
noun .plan, .way, .strategy, system, method, program,
scheme, .solution, policy, means, formula, team.,
.experiment, researcher., theory *misc* .new, help,
ever., must., yet.
4696 | 0.93 A

4912 premium *n*
adj high, annual, monthly, due, average, medical,
increased, private, additional, hefty *noun* insurance.,
percent, health., year, cost, price, company, plan,
malpractice., risk *verb* pay, place, put., increase, raise.,
rise, charge, reduce, sell., offer
4916 | 0.89 M

4913 chemistry *n*
adj organic, physical, atmospheric, environmental,
sexual, medicinal, biological *noun* physics, biology,
brain., professor, team., science, .lab, prize., .class,
.teacher *verb* change., teach., study., develop, alter.,
affect, lack., .enable
4773 | 0.92

4914 bureaucracy *n*
adj federal, large, military, bloated, huge, central, vast,
entrenched, massive, powerful *noun* government.,
state., layer., art., education, service, security, agency,
welfare, interest *verb* create, cut., reduce., deal,
expand., streamline., control, navigate., administer,
.operate
4816 | 0.91

4915 inherent *j*
noun problem, risk, value, danger, power, right,
limitation, contradiction, difficulty, conflict, nature,
system *misc* in, between, human, because, recognize,
social, natural
4975 | 0.88 A

4916 hazard *n*
adj environmental, potential, occupational, natural,
moral, serious, possible, real, human, choking
noun health., fire., safety., .analysis, water., .ratio,
control, paint. *verb* pose., present., create., identify,
avoid, reduce., constitute., protect, result
4903 | 0.89 A

4917 swell *v*
noun eye., face., foot., rank, number, population,
heart., chest, brain., .pride, head, river, throat, breast.,
body *misc* begin., cause., red, .shut, .around, .million,
already, whose., .fill, slightly
4725 | 0.93 F

4918 bride *n*
adj new, young, runaway, beautiful, future, modern, blushing *noun* .groom, father, wedding, family, mother, war., .price *verb* .wear, kiss., choose, dress, marry, dance, photograph., .emerge, accompany, promise
5233 | 0.84 F

4919 bow *v*
noun head, .pressure, .prayer, .waist, king, .weight, forehead, string, .shame, .return, instrument
misc .out, slightly, .low, .again, .deeply
4864 | 0.90 F

4920 processor *n*
adj faster, central, multiple, single, fast, main, embedded, neural *noun* food., word., blender, bowl, .blade, .pulse, .metal, data, puree, computer
verb use, .add, .fit, .combine, .whirl, .blend, transfer, contain, operate, .generate
5496 | 0.79 M

4921 bucket *n*
adj full, five-gallon, empty, wooden, galvanized, leaky, overturned *noun* water, drop., ice, plastic., .seat, mop., .brigade, paint, money, chicken
verb fill, carry., put., bring, pour, throw, kick., lift., .compare
4760 | 0.92 F

4922 timber *n*
adj big, federal, thick, commercial, old-growth, tropical, massive, flooded *noun* .industry, .company, forest, .sales, land, .harvest, resource, .production, .wolf, .worker *verb* cut, sell, fall, buy, own, support, produce, manage., haul., decline
4871 | 0.90 M

4923 feminist *j*
noun movement, theory, woman, study, scholar, critic, group, perspective, theology, issue, activist, analysis
misc American, political, radical, contemporary, literary, critical, recent, sexual
5468 | 0.8 A

4924 till *i*
wait., .get, up., .now, .see, morning, .then, .end, day, .after, .next, last, stay.
4763 | 0.92 F

4925 tumor *n*
adj malignant, benign, primary, rare, cancerous, aggressive, fibrous, fibroid, pituitary *noun* brain., cell, patient, growth, cancer, breast, size, gland, doctor, surgery *verb* remove, .grow, shrink, develop, cause, die, diagnose, treat, reveal, kill
5970 | 0.73 M A

4926 apology *n*
adj public, sincere, formal, official, written, personal, simple *noun* letter., explanation, note, sort, reparation, gesture., .slavery *verb* make., accept, offer., owe., issue., demand., write., .acknowledge
4602 | 0.95

4927 screening *n*
adj final, universal, early, initial, genetic, medical, newborn, private *noun* test, cancer., .process, .room, .program, film, .script, health., .procedure, .tool
verb provide, offer, attend., require, complete, receive, undergo., .reduce, measure, .consist
4839 | 0.90

4928 arrow *n*
adj straight, broken, black, white, green, directional, yellow, down, flaming *noun* bow., .right, quiver, sling., .maker, direction, heart, shaft, .key *verb* .point, shoot, indicate, .fly, fire., draw, hit, pierce, follow., pull.
4814 | 0.90 F

4929 marker *n*
adj magic, genetic, black, historical, grave, permanent, red, historic, cultural, clear *noun* mile., gene, DNA, stone., pen, disease, table, boundary., buoy, bone *verb* identify, serve., place, draw, .indicate, pick., label, express., grab., toss.
4721 | 0.92 A

4930 sunny *j*
noun day, afternoon, morning, side, sky, room, spot, weather, window, disposition, spring, beach *misc* warm, bright, hot, beautiful, clear, yellow, cold
4715 | 0.92 M

4931 technician *n*
adj medical, skilled, chief, dental, biological, experienced, x-ray *noun* lab., emergency., computer., engineer, scientist, electronics., sound., room., doctor
verb train, watch, send., monitor, hire, .perform, employ, supervise, analyze
4787 | 0.91

4932 homework *n*
adj daily, assigned, incomplete, weekly, Latin *noun* .assignment, school, student, child, kid, math., teacher, night, parent, class *verb* do., complete., finish., assign, read, eat, check
4709 | 0.92

4933 fog *n*
adj thick, dense, heavy, white, gray, coastal, mental *noun* morning., .war, rain, cloud, night, bank, light, mist, smoke, wind *verb* .lift, .roll, rise, disappear., shroud, .hang, clear, swirl, emerge., burn
4785 | 0.91 F

4934 soak *v*
noun water, blood, .sweat, rain, foot, .sun, .tub, minute, hour, bean, bread, ground, clothes, hair, bath *misc* .up, .into, .through, .hot, .overnight, .rich
4707 | 0.92 F M

4935 mortality *n*
adj high, low, maternal, natural, increased, overall, excess *noun* .rate, infant., morbidity, child, cancer, fishing., risk, study, disease, reduction. *verb* reduce., associate, decline, decrease, face., suffer., .drop
5366 | 0.81 A

4936 flying *j*
noun saucer, machine, color, fish, squirrel, object, lesson, public, glass, plane, car, insect *misc* pass, distinguished, unidentified, fly, catch, through, injure
4686 | 0.93

4937 accountability *n*
adj public, great, political, increased, individual, financial, corporate, personal *noun* government., system, school, .office, responsibility, education, standard, program, lack., transparency *verb* ensure, increase, establish, create, develop, demonstrate, promote., avoid., strengthen, imply
4984 | 0.87 A

4938 skilled *j*
noun worker, labor, people, job, student, work, player, care, force, professional, hand, craftsman *misc* highly, more, become, most, less, low, nursing, unskilled
4686 | 0.93 A

4939 straighten *v*
noun .leg, .arm, hair, shoulder, .tie, back, knee, head, room, spine, foot, floor., .clothes, .seat, tooth *misc* .out, then, slowly, right, .himself, .left, .repeat, quickly, push, .smile, suddenly., abruptly, carefully., fully
4902 | 0.88 F

4940 sprinkle *v*
noun .salt, .cheese, .sugar, pepper, top, mixture, .parsley, water, oil., dish., pan., chicken, .sesame *misc* .remaining, .evenly, each, .chopped
   over .top, cheese, .salad, cinnamon., mixture, .vegetable, .apple
5090 | 0.85 M

4941 cue *n*
adj visual, verbal, social, environmental, subtle, specific, external, sexual, motivational, contextual *noun* pool., .card, .ball, performance, information, music, use., .environment, .condition *verb* take., give, provide, respond., miss., follow., pick., suggest, serve., focus
4824 | 0.90 A

4942 epidemic *n*
adj global, growing, deadly, worldwide, silent, hidden, terrible *noun* AIDS., disease, obesity, .proportion, cholera., flu., drug, diabetes, cancer, crack. *verb* become, reach., cause, spread, .kill, die., stop., occur, .sweep, control.
4660 | 0.93

4943 articulate *v*
noun .vision, position, principle, view, value, goal, idea, need, .interest, role, relationship *misc* clearly, able., political, fully., best., better
4891 | 0.89 A

4944 rehabilitation *n*
adj vocational, physical, social, psychiatric, cardiac, visual, successful, extensive *noun* .program, .center, .service, vision., drug., education, .research, .counselor, hospital *verb* provide, enter., undergo., support, complete., promote., emphasize, assist., ensure, specialize
5193 | 0.83 A

4945 diplomat *n*
adj western, American, senior, foreign, European, top, military, veteran, chief *noun* US., official, career., country, nation, government, politician, journalist, leader, analyst *verb* expel, order., negotiate, train, quote, .predict, .gather, withdraw, kidnap.
4862 | 0.89 N

4946 ribbon *n*
adj blue, yellow, red, white, pink, black, green, thin, wide, narrow *noun* hair, paper, satin., bow, silk., gold, .panel, velvet., color, light *verb* tie, cut., wear., wrap, hang, win., thread, pull, .flutter, drape
4721 | 0.92 F

4947 transit *n*
adj mass, public, rapid, metropolitan, federal, regional, urban, light-rail *noun* .system, .authority,

bus, city, area., rail, .agency, .police, service *verb* use., observe., build, ride., support, improve, connect.
4929 | 0.88 N

4948 militia *n*
adj local, armed, private, well-regulated, sectarian, radical, various, unorganized, colonial, organized *noun* .group, member, .leader, state, force, .movement, .commander, government, .unit *verb* fight, disarm., form, disband, join, organize, regulate., .guard
4838 | 0.89

4949 kneel *v*
noun floor, bed, .side, hand, .prayer, ground, head, mother, room., body, father, boy, altar, .edge, pew *misc* .beside, .before, .front, .next, over, .pray, .behind, stand, .kiss, .face
5053 | 0.86 F

4950 seller *n*
adj best, big, top, short, hot, willing, direct, private, leading *noun* buyer., market, .list, home, book, ticket., property, flower. *verb* represent., become., .sell, pay, buy, match, .accept, trade, arrest., .finance
4719 | 0.92 N

4951 fatal *j*
noun accident, disease, crash, flaw, attraction, mistake, shooting, attack, heart, blow, illness, injury *misc* potentially, prove, cause, suffer, often, sometimes, fire, involve
4525 | 0.96

4952 twist *n*
adj new, ironic, interesting, late, strange, bizarre, different *noun* .turn, .fate, story, plot., tale, lemon, .theme, surprise, .tie, .irony *verb* add., put., offer., introduce
4913 | 0.95

4953 compelling *j*
noun reason, evidence, interest, story, case, argument, state, need, way, vision, image, example *misc* most, more, there, so, very, provide, less, offer
4556 | 0.95

4954 praise *n*
adj high, critical, faint, verbal, full, effusive, special, universal *noun* song, word., teacher., criticism, hymn., .glory, letter., .blame, behavior, encouragement *verb* sing., win., give, receive., earn., deserve., draw., heap, offer., lavish.
4543 | 0.95

4955 copy *v*
noun file, book, work, painting, .document, other, data, artist, style, idea, .name, .photograph, .address, software, music *misc* .from, try., simply., hard., directly, widely.
4645 | 0.93

4956 well-being *n*
adj psychological, economic, physical, emotional, social, human, mental, spiritual, subjective, overall *noun* health., sense., child, family, level., community, concern., individual, material., feeling. *verb* improve., affect., promote., enhance., contribute., relate, threaten., .constitute
4894 | 0.88 A

4957 laundry *n*
adj dirty, wet, coin-operated, folded, industrial *noun* .room, .list, .detergent, .basket, .line, bag,

.service, load., power. _verb_ do., hang, wash, fold, dry, clean, sort., carry., flap
4690 | 0.92 F

4958 screen _v_
noun film, cancer, .call, .applicant, patient, program, movie, candidate, room, passenger, compost, process, data, employee, doctor _misc_ carefully, potential, early, routinely.
4640 | 0.93

4959 confession _n_
adj videotaped, full, public, coerced, taped, voluntary, alleged _noun_ evidence, .faith, police, sin, murder, priest, crime, communion, creed., interrogation.
verb make, hear., sign., obtain, write, read., recant., exclude, demand., corroborate
4680 | 0.92

4960 twentieth _m_
.century, early, late., nineteenth., decade., first., half., end., during., beginning., turn., .fox, second., throughout.
5101 | 0.84 A

4961 dense _j_
noun forest, cloud, tree, fog, foliage, air, wood, area, vegetation, smoke, jungle, population _misc_ through, less, form, hot, create, grow, heavy, urban
4662 | 0.92 M

4962 accelerate _v_
noun process, growth, pace, .development, trend, year, change, car., rate, program, effort, progress, reform, inflation., field _misc_ .toward, economic, greatly, rapidly, quickly
4569 | 0.94

4963 tribute _n_
adj special, fitting, musical, dead, final, annual, moving, loving _noun_ .album, .hero, memorial., band, .concert, song, birthday., payment _verb_ pay., receive, collect, sing., present., demand., feature, honor, exact.
4613 | 0.93

4964 smoking _n_
adj passive, teenage, maternal, parental, heavy, active, adolescent _noun_ cigarette., scene., drinking, health, cancer, alcohol, risk, lung, effect., teen.
verb quit., stop., cause, start., ban, reduce, allow
4706 | 0.92

4965 aboard _i_
.ship, .space, .boat, .plane, climb., .flight, .USS, .air, .shuttle, cruise, .force, .aircraft, .vessel, .station
4641 | 0.93

4966 marble _n_
adj white, black, polished, Italian, green, smooth, cool, carved _noun_ .floor, .statue, slab, wall, granite, .step, .table, glass, stone, .column _verb_ lose., carve., walk., roll, chisel., shine, resemble, climb., feature, .sink
4723 | 0.91 F

4967 entertain _v_
noun .idea, .guest, .thought, .friend, .notion, .audience, .possibility, kid, .visitor, .tale, .crowd, .troop, doubt, .client, fan _misc_ keep., while, .themselves, love., willing., .ourselves, seriously.
4481 | 0.96

4968 boring _j_
noun life, job, stuff, work, story, machine, place, meeting, speech, routine, task, part _misc_ so, find, too, become, really, most, pretty, never
4506 | 0.96

4969 scrutiny _n_
adj public, intense, close, strict, closer, great, increased, careful, judicial _noun_ media., kind., level., government, court, press, .criticism, bureau.
verb come., face., receive., subject., withstand., stand., apply, deserve., require, survive.
4545 | 0.95

4970 bizarre _j_
noun behavior, story, case, kind, event, twist, life, scene, series, situation, circumstance, incident _misc_ most, seem, sound, rather, strange, little, truly, pretty
4526 | 0.95

4971 bargain _n_
adj best, great, grand, hard, real, better, relative, available, fair _noun_ plea., .price, part., end., .hunter, stock, .basement, .rate, .hunting, deal _verb_ find, look., strike, offer., drive., .compare, accept., agree, shop., .abound
4601 | 0.93

4972 deeper _r_
.into, .than, go., dig., much., even., sink, little., run., something., far., move., ever, grow.
4520 | 0.95 F

4973 drown _v_
noun child, water, .sea, sound, river, noise, word, mother, .sorrow, son, .blood, music, .bathtub, wave, .debt _misc_ .out, try, almost., nearly., dead, threaten., accidentally
4667 | 0.92 F

4974 biography _n_
adj new, unauthorized, recent, brief, authorized, literary, official, definitive, critical, short _noun_ type., author, history, book, artist, autobiography, film., dictionary., fiction, series _verb_ write, read., publish, include, research., complete., cite, .expose, edit, recount
4624 | 0.93

4975 naval _j_
noun US, base, academy, officer, station, force, center, research, operation, observatory, war, blockade _misc_ military, medical, British, former, investigative, Japanese, near
4667 | 0.92

4976 nationwide _r_
store., school., percent, million., about, number, program., open., available., department., among., nearly., .including, theater.
4702 | 0.91 N

4977 skeptical _j_
noun claim, eye, public, reason, expert, view, scientist, look, analyst, critic, voter, official _misc_ about, more, remain, very, many, little
4484 | 0.96

4978 shorts _n_
adj white, baggy, khaki, black, blue, red, running, yellow, green, tight _noun_ T-shirt, shirt, boxer., pair.,

.story, sock, tank, gym., jeans, shoe *verb* wear., pull, dress., .cut, change., strip., unzip., zip.
4655 | 0.92 F

4979 lens *n*
adj long, critical, wide-angle, objective, focal, optical, magnifying, single, fish-eye *noun* camera, zoom., eye, telephoto., contact., .media, glass, image, film, aperture *verb* use, turn., view, provide, cover, act., remove., attach
5150 | 0.83 M A

4980 spit *v*
noun .word, .face, .blood, mouth, tobacco, water, .fire, head., tooth, .seed, .stream, .juice, food, window, dust *misc* .out, .into, then, chew., .onto, .upon, cough.
4829 | 0.89 F

4981 sexuality *n*
adj human, female, male, sexual, adolescent, teenage, healthy, emerging *noun* woman, gender, .education, issue, attitude, study, class, research, relationship, race *verb* explore., understand., express, control., relate., deal., teach., emphasize
5252 | 0.82 A

4982 rape *v*
noun woman, girl, daughter, wife, mother, father, sister, prison, police, player, girlfriend, .gunpoint *misc* .her, .by, .murder, beat, kill, repeatedly
4768 | 0.90 S

4983 warehouse *n*
adj old, abandoned, full, empty, converted, huge, central, renovated, nondescript *noun* store, data., .club, .district, .night, .space, food, street, door, .worker *verb* build, fill, convert, rent, enter., .contain, lock., .feature
4658 | 0.92 N

4984 paradise *n*
adj tropical, earthly, lost, rural, terrestrial, rainy, absolute *noun* island, bird., day, .earth, .venture, garden, trouble., hotel, piece. *verb* .lose, create., promise, discover, enter, welcome., envision, land.
4627 | 0.95

4985 nominate *v*
noun president, .Oscar, .candidate, party, year, Republican, film, convention, .court, student, Democrat, member, .Emmy, picture, judge *misc* .for, .by, .best, also., .national, .someone, .support, secondary, select, formally.
4647 | 0.92 S

4986 developed *j*
noun country, world, nation, system, area, region, society, program, economy, sense, skill, market *misc* less, more, highly, developing, most, newly, fully, least, among
4844 | 0.88 A

4987 campaign *v*
noun president, candidate, state, year, Republican, day, issue, governor, Democrat, party, office, .tax, .presidency, politician, fall *misc* .for, .against, while., .hard, actively
4697 | 0.91 S

4988 unfortunate *j*
noun thing, event, situation, people, incident, consequence, result, accident, fact, circumstance,

effect, choice *misc* it, think, very, because, most, happen, enough
4429 | 0.97

4989 grandchild *n*
adj future, numerous, visiting, surviving, great-great *noun* child., .great-grandchildren, grandparent, daughter., son, parent, sister., generation *verb* raise., .live, grow, visit, enjoy, care., dote., benefit, spoil., baby-sit.
4729 | 0.90 N

4990 tenure *n*
adj long, average, academic, brief, short, five-year, judicial *noun* promotion, land., life., system, job, .decision, justice, faculty, .office, end. *verb* deny., achieve., abolish., grant., receive., enjoy., mark, .last, coincide, ensure
4780 | 0.89 A

4991 preach *v*
noun .gospel, sermon, church, .word, .message, .choir, Jesus, pulpit, pastor., minister., religion, .value, .abstinence, .virtue, .peace *misc* practice., .against, teach, Christian, .converted
4673 | 0.91

4992 slot *n*
adj top, empty, narrow, coveted, Olympic, guaranteed, late-night, permanent, speaking *noun* .machine, time., card., mail., expansion., .canyon, video, number., quarter., coin. *verb* fill, cut, play., fit., open, drop, push, occupy, earn.
4732 | 0.90 M

4993 stereotype *n*
adj negative, racial, old, cultural, black, ethnic, social, popular, white, common *noun* gender., .woman, .threat, group, prejudice, role, .American, sex, culture, media *verb* fit., reinforce., perpetuate., base, defy., play., dispel., .exist, reflect, fight
4650 | 0.92 A

4994 bulb *n*
adj fluorescent, incandescent, bare, single, small, electric, dim, naked, flash, overhead *noun* light., fennel., spring, flower, tulip., ceiling, garlic, halogen. *verb* plant, use, replace., .hang, change., .burn, buy, screw, remove, dig.
4770 | 0.89 M

4995 weave *v*
noun .way, .fabric, story, thread, basket, web, pattern, .tale, .traffic, color, .crowd, loom, piece, finger, culture *misc* .into, .through, .together, .around, .out, tightly.
4605 | 0.93

4996 merger *n*
adj proposed, recent, corporate, large, possible, planned, pending, potential, friendly *noun* .acquisition, company, bank, wave, .talk, .mania, .partner *verb* announce, create, approve, complete, expect, form., result, block., oppose., .boost
4873 | 0.87 N

4997 inadequate *j*
noun care, system, health, training, problem, facility, resource, response, education, water, supply, funding *misc* feel, woefully, prove, because, poor, often, totally, due
4677 | 0.91 A

4998 objective *j*
noun measure, reality, criterion, truth, test, standard, information, function, value, fact, data, assessment
misc more, subjective, provide, both, base, than, such
4838 | 0.88 A

4999 electronics *n*
adj electrical, digital, modern, sophisticated, advanced, high-tech, state-of-the-art, mobile
noun consumer•, •industry, computer, company, •store, •show, •firm, product, •engineer, •manufacturer
verb sell, design, own, integrate, contain•, purchase•, fry•, enable, destroy•, eliminate
4776 | 0.89 M

5000 trim *v*
noun •fat, hair, end, tree, beard, stem, budget, •edge, •cost, hedge, •gold, fur, beef, tax *misc* cut, green, •off, neatly•, white, •away
4657 | 0.91 M

Alphabetical index

Format of entries

A

a *a* 5

abandon *v* 2216

ability *n* 794

able *j* 388

aboard *i* 4965

abortion *n* 1966

about *i* 47

about *r* 182

above *r* 1606

above *i* 903

abroad *r* 3431

absence *n* 2540

absolute *j* 3180

absolutely *r* 1164

absorb *v* 3150

abstract *j* 3991

abuse *v* 3755

abuse *n* 1595

academic *j* 1557

academy *n* 2262

accelerate *v* 4962

accent *n* 4226

accept *v* 762

acceptable *j* 3406

acceptance *n* 3463

access *v* 4605

access *n* 1131

accessible *j* 4381

accident *n* 1711

accommodate *v* 3710

accompany *v* 2450

accomplish *v* 2335

accomplishment *n* 4267

according *i* 483

account *v* 1935

account *n* 1088

accountability *n* 4937

accounting *n* 4199

accuracy *n* 4054

accurate *j* 2730

accurately *r* 4905

accusation *n* 4889

accuse *v* 2017

achieve *v* 1157

achievement *n* 2126

acid *n* 3357

acknowledge *v* 1673

acquire *v* 2062

acquisition *n* 3882

acre *n* 2403

across *r* 3158

across *i* 385

act *v* 839

act *n* 730

action *n* 502

active *j* 1464

actively *r* 4311

activist *n* 2653

activity *n* 552

actor *n* 1544

actress *n* 3365

actual *j* 1749

actually *r* 402

ad *n* 1761

adapt *v* 2983

add *v* 351

added *j* 4567

addition *n* 3994

addition *i* 2061

additional *j* 1349

address *n* 1864

address *v* 1049

adequate *j* 3305

adjust *v* 2348

adjustment *n* 3161

administer *v* 3730

administration *n* 644

administrative *j* 3524

administrator *n* 2574

admire *v* 3312

admission *n* 3116

admit *v* 1106

adolescent *n* 3753

adopt *v* 1636

adoption *n* 3757

adult *n* 1003

advance *n* 2309

advance *v* 2706

advanced *j* 2856

advantage *n* 1319

adventure *n* 2956

advertising *n* 2661

advice *n* 1657

advise *v* 2582

adviser *n* 2803

advocate *v* 3949

advocate *n* 2634

aesthetic *j* 4384

affair *n* 1378

affect *v* 972

affiliation *n* 2966

affirmative *j* 4771

afford *v* 1875

afraid *j* 1404

African *j* 1395

African-American *j* 3650

after *c* 264

after *i* 120

afternoon *n* 1202

afterward *r* 4233

again *r* 187

against *i* 177

age *v* 4014

age *n* 395

agency *n* 693

agenda *n* 2137

agent *n* 1034

aggression *n* 4465

aggressive *j* 2541

ago *r* 312

agree *v* 523

agreement *n* 1078

agricultural *j* 3242

agriculture *n* 3215

ah *u* 3298

ahead *r* 1036

ahead *i* 2674

aid *v* 4538

aid *n* 1643

aide *n* 3127

AIDS *n* 1808

aim *n* 3676

aim *v* 1968

air *n* 370

aircraft *n* 2790

airline *n* 2133

airplane *n* 3438

airport *n* 1743

aisle *n* 4531

alarm *n* 3739

album *n* 2452

alcohol *n* 2286

alien *n* 4196

alike *r* 4387

alive *j* 1543

all *r* 227

all *d* 43

allegation *n* 3450

alleged *j* 4075

allegedly *r* 4726

alley *n* 4420

alliance *n* 2417

allow *v* 344

ally *n* 2436

almost *r* 295

alone *j* 1617

alone *r* 1115

along *r* 1201

along *i* 454

alongside *i* 4277

already *r* 339

also *r* 89

alter *v* 2885

alternative *n* 2072

alternative *j* 2600

although *c* 362

altogether *r* 3806

aluminum *n* 4423

always *r* 213

AM *r* 1277

amazing *j* 2364

ambassador *n* 3238

ambition *n* 4320

ambitious *j* 4310

amendment *n* 2165

American *n* 553

American *j* 179

amid *i* 3904

among *i* 286

amount *n* 784

analysis *n* 829

analyst *n* 1710

analyze *v* 2329

ancestor *n* 4296

ancient *j* 1891

and *c* 3

and/or *c* 3684

angel *n* 2607

anger *n* 2369

angle *n* 2486

angry *j* 1709

animal *n* 741

ankle *n* 3917

anniversary *n* 3396

announce *v* 1187

announcement *n* 3669

annual *j* 1408

annually *r* 4051

anonymous *j* 4351

another *p* 2346

another *d* 146

answer *v* 831

answer *n* 769

anticipate *v* 3181

anxiety *n* 2679

anxious *j* 3863

any *r* 4708

any *d* 110

anybody *p* 1387

anymore *r* 1705

anyone *p* 665

anything *p* 336

anyway *r* 1426

anywhere *r* 1871

apart *r* 1974

apart *i* 4737

apartment *n* 1304

apologize *v* 3807

apology *n* 4926

apparent *j* 2484

apparently *r* 1429

appeal *v* 2899

appeal *n* 1843

appear *v* 394

appearance *n* 1714

apple *n* 1983

application *n* 1559

apply *v* 956

appoint *v* 3197

appointment *n* 3084

appreciate *v* 1780

appreciation *n* 4374

approach *v* 1401

approach *n* 764

appropriate *j* 1498

approval *n* 2560

approve *v* 2044

approximately *r* 2378

Arab *n* 4114

Arab *j* 2415

architect *n* 3422

architecture *n* 3576

area *n* 233

arena *n* 3645

argue *v* 785

argument *n* 1196

arise *v* 2573

arm *v* 4670

arm *n* 495

armed *j* 2669

army *n* 821

around *r* 332

around *i* 266

arrange *v* 2233

arrangement *n* 2343

array *n* 3656

arrest *n* 3059

arrest *v* 2155

arrival *n* 3219

arrive *v* 813

arrow *n* 4928

art *n* 373

article *n* 736

articulate *v* 4943

artifact *n* 4868

artificial *j* 4012

artist *n* 865

artistic *j* 3383

as *r* 130

as *i* 50
as *c* 34
ash *n* 4727
Asian *j* 2410
aside *r* 1910
ask *v* 132
asleep *j* 3098
aspect *n* 1369
ass *n* 4383
assault *n* 2861
assemble *v* 3599
assembly *n* 2783
assert *v* 3166
assess *v* 2100
assessment *n* 1640
asset *n* 2207
assign *v* 2613
assignment *n* 3192
assist *v* 2521
assistance *n* 2095
assistant *j* 2847
assistant *n* 2728
associate *n* 3245
associate *j* 4607
associate *v* 1392
associated *j* 4366
association *n* 822
assume *v* 1104
assumption *n* 2605
assure *v* 2571
astronomer *n* 4668
at *i* 24
athlete *n* 2070
athletic *j* 3287
atmosphere *n* 2271
atop *i* 4662
attach *v* 2340
attack *v* 1541
attack *n* 766
attempt *n* 1226
attempt *v* 1627
attend *v* 1194
attendance *n* 4542
attention *n* 596
attitude *n* 1170
attorney *n* 1079
attract *v* 1870
attraction *n* 3821
attractive *j* 2817

attribute *v* 3333
auction *n* 4645
audience *n* 1092
audio *j* 4473
aunt *n* 2657
author *n* 686
authority *n* 835
authorize *v* 4836
auto *n* 3272
automatic *j* 4135
automatically *r* 4003
automobile *n* 3977
autonomy *n* 4826
availability *n* 4859
available *j* 622
avenue *n* 2172
average *v* 3738
average *n* 1698
average *j* 1322
avoid *v* 912
await *v* 3702
awake *j* 4650
award *v* 3743
award *n* 1626
aware *j* 1453
awareness *n* 2853
away *i* 742
away *r* 272
awful *j* 3249

B

baby *n* 599
back *v* 1863
back *n* 328
back *r* 109
background *n* 1431
backyard *n* 4553
bacteria *n* 3756
bad *j* 290
badly *r* 3135
bag *n* 1045
bake *v* 2978
balance *n* 1659
balance *v* 2747
balanced *j* 4641
ball *n* 951
balloon *n* 4764
ballot *n* 3412
ban *n* 3927

ban *v* 3276
banana *n* 4795
band *n* 1389
bank *n* 701
banker *n* 4537
banking *n* 4086
bankruptcy *n* 4322
bar *n* 1021
bare *j* 3486
barely *r* 2013
bargain *n* 4971
barn *n* 4155
barrel *n* 3218
barrier *n* 2612
base *n* 939
base *v* 544
baseball *n* 1397
basement *n* 3641
basic *j* 1145
basically *r* 1696
basin *n* 4869
basis *n* 1303
basket *n* 3338
basketball *n* 1859
bat *n* 3793
bath *n* 3915
bathroom *n* 2441
battery *n* 3381
battle *n* 1233
battle *v* 4838
be *v* 2
beach *n* 1216
beam *n* 3907
bean *n* 2390
bear *v* 1623
bear *n* 1894
beard *n* 4733
beast *n* 4482
beat *n* 3021
beat *v* 1061
beautiful *j* 1015
beauty *n* 1752
because *i* 516
because *c* 91
become *v* 138
bed *n* 680
bedroom *n* 1889
bee *n* 4449
beef *n* 3622

beer *n* 1924

before *r* 707

before *i* 224

before *c* 372

beg *v* 3510

begin *v* 164

beginning *n* 1213

behalf *i* 4466

behave *v* 3692

behavior *n* 690

behavioral *j* 4028

behind *r* 2079

behind *i* 427

being *n* 1717

belief *n* 1427

believe *v* 215

bell *n* 2708

belly *n* 3875

belong *v* 1653

below *r* 1547

below *i* 1943

belt *n* 2449

bench *n* 2808

bend *v* 2231

beneath *i* 2010

benefit *v* 2270

benefit *n* 819

beside *i* 1973

besides *r* 3048

besides *i* 4171

best *r* 988

best *j* 316

bet *n* 4514

bet *v* 2705

better *r* 507

better *j* 461

between *i* 141

beyond *i* 752

beyond *r* 4894

bias *n* 3936

Bible *n* 2844

bicycle *n* 4584

bid *n* 4048

big *j* 165

bike *n* 3012

billion *m* 714

bind *v* 2513

biography *n* 4974

biological *j* 2583

biology *n* 4490

bird *n* 1176

birth *n* 1518

birthday *n* 2496

bishop *n* 3675

bit *n* 975

bite *v* 3189

bite *n* 3914

bitter *j* 3502

bizarre *j* 4970

black *n* 1939

black *j* 259

blade *n* 3231

blame *v* 1814

blank *j* 4618

blanket *n* 3341

blast *n* 4798

blend *v* 4037

bless *v* 4245

blessing *n* 4790

blind *j* 2782

blink *v* 4722

block *v* 2446

block *n* 1340

blood *n* 715

bloody *j* 4154

blow *n* 3841

blow *v* 1422

blue *j* 849

blue *n* 2829

board *n* 664

boast *v* 4561

boat *n* 1326

body *n* 320

boil *v* 4335

bold *j* 3963

bomb *n* 1942

bomb *v* 4742

bomber *n* 4824

bombing *n* 2987

bond *n* 1927

bone *n* 1487

bonus *n* 4460

book *n* 245

boom *n* 3198

boost *v* 3835

boot *n* 2476

booth *n* 4370

border *n* 1366

boring *j* 4968

born *v* 1102

borrow *v* 3279

boss *n* 2367

both *d* 261

both *r* 377

bother *v* 2199

bottle *n* 1772

bottom *n* 1522

bottom *j* 2688

bounce *v* 3819

boundary *n* 2795

bow *n* 4147

bow *v* 4919

bowl *n* 1357

box *n* 802

boy *n* 382

boyfriend *n* 3609

brain *n* 1269

branch *n* 1824

brand *n* 2625

brave *j* 4388

bread *n* 2142

break *n* 1089

break *v* 501

breakfast *n* 2433

breast *n* 1667

breath *n* 1670

breathe *v* 2290

breathing *n* 4555

breeze *n* 4349

brick *n* 3370

bride *n* 4918

bridge *n* 1719

brief *j* 2181

briefly *r* 3028

bright *j* 1548

brilliant *j* 3196

bring *v* 221

British *j* 1208

broad *j* 1438

broadcast *n* 3613

broadcast *v* 4851

broken *j* 2715

broker *n* 4056

brother *n* 623

brown *j* 1695

brush *v* 3275

brush *n* 3705

brutal *j* 4747

bubble *n* 4222

buck *n* 2593

bucket *n* 4921

buddy *n* 4326

budget *n* 1043

bug *n* 4188

build *v* 416

builder *n* 4649

building *n* 508

bulb *n* 4994

bulk *n* 4669

bull *n* 3184

bullet *n* 2809

bunch *n* 2727

burden *n* 2696

bureau *n* 2338

bureaucracy *n* 4914

burn *v* 1451

burning *j* 4066

burst *v* 3574

bury *v* 2422

bus *n* 1479

business *n* 254

businessman *n* 3814

busy *j* 1945

but *i* 1720

but *c* 23

butt *n* 4740

butter *n* 2551

button *n* 2738

buy *v* 403

buyer *n* 2984

by *r* 1188

by *i* 31

C

cab *n* 4278

cabin *n* 3205

cabinet *n* 2713

cable *n* 2004

cafe *n* 3772

cage *n* 4175

cake *n* 2637

calculate *v* 3074

calculation *n* 4666

calendar *n* 4785

call *n* 663

call *v* 121

calm *v* 4223

calm *j* 4769

camera *n* 1018

camp *n* 1235

campaign *n* 650

campaign *v* 4987

campus *n* 2113

can *n* 3038

can *v* 40

Canadian *j* 2974

canal *n* 4211

cancel *v* 3902

cancer *n* 1066

candidate *n* 985

candle *n* 3948

candy *n* 3518

canvas *n* 4182

cap *n* 2319

capability *n* 2973

capable *j* 2393

capacity *n* 1792

capital *n* 1080

captain *n* 2039

capture *v* 1747

car *n* 296

carbon *n* 3235

card *n* 917

care *v* 920

care *n* 472

career *n* 768

careful *j* 1970

carefully *r* 1599

carrier *n* 3266

carrot *n* 4744

carry *v* 487

cart *n* 4105

cartoon *n* 4120

carve *v* 3932

case *c* 4481

case *n* 189

cash *n* 1768

casino *n* 4332

cast *n* 4375

cast *v* 2053

castle *n* 4356

casual *j* 4027

casualty *n* 4152

cat *n* 1786

catalog *n* 4451

catch *v* 590

catch *n* 4796

category *n* 1471

Catholic *n* 3393

Catholic *j* 1955

cattle *n* 3689

cause *v* 602

cause *n* 1000

cave *n* 3649

cease *v* 4455

ceiling *n* 2654

celebrate *v* 2057

celebration *n* 3037

celebrity *n* 3017

cell *n* 949

cemetery *n* 4648

census *n* 4339

center *n* 302

central *j* 746

century *n* 609

ceremony *n* 2737

certain *j* 576

certainly *r* 658

chain *n* 1825

chair *n* 959

chairman *n* 1382

challenge *n* 1032

challenge *v* 1793

chamber *n* 2701

champion *n* 2812

championship *n* 2425

chance *n* 620

change *v* 309

change *n* 361

changing *j* 3344

channel *n* 1888

chaos *n* 3777

chapter *n* 2198

character *n* 820

characteristic *n* 2059

characterize *v* 2867

charge *i* 4318

charge *n* 915

charge *v* 1446

charity *n* 3400

charm *n* 4875

chart *n* 2769

charter *n* 4411

chase *n* 4693

chase *v* 3052

cheap *j* 1972

cheat *v* 4472

check *v* 830

check *n* 1897

cheek *n* 2731

cheer *v* 4640

cheese *n* 2222

chef *n* 3318

chemical *j* 2680

chemical *n* 2633

chemistry *n* 4913

chest *n* 1750

chew *v* 4663

chicken *n* 1596

chief *j* 1481

chief *n* 1298

child *n* 116

childhood *n* 2158

chill *n* 4898

chin *n* 4034

Chinese *j* 1291

chip *n* 2218

chocolate *n* 2736

choice *n* 636

cholesterol *n* 3626

choose *v* 605

chop *v* 4201

Christian *n* 3425

Christian *j* 1400

Christianity *n* 4608

Christmas *n* 1385

chronic *j* 3888

chunk *n* 4614

church *n* 512

cigarette *n* 2103

circle *n* 1533

circle *v* 4788

circuit *n* 3123

circumstance *n* 1781

cite *v* 1946

citizen *n* 1091

citizenship *n* 4909

city *n* 188

civic *j* 4023

civil *j* 1050

civilian *n* 3708

civilian *j* 3476

civilization *n* 3536

claim *v* 876

claim *n* 1358

class *n* 438

classic *n* 3945

classic *j* 2643

classical *j* 3537

classify *v* 4528

classroom *n* 1614

clay *n* 3505

clean *j* 1542

clean *v* 1925

clear *j* 563

clear *v* 1908

clearly *r* 842

clerk *n* 3859

click *v* 4184

client *n* 1281

cliff *n* 4424

climate *n* 2267

climb *v* 1588

cling *v* 4714

clinic *n* 2423

clinical *j* 2822

clip *n* 4261

clock *n* 2655

close *r* 1600

close *j* 883

close *v* 653

closed *j* 3716

closely *r* 2063

closer *j* 3046

closer *r* 2036

closest *j* 4598

closet *n* 3515

cloth *n* 3728

clothes *n* 1458

clothing *n* 2684

cloud *n* 1956

club *n* 866

clue *n* 3401

cluster *n* 3414

coach *n* 1109

coal *n* 3441

coalition *n* 2193

coast *n* 1476

coastal *j* 4176

coat *n* 2284

cocaine *n* 4314

code *n* 1680

coffee *n* 1425

cognitive *j* 3465

coin *n* 4433

cold *j* 902

collaboration *n* 4260

collapse *n* 3532

collapse *v* 3257

collar *n* 4554

colleague *n* 1567

collect *v* 1343

collection *n* 1116

collective *j* 3369

collector *n* 4064

college *n* 449

colonel *n* 3871

colonial *j* 3473

colony *n* 3856

color *v* 4574

color *n* 470

colorful *j* 4551

column *n* 2119

columnist *n* 4488

combat *n* 3490

combination *n* 1818

combine *v* 1474

combined *j* 4195

come *v* 70

comedy *n* 3326

comfort *n* 2998

comfortable *j* 1726

coming *j* 4787

command *v* 4040

command *n* 2405

commander *n* 2400

comment *v* 2569

comment *n* 1428

commerce *n* 2976

commercial *j* 1038

commission *n* 1271

commissioner *n* 3154

commit *v* 1411

commitment *n* 1628

committee *n* 748

commodity *n* 4772

common *j* 712

commonly *r* 3778

communicate *v* 2703

communication *n* 1261

communist *j* 2871

community *n* 315
companion *n* 3618
company *n* 195
comparable *j* 4603
compare *v* 844
comparison *n* 2194
compel *v* 4454
compelling *j* 4953
compensation *n* 3827
compete *v* 2087
competition *n* 1402
competitive *j* 2409
competitor *n* 3330
complain *v* 1849
complaint *n* 2318
complete *j* 1461
complete *v* 1239
completely *r* 1189
complex *n* 3174
complex *j* 1603
complexity *n* 3770
compliance *n* 4657
complicated *j* 2765
comply *v* 4689
component *n* 1779
compose *v* 3410
composition *n* 3162
compound *n* 3485
comprehensive *j* 2935
comprise *v* 4414
compromise *v* 4655
compromise *n* 3733
computer *n* 586
concede *v* 4153
conceive *v* 4165
concentrate *v* 2334
concentration *n* 2799
concept *n* 1230
conception *n* 4624
concern *v* 3416
concern *n* 717
concerned *j* 1126
concerning *i* 3390
concert *n* 2618
conclude *v* 1662
conclusion *n* 1650
concrete *j* 3375
condemn *v* 4130
condition *n* 631

conduct *n* 3671
conduct *v* 1191
conference *n* 983
confess *v* 3981
confession *n* 4959
confidence *n* 1909
confident *j* 2936
confirm *v* 1881
conflict *n* 1192
confront *v* 2432
confrontation *n* 4429
confuse *v* 3525
confusion *n* 3332
congress *n* 630
congressional *j* 2320
congressman *n* 3102
connect *v* 1682
connection *n* 1456
conscience *n* 4783
conscious *j* 3870
consciousness *n* 3260
consensus *n* 3324
consent *n* 4495
consequence *n* 1629
consequently *r* 4316
conservation *n* 4601
conservative *n* 2859
conservative *j* 1861
consider *v* 397
considerable *j* 2824
considerably *r* 4620
consideration *n* 2465
consist *v* 2201
consistent *j* 2285
consistently *r* 3651
conspiracy *n* 4216
constant *j* 2394
constantly *r* 2512
constitute *v* 2883
constitution *n* 2147
constitutional *j* 2712
constraint *n* 4656
construct *v* 2495
construction *n* 1444
consult *v* 3617
consultant *n* 2491
consume *v* 3077
consumer *n* 1097
consumption *n* 3252

contact *n* 1502
contact *v* 2307
contain *v* 933
container *n* 3508
contemplate *v* 4835
contemporary *j* 2016
contend *v* 3558
content *n* 1778
contest *n* 3140
context *n* 1463
continent *n* 4167
continue *v* 305
continued *j* 3340
continuing *j* 3629
continuous *j* 3749
contract *n* 1283
contractor *n* 3752
contrast *n* 1771
contribute *v* 1324
contribution *n* 1769
control *v* 937
control *n* 435
controversial *j* 3100
controversy *n* 2873
convenience *n* 4897
convention *n* 1794
conventional *j* 2552
conversation *n* 1211
conversion *n* 4720
convert *v* 2919
convey *v* 3826
convict *v* 3699
conviction *n* 3086
convince *v* 2071
convinced *j* 3721
cook *n* 4291
cook *v* 1488
cookie *n* 3386
cooking *n* 3372
cool *v* 3411
cool *j* 1492
cooperate *v* 4026
cooperation *n* 2756
cooperative *j* 4419
coordinate *v* 4853
coordinator *n* 4275
cop *n* 2288
cope *v* 3354
copy *n* 1916

copy *v* 4955

cord *n* 4329

core *n* 1994

corn *n* 2542

corner *n* 1144

corporate *j* 1581

corporation *n* 1947

corps *n* 3172

correct *v* 3261

correct *j* 1790

correction *n* 4340

correctly *r* 4393

correlation *n* 3642

correspondent *n* 2915

corridor *n* 3540

corruption *n* 3845

cost *n* 558

cost *v* 1135

costly *j* 4280

costume *n* 4243

cottage *n* 4864

cotton *n* 3227

couch *n* 3408

could *v* 73

council *n* 1059

counsel *n* 3244

counseling *n* 3707

counselor *n* 3481

count *v* 1317

count *n* 2538

counter *v* 4450

counter *n* 2843

counterpart *n* 3825

country *n* 168

county *n* 671

coup *n* 4352

couple *n* 542

courage *n* 3362

course *n* 646

court *n* 366

courtesy *n* 4502

courtroom *n* 4122

cousin *n* 2766

cover *v* 564

cover *n* 1658

coverage *n* 1892

cow *n* 3107

cowboy *n* 3551

crack *v* 3284

crack *n* 3027

craft *n* 3093

crash *n* 2882

crash *v* 3339

crawl *v* 3869

crazy *j* 1839

cream *n* 2074

create *v* 342

creation *n* 2138

creative *j* 2109

creativity *n* 4435

creature *n* 2413

credibility *n* 4033

credit *v* 4112

credit *n* 1182

creek *n* 2474

crew *n* 1736

crime *n* 825

criminal *n* 3307

criminal *j* 1975

crisis *n* 1255

criteria *n* 2609

critic *n* 1363

critical *j* 1143

criticism *n* 2106

criticize *v* 2558

crop *n* 2611

cross *n* 2407

cross *v* 1419

crowd *n* 1299

crowd *v* 4885

crowded *j* 4766

crown *n* 3751

crucial *j* 2402

cruel *j* 4823

cruise *n* 3740

crush *v* 4325

cry *n* 3453

cry *v* 1365

crystal *n* 3694

Cuban *j* 4107

cue *n* 4941

cultural *j* 958

culture *n* 617

cup *n* 827

cure *n* 4628

cure *v* 4569

curiosity *n* 4570

curious *j* 3156

currency *n* 3789

current *j* 699

currently *r* 1715

curriculum *n* 2200

curtain *n* 3658

curve *n* 3513

custody *n* 4436

custom *n* 3015

customer *n* 1142

cut *n* 1493

cut *v* 425

cute *j* 4517

cycle *n* 2246

D

dad *n* 1159

daddy *n* 2659

daily *r* 3590

daily *j* 1523

dam *n* 4443

damage *v* 3011

damage *n* 1520

damn *j* 4442

dance *n* 1724

dance *v* 1993

dancer *n* 3746

dancing *n* 4758

danger *n* 1554

dangerous *j* 1472

dare *v* 3379

dark *j* 1006

dark *n* 2185

darkness *n* 2658

data *n* 572

database *n* 3858

date *n* 1220

date *v* 2589

daughter *n* 654

dawn *n* 4005

day *n* 92

dead *j* 729

deadline *n* 3286

deadly *j* 3526

deal *v* 666

deal *n* 803

dealer *n* 2549

dear *j* 3433

death *n* 420

debate *v* 3954

debate *n* 1096

debris *n* 4690

debt *n* 1929

debut *n* 4652

decade *n* 735

decent *j* 3916

decide *v* 455

decision *n* 485

deck *n* 2814

declaration *n* 4242

declare *v* 1759

decline *v* 2027

decline *n* 2763

decorate *v* 4457

decrease *v* 3419

dedicate *v* 3860

deem *v* 4592

deep *j* 1179

deep *r* 2152

deeper *j* 4249

deeper *r* 4972

deeply *r* 2156

deer *n* 3056

defeat *n* 4143

defeat *v* 3363

defend *v* 1754

defendant *n* 3409

defender *n* 4903

defense *n* 647

defensive *j* 2986

deficit *n* 2332

define *v* 1221

definitely *r* 2035

definition *n* 2114

degree *n* 789

delay *n* 3119

delay *v* 3444

deliberately *r* 4583

delicate *j* 3842

delight *n* 4879

deliver *v* 1316

delivery *n* 2834

demand *n* 1308

demand *v* 1475

democracy *n* 1512

Democrat *n* 938

democratic *j* 888

demographic *j* 4809

demonstrate *v* 1398

demonstration *n* 3142

denial *n* 4729

dense *j* 4961

density *n* 4639

deny *v* 1412

depart *v* 4862

department *n* 496

departure *n* 3884

depend *v* 1483

dependent *j* 3234

depending *i* 2995

depict *v* 3295

deploy *v* 4590

deposit *n* 4702

depressed *j* 4588

depression *n* 2213

depth *n* 2596

deputy *n* 2588

derive *v* 3029

descend *v* 4058

describe *v* 565

description *n* 2184

desert *n* 2206

deserve *v* 2255

design *v* 882

design *n* 860

designer *n* 2482

desire *v* 3903

desire *n* 1578

desk *n* 1668

desperate *j* 3138

desperately *r* 4469

despite *i* 754

dessert *n* 4385

destination *n* 3973

destroy *v* 1423

destruction *n* 2602

detail *n* 1030

detailed *j* 3131

detect *v* 2823

detective *n* 3045

determination *n* 3861

determine *v* 774

devastating *j* 4881

develop *v* 488

developed *j* 4986

developer *n* 3545

developing *j* 2666

development *n* 452

developmental *j* 4832

device *n* 1538

devil *n* 3432

devise *v* 4911

devote *v* 3211

diabetes *n* 4360

diagnose *v* 3984

diagnosis *n* 3900

diagram *n* 4890

dialogue *n* 2848

diamond *n* 3155

diary *n* 4342

dictate *v* 4901

die *v* 405

diet *n* 2228

differ *v* 3003

difference *n* 511

different *j* 241

differently *r* 3157

difficult *j* 608

difficulty *n* 1693

dig *v* 2516

digital *j* 2518

dignity *n* 4133

dilemma *n* 4090

dimension *n* 2445

diminish *v* 3967

dining *n* 3013

dinner *n* 1094

dip *v* 4609

diplomat *n* 4945

diplomatic *j* 3944

direct *v* 1579

direct *j* 1490

direction *n* 944

directly *r* 1147

director *n* 521

dirt *n* 2793

dirty *j* 2889

disability *n* 2601

disabled *j* 4449

disagree *v* 2710

disappear *v* 1594

disappointed *j* 3996

disappointment *n* 4610

disaster *n* 2316

discipline *n* 2298

disclose *v* 4447

discount *n* 4559

discourage *v* 4210

discourse *n* 3394

discover *v* 962

discovery *n* 2260

discrimination *n* 3167

discuss *v* 896

discussion *n* 1052

disease *n* 797

dish *n* 2009

disk *n* 3898

dismiss *v* 2813

disorder *n* 2481

display *v* 2112

display *n* 2245

dispute *n* 2741

dissolve *v* 4431

distance *n* 1262

distant *j* 2665

distinct *j* 3269

distinction *n* 2932

distinctive *j* 4752

distinguish *v* 3247

distract *v* 4575

distribute *v* 2963

distribution *n* 2051

district *n* 875

disturb *v* 4535

disturbing *j* 4867

diverse *j* 2855

diversity *n* 2580

divide *v* 1967

divine *j* 4337

division *n* 1275

divorce *n* 2985

divorce *v* 4250

do *v* 18

doctor *n* 569

doctrine *n* 3874

document *v* 3374

document *n* 1525

documentary *n* 4317

dog *n* 770

doll *n* 3820

dollar *n* 795

domain *n* 3648

domestic *j* 1573

dominant *j* 3183

dominate *v* 2314

donate *v* 4156

donation *n* 4468

donor *n* 3939

door *n* 349

doorway *n* 3899

dose *n* 3704

dot *n* 4518

double *v* 2874

double *j* 2219

doubt *v* 3006

doubt *n* 1918

dough *n* 4704

down *i* 1041

down *r* 118

downtown *j* 3160

downtown *r* 4746

dozen *m* 1758

draft *v* 4255

draft *n* 2650

drag *v* 2139

drain *v* 3744

drama *n* 2691

dramatic *j* 2121

dramatically *r* 3388

draw *v* 601

drawer *n* 4244

drawing *n* 2770

dream *v* 2603

dream *n* 1004

dress *n* 1799

dress *v* 1469

dried *j* 4558

drift *v* 3646

drink *v* 1258

drink *n* 2054

drinking *n* 3584

drive *n* 1514

drive *v* 493

driver *n* 1246

driveway *n* 4849

driving *j* 3768

drop *v* 691

drop *n* 2604

drown *v* 4973

drug *n* 480

drum *n* 4206

drunk *j* 3723

dry *v* 3262

dry *j* 1593

duck *n* 3592

due *i* 1820

due *j* 2469

dumb *j* 4686

dump *v* 3685

during *i* 200

dust *n* 2303

Dutch *j* 4362

duty *n* 1776

dying *j* 4550

dynamic *j* 3999

dynamics *n* 4728

E

e-mail *n* 1990

each *p* 721

each *d* 196

eager *j* 3152

eagle *n* 3343

ear *n* 1390

early *r* 522

early *j* 368

earn *v* 1329

earnings *n* 3096

earth *n* 836

earthquake *n* 4179

ease *v* 3265

ease *n* 4270

easily *r* 1232

east *n* 740

eastern *j* 1508

easy *r* 2937

easy *j* 559

eat *v* 554

eating *n* 3988

echo *v* 3487

ecological *j* 4794

economic *j* 474

economically *r* 4899

economics *n* 3204

economist *n* 3069

economy *n* 677

edge *n* 995

edit *v* 4354

edition *n* 2428

editor *n* 1047

educate *v* 3082

education *n* 400

educational *j* 1678

educator *n* 2636

effect *n* 432

effective *j* 1152

effectively *r* 2590

effectiveness *n* 3654

efficiency *n* 3132

efficient *j* 3070

effort *n* 459

egg *n* 1445

ego *n* 4872

eight *m* 756

eighth *m* 4546

either *r* 577

either *d* 2031

elaborate *j* 4661

elbow *n* 3585

elder *n* 4174

elderly *j* 3036

elect *v* 2266

election *n* 800

electric *j* 2326

electrical *j* 3913

electricity *n* 2854

electronic *j* 2440

electronics *n* 4999

elegant *j* 3970

element *n* 1225

elementary *j* 2614

elephant *n* 4626

elevator *n* 3957

eleven *m* 4293

eligible *j* 4698

eliminate *v* 1846

elite *n* 2762

else *r* 443

elsewhere *r* 2295

embarrassed *j* 4582

embassy *n* 4218

embrace *v* 2526

emerge *v* 1323

emergency *n* 1760

emerging *j* 4659

emission *n* 3137

emotion *n* 2166

emotional *j* 1689

emotionally *r* 4755

emphasis *n* 2333

emphasize *v* 1991

empire *n* 3130

employ *v* 1976

employee *n* 953

employer *n* 2349

employment *n* 2522

empty *j* 1661

enable *v* 2203

enact *v* 4806

encounter *n* 3619

encounter *v* 2711

encourage *v* 1204

encouraging *j* 4396

end *v* 543

end *n* 284

endless *j* 3779

endorse *v* 3979

endure *v* 3706

enemy *n* 1621

energy *n* 649

enforce *v* 3548

enforcement *n* 2328

engage *v* 1437

engagement *n* 3971

engine *n* 1690

engineer *n* 2130

engineering *n* 2683

English *j* 1836

English *n* 1931

enhance *v* 2360

enjoy *v* 893

enormous *j* 1988

enough *d* 881

enough *r* 380

ensure *v* 1801

enter *v* 719

enterprise *n* 2468

entertain *v* 4967

entertainment *n* 2355

enthusiasm *n* 3769

entire *j* 879

entirely *r* 1874

entitle *v* 3443

entity *n* 3960

entrance *n* 2922

entrepreneur *n* 4475

entry *n* 2387

envelope *n* 3905

environment *n* 859

environmental *j* 886

envision *v* 4522

epidemic *n* 4942

episode *n* 2923

equal *j* 1835

equality *n* 4646

equally *r* 2358

equation *n* 4126

equip *v* 4169

equipment *n* 1351

equity *n* 4085

equivalent *n* 4331

era *n* 1903

error *n* 2182

escape *n* 4190

escape *v* 2049

especially *r* 525

essay *n* 2585

essence *n* 3565

essential *j* 1959

essentially *r* 2297

establish *v* 887

establishment *n* 2904

estate *n* 1832

estimate *v* 1816

estimate *n* 2525

estimated *j* 3478

etc *r* 3122

ethical *j* 3522

ethics *n* 3346

ethnic *j* 1765

European *n* 3785

European *j* 1293

evaluate *v* 2380

evaluation *n* 2444

eve *n* 4497

even *c* 492

even *r* 107

evening *n* 969

event *n* 537

eventually *r* 1119

ever *r* 288

every *a* 174

everybody *p* 798

everyday *j* 3349

everyone *p* 541

everything *p* 393

everywhere *r* 1949

evidence *n* 606

evident *j* 3461

evil *n* 3501

evil *j* 3889

evolution *n* 3039

evolve *v* 2890

exact *j* 3380

exactly *r* 753

exam *n* 4345

examination *n* 3177

examine *v* 1210

example *n* 850

exceed *v* 3283

excellent *j* 2149

except *c* 1886

except *i* 1840

exception *n* 2399

excessive *j* 4536

exchange *v* 4146

exchange *n* 1521

excited *j* 3499

excitement *n* 3547

exciting *j* 2958

exclude *v* 3472

exclusive *j* 3829

exclusively *r* 4459

excuse *n* 3771

excuse *v* 3495

execute *v* 3695

execution *n* 4324

executive *n* 874

exercise *n* 1552

exercise *v* 2384

exhaust *v* 4750

exhibit *v* 3352

exhibit *n* 3920

exhibition *n* 2724

exist *v* 1025

existence *n* 2221

existing *j* 2167

exit *n* 3911

exotic *j* 4299

expand *v* 1591

expansion *n* 2725

expect *v* 409

expectation *n* 1914

expected *j* 4334

expedition *n* 4781

expense *n* 2134

expensive *j* 1688

experience *v* 1215

experience *n* 424

experienced *j* 4355

experiment *n* 2028

experimental *j* 3535

expert *n* 909

expertise *n* 3929

explain *v* 486

explanation *n* 2047

explicit *j* 4811

explode *v* 3148

exploit *v* 4358

exploration *n* 3931

explore *v* 1634

explosion *n* 3001

export *n* 3503

expose *v* 2021

exposure *n* 2317

express *v* 1265

expression *n* 1546

extend *v* 1473

extended *j* 4139

extension *n* 3217

extensive *j* 2816

extent *n* 1753

external *j* 2851

extra *j* 1576

extraordinary *j* 2630

extreme *j* 2529

extremely *r* 1745

eye *n* 246

eyebrow *n* 4593

F

fabric *n* 3165

face *v* 561

face *n* 335

facilitate *v* 3640

facility *n* 1327

fact *n* 232

factor *n* 745

factory *n* 2170

faculty *n* 2204

fade *v* 2949

fail *v* 816

failure *n* 1372

faint *j* 4269

fair *j* 1348

fairly *r* 2160

faith *n* 1434

fall *n* 1040

fall *v* 418

false *j* 2537

fame *n* 3293

familiar *j* 1511

family *n* 149

famous *j* 1499

fan *n* 1253

fantastic *j* 4861

fantasy *n* 3008

far *j* 977

far *c* 2168

far *r* 257

fare *n* 4789

farm *n* 1305

farmer *n* 1655

fascinating *j* 4252

fashion *n* 1981

fast *r* 1570

fast *j* 2591

faster *j* 4622

faster *r* 2858

fat *j* 2381

fat *n* 1675

fatal *j* 4951

fate *n* 2959

father *n* 278

fatigue *n* 4880

fault *n* 2821

favor *n* 3407

favor *i* 3468

favor *v* 2493

favorable *j* 4807

favorite *n* 2913

favorite *j* 1633

fear *v* 1681

fear *n* 1005

feather *n* 4625

feature *v* 1775

feature *n* 1222

federal *j* 500

federation *n* 4464

fee *n* 408

feed *v* 1355

feedback *n* 4160

feel *n* 4008

feel *v* 136

feeling *n* 809

fellow *n* 3004

fellow *j* 2461

female *n* 2102

female *j* 1448
feminist *j* 4923
fence *n* 2673
festival *n* 2649
fever *n* 4409
few *d* 191
fewer *d* 2003
fiber *n* 2686
fiction *n* 2930
field *n* 448
fierce *j* 4513
fifteen *m* 3032
fifth *m* 2536
fifty *m* 3071
fight *v* 672
fight *n* 1580
fighter *n* 3040
fighting *n* 3278
figure *v* 1108
figure *n* 557
file *n* 1905
file *v* 1879
fill *v* 685
film *n* 604
filter *n* 4520
final *n* 3653
final *j* 898
finally *r* 479
finance *n* 2863
finance *v* 3467
financial *j* 892
find *v* 97
finding *n* 1551
fine *j* 708
finger *n* 1067
finish *n* 3891
finish *v* 923
fire *n* 652
fire *v* 1489
firm *j* 3303
firm *n* 925
firmly *r* 3848
first *m* 88
fiscal *j* 3713
fish *n* 992
fisherman *n* 4500
fishing *n* 2141
fist *n* 3925
fit *j* 3557

fit *v* 1381
fitness *n* 3872
five *m* 301
fix *v* 1873
fixed *j* 4330
flag *n* 2480
flame *n* 3202
flash *n* 4125
flash *v* 3553
flat *j* 2597
flavor *n* 3221
flee *v* 2982
fleet *n* 4600
flesh *n* 3224
flexibility *n* 4312
flexible *j* 4241
flight *n* 1306
flip *v* 4042
float *v* 3168
flood *n* 3561
flood *v* 4545
floor *n* 640
flour *n* 3637
flow *n* 2002
flow *v* 2794
flower *n* 1537
fluid *n* 3910
fly *n* 3233
fly *v* 945
flying *j* 4936
focus *v* 704
focus *n* 1465
fog *n* 4933
fold *v* 3538
folk *n* 1388
follow *v* 331
following *j* 1482
food *n* 384
fool *n* 4068
foot *n* 1399
football *n* 1571
for *c* 2324
for *i* 13
forbid *v* 4741
force *v* 855
force *n* 367
forehead *n* 3852
foreign *j* 698
foreigner *n* 4907

forest *n* 1158
forever *r* 2099
forget *v* 877
forgive *v* 3672
fork *n* 4116
form *v* 897
form *n* 526
formal *j* 2215
format *n* 3817
formation *n* 3079
former *d* 451
formerly *r* 4687
formula *n* 3351
forth *r* 1833
fortunately *r* 4309
fortune *n* 2832
forty *m* 3790
forum *n* 3458
forward *r* 834
foster *v* 4413
found *v* 2681
foundation *n* 1338
founder *n* 2865
four *m* 253
fourth *m* 1592
fraction *n* 4753
fragile *j* 4784
fragment *n* 4856
frame *v* 3956
frame *n* 1952
framework *n* 3020
franchise *n* 4494
frankly *r* 3580
fraud *n* 3603
free *v* 2857
free *j* 490
freedom *n* 1166
freely *r* 4774
freeze *v* 2875
French *n* 3095
French *j* 1396
frequency *n* 3117
frequent *j* 3291
frequently *r* 1813
fresh *j* 1173
freshman *n* 4760
friend *n* 273
friendly *j* 2757
friendship *n* 3091

from *i* 27
front *j* 1252
front *n* 1516
front *i* 1107
frontier *n* 4621
frozen *j* 3865
fruit *n* 1723
frustrate *v* 4866
frustration *n* 3263
fuel *n* 1651
full *j* 513
full-time *j* 4024
fully *r* 1503
fun *n* 1919
fun *j* 2127
function *v* 3259
function *n* 1443
functional *j* 4321
fund *v* 3085
fund *n* 805
fundamental *j* 2341
funding *n* 2189
funeral *n* 2917
funny *j* 1841
fur *n* 4773
furniture *n* 2743
furthermore *r* 3213
future *j* 1285
future *n* 660

G

gain *v* 1264
gain *n* 2232
galaxy *n* 3805
gallery *n* 2379
gallon *n* 4307
game *n* 287
gang *n* 2623
gap *n* 2136
garage *n* 3226
garbage *n* 3926
garden *n* 1130
garlic *n* 3139
gas *n* 1083
gasoline *n* 4141
gate *n* 2005
gather *v* 1375
gathering *n* 4049
gay *j* 2098

gaze *v* 4452
gaze *n* 3531
gear *n* 2734
gender *n* 1922
gene *n* 2376
general *j* 585
general *n* 1416
generally *r* 1212
generate *v* 1706
generation *n* 1037
generous *j* 3950
genetic *j* 2797
genius *n* 4101
genre *n* 4673
gentle *j* 3717
gentleman *n* 2506
gently *r* 2772
genuine *j* 3783
German *n* 3179
German *j* 1829
gesture *n* 2989
get *v* 41
ghost *n* 3348
giant *j* 2579
gift *n* 1424
girl *n* 381
girlfriend *n* 3232
give *v* 98
given *j* 3019
glad *j* 2281
glance *n* 3762
glance *v* 2510
glass *n* 833
glimpse *n* 4633
global *j* 1223
globe *n* 3625
glory *n* 4148
glove *n* 3080
go *v* 36
goal *n* 689
goat *n* 4779
God *n* 3010
gold *n* 1284
golden *j* 1883
golf *n* 1998
good *j* 111
goods *n* 2282
gospel *n* 4272
govern *v* 3750

government *n* 208
governor *n* 1228
grab *v* 1532
grade *n* 1507
gradually *r* 2971
graduate *n* 2169
graduate *v* 2656
graduation *n* 4892
grain *n* 3268
gram *n* 4425
grand *j* 1526
grandchild *n* 4989
grandfather *n* 2977
grandmother *n* 2545
grant *v* 1904
grape *n* 4871
graph *n* 4532
grasp *v* 4227
grass *n* 2034
grateful *j* 3734
grave *n* 3402
gravity *n* 4142
gray *j* 2115
great *j* 163
greatest *j* 1602
greatly *r* 3437
Greek *j* 4137
green *n* 2243
green *j* 935
greet *v* 3512
grief *n* 4161
grill *n* 4548
grin *n* 4680
grin *v* 4229
grip *n* 3763
grocery *n* 3377
gross *j* 4379
ground *n* 529
group *n* 167
grow *v* 356
growing *j* 1441
growth *n* 792
guarantee *v* 2735
guarantee *n* 4757
guard *v* 3719
guard *n* 1314
guess *v* 853
guest *n* 1344
guidance *n* 3943

guide *v* 3014
guide *n* 1807
guideline *n* 3076
guilt *n* 3688
guilty *j* 2089
guitar *n* 3928
gulf *n* 2909
gun *n* 856
gut *n* 4373
guy *n* 386
gym *n* 3993

H

habit *n* 2356
habitat *n* 3440
hair *n* 618
half *d* 551
half *n* 1639
halfway *r* 4715
hall *n* 990
hallway *n* 3703
hammer *n* 4857
hand *v* 2043
hand *n* 175
handful *n* 3147
handle *n* 4011
handle *v* 1250
handsome *j* 3890
hang *v* 878
happen *v* 220
happily *r* 4724
happiness *n* 3985
happy *j* 755
harassment *n* 4406
harbor *n* 3477
hard *j* 531
hard *r* 929
harder *j* 3544
harder *r* 3881
hardly *r* 1742
hardware *n* 4168
harm *n* 3727
harm *v* 4364
harmony *n* 4745
harsh *j* 3541
hat *n* 2030
hate *v* 1545
haul *v* 4213
have *v* 8

hazard *n* 4916
he *p* 15
head *v* 954
head *n* 256
headache *n* 4845
headline *n* 3313
headquarters *n* 2880
heal *v* 4480
health *n* 365
healthy *j* 1515
hear *v* 198
hearing *n* 1722
heart *n* 471
heat *v* 4191
heat *n* 1058
heaven *n* 2651
heavily *r* 2370
heavy *j* 1012
heel *n* 3175
height *n* 2092
helicopter *n* 3129
hell *n* 1485
hello *u* 2456
helmet *n* 4510
help *n* 901
help *v* 176
helpful *j* 3114
hence *r* 3631
her *a* 45
her *p* 108
herb *n* 3683
here *r* 96
heritage *n* 3236
hero *n* 1941
hers *p* 3942
herself *p* 804
hesitate *v* 3964
hey *u* 1480
hi *u* 2143
hidden *j* 4198
hide *v* 1279
high *r* 3347
high *j* 142
high-tech *j* 4471
highlight *v* 3482
highly *r* 1330
highway *n* 1951
hill *n* 1024
him *p* 69

himself *p* 369
hint *n* 3987
hip *n* 2694
hire *v* 1500
his *p* 1896
his *a* 26
Hispanic *j* 3735
historian *n* 2587
historic *j* 2561
historical *j* 1495
historically *r* 3878
history *n* 354
hit *v* 549
hit *n* 2264
hockey *n* 4552
hold *n* 2905
hold *v* 217
hole *n* 1251
holiday *n* 1989
holy *j* 2467
home *r* 413
home *n* 229
homeland *n* 4140
homeless *j* 3316
homework *n* 4932
honest *j* 2577
honey *n* 2980
honor *v* 2761
honor *n* 2108
hook *n* 3846
hook *v* 4052
hope *n* 1186
hope *v* 491
hopefully *r* 4057
horizon *n* 3178
hormone *n* 4587
horn *n* 3667
horrible *j* 3797
horror *n* 3334
horse *n* 1292
hospital *n* 667
host *v* 3439
host *n* 1895
hostage *n* 3638
hostile *j* 4138
hot *j* 725
hotel *n* 1022
hour *n* 279
house *v* 2678

house *n* 151
household *n* 2056
housing *n* 2209
how *r* 78
however *r* 274
hug *v* 3892
huge *j* 926
huh *u* 4032
human *n* 1744
human *j* 406
humanity *n* 3661
humor *n* 3133
hundred *m* 1203
hunger *n* 4638
hungry *j* 3200
hunt *v* 3608
hunter *n* 3145
hunting *n* 2967
hurricane *n* 2896
hurry *v* 3643
hurt *v* 1160
husband *n* 656
hypothesis *n* 3404

I

I *p* 11
ice *n* 1267
icon *n* 4596
idea *n* 318
ideal *n* 4456
ideal *j* 2792
identical *j* 3839
identification *n* 3321
identify *v* 780
identity *n* 1361
ideological *j* 4209
ideology *n* 3664
if *c* 42
ignore *v* 1406
ill *j* 3016
illegal *j* 2085
illness *n* 2424
illusion *n* 4350
illustrate *v* 2357
illustration *n* 3057
image *n* 566
imagination *n* 2944
imagine *v* 922
immediate *j* 2186

immediately *r* 1156
immigrant *n* 2202
immigration *n* 2575
immune *j* 4372
impact *n* 940
implement *v* 2327
implementation *n* 3607
implication *n* 2451
imply *v* 2777
import *n* 4123
importance *n* 1589
important *j* 270
importantly *r* 4908
impose *v* 2325
impossible *j* 1610
impress *v* 3068
impression *n* 2534
impressive *j* 3317
improve *v* 1019
improved *j* 4131
improvement *n* 1961
impulse *n* 4709
in *c* 3035
in *i* 6
in *r* 128
inadequate *j* 4997
incentive *n* 2775
inch *n* 1393
incident *n* 1965
include *v* 300
including *i* 398
income *n* 1146
incorporate *v* 2624
increase *n* 1273
increase *v* 659
increased *j* 2011
increasing *j* 2366
increasingly *r* 1601
incredible *j* 3067
incredibly *r* 4315
indeed *r* 845
independence *n* 2306
independent *j* 1266
index *n* 2732
Indian *n* 2472
Indian *j* 1565
indicate *v* 791
indication *n* 3385
indicator *n* 3959

indigenous *j* 4022
individual *n* 767
individual *j* 984
industrial *j* 1913
industry *n* 550
inevitable *j* 3564
inevitably *r* 4634
infant *n* 3106
infection *n* 2872
inflation *n* 3212
influence *v* 1806
influence *n* 1415
influential *j* 4288
inform *v* 2214
informal *j* 4543
information *n* 313
infrastructure *n* 3809
ingredient *n* 2693
inherent *j* 4915
inherit *v* 4573
initial *j* 1957
initially *r* 2729
initiate *v* 3520
initiative *n* 2192
injure *v* 3741
injury *n* 1619
inmate *n* 4108
inn *n* 4259
inner *j* 2470
innocent *j* 2776
innovation *n* 3786
innovative *j* 4492
input *n* 4181
inquiry *n* 3392
insect *n* 3644
insert *v* 4319
inside *n* 3968
inside *i* 976
inside *r* 1318
insight *n* 2879
insist *v* 1386
inspection *n* 3595
inspector *n* 3457
inspiration *n* 4134
inspire *v* 2368
install *v* 2647
installation *n* 4539
instance *n* 2965
instant *j* 4506

instant *n* 4738

instantly *r* 4221

instead *i* 1084

instead *r* 1023

instinct *n* 4283

institute *n* 1288

institution *n* 1027

institutional *j* 3315

instruct *v* 4262

instruction *n* 1630

instructional *j* 4882

instructor *n* 3445

instrument *n* 1684

insurance *n* 1238

intact *j* 4682

integrate *v* 3488

integrated *j* 4812

integration *n* 3610

integrity *n* 3446

intellectual *j* 2870

intellectual *n* 4630

intelligence *n* 1413

intelligent *j* 3758

intend *v* 1560

intense *j* 2322

intensity *n* 3387

intent *n* 3975

intention *n* 2554

interact *v* 4441

interaction *n* 2120

interest *n* 422

interested *j* 1297

interesting *j* 1099

interfere *v* 4437

interior *j* 3961

interior *n* 3516

internal *j* 1734

international *j* 517

Internet *n* 1470

interpret *v* 2754

interpretation *n* 2354

interrupt *v* 3421

interval *n* 4671

intervention *n* 2084

interview *v* 2253

interview *n* 997

intimate *j* 4285

into *i* 67

introduce *v* 1236

introduction *n* 2916

invade *v* 4428

invasion *n* 3239

invent *v* 3426

invention *n* 4819

inventory *n* 4067

invest *v* 2080

investigate *v* 1828

investigation *n* 1185

investigator *n* 2344

investment *n* 1087

investor *n* 1819

invisible *j* 3851

invitation *n* 4117

invite *v* 1620

involve *v* 655

involved *j* 1174

involvement *n* 2374

Iraqi *n* 4820

Iraqi *j* 1539

Irish *j* 3144

iron *n* 2305

ironically *r* 4770

irony *n* 4365

Islam *n* 3748

Islamic *j* 2751

island *n* 828

isolate *v* 3980

isolated *j* 4576

isolation *n* 4279

Israeli *n* 3823

Israeli *j* 2097

issue *v* 1857

issue *n* 251

it *p* 10

Italian *j* 2700

item *n* 1075

its *a* 79

itself *p* 555

J

jacket *n* 2321

jail *n* 2547

Japanese *n* 3736

Japanese *j* 1685

jar *n* 4313

jaw *n* 4128

jazz *n* 3034

jeans *n* 3591

jet *n* 2455

jewelry *n* 4359

Jewish *j* 1851

job *n* 248

join *v* 514

joint *j* 2224

joke *v* 4632

joke *n* 2272

journal *n* 1527

journalism *n* 4707

journalist *n* 2146

journey *n* 2479

joy *n* 2893

judge *v* 1757

judge *n* 1140

judgment *n* 1912

judicial *j* 4065

juice *n* 2429

jump *n* 4341

jump *v* 1376

jungle *n* 4527

junior *j* 2527

jurisdiction *n* 4887

juror *n* 3866

jury *n* 1607

just *j* 1856

just *r* 68

justice *n* 961

justify *v* 2806

K

keep *v* 161

key *j* 1120

key *n* 1484

kick *v* 1852

kid *n* 322

kill *v* 426

killer *n* 2672

killing *n* 3285

kind *n* 249

king *n* 947

kingdom *n* 4696

kiss *n* 4001

kiss *v* 2304

kit *n* 4072

kitchen *n* 1074

knee *n* 1528

kneel *v* 4049

knife *n* 2269

knock *v* 2111
know *v* 49
knowledge *n* 847
known *j* 4415
Korean *j* 3614

L

lab *n* 2154
label *v* 3602
label *n* 2619
labor *n* 1153
laboratory *n* 2339
lack *n* 1245
lack *v* 1999
ladder *n* 4511
lady *n* 1093
lake *n* 1068
lamp *n* 3938
land *n* 583
land *v* 2075
landing *n* 3873
landmark *n* 4736
landscape *n* 1996
lane *n* 2931
language *n* 727
lap *n* 3391
large *j* 225
largely *r* 1703
laser *n* 4096
last *v* 1697
last *m* 131
late *r* 1812
late *j* 439
lately *r* 4095
later *j* 2178
later *r* 297
Latin *j* 2564
latter *d* 2716
laugh *n* 3680
laugh *v* 858
laughter *n* 3395
launch *v* 1773
laundry *n* 4957
law *n* 294
lawmaker *n* 4840
lawn *n* 2994
lawsuit *n* 2646
lawyer *n* 862
lay *v* 810

layer *n* 2258
lead *n* 1605
lead *v* 319
leader *n* 466
leadership *n* 1325
leading *j* 2188
leaf *n* 1613
league *n* 1234
lean *v* 1534
leap *v* 3652
learn *v* 321
learning *n* 1587
least *r* 306
leather *n* 3018
leave *v* 152
leave *n* 4822
lecture *n* 3589
left *j* 788
leg *n* 880
legacy *n* 3216
legal *j* 900
legally *r* 4594
legend *n* 3546
legislation *n* 2029
legislative *j* 3588
legislator *n* 4644
legislature *n* 3337
legitimate *j* 3187
lemon *n* 3378
lend *v* 3632
length *n* 1876
lens *n* 4979
less *d* 621
less *r* 481
lesson *n* 1384
let *v* 158
letter *n* 629
level *n* 345
level *j* 4815
liability *n* 4380
liberal *n* 4675
liberal *j* 2037
liberation *n* 4791
liberty *n* 2692
library *n* 1687
license *n* 2845
lid *n* 4705
lie *n* 2866
lie *v* 751

lieutenant *n* 3847
life *n* 115
lifestyle *n* 3241
lifetime *n* 2815
lift *v* 1367
light *j* 1341
light *v* 2395
light *i* 4775
light *n* 467
lightly *r* 3500
lightning *n* 4557
like *c* 1168
like *j* 1713
like *r* 2742
like *i* 75
like *v* 212
likelihood *n* 4674
likely *r* 2840
likely *j* 633
likewise *r* 4579
limb *n* 3962
limit *n* 1665
limit *v* 1360
limitation *n* 3047
limited *j* 1987
line *v* 2515
line *n* 283
link *n* 2223
link *v* 1740
lion *n* 3193
lip *n* 1624
liquid *n* 4446
liquid *j* 4793
list *n* 758
list *v* 2093
listen *v* 619
listener *n* 4768
literally *r* 2483
literary *j* 2918
literature *n* 1575
little *d* 843
little *r* 440
little *j* 262
live *j* 2094
live *v* 219
liver *n* 4767
living *j* 2090
living *n* 1345
load *v* 2961

load *n* 3026
loan *n* 1767
lobby *n* 3791
local *j* 430
locate *v* 1701
location *n* 1467
lock *v* 2237
lock *n* 3824
log *n* 3493
logic *n* 3506
logical *j* 4556
lonely *j* 4020
long *c* 1826
long *r* 267
long *j* 258
long-term *j* 1844
longtime *j* 4077
look *n* 612
look *v* 87
loop *n* 4389
loose *j* 2850
lord *n* 2565
lose *v* 289
loss *n* 801
lost *j* 2702
lot *n* 244
lots *p* 1564
loud *j* 4282
loud *r* 3896
love *n* 594
love *v* 401
lovely *j* 3325
lover *n* 2787
low *r* 4844
low *j* 371
lower *v* 2086
loyal *j* 4782
loyalty *n* 4070
luck *n* 2420
lucky *j* 2148
lunch *n* 1616
lung *n* 3294

M

machine *n* 1031
mad *j* 2599
magazine *n* 1010
magic *j* 3469
magic *n* 3965

magnitude *n* 4232
mail *n* 2502
main *j* 890
mainly *r* 2789
mainstream *j* 3579
maintain *v* 918
maintenance *n* 3078
major *n* 3246
major *j* 441
majority *n* 1098
make *v* 46
maker *n* 2373
makeup *n* 3794
male *j* 1561
male *n* 1803
mall *n* 3112
mama *n* 3103
man *n* 95
manage *v* 965
management *n* 914
manager *n* 873
mandate *n* 3737
manipulate *v* 4236
manner *n* 1822
mansion *n* 4831
manufacturer *n* 2252
manufacturing *n* 3251
many *d* 101
map *n* 1598
marble *n* 4966
march *v* 3534
margin *n* 3367
marine *j* 2744
marine *n* 4055
mark *n* 2345
mark *v* 1700
marker *n* 4929
market *v* 2786
market *n* 414
marketing *n* 2315
marketplace *n* 4568
marriage *n* 1070
married *j* 1648
marry *v* 1370
mask *n* 3188
mass *n* 2022
mass *j* 2150
massive *j* 2033
master *n* 1420

match *v* 1995
match *n* 2721
mate *n* 4186
material *n* 642
math *n* 3170
mathematics *n* 4837
matter *v* 1784
matter *n* 524
matter *d* 3788
maximum *j* 3655
may *v* 122
maybe *r* 390
mayor *n* 1625
me *p* 65
meal *n* 1751
mean *j* 1937
mean *v* 157
meaning *n* 1618
meaningful *j* 3854
means *n* 1452
meanwhile *r* 1885
measure *v* 1403
measure *n* 963
measurement *n* 3320
meat *n* 1842
mechanic *n* 4382
mechanical *j* 4007
mechanism *n* 2670
medal *n* 3529
media *n* 771
medical *j* 662
medication *n* 3289
medicine *n* 1505
medium *n* 3492
medium *j* 3887
meet *v* 292
meeting *n* 776
melt *v* 3556
member *n* 291
membership *n* 3092
memorial *n* 2903
memory *n* 913
mental *j* 1692
mentally *r* 4427
mention *v* 994
mention *n* 4893
mentor *n* 4732
menu *n* 3248
merchant *n* 4136

mere *j* 2946

merely *r* 1992

merger *n* 4996

merit *n* 4484

mess *n* 3448

message *n* 812

metal *n* 1604

metaphor *n* 3976

meter *n* 3186

method *n* 1008

metropolitan *j* 4346

Mexican *j* 2300

middle *j* 999

middle *n* 1280

middle-class *j* 4891

midnight *n* 3480

midst *n* 4353

might *v* 184

migration *n* 4743

mild *j* 3912

mile *n* 643

military *j* 499

military *n* 3436

militia *n* 4948

milk *n* 2091

mill *n* 3514

million *m* 260

mind *v* 2081

mind *n* 477

mine *p* 2261

mine *n* 2531

mineral *n* 4786

minimal *j* 4300

minimize *v* 3983

minimum *n* 4371

minimum *j* 3552

minister *n* 1249

ministry *n* 2801

minor *j* 2610

minority *n* 1536

minute *n* 323

miracle *n* 3314

mirror *n* 1865

miss *v* 806

missile *n* 2265

missing *j* 3600

mission *n* 1121

mistake *n* 1454

mix *v* 1809

mix *n* 2947

mixed *j* 4231

mixture *n* 2543

mm-hmm *u* 3060

mobile *j* 4800

mode *n* 2810

model *n* 518

model *v* 4549

moderate *j* 3323

modern *j* 1063

modest *j* 3128

modify *v* 4228

mom *n* 1054

moment *n* 375

momentum *n* 4485

money *n* 236

monitor *v* 2363

monitor *n* 3104

monkey *n* 4580

monster *n* 3620

month *n* 243

monthly *j* 3577

monument *n* 4238

mood *n* 2389

moon *n* 1718

moral *j* 1496

more *d* 93

more *r* 82

moreover *r* 2283

morning *n* 358

mortality *n* 4935

mortgage *n* 3543

most *d* 190

most *r* 145

mostly *r* 1352

mother *n* 240

motion *n* 1848

motivate *v* 3582

motivation *n* 3299

motive *n* 3697

motor *n* 2312

mount *v* 2900

mountain *n* 852

mouse *n* 3345

mouth *n* 1077

move *n* 1435

move *v* 211

movement *n* 711

movie *n* 587

much *r* 298

much *d* 147

mud *n* 3635

multiple *j* 2023

municipal *j* 4700

murder *n* 1449

murder *v* 3549

muscle *n* 1823

museum *n* 986

mushroom *n* 4448

music *n* 464

musical *j* 2567

musician *n* 3124

Muslim *j* 2707

Muslim *n* 3674

must *v* 226

mutual *j* 2849

my *a* 48

myself *p* 670

mysterious *j* 4113

mystery *n* 2386

myth *n* 3087

N

n't *x* 30

nail *n* 3615

naked *j* 3199

name *v* 826

name *n* 299

narrative *n* 3403

narrator *n* 3274

narrow *j* 2014

nasty *j* 4530

nation *n* 417

national *j* 234

nationwide *r* 4976

native *j* 1491

natural *j* 724

naturally *r* 2800

nature *n* 692

naval *j* 4975

navy *n* 2507

near *i* 709

near *r* 4629

near *j* 4144

nearby *j* 2464

nearby *r* 3761

nearly *r* 610

neat *j* 4694

necessarily *r* 1963

necessary *j* 982

necessity *n* 3952

neck *n* 1555

need *n* 556

need *v* 134

needle *n* 3822

negative *j* 1504

negotiate *v* 2533

negotiation *n* 2251

neighbor *n* 1468

neighborhood *n* 1151

neighboring *j* 4805

neither *r* 1787

neither *d* 2951

nerve *n* 3353

nervous *j* 2406

nest *n* 4343

net *j* 3498

net *n* 2940

network *n* 894

neutral *j* 4251

never *r* 140

nevertheless *r* 2559

new *j* 90

newly *r* 2791

news *n* 364

newspaper *n* 1123

next *i* 1524

next *m* 222

nice *j* 911

night *n* 214

nightmare *n* 3621

nine *m* 1183

no *r* 627

no *p* 732

no *d* 3787

no *u* 276

no *a* 86

nobody *p* 1154

nod *v* 1586

noise *n* 2020

nominate *v* 4985

nomination *n* 3331

nominee *n* 4298

none *p* 1105

nonetheless *r* 3306

nonprofit *j* 4799

noon *n* 4038

nor *c* 1062

norm *n* 3449

normal *j* 1247

normally *r* 2606

north *n* 593

northeast *n* 4192

northern *j* 1577

northwest *n* 3470

nose *n* 1766

not *c* 2887

not *x* 29

note *n* 943

note *v* 706

notebook *n* 4672

nothing *p* 314

notice *v* 1060

notice *n* 3647

notion *n* 1729

novel *n* 1774

now *c* 1887

now *r* 72

nowhere *r* 2953

nuclear *j* 1199

number *n* 206

numerous *j* 2276

nurse *n* 1964

nut *n* 3229

nutrition *n* 4348

O

o'clock *r* 4018

oak *n* 3110

object *n* 1197

object *v* 4266

objection *n* 4711

objective *n* 2392

objective *j* 4998

obligation *n* 3009

observation *n* 2135

observe *v* 1315

observer *n* 2511

obstacle *n* 3581

obtain *v* 1597

obvious *j* 1708

obviously *r* 1302

occasion *n* 2277

occasional *j* 3550

occasionally *r* 2509

occupation *n* 3361

occupy *v* 2733

occur *v* 747

ocean *n* 1906

odd *j* 2774

odds *n* 3300

of *i* 4

off *r* 210

off *i* 392

offender *n* 4735

offense *n* 2897

offensive *j* 3255

offer *n* 2110

offer *v* 376

offering *n* 4031

office *n* 343

officer *n* 681

official *n* 534

official *j* 1845

officially *r* 4110

often *r* 280

oh *u* 419

oil *n* 578

ok *r* 872

ok *j* 3058

okay *r* 1730

okay *j* 3454

old *j* 154

old-fashioned *j* 4839

Olympic *j* 2746

Olympics *n* 3843

on *r* 155

on *i* 17

once *c* 1209

once *r* 303

one *n* 838

one *m* 52

one *p* 106

one-third *m* 4833

ongoing *j* 3115

onion *n* 2709

online *j* 2860

online *r* 3686

only *r* 102

only *j* 333

onto *i* 946

open *j* 589

open *v* 359

opening *n* 1962

openly *r* 4512

opera *n* 3073

operate *v* 1311

operating *n* 3264

operation *n* 823

operator *n* 3228

opinion *n* 1138

opponent *n* 2196

opportunity *n* 634

oppose *v* 1954

opposed *i* 4207

opposite *j* 2287

opposition *n* 1858

opt *v* 4765

optimistic *j* 4150

option *n* 1139

or *c* 32

oral *j* 4017

orange *j* 3207

orange *n* 3342

orbit *n* 4586

orchestra *n* 4304

order *v* 1353

order *n* 675

ordinary *j* 2274

organ *n* 3430

organic *j* 3237

organism *n* 4589

organization *n* 598

organizational *j* 4571

organize *v* 1649

organized *j* 4874

orientation *n* 3335

origin *n* 2578

original *j* 1141

originally *r* 2864

other *p* 713

other *i* 2362

other *j* 76

otherwise *r* 1530

ought *v* 1732

ounce *n* 4257

our *a* 81

ours *p* 4098

ourselves *p* 1789

out *r* 66

out *i* 150

outcome *n* 1831

outdoor *j* 3724

outer *j* 3760

outfit *n* 4496

outlet *n* 4692

outline *v* 4426

outlook *n* 4412

output *n* 4172

outside *j* 2060

outside *r* 1756

outside *i* 815

outsider *n* 4508

outstanding *j* 4013

oven *n* 3050

over *r* 183

over *i* 124

overall *j* 1997

overall *r* 4004

overcome *v* 2717

overlook *v* 3171

overnight *r* 4804

oversee *v* 4462

overwhelm *v* 4852

overwhelming *j* 3598

owe *v* 3022

own *v* 1148

own *d* 148

owner *n* 1033

ownership *n* 3639

oxygen *n* 3923

P

pace *n* 2553

pack *n* 2773

pack *v* 2313

package *n* 1731

pad *n* 3798

page *n* 716

pain *n* 968

painful *j* 3101

paint *v* 1783

paint *n* 2969

painter *n* 3698

painting *n* 1354

pair *n* 1513

palace *n* 3483

pale *j* 2968

Palestinian *j* 2642

Palestinian *n* 3203

pan *n* 2570

panel *n* 1686

panic *n* 4410

pants *n* 2759

paper *n* 533

parade *n* 3930

paradise *n* 4984

parent *n* 340

parental *j* 4303

park *v* 3399

park *n* 615

parking *n* 2371

parliament *n* 3627

part *n* 180

part *i* 4643

partial *j* 4524

partially *r* 4391

participant *n* 1195

participate *v* 1506

participation *n* 2268

particle *n* 3997

particular *j* 952

particularly *r* 782

partly *r* 2826

partner *n* 1110

partnership *n* 2972

party *n* 355

pass *v* 444

pass *n* 2351

passage *n* 2236

passenger *n* 2105

passing *j* 4390

passion *n* 2301

past *r* 3673

past *i* 1417

past *j* 687

past *n* 991

pasta *n* 4751

pastor *n* 4289

pat *v* 4597

patch *n* 3366

patent *n* 4525

path *n* 1368

patience *n* 4177

patient *j* 3726

patient *n* 639

patrol *n* 4202

patron *n* 4848

pattern *n* 1029

pause *n* 3850

pause *v* 2839

pay *v* 293

pay *n* 2740

payment *n* 2151

peace *n* 934

peaceful *j* 3660

peak *n* 2431

peanut *n* 4860

peasant *n* 4691

peel *v* 4015

peer *v* 3475

peer *n* 2555

pen *n* 3616

penalty *n* 2664

pencil *n* 4665

pension *n* 3782

people *n* 63

pepper *n* 2073

perceive *v* 2212

perceived *j* 4821

percent *n* 197

percentage *n* 1830

perception *n* 1900

perfect *j* 1205

perfectly *r* 2453

perform *v* 981

performance *n* 700

performer *n* 4071

perhaps *r* 436

period *n* 616

permanent *j* 2485

permission *n* 3253

permit *n* 4863

permit *v* 2104

Persian *j* 4302

persist *v* 4399

person *n* 348

personal *j* 581

personality *n* 2096

personally *r* 2640

personnel *n* 2448

perspective *n* 1439

persuade *v* 3296

pet *n* 3359

phase *n* 2248

phenomenon *n* 2460

philosophical *j* 4723

philosophy *n* 2278

phone *n* 574

photo *n* 445

photograph *n* 832

photograph *v* 1884

photographer *n* 3328

photography *n* 4491

phrase *n* 2638

physical *j* 930

physically *r* 3310

physician *n* 2118

physics *n* 4035

piano *n* 3389

pick *v* 532

pickup *n* 4132

picture *n* 562

pie *n* 3415

piece *n* 575

pig *n* 3527

pile *v* 4616

pile *n* 3064

pill *n* 3451

pillow *n* 4092

pilot *n* 1800

pin *n* 4394

pine *n* 3214

pink *j* 2539

pioneer *n* 4489

pipe *n* 3055

pit *n* 3921

pitch *v* 3575

pitch *n* 3360

pitcher *n* 3566

pizza *n* 4044

place *n* 186

place *v* 638

placement *n* 4541

plain *n* 3456

plain *j* 3605

plan *n* 421

plan *v* 694

plane *n* 1169

planet *n* 1763

planner *n* 4577

planning *n* 2176

plant *v* 2576

plant *n* 648

plastic *n* 1553

plate *n* 1540

platform *n* 2827

play *v* 209

play *n* 973

player *n* 540

playoff *n* 3879

plaza *n* 4910

plea *n* 4883

plead *v* 3559

pleasant *j* 3795

please *v* 4089

please *r* 1198

pleased *j* 3455

pleasure *n* 1878

plenty *p* 2078

plot *n* 2999

plunge *v* 4636

plus *i* 1928

PM *r* 960

pocket *n* 1642

poem *n* 2550

poet *n* 2970

poetry *n* 2990

point *n* 218

point *v* 613

poke *v* 4756

pole *n* 2869

police *n* 473

policeman *n* 4710

policy *n* 396

political *j* 282

politically *r* 2818

politician *n* 1795

politics *n* 964

poll *n* 1632

pollution *n* 2993

pond *n* 3670

pool *n* 1574

poor *j* 718

pop *n* 3630

pop *v* 2608

pope *n* 3876

popular *j* 928

popularity *n* 3958

population *n* 651

porch *n* 3099

pork *n* 4504

port *n* 2764

portfolio *n* 4187

portion *n* 2195

portrait *n* 2876

portray *v* 3277

pose *v* 2247

position *v* 4248

position *n* 519

positive *j* 1085

possess *v* 2895

possession *n* 3666

possibility *n* 1206

possible *j* 458

possibly *r* 1704

post *v* 4194

poster *n* 3880

pot *n* 2310

potato *n* 2311

potential *n* 2082

potential *j* 1286

potentially *r* 2888

pound *n* 1332

pour *v* 1921

poverty *n* 2365

powder *n* 3459

power *n* 275

powerful *j* 1175

practical *j* 2291

practically *r* 3922

practice *v* 2912

practice *n* 573

practitioner *n* 4395

praise *n* 4954

praise *v* 3759

pray *v* 2473

prayer *n* 2191

preach *v* 4991

precious *j* 4039

precise *j* 3831

precisely *r* 2598

predict *v* 1635

prediction *n* 3662

prefer *v* 1735

preference *n* 3075

pregnancy *n* 3364

pregnant *j* 2663

preliminary *j* 4403

premise *n* 4547

premium *n* 4912

preparation *n* 2563

prepare *v* 779

prescription *n* 3427

presence *n* 1287

present *j* 1328

present *v* 824

present *n* 2240

presentation *n* 2939

preserve *v* 2227

presidency *n* 3466

president *n* 160

presidential *j* 1664

press *v* 1549

press *n* 781

pressure *n* 761

presumably *r* 4290

pretend *v* 2945

pretty *r* 807

pretty *j* 2530

prevail *v* 4748

prevent *v* 1100

prevention *n* 3185

previous *j* 1321

previously *r* 2336

price *n* 498

pride *n* 2852

priest *n* 2352

primarily *r* 2124

primary *n* 4104

primary *j* 1529

prime *j* 1666

prince *n* 2416

princess *n* 3947

principal *j* 3302

principal *n* 3358

principle *n* 1356

print *v* 3206

print *n* 2372

prior *i* 2902

prior *j* 4212

priority *n* 2125

prison *n* 1300

prisoner *n* 2426

privacy *n* 3120

private *j* 626

privately *r* 4713

privilege *n* 3573

prize *n* 2722

pro *j* 4509

pro *n* 4158

probably *r* 399

problem *n* 170

procedure *n* 1391

proceed *v* 2685

process *n* 391

process *v* 2788

processing *n* 4088

processor *n* 4920

proclaim *v* 4476

produce *v* 546

producer *n* 1854

product *n* 571

production *n* 974

productive *j* 3978

productivity *n* 4164

profession *n* 2957

professional *j* 1127

professional *n* 2622

professor *n* 891

profile *n* 2758

profit *n* 1738

profound *j* 3764

program *n* 203

programming *n* 4685

progress *n* 1519

progressive *j* 4235

prohibit *v* 4099

project *v* 3633

project *n* 545

projection *n* 4802

prominent *j* 2938

promise *v* 1459

promise *n* 2008

promising *j* 3897

promote *v* 1350

promotion *n* 3803

prompt *v* 3149

proof *n* 2877

proper *j* 2064

properly *r* 2908

property *n* 1014

proportion *n* 3083

proposal *n* 1609

propose *v* 1691

proposed *j* 3108

proposition *n* 4338

prosecution *n* 3464

prosecutor *n* 2161

prospect *n* 2359

protect *v* 757

protection *n* 1347

protective *j* 4214

protein *n* 2682

protest *n* 2868

protest *v* 3606

protocol *n* 4642

proud *j* 2007

prove *v* 867

provide *v* 268

provided *c* 3855

provider *n* 3311

province *n* 3322

provision *n* 2695

provoke *v* 4825

psychological *j* 2443

psychologist *n* 3356

psychology *n* 3281

public *j* 337

public *n* 846

publication *n* 2463

publicity *n* 4453

publicly *r* 3041

publish *v* 1132

publisher *n* 3273

publishing *n* 4827

pull *v* 484

pulse *n* 4507

pump *v* 4000

pump *n* 3636

punch *v* 4378

punish *v* 3868

punishment *n* 3113

purchase *n* 3126

purchase *v* 2187

pure *j* 2437

purple *j* 3946

purpose *n* 1028

purse *n* 4493

pursue *v* 1796

pursuit *n* 3894

push *v* 703

put *v* 153

puzzle *n* 4595

Q

qualify *v* 3094

quality *n* 760

quantity *n* 4074

quarter *n* 1432

quarterback *n* 3509

queen *n* 2375

quest *n* 4091

question *n* 201

question *v* 1971

questionnaire *n* 3812

quick *j* 1339

quickly *r* 678

quiet *j* 1455

quietly *r* 2546

quit *v* 2517

quite *r* 560

quote *n* 4408

quote *v* 2254

R

rabbit *n* 4368

race *n* 726

race *v* 2447

racial *j* 2294

racism *n* 3924

rack *n* 4246

radar *n* 4842

radiation *n* 3816

radical *j* 2955

radio *n* 910

rage *n* 3972

rail *n* 3418

railroad *n* 3665

rain *v* 4627

rain *n* 1569

raise *v* 437

rally *n* 4717

ranch *n* 3270

random *j* 3682

range *n* 978

range *v* 1867

rank *v* 3434

rank *n* 2671

rape *v* 4982

rape *n* 3420

rapid *j* 3051

rapidly *r* 2524

rare *j* 1901

rarely *r* 2296

rat *n* 3611

rate *n* 462

rate *v* 3230

rather *c* 2466

rather *i* 970

rather *r* 864

rating *n* 1944

ratio *n* 3118

rational *j* 4487

raw *j* 2820

reach *v* 428

reach *n* 3604

react *v* 2687

reaction *n* 1418

read *v* 346

reader *n* 1342

readily *r* 3969

reading *n* 1644

ready *j* 763

real *j* 307

realistic *j* 3974

reality *n* 1046

realize *v* 625

really *r* 144

realm *n* 3933

rear *j* 4258

reason *n* 357

reasonable *j* 2501

rebel *n* 3837

rebuild *v* 3796

recall *v* 1133

receive *v* 509

receiver *n* 3530

recent *j* 570

recently *r* 695

reception *n* 4030

recession *n* 3701

recipe *n* 2626

recipient *n* 3934

recognition *n* 2434

recognize *v* 786

recommend *v* 1721

recommendation *n* 2804

record *v* 1669

record *n* 527

recording *n* 3417

recover *v* 2163

recovery *n* 2532

recruit *v* 3376

red *j* 611

reduce *v* 705

reduction *n* 2250

refer *v* 1172

reference *n* 1934

reflect *v* 1011

reflection *n* 2836

reform *n* 1125

refrigerator *n* 4189

refuge *n* 4617

refugee *n* 2595

refuse *v* 1257

regain *v* 4870

regard *n* 4777

regard *i* 4215

regard *v* 2083

regarding *i* 2211

regardless *r* 2960

regime *n* 1872

region *n* 808

regional *j* 1707

register *v* 3220

regret *v* 4699

regular *j* 1414

regularly *r* 2819

regulate *v* 3471

regulation *n* 1739

regulator *n* 4902

regulatory *j* 4119

rehabilitation *n* 4944

reinforce *v* 3368

reject *v* 2026

relate *v* 1103

related *j* 3413

relation *n* 1128

relationship *n* 505

relative *j* 3163

relative *n* 2458

relatively *r* 1477

relax *v* 2898

release *v* 1149

release *n* 2217

relevant *j* 2837

reliability *n* 4333

reliable *j* 3554

relief *n* 1817

relieve *v* 3800

religion *n* 1460

religious *j* 950

reluctant *j* 3908

rely *v* 1860

remain *v* 431

remaining *j* 2220

remark *v* 4754

remark *n* 3424

remarkable *j* 2714

remember *v* 378

remind *v* 1494

reminder *n* 4479

remote *j* 2828

removal *n* 4776

remove *v* 889

render *v* 3578

rent *v* 3474

rent *n* 4225

rental *n* 4846

repair *n* 3940

repair *v* 3998

repeat *v* 1622

repeatedly *r* 3290

replace *v* 1193

replacement *n* 3668

reply *v* 2299

report *v* 465

report *n* 478

reportedly *r* 4407

reporter *n* 1312

reporting *n* 3919

represent *v* 682

representation *n* 2928

representative *j* 4046

representative *n* 1948

republic *n* 2123

Republican *n* 607

reputation *n* 2427

request *v* 3169

request *n* 2128

require *v* 453

required *j* 4515

requirement *n* 1890

rescue *n* 4016

rescue *v* 3883

research *n* 379

research *v* 3808

researcher *n* 1259

resemble *v* 3066

reservation *n* 3159

reserve *v* 4149

reserve *n* 2991

residence *n* 3895

resident *n* 1282

residential *j* 3935

resign *v* 3497

resist *v* 2478

resistance *n* 2239

resolution *n* 1915

resolve *v* 2234

resort *n* 2796

resource *n* 783

respect *v* 2830

respect *i* 4287

respect *n* 1566

respectively *r* 3802

respond *v* 927

respondent *n* 2641

response *i* 3693

response *n* 733

responsibility *n* 1076

responsible *j* 1374

rest *n* 668

rest *v* 1940

restaurant *n* 1150

restore *v* 2556

restrict *v* 3519

restriction *n* 3143

result *n* 374

result *v* 1379

resume *v* 3801

retail *j* 3542

retailer *n* 4651

retain *v* 2720

retire *v* 2331

retired *j* 3715

retirement *n* 2504

retreat *n* 4828

return *v* 482

return *n* 1274

reveal *v* 948

revelation *n* 4265

revenue *n* 1728

reverse *v* 3521

review *v* 2122

review *n* 1433

revolution *n* 2040

revolutionary *j* 3992

reward *v* 4470

reward *n* 3428

rhetoric *n* 3780

rhythm *n* 3479

rib *n* 4677

ribbon *n* 4946

rice *n* 2131

rich *j* 1090

rid *v* 3044

ride *v* 1373

ride *n* 2174

rider *n* 4264

ridiculous *j* 4087

rifle *n* 3195

right *j* 317

right *r* 202

right *n* 237

rigid *j* 4097

rim *n* 4877

ring *n* 1699

ring *v* 2388

riot *n* 4730

rip *v* 3681

rise *v* 734

rise *n* 1984

risk *v* 3223

risk *n* 674

risky *j* 4647

ritual *n* 3496

rival *n* 4478

river *n* 728

road *n* 515

robot *n* 4719

rock *v* 4205

rock *n* 904

rocket *n* 3292

rod *n* 3517

role *n* 460

roll *v* 1278

roll *n* 2586

rolling *j* 4440

Roman *j* 3663

romance *n* 4073

romantic *j* 3210

roof *n* 2164

room *n* 231

root *v* 4234

root *n* 1777

rope *n* 3350

rough *j* 2662

roughly *r* 2690

round *v* 4778

round *j* 2981

route *n* 2001

routine *n* 2620

routinely *r* 4739

row *n* 1850

royal *j* 2660

rub *v* 2921

rubber *j* 4803

ruin *v* 4204

rule *n* 635

rule *v* 2226

ruling *n* 4006

rumor *n* 3586

run *v* 205

run *n* 1290

runner *n* 4323

running *j* 3355

rural *j* 2052

rush *v* 1977

Russian *n* 3995

Russian *j* 1585

S

sack *n* 4544

sacred *j* 3429

sacrifice *v* 4430

sacrifice *n* 4109

sad *j* 2157

safe *j* 1217

safely *r* 4297

safety *n* 1163

sail *v* 4118

salad *n* 2911

salary *n* 2439

sale *n* 2257

salmon *n* 3511

salt *n* 1654

same *d* 162

sample *n* 1377

sanctions *n* 3134

sand *n* 2263

sandwich *n* 3659

satellite *n* 2629

satisfaction *n* 2878

satisfy *v* 2992

sauce *n* 2430

save *v* 744

savings *n* 2225

say *v* 20

scale *n* 1268

scan *v* 4129

scandal *n* 3031

scare *v* 3818

scared *j* 2988

scary *j* 4043

scatter *v* 3836

scenario *n* 2780

scene *n* 777

scent *n* 4678

schedule *n* 2171

schedule *v* 2592

scheme *n* 3033

scholar *n* 2132

scholarship *n* 3081

school *n* 129

science *n* 628

scientific *j* 1611

scientist *n* 1112

scope *n* 3267

score *n* 1122

score *v* 1926

scout *n* 3901

scramble *v* 4376

scratch *v* 4718

scream *v* 2145

screen *n* 1289

screen *v* 4958

screening *n* 4927

screw *v* 4817

script *n* 3371

scrutiny *n* 4969

sculpture *n* 3742

sea *n* 1026

seal *n* 4268

seal *v* 4081

search *n* 1702

search *v* 1737

season *n* 535

seat *v* 4284

seat *n* 906

second *n* 696

second *m* 387

secondary *j* 3523

secret *j* 2032

secret *n* 1877

secretary *n* 1214

section *n* 868

sector *n* 2042

secular *j* 4422

secure *j* 4247

secure *v* 2562

security *n* 456

see *v* 58

seed *n* 2025

seek *v* 669

seem *v* 166

seemingly *r* 3601

segment *n* 2933

seize *v* 3280

seldom *r* 4843

select *v* 1764

selection *n* 2153

self *n* 2177

self-esteem *n* 4402

sell *v* 446

seller *n* 4950

seminar *n* 4858

senate *n* 1137

senator *n* 1044

send *v* 407

senior *n* 4159

senior *j* 1113

sensation *n* 4474

sense *v* 3194

sense *n* 411

sensitive *j* 2505

sensitivity *n* 4501

sentence *n* 2048

sentiment *n* 4079

separate *j* 1882

separate *v* 1936

separation *n* 3718

sequence *n* 3173

sergeant *n* 4151

series *n* 722

serious *j* 749

seriously *r* 1907

servant *n* 4021

serve *v* 410

service *n* 269

serving *n* 3624

session *n* 1582

set *n* 871

set *v* 310

setting *n* 1797

settle *v* 1335

settlement *n* 2190

seven *m* 738

seventh *m* 4193

several *d* 311

severe *j* 2361

severely *r* 4808

sex *n* 863

sexual *j* 1171

sexuality *n* 4981

sexually *r* 4200

sexy *j* 4534

shade *n* 3072

shadow *n* 1716

shake *v* 957

shall *v* 2280

shallow *j* 4178

shame *n* 3840

shape *n* 1307

shape *v* 2457

share *n* 1313

share *v* 720

shared *j* 4084

shareholder *n* 4780

shark *n* 4683

sharp *j* 2244

sharply *r* 3941

she *p* 33

shed *v* 4418

sheep *n* 4224

sheer *j* 4208

sheet *n* 1815

shelf *n* 2979

shell *n* 2584

shelter *n* 2914

sheriff *n* 3691

shield *n* 4818

shift *v* 1725

shift *n* 2293

shine *v* 3447

ship *v* 3828

ship *n* 1263

shirt *n* 1805

shit *n* 3384

shock *v* 4094

shock *n* 2347

shoe *n* 1457

shoot *v* 739

shooting *n* 2781

shop *v* 3491

shop *n* 1371

shopping *n* 2739

shore *n* 3327

short *r* 3731

short *j* 632

short-term *j* 4417

shortage *n* 4029

shortly *r* 2862

shorts *n* 4978

shot *n* 1111

should *v* 125

shoulder *n* 1020

shout *v* 2179

shove *v* 4499

show *n* 476

show *v* 181

shower *n* 3256

shrimp *n* 4572

shrink *v* 4516

shrug *v* 3243

shut *v* 1563

shuttle *n* 3810

shy *j* 4432

sibling *n* 4563

sick *j* 1746

side *n* 252

sidewalk *n* 3813

sigh *v* 3423

sight *n* 1637

sign *v* 1007

sign *n* 765

signal *v* 3862

signal *n* 2116

signature *n* 3857

significance *n* 2943

significant *j* 731

significantly *r* 1868

silence *n* 1821

silent *j* 2180

silk *n* 4047

silly *j* 4010

silver *n* 2503

similar *j* 743

similarity *n* 4664

similarly *r* 2805

simple *j* 793

simply *r* 579

simultaneously *r* 3700

sin *n* 3460

since *r* 2997

since *i* 885

since *c* 265

sing *v* 1065

singer *n* 2962

single *j* 637

sink *n* 4078

sink *v* 2842

sister *n* 854

sit v 271
site n 547
situation n 548
six m 429
sixth m 3634
size n 759
skeptical j 4977
skill n 869
skilled j 4938
skin n 1057
skip v 4292
skirt n 3754
skull n 4328
sky n 1200
slam v 3570
slap v 4111
slave n 2833
slavery n 4763
sleep v 1184
sleep n 2055
sleeve n 4611
slice n 3489
slice v 4093
slide n 4183
slide v 2242
slight j 3023
slightly r 1440
slip v 1810
slope n 3593
slot n 4992
slow j 1770
slow v 2208
slowly r 1227
small j 207
smart j 1930
smell n 2894
smell v 2435
smile n 1478
smile v 1082
smoke n 2414
smoke v 2490
smoking n 4964
smooth j 2487
snake n 3533
snap v 2644
sneak v 4599
snow n 1853
so c 199
so r 56

so-called j 2408
soak v 4934
soap n 4369
soar v 4731
soccer n 3442
social j 338
socially r 4612
society n 510
sock n 4263
sodium n 4080
sofa n 4816
soft j 1407
softly r 4050
software n 1676
soil n 1950
solar j 3088
soldier n 1013
sole j 4560
solely r 4697
solid j 2015
solution n 1241
solve v 1855
some d 61
somebody p 1009
someday r 4445
somehow r 1663
someone p 423
something p 143
sometime r 4873
sometimes r 450
somewhat r 1869
somewhere r 1590
son n 494
song n 908
soon r 683
soon c 2497
sooner r 3906
sophisticated j 3053
sorry j 1231
sort v 4357
sort n 840
soul n 1646
sound v 895
sound n 702
soup n 3049
source n 600
south n 661
southeast n 3833
southern j 1136

southwest n 3722
Soviet j 1134
space n 539
Spanish j 2308
spare v 4654
spark v 4896
speak v 341
speaker n 3030
special j 528
specialist n 2548
specialize v 4115
specialty n 4529
species n 1276
specific j 987
specifically r 1986
specify v 4865
spectacular j 4256
spectrum n 3986
speculate v 4878
speculation n 4434
speech n 1118
speed v 3596
speed n 1436
spell v 4271
spend v 347
spending n 2401
sphere n 4637
spill v 3712
spin v 2689
spirit n 1218
spiritual j 2173
spit v 4980
spite i 4162
split v 2927
spokesman n 2749
sponsor n 4658
sponsor v 3462
spoon n 4438
sport n 750
spot v 2948
spot n 1254
spouse n 3909
spray n 4498
spread n 4083
spread v 1405
spring v 4063
spring n 916
sprinkle v 4940
spy n 4847

squad *n* 4688

square *j* 2811

square *n* 2077

squeeze *v* 2941

stability *n* 3007

stable *j* 2926

stack *n* 4503

stadium *n* 2779

staff *n* 818

stage *n* 837

stair *n* 2881

stake *n* 2617

stance *n* 4585

stand *n* 1898

stand *v* 285

standard *j* 1788

standard *n* 814

standing *n* 3146

star *v* 4347

star *n* 582

stare *v* 1155

start *n* 1558

start *v* 178

starter *n* 4102

starting *n* 3966

state *v* 848

state *n* 139

statement *n* 924

station *n* 841

statistical *j* 4392

statistics *n* 2745

statue *n* 3955

status *n* 1237

statute *n* 4344

stay *n* 4404

stay *v* 415

steadily *r* 4797

steady *j* 2950

steak *n* 4792

steal *v* 1811

steam *n* 4217

steel *n* 2205

steep *j* 4163

steer *v* 4681

stem *v* 4103

stem *n* 3563

step *n* 595

step *v* 1051

stereotype *n* 4993

stick *v* 1240

stick *n* 2798

stiff *j* 4121

still *j* 2391

still *r* 126

stimulate *v* 4486

stir *v* 2038

stock *n* 790

stomach *n* 2528

stone *n* 1244

stop *n* 2419

stop *v* 334

storage *n* 3063

store *v* 3042

store *n* 697

storm *n* 1638

story *n* 238

stove *n* 4564

straight *r* 1656

straight *j* 2519

straighten *v* 4939

strain *n* 3690

strain *v* 4701

strange *j* 1647

stranger *n* 2719

strategic *j* 2767

strategy *n* 851

straw *n* 4801

streak *n* 4676

stream *n* 2241

street *n* 352

strength *n* 1309

strengthen *v* 3141

stress *v* 2929

stress *n* 1834

stretch *n* 3569

stretch *v* 1953

strict *j* 3597

strictly *r* 4591

strike *v* 1162

strike *n* 2454

striking *j* 4606

string *n* 2723

strip *v* 3951

strip *n* 2785

stroke *n* 3191

strong *j* 463

strongly *r* 2398

structural *j* 3849

structure *n* 941

struggle *n* 1902

struggle *v* 1727

student *n* 173

studio *n* 1584

study *v* 884

study *n* 247

stuff *v* 3766

stuff *n* 1017

stumble *v* 4061

stupid *j* 2704

style *n* 998

subject *i* 3679

subject *n* 673

submit *v* 3225

subsequent *j* 3282

subsidy *n* 4421

substance *n* 2396

substantial *j* 2544

substantially *r* 4830

subtle *j* 3568

suburb *n* 3555

suburban *j* 3528

succeed *v* 2012

success *n* 778

successful *j* 1117

successfully *r* 3176

such *d* 185

such *i* 353

suck *v* 3709

sudden *j* 2886

suddenly *r* 955

sue *v* 3125

suffer *v* 1114

suffering *n* 4053

sufficient *j* 3109

sugar *n* 1677

suggest *v* 433

suggestion *n* 2523

suicide *n* 2279

suit *v* 3190

suit *n* 1421

suitable *j* 4761

suite *n* 3628

sum *n* 3864

summary *n* 3885

summer *n* 624

summit *n* 3240

sun *n* 861

sunlight *n* 3937

sunny *j* 4930

sunset *n* 4405

super *j* 2750

superior *j* 3435

supermarket *n* 4721

supervisor *n* 3732

supplier *n* 4477

supply *n* 1509

supply *v* 2475

support *n* 592

support *v* 538

supporter *n* 2499

supportive *j* 4602

suppose *v* 2159

supposed *j* 1256

supposedly *r* 4578

supreme *j* 1583

sure *r* 2330

sure *j* 350

surely *r* 2442

surface *n* 1042

surgeon *n* 3494

surgery *n* 1899

surprise *v* 3105

surprise *n* 1631

surprised *j* 1923

surprising *j* 2802

surprisingly *r* 3382

surround *v* 1615

surrounding *j* 4458

survey *v* 3773

survey *n* 1296

survival *n* 2698

survive *v* 1364

survivor *n* 3065

suspect *n* 3151

suspect *v* 2140

suspend *v* 3799

suspicion *n* 3832

suspicious *j* 4623

sustain *v* 3005

swallow *v* 3587

swear *v* 3398

sweat *n* 3784

sweater *n* 4876

sweep *v* 2648

sweet *j* 1608

swell *v* 4917

swim *v* 2907

swimming *n* 4540

swing *n* 3504

swing *v* 2498

switch *n* 4100

switch *v* 2652

sword *n* 4185

symbol *n* 2337

symbolic *j* 4203

sympathy *n* 4254

symptom *n* 2421

syndrome *n* 4397

system *n* 192

T

t-shirt *n* 3594

table *n* 324

tablespoon *n* 2489

tackle *v* 4219

tactic *n* 3319

tag *n* 4562

tail *n* 3002

take *v* 64

tale *n* 2302

talent *n* 2088

talented *j* 4276

talk *n* 931

talk *v* 169

tall *j* 1562

tank *n* 1866

tap *v* 2906

tape *n* 1450

target *v* 2952

target *n* 1294

task *n* 1072

taste *n* 2058

taste *v* 2778

tax *n* 520

taxpayer *n* 3209

tea *n* 2230

teach *v* 567

teacher *n* 412

teaching *n* 1782

team *n* 327

teammate *n* 4505

tear *v* 2238

tear *n* 1911

teaspoon *n* 2566

tech *n* 2975

technical *j* 2076

technician *n* 4931

technique *n* 1359

technological *j* 3804

technology *n* 597

teen *n* 2697

teenage *j* 4401

teenager *n* 2891

telephone *n* 1827

telescope *n* 3397

television *n* 775

tell *v* 104

temperature *n* 1660

temple *n* 3745

temporary *j* 3153

ten *m* 1001

tend *v* 1048

tendency *n* 3025

tender *j* 4166

tennis *n* 3136

tens *m* 4294

tension *n* 2197

tent *n* 3297

tenure *n* 4990

term *n* 641

terms *i* 1301

terrain *n* 4810

terrible *j* 1932

terribly *r* 4813

terrific *j* 4253

territory *n* 2229

terror *n* 2676

terrorism *n* 2508

terrorist *j* 3111

terrorist *n* 2768

test *n* 580

test *v* 1053

testify *v* 2755

testimony *n* 2616

testing *n* 2500

text *n* 1180

textbook *n* 4631

texture *n* 4604

than *i* 710

than *c* 74

thank *v* 504

thanks *n* 936

Thanksgiving *n* 4416

that *r* 905

that *c* 12

that *d* 28

the *a* 1

theater *n* 1671

theatre *n* 4274

their *a* 37

them *p* 62

theme *n* 1674

themselves *p* 447

then *r* 77

theology *n* 4829

theoretical *j* 3792

theory *n* 919

therapist *n* 4076

therapy *n* 2292

there *e* 51

there *r* 117

thereby *r* 3877

therefore *r* 1165

these *d* 83

they *p* 21

thick *j* 1785

thigh *n* 4308

thin *j* 1645

thing *n* 99

think *v* 57

thinking *n* 1741

third *m* 584

thirty *m* 2884

this *r* 4660

this *d* 22

thoroughly *r* 4145

those *d* 103

though *r* 2771

though *c* 255

thought *n* 772

thousand *m* 1679

thread *n* 4725

threat *n* 1081

threaten *v* 1410

three *m* 135

threshold *n* 4841

thrive *v* 4712

throat *n* 2494

through *r* 1229

through *i* 113

throughout *i* 989

throw *v* 679

thumb *n* 3811

thus *r* 737

ticket *n* 1612

tide *n* 4059

tie *v* 1517

tie *n* 2006

tiger *n* 3164

tight *j* 3201

tight *r* 3452

tighten *v* 4653

tightly *r* 4124

tile *n* 4906

till *i* 4924

till *c* 4850

timber *n* 4922

time *n* 54

timing *n* 3867

tiny *j* 1333

tip *v* 3567

tip *n* 1982

tired *j* 1969

tissue *n* 2841

title *n* 1362

to *t* 7

to *i* 9

tobacco *n* 2942

today *r* 216

together *r* 330

toilet *n* 4045

tolerance *n* 4667

tolerate *v* 4306

toll *n* 4581

tomato *n* 2581

tomorrow *r* 1337

ton *n* 2964

tone *n* 2065

tongue *n* 2910

tonight *r* 942

too *r* 133

tool *n* 1346

tooth *n* 1880

top *i* 2831

top *v* 3677

top *n* 684

top *j* 979

topic *n* 2066

toss *v* 2462

total *n* 2397

total *j* 1056

totally *r* 1920

touch *n* 2323

touch *v* 1177

touchdown *n* 4463

tough *j* 1035

tour *n* 1550

tourism *n* 4884

tourist *n* 2459

tournament *n* 2924

toward *i* 389

towards *i* 2067

towel *n* 3747

tower *n* 2411

town *n* 506

toxic *j* 4230

toy *n* 2438

trace *v* 3043

trace *n* 4239

track *v* 2752

track *n* 1086

trade *n* 817

trade *v* 2382

trading *n* 3484

tradition *n* 1260

traditional *j* 932

traditionally *r* 3711

traffic *n* 1733

tragedy *n* 2846

tragic *j* 4281

trail *v* 4060

trail *n* 1893

trailer *n* 4082

train *n* 1694

train *v* 1531

trainer *n* 4565

training *n* 811

trait *n* 3781

transaction *n* 3918

transfer *n* 2934

transfer *v* 2383

transform *v* 2210

transformation *n* 3309

transit *n* 4947

transition *n* 2249

translate *v* 2753

translation *n* 4361

transmission *n* 3062

transmit *v* 4834

transport *v* 4703

transport *n* 4855

transportation *n* 2418

trap *n* 4106

trap *v* 3583

trash *n* 4400

travel *n* 1960

travel *v* 1101

traveler *n* 3853

tray *n* 4526

treasure *n* 4127

treasury *n* 4305

treat *v* 966

treatment *n* 787

treaty *n* 2901

tree *n* 603

tremendous *j* 2726

trend *n* 1712

trial *n* 899

tribal *j* 4398

tribe *n* 3054

tribute *n* 4963

trick *n* 3121

trigger *v* 3765

trim *v* 5000

trip *n* 993

triumph *n* 4635

troops *n* 1129

tropical *j* 4220

trouble *n* 996

trouble *v* 4759

truck *n* 1248

true *j* 497

truly *r* 1762

trunk *n* 3572

trust *v* 1862

trust *n* 2256

truth *n* 870

try *v* 127

tube *n* 2594

tuck *v* 3953

tumor *n* 4925

tune *v* 3725

tune *n* 3989

tunnel *n* 3373

turn *n* 1207

turn *v* 172

twelve *m* 3254

twentieth *m* 4960

twenty *m* 2107

twice *r* 1430

twin *n* 2492

twist *v* 3830

twist *n* 4952

two *m* 80

two-thirds *m* 4615

type *n* 591

typical *j* 1838

typically *r* 2041

U

ugly *j* 3304

uh *u* 4684

ultimate *j* 2632

ultimately *r* 1802

unable *j* 2144

uncertain *j* 4301

uncertainty *n* 3767

uncle *n* 2045

uncomfortable *j* 3678

uncover *v* 4483

under *r* 1672

under *i* 230

undergo *v* 3258

undergraduate *n* 4900

underlying *j* 4286

undermine *v* 3775

understand *v* 326

understanding *n* 1334

undertake *v* 4019

unemployment *n* 3571

unexpected *j* 3657

unfair *j* 4444

unfold *v* 4619

unfortunate *j* 4988

unfortunately *r* 2018

unhappy *j* 4716

uniform *n* 3061

union *n* 796

unique *j* 1748

unit *n* 971

unite *v* 4157

united *j* 1462

unity *n* 3776

universal *j* 2675

universe *n* 2289

university *n* 304

unknown *j* 2838

unless *c* 1336

unlike *j* 3562

unlike *I* 2488

unlikely *j* 2699

unprecedented *j* 4461

until *i* 1383

until *c* 281

unusual *j* 2050

up *i* 457

up *r* 53

update *v* 4888

upon *i* 688

upper *j* 1979

upset *v* 3405

upset *j* 4363

upstairs *r* 4377

urban *j* 1652

urge *v* 2273

us *p* 112

use *v* 94

use *n* 434

used *j* 1847

useful *j* 2019

user *n* 1978

usual *j* 2385

usually *r* 723

utility *n* 2628

utilize *v* 4367

V

vacation *n* 2627

vaccine *n* 4237

valid *j* 4695

validity *n* 4679

valley *n* 1556

valuable *j* 2615

value *v* 4002

value *n* 503

van *n* 3838

vanish *v* 4036

variable *n* 1958

variation *n* 2954

variety *n* 1178

various *j* 857

vary *v* 2377

vast *j* 1985

vegetable *n* 2024

vehicle *n* 1331

vendor *n* 4854

venture *n* 3329

verbal *j* 4062

verdict *n* 4240

version *n* 1167

versus *i* 3222

vertical *j* 4566

very *j* 1224

very *r* 105

vessel *n* 3089

veteran *n* 2412

veteran *j* 4814

via *i* 2645

vice *j* 1938

victim *n* 1071

victory *n* 1501

video *n* 1161

videotape *n* 4523

view *v* 1442

view *n* 489

viewer *n* 2572

village *n* 1310

violate *v* 2920

violation *n* 2892

violence *n* 1055

violent *j* 2162

virtual *j* 3774

virtually *r* 2000

virtue *n* 3507

virus *n* 2718

visible *j* 2350

vision *n* 1243

visit *n* 1486

visit *v* 921

visitor *n* 1755

visual *j* 2275

vital *j* 2925

vitamin *n* 4009

voice *n* 469

volume *n* 2046

voluntary *j* 4706

volunteer *v* 3990

volunteer *n* 2353

vote *n* 1064

vote *v* 1190

voter *n* 1497

voting *n* 4180

vs *i* 2520

vulnerable *j* 3000

W

wage *n* 2535

wagon *n* 4170

waist *n* 4386

wait *v* 404

wake *n* 4041

wake *v* 1804

walk *n* 2235

walk *v* 363

walking *n* 3834

wall *n* 568

wander *v* 3208

want *v* 84

war *n* 228

warehouse *n* 4983

warm *v* 3687

warm *j* 1394

warmth *n* 4886

warn *v* 1791

warning *n* 2117

warrior *n* 3720

wash *v* 2175

waste *v* 3097

waste *n* 2068

watch *n* 2471

watch *v* 329

water *n* 239

wave *n* 1447

wave *v* 2631

way *r* 4069

way *n* 85

we *p* 25

weak *j* 2101

weaken *v* 4519

weakness *n* 3539

wealth *n* 2621

wealthy *j* 3090

weapon *n* 907

wear *v* 536

weather *n* 1641

weave *v* 4995

web *n* 1242

wedding *n* 2259

weed *n* 4749

week *n* 193

weekend *n* 1219

weekly *j* 3336

weigh *v* 2568

weight *n* 1002

weird *j* 3815

welcome *j* 3714

welcome *v* 1572

welfare *n* 1837

well *i* 645

well *r* 100

well-being *n* 4956

well-known *j* 4467

west *n* 676

western *j* 1095

wet *j* 2514

whale *n* 4273

what *d* 35

whatever *d* 773

wheat *n* 4613

wheel *n* 2069

when *c* 60

when *r* 137

whenever *r* 2342

where *r* 194

where *c* 171

whereas *c* 2760

wherever *r* 3729

whether *c* 325

which *d* 59

while *c* 156

whip *v* 4336

whisper *v* 2477

white *j* 308

who *p* 39

whoever *p* 4295

whole *j* 468

whom *p* 1039

whose *d* 530

why *r* 159

wide *j* 1181

widely *r* 2183

wider *j* 3844

widespread *j* 3308

widow *n* 4734

wife *n* 475

wild *j* 1320

wilderness *n* 3982

wildlife *n* 2807

will *v* 38

willing *j* 1295

willingness *n* 4197

win *n* 3623

win *v* 383

wind *n* 1124

wind *v* 2668

window *n* 614

wine *n* 1535

wing *n* 1917

winner *n* 1980

winter *n* 1270

wipe *v* 2748

wire *n* 2404
wisdom *n* 2996
wise *j* 3288
wish *n* 3612
wish *v* 1069
with *i* 16
withdraw *v* 2784
withdrawal *n* 4173
within *i* 360
within *r* 4895
without *i* 223
witness *v* 3024
witness *n* 1933
wolf *n* 2677
woman *n* 114
wonder *n* 2635
wonder *v* 799
wonderful *j* 1409
wood *n* 1272
wooden *j* 2557
word *n* 250
work *v* 119
work *n* 204
worker *n* 588

working *j* 2825
workout *n* 4904
workplace *n* 4327
workshop *n* 3271
world *n* 123
worldwide *r* 4521
worried *j* 3301
worry *n* 4025
worry *v* 980
worth *i* 1380
worth *n* 2835
would *v* 44
wound *v* 4533
wound *n* 3250
wow *u* 3893
wrap *v* 2129
wrist *n* 3696
write *v* 235
writer *n* 1016
writing *n* 1568
written *j* 3560
wrong *r* 3886
wrong *j* 657

Y

yard *n* 1073
yeah *u* 442
year *n* 55
yell *v* 2639
yellow *j* 1683
yes *u* 263
yesterday *r* 1510
yet *r* 277
yield *v* 2667
you *p* 14
young *j* 242
youngster *n* 4762
your *a* 71
yours *p* 3182
yourself *p* 967
youth *n* 1466

Z

zone *n* 1798

,

's *g* 19

Part of speech index

Format of entries

rank order (1 – 5000), **headword**

Verb

2	be	176	help	376	offer
8	have	178	start	378	remember
18	do	181	show	383	win
20	say	184	might	394	appear
36	go	198	hear	397	consider
38	will	205	run	401	love
40	can	209	play	403	buy
41	get	211	move	404	wait
44	would	212	like	405	die
46	make	215	believe	407	send
49	know	217	hold	409	expect
57	think	219	live	410	serve
58	see	220	happen	415	stay
64	take	221	bring	416	build
70	come	226	must	418	fall
73	could	235	write	425	cut
84	want	268	provide	426	kill
87	look	271	sit	428	reach
94	use	285	stand	431	remain
97	find	289	lose	433	suggest
98	give	292	meet	437	raise
104	tell	293	pay	444	pass
119	work	300	include	446	sell
121	call	305	continue	453	require
122	may	309	change	455	decide
125	should	310	set	465	report
127	try	319	lead	482	return
132	ask	321	learn	484	pull
134	need	326	understand	486	explain
136	feel	329	watch	487	carry
138	become	331	follow	488	develop
152	leave	334	stop	491	hope
153	put	341	speak	493	drive
157	mean	342	create	501	break
158	let	344	allow	504	thank
161	keep	346	read	509	receive
164	begin	347	spend	514	join
166	seem	351	add	523	agree
169	talk	356	grow	532	pick
172	turn	359	open	536	wear
		363	walk	538	support

543	end	810	lay	1025	exist
544	base	813	arrive	1048	tend
546	produce	816	fail	1049	address
549	hit	824	present	1051	step
554	eat	826	name	1053	test
561	face	830	check	1060	notice
564	cover	831	answer	1061	beat
565	describe	839	act	1065	sing
567	teach	844	compare	1069	wish
590	catch	848	state	1082	smile
601	draw	853	guess	1100	prevent
602	cause	855	force	1101	travel
605	choose	858	laugh	1102	born
613	point	867	prove	1103	relate
619	listen	876	claim	1104	assume
625	realize	877	forget	1106	admit
638	place	878	hang	1108	figure
653	close	882	design	1114	suffer
655	involve	884	study	1132	publish
659	increase	887	establish	1133	recall
666	deal	889	remove	1135	cost
669	seek	893	enjoy	1148	own
672	fight	895	sound	1149	release
679	throw	896	discuss	1155	stare
682	represent	897	form	1157	achieve
685	fill	912	avoid	1160	hurt
691	drop	918	maintain	1162	strike
694	plan	920	care	1172	refer
703	push	921	visit	1177	touch
704	focus	922	imagine	1184	sleep
705	reduce	923	finish	1187	announce
706	note	927	respond	1190	vote
719	enter	933	contain	1191	conduct
720	share	937	control	1193	replace
734	rise	945	fly	1194	attend
739	shoot	948	reveal	1204	encourage
744	save	954	head	1210	examine
747	occur	956	apply	1215	experience
751	lie	957	shake	1221	define
757	protect	962	discover	1236	introduce
762	accept	965	manage	1239	complete
774	determine	966	treat	1240	stick
779	prepare	972	affect	1250	handle
780	identify	980	worry	1257	refuse
785	argue	981	perform	1258	drink
786	recognize	994	mention	1264	gain
791	indicate	1007	sign	1265	express
799	wonder	1011	reflect	1278	roll
806	miss	1019	improve	1279	hide

1993 dance	2233 arrange	2478 resist
1995 match	2234 resolve	2490 smoke
1999 lack	2237 lock	2493 favor
2012 succeed	2238 tear	2495 construct
2017 accuse	2242 slide	2498 swing
2021 expose	2247 pose	2510 glance
2026 reject	2253 interview	2513 bind
2027 decline	2254 quote	2515 line
2038 stir	2255 deserve	2516 dig
2043 hand	2266 elect	2517 quit
2044 approve	2270 benefit	2521 assist
2049 escape	2273 urge	2526 embrace
2053 cast	2280 shall	2533 negotiate
2057 celebrate	2290 breathe	2556 restore
2062 acquire	2299 reply	2558 criticize
2071 convince	2304 kiss	2562 secure
2075 land	2307 contact	2568 weigh
2080 invest	2313 pack	2569 comment
2081 mind	2314 dominate	2571 assure
2083 regard	2325 impose	2573 arise
2086 lower	2327 implement	2576 plant
2087 compete	2329 analyze	2582 advise
2093 list	2331 retire	2589 date
2100 assess	2334 concentrate	2592 schedule
2104 permit	2335 accomplish	2603 dream
2111 knock	2340 attach	2608 pop
2112 display	2348 adjust	2613 assign
2122 review	2357 illustrate	2624 incorporate
2129 wrap	2360 enhance	2631 wave
2139 drag	2363 monitor	2639 yell
2140 suspect	2368 inspire	2644 snap
2145 scream	2377 vary	2647 install
2155 arrest	2380 evaluate	2648 sweep
2159 suppose	2382 trade	2652 switch
2163 recover	2383 transfer	2656 graduate
2175 wash	2384 exercise	2667 yield
2179 shout	2388 ring	2668 wind
2187 purchase	2395 light	2678 house
2199 bother	2422 bury	2681 found
2201 consist	2432 confront	2685 proceed
2203 enable	2435 smell	2687 react
2208 slow	2446 block	2689 spin
2210 transform	2447 race	2703 communicate
2212 perceive	2450 accompany	2705 bet
2214 inform	2457 shape	2706 advance
2216 abandon	2462 toss	2710 disagree
2226 rule	2473 pray	2711 encounter
2227 preserve	2475 supply	2717 overcome
2231 bend	2477 whisper	2720 retain

3510	beg	3730	administer	4002	value
3512	greet	3738	average	4014	age
3519	restrict	3741	injure	4015	peel
3520	initiate	3743	award	4019	undertake
3521	reverse	3744	drain	4026	cooperate
3525	confuse	3750	govern	4036	vanish
3534	march	3755	abuse	4037	blend
3538	fold	3759	praise	4040	command
3548	enforce	3765	trigger	4042	flip
3549	murder	3766	stuff	4052	hook
3553	flash	3773	survey	4058	descend
3556	melt	3775	undermine	4060	trail
3558	contend	3796	rebuild	4061	stumble
3559	plead	3799	suspend	4063	spring
3567	tip	3800	relieve	4081	seal
3570	slam	3801	resume	4089	please
3574	burst	3807	apologize	4093	slice
3575	pitch	3808	research	4094	shock
3578	render	3818	scare	4099	prohibit
3582	motivate	3819	bounce	4103	stem
3583	trap	3826	convey	4111	slap
3587	swallow	3828	ship	4112	credit
3596	speed	3830	twist	4115	specialize
3599	assemble	3835	boost	4118	sail
3602	label	3836	scatter	4129	scan
3606	protest	3860	dedicate	4130	condemn
3608	hunt	3862	signal	4146	exchange
3617	consult	3868	punish	4149	reserve
3632	lend	3869	crawl	4153	concede
3633	project	3883	rescue	4156	donate
3640	facilitate	3892	hug	4157	unite
3643	hurry	3902	cancel	4165	conceive
3646	drift	3903	desire	4169	equip
3652	leap	3932	carve	4184	click
3672	forgive	3949	advocate	4191	heat
3677	top	3951	strip	4194	post
3681	rip	3953	tuck	4201	chop
3685	dump	3954	debate	4204	ruin
3687	warm	3956	frame	4205	rock
3692	behave	3964	hesitate	4210	discourage
3695	execute	3967	diminish	4213	haul
3699	convict	3979	endorse	4219	tackle
3702	await	3980	isolate	4223	calm
3706	endure	3981	confess	4227	grasp
3709	suck	3983	minimize	4228	modify
3710	accommodate	3984	diagnose	4229	grin
3712	spill	3990	volunteer	4234	root
3719	guard	3998	repair	4236	manipulate
3725	tune	4000	pump	4245	bless

Noun

123 world	273 friend	396 policy
129 school	275 power	400 education
139 state	278 father	408 fee
149 family	279 hour	411 sense
151 house	283 line	412 teacher
160 president	284 end	414 market
167 group	287 game	417 nation
168 country	291 member	420 death
170 problem	294 law	421 plan
173 student	296 car	422 interest
175 hand	299 name	424 experience
180 part	302 center	432 effect
186 place	304 university	434 use
188 city	313 information	435 control
189 case	315 community	438 class
192 system	318 idea	445 photo
193 week	320 body	448 field
195 company	322 kid	449 college
197 percent	323 minute	452 development
201 question	324 table	456 security
203 program	327 team	459 effort
204 work	328 back	460 role
206 number	335 face	462 rate
208 government	340 parent	464 music
214 night	343 office	466 leader
218 point	345 level	467 light
228 war	348 person	469 voice
229 home	349 door	470 color
231 room	352 street	471 heart
232 fact	354 history	472 care
233 area	355 party	473 police
236 money	357 reason	475 wife
237 right	358 morning	476 show
238 story	361 change	477 mind
239 water	364 news	478 report
240 mother	365 health	480 drug
243 month	366 court	485 decision
244 lot	367 force	489 view
245 book	370 air	494 son
246 eye	373 art	495 arm
247 study	374 result	496 department
248 job	375 moment	498 price
249 kind	379 research	502 action
250 word	381 girl	503 value
251 issue	382 boy	505 relationship
252 side	384 food	506 town
254 business	386 guy	508 building
256 head	391 process	510 society
269 service	395 age	511 difference

781 press	861 sun	969 evening
783 resource	862 lawyer	971 unit
784 amount	863 sex	973 play
787 treatment	865 artist	974 production
789 degree	866 club	975 bit
790 stock	868 section	978 range
792 growth	869 skill	983 conference
794 ability	870 truth	985 candidate
795 dollar	871 set	986 museum
796 union	873 manager	990 hall
797 disease	874 executive	991 past
800 election	875 district	992 fish
801 loss	880 leg	993 trip
802 box	891 professor	995 edge
803 deal	894 network	996 trouble
805 fund	899 trial	997 interview
808 region	901 help	998 style
809 feeling	904 rock	1000 cause
811 training	906 seat	1002 weight
812 message	907 weapon	1003 adult
814 standard	908 song	1004 dream
817 trade	909 expert	1005 fear
818 staff	910 radio	1008 method
819 benefit	913 memory	1010 magazine
820 character	914 management	1013 soldier
821 army	915 charge	1014 property
822 association	916 spring	1016 writer
823 operation	917 card	1017 stuff
825 crime	919 theory	1018 camera
827 cup	924 statement	1020 shoulder
828 island	925 firm	1021 bar
829 analysis	931 talk	1022 hotel
832 photograph	934 peace	1024 hill
833 glass	936 thanks	1026 sea
835 authority	938 Democrat	1027 institution
836 earth	939 base	1028 purpose
837 stage	940 impact	1029 pattern
838 one	941 structure	1030 detail
840 sort	943 note	1031 machine
841 station	944 direction	1032 challenge
846 public	947 king	1033 owner
847 knowledge	949 cell	1034 agent
850 example	951 ball	1037 generation
851 strategy	953 employee	1040 fall
852 mountain	959 chair	1042 surface
854 sister	961 justice	1043 budget
856 gun	963 measure	1044 senator
859 environment	964 politics	1045 bag
860 design	968 pain	1046 reality

1309 strength	1418 reaction	1514 drive
1310 village	1420 master	1516 front
1312 reporter	1421 suit	1518 birth
1313 share	1424 gift	1519 progress
1314 guard	1425 coffee	1520 damage
1319 advantage	1427 belief	1521 exchange
1325 leadership	1428 comment	1522 bottom
1326 boat	1431 background	1525 document
1327 facility	1432 quarter	1527 journal
1331 vehicle	1433 review	1528 knee
1332 pound	1434 faith	1533 circle
1334 understanding	1435 move	1535 wine
1338 foundation	1436 speed	1536 minority
1340 block	1439 perspective	1537 flower
1342 reader	1443 function	1538 device
1344 guest	1444 construction	1540 plate
1345 living	1445 egg	1544 actor
1346 tool	1447 wave	1546 expression
1347 protection	1449 murder	1550 tour
1351 equipment	1450 tape	1551 finding
1354 painting	1452 means	1552 exercise
1356 principle	1454 mistake	1553 plastic
1357 bowl	1456 connection	1554 danger
1358 claim	1457 shoe	1555 neck
1359 technique	1458 clothes	1556 valley
1361 identity	1460 religion	1558 start
1362 title	1463 context	1559 application
1363 critic	1465 focus	1566 respect
1366 border	1466 youth	1567 colleague
1368 path	1467 location	1568 writing
1369 aspect	1468 neighbor	1569 rain
1371 shop	1470 Internet	1571 football
1372 failure	1471 category	1574 pool
1377 sample	1476 coast	1575 literature
1378 affair	1478 smile	1578 desire
1382 chairman	1479 bus	1580 fight
1384 lesson	1484 key	1582 session
1385 Christmas	1485 hell	1584 studio
1388 folk	1486 visit	1587 learning
1389 band	1487 bone	1589 importance
1390 ear	1493 cut	1595 abuse
1391 procedure	1497 voter	1596 chicken
1393 inch	1501 victory	1598 map
1397 baseball	1502 contact	1604 metal
1399 foot	1505 medicine	1605 lead
1402 competition	1507 grade	1607 jury
1413 intelligence	1509 supply	1609 proposal
1415 influence	1512 democracy	1612 ticket
1416 general	1513 pair	1613 leaf

1905 file	2005 gate	2116 signal
1906 ocean	2006 tie	2117 warning
1909 confidence	2008 promise	2118 physician
1911 tear	2009 dish	2119 column
1912 judgment	2020 noise	2120 interaction
1914 expectation	2022 mass	2123 republic
1915 resolution	2024 vegetable	2125 priority
1916 copy	2025 seed	2126 achievement
1917 wing	2028 experiment	2128 request
1918 doubt	2029 legislation	2130 engineer
1919 fun	2030 hat	2131 rice
1922 gender	2034 grass	2132 scholar
1924 beer	2039 captain	2133 airline
1927 bond	2040 revolution	2134 expense
1929 debt	2042 sector	2135 observation
1931 English	2045 uncle	2136 gap
1933 witness	2046 volume	2137 agenda
1934 reference	2047 explanation	2138 creation
1939 black	2048 sentence	2141 fishing
1941 hero	2051 distribution	2142 bread
1942 bomb	2054 drink	2146 journalist
1944 rating	2055 sleep	2147 constitution
1947 corporation	2056 household	2151 payment
1948 representative	2058 taste	2153 selection
1950 soil	2059 characteristic	2154 lab
1951 highway	2065 tone	2158 childhood
1952 frame	2066 topic	2161 prosecutor
1956 cloud	2068 waste	2164 roof
1958 variable	2069 wheel	2165 amendment
1960 travel	2070 athlete	2166 emotion
1961 improvement	2072 alternative	2169 graduate
1962 opening	2073 pepper	2170 factory
1964 nurse	2074 cream	2171 schedule
1965 incident	2077 square	2172 avenue
1966 abortion	2082 potential	2174 ride
1978 user	2084 intervention	2176 planning
1980 winner	2088 talent	2177 self
1981 fashion	2091 milk	2182 error
1982 tip	2092 height	2184 description
1983 apple	2095 assistance	2185 dark
1984 rise	2096 personality	2189 funding
1989 holiday	2102 female	2190 settlement
1990 e-mail	2103 cigarette	2191 prayer
1994 core	2105 passenger	2192 initiative
1996 landscape	2106 criticism	2193 coalition
1998 golf	2108 honor	2194 comparison
2001 route	2110 offer	2195 portion
2002 flow	2113 campus	2196 opponent
2004 cable	2114 definition	2197 tension

2455 jet	2554 intention	2641 respondent
2458 relative	2555 peer	2646 lawsuit
2459 tourist	2560 approval	2649 festival
2460 phenomenon	2563 preparation	2650 draft
2463 publication	2565 lord	2651 heaven
2465 consideration	2566 teaspoon	2653 activist
2468 enterprise	2570 pan	2654 ceiling
2471 watch	2572 viewer	2655 clock
2472 Indian	2574 administrator	2657 aunt
2474 creek	2575 immigration	2658 darkness
2476 boot	2578 origin	2659 daddy
2479 journey	2580 diversity	2661 advertising
2480 flag	2581 tomato	2664 penalty
2481 disorder	2584 shell	2670 mechanism
2482 designer	2585 essay	2671 rank
2486 angle	2586 roll	2672 killer
2489 tablespoon	2587 historian	2673 fence
2491 consultant	2588 deputy	2676 terror
2492 twin	2593 buck	2677 wolf
2494 throat	2594 tube	2679 anxiety
2496 birthday	2595 refugee	2682 protein
2499 supporter	2596 depth	2683 engineering
2500 testing	2601 disability	2684 clothing
2502 mail	2602 destruction	2686 fiber
2503 silver	2604 drop	2691 drama
2504 retirement	2605 assumption	2692 liberty
2506 gentleman	2607 angel	2693 ingredient
2507 navy	2609 criteria	2694 hip
2508 terrorism	2611 crop	2695 provision
2511 observer	2612 barrier	2696 burden
2522 employment	2616 testimony	2697 teen
2523 suggestion	2617 stake	2698 survival
2525 estimate	2618 concert	2701 chamber
2528 stomach	2619 label	2708 bell
2531 mine	2620 routine	2709 onion
2532 recovery	2621 wealth	2713 cabinet
2534 impression	2622 professional	2718 virus
2535 wage	2623 gang	2719 stranger
2538 count	2625 brand	2721 match
2540 absence	2626 recipe	2722 prize
2542 corn	2627 vacation	2723 string
2543 mixture	2628 utility	2724 exhibition
2545 grandmother	2629 satellite	2725 expansion
2547 jail	2633 chemical	2727 bunch
2548 specialist	2634 advocate	2728 assistant
2549 dealer	2635 wonder	2731 cheek
2550 poem	2636 educator	2732 index
2551 butter	2637 cake	2734 gear
2553 pace	2638 phrase	2736 chocolate

3017 celebrity	3102 congressman	3184 bull
3018 leather	3103 mama	3185 prevention
3020 framework	3104 monitor	3186 meter
3021 beat	3106 infant	3188 mask
3025 tendency	3107 cow	3191 stroke
3026 load	3110 oak	3192 assignment
3027 crack	3112 mall	3193 lion
3030 speaker	3113 punishment	3195 rifle
3031 scandal	3116 admission	3198 boom
3033 scheme	3117 frequency	3202 flame
3034 jazz	3118 ratio	3203 Palestinian
3037 celebration	3119 delay	3204 economics
3038 can	3120 privacy	3205 cabin
3039 evolution	3121 trick	3209 taxpayer
3040 fighter	3123 circuit	3212 inflation
3045 detective	3124 musician	3214 pine
3047 limitation	3126 purchase	3215 agriculture
3049 soup	3127 aide	3216 legacy
3050 oven	3129 helicopter	3217 extension
3054 tribe	3130 empire	3218 barrel
3055 pipe	3132 efficiency	3219 arrival
3056 deer	3133 humor	3221 flavor
3057 illustration	3134 sanctions	3224 flesh
3059 arrest	3136 tennis	3226 garage
3061 uniform	3137 emission	3227 cotton
3062 transmission	3139 garlic	3228 operator
3063 storage	3140 contest	3229 nut
3064 pile	3142 demonstration	3231 blade
3065 survivor	3143 restriction	3232 girlfriend
3069 economist	3145 hunter	3233 fly
3072 shade	3146 standing	3235 carbon
3073 opera	3147 handful	3236 heritage
3075 preference	3151 suspect	3238 ambassador
3076 guideline	3154 commissioner	3239 invasion
3078 maintenance	3155 diamond	3240 summit
3079 formation	3159 reservation	3241 lifestyle
3080 glove	3161 adjustment	3244 counsel
3081 scholarship	3162 composition	3245 associate
3083 proportion	3164 tiger	3246 major
3084 appointment	3165 fabric	3248 menu
3086 conviction	3167 discrimination	3250 wound
3087 myth	3170 math	3251 manufacturing
3089 vessel	3172 corps	3252 consumption
3091 friendship	3173 sequence	3253 permission
3092 membership	3174 complex	3256 shower
3093 craft	3175 heel	3260 consciousness
3095 French	3177 examination	3263 frustration
3096 earnings	3178 horizon	3264 operating
3099 porch	3179 German	3266 carrier

3517 rod	3621 nightmare	3701 recession
3518 candy	3622 beef	3703 hallway
3527 pig	3623 win	3704 dose
3529 medal	3624 serving	3705 brush
3530 receiver	3625 globe	3707 counseling
3531 gaze	3626 cholesterol	3708 civilian
3532 collapse	3627 parliament	3718 separation
3533 snake	3628 suite	3720 warrior
3536 civilization	3630 pop	3722 southwest
3539 weakness	3635 mud	3727 harm
3540 corridor	3636 pump	3728 cloth
3543 mortgage	3637 flour	3732 supervisor
3545 developer	3638 hostage	3733 compromise
3546 legend	3639 ownership	3736 Japanese
3547 excitement	3641 basement	3737 mandate
3551 cowboy	3642 correlation	3739 alarm
3555 suburb	3644 insect	3740 cruise
3561 flood	3645 arena	3742 sculpture
3563 stem	3647 notice	3745 temple
3565 essence	3648 domain	3746 dancer
3566 pitcher	3649 cave	3747 towel
3569 stretch	3653 final	3748 Islam
3571 unemployment	3654 effectiveness	3751 crown
3572 trunk	3656 array	3752 contractor
3573 privilege	3658 curtain	3753 adolescent
3576 architecture	3659 sandwich	3754 skirt
3581 obstacle	3661 humanity	3756 bacteria
3584 drinking	3662 prediction	3757 adoption
3585 elbow	3664 ideology	3762 glance
3586 rumor	3665 railroad	3763 grip
3589 lecture	3666 possession	3767 uncertainty
3591 jeans	3667 horn	3769 enthusiasm
3592 duck	3668 replacement	3770 complexity
3593 slope	3669 announcement	3771 excuse
3594 t-shirt	3670 pond	3772 cafe
3595 inspection	3671 conduct	3776 unity
3603 fraud	3674 Muslim	3777 chaos
3604 reach	3675 bishop	3780 rhetoric
3607 implementation	3676 aim	3781 trait
3609 boyfriend	3680 laugh	3782 pension
3610 integration	3683 herb	3784 sweat
3611 rat	3688 guilt	3785 European
3612 wish	3689 cattle	3786 innovation
3613 broadcast	3690 strain	3789 currency
3615 nail	3691 sheriff	3791 lobby
3616 pen	3694 crystal	3793 bat
3618 companion	3696 wrist	3794 makeup
3619 encounter	3697 motive	3798 pad
3620 monster	3698 painter	3803 promotion

4073 romance	4161 grief	4263 sock
4074 quantity	4164 productivity	4264 rider
4076 therapist	4167 continent	4265 revelation
4078 sink	4168 hardware	4267 accomplishment
4079 sentiment	4170 wagon	4268 seal
4080 sodium	4172 output	4270 ease
4082 trailer	4173 withdrawal	4272 gospel
4083 spread	4174 elder	4273 whale
4085 equity	4175 cage	4274 theatre
4086 banking	4177 patience	4275 coordinator
4088 processing	4179 earthquake	4278 cab
4090 dilemma	4180 voting	4279 isolation
4091 quest	4181 input	4283 instinct
4092 pillow	4182 canvas	4289 pastor
4096 laser	4183 slide	4291 cook
4100 switch	4185 sword	4296 ancestor
4101 genius	4186 mate	4298 nominee
4102 starter	4187 portfolio	4304 orchestra
4104 primary	4188 bug	4305 treasury
4105 cart	4189 refrigerator	4307 gallon
4106 trap	4190 escape	4308 thigh
4108 inmate	4192 northeast	4312 flexibility
4109 sacrifice	4196 alien	4313 jar
4114 Arab	4197 willingness	4314 cocaine
4116 fork	4199 accounting	4317 documentary
4117 invitation	4202 patrol	4320 ambition
4120 cartoon	4206 drum	4322 bankruptcy
4122 courtroom	4211 canal	4323 runner
4123 import	4216 conspiracy	4324 execution
4125 flash	4217 steam	4326 buddy
4126 equation	4218 embassy	4327 workplace
4127 treasure	4222 bubble	4328 skull
4128 jaw	4224 sheep	4329 cord
4132 pickup	4225 rent	4331 equivalent
4133 dignity	4226 accent	4332 casino
4134 inspiration	4232 magnitude	4333 reliability
4136 merchant	4237 vaccine	4338 proposition
4140 homeland	4238 monument	4339 census
4141 gasoline	4239 trace	4340 correction
4142 gravity	4240 verdict	4341 jump
4143 defeat	4242 declaration	4342 diary
4147 bow	4243 costume	4343 nest
4148 glory	4244 drawer	4344 statute
4151 sergeant	4246 rack	4345 exam
4152 casualty	4254 sympathy	4348 nutrition
4155 barn	4257 ounce	4349 breeze
4158 pro	4259 inn	4350 illusion
4159 senior	4260 collaboration	4352 coup
4160 feedback	4261 clip	4353 midst

4644 legislator	4730 riot	4827 publishing
4645 auction	4732 mentor	4828 retreat
4646 equality	4733 beard	4829 theology
4648 cemetery	4734 widow	4831 mansion
4649 builder	4735 offender	4837 mathematics
4651 retailer	4736 landmark	4840 lawmaker
4652 debut	4738 instant	4841 threshold
4656 constraint	4740 butt	4842 radar
4657 compliance	4743 migration	4845 headache
4658 sponsor	4744 carrot	4846 rental
4664 similarity	4745 harmony	4847 spy
4665 pencil	4749 weed	4848 patron
4666 calculation	4751 pasta	4849 driveway
4667 tolerance	4753 fraction	4854 vendor
4668 astronomer	4757 guarantee	4855 transport
4669 bulk	4758 dancing	4856 fragment
4671 interval	4760 freshman	4857 hammer
4672 notebook	4762 youngster	4858 seminar
4673 genre	4763 slavery	4859 availability
4674 likelihood	4764 balloon	4860 peanut
4675 liberal	4767 liver	4863 permit
4676 streak	4768 listener	4864 cottage
4677 rib	4772 commodity	4868 artifact
4678 scent	4773 fur	4869 basin
4679 validity	4776 removal	4871 grape
4680 grin	4777 regard	4872 ego
4683 shark	4779 goat	4875 charm
4685 programming	4780 shareholder	4876 sweater
4688 squad	4781 expedition	4877 rim
4690 debris	4783 conscience	4879 delight
4691 peasant	4785 calendar	4880 fatigue
4692 outlet	4786 mineral	4883 plea
4693 chase	4789 fare	4884 tourism
4696 kingdom	4790 blessing	4886 warmth
4702 deposit	4791 liberation	4887 jurisdiction
4704 dough	4792 steak	4889 accusation
4705 lid	4795 banana	4890 diagram
4707 journalism	4796 catch	4892 graduation
4709 impulse	4798 blast	4893 mention
4710 policeman	4801 straw	4897 convenience
4711 objection	4802 projection	4898 chill
4717 rally	4810 terrain	4900 undergraduate
4719 robot	4816 sofa	4902 regulator
4720 conversion	4818 shield	4903 defender
4721 supermarket	4819 invention	4904 workout
4725 thread	4820 Iraqi	4906 tile
4727 ash	4822 leave	4907 foreigner
4728 dynamics	4824 bomber	4909 citizenship
4729 denial	4826 autonomy	4910 plaza

Adjective

950 religious	1285 future	1529 primary
952 particular	1286 potential	1539 Iraqi
958 cultural	1291 Chinese	1542 clean
977 far	1293 European	1543 alive
979 top	1295 willing	1548 bright
982 necessary	1297 interested	1557 academic
984 individual	1320 wild	1561 male
987 specific	1321 previous	1562 tall
999 middle	1322 average	1565 Indian
1006 dark	1328 present	1573 domestic
1012 heavy	1333 tiny	1576 extra
1015 beautiful	1339 quick	1577 northern
1035 tough	1341 light	1581 corporate
1038 commercial	1348 fair	1583 supreme
1050 civil	1349 additional	1585 Russian
1056 total	1374 responsible	1593 dry
1063 modern	1394 warm	1602 greatest
1085 positive	1395 African	1603 complex
1090 rich	1396 French	1608 sweet
1095 western	1400 Christian	1610 impossible
1099 interesting	1404 afraid	1611 scientific
1113 senior	1407 soft	1617 alone
1117 successful	1408 annual	1633 favorite
1120 key	1409 wonderful	1645 thin
1126 concerned	1414 regular	1647 strange
1127 professional	1438 broad	1648 married
1134 Soviet	1441 growing	1652 urban
1136 southern	1448 female	1661 empty
1141 original	1453 aware	1664 presidential
1143 critical	1455 quiet	1666 prime
1145 basic	1461 complete	1678 educational
1152 effective	1462 united	1683 yellow
1171 sexual	1464 active	1685 Japanese
1173 fresh	1472 dangerous	1688 expensive
1174 involved	1481 chief	1689 emotional
1175 powerful	1482 following	1692 mental
1179 deep	1490 direct	1695 brown
1181 wide	1491 native	1707 regional
1199 nuclear	1492 cool	1708 obvious
1205 perfect	1495 historical	1709 angry
1208 British	1496 moral	1713 like
1217 safe	1498 appropriate	1726 comfortable
1223 global	1499 famous	1734 internal
1224 very	1504 negative	1746 sick
1231 sorry	1508 eastern	1748 unique
1247 normal	1511 familiar	1749 actual
1252 front	1515 healthy	1765 ethnic
1256 supposed	1523 daily	1770 slow
1266 independent	1526 grand	1785 thick

2615 valuable	2850 loose	3152 eager
2630 extraordinary	2851 external	3153 temporary
2632 ultimate	2855 diverse	3156 curious
2642 Palestinian	2856 advanced	3160 downtown
2643 classic	2860 online	3163 relative
2660 royal	2870 intellectual	3180 absolute
2662 rough	2871 communist	3183 dominant
2663 pregnant	2886 sudden	3187 legitimate
2665 distant	2889 dirty	3196 brilliant
2666 developing	2918 literary	3199 naked
2669 armed	2925 vital	3200 hungry
2675 universal	2926 stable	3201 tight
2680 chemical	2935 comprehensive	3207 orange
2688 bottom	2936 confident	3210 romantic
2699 unlikely	2938 prominent	3234 dependent
2700 Italian	2946 mere	3237 organic
2702 lost	2950 steady	3242 agricultural
2704 stupid	2955 radical	3249 awful
2707 Muslim	2958 exciting	3255 offensive
2712 constitutional	2968 pale	3269 distinct
2714 remarkable	2974 Canadian	3282 subsequent
2715 broken	2981 round	3287 athletic
2726 tremendous	2986 defensive	3288 wise
2730 accurate	2988 scared	3291 frequent
2744 marine	3000 vulnerable	3301 worried
2746 Olympic	3016 ill	3302 principal
2750 super	3019 given	3303 firm
2751 Islamic	3023 slight	3304 ugly
2757 friendly	3036 elderly	3305 adequate
2765 complicated	3046 closer	3308 widespread
2767 strategic	3051 rapid	3315 institutional
2774 odd	3053 sophisticated	3316 homeless
2776 innocent	3058 ok	3317 impressive
2782 blind	3067 incredible	3323 moderate
2792 ideal	3070 efficient	3325 lovely
2797 genetic	3088 solar	3336 weekly
2802 surprising	3090 wealthy	3340 continued
2811 square	3098 asleep	3344 changing
2816 extensive	3100 controversial	3349 everyday
2817 attractive	3101 painful	3355 running
2820 raw	3108 proposed	3369 collective
2822 clinical	3109 sufficient	3375 concrete
2824 considerable	3111 terrorist	3380 exact
2825 working	3114 helpful	3383 artistic
2828 remote	3115 ongoing	3406 acceptable
2837 relevant	3128 modest	3413 related
2838 unknown	3131 detailed	3429 sacred
2847 assistant	3138 desperate	3433 dear
2849 mutual	3144 Irish	3435 superior

3454 okay
3455 pleased
3461 evident
3465 cognitive
3469 magic
3473 colonial
3476 civilian
3478 estimated
3486 bare
3498 net
3499 excited
3502 bitter
3522 ethical
3523 secondary
3524 administrative
3526 deadly
3528 suburban
3535 experimental
3537 classical
3541 harsh
3542 retail
3544 harder
3550 occasional
3552 minimum
3554 reliable
3557 fit
3560 written
3562 unlike
3564 inevitable
3568 subtle
3577 monthly
3579 mainstream
3588 legislative
3597 strict
3598 overwhelming
3600 missing
3605 plain
3614 Korean
3629 continuing
3650 African-American
3655 maximum
3657 unexpected
3660 peaceful
3663 Roman
3678 uncomfortable
3682 random
3713 fiscal
3714 welcome
3715 retired

3716 closed
3717 gentle
3721 convinced
3723 drunk
3724 outdoor
3726 patient
3734 grateful
3735 Hispanic
3749 continuous
3758 intelligent
3760 outer
3764 profound
3768 driving
3774 virtual
3779 endless
3783 genuine
3792 theoretical
3795 pleasant
3797 horrible
3804 technological
3815 weird
3829 exclusive
3831 precise
3839 identical
3842 delicate
3844 wider
3849 structural
3851 invisible
3854 meaningful
3863 anxious
3865 frozen
3870 conscious
3887 medium
3888 chronic
3889 evil
3890 handsome
3897 promising
3908 reluctant
3912 mild
3913 electrical
3916 decent
3935 residential
3944 diplomatic
3946 purple
3950 generous
3961 interior
3963 bold
3970 elegant
3974 realistic

3978 productive
3991 abstract
3992 revolutionary
3996 disappointed
3999 dynamic
4007 mechanical
4010 silly
4012 artificial
4013 outstanding
4017 oral
4020 lonely
4022 indigenous
4023 civic
4024 full-time
4027 casual
4028 behavioral
4039 precious
4043 scary
4046 representative
4062 verbal
4065 judicial
4066 burning
4075 alleged
4077 longtime
4084 shared
4087 ridiculous
4097 rigid
4107 Cuban
4113 mysterious
4119 regulatory
4121 stiff
4131 improved
4135 automatic
4137 Greek
4138 hostile
4139 extended
4144 near
4150 optimistic
4154 bloody
4163 steep
4166 tender
4176 coastal
4178 shallow
4195 combined
4198 hidden
4203 symbolic
4208 sheer
4209 ideological
4212 prior

4214 protective
4220 tropical
4230 toxic
4231 mixed
4235 progressive
4241 flexible
4247 secure
4249 deeper
4251 neutral
4252 fascinating
4253 terrific
4256 spectacular
4258 rear
4269 faint
4276 talented
4280 costly
4281 tragic
4282 loud
4285 intimate
4286 underlying
4288 influential
4299 exotic
4300 minimal
4301 uncertain
4302 Persian
4303 parental
4310 ambitious
4321 functional
4330 fixed
4334 expected
4337 divine
4346 metropolitan
4351 anonymous
4355 experienced
4362 Dutch
4363 upset
4366 associated
4372 immune
4379 gross
4381 accessible
4384 aesthetic
4388 brave
4390 passing
4392 statistical
4396 encouraging
4398 tribal
4401 teenage
4403 preliminary
4415 known
4417 short-term

4419 cooperative
4422 secular
4432 shy
4440 rolling
4442 damn
4444 unfair
4449 disabled
4458 surrounding
4461 unprecedented
4467 well-known
4471 high-tech
4473 audio
4487 rational
4492 innovative
4506 instant
4509 pro
4513 fierce
4515 required
4517 cute
4524 partial
4530 nasty
4534 sexy
4536 excessive
4543 informal
4550 dying
4551 colorful
4556 logical
4558 dried
4560 sole
4566 vertical
4567 added
4571 organizational
4576 isolated
4582 embarrassed
4588 depressed
4598 closest
4602 supportive
4603 comparable
4606 striking
4607 associate
4618 blank
4622 faster
4623 suspicious
4641 balanced
4647 risky
4650 awake
4659 emerging
4661 elaborate
4682 intact
4686 dumb

4694 neat
4695 valid
4698 eligible
4700 municipal
4706 voluntary
4716 unhappy
4723 philosophical
4747 brutal
4752 distinctive
4761 suitable
4766 crowded
4769 calm
4771 affirmative
4782 loyal
4784 fragile
4787 coming
4793 liquid
4794 ecological
4799 nonprofit
4800 mobile
4803 rubber
4805 neighboring
4807 favorable
4809 demographic
4811 explicit
4812 integrated
4814 veteran
4815 level
4821 perceived
4823 cruel
4832 developmental
4839 old-fashioned
4861 fantastic
4867 disturbing
4874 organized
4881 devastating
4882 instructional
4891 middle-class
4915 inherent
4923 feminist
4930 sunny
4936 flying
4938 skilled
4951 fatal
4953 compelling
4961 dense
4968 boring
4970 bizarre
4975 naval
4977 skeptical

1802 ultimately	2559 nevertheless	3601 seemingly
1812 late	2590 effectively	3631 hence
1813 frequently	2598 precisely	3651 consistently
1833 forth	2606 normally	3673 past
1868 significantly	2640 personally	3686 online
1869 somewhat	2690 roughly	3700 simultaneously
1871 anywhere	2729 initially	3711 traditionally
1874 entirely	2742 like	3729 wherever
1885 meanwhile	2771 though	3731 short
1907 seriously	2772 gently	3761 nearby
1910 aside	2789 mainly	3778 commonly
1920 totally	2791 newly	3802 respectively
1949 everywhere	2800 naturally	3806 altogether
1963 necessarily	2805 similarly	3848 firmly
1974 apart	2818 politically	3877 thereby
1986 specifically	2819 regularly	3878 historically
1992 merely	2826 partly	3881 harder
2000 virtually	2840 likely	3886 wrong
2013 barely	2858 faster	3896 loud
2018 unfortunately	2862 shortly	3906 sooner
2035 definitely	2864 originally	3922 practically
2036 closer	2888 potentially	3941 sharply
2041 typically	2908 properly	3969 readily
2063 closely	2937 easy	4003 automatically
2079 behind	2953 nowhere	4004 overall
2099 forever	2960 regardless	4018 o'clock
2124 primarily	2971 gradually	4050 softly
2152 deep	2997 since	4051 annually
2156 deeply	3028 briefly	4057 hopefully
2160 fairly	3041 publicly	4069 way
2183 widely	3048 besides	4095 lately
2283 moreover	3122 etc.	4110 officially
2295 elsewhere	3135 badly	4124 tightly
2296 rarely	3157 differently	4145 thoroughly
2297 essentially	3158 across	4200 sexually
2330 sure	3176 successfully	4221 instantly
2336 previously	3213 furthermore	4233 afterward
2342 whenever	3290 repeatedly	4290 presumably
2358 equally	3306 nonetheless	4297 safely
2370 heavily	3310 physically	4309 fortunately
2378 approximately	3347 high	4311 actively
2398 strongly	3382 surprisingly	4315 incredibly
2442 surely	3388 dramatically	4316 consequently
2453 perfectly	3431 abroad	4377 upstairs
2483 literally	3437 greatly	4387 alike
2509 occasionally	3452 tight	4391 partially
2512 constantly	3500 lightly	4393 correctly
2524 rapidly	3580 frankly	4407 reportedly
2546 quietly	3590 daily	4427 mentally

Function words

Article

Determiner

Number

Pronoun

112 us
143 something
314 nothing
336 anything
369 himself
393 everything
423 someone
447 themselves
541 everyone
555 itself
665 anyone
670 myself
713 other
721 each
732 no
798 everybody
804 herself
967 yourself
1009 somebody
1039 whom
1105 none
1154 nobody
1387 anybody
1564 lots
1789 ourselves
1896 his
2078 plenty
2261 mine
2346 another
3182 yours
3942 hers
4098 ours
4295 whoever

Preposition

4 of
6 in
9 to
13 for
16 with
17 on
24 at
27 from
31 by
47 about
50 as
67 into
75 like

113 through
120 after
124 over
141 between
150 out
177 against
200 during
223 without
224 before
230 under
266 around
286 among
353 such
360 within
385 across
389 toward
392 off
398 including
427 behind
454 along
457 up
483 according
516 because
645 well
688 upon
709 near
710 than
742 away
752 beyond
754 despite
815 outside
885 since
903 above
946 onto
970 rather
976 inside
989 throughout
1041 down
1084 instead
1107 front
1301 terms
1380 worth
1383 until
1417 past
1524 next
1720 but
1820 due
1840 except

1928 plus
1943 below
1973 beside
2010 beneath
2061 addition
2067 towards
2211 regarding
2362 other
2488 unlike
2520 vs
2645 via
2674 ahead
2831 top
2902 prior
2995 depending
3222 versus
3390 concerning
3468 favor
3679 subject
3693 response
3904 amid
4162 spite
4171 besides
4207 opposed
4215 regard
4277 alongside
4287 respect
4318 charge
4466 behalf
4643 part
4662 atop
4737 apart
4775 light
4924 till
4965 aboard

Conjunction

3 and
12 that
23 but
32 or
34 as
42 if
60 when
74 than
91 because
156 while
171 where

Related titles from Routledge

The Routledge Dictionary of Modern American Slang and Unconventional English

Tom Dalzell

The Routledge Dictionary of Modern American Slang and Unconventional English offers the ultimate record of modern American Slang.

The 25,000 entries are accompanied by citations that authenticate the words as well as offer lively examples of usage from popular literature, newspapers, magazines, movies, television shows, musical lyrics, and Internet user groups. Etymology, cultural context, country of origin, and the date the word was first used are also provided.

This informative, entertaining, and sometimes shocking dictionary is an unbeatable resource for all language aficionados out there.

Hb: 978-0-415-37182-7
Ebk: 978-0-203-89513-9

Available at all good bookshops
For ordering and further information please visit:
www.routledge.com

Atlas of the World's Languages
2nd edition

Ron Asher and Christopher Moseley

The second edition of this highly successful atlas has been fully updated to provide a truly comprehensive, one-of-a-kind resource. The ten expanded sections feature a total of 140 maps, all of which have been revised to give the most accurate picture of the world language situation, and redesigned for greater ease of use. With an emphasis on the contemporary world linguistic situation, the *Atlas of the World's Languages* features:

- New information on population density, immigrant use, and contemporary linguistic practices as found in global business activity, diplomatic work, and internet language use

- Over twenty-five brand new maps plus a selection of pie charts indicating language diversity in key cities around the world

- An entirely new North American section featuring twelve maps giving both historical and contemporary language information.

Developed by the leading experts from around the world, this new edition of the *Atlas* is undoubtedly an important and unique work in its field.

Hb: 0-415-31074-1

For ordering and further information please visit:
www.routledge.com

The Concise Compendium of the World's Languages

George Campbell and Gary King

Forthcoming, in 2010

The Concise Compendium of the World's Languages provides brief descriptions in non-technical language of a wide cross-section of natural-language systems. The languages selected for this concise edition have been chosen on the basis of both numbers of speakers and socio-political interest and importance.

This new edition of the abridged two-volume classic has been extensively revised ensuring all statistics are completely up to date. An index and cross references throughout make this new edition even more user-friendly.

The Concise Compendium of the World's Languages remains the ideal compact reference for all interested linguistics and professionals alike.

Hb: 978-0-415-47841-0

Encyclopedia of the World's Endangered Languages

Christopher Moseley

The concern for the fast-disappearing language stocks of the world has arisen particularly in the past decade, as a result of the impact of globalization. This book appears as an answer to a felt need: to catalogue and describe those languages – making up the vast majority of the world's six thousand or more distinct tongues – which are in danger of disappearing within the next few decades.

Endangerment is a complex issue, and the reasons why so many of the world's smaller, less empowered languages are not currently being passed on to future generations are discussed in the book's introduction. The introduction is followed by regional sections, each authored by a notable specialist, all combining to provide a comprehensive listing of every language which, by the criteria of endangerment set out in the introduction, is likely to disappear within the next few decades. These languages make up ninety per cent of the world's remaining language stocks.

The book therefore provides in a single resource: expert analysis of the current language policy situation in every multilingual country and on every continent, detailed descriptions of little-known languages from all over the world, and clear alphabetical entries, region by region, of all the world's languages currently thought to be in danger of extinction.

The *Encyclopedia of the World's Endangered Languages* will be a necessary addition to all academic linguistics collections and will be a useful resource for a range of readers with an interest in development studies, cultural heritage, and international affairs.

Pb: 9780-415-56331-4
Hb: 978-0-70071197-0

Available at all good bookshops
For ordering and further information please visit:
www.routledge.com

Origins

A Short Etymological Dictionary of Modern English

Eric Partridge

This dictionary gives the origins of some 20,000 items from the modern English vocabulary, discussing them in groups that make clear the connections between words derived by a variety of routes from originally common stock. As well as giving the answers to questions about the derivation of individual words, it is a fascinating book to browse through, since every page points out links with other entries. It is easy to pursue such trails as the longer articles are written as continuous prose clearly divided up by means of numbered paragraphs and subheadings, and there is a careful system of cross-references. In addition to the main A–Z listing, there are extensive lists of prefixes, suffixes, and elements used in the creation of new vocabulary.

Hb: 978-0-415-05077-7
Pb: 978-0-415-47433-7